Expert Oracle Practices

Oracle Database Administration
from the Oak Table

Melanie Caffrey, Pete Finnigan, Randolf Geist, Alex Gorbachev,
Tim Gorman, Connie Green, Charles Hooper, Jonathan Lewis,
Niall Litchfield, Karen Morton, Robyn Sands, Jože Senegačnik,
Uri Shaft, Riyaj Shamsudeen, Jeremiah Wilton, Graham Wood

Apress®

ISBN-13 (pbk): 978-1-4302-2668-0

ISBN-13 (electronic): 978-1-4302-2669-2

Printed and bound in the United States of America 9 8 7 6 5 4 3 2 1

Trademarked names may appear in this book. Rather than use a trademark symbol with every occurrence of a trademarked name, we use the names only in an editorial fashion and to the benefit of the trademark owner, with no intention of infringement of the trademark.

President and Publisher: Paul Manning
Lead Editor: Jonathan Gennick
Technical Reviewers: Melanie Caffrey, Arup Nanda, Peter Sharman
Editorial Board: Clay Andres, Steve Anglin, Mark Beckner, Ewan Buckingham, Gary Cornell, Jonathan Gennick, Michelle Lowman, Matthew Moodie, Jeffrey Pepper, Frank Pohlmann, Ben Renow-Clarke, Dominic Shakeshaft, Matt Wade, Tom Welsh
Coordinating Editor: Fran Parnell
Copy Editors: Sharon Wilkey, James A. Compton
Compositor: Molly Sharp
Indexer: Brenda Miller
Artist: April Milne
Cover Designer: Anna Ishchenko

Distributed to the book trade worldwide by Springer-Verlag New York, Inc., 233 Spring Street, 6th Floor, New York, NY 10013. Phone 1-800-SPRINGER, fax 201-348-4505, e-mail orders-ny@springer-sbm.com, or visit www.springeronline.com.

For information on translations, please e-mail info@apress.com, or visit www.apress.com.

Apress and friends of ED books may be purchased in bulk for academic, corporate, or promotional use. eBook versions and licenses are also available for most titles. For more information, reference our Special Bulk Sales–eBook Licensing web page at www.apress.com/info/bulksales.

The information in this book is distributed on an "as is" basis, without warranty. Although every precaution has been taken in the preparation of this work, neither the author(s) nor Apress shall have any liability to any person or entity with respect to any loss or damage caused or alleged to be caused directly or indirectly by the information contained in this work.

The source code for this book is available to readers at www.apress.com. You will need to answer questions pertaining to this book in order to successfully download the code.

Contents at a Glance

Contents

Foreword

Like many red-blooded Americans, my friend—let's call him John—dabbles in carpentry whenever he can motivate himself to move from the computer to produce something more tangible. Recently he discovered that although motivation can be a great catalyst, it can never replace skills. In a grand testimony to that truth, he has never been able to produce anything more than a hole in a board or two pieces of wood out of one. His most recent story parallels the teachings of this book.

Embarrassed by the incessant boasting of neighbors and friends about their great accomplishments in the fine art of carpentry, John woke up one day determined to turn the tide—become skilled at carpentry. He even picked out a project—a garden shed to store all the mysterious but seemingly useful stuff that occupied the modest real-estate of his garage, forcing his cars to become refugees on the driveway. No way, no sir, he told the cars—pretty soon they would be able to go back to their promised homeland, just as soon as he banished the clutter to the garden shed, which he would build with his newly acquired skill. The cars seemed to honk in agreement, or perhaps he imagined it.

Charged with new passion, he rushed off to a store for homebuilders full of other trumped-up newbies like himself. He chose a book on do-it-yourself garden sheds. He bought the materials and the all-important tools. He did everything by the book. But two years have passed by, and all he has been able to produce are numerous cuts, bruises, scratches, and countless pieces of wood wasted as a result of not being cut properly—either cut too short or angled too acutely. In the course of these years, my friend added more tools to the collection—tools that supposedly make a carpenter out of anyone with the right inclination and bent of mind—and more wasted wood, drill bits, and saw dust. The shed, not even a remote resemblance of it, never saw the light of the day.

What went wrong? The missing ingredient was the right foundation. My friend was not a skilled carpenter. All the good intentions and excellent tools didn't do a thing to get him the right skills. What he should have invested in early on was time in learning the trade. He should have spent time in small but sure ways, learning how to use the tools he acquired. He should have learned how to measure pieces of wood before cutting them. No, he should have learned how to measure twice before cutting! He should have learned how to master the tools before actually using them on a project. But, above all, he should have realized that sophisticated tools and do-it-yourself books are not substitutes for a conceptual foundation on anything that requires expertise—the building of garden sheds included.

I tried to persuade my friend to give up on that project and hire a professional. But John doesn't give up easily. Instead, he began anew. This time he invested in learning the craft, in making small cuts and completing small projects to build up his skills. Once he was confident, he started on the shed. Finally, late one fall and after an embarrassing amount of time, the shed was done. John put it on concrete slabs and stored all his lawn and garden tools in it. For the first time in years, John's cars went inside his garage. The neighbors and I gathered. Everyone was smiling. John was beaming as he showed his handiwork to us all.

Then, the snow came.

You see, it was fall 2008, and the 2008–2009 winter turned into one of worst we had seen, with snowfalls going up to 13 inches or so every other day. The snow and ensuing cold spell left a huge pile of ice on John's beloved shed. One day, after days of enduring under the heavy accumulation, the shed buckled under the weight. We all watched helplessly as his blood and sweat just went up in a pile of wood, exposing everything inside it.

We neighbors tried to enlighten John on the futility of his attempts, but he won't budge. He spent hours and hours fixing the broken shed, but after every effort it would break. His attempts drew mixed emotions from the neighbors. Most people applauded his attempts at a positive attitude by making these efforts to fix the shed. But there were a few well-wishers who advised him to give up, to admit failure, and to have a prebuilt shed installed by professionals.

Where did John go wrong this second time? At least he started off in the right way, but he didn't have the expertise in the business of sustenance. Building a shed is only half the story; making it tough enough to withstand the elements is the other half—one that proverbially separates the men from the boys.

How does John's story parallel the teachings in the book? In many ways, John's experience paraphrases the activity of many professionals engaged in the technology trade—Oracle technology included. Even some so-called experts are not immune to the temptations of a shortcut. The dependence on tools is a foregone conclusion in many cases, with greater emphasis on seemingly sophisticated ones. What's worse, it is a common belief in the corporate world that a go-getter attitude coupled with the right tools enables one to do any job, and do it well. That belief often leads to a reinforcement of the pattern of behavior that rewards an effort—not necessarily the right effort.

The expert must have the right tools, but the sophistication of the tools is not as important as their right use. Using the handle end of a screwdriver to drive a nail when a hammer is lying right in front of you is not just idiotic but goes against the "no screwdrivers were harmed in the making of this project" theme. Using the right tool for the right job is what makes an expert an expert. Consider Chapter 3, in which Connie, Uri, and Graham show you how to use ADDM to resolve some thorny issues in performance. Many people I meet often balk at using a tool such as ADDM. Why? Their reasons are often a mixture of ignorance, skepticism, and masochistic viewpoints that a tool can't be better than their bare hands. But for a DBA to avoid using ADDM is like a nurse in a busy hospital wanting to throw away the automatic blood-pressure monitor. Sure, a nurse can get by with a manual cuff. So can an expert DBA get by without ADDM. But ADDM makes life easier and more efficient, and an expert will take advantage of ADDM in order to get those benefits.

Getting back to the story, Alex shows in Chapter 1 how the behavior of doing just *something*, even doing something completely ineffective, is often rewarded. Work that does not get results represents lost productivity and delayed execution. Alex painstakingly demonstrates how it hurts productivity to make assumptions rather than to take accurate measurements, and that a major impediment to the resolution of any problem is the presence of assumptions. Many chapters in this book try to drive home the point that the practice of measuring instead of assuming should be the first order of business in any resolution process. In Chapter 6, Karen shows how to instrument and measure code for hidden issues, and to rely on proper measurement techniques. In Chapters 8 and 9, Charles and Randolf describe how to develop a system that measures performance and practically puts the culprit of a performance problem right in front of you. And Robyn shows in Chapter 13 how to use statistics to find the proverbial "red rock" representing a performance problem buried under a mountain of collapsed rubble.

About eight years ago, I was delivering a technical session on buffer busy waits, how to diagnose them, and how resolve them. At the end of the session, during the question-and-answer period, an attendee asked me a very interesting question: SQL Server didn't suffer conditions such as buffer busy waits, so did that mean that SQL Server was better than Oracle? I resorted to an allegory as a response. I said that I took my car for oil changes, but not my bicycle; so did it mean that my bicycle is technologically superior to my car? The response, as expected, drew a chuckle from the audience and drove home the point about the futility of comparison between those two databases. In the audience was Tim Gorman, one of the authors of this book, who also responded to the question from the attendee. Tim asked the attendee how he knew that SQL Server did not indeed have the condition known as buffer busy waits. Perhaps SQL Server did suffer from those, but he just didn't know how to measure them and resolve them.

While the audience was mulling over the response, I realized the enormous universal truth behind Tim's response. Most of the audience, even seasoned DBAs, weren't even aware of the buffer busy waits in Oracle, or were quite hazy in their understanding of them. The point was not about the specific condition or what it is called. The point was about the universal acceptance of the absence of something that has not been characterized yet. The questioning of accepted knowledge is the key to getting closer to the truth. But it is not just the act of skepticism, but the examination of the knowledge that matters. Centuries ago, many believed the world was flat. Had Newton not discovered gravity, the concept of a round earth might have defied logic and been relegated to the category of myth. Instead, the ability to understand gravity and correlate that understanding with other observations about the world led to widespread acceptance that the world was, in fact, round.

In Chapter 12, Riyaj explains the little known and often misunderstood concept of latch contention. Lack of understanding of latch contention leads to design of systems that do not scale well, and to issues that remain unresolved for quite long periods of time. Riyaj's chapter should also educate readers enough to explain some of the other mysteries that have plagued them. The concept of deeper understanding to dispel myths is reinforced in Jonathan's Chapter 11 on statistics. These chapters highlight the need to build a system for scalability, which was the precise cause of the failure in the case of the garden shed made by my friend John.

Many of the authors, such as Jonathan and Jože, portray themselves not as consultants or DBAs extraordinaire, but merely as researchers. This self-attribution is a testimony to the fact that they are still learning and will continue to do so. They have epitomized the belief that knowledge is never a destination; it's a journey. It is not supposed to end. Any pretense of accomplishing the end is exactly that—a pretense. The other authors hold different titles, but all of them espouse the same principle: they never seek the end of knowledge; they create it, encourage others to create ever more, and then they absorb it all like a sponge. As a famous contemporary author once wrote, the worst part of knowledge is that the more you know, the more you learn how much you don't know. The best part is that this realization results in the creation of knowledge exponentially. The enlightened group of authors behind this book have attempted to kick off that very process. By filling in some voids in your knowledge, they hopefully tickle your imagination and inspire you to explore more, to add to the entire gamut of knowledge as a whole.

Going back to the original discussion, what makes an expert? Is it winning some titles or passing some certification tests? Many of these authors have been honored for their excellence in some form or other. Some are formally recognized by Oracle (as Administrator Certified Expert and ACE Directors, and as an Author of the Year, for example). Others are recognized by by formal certification authorities (as Oracle Certified Professionals and Oracle Certified Masters). All are recognized by the strictest body of all—the OakTable Network itself. But all these recognitions pale in comparison to the biggest accomplishment of all—their recognition by their peer group: the user community. Ultimately, what makes the difference is the acceptance of their excellence by you, the reader and the user of Oracle technology. All of these authors participate heavily in the user community, give knowledge back to the community—internationally or in their local spheres—and shape the progress of accumulation of collective knowledge. When they come together to pen their thoughts in the format of a book, the result can be nothing short of sheer pleasure.

An expert also must be well rounded, albeit is expected to be an expert in a subset of the technologies. The dissemination of knowledge is not complete without a deeper understanding of some of the supporting technologies. In Chapter 5, Niall shows how to effectively manage Oracle on Windows through a thorough explanation of the subtle nuances of Windows and how to get around them. In Chapter 7, Jože shows how to exploit a little known but powerful feature of the cost-based optimizer called the *extensible optimizer*. In Chapters 14 and 15, world-renowned security expert Pete shows how to deviate from performance aspects and bulletproof your database from security threats—a goal that attained considerable importance lately. In Chapter 10, another renowned expert named Tim takes a detour to the world of superlatives—big databases, longer load times, and so on, to educate readers in the fine art of managing beasts of databases.

Technology changes faster than you can spell it, and most of us are stuck in a loop of understanding deeply and then becoming obsolete. However, there is no substitute to solid foundation in design, as Melanie describes in Chapter 4. Changes are inevitable, and keeping up with the pace of change often poses challenges for experts in any domain. Pace of change is one of the factors leading to the pollution of knowledge, as performance-tuning guru Jonathan explains in Chapter 11 in relation to the gathering of statistics. And Jeremiah's Chapter 2 is the result of change; it explains the newest phenomenon to hit the experts—Oracle in the cloud.

As a part of my extra-curricular activities, I often travel outside my native United States to other countries to provide seminars, trainings, sessions, and to participate in discussion forums. In fact, I am writing this foreword in the middle of a two-week, four-country tour across Europe. While on the plane from Estonia to Germany, I was reflecting on the lesser-appreciated aspects of knowledge processing, the ones too subtle to notice but too important to ignore. Cultural aspects play a huge role in the collection and dissemination of knowledge. Mankind is far from being homogeneous; it's submerged in plurality—languages, cultures, customs, and expressions shaped by traditions. Ignoring this plethora of differences is not only detrimental to synergy, but also to the very essence of the knowledge-begets-knowledge belief. Not understanding cultural and customary differences can only lead to the inefficiency of the process, if not to a more dangerous reversal and creation of ignorance puddles. A vital characteristic of this cast of authors is that they represent many parts of the globe. The ideas they propound, the mannerisms they convey, are shaped and influenced—some more than the other—by the customs and traditions they uphold. A profound example is the United States, a melting pot of many cultures in which diversity gives strength to the society and is celebrated. It's diversity of the authors that gives this book an all-round perspective, something that is literally world-class.

Finally, it's the supporting cast that makes the last run of the technical aspect of the book a huge success. The authors didn't just get a free rein in whatever they wanted to write; their work was thoroughly scrutinized by a team of technical reviewers—also members of the OakTable Network and respected professionals in their own right. Even the editor—Jonathan Gennick—is an Oakie as well, making it an Oakie production end to end.

While I have been honored to write the foreword, I stoop under the weight of the huge expectation of summarizing the essence of these chapters from the stalwarts of the Oracle user community into a few pages. In conclusion, I will reiterate the message that has been delivered by many authors in many shapes or forms—excellence is not an end or even a journey. It is not about gathering as much knowledge as possible; it's about building a very strong foundation on whatever you know, expanding the horizon but not at the cost of a weakened foundation. It is about refining your foundation, and reinforcing it by constantly subjecting it to assessment and analysis, and finally providing evidence (quantifiable or otherwise), not opinions based on perceptions.

Happy reading!

Arup Nanda
Chief database architect, Starwood Hotels and Resorts
OakTable Network member
Oracle ACE Director

About the Authors

Melanie Caffrey, Pete Finnigan, Randolf Geist, Alex Gorbachev, Tim Gorman, Connie Green, Charles Hooper, Jonathan Lewis, Niall Litchfield, Karen Morton, Robyn Sands, Jože Senegačnik, Uri Shaft, Riyaj Shamsudeen, Jeremiah Wilton, Graham Wood

Melanie Caffrey

Melanie Caffrey is a senior development manager for Oracle Corporation, providing front-end and back-end Oracle solutions for the business needs of various clients. She is co-author of several technical publications, including *Oracle Web Application Programming for PL/SQL Developers*, *Oracle DBA Interactive Workbook*, and *Oracle Database Administration: The Complete Video Course*, all published by Prentice Hall. She has instructed students in Columbia University's Computer Technology and Applications program in New York City, teaching advanced Oracle database administration and PL/SQL development. She is a frequent Oracle conference speaker.

Pete Finnigan

Pete is a world-renowned expert in the area of Oracle security, providing consultancy, design expertise, security audits, and training, all in the area of Oracle security. Pete is a member of the OakTable Network. He has spoken regularly all over the world at various conferences such as those of the United Kingdom Oracle Users Group (UKOUG), PSOUG, Black Hat, and Risk. Pete is a published author on Oracle security, and researches and writes about the subject regularly. Pete also runs his website, www.petefinnigan.com, dedicated to Oracle security and providing help and free tools to the community.

Randolf Geist

Randolf Geist has been working with Oracle software for 15 years now. Since 2000 he has operated as a freelance database consultant focusing primarily on performance-related issues, and in particular helping people to understand and unleash the power of the Oracle cost-based optimizer (CBO). He is writing on his blog about CBO-related issues and is also regularly contributing to the official Oracle Technology Network (OTN) forums. Randolf is a member of the OakTable Network, the Oracle ACE program, and is an Oracle Certified Professional DBA for Oracle Versions 8i, 9i, and 10g. He also maintains SQLTools++, an open source Oracle GUI for Windows.

Alex Gorbachev

Alex Gorbachev is a respected figure in the Oracle world, and a sought-after leader and speaker at Oracle conferences around the globe. He is an OakTable Network member, and has been recognized as an Oracle ACE Director for his contributions to the community and unmatched set of skills. He is the founder of the *Battle Against Any Guess* movement, promoting scientific troubleshooting techniques. He is currently the chief technology officer at The Pythian Group.

Alex has worked for The Pythian Group in several roles. He began by leading a team of database experts in Ottawa. He then moved to Australia to build the company's presence in the East Asia Pacific region. Now he is back in Ottawa as The Pythian Group's chief technology officer. In all his work, Alex continues to work toward bridging the gap between business and technology. The search for the perfect fit between technology, engineering talents, and business process is what keeps him up at night.

Tim Gorman

Tim Gorman began his IT career in 1984 as a C programmer on Unix and VMS systems, working on medical and financial systems as an application developer, systems programmer, and systems administrator. He joined Oracle Corporation in 1990 as a consultant, became an independent consultant in 1998, and has worked for SageLogix since 2000. Gorman is the co-author of *Essential Oracle8i Data* Warehousing and *Oracle8 Data Warehousing*. He specializes in performance-tuning applications, databases, and systems, as well as data warehouse design and implementation, backup and recovery, architecture and infrastructure, and database administration. Gorman still considers himself a pretty good coder, although the market for C programs has dried up somewhat lately.

Connie Green

Connie Green has 20 years of experience with Oracle products, the last 12 years working for Oracle U.S. Server Development. Connie's expertise is in database performance tuning. She designed and developed Statspack from its initial release. Over the years Connie has been privileged to work with many talented kernel developers, performance engineers, and support engineers, having been involved with library cache development, buffer cache development, and the query optimizer.

Charles Hooper

Charles Hooper is the IT manager and an Oracle database administrator at K&M Machine Fabricating, where he has been employed since 2000. His role in the company extends well beyond Oracle database administration responsibilities, providing opportunities for database performance tuning, network administration, programming, hardware/software troubleshooting, mentoring fellow IT staff, and end-user training for the Infor ERP Visual system as well as other custom-developed applications. Charles is well known among the user community of Infor Visual Enterprise because of his years of participation in various user forums answering technical questions, providing the only Oracle presentation at Infor's 2008 user's conference, and providing presentations to regional user groups. Prior to joining K&M, he was a computer/technology instructor and Novell NetWare administrator. He holds a bachelor of science in mathematics and computer science. Much has changed in the computer industry since his first home computer in 1981, which offered 5KB of memory, a surprisingly small amount today as manufacturers offer home computers with as much as 24GB of memory.

Jonathan Lewis

Jonathan Lewis has been working in the IT industry for nearly 25 years, and has been using the Oracle RDBMS for more than 20. For the last 16 years he has been working as a freelance consultant, often spending only one or two days at a time with any client to address critical performance problems. He also advises on design and implementation problems, and on how to make best use of the most appropriate Oracle features for a given project.

Jonathan is renowned throughout the world (having visited 42 countries at last count) for his tutorials and seminars about the Oracle database engine and how to make best use of it. His exceptional ability has earned him an O-1 visa from the United States, allowing him to do consultancy and lecture work there.

Jonathan has written two books about Oracle (*Practical Oracle8i*, Addison-Wesley, 2000; *Cost-Based Oracle Fundamentals*, Apress, 2005) as well as contributing to two others (*Oracle Insights*, Apress, 2004; *Oracle Database 10g New Features*, McGraw-Hill, 2004). He also writes regularly for the UKOUG magazine, and occasionally for other publications around the world. In the limited amount of time he has left over, Jonathan also publishes high-tech Oracle articles on his blog at http://jonathanlewis.wordpress.com.

Niall Litchfield

Niall Litchfield is a DBA of 15 years standing, with extensive experience of running databases on various x86(64) platforms, and with a particular bias toward Microsoft Windows. Niall began professional life as a "bean-counter" for KPMG; consequently he is a DBA who respects auditors, not least because they have to stand in unheated warehouses in the middle of winter watching other people count things, something he never wants to do again. His dad was a *real* engineer crafting genuinely useful objects with fine tolerances and that, coupled with an early experience in which he showed that the two competing macro-economic theories of the time both explained actual behavior equally well, and that neither explained it adequately, rather explains his evidence-based approach to databases in general and performance tuning in particular.

Karen Morton

Karen Morton is a consultant and educator specializing in application optimization in both shoulder-to-shoulder consulting engagements and classroom settings. She is a senior principal database engineer for Agilex Technologies (http://agilex.com), a Chantilly, Virginia company founded by Bob LaRose and Jay Nussbaum. Agilex offers customers innovative thinking on leveraging advanced technologies within the healthcare, federal, intelligence, commercial, and public sectors to fully realize the value of information.

For over 20 years, Karen has worked in information technology, starting out as a mainframe programmer, developer, DBA, data architect, and now as a researcher, educator, and consultant. Having used Oracle since the early 90s, she began teaching others how to use Oracle over a decade ago.

She is a frequent speaker at conferences and user groups, an Oracle ACE, and a member of the OakTable network. She blogs at http://karenmorton.blogspot.com.

Robyn Sands

Robyn Anderson Sands is a software engineer for Cisco Systems. In a previous incarnation, she worked in industrial engineering, manufacturing development, and quality engineering at Lockheed Martin, supporting the P-7, F-22, and C-130J programs. Robyn has been working with databases and Oracle software since around 1996. She began her work with Oracle by developing tools for scheduling, composite fabrication capacity modeling, and engineering workflow, and progressing to the implementation and administration of data warehouse, PeopleSoft, and SAP systems. Current projects include "architecting" and managing the development of embedded database systems for Cisco customers, and searching for new ways to design and develop database systems with consistent performance and minimal maintenance requirements. She has been a speaker at UKOUG, Miracle conferences, Oracle OpenWorld, and the Hotsos Symposium. She occasionally posts random blog entries at adhdocddba.blogspot.com.

Jože Senegačnik

Jože Senegačnik has more than 20 years of experience in working with Oracle products. He began in 1988 with Oracle Database version 4 while working for the City of Ljubljana, Slovenia, where he had charge over the city's municipal and geographic information systems. From 1993 to 2003, he worked in developing GIS systems for the Surveying and Mapping Authority of the Republic of Slovenia, and in the development of applications for other governmental institutions, all based on the Oracle database. More recently, he has specialized in performance optimization, having developed his own toolset for monitoring performance and analyzing trace files.

Jože is an internationally recognized speaker, and a member of the highly respected OakTable Network (oaktable.net). He is a regular speaker at user-group conferences, especially those put on by the Slovenian Oracle Users Group (SIOUG), the Independent Oracle Users Group (IOUG), and the United Kingdom Oracle Users Group (UKOUG). He also speaks routinely at the Hotsos Symposium and Oracle OpenWorld. In addition to sharing his knowledge through conference talks, Jože conducts technical seminars organized either by Oracle University or himself. He was awarded Oracle ACE membership for his long record of positive contributions to the Oracle community.

Uri Shaft

Uri Shaft received a Ph.D. from the University of Wisconsin-Madison, specializing in database systems. He was the lead developer of the innovative QUIQ hybrid database and information retrieval system. Currently, Uri works for Oracle USA in the server manageability group. He is the developer in charge of the Automatic Database Diagnostic Monitor (ADDM), and of components that analyze the Active Session History (ASH) sampled data. Uri's areas of expertise include multimedia support in database systems, multidimensional indexing theory (and practice), and database performance diagnosis and tuning.

Riyaj Shamsudeen

Riyaj Shamsudeen is the principal DBA and president of OraInternals (www.orainternals.com), a performance/recovery/EBS11i consulting company. He specializes in RAC, performance tuning, and database internals. He also frequently blogs about these technology areas in his blog, http://orainternals.wordpress.com. He is a regular presenter in many international conferences such as Hotsos, COLLABORATE, RMOUG, SIOUG, and UKOUG. He is a proud member of OakTable network. He has more than 16 years of experience using Oracle technology products and more than 15 years as an Oracle DBA/Oracle Applications DBA.

Jeremiah Wilton

Jeremiah Wilton has worked with Oracle technology since 1994. His main claim to fame is having been Amazon.com's first database administrator, back in the pre-IPO days. For seven years, he helped Amazon.com survive exponential scaling and a wide variety of nearly catastrophic technology failures. Jeremiah owned and ran ORA-600 Consulting for a number of years, until it was acquired by Blue Gecko, a global provider of remote administration for Oracle, MySQL, and E-Business Suite. Jeremiah also teaches the Oracle certificate program for the University of Washington. Jeremiah is an Oracle Certified Master, a member of the OakTable, and a frequent presenter at industry conferences and user groups. His publications and whitepapers can be found at www.bluegecko.net.

Graham Wood

Graham Wood is an architect in the database development group at Oracle. Most of his 20 years at Oracle have been spent in performance-related areas, including designing and tuning large high-performance systems, building monitoring tools such as Statspack, and in architecting performance and scalability features into the database engine itself. More recently Graham was the architect of the Oracle Manageability team tasked with simplifying the process of tuning the operation of the database, which resulted in the development of AWR, ASH, and ADDM to provide automatic tuning.

About the Technical Reviewers

Melanie Caffrey

Melanie Caffrey is a senior development manager for Oracle Corporation, providing front-end and back-end Oracle solutions for the business needs of various clients. She is co-author of several technical publications, including *Oracle Web Application Programming for PL/SQL Developers*, the *Oracle DBA Interactive Workbook*, and *Oracle Database Administration: The Complete Video Course*, all published by Prentice Hall. She has instructed students in Columbia University's Computer Technology and Applications program in New York City, teaching advanced Oracle database administration and PL/SQL development. She is a frequent Oracle conference speaker.

Arup Nanda

Arup Nanda has been an Oracle DBA for more than 16 years—touching all aspects of database management and architecture—from modeling to performance tuning and disaster recovery. He has written more than 300 articles, co-authored 4 books, spoken at 150 technical conferences, and delivered a number of full-length training sessions. In 2003, he was awarded DBA of the Year by Oracle. He is an Oracle Certified Professional DBA, an OTN ACE Director, and a member of the OakTable Network. He lives in Connecticut with his wife Anu and son Anish.

Peter Sharman

Peter Sharman is a curriculum developer with Server Technologies Curriculum Development at Oracle Corporation. He has over 20 years of Oracle experience, and has been a speaker at several Oracle OpenWorld, Miracle Database Forum, and RMOUG Training Days conferences. Pete has multiple OCP and OCM certifications, and is currently responsible for developing training on the Oracle Enterprise Manager product family.

CHAPTER 1

■ ■ ■

Battle Against Any Guess

by Alex Gorbachev

During my experience with Oracle, I have become very engaged in the user community. I've been a frequent visitor on the Oracle Technology Network forums and the Oracle-L list and have become a regular participant and contributor at user group conferences and other events. My experience started with seeking help and gradually shifted towards helping others with their issues. My growth in Oracle has correlated with the booming popularity of the Internet, over which it becomes very easy to both seek and give advice.

While the Internet increases community participation, it also causes some dysfunction that can lower the quality of the information. Many times I have seen online discussions branch into controversial arguments in which the "combatants" are going by guesswork. It is surprising how few people will stop to test what really happens, and instead will battle endlessly over what might happen or what they believe ought to happen.

While my contributions to the community have been usually rather technical, this chapter is more generic and rather motivational reading. My first attempt at a motivational contribution was creating BattleAgainstAnyGuess.com, or the BAAG Party for short, in June 2007. This is where the title of the chapter comes from. The trigger to establish the BAAG Party was coming across yet another quest for guess-based solutions on the Internet; and I wanted something generic to refer to every time I see such symptoms. Thus, I want to start this chapter by showing some examples of guess-provoking questions.

Guess Hunting

The way you ask a question is crucial. A badly formed inquiry is almost guaranteed to attract guess-based solutions. Here is one example of seeking a quick solution from the Oracle-L list:

> *"I'm also having performance issues with 10g. Why would my dictionary queries take a long time to return? ... In 9i they used to take seconds, now they take minutes or they just never come back..."*

When reading this question, it is difficult to divine precisely what the problem is that the writer is experiencing. Without a clear understanding of the problem, the proposed solutions were all over the map. Here are some of the suggestions that turned up quickly:

> *"You might need to analyze the system tables."*

"There are a few known bugs with DD queries in 10g. Few of them involved the CDEF$ table so you might want to do a search for that and/or for the particular views you're having trouble with. The solution was to delete statistics from the involved tables and then lock the stats."

"Remove any initialization parameters set for Oracle 9i."

"Apply application vendor suggestions (like _optimizer_cost_based_transformation=false, NLS_LENGTH_SEMANTICS=CHAR, _gby_hash_aggregation_enabled=false)."

"Disable sub-query unnesting (_UNNEST_SUBQUERY = FALSE)."

"Don't use FIRST_ROWS optimizer goal."

All these might be absolutely valid solutions for different people's own problems. One could very well be the solution the original poster needs, but we don't know which one. A couple of these solutions actually contradict each other (collect vs. delete statistics). These recommendations are based on the previous experience (often quite extensive) of those who proposed them, and they might match well the symptom observed, that "dictionary queries take a long time to return." However, there is one common problem to all of the proposed solutions: the analysis phase is missing. No one has done any analysis or testing to verify the problem, or to verify that their proposed solution even addresses the problem. Everyone is, in essence, guessing.

To show you the magnitude of guesswork and where it leads, here is another example, this time from the OTN Forums:

"My database running on AIX 5.3, oracle getting the version 9.2.0.5.0, after migration it is getting very slow. Kindly provide a solution to tune the database and increase performance."

This is probably an extreme example of ignorance and/or laziness that pushes the author to search for a quick fix solution. Now let's see how this plea for help is being followed up. First of all, a number of people asked for clarification on what is actually running slowly, and for more details about the environment—fair enough. However, there was also a shower of well-meaning advice. One well-intended bit of advice was:

"You can delete and re-gather dbms stats for your application schemas after the upgrade."

And these were the results after the original poster tried implementing the advice:

"getting same problem
continuously database have lock and the
dbcache hit ratio is 60% only.
total sga size is 20GB
db_cache_size 13gb"

This next proposed solution is a bit better. It's hinting towards actually analyzing the problem:

"From OEM you can view the performance and the SQL statements which are being fired every moment and then find out about missing indexes or tune the SQL."

Then follows advice from someone who is seemingly a guru in Oracle database performance tuning. That advice comes in the form of 11 bullet points. Applied, each of them could fix certain problems, or make performance worse in this particular case. Making 11 changes and hoping that one of them fixes a problem is not an optimal approach.

Following is yet another suggestion on configuring asynchronous input/output. It could be a valid path in certain cases, but is it valid in this case?

"Have you got asynch I/O configured on AIX?"

The original poster did enable ASYNC I/O and, of course, it didn't help.

The list of randomly proposed solutions went on and on, and the discussion ended up sidetracked far from solving the original problem. Did the original poster ever get the help s/he was after? I don't know. It didn't appear so.

Why Do We Guess?

The most trivial factor leading to guess-based solutions is laziness, a natural human quality. Why embark on a path of investigation when there is a chance that one of the proposed solutions just fixes the problem? The reason is that while a random fix might actually work for some commonplace issues, it introduces a significant chance of fixing the wrong problem, making things worse, or simply hiding the symptoms. Fortunately, in my professional life I've met very few DBAs who are too lazy to analyze a problem. Most prefer to troubleshoot and fix a problem once and for all.

■ **Note** One can almost argue that taking the time to analyze a problem and implement a true solution is also a way of being lazy, because you save all the work of randomly guessing and trying. But it's a "good" lazy.

Unfortunately, there are other factors besides laziness. Often, companies are not investing enough to provide their support engineers with the right tools and knowledge. Spending money on a performance-tuning tool or on the Diagnostic Pack option will pay back in spades when it comes to, say, troubleshooting an issue that causes online orders to time out, or that causes the factory floor to be idle. The same goes with investing in education and hiring qualified performance consultants or services. The investment pays back the next time a problem is experienced with a business-critical function, and such problems are solved many times more quickly than otherwise.

An Example from Cycling

by Jonathan Gennick

The idea of "knowing" something rather than "guessing" it is near and dear to my heart. The concept applies beyond just Oracle. I do an increasing amount of bicycle maintenance for myself and for friends. A common problem that I encounter is the bent derailleur hanger. To diagnose that problem reliably, one must purchase a $50 tool. Many get by without the tool. They derive the diagnosis of "bent hanger" based upon the absence of any other problem that they can think of. I much prefer to measure and "know" for certain that a shifting problem is due to a bent hanger rather than to infer the problem based upon my inability to lay the blame elsewhere. So I spent $50 so that I can know something for certain rather than having to guess at it.

My investment has paid off in an unexpected way too. Once I had the tool, I read the instructions and realized that I can use it to straighten hangers that are not too badly bent. (I had been throwing all bent hangers in the trash). Hangers range in price from $20 to $30 each. Repairing rather than replacing just a couple or three hangers easily covers my investment in the proper tool. Perhaps the ultimate benefit is that my bikes shift very, very well.

Another common factor is the time pressure. A very common attitude is this: "we don't have time to analyze; we just need to fix it now." That attitude is a siren song. The reality is that the guess-and-try path is much longer on average than a targeted scientific analysis of a problem situation. It often takes a number of guess-and-try iterations until you find the one that works, and there is still a danger of not fixing the root cause—simply because the root cause wasn't identified in the first place.

Yet another reason for premature decisions is the "call for action from above." A loud call for action from management is a variation of the time-pressure problem. Management pressure can be very intense, and it's usually more the effect of the political atmosphere in a company than of anything else. A prime example is when a DBA is pressured to DO SOMETHING NOW to fix a problem and leave the understanding part for later. Such enormous pressure comes from the business because, for example, it might cost millions of dollars for each hour of a factory floor being idle. In such cases, it is reasonable to take measures to reduce business impact to acceptable levels while also undertaking a full investigation into the root problem. Too much management pressure often leads to what I term "blame-storm" meetings, in which fingers are pointed and everyone tries their best to deflect blame. A factor that's often most visible during blame-storm sessions is unwillingness to admit that one does not know where a problem really lies, that one does not really know the root cause. Nobody wants to look stupid, and not knowing what we are supposed to know as professionals tends to make us feel that way. Management often takes advantage of that feeling to add yet more pressure, which ends up as more fuel for the fire.

The best way to address the management pressure is to show that you *know* what to do, and that you have a clear action plan in place that is being followed and that will lead to clearly identified deliverables. It does require some good communication and persuasion skills to calm management, and to present a plan in a way that management will buy in, but the effort does pay off.

A very efficient "play" is to buy time—let someone implement a harmless guess-based solution (providing you are not to be blamed for its failure) while you are focused on the real troubleshooting. In the meantime, focus all your energy on proper analysis.

If you've caught yourself smiling reading these lines, you know what I'm talking about. For the rest of you, be very careful with the strategy of buying time. It might backfire—I warned you!

Efficiency vs. Effectiveness

One good strategy to fight a demand for immediate action is to distinguish between efficiency and effectiveness. Efficiency is all about the process; it means to act so that you save time, money, and effort. Effectiveness is all about the result—how well the job gets done, and the quality of the output.

While a production engineer always needs to find the balance between both, it's often that effectiveness does prevail, and that efficiency becomes a secondary target. Let's compare these two approaches:

1. An engineer identifies 10 configuration changes that are likely to fix a given problem. The DBA team collaborates with the QA team, making a great effort and managing to validate all 10 changes in 2 days. They are efficient—they managed to validate and implement 10 changes in a short period of time—but does that effort solve the problem at hand?

2. An engineer spends two days to analyze the problem and come up with a narrowly scoped solution by changing one `init.ora` variable for affected sessions. He only performs the one change in those two days, so he is not as efficient as the DBA team in the first scenario, if we measure efficiency as the number of changes per day. However, he has addressed the problem precisely. He is effective.

Understanding a Problem

When faced with a problem, the number-one thing we need to understand is the problem itself. Understanding a problem is the very first step toward a successful solution. Nothing is worse than spinning wheels solving a completely wrong problem. That is why we want business owners and end users to provide some input into our discussion about a problem, even though that input brings with it some pressure to solve the issue.

A great example of what I'm talking about was brought to my attention by Niall Litchfield, a coauthor of this book and fellow member of the OakTable Network. The quote below is published on BattleAgainstAnyGuess.com:

"One of the great problems with guesswork is that you can be led down some very blind alleys indeed. This commonly occurs when you guess what a problem is, rather than diagnose it, and then embark upon a solution. Every time you find yourself doing this, think of Miriam."

Miriam in this case refers to a woman who wrote in to an advice columnist. She had left for work. Her car had stalled. She walked back home to find her husband wearing her underwear and makeup. Completely put out by that turn of events, she wrote to an advice columnist. And the answer came back:

A car stalling after being driven a short distance can be caused by...

Clearly the columnist failed to read far enough to understand the true problem at hand.

■ **Note** See `http://www.battleagainstanyguess.com/2007/06/missing-the-point/` for the full story.

When you are defining a problem for others to solve, think whether it's explained clearly, and take care of any possible dual meaning in your words. Even the most obvious explanation can be misunderstood. Be direct. Keep things simple. Speak in short sentences. Try to distill your initial problem statement to one succinct sentence. All these things will help.

But there is responsibility on the other side as well! When you start to solve a problem, don't immediately assume that you understand it. Always double-check what the real issue is. Agree on some tests, or examples to demonstrate the problem, that you can later use to prove the problem fixed. There is no point, for example, in fixing a heavy batch process when the real problem is that interactive users are suffering from timeouts on their order-entry screens.

Another Cycling Example

by Jonathan Gennick

My neighbor boy once asked about a problem with his bike. He described the problem as the chain jumping between gears. Having recently solved such a problem on my own bike by adjusting the derailleur, I practically assured the boy that I could fix the problem by making some simple adjustments. I asked him to leave the bike with me for a couple hours.

I took the bike into my workshop, and the "couple hours" turned into "all evening." Then one evening turned into two, and then into three as I decided to also clean the bike and fix some unrelated problems. Finally, at about 1:30 AM after three long evenings of tearing apart and rebuilding the drive train multiple times, I had the bike all back together and again and working.

My guess about adjusting the derailleur was completely wrong. The root problem was a worn drive train. Unable to bring myself to disappoint an 11-year-old by not fixing his bike, I scavenged a very nice chain, rear cog set, and chain ring set from one of my own bikes. My new cog set had a larger-diameter gear on it, forcing me to also throw in a new derailleur. As an extra, I threw in a bash guard. And I replaced brake and shifter cables, brake pads, and also a broken left-shifter.

The bike worked. The kid was very happy. And I learned an important lesson about guessing versus diagnosing.

Logical Conclusions vs. Historical Observations

Munich, May 2006. Tom Kyte, a fellow member of OakTable Network, was doing a two-day seminar. One of his topics was about bind variables. He shared a very interesting example he observed at one Oracle customer site that I am borrowing with his permission.

According to the end-users' observations, if it was raining heavily Monday morning, then database performance was terrible. Any other day of the week, or on Mondays without rain, there were no problems. Talking to the DBA responsible for the system, Tom found that the performance problems continued until the DBA restarted the database, at which point performance went back to normal. That was the workaround: Rainy Mondays = Reboots.

Any analyst approaching a new performance problem should always gather users' feedback to determine the scope of the issue and the impact on the business. However, one should be very careful in making conclusions from those discoveries. In this case, it was very easy to get sidetracked into environmental causes such as humidity, water levels, and so forth.

What a savvy analyst would learn from these observations is the exact pattern of occurrences in the past, as well as how to reliably catch the issue on the live system in the future. He would also learn that the issue is intermittent, and there is likely some correlation with Mondays' rains.

It turned out that one of the application users was typically starting the day very early, before 7 AM, and the first thing she did was to log into the system and open her main screen—the very screen that she and all her colleagues would be using all the time during the day. Let's call this user Mrs. Early Bird.

Unfortunately, if it's raining heavily on Monday, she must take her children to school, and then fight traffic, causing her to be later to work than otherwise. When it rained on other days, she had other arrangements.

Nonsense Correlation

As I was writing this section of the chapter, a fellow member of the OakTable Network, Robyn Sands, posted a blog entry that taught me a very interesting statistics term: *nonsense correlation*. I can't resist mentioning it. So thanks to Robyn, here is the definition from the *Oxford Dictionary of Statistics* by Graham Upton and Ian Cook (Oxford University Press, 2nd ed. 2008):

> **nonsense correlation:** A term used to describe a situation where two variables (X and Y, say) are correlated without being causally related to one another. The usual explanation is that they are both related to a third variable, Z. Often the third variable is time. For example, if we compare the price of a detached house in Edinburgh in 1920, 1930, ... with the size of the population of India at those dates, a 'significant' positive correlation will be found, since both variables have increased markedly with time.

The situation I'm describing involving the early-arriving user is essentially a nonsense correlation.

In the meantime, another department was starting the day at 8 AM, each day preparing a special report for the 9 AM Monday meeting based on some historical data. One component of that report was using exactly the same statement as the screen opened by Mrs. Early Bird and later by tens of her colleagues. That statement was using bind variables, which many consider a "best practice" (ding!) of database development. The only difference between the statement used by the interactive application and that used in the report was in the bind variables' values.

Furthermore, a cold database backup was performed each weekend that involved an instance bounce. Thus, all cached SQL and execution plans were, of course, lost. Now, if you know what bind variable peeking is, you are likely to already be on to the true cause and effect chain here. If Mrs. Early Bird starts her Monday early, she executes the key statement first. When Oracle executes an SQL statement with bind variables the first time, it tries to peek into the values of the real variables in an attempt to do a better estimate of cardinalities based on the assumption that most of the following executions will be of the same nature. The application screen produced an execution plan using a nested-loop join with index range scan that performed very quickly for the set of bind variable values that application users tended to use all day long.

However, the statement executed with values from the historical report performed better with a full table scan and a hash join, because it involves rows from a significant part of the table. It was thus much faster and cheaper to perform a full scan rather than a nested-loop join, and the optimizer recognized that. The problem was that the bind variables values used by the report were unique and were used literally once a week—in preparations for that 9 AM Monday report. Unfortunately, that report, executed first in the week, set the tone for the rest of the users of that environment. On days when Mrs. Early Bird did not come in early, the execution plan for the statement would be set by the report, and all havoc broke loose with performance.

Heavy rains on Monday and performance problems on that particular system led to a perfect example of what is called nonsense correlation. The correlation could lead one to a solution, but only if one took care to avoid assuming a causal relationship.

■ **Note** Another example of nonsense correlation from the OakTable Network mailing list is how the World Cup made one SAP system with lots of remote users run very slowly. Apparently, a mind-boggling number of people use online streaming to watch World Cup football (yes, I mean soccer) matches, and it turns out that Internet throughput is still not unlimited in our universe.

Knowledge Is Power

Nothing helps in troubleshooting as much as knowledge of a problem domain and the technical products used in the system. For a database engineer, the problem domain means application design, business process, maintenance process (such as upgrade or backup), and so forth. Of course, the product we are talking about is Oracle Database, but often the technical stack includes several other products working together.

Broad and up-to-date knowledge is the key to success for a seasoned database administrator these days. Let's take something other than performance troubleshooting as an example. When troubleshooting a failed Oracle RMAN restore, it is crucial to understand how RMAN works with backup pieces and sets, how SCNs are tracked and why they are needed, how Oracle redo is generated and applied to the database during restore, and all other bells and whistles such as incremental restores and RESETLOGS incarnations. That level of knowledge and understanding comes from studying available materials, as well as experience.

Likewise, troubleshooting sporadic node reboots in an Oracle RAC cluster requires knowledge of cluster design, and it requires knowledge of components in Oracle Clusterware and how they operate. Successful troubleshooting of Oracle Data Guard requires understanding of the processes behind Oracle Grid Control configuration screens and wizards.

But it's not enough to know only core database technology. In the first example, in order to troubleshoot failing RMAN tape backups successfully, a DBA often needs a good working knowledge of tape management software. If hands-on knowledge isn't there, it helps to at least be capable of talking to the storage administration team in the terms they understand.

Understanding of storage technologies is crucial to designing a database environment that is scalable and reliable. A modern DBA need to know about the different RAID levels, how SAN arrays are connected via the SAN network, what the implications are of using advanced features such as snapshots and cloning, and more.

Understanding of the development tools and methods has always been crucial, and it's even more important these days. As time-to-market for products and solutions is decreasing more and more, DBAs have fewer and fewer opportunities to engage in the development life-cycle.

DBAs often have no time to learn the specifics of a particular environment. In the past, knowledge of Oracle Forms would cover a significant portion of what a DBA needed to know about development tools. Those days are long gone. These days, there are dozens of frameworks and languages used by developers. A savvy DBA will want to have at least general understanding of those frameworks and languages.

There are a number of ways to keep yourself updated on new technologies and learn how things work. Here are some to consider:

- Books are a traditional source of knowledge for Oracle DBA. These days more and more books are published, so readers need to do a bit of research to make sure a particular book is a reliable source of high-quality information. Be careful to base your decisions on the quality rather than the number of books published; quantity doesn't automatically translate into quality.

- The Internet has made it possible to access thousands of articles that people share via blogs, forums, email lists, and other social networks. Just as with books, but to the greater extent, be careful not to trust blindly everything written on the Internet. Always question what you read, even if it comes from a known expert in the field. This chapter, of course, is an exception.

- Experience is something that a seasoned DBA can never replace with books and other reading. Just as solders develop their skills in battle, DBAs acquire critical skills by managing real database environments. This is the chance to apply the theory in the real life.

- A personal playground is something every DBA should create for themselves. These days, every workstation or laptop is capable of running a minimal database configuration. Availability of virtualization software makes it even easier; on my laptop with 4 GB of memory and a dual-core CPU, I'm able to run up to three nodes in a mini-RAC cluster. Of course, when it comes to real workloads, nothing beats a dedicated lab environment, but you wouldn't believe how much you can learn on a small database environment installed on your laptop.

RTFM

One source of knowledge that I want to emphasize specifically is vendor documentation. Yes, I'm talking about Oracle documentation that is freely available with any recent Oracle database release. Reading vendor documentation is often referred as RTFM or "Read The Fine Manual" (though people argue what F exactly stands for).

The *Oracle Database Concepts Guide* has become my favorite book from Oracle's documentation set. It's a great starting point for learning the basic concepts of all database components and how they fit together. The Oracle Database product has become very complex in the past years, and it's become impossible to know in depth every feature and how it works, but every DBA should know where to start when it comes to something new. The *Oracle Database Concepts Guide* often serves as that starting point.

Oracle's *SQL Language Reference* is another guide that you should keep handy and review with every new database release. Its syntax diagrams and comments are priceless, and many times have clued me in to important features that I never knew existed.

The *Oracle Database Reference* is where you'll find information about all of the dynamic and static dictionary views, init.ora parameters, wait events, and other goodies. I have learned to consult the version of this manual from the latest release even when working with a previous version. That's because the *Oracle Database Reference* is often updated more slowly than the features themselves. You can sometimes glean precious information by looking at the documentation for the latest Oracle software release even if you are working with previous versions.

Finally, while Oracle Metalink (or My Oracle Support as it's called these days) is not part of the official documentation, every Oracle DBA should be able to navigate in support articles and know how to research Oracle Support notes and bug reports. Those often help to fill the blanks in the puzzle when standard documentation doesn't provide enough detail.

Oracle Database is a complex product. It's physically impossible for a single person to know all its bells and whistles and to have in-depth knowledge of each feature and area. Take Oracle XMLDB, Oracle Streams, and Oracle Spatial as examples. Unless you have worked with these features, you are unlikely to know in detail how they work. However, you do want to have a general idea of such features. Most importantly, you want an idea of where to go to learn more. Just knowing where to go can help you get up to speed relatively quickly in any area of Oracle Database.

Understand vs. Memorize

As I finished this chapter, Jared Still, a fellow OakTable Network member, pointed me to the excellent visual chart courtesy of Kathy Sierra from the Creating Passionate Users blog (visit `http://headrush.typepad.com/creating_passionate_users/2006/09/how_to_get_user.html`). Learning to understand saves you time in the long term and lets you make educated decisions as opposed to decisions powered by guesswork, which happens when you simply try to memorize (as in preparing for a certification exam).

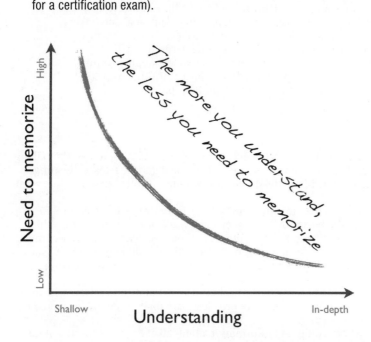

You want to read Oracle documentation to grasp the principles of Oracle Database and how it works. You should also learn where to look for particular details. You want to read Oracle Database Concepts guide in full, but you peek into references books on a demand basis.

You want to use Google to assist in your research and help understand a given problem, and why the problem happens. You don't want to use Google for ready-to-apply solutions; use it for understanding instead. You want to ask questions to understand why, before asking questions about what to do to fix something.

Facing the Unknown

Oracle Database is not only a complex product, it's also proprietary software. Oracle Corporation introduced significant instrumentation and provided lots of new documentation in the last decade, but there are still many blanks about how the product works, especially when it comes to the implementation of new features and of some advanced deployments that hit the boundaries of software and hardware. Whether it's because Oracle wants to keep some of its software secrets or because documentation and instrumentation are simply lagging, we always face situations that are somewhat unique and require deeper research into the software internals.

When I established the Battle Against Any Guess Party, a number of people argued that guesswork is the cruel reality with Oracle databases because sometimes we do hit the wall of the unknown. The argument is that at such point, there is nothing else left but to employ guesswork. Several times people have thrown out the refined term "educated guess." However, I would argue that even in these cases, or especially in these cases, we should be applying scientific techniques. Two good techniques are deduction and induction.

When we have general knowledge and apply it to the particular situation, we use deductive reasoning or deductive logic. Deduction is often known as a "top-down" method. It's easy to use when we have no gaps in our understanding. Deduction is often the path we take when we know a lot about the problem domain and can formulate a hypothesis that we can confirm or deny by observation (problem symptoms).

Inductive reasoning is often considered the opposite of deductive reasoning and represents a bottom-up approach. We start with particular observations, then recognize a pattern, and based on that pattern we form a hypothesis and a new general theory.

While these techniques are quite different, we can find ourselves using both at different stages as verification that our conclusions are correct. The more unknowns we face, the more we favor inductive reasoning when we need to come up with the generic theory while explaining a particular problem. However, when we form the theory via inductive logic, we often want to prove it with additional experiments, and that's when we enter into a deduction exercise.

When taking a deductive approach first, when applying known knowledge and principles, we often uncover some inconsistencies in the results that require us to review existing theories and formulate new hypothesis. This is when research reverts into inductive reasoning path.

Deduction and induction each have their place; they are both tools in your arsenal. The trick is to use the correct tool at the correct time.

Paradigm Shifts

The term *paradigm shift* was originally introduced by Thomas Kuhn in his book *The Structure of Scientific Revolutions* (University of Chicago Press, 3rd edition 1996). A paradigm is our perception of reality as we see it—our view of the world. Based on our previous experience, we interpret current observations and make seemingly logical conclusions. A paradigm shift is a sudden change in the point of view of how we see and interpret things.

Centuries ago, people used to think that Earth was the center of the universe. The realization that neither the Earth nor even the sun is the center of the universe is a typical paradigm shift. Another great example of a paradigm shift is Stephen Covey's story from *The 7 Habits of Highly Effective People* (Free Press, 2004). While traveling, he observed a quiet man with two sons running like headless chickens and behaving provocatively so as to irritate everyone around. When Covey finally asked the man why he didn't do something to control the kids, the answer followed "We just got back from the hospital where their mother died. I don't know how to handle it and I guess they don't either." This realization throws everything upside down and completely transforms one's perception of the situation.

One of the most revolutionary paradigm shifts that I personally had about Oracle Databases came from reading the book *Optimizing Oracle Performance* (O'Reilly, 2003) by Cary Millsap and Jeff Holt, fellow members of OakTable Network. That book is what shifted my paradigm of performance troubleshooting. Performance is all about time, so time is what you need to focus on and analyze. It is response time that matters. Now that I understand the idea, it seems so natural that I can't imagine why I ever believed in relying upon indirectly related counters to troubleshoot Oracle database performance problems.

As much as you want to use generally known principles and knowledge, do question these principles regularly even if the questioning seems crazy at the moment. Stepping away from deductive reasoning doesn't mean you are guessing as long as you realize what you are doing—maybe you are about to make the next paradigm shift! However, don't forget that thousands of times, you'll likely just be wrong.

Experience Is Danger

I hear very often that nothing helps in troubleshooting so much as years and years of real-world experience in the field. While this is generally true, experienced analysts tend to fall into a trap of quick guessing based on previous situations.

Top-notch DBAs sometimes have successfully used their gut feeling and intuition to lead them towards the right solutions quickly. However, intuition should never dictate a solution, because there is always a danger that the particular case could be in some way different from what has been experienced so far. I've been in such situations a few times, and I've observed a number of very smart and experienced DBAs falling into the same trap.

■ **Note** An example of this outside the database sphere is the trap I fell into with the neighbor boy's bicycle. (See the earlier sidebar "Another Cycling Example.") I made a quick assumption based upon my past experience. And that assumption was badly wrong. – Jonathan Gennick.

It's very easy to reach erroneous conclusions based on previous experience. Let me give you an example. Working a lot with Oracle Real Application Clusters (RAC), I learned pretty much all the common symptoms and causes for node evictions in an Oracle RAC cluster. I knew there are a few components that cause node eviction, and I could always quickly determine by running Oracle 10g Release 2 on Linux (let's be specific) that it's one of three Clusterware components that can evict a node: the `CSSD` daemon, the `OCLSOMON` daemon, and the `hangcheck-timer` module (which is actually part of the Linux operating system).

If I blindly follow my experience, I could easily miss that the Oracle 10.2.0.4 patchset on Linux introduced a new OPROCD daemon, which becomes responsible for suicidal self-evictions instead of hangcheck-timer. Furthermore, I might never think about the OCFS cluster filesystem that has eviction functionality as well.

The weirdest node eviction case I ever experienced would have been extremely difficult to find by relying purely on my experience. It was when one client had an infrastructure platform that had its own watchdogs for server health. When a server's watchdog failed, a server reset was initiated remotely by a central watchdog. God knows how far I would have gone assuming that such a node eviction represented one of the "standard" RAC evictions.

■ **Note** Another classical example of the danger of experience is troubleshooting CPU starvation. I know one very sharp DBA who was battling developers in his organization because they kept delivering application code that caused lots of excessive hard parsing, which in turn brought production database servers to their knees after almost every new application release. Going further, this DBA also identified that even soft parsing was causing a lot of grief when it came to scaling the applications further. From his experience, excessive parsing was the root cause of all cases of CPU starvation he'd seen recently on his databases. Naturally, his troubleshooting of an application release was always focused on identifying excessive parsing. However, when database size had grown and developers finally learned to avoid excessive parsing, the cause of CPU consumption moved toward excessive logical I/Os caused by very inefficient SQL statements. For some time, this DBA kept asking developers to reduce parsing more and more as CPU utilization was going through the roof. It took a while for him to realize that he'd fallen into the trap of his past experience.

We should use our experience to aid in scientific troubleshooting. We should never rely on ready-made solutions from past experience, but we can use that experience to take some shortcuts and save time and effort in analysis phase of a new problem. Our experience should help us narrow down the search for the root cause. We can't skip cause and effect analysis and, most importantly, validation of our conclusions.

Fixing the Root Cause?

We always talk about the root cause to fix. However, is it always crystal-clear what the root cause of a given problem actually is? Not really! There are always problems of the chicken-and-egg type.

Let's say we are troubleshooting a significant slowdown in application performance (online orders in the Internet book shop), including timeouts that happen regularly around lunch time. We've gone through the required troubleshooting and documented our conclusions:

- User activity is growing by 50 percent during the lunch-hour; that is, there are 50 percent more new orders during that time period.

- The number of online orders is growing steadily every month.

- The time spent on physical I/O contributes 90 percent to response time based on a performance profile we've built.

- Three SQL statements are responsible for about 90 percent of the I/O.

- Random single-block I/O time almost doubles during the lunch period, from 8 ms to 15 ms.

Can we identify the root cause from all these items?

On the surface, it seems clear that performance issues are caused by increased user activity. So would it be fair to attempt to decrease user activity and address the root cause in that way? Probably not, because it means sacrificing business growth and revenue from online orders. The business presumably wants the growth.

Perhaps, the root cause is the random I/O response time increase. If we dig further, we might realize that our I/O subsystem is working at the limit of its capacity, and that additional I/O activity simply cannot be handled without significant degradation in performance. We could also find out that there is a heavy batch running on another database that apparently uses the same physical disks on the same SAN. Is I/O capacity our root cause? Or could the root cause be bad scheduling for the batch? Does all this mean we need to scale I/O, or can we reschedule the batch job or separate the databases to different disks?

Don't forget about our three top SQL statements consuming 90 percent of I/O in the database. Perhaps the root cause is inefficient SQL that needs fixing. Or perhaps we require a heavy redesign of the data model to make that SQL scalable.

How do we choose what areas to improve without taking a guess? The answer is in the requirements—never lose sight of the business requirements. In this case, our requirement is to handle the current peak number of online orders. We might also have a requirement to be capable of handling three times the current order rate in one year as our business keeps growing.

The next factor is the cost and—often forgotten—common sense. If that heavy batch can be moved to another time, then moving it is probably the cheapest approach to a solution. If SQL tuning is not an option or requires a costly redesign of the underlying database, then adding I/O capacity could be easier at the moment. On the other hand, sustaining three times more traffic next year might change the equation, and redesigning the data model might end up being the most reasonable thing to do after all. In fact, it might be the only option, as otherwise the bottleneck could move from the I/O subsystem to contention in the database instance caused by inefficient SQL.

Whenever you meet a chicken-and-egg problem such as I've described, make sure you keep the requirements in mind. Think about the requirements and the cost, and apply common sense.

Best Practices and Myths

"Best practices" has become an extremely popular concept in recent years, and the way IT best practices are treated these days is very dangerous. Initially, the concept of best practices came around to save time and effort on a project. Best practices represent a way to reuse results from previous, similar engagements. Current application of best practices has changed radically as the term has come into vogue.

What are now called best practices used to be called "rules of thumb," or "industry standards," or "guidelines." They were valuable in the initial phase of a project to provide a reasonable starting point for analysis and design. Unfortunately, modern best practices are often treated as IT law—if your system doesn't comply, you are clearly violating that commonly accepted law.

Blindly implementing best practices is nothing different from guesswork; we are applying some past-proven solutions without measuring how they stand against our requirements, and without testing whether they bring us any closer to the targets we have. Industry has become so obsessed with best practices that we commonly see projects in which reviewing an environment for compliance with best practices is the ultimate goal.

Implementing and complying with best practices in the field is becoming an inherent part of an IT support engineer's job description. Just look at job postings for DBAs, or search for "DBA best practices" on any online job board.

So how do we put best practices to good use? The key is to understand best practices, how they work, and why each of them is applied. What problems is a best practice solving, and what are the side-effects? We can then map best practices to our environments and see whether any of them bring us closer to satisfying our requirements.

Best practices might be useful during the initial phases of the project to come up with the most reasonable initial configuration and design with the least efforts and costs. Solving existing problems by blindly implementing best practices is pure guesswork and is generally more expensive than focusing on the problem and walking a scientific troubleshooting path.

Here is a recent example from my company. One of the clients recently asked their DBA team to perform a health check on their new environment to see if it is compliant with best practices, and to understand why they have regular performance problems. It was a complex environment with Oracle E-Business Suite on Oracle RAC, and four areas of focus were identified. The client insisted on a best-practices review.

The team initiated two streams for this client. In the first stream, they reviewed configuration for compliance to best practices and documented all findings and the potential benefits of implementing missing best practices. None of those findings directly solved the performance problems of that client, according to our analysis.

In another parallel stream, one of my colleagues engaged the end-users and analyzed their problems. This engineer found very inefficient SQL. Apparently, the environment was customized heavily and that was done pretty sloppily, resulting in many layers of views.

The best-practices review stream took about 90 percent of the time, without getting us any closer to solving the client's most critical problem, regular performance issues. Implementing any of the best practices that the team identified would be nothing but pure guesswork. Possibly some of them could make a slight improvement, but guessing is still guessing.

The second danger of best practices is that they easily become myths. The technology keeps improving and issues addressed by certain best practices might not be relevant anymore in the next software version. A typical example of old guidelines (that is, best practices) is keeping checkpoint frequency low or using raw devices to get the best possible performance. The life-span of best practices is generally longer than their applicability time-frame. Inertia is part of human nature.

BattleAgainstAnyGuess.com

BattleAgainstAnyGuess.com is a web site I've created for everyone in the community to unite and stand against guess-based troubleshooting. You'll find stories, articles, and even the occasional video to help you in your efforts to take a rigorous and scientific approach to problem-solving.

Those of us who have signed up as members of the site lightheartedly refer to ourselves as the BAAG Party. We welcome you to join us. Join as a member. And if you have something to share, let me know that you wish to post it.

BattleAgainstAnyGuess.com can be a good reference whenever you see others guessing too much, or starting to ask guess-provoking questions. Every time you are about to guess the cause and solution to a problem, stop and think of the BAAG Party.

CHAPTER 2

■ ■ ■

A Partly Cloudy Future

by Jeremiah Wilton

What the hell is cloud computing?…I don't know what we would do differently in the light of cloud computing…other than change our ads.

—Larry Ellison

Regardless of his own relentless use of the terms *grid*, *real*, and *flashback* in ways that are less than exact, I can't really blame Oracle founder and CEO Larry Ellison for being irritated by the term *cloud computing*. Lately, you see it everywhere. Marketing departments, bloggers, and the industry press toss around the term without a clear understanding of what it is. The confusion among pundits is resulting in widespread public confusion over cloud computing. If we are to believe vendor behemoths Amazon.com, Google, Salesforce.com, Sun Microsystems, Oracle, and best of all, Microsoft, each possesses the one true *cloud* solution. Never mind that each is referring to completely dissimilar offerings.

Indeed, for aging and jaded IT professionals, the cloud computing hubbub has a familiar ring to it. It has all the hallmarks of yet another fad-driven buzzword, hyped by marketing people who don't understand what they are talking about. It seems to be just another in-vogue term bandied about by sales consultants, signifying no genuine deployable or applicable technology. The assertion that the cloud will change how companies and technology professionals do business is hard to believe when our industry leaders are still asking, "What the hell is cloud computing?"

In Larry's defense, he voices a sentiment shared by many in our field. Technology implementers know that high-tech fads have inflicted pain and resulted in real failed projects and wasted millions. Organizations have a long track record of designing system architectures based on buzzwords and PowerPoint slides instead of sound engineering.

Much of the confusion over cloud computing arises from the many and various forms that it takes as promoted by various vendors. It might help to start with what they all have in common.

What Is Cloud Computing?

Cloud computing is an umbrella term for a set of methods for delivering computing resources over networks. Most companies touting cloud solutions are referring to some kind of managed computing resource provided over a network that can be provisioned incrementally based on demand, and with which applications and tools can interact by using a uniform published web API. Generally (but not universally), the cost model is also incremental, enabling consumers of cloud technology to pay as they go and avoid large capital expenditures.

Arguably, the term *cloud* is a poor term for flexible managed services that can be provisioned on demand. Clouds in the sky come and go as they please. If computing resources came and went like clouds, life for IT professionals would be very difficult. Maybe this emerging computing model should be named for something IT professionals more commonly provision incrementally, like beer or pizza.

Cloud computing service offerings generally fall into three categories:

- Software as a service (SAAS)

- Platform as a service (PAAS)

- Infrastructure as a service (IAAS)

Software as a Service (SAAS)

SAAS is an easy concept to understand. In essence, a SAAS provider provides an application service and allows users, such as the general public, to use those applications. Web mail sites are the most common example of SAAS. Instead of running your own mail program on your personal computer, Google or Hotmail runs one for you and lets you access it via a web browser. There are many more complex examples of SAAS, including enterprise applications such as accounting and customer relationship management (CRM) tools.

Platform as a Service (PAAS)

A handful of providers offer a cloud service on which customers develop custom applications on hosted infrastructure by using a provided set of application building blocks. PAAS provides cloudlike flexibility in terms of incremental scaling, managed services, and reliability, but generally locks the customer into a proprietary application development environment. Some PAAS providers support widely used application development frameworks such as .NET. This allows you the freedom of either running your application on your own infrastructure or on the cloud. Others have proprietary and closed application development frameworks. After your enterprise is on board with a particular proprietary PAAS platform, you will be with that provider for the lifetime of the application. It reminds me of those old TV ads for the Roach Motel, where "roaches check in, but they don't check out." With proprietary PAAS platforms, applications check in but they never check out.

Infrastructure as a Service (IAAS)

If you have ever wished you could borrow someone's enterprise-class server and storage for a few days, run anything you want on it, and then give it back (and pay almost nothing), IAAS is a model you will appreciate. IAAS providers allow instant provisioning of virtual servers, storage, and other resources. The method for provisioning and managing these resources is generally a uniform published web API. Organizations needing temporary or long-term hosting infrastructure on short notice and at low cost can simply provision a server and reliable storage on the operating system of their choice and use it for whatever length of time they desire.

Who Are the Cloud Providers?

Judging by Google rankings in late 2009, a few companies seem to have successfully associated themselves with cloud computing. The following five are not all cloud computing providers in the strictest sense, but the list is useful for illustrating how cloud computing can mean different things to different companies.

- Sun Microsystems

- Salesforce.com

- Google

- Microsoft

- Amazon.com

These companies provide a wide variety of products that they market as cloud computing. By examining each of them, we can compare offerings, contrast, and focus on where Oracle fits in.

Sun

We can eliminate Sun immediately from our discussion, because it is not really a cloud provider. Sun's offering is called BLOOHP, which stands for *buy lots of our hardware, please.* Sun's idea is that you should buy massive numbers of their servers and storage. Then you will own your very own computing cloud. This may be appropriate if you are suddenly going to start a massive corporation from scratch, but for everyone else, it is the antithesis of cloud computing. Rather than saving resources by incrementally allocating resources professionally managed by others, Sun suggests you buy large amounts of equipment and hire many people to manage it.

Salesforce.com

If cloud computing market position were proportional to display size on the Oracle OpenWorld 2009 exhibition hall floor, Salesforce.com would have a cloud offering roughly 20 times the size of Amazon.com's. Indeed, Salesforce's SAAS CRM offerings are popular, but not massive on a scale even approaching that of Amazon. Firmly on the cloud bandwagon, Salesforce.com emphasizes the buzzword heavily in their marketing messages. Their PAAS offering, Force.com, is a development environment on which customers can build a variety of web-based applications. It is appropriately named, because once deployed on Force.com, an application is "forced" to remain there for its functional lifetime.

Google

Google is the hands-down leader in SAAS. Their offerings such as search, Gmail, calendar, groups, and documents are not only available to the general public, but also to organizations that want Google's simple, reliable web-based interface for their internal business operations. Google's enterprise mail, calendar, and document sharing can completely replace Microsoft's expensive PC-based Exchange and Office suites. With these services hosted by Google, organizations can save significantly on internal IT and support costs that have traditionally come along with Microsoft desktop productivity. Google also has a competitive PAAS offering called App Engine. Unlike Force.com, Google App Engine runs applications written in Java and Python. That means that there is no lock-in. You can move applications off Google at any time and host them yourself.

Microsoft

Microsoft's Windows Azure is a relatively new .NET PAAS service. It boasts low-maintenance pay-as-you-go .NET services and SQL services. Microsoft is late to the game but has a lot of financial resources at its disposal. For pure SQL Server and .NET environments, Azure could be a preferable option to hosting your own servers.

Amazon.com

Amazon Web Services (AWS) is the premier provider of infrastructure as a service. AWS's IAAS offering is referred to as the *Elastic Compute Cloud* (EC2). It allows you to instantly provision running virtual server hosts, storage, and a variety of other computing resources via Amazon's API. These servers run real operating systems such as Linux and Windows, to serve whatever applications you want. Currently, Amazon's offering is the only leading cloud service that can run Oracle. Amazon and Oracle have collaborated on certification, special software, operating system environments, and licensing. Some components of Amazon's offering blur the line between IAAS and SAAS. For instance, Amazon offers RDS, a cloud-based relational database service based on MySQL.

Running Oracle on Amazon's Cloud

Because AWS is the only leading cloud service capable of actually running an Oracle database, the remainder of this chapter focuses on how exactly to do that. AWS has several features, services, and components that help installation, performance, and security of a running Oracle service in the cloud. In order to make valid architecture decisions, a thorough understanding of Amazon's platform is essential.

Why would you want to use something like EC2 rather than your own servers? Well, maybe you wouldn't. This depends on what you want to do and what kind of resources you have. The pros and cons of using EC2 as an Oracle hosting solution can be complex. Here are just a few of the questions you must answer to your own satisfaction to help justify EC2 as an Oracle hosting solution:

- Is EC2's storage I/O performance adequate for my database?

- How reliable is my Internet connection?

- Will it cost less than my current or an alternate solution?

I use EC2 for my own Oracle-related research and development efforts, and as a sandbox for students who attend my Oracle classes. For R&D, it allows me to run as many or as few Oracle databases as I want at any time. I can get a server instantly that normally I would have to ask someone for or buy myself. Best of all, I can provision some fairly high-end hardware for short amounts of time, and pay only for what I use. I would not normally be able to afford a 26-CPU 64-bit server with 68GB of RAM. With EC2 I can provision a generous server like that for $2.40 per hour. If I don't need that degree of performance, I can provision a 4-CPU 64-bit server with 7.5GB of RAM (still enterprise class) for 40 cents per hour.

Each of my students creates and maintains a database that they maintain throughout the duration of a class. When they are not using it, they shut down their AWS server and pay only 15 cents per gigabyte each month for persistent storage where the database is kept. This is by far the most affordable way for my students to gain experience and hands-on skills with enterprise-class systems.

Beyond these temporary needs, Amazon tries to encourage permanent hosting on their platform with special pricing structures for such customers. They tout the ability to scale incrementally and the proven reliability of Amazon's platform among the advantages of this approach. The general public would never realize the many services that are hosted on AWS. Many Facebook apps, iPhone apps, parts of the infrastructure of Virgin Atlantic Airways, The Washington Post, Harvard Medical School, Second Life, Autodesk, and many others run on AWS.

But Is It Supported?

Amazon Web Services supports EC2 as a platform to run Oracle. Conversely, Oracle will support Oracle software running on AWS to the same degree that they support it on other non-Oracle virtualization platforms. According to Oracle, "Oracle fully supports deploying Oracle Database, Middleware, and Enterprise Manager products on the Amazon EC2 platform. However, it may be noted that Amazon EC2 is a virtualized environment and uses a virtualization engine that is not supported by Oracle. Users will therefore be directed to Amazon for any virtualization-related issues."[1]

Making the Cloud Concrete

At its simplest, AWS allows you to provision virtual hosts, called *instances*, on demand. As I stated earlier, this service is called the Elastic Compute Cloud (EC2). An EC2 instance is composed of a running virtual host with a specific amount of CPU and I/O capacity, a specific amount of memory (RAM), 32- or 64-bit architecture, and a specific amount of *ephemeral storage*. This is a set of virtual storage devices and a file system containing the operating system and other preinstalled software. You can read and write to this storage, but it is not persistent after the instance is terminated. In other words, if you store important data on the ephemeral storage, you will lose it when you terminate your EC2 instance. AWS also has persistent storage available, which I will discuss shortly. When you ask EC2 to start an instance, you must specify several parameters that control what the instance is like after it is running:

Amazon Machine Image (AMI): EC2 instances are fully functioning virtual hosts and as such, need an operating system to run. You may have a particular version of Ubuntu or Red Hat that you prefer, with all of your needed software installed and functioning. AWS allows you to build your favorite Linux or Windows host into a bootable image (AMI) for starting an EC2 instance. In addition, Amazon has an extensive library of prebuilt AMIs for Linux and Windows, including Oracle Enterprise Linux with Oracle Database software preinstalled.

AWS Region: Most cloud users want their servers to be running geographically close to where they are. As of Q4 2009, AWS offers two regions, the United States and Europe. When you run your instance on EC2, you specify the region in which you want it to run.

---

[1] Oracle in the Cloud Frequently Asked Questions, www.oracle.com/technology/tech/cloud/faq.html, accessed Nov. 2, 2009.

Security Group: Security groups on EC2 are a bit like firewall configurations. By default, EC2 allows no ingress on any TCP port to your instance from the public Internet. Security groups contain the exceptions to that rule. Typically, a Linux instance would be started with a security group that allows at least port 22 (SSH) access. As you need an instance to accept connections on other ports, such as 80 for HTTP or 1521 for the Oracle listener, you can add those ports to one of your instance's security groups. A security group can be used by any number of instances in your EC2 account.

Key Pair: In order to provide secure authentication via SSH, Amazon provides the ability for an SSH key to be preinstalled in the root account of any new Linux instance. When you create a key pair via one of the management tools, you download the private key to your local machine, and EC2 retains the public key. When starting instances, you specify the key-pair name. You then may log into the instance via SSH as root by specifying the local private key file.

Instance Type: As of Q4 2009, EC2 instances are available in many capacities, ranging from *small* to *quadruple extra large*. For the purposes of providing performance expectations for instances, Amazon has devised a compute power factor called the *EC2 Compute Unit*, roughly equivalent to one 1GHz 2007 Opteron or Xeon processor. Table 2-1 illustrates the different instance types available, and lends support to the idea that pizza is a better model than clouds for cloud computing.

Table 2-1. Instance Types and Available Resources

Instance Type	Memory	Compute Units	Virtual Cores	Ephemeral Storage	Architecture	I/O Performance
Small	1.7GB	1	1	160GB	32-bit	Moderate
Large	7.5GB	4	2	850GB	64-bit	High
Extra Large	15GB	8	4	1690GB	64-bit	High
High Mem. 2 × Extra Lg.	34.2GB	13	4	850GB	64-bit	High
High Mem. 4 × Extra Lg.	68.4GB	26	8	1,690GB	64-bit	High
High CPU Medium	1.7GB	5	2	350GB	32-bit	Moderate
High CPU Extra Large	7GB	20	8	1,690GB	64-bit	High

Availability Zone: Within each geographic region (United States, Europe), there are multiple availability zones, which Amazon states we should think of roughly as distinct data centers. If you were building a system in which you wanted services to run from separate data centers for the purposes of redundancy or availability, you could run them in distinct EC2 availability zones.

AWS also allows you to provision virtual storage and a variety of supporting services and features that make using the instances and storage easier and more secure. For example, when you need a Linux host, you ask AWS to start one for you. Then you ask AWS for some storage, which you attach to your instance and use like disks.

In this chapter, you will follow the steps to provision a host running Oracle 11*g* on Red Hat Enterprise Linux 5. As you follow the steps to accomplish this end, I will discuss the various options and features available, and how I arrived at the architecture choices I did.

Prerequisites

To use AWS, you need an account on Amazon.com. You can use your existing Amazon.com retail account, but you must also visit Amazon Web Services at `http://aws.amazon.com` and explicitly sign up for the various cloud services, such as EC2, that you intend to use.

How Do You Work This Thing?

All of the functions of managing AWS are controlled via either of two web services APIs: SOAP and Query. For example, when you ask AWS to start a virtual host (instance) for you, it could take the form of an HTTP query such as the following:

```
https://ec2.amazonaws.com/?Action=RunInstances&<parameters>
```

This will cause AWS to reply with XML containing the information on the instance just created. In practice, it is cumbersome to formulate by hand the precise web services requests and read the XML responses, so Amazon has built a number of tools and libraries to enable people and software to manage AWS resources.

AWS Management Console

For those who don't care to download, install, or write additional software to manage AWS resources, Amazon provides a web GUI that makes it simple to provision and manage instances, storage, and more (see Figure 2-1). The AWS management console can be found at `http://console.aws.amazon.com/ec2`. It boasts simplicity and ease of use. Users quickly discover a few odd quirks. As you navigate around the screens, you will discover that you must click Reload frequently to register changes in your environment. Because the screens appear to be dynamically generated, this is unintuitive. Another drawback to the console is that it operates on only one AWS account at a time. If you have multiple AWS accounts, you must log out and log back in to see other account resources.

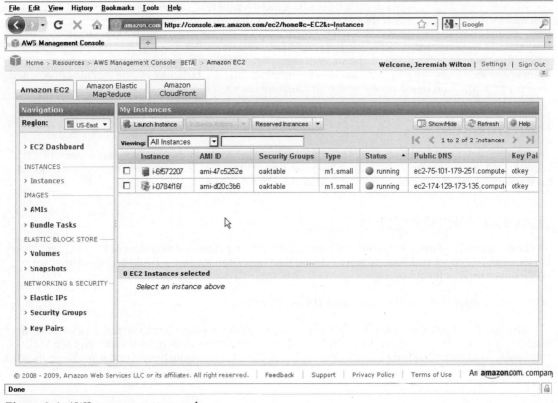

Figure 2-1. AWS management console

Elasticfox

A Firefox browser add-on called Elasticfox is probably the most popular GUI tool for managing AWS resources (see Figure 2-2). Both intuitive and fast, it makes AWS easy to use. It supports multiple accounts and almost all of AWS's many cloud features. It is developed and made available by Amazon.

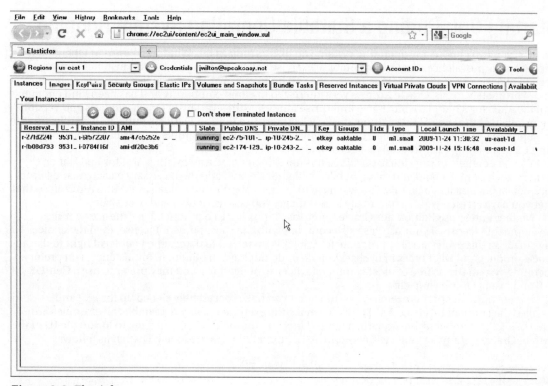

Figure 2-2. Elasticfox

Command-Line Tools

GUI tools are not suitable for tasks that must be repeatable, scripted, or logged. In addition, neither the AWS management console nor Elasticfox support all of the functions, options, and features available on AWS. For these more comprehensive requirements, Amazon provides a suite of command-line tools. The tools are Java based, so they can run on the command line of almost any system connected to the Internet. I run mine on a Mac.

The command-line tools are preinstalled on most of the AMIs provided by AWS. You can invoke these tools remotely from your own machine, or from the EC2 instance itself, to manage that instance or other cloud resources.

Perl/Java/Ruby Libraries

Although some repetitive AWS management tasks can simply be scripted to call external command-line tools, more-sophisticated software development requires libraries and classes for programming languages. Amazon provides libraries that are very easy to install and use for Perl, Java, and Ruby. These libraries expose the complete set of AWS features to software developers.

Starting Out: Getting a Suitable Operating System Running

On EC2, you can choose any operating system you like, as long as it is Windows, Linux, or OpenSolaris. Because of its prevalence, our Oracle database exercise will be on Linux. To get an instance started, we need to choose an Amazon Machine Image. We can build our own or use one that has already been built. Fortunately for us, Oracle Corp. is very interested in cloud computing and has been kind enough to provide AMIs for 32- and 64-bit Oracle Enterprise Linux 5, with a variety of Oracle editions and versions preinstalled. At the time of this writing, the Oracle Enterprise Edition 11*g* R2 is publicly available, but the latest prebuilt AMI has only Oracle 11.1.0.7 preinstalled. This is not a problem, because if you want to run 11.2 or anything else, you can just download it.

You do not have to run Oracle on OEL5. It is not difficult to use an existing AMI for Red Hat or CentOS, such as those built and made public by RightScale, and add the necessary packages and kernel parameters for Oracle. To do this, you will have to learn to bundle and upload an AMI to Amazon so that after you have created your Oracle-ready Linux image, you can use it over and over again.

Neither Enterprise Edition nor Oracle Enterprise Linux is a free product. I use these under the Development License. If your use case also complies with the Development License, then the choices I have made in this exercise are appropriate for you. It is up to you to determine your legal right to use an Oracle product and what types of licenses you do or do not have to obtain. If, for instance, you prefer an operating system that is free of most commercial license obligations, you may prefer to use a CentOS AMI and install Oracle yourself.

For the purposes of this exercise, I assume that you have successfully signed up for EC2 and installed the command-line EC2 API tools. To make the exercise reliably repeatable, all examples are given using the command-line tools in a Linux/Unix environment. First, you need to locate the ID of the AMI for Oracle Enterprise Linux with Enterprise Edition 11.1.0.7 preinstalled. Do that as follows:

```
$ ec2-describe-images --all | grep -i oracle | grep 11107
IMAGE  ami-47c5252e  oracle-corporation/database-ami/32-bit/oracle_11107_EE_32Bit-
  image.manifest.xml  725966715235  available  public  i386  machine  aki-c5e703ac
  ari-c2e703ab
IMAGE  ami-3dc62654  oracle-corporation/database-ami/32-bit/oracle_11107_SE_SE1_32
  Bit-image.manifest.xml  725966715235  available  public  i386  machine
  aki-c5e703ac  ari-c2e703ab
IMAGE  ami-c3e808aa  oracle-corporation/database-ami/64-bit/oracle_11107_EE_64Bit-
  image.manifest.xml  725966715235  available  public  x86_64  machine
  aki-0d9f7b64  ari-369f7b5f
IMAGE  ami-67ea0a0e  oracle-corporation/database-ami/64-bit/oracle_11107_SE_SE1_64
  Bit-image.manifest.xml  725966715235  available  public  x86_64  machine
  aki-0d9f7b64  ari-369f7b5f
```

Here you see four images, two (32- and 64-bit) for 11.1.0.7 Standard Edition One, and two for Enterprise Edition. Because we will be experimenting with Enterprise Edition, we will select AMI ID ami-c3e808aa.

Before you can start an instance, you need a security group so that you can open at least port 22 to allow access to the server. You also need a key pair so that you can authenticate as root on the server via SSH. If you already have a suitable security group and key pair in your EC2 account, you can use those. Otherwise, create them, and open TCP port 22 for access by all IP addresses. For better security, you may want to restrict access to your own local IP address or subnet. In that case, you would specify that IP address or subnet in place of 0.0.0.0/0. The following example shows how to create our security group:

```
$ ec2-add-group oaktable -d 'Security group for 42 clowns'
GROUP  oaktable  Security group for 42 clowns

$ec2-authorize oaktable -P tcp -p 22 -s0.0.0.0/0
GROUP  oaktable
PERMISSION  oaktable  ALLOWS  tcp  22  22  FROM  CIDR  0.0.0.0/0

$ ec2-add-keypair otkey
KEYPAIR  otkey  09:13:b6:d0:34:b8:b0:28:57:fd:c6:2a:e4:b5:ea:6b:d6:3e:35:4c
-----BEGIN RSA PRIVATE KEY-----
MIIEogIBAAKCAQEAmAsfDtQ6O5nVWMkRbndQNM9VvKMgVdYVZCaStl4FDiinJEUXTHb2HDlgeL
…
Q6rOYtCmqHiBdvsngcCKKEKGQhkddxyd6+oRsQ8RT9u8egCppHTwNlp8U9KNdzxoDIO=
-----END RSA PRIVATE KEY-----
```

The ec2-add-keypair command displays the private-key component of the key pair. You then copy and save everything from the BEGIN… line through the END… line into a private-key file with permissions set to 600. If you have mad shell skills, you can write the private key directly to a file. For example:

```
$ ec2-add-keypair otkey | grep -A 100 BEGIN > id-otkey
$ chmod 600 id-otkey
```

Now you are ready to start one *large* EC2 instance with the oaktable security group and the otkey key pair. I chose large because it is the least expensive 64-bit instance available, and I want to run Oracle in a production-like environment.

```
$ ec2-run-instances ami-c3e808aa -n 1 -g oaktable -k otkey -t m1.large
RESERVATION  r-f43ec29c  953101432481  oaktable
INSTANCE  i-3ca42654  ami-c3e808aa  pending  otkey  0  m1.large  2009-10-28
  T23:06:52+0000  us-east-1b  aki-0d9f7b64  ari-369f7b5f  monitoring-disabled
```

The output indicates that EC2 is starting an instance. The instance ID is i-3ca42654. We did not specify an availability zone, so EC2 chose us-east-1b for us. The current status is *pending*, which means it is starting up. The instance will take up to 15 minutes to start. Most of this time is spent copying the AMI to the ephemeral storage. There are other options for booting an instance, including booting from a persistent storage volume, that eliminate the time spent performing the copy.

To determine whether the instance is up, you can query EC2 for the status. Do that by issuing the ec2-describe-instances command as follows:

```
$ ec2-describe-instances i-3ca42654
RESERVATION  r-f43ec29c  953101432481  oaktable
INSTANCE  i-3ca42654  ami-c3e808aa  ec2-174-129-59-250.compute-1.amazonaws.com
  domU-12-31-39-00-16-02.compute-1.internal  running  otkey  0m1.large2009-10-28
  T23:06:52+0000  us-east-1b  aki-0d9f7b64  ari-369f7b5f  monitoring-disabled
```

The output tells us the instance is up (running) and that the address of the server is ec2-174-129-59-250.compute-1.amazonaws.com. You can connect directly to that address, but it is not permanent. It is available only for the lifetime of your instance. You can allocate a permanent IP address to represent a particular service (such as an Oracle database), and associate it with any instance. If that instance is terminated and replaced by a new instance, you can associate the IP address with the new instance. This service is called Elastic IP. Allocate one for our instance as follows:

```
$ ec2-allocate-address
ADDRESS   75.101.164.116

$ ec2-associate-address 75.101.164.116 -i i-3ca42654
ADDRESS   75.101.164.116   i-3ca42654
```

Now it is time to try connecting to our server:

```
$ ssh -i id-otkey root@75.101.164.116
Last login: Wed Aug 19 16:26:44 2009 from 148.87.1.171
=========================================================================
 Oracle Database 11g Release 1 (11.1.0.7) Enterprise Edition 64 bit AMI
=========================================================================
                      Terms of Use
...
```

At this point, you have a functioning server ready to run Oracle. On first login, the Oracle-built AMIs will ask you to agree to their Terms of Service and will ask whether you want to create a new database. We will be setting up Oracle Automatic Storage Management (ASM) and Oracle's Linux libraries for ASM (ASMLib) first, so don't allow the script to create a database yet. The next steps will be to add storage.

It is important to note that this server is on the public Internet. Although EC2 restricts the access to the ports and subnets specified in your security group, a higher level of protection is available. EC2 allows you to connect your instances to your local internal network via a virtual private network (VPN), using a feature called *Virtual Private Cloud* (VPC). VPC is likely the only acceptable security model for many enterprise-class customers moving their internal IT systems to EC2.

With VPC, your EC2 cloud resources appear as though they are on your internal network. For most users, cloud systems would be indistinguishable from internally hosted systems.

Persistent Storage

The devices and file systems you get with a new EC2 instance are ephemeral. They disappear and release all data when the instance terminates. This vanishing quality makes it downright poor storage for databases, if you prefer keeping your data. For reliable, persistent storage, AWS provides two services: Simple Storage Service (S3) and Elastic Block Storage (EBS).

Simple Storage Service (S3)

AWS's oldest cloud service is S3, the Simple Storage Service. This inexpensive data storage service allows you to write and read files up to 5GB in size via HTTP. Amazon uses the terms *bucket* and *object* to describe data stored in S3. A bucket is analogous to a top-level directory, and an object is essentially a file.

S3 data is replicated three ways within a geographic region, making it extremely reliable. It is secure, requiring authentication to access data. Depending on the use case, you can also make S3 objects available to the public.

Although third-party software exists that can present S3 to Linux as a mounted file system, we do not store live Oracle data files and file systems on S3. It is used to store AMIs, offline data such as backups, and other low-priority data. S3 is the cheapest place you can store your data on the Amazon cloud.

S3 is available to machines both inside and outside EC2. For instance, many people back up their personal computers to S3 by using third-party backup tools such as Jungle Disk. Access to S3 from inside EC2 is naturally very fast, making it a useful destination for EC2 file system and Oracle backups. Oracle even provides the Oracle Secure Backup Cloud Module, a media management layer (MML) for Recovery Manager to back up directly to Amazon S3 via the SBT interface.

Just as with EC2, there is a very useful Firefox add-on for managing and interacting with S3. S3Fox presents buckets and objects in a familiar directory and file format and allows drag-and-drop upload and download from S3.

Elastic Block Storage (EBS)

EBS is the primary high-performance persistent storage method for EC2 instances. EBS allows you to create block volumes from 1GB to 1TB and present them to your instances as devices. In Linux, they appear as SCSI devices (`/dev/sdf`, `/dev/sdg`, and so forth). You can do anything with these devices that you can do with any Linux storage device. You can partition them, stripe them with Linux software RAID, present them to a logical volume manager (LVM), format them as file systems, or present them to ASM with or without ASMLib.

EBS volumes are replicated within the same EC2 availability zone (that is, data center) for availability and durability. Volumes can be detached from one instance and attached to another seamlessly, but you can attach volumes only to instances within the same availability zone. You can also attach a volume to only one instance at a time. Therefore, as of Q4 2009, Real Application Clusters (RAC) are not supported on EC2 (which doesn't mean they are an impossibility).

Amazon provides a very useful capability for EBS volumes that allows you to snapshot them to S3. You can subsequently create new volumes from these snapshots. I use snapshots to store my installed, ready-to-run Oracle versions.

EBS Performance for Oracle

I/O performance is one of the limiting factors to scaling Oracle on EC2. This doesn't mean that I/O performance is poor. It is probably better than required by 90 percent of applications. However, this limiting factor is one that you must confront before deploying an application on EC2.

Remember that AWS performance capabilities and features are always improving. So I/O results that I measured at the time of this writing may not be reflective of capabilities at the time you are reading this. When you are considering your own deployment, first thoroughly review the available I/O options, test them with an I/O load-testing tool, and then examine your existing AWR data to determine whether your application's I/O needs are within EC2's capabilities. The AWR view DBA_HIST_IOSTAT_FILETYPE can provide historical information on peak I/O rates for an existing application.

Because EC2 presents EBS volumes to an instance as block devices, you can manage your EC2 storage in whatever way best suits your application. File systems, logical volume managers, ASM, and raw devices are all possible. The standard file system on Linux is EXT3, which includes journaling and a cache. Whether a file system cache is a benefit for Oracle depends on the I/O intensiveness of the application and degree of concurrency. In load testing against noncaching solutions such as Oracle Cluster File System (OCFS) and ASM, the usefulness of file system caching decreased as concurrency and transaction rates increased.[2] ASM also offers many features around performance and flexibility, such as volume migration and rebalancing, that are not present in most file systems and volume managers. For these reasons and because of the prevalence of ASM as an Oracle storage option, our exercise will demonstrate deploying Oracle storage on ASM.

As currently architected, EBS volumes are essentially network-attached storage and behave much like iSCSI initiated devices. That means the performance of EBS storage is limited by the capabilities of the network interface. There is a limited set of measures you can take to maximize Oracle's use of these resources.

The I/O (network) capacities of the various instance types (small, large) are different from one another. Amazon lists the I/O performance of a small instance as "moderate" while a large instance is "high." To test the capabilities of the high-performance I/O option, I ran a series of tests using Oracle's ORION tool. ORION is an I/O load-testing package that simulates a broad range of I/O that would be typical from an Oracle database. My results showed that striping across five EBS volumes provided up to 600 8KB IOPS, a six-fold benefit over a single EBS volume (see Figure 2-3). Because of these results, I use some degree of ASM striping across EBS volumes as a standard for deploying Oracle on EC2.

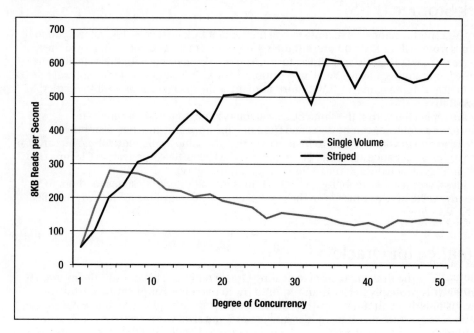

Figure 2-3. 8KB read performance under load

---

[2] "Linux Filesystem Performance Comparison for OLTP: An Oracle White Paper," January, 2004, http://otn.oracle.com/tech/linux/pdf/Linux-FS-Performance-Comparison.pdf.

Attaching and Configuring EBS Storage

EC2 instances can attach only EBS volumes that are in their same availability zone. Because our instance was created in zone us-east-1b, we will create our EBS volumes there too (-z argument). We can run these commands from our local machine, as we did with the first exercise, or from the EC2 instance itself. Here we create five volumes of size 20G (-s argument):

```
$ ec2-create-volume -s 20 -z us-east-1b
VOLUME    vol-31de2058    20    us-east-1b    creating    2009-10-24T23:27:41+0000
VOLUME    vol-2835c941    20    us-east-1b    creating    2009-10-24T23:27:51+0000
VOLUME    vol-f7c23d9e    20    us-east-1b    creating    2009-10-24T23:28:01+0000
VOLUME    vol-2a35c943    20    us-east-1b    creating    2009-10-24T23:28:11+0000
VOLUME    vol-2c35c945    20    us-east-1b    creating    2009-10-24T23:28:21+0000
```

Now we attach the storage to our instance as devices:

```
$ ec2-attach-volume vol-31de2058 -i i-24d1614c -d /dev/sdmsdh
ATTACHMENT   vol-31de2058   i-24d1614c   /dev/sdh   attaching   2009-10-24T23:35:12+0000
$ ec2-attach-volume vol-2835c941 -i i-24d1614c -d /dev/sdi
ATTACHMENT   vol-2835c941   i-24d1614c   /dev/sdi   attaching   2009-10-24T23:35:31+0000
$ ec2-attach-volume vol-f7c23d9e -i i-24d1614c -d /dev/sdj
ATTACHMENT   vol-f7c23d9e   i-24d1614c   /dev/sdj   attaching   2009-10-24T23:35:47+0000
$ ec2-attach-volume vol-2a35c943 -i i-24d1614c -d /dev/sdk
ATTACHMENT   vol-2a35c943   i-24d1614c   /dev/sdk   attaching   2009-10-24T23:35:58+0000
$ ec2-attach-volume vol-2c35c945 -i i-24d1614c -d /dev/sdl
ATTACHMENT   vol-2c35c945   i-24d1614c   /dev/sdl   attaching   2009-10-24T23:36:10+0000
```

On the instance, we can see the devices:

```
# ls -l /dev/sd?
brw-r----- 1 root disk 8, 112 Oct 24 23:35 /dev/sdh
brw-r----- 1 root disk 8, 128 Oct 24 23:35 /dev/sdi
brw-r----- 1 root disk 8, 144 Oct 24 23:35 /dev/sdj
brw-r----- 1 root disk 8, 160 Oct 24 23:35 /dev/sdk
brw-r----- 1 root disk 8, 176 Oct 24 23:36 /dev/sdl
```

Each of these volumes must be partitioned with fdisk in order to be usable to ASMLib. However, to use ASM on Linux, you do not need to use ASMLib. Just as in non-cloud deployments, you do not need ASMLib if you already have a reliable way to attach storage to the correct Linux device, and set permissions to be owned by the Oracle Linux user. To prepare a volume using ASMLib, the procedure would be as follows:

```
$ fdisk /dev/sdh
Command (m for help): n
Command action
   e   extended
   p   primary partition (1-4)
p
Partition number (1-4): 1
First cylinder (1-2610, default 1): 1
Last cylinder or +size or +sizeM or +sizeK (1-2610, default 2610): 2610
```

```
Command (m for help): w
The partition table has been altered!
Calling ioctl() to re-read partition table.
Syncing disks.

$ /etc/init.d/oracleasm createdisk E01 /dev/sdh1
```

To prepare a volume without using ASMLib, use the following:

```
$ chown oracle:oinstall /dev/sdh
```

With the volumes ready, you can start the ASM instance and create a disk group using the volumes you have attached. Because EBS is already redundant within an availability zone, I recommend specifying external redundancy when creating the disk groups. From this point forward, the creation of an ASM instance and a database are not significantly different from any other Linux server.

Persistence Approaches

With all the work of configuring storage complete, it is disturbing to realize that we have not addressed the potential impact of simply halting the server, which will result in the destruction of all ephemeral storage. Although the database itself is stored in persistent EBS volumes, we have several pieces of data stored in ephemeral storage that could hamper us restarting the Oracle services if they were lost. Among the data we would lose along with the ephemeral storage are the following:

- /etc/oratab
- $ORACLE_HOME/dbs/init<sid>.ora, spfile<sid>
- Mapping of EBS volume ID to Linux device (/dev/sd<x>)

In order for these items to survive instance shutdown, we need some kind of persistent way of storing them. EC2 users have developed several approaches over the years, and Amazon has responded by adding important features to EC2 that make persistence simpler.

Method A: Generic AMI and EBS File System

If we are using a generic AMI like the Oracle-built ones, we can store oratab and (s)pfiles on an EBS volume with a file system. Every time we start an EC2 instance, before we start any Oracle services, we add symbolic links under /etc/ and $ORACLE_HOME/dbs/ pointing to the persistent versions of these files on the EBS file system. This is a manual approach that requires someone to decide what an instance is going to be used for, attach the appropriate EBS volume, mount the file system, and create the symbolic links. This can be automated by using scripts.

For EBS volumes, there must be some way to attach the right volumes to the right instance. Also, each volume needs to appear as the correct Linux device, so that file systems and ASM disks show up as the same devices (/dev/sd<x>), as originally configured. With a generic AMI, we must store this data externally. I have sometimes used Amazon's SimpleDB service to store data on EBS volume attach order. This has the added advantage of allowing the attach operations for a given instance to be scripted.

Method B: Custom AMI

One of the nice features of EC2 is the ability to bundle your own AMI from a running instance. This means that you can build a custom AMI for each instance you use for Oracle on EC2. With this method, you completely set up a database and ASM instance, and then bundle and upload the instance into a bootable AMI. From that point forward, you boot from the custom AMI whenever you start that particular database host. This preserves the state of the oratab and Oracle parameter files, but does not provide a complete solution for EBS volume attach order.

To correctly attach the EBS volumes as devices, you can write an init script that attaches the volumes. The script can call the command-line utilities such as ec2-attach-volume, or it can use one of the programming libraries such as the Perl modules. Install the script in /etc/init.d/ and link to it from the appropriate /etc/rc<n>.d/ directories. The links should be numbered to cause the attach script to be invoked during boot before the file systems are mounted.

Method C: Boot from EBS

For the first two years or so that EC2 has been available, users have been employing a trick that allows them to boot a minimal Linux AMI that invokes pivot_boot during init and attaches and boots off an EBS volume rather than the ephemeral storage. This method was pioneered by several EC2 forum participants, and popularized by Shlomo Swidler in his blog clouddevelopertips.blogspot.com.

Booting from an EBS volume instead of an AMI has many advantages. The copy time from S3 to ephemeral storage is eliminated, resulting in instances that boot much faster. Configuration changes such as new O/S packages, software, init scripts for EBS boot order, and files like oratab and (s)pfiles remain on a persistent bootable volume, and eliminate the tedious and repetitive process of rebundling an AMI. Essentially, with an EBS volume as the root disk, an EC2 server lives a normal life like a physical server in the real world.

The pivot_boot approach is a bit of a hack, and EC2 users have been lobbying Amazon heavily for an EC2 feature to provide the ability to boot from EBS. Many believe that this feature is likely to be available before this book's publication date.

Oracle Backup on EC2: The OSB Cloud Module

Tape backup has been the dominant backup paradigm for customers hosting Oracle for some time. A shift in thinking is needed to see how hosting production Oracle services on EC2 is safe and reliable, despite there being no exact equivalent of tape backup. Both Oracle and Amazon intend for cloud-deployed Oracle databases to be backed up to S3, the Simple Storage Service. To this end, Oracle has provided the *Oracle Secure Backup Cloud Module*, an MML for Oracle Recovery Manager. In addition to backups of EC2-hosted databases, the OSB cloud module can be used to back up conventionally hosted databases to S3.

MMLs such as Symantec's Veritas NetBackup and EMC NetWorker give RMAN the ability to back up to tape libraries via the SBT interface. Similarly, the OSB cloud module allows RMAN to back up to S3 as though it were a tape library. Because S3 is geographically replicated and inexpensive, it is well suited as a substitute for tape backups and vaulting.

Oracle backups on EC2 can be made directly to S3, or make use of disk backups. On EC2, disk backups would be to an EBS-based file system or ASM storage. Using a combination of the Flash Recovery Area (db_recovery_file_dest) and RMAN, backup optimization can minimize the size of subsequent Flash Recovery Area backups to S3 storage. As with all backups, a solution using S3 and the OSB cloud module should be thoroughly tested for both functionality and time to recovery (TTR).

33

Especially for systems hosted outside the Amazon cloud, TTR for backups stored on S3 may be unacceptably long.

The OSB cloud module is available from the Oracle Cloud Computing Center at `www.oracle.com/technology/tech/cloud`. It is a licensed option, requiring one license per concurrently used SBT channel.

Summary

Although it is true that *cloud computing* as a term suffers from overuse and abuse, there are real platforms that are of note and importance for Oracle and other database technology professionals. Amazon Web Services, above all, provides a real platform for hosting a wide range of Oracle services. Cloud computing promotes flexibility in infrastructure deployment and design. New ideas are easy to execute, because EC2 allows you to build enterprise-class systems with no capital outlay and miniscule ongoing costs.

To fully embrace cloud computing, we must make changes to our conventional approaches to hosting, infrastructure, and storage. As Amazon and the other cloud providers broaden and improve their offerings, current roadblocks such as I/O performance, lack of shared storage, and geography will fall. Then, maybe Larry Ellison will see how Oracle can do more to embrace this emerging architecture than changing their ads.

■ ■ ■

CHAPTER 3

Developing a Performance Methodology

by Connie Green, with Graham Wood and Uri Shaft

We believe that performance is best managed systematically and methodically. Too frequently, people approach performance management by using what might be called the *Keystone Kops Method*. Everything is calm until a problem occurs. And then much energy is expended in trying this and trying that, causing chaos, and only infrequently is an acceptable solution found in a timely manner. Chaos is avoidable, as is stress. We wrote this chapter to lay out a calmer, more systematic approach to performance. We want you to be able to hone in on the cause of a problem by using a repeatable process. Most importantly, we want you to be home by dinnertime.

What Is Performance?

Performance is a measure of the responsiveness of a system. A performance problem by definition is a lack of response within an expected time frame. So performance is *always* about time—for example, how long a user waits for a response after saving a change, how long a report takes to complete, or how long data loads take to process.

Therefore, it makes sense that the common currency of performance is time itself, however it is measured. A common currency makes it easier to prioritize the resolution of one problem compared to another. For example, it is logical to attempt to first rectify the problem that is inflicting the biggest delay. Enacting a performance improvement means doing the same work in less time.

The Early Days

In the early days of Oracle, performance statistics were sparse and there were few ways to tweak the system. The available statistics were counter-based and measured the number of times a certain action was performed—the implication being that if you're doing something a lot, such as disk I/O, it may be a candidate for tuning. The major limitation with this method was that some operations consume significantly more resources than others, so there was no way to know which "problem" was more important (or if there was a problem at all). Indeed, not all increments of a single counter represent the same resource usage. For example, a buffer get for a row access via `rowID` uses much less CPU than a buffer get applying many filters to all rows in a block as part of a table scan; both count as a buffer get.

The next major tuning enhancement occurred in Oracle 7, with the addition of more counter-based performance views, and notably the introduction of the first time-based statistics via the wait interface (in views such as V$SESSION_WAIT and V$SYSTEM_EVENT and V$LATCH). These views showed how long sessions waited for specific resources, allowing the method to focus on reducing the *wait time* in the system. Whichever wait event composed the majority of the wait time dictated where tuning was needed. For example, if there was a lot of wait time for I/O-related wait events, it could be that SQL was consuming a lot of resources. The response was to tune in this specific order: SQL, memory, I/O, contention, sorts, freelists, and checkpoints! This "method" originated from a benchmark of a small application and was not applicable to general use. Note that the application and data design was not included as a part of this tuning method.

There weren't any statistics to measure the CPU utilization of SQL statements, so the SQL statistic BUFFER_GETS was used as a proxy or estimate for CPU utilization (the more buffer gets, the larger the CPU utilization), and PHYSICAL_READS was used to as a proxy for I/O utilization.

The limitations of counter-based statistics and ratios (such as the buffer cache hit ratio) were recognized, even in early Oracle releases, and so the emphasis on using these statistics as definitive diagnostics was significantly reduced. Instead, each new subsequent Oracle server release enhanced the wait and CPU timing data available.

Time-Based Performance Analysis

The most important advance in instrumentation came in Oracle 10g, which introduced significant changes in order to support automated performance diagnosis via the Automated Database Diagnostic Monitor (ADDM). These additions included the Time Model data and Active Session History (ASH), a record of sessions working in the database sampled every second. Time was captured for CPU utilization and waits at many levels, including instance-wide, drilling down to dimensions such as SQL, module, and server operation type (for example, parse). This data made it easier to determine what was consuming resources in the database and to quantitatively measure the effects of tuning.

Performance diagnosis and tuning is now heavily reliant on *time-based* data. Counters are still used in certain situations, such as to calculate average response times for an operation (this is done by dividing the total time for an operation by the count of occurrences). Counters are also used when no alternative time-based data is available—for example, by kernel development staff when attempting to diagnose certain types of defects.

Performance Strategy

Many believe that developing and attaining a robust performance strategy is unattainable, either because of time constraints or perceived complexity. This is not the case. It doesn't take much time to configure the minimum data capture and put in place simple procedures to start on the road to developing an excellent performance method; having the basics in place will go a long way when something goes wrong. Similarly, although computer software and hardware environments are becoming more complex, the high-level method for investigating and resolving reactive performance problems remains constant across Oracle releases, and is in fact valid in all disciplines that require a rigorous problem-solving strategy.

Developing a performance methodology and reactive performance tuning requires being organized and responding in a logical manner. You must know what data to gather and how long it is retained. Problem solving requires thinking a problem through by using common sense and looking at all evidence provided, including the performance data available, variables such as configuration changes, and even hearsay. This must be done without preconceptions of what may or may not be causing a particular problem, or indeed, what the actual problem may be. The procedure is systematic and the results quantifiable.

Unfortunately, myths and legends often are exchanged on bulletin boards or similar forums, which may lure you away from such a systematic approach. Instead of matching problem to symptom and using rigorous (and non-glamorous) methods for solving problems, the advice proffered is often dangerous, and includes trying out undocumented underscore (_) parameters, fiddling with configuration options that in 99 percent of cases should not be changed, and other black magic. This type of method often promises a "silver bullet" solution, whereby one quick fix resolves the problem. In some unfortunate cases, applying silver-bullet advice has made the situation significantly worse. Remember, silver bullets very infrequently fix the problem, but they often make it easy to shoot yourself in the foot.

This chapter intends to debunk these mysteries, instead showing how any DBA can start on the road to excellent performance, and look extremely competent and confident while doing so. We will briefly cover design and development, and concentrate mainly on performance methods and tuning activities post-production, when unfortunately, most tuning occurs.

Design and Development

You probably know that the most effective way to write a consistent and well-performing application is to build in performance during application design and development. The opportunities available to improve performance reduce considerably as the application moves to quality assurance (QA) and then reaches production. As the potential benefit reduces, the cost of making improvements increases significantly.

Unfortunately, it is not uncommon to get kick-back from the development organization when attempting to recommend changes needed to ensure solid performance. The following, which was said to a performance advisor making design recommendations during the development phase, demonstrates admirably:

You're picking holes in it before we've even built it!

— A. Developer

This is exactly when design changes need to be made—during design and development, which is much simpler and faster than making changes in production. In production, the cost is measured not only in terms of the number of development hours required to correct the problem, but also in the loss of productivity and service to the end user. That is assuming it is possible to implement a redesign without loss of data. Tweaking the database post-production can provide improvements, but nothing as significant as a good initial design.

Building in performance may be facilitated by prototyping if there is a particularly tricky part of the application. For example, when there are extremely high data volumes or requirements for subsecond response time, prototyping can be a great method to shake out and fix problems during the design phase.

Common Design Pitfalls

A number of common mistakes are made during design and coding, and these can be on all levels, from very high-level architectural issues, down to individual features' implementation and usage. Watch for these mistakes and try to avoid them whenever possible:

Lack of database design: Designing a database that is capable of running efficiently with high throughput and fast performance is not the same as designing the objects used in the application server tier. It is necessary to design both the objects and the database; one is not a replacement for the other. For example, some developers erroneously assume that because XML is self-describing, they don't need to design the database schema. Invariably for large systems, this results in danger dead ahead. Of course in these days of agile development, by the time the performance problems surface in production, the development team has already been redeployed onto other projects, which only makes resolving the problem harder.

Developing a database-agnostic application: *Database agnostic* often means using the lowest-common-denominator features. Such applications normally ignore the extensive features Oracle has incorporated over many releases to aid or improve scalability. The result is bad performance and complaints that Oracle doesn't scale. If the application will be used by a large user population, will have strict response time requirements, must process a large number of transactions, or perform extensive reporting analysis, then significant thought must be given to the database features best leveraged to support the requirements.

Complex data design: Sometimes we are forced to make a design more complex than we would like. However, doing so from the outset, without a clear understanding of how the database server functions, indicates that design reconsideration is needed.

Flexible design: Decisions that result in a "flexible" or "generic" design that allows for future features that may or may not be implemented, often result in a significant performance cost.

The misuse and overuse of global unique identifiers (GUIDs): The concept of a global unique identifier is to have an identifier that can be guaranteed to be unique—globally. The problem is that GUIDs are misused as unique keys, instead of using a representative unique (or primary) key. Using GUIDs in this way results in the inadvertent insertion of duplicate data and joining more tables.

Designing without regard to multirow performance: An extreme example is storing data in long, narrow tables using name-value pairs. The application must do multiple queries to the same table to retrieve data, which would better be served by being stored in one row. The unfortunate side effect is poor performance.

Unnecessary feature usage: Sometimes new database features are used because they are cool, and because they exist, rather than because they are necessary to optimal application function.

Not using standard, proven database features: Examples include writing your own locking code or writing home-grown sequence-generation code, rather than using those inherent in the database.

■ **Tip** Don't assume faster hardware will compensate for not building performance into the application design. Optimistic development staff often assume that future hardware innovation will cope with any "designed" performance problems. Solutions such as upgrading hardware may temporarily provide some headroom. However, some scalability issues can be made worse by upgrading hardware. For example, adding more CPUs to a system that is experiencing high CPU utilization and significant latch contention (for example, due to logon storms) will make the problem worse, because more processes will be vying for the same latch, all spinning consuming CPU (in an active wait).

Lightweight Performance Measures

The design and development phase of a system is the right time to build in lightweight performance measures for critical end-user functions. This type of feature-specific application-performance measure can be used to trigger alerts and warnings if a significant deviation from the expected behavior occurs in production. The data captured doesn't need to be complex. Instead, simple measures such as elapsed job execution time can be very useful when kept over time, allowing performance trending and rapid identification of problems.

Quality Assurance

After an application has taken form, it is time to put it through its paces. Not only should your application be quality-assurance tested for functional completeness, the application must be stress tested with realistic and representative transaction, reporting, and data volumes.

Testing for Performance

The tests and test environment should replicate as closely as possible what will actually occur in production, including hardware (such as CPUs and disks), the usernames connected, number of connections, optimizer statistics, workload mix, and the configuration. An important test factor is running a concurrent workload that is a reasonable representation of the production system. The intention is to determine where the limitations are prior to production, in order that they can be resolved. Questions your testing should address include the following:

- How will load caused by batch-job queuing and release be managed?

- How will performance fare with high concurrent user count performing the same, and disparate, actions?

- Which are the most critical features? How do they respond to limited resources and high loads?

- How do the most commonly used features perform under limited resources and high loads? Do they scale?

In practice, testing and capturing results for the entire application isn't feasible. However you *can* identify the minimum set of important queries and reports; the performance of these must be known and tested. Include testing and capturing results for the following:

- SQL run frequently

- Short-duration online reports

- Long-running reports

- Any time-critical or vital infrequently run SQL (such as monthly reports, CEO reports)

You must verify specific and mandatory performance requirements during QA. The simplest situation is to run a single-user functional test. If the test is failing to meet its performance requirements, there is little point in ramping up the load to multiple users. Illogically, some engineers believe that if a single user test is running in 10 seconds rather than the required 2 seconds, adding more users to the test may help the application reach its performance goals! It won't. It may, however, delay starting the work required to actually fix the problem. A similar test should be performed with varying data volumes. For example, if the application has a subsecond response-time requirement, and the testing shows a 2-second response time with a quarter of the initial production data volume (or load), there is an issue that needs to be addressed immediately.

Capturing Resource Utilization and Outlines

Another important measure of SQL performance is the resource utilization per execution (DB time/execute, CPU/execute). The values in testing will be compared to those in production to verify that no significant changes are evident.

This data should be saved for future reference, along with the statement's execution plans. If possible, save important queries' stored outlines; these are often a "fast track" for developers, which can be used during problem debugging. This way, should anything not perform as expected in production, some diagnostic data is already available so you can work out what has changed and why the performance has degraded.

Set Up and Verify Monitoring

The QA phase is the right time to set up procedures to gather systemwide performance data. You'll want to do do these things for all hardware and software resources. These procedures can then be rolled into production. Optimally, performance data should be captured from the database, the database server host, the network, the application servers, and (if it has been instrumented in development) the application performance by module or function. Consider the frequency with which the information should be polled, the amount of data captured, how long to retain data online, and how to archive important representative sets of data (that is, baselines) for future use and comparison. A good way to start is by using the default performance tool setup; then monitor to determine whether the amount of data captured and retention policy will suffice.

For the database, a good first start is to capture performance statistics every hour. Statspack is currently available in all releases (8.1.7 and above). Check spdoc.txt in the $ORACLE_HOME/RDBMS/ADMIN directory for more information. If your site is licensed for the Server Diagnostics Pack, use the Automatic Workload Repository (AWR) to take performance snapshots instead of Statspack. The Diagnostics Pack includes licensing for the ADDM, which identifies the cause of many performance issues with little or no effort. We recommend changing the AWR retention period, because it defaults to a week, which is not sufficient for most production sites: anywhere from 4 weeks to 13 months may be needed in order to retain sufficient data to do a comparison for infrequently used operations, such as monthly or yearly processing. Note that a longer retention period will require more disk space in the SYSAUX tablespace. Alternatively, when disk space is limited, determine how much disk space you are willing to dedicate to the AWR repository, and change the retention period to allow that much data to be saved.

■ **Note** Some performance engineers and DBAs move the AWR data to a different database to maintain a historical repository. The repository is an amazing source of data that has many uses, such as capacity planning or finding patterns.

Do not wait until you have "good" performance before collecting a baseline. If you do not have baseline performance data, the time to begin collecting is now! Also, ensure that you have baseline statistics when the system is stable with good performance. The good baseline can be kept for future comparison. You should take baselines for each important period, so you have representative data for all types of workloads on your system. In addition, you can define alert warning thresholds based on systemwide statistics (SYSMETRICs such as Average Active Sessions and SQL Service Response Time; in 10g, Average Active Sessions was called Database Time Per Sec).

Performance statistics to be collected include AWR (or Statspack) and OS statistics (such as sar or vmstat) for the following:

- Typical peak load times

- Periodic peak load times (for example, month-end queries)

- Off-peak times

For easier comparison, the database and OS statistics should correlate time-wise. Having data that does not easily correlate means you will have to match statistics from differing time periods, which can complicate and delay problem investigation. Also verify that the retention period for the Oracle and non-Oracle statistics are similar, so you can have data from both when resolving problems.

■ **Tip** Rather than keeping only reports, ensure that you have the AWR data available for ease of future analysis. It is a lot easier to aggregate data and do data comparisons by using SQL queries, rather than cutting and pasting from a number of reports into a spreadsheet.

New Software and Upgrades

New software installations are inevitable. Upgrades are inevitable. Preparation is the key to success in either case. Prepare properly, and you'll be home for dinner at night. Don't prepare, and it'll feel like you've hired the Three Stooges to assist the Keystone Kops in resolving the issues that arise. Following are some common-sense actions to consider when preparing the production database for new software or upgrades.

Know Your Hardware

Whether your site is installing new software or your existing system is undergoing a software and/or hardware upgrade, it is important to know your hardware and configuration and what it is capable of.

This sounds simple, but because of new hardware features, or usability features enabled by default, this can be difficult (or deceiving).

■ **Case** A site spent copious time investigating an intermittent and unpredictable performance degradation that occurred after they had upgraded their software and hardware. The site engaged support, and ultimately our performance team was asked to resolve the highly escalated situation. We identified that the hardware was automatically enabling power-saving mode at seemingly random times. This reduced the effective clock speed and therefore the throughput of work. The system administrators were aware of this feature, but the DBAs were not. It also took time for the hardware folks to determine how to work out what the clock speed was at any given time so we could verify the clock-speed-to-performance relationship.

You must be familiar with your hardware. What type of CPUs do you have, and how many physical CPUs are there? What is the effective clock speed? How much memory is there, and how much of that memory will be allocated to the SGA? What are the logical and physical disk configurations, the maximum I/O rate and random I/O rate, and what else uses those disks? In a RAC environment, you must know what speed the interconnect is rated for and what it is capable of. What about the network? You must also know which tools to use to verify the configuration.

Virtualization leads to all sorts of problems. Your storage is virtualized on a SAN that is shared with several other systems. Your performance degrades, and you diagnose that disk I/O has gotten slower. What is harder to see is that the administrator for one of the other systems that is sharing the SAN is running ten concurrent FTPs together and soaking up all of the available I/O bandwidth. As a DBA, you probably have no visibility into what else is happening on the physical storage, only on the part of it that is in use by the database.

■ **Case** A test application on a virtual machine (VM) intermittently took 8 hours to complete, but at other times completed in 2 hours. This time difference occurred because the entire VM was being swapped out for minutes at a time. So the OS statistics and Oracle statistics did not show any problems; the only small clue was missing time sequences.

Verify Statistics Collection

Prior to the system going live, you must verify that the statistics-collection procedures you configured and tested during QA have been rolled into production and are working as expected. Diagnosing performance issues without statistics gathering in place takes significantly longer and inflicts more pain on the users.

Back Up the Optimizer Statistics

Software performance emergencies are often caused by changes in SQL execution plans, so it is always a good idea to keep an export of known "good performance" optimizer statistics from your production system. Similarly, in order to better diagnose performance problems, ensure that performance statistics (DB time, CPU time, and so forth) prior to the change are saved. Keeping this data will help determine whether any important changes have occurred in the workload, the execution plan, or application use.

Implement Change Incrementally

For maximum stability, it is best to keep functionality as similar to the existing environment as possible when upgrading an existing production system to a new release. Unless a new feature has been *rigorously exercised* during testing, it is not advisable to enable new features when upgrading an existing production system to a new release.

To minimize risk, it is best to use a similar configuration to what you are currently using, and to introduce changes and new features gradually over time, after the production system has stabilized, and after exercising the features in the test environment. For example:

- Do not change the values for init.ora parameters (unless required by the upgrade). There is one exception here: determine whether events and underscore (_) parameters used in the init file are still needed, and if not, remove them. For example, an underscore (_) parameter or an event may have been set to work around a bug that your site encountered. If the bug is fixed in the new release, the parameter or event is no longer required. Leaving the event set may result in unexpected side effects, such as the production of longer traces, or traces occurring more often. There is no guarantee of what impact or effect the parameter setting will have in the new release.

- Do not alter your method for gathering and retaining optimizer statistics. In fact, consider temporarily suspending statistics gathering until production has been upgraded and performance is stable.

- Set optimizer_features_enable to the pre-upgrade release until the system is stable.

Post Installation or Upgrade

After a system has been installed or upgraded, it is important to examine the application's and instance's vital statistics. From an application perspective, verify that the execution times for key jobs or transactions are as expected. From a database perspective, check the Load Profile section of the instance report (see the "Using and Interpreting the AWR and Statspack Instance Reports" section later in this chapter). Such a health check would include looking at the following:

- DB time per instance

- Average number of active sessions per instance (and per database in RAC)

- DB time per second (How much working and active waiting are we doing per second and per transaction?)

- CPU time per second (Are we taking more resources per second, and per transaction?)

If performance is not acceptable, you must start reactive tuning efforts (see the following "Reactive Tuning" section). To ensure that the diagnostic data is not automatically "aged out" by the AWR, create an AWR baseline. This will cause the data to be retained until it is explicitly purged or the baseline is dropped.

In the unlikely event that you need to revert to an earlier release of the database, copy the existing performance and diagnostic data from the production system first, to avoid loss of vital diagnostic information. This would include an AWR export of the entire schema (which can be loaded elsewhere for analysis), and saving alert logs, trace files, and the related OS statistics.

■ **Case** One site reported a serious performance regression after upgrade, and after attempting a number of silver-bullet solutions, decided to downgrade. Unfortunately, they did not back up the captured performance data prior to restoring the database and reverting to the older release. This valuable data was lost. The only evidence remaining for analysis were six AWR reports, taken from various unrelated times. The site could not identify the application configuration, their database configuration, nor what was running during the AWR reports' runtime, because so many "quick fix" configurations had been attempted. Needless to say, identifying the various problems was time-consuming and as easy as piecing together a jigsaw puzzle with missing pieces.

After the system is stable, you can begin making systematic changes, preferably one change at a time. After each change is made, the impact in terms of response time and system resources must be observed and recorded for comparison.

You can begin gathering optimizer statistics, as per your existing strategy. If the system remains stable, the next step would be to let `optimizer_features_enable` default to the current release. And following that, if a new method for gathering optimizer statistics is available, consider using that (after testing, of course). Subsequently introduce new features pertinent to your application and needs.

Reactive Tuning

Reactive tuning is defined as responding to a lack of performance in an application. Whether the application is in testing or production, the investigation steps are the same. However, in production there is often intense pressure, and fewer opportunities, to implement effective change.

Those who do not understand the importance of systematically making changes demand immediate resolution. This is almost impossible to do successfully, especially when the exact nature of the problem hasn't yet been identified and clearly specified. This problem occurs more often than you might expect.

There is great value in using rigorous, systematic, and quantifiable methods. You know exactly which changes you are making, understand the intended outcome, and can measure how far you have traveled toward that outcome.

The steps of reactive tuning are as follows:

1. Define the problem. Identify the performance issue, determine the scope of the problem, set goals.

2. Formulate a theory. Piece together the evidence into a coherent picture and then determine remedial action.

3. Implement and verify the solution. Modify the system, application, or configuration, remembering the aim is to tune for the largest gain (that is directly relevant to the performance issue experienced). Evaluate your results against the performance target.

4. Repeat from step 2 if your goals are not met.

It is easy to lose sight of the goal while investigating a performance problem. Here are some ways to avoid falling into some of the most common traps:

*   Stay within the defined scope for the problem analysis. Do not fix a problem external to the problem definition.

*   Stay within the defined scope for the problem resolution. Do not make an instance-wide change to fix the performance of a few SQL statements (that is, don't tweak database or optimizer parameters before tuning SQL).

*   Apply fixes iteratively, one at a time (where practical). If fixes must be applied together, concurrent fixes should be orthogonal so the result of applying each fix separately is distinguishable.

*   Measure results after each change, and compare them to the results you expected when applying the changes.

*   Stop when your goals are met.

Step 1: Define the Problem

To some, this section is superfluous—there is a performance problem, so surely that *is* the problem definition! The following quote illustrates why this is not the case.

> *A well-defined problem is a problem half-solved.*
>
> — John Dewey

Pressure from users, management, salespeople, and even outside sources can create an intense environment in which the push is for immediate satisfaction. Jumping directly to fixes in this environment may at best keep the situation as is, but could render a worse problem (such as total loss of availability). To be fair, in a few rare cases the appropriate solution was accidentally stumbled upon, but this is not typical. Instead, you must clearly understand the exact nature of the issue you are dealing with, prior to engaging in analysis and resolution.

Be prepared to look at the problem laterally. The issue is often obfuscated in any number of ways, such as in erroneous initial preconceptions (that is, guesses). Other redirections commonly occur when secondhand (or thirdhand) descriptions of the problem are taken at face value. You must ascertain an accurate, quantifiable definition of the problem before any useful analysis of data can take place.

■ **Tip** Symptom or problem? Sometimes the main symptom is actually a side effect of the real problem. For example, in one case `cache buffers chains` latch contention increased CPU utilization to 100 percent, which resulted in `library cache` latch wait times increasing to the point that they were the top wait event. Although the symptom pointed to a `library cache` problem, it was actually the result of `cache buffers chains` latch contention, which itself was induced by inefficient SQL.

The User Experience

When gathering user feedback, be prepared to ask the same question several ways. Sometimes end users or less-senior technicians will provide their analysis of the problem and *present it as the actual symptoms.*

In many situations, the purported user experience does not match the actual experience, when verified with the user. This misunderstanding has resulted in a lot of wasted time as (even expert) diagnosticians have been assured that the definition of the problem is clear, when in fact it is based on someone's incomplete understanding. Instead try to focus on obtaining an accurate and quantifiable description of the symptoms.

■ **Case** A site was adamant that they had a scalability issue and that the solution was to add more middle-tier servers. Upon analysis, the situation was very different: the database server was severely I/O bound, with an average I/O read time of 40ms–60ms. Adding middle-tier hardware to this problem would have made the problem much worse. It took considerable effort to convince the site there was a real I/O issue. Once convinced, the site immediately wanted to add more disks. Although this is often a valid remedial action, it was not applicable here because the application SQL would not scale; the SQL had to be corrected in order to get a scalable application. You should be similarly cautious in confirming an accurate problem definition when beginning analysis for a problem that has been ongoing prior to your engagement. In many situations, end users are initially irate because they have been asked to re-explain the problem for the nth time. Their ire transforms into support when they comprehend that their problem had been misunderstood and that the effort so far had been geared toward resolving an issue that was not their actual problem. This is not uncommon in large organizations that have multitiered support groups involved in problem resolution.

For any useful analysis to take place, you must ascertain answers to questions in the following areas:

Scope: Who is complaining? Is the problem related to a single user, a single function, a single division, or is it company-wide? What is the end user's definition of the problem, and how is this behavior different from what is normal? Is the problem constantly present or intermittent? Is it dependent on data entered? Is it a specific transaction or report? This then translates to the scope: whether the problem may be local to the host, database/instance, a particular `Service/Module/Action`, a single session or `client id`, or a single `SQL id`.

Time frame: When did the problem occur? How frequently? Is the problem apparent only during peak periods? Does performance slow gradually, or is there a specific identifiable tipping point?

Performance problem: How long did the function take previously? Compare the current performance to the typical and expected performance. Knowing the current time and the expected time gives an indication of the regression and also gives you the target response time.

Evidence: Request evidence that demonstrates the issue, if the evidence is available. Sometimes there is resistance to a request for concrete data (often because the person reporting the issue may not be aware that logs exist). Gathering the actual logs is useful, because experience shows that the actual performance data sometimes differs from what is initially reported. For example, the data may indicate that the performance problem is not in the module reported—it may be in a different area.

Context: Understand the context of the evidence provided. For example, in the case of a batch job, there may be many phases, of which the provided data is only a small part (and this part might not be the problem area). Or the particular log examined may not be representative of what happened during the problem time. Another example: the log provided may represent significantly different data volumes or user load as compared to what was happening during the problem time. Ensure that the data you have is representative of the bad run. (Sometimes users accidentally mix and match evidence from different days, which may have different problems.)

User configuration feedback: Determine whether the users are aware of any recent changes. This may help track down possible culprits. Things to ask include whether the user count has increased, whether different applications or features have been enabled recently, or whether any new data loads have occurred.

A good run: Problem drill-down is easier if you have a "good" run to compare against. It is also useful to have a couple of "good" runs and "bad" runs to determine whether the nature of the problem is consistent. Sometimes a single consistent problem will emerge; at other times more than one problem will be identified.

The answers will give you information on the range of the problem, and therefore which data and tools are appropriate to use for this situation.

■ **Tip** Sometimes when questioning experienced end users about recent changes, they may divulge some suspicions they have about the nature or cause of the problems. The more questions you ask, the higher the likelihood these ideas will be shared.

An Agreed-Upon Problem Definition

You now have sufficient information to form the problem definition. You know whether the problem is systemwide or limited to a particular set of users or jobs. You know whether it is intermittent, short-lived, or ongoing. You also have a quantified performance target.

Prior to proceeding, ensure that representatives from all key areas agree on the problem definition. This includes users, management, system administrators, and DBAs. Lack of agreement means resources such as system administrators and DBAs may be working at cross-purposes to prove different theories.

The definition doesn't need to be long-winded or time-consuming. The intent is to create a dump of accurate information, which can be referred to by all involved. Goals should be business-oriented and quantifiable, such as "perform x transactions per minute" or "complete execution in n seconds or less." To contrast, "just fix it" or "make it run as fast as possible" are not quantifiable aims.

This is also a good time to set expectations for how long initial analysis may take (setting realistic expectations will avoid misconceptions).

Hardware and Database Data

You must also collect relevant data from the database and host hardware. Data collected must encompass the problem time. Knowing the times, you can determine which data points are most likely going to provide the most pertinent information, and allow you to work out the interval of data to examine. For example, if the slowdown occurred at 10:15 a.m. and lasted for 10 minutes, assuming your site gathers statistics every half hour, it would be prudent to initially look at the 10 a.m. to 10.30 a.m. window. Looking at a wider 9 a.m. to 12 p.m. period, may average out, and thereby hide, the problem.

For the operating system, you need to look at the CPU utilization, memory, I/O subsystem, and network statistics to ensure that they are performing as expected. Looking here could help determine possible areas to drill down.

■ **Tip** Systemwide problems require looking at the entire stack, not just at the database or host. Often the finger of blame is pointed at the database before any analysis has taken place. For example, the database may be blamed for poor performance when it is actually the middle tier struggling and not serving requests fast enough, or the database host may be performing CPU-intensive nondatabase work.

If the problem has been scoped to the database, you will need to look at the database statistics. This will also provide clues as to whether the operating system and hardware need to be investigated in detail. Gather reports from ADDM and AWR and ASH, or SP. Also gather the init.ora file and alert log messages.

If the problem occurred within a relatively short interval, ASH data (which is granular) is a good place to investigate the nature of the problem.

■ **Tip** If the time the problem occurred can't be pinpointed, and it was systemwide, use the ASH data available through Enterprise Manager to view the resource utilization graphically. Look for spikes that will identify when the issue may have occurred.

If the problem is related to a particular module or job, the execution of that module must be investigated. Locate statistics related to the module or SQL's performance, response time, and resource utilization (if necessary, lower the SP thresholds to capture these in the repository, or increase the number of SQL statements that AWR captures). Find corresponding data for the module or SQL prior to the performance problem, for comparison.

Determine what changes have occurred since the performance was acceptable; this may help track down the problem. Having data available that allows the identification of changes is a major advantage. The first response to this question from users, DBAs, and system administrators often is, "It was working fine yesterday, and nothing has been changed." The response from a very experienced support analyst (usually muttered while the call is on mute), is, "Well if nothing has changed, then there can't be a problem!" This makes perfect sense: something *must* have changed.

Check whether modifications have been made in the following areas: hardware additions or reconfigurations, database and operating system patches or new releases, configuration changes, application patches or new releases, more workload, new workload (of a previously unused feature), changes in data loads, changes in data volumes, new optimizer statistics whose values differ considerably from previous statistics.

Step 2: Examine the Performance Data

All relevant performance data is examined in this step. However, before diving deeply into the statistics, it is always a good idea to check the fundamental areas first, to ensure that no configuration changes have been made without your knowledge. It is also important to check the basic evidence such as log files.

Sanity Check

It is always a good idea to do the following:

- Examine the OS statistics to determine whether non-Oracle programs are consuming excessive resources that are shared with the database (such as CPU).

- Check for error messages occurring at the same time as the problem in all logs (application, middle-tier, alert log).

- Check the `init.ora` parameter settings for any unusual parameter values or new parameters.

■ **Case** A site experienced a significant increase in CPU utilization after applying a patch. There were no discernable differences in the type of workload or the quantity of work requested. The SQL statement statistics were almost identical, and there were no execution plan changes (other than ones that resulted in lower resource utilization). After significant investigation, a lateral thinker went back to basics, checked the init.ora file, and spotted that pre_page_sga was set to TRUE. This is not a typical setting on most sites. He quietly checked the the list of bugs that were fixed in the patch that had just been applied, and determined that in the prior release, Oracle had ignored a TRUE setting for pre_page_sga, and this patch set included a bug fix that enabled this feature. After upgrade, the user sessions began pre-paging the SGA at connection time, which resulted in an unexpected but significant increase in CPU usage. The customer decided to turn off this feature to return to the prior CPU utilization. Similar situations have also been seen with diagnostic "events" that suddenly started working, or doing more work than in prior releases, so it is a good idea to know why unusual events (or _ parameters) are set and when they need to be removed.

Analysis

You have defined the problem and are ready to examine the data for evidence. The aim when examining performance data is to identify where the majority of time is spent within the defined scope (that is, database, instance, session, or SQL level). Next identify what actions performed in the database may be using the associated resources. Then look at additional related data to find and confirm patterns. The user experience, resource usage, and diagnostic data together form a theory of what is occurring on the system.

Scope: Local Issue

For problems local to a single user or functionality (such as a service, module, or action), it is likely that the application is no longer performing optimally, and the solution will be related to the application design or coding (or changes in optimizer statistics).

To determine the cause of the problem, use ASH to identify what the user or function was waiting for and the resources it was consuming (query ASH by module or action or user). Alternatively, SQL-trace the server process to examine the SQL statements being executed and the flow of work.

If an application programming language is used, this is also the time to look at the code. Is the program flow efficient, for example, can it be improved by avoiding executing code in loops when it needs to be executed only once? Is it possible to reduce the database load, for example, by caching data locally?

If a specific SQL execution is inefficient, determine how the SQL (or underlying schema structure) can be tuned. Gather the complete SQL text, the execution plan, the data volumes, the indexing (including column ordering), any view definitions and the table structure. Check whether the optimizer statistics for the objects involved in the SQL statement have been recently updated.

To more easily identify changes, it is helpful to have a prior "good" execution plan and the associated expected resource usage statistics. Compare the current execution plan with that of the "good" plan to determine what is different. If the plan is unchanged, the plan might no longer be optimal for the data volume and distribution in the related segments. If the plan is different, determine what has changed and what is the most appropriate remedial action. This includes modifying the SQL or the indexing or the design, and considering any specific features that may be beneficial.

Scope: Instance-Wide

For instance-wide issues, first look to ADDM (for information on ADDM, see the "Using and Interpreting ADDM" section later in this chapter). If ADDM does not identify the problem, you will need to manually investigate the issue by using ASH and AWR (or just SP).

It is often helpful to generate an ASH report, as the Activity Over Time section of the ASH report shows a breakdown of the top events into smaller time slices. For example:

Time (Duration)	Slot Count	Event	Event Count	% Event
12:07:55 (2.1 min)	18	enq: TX - row lock contention	18	2.04
12:10:00 (5.0 min)	120	enq: TX - row lock contention	119	13.49
12:15:00 (5.0 min)	109	enq: TX - row lock contention	110	12.47
12:20:00 (5.0 min)	104	enq: TX - row lock contention	99	11.22
		latch: cache buffers chains	4	0.45
12:25:00 (5.0 min)	117	enq: TX - row lock contention	117	13.27
12:30:00 (5.0 min)	280	enq: TX - row lock contention	270	30.61
12:35:00 (3.9 min)	144	enq: TX - row lock contention	144	16.33

■ **Note** ASH allows you to pinpoint when a problem started. You will be able to see peaks and valleys, spurts of waits by time (or by resource or user). You can also see the progression of the problem, which may indicate how the problem originated (which is not necessarily what the main symptom looks like!). For example, a slow interconnect in a RAC cluster may result in extremely long waits for library-cache-related resources and buffer-cache-related resources. However, the problem itself may not be obvious from the waits. Instead it is important to see how the problem built up: which events the sessions were waiting on before the more obvious symptoms arose.

Examining the ASH data allows you to determine whether the problem was long-lived—that is, whether it appeared throughout the interval or whether there was a temporary peak. For peaks, it is useful to generate a second more-granular ASH report for the smaller peak interval to see how the problem built up, the objects involved, the users involved, and so forth. For detailed information on how to leverage ASH, see the "Using and Interpreting the ASH Report" section later in this chapter.

If the problem is evident over a significant portion of the interval, it is useful to look at an AWR (or SP) instance report. To identify the component accounting for the majority of database time and to get a good indication of the nature of the problem, examine the top-level summary data on the first two pages of the instance report.

An instance report is voluminous, which is intimidating to those who erroneously assume that the report must be read from cover to cover. The usage model is to examine the summary data first, determine the high-level characteristics of the problem, and then drill down to key areas to investigate further. Usually only a few sections of the report are relevant to a specific problem, and you skip from one to another, comparing data as needed.

The drill-down statistics are examined and analyzed for consistency or inconsistency when compared to the information you have so far. They also provide further evidence about the nature of the problem. For information on using instance reports, see "Using and Interpreting the AWR and Statspack Instance Reports" later in this chapter.

Step 3: Formulate a Theory

The data you have examined will lead you to formulate a theory about the nature of the problem. This is the time to discuss your theory and findings with others. Work through the data with colleagues; discuss the evidence found, contradictory data, and possible conclusions. Listen to opinions without bias.

If you are working on your own, think through the problem as if you were describing it to someone. A well-known performance expert was known to approach a life-sized cardboard cutout advertisement for Kodak (called the Kodak lady) to discuss the data found, the theory, and the conclusions. (British people are typically eccentric, so this type of behavior was not *that* strange.) Explaining the problem to someone does help, even if they don't, or can't, respond!

■ **Tip** Avoid making the facts fit the theory. When a technician is comfortable with solving a particular type of problem, his attention is drawn toward data relevant to that issue. For example, some people are fond of library cache latch issues, so if `latch: library cache` appears in the top timed events (even if it is only a small percentage of the total wait time), they may focus on that "problem." Don't fall into that trap. Instead, let the time-based data lead you to the issue.

Test any theories with known facts to determine whether the theory meshes with the data. This will involve directing your thought processes to ask questions such as "If this theory is true, then I should also see the following evidence...."

If your investigation indicates that the instance-wide issue is caused by a class of similarly structured SQL statements (or a particular application), the resolution is the same as that for problems of local scope.

For issues that cannot be improved by making the SQL, the schema, or the application code more efficient, available options include changing the configuration of the instance or adding hardware resources. The addition of hardware is not always a solution, and for applications that are inherently nonscalable, adding hardware will not resolve the issue long-term. Hardware should be added only if it is not possible to resolve the issue any other way.

The theory of what is contributing to or causing the problem will direct you to the issue that you must resolve. For example, if the evidence consistently points to a specific problem, the solution is to resolve that problem. If the statistics indicate excessive CPU usage for hard parsing, and there is latch contention for parse-related latches (such as library cache and shared pool), the solution is to reduce the hard parsing.

There are a number of different ways to resolve most problems. You should identify and carefully consider one or more potential solutions. Choose the solution that gives the best value (implementation cost vs. benefit), which is as close as possible to the scope of the problem identified. For example, in the hard-parse case, options to reduce hard parsing include modifying the application to soft-parse, setting cursor_sharing to FORCE, and if the application has many different versions of the schema in one database, you should consider amalgamating the schema copies into one user.

Also look at the costs and benefits of temporary and permanent solutions; it may be necessary to implement a suboptimal solution for a short time (such as setting cursor_sharing to FORCE instance-wide), while a longer-term solution is implemented. Knowing business-specific targets will help direct what needs to be done and how quickly.

Step 4: Implement and Verify the Solution

Hopefully, implementing the solution you have identified will resolve the issue. To determine whether this is the case, you must identify whether the tuning aims have been met and how much of an improvement (quantitatively speaking) has been achieved. Check the statistics that are relevant to the changes implemented. Compare the target response time to the current response time, and ascertain the users' perception of the performance improvement (if any). Is performance acceptable? If so, the tuning exercise is complete.

If you have not met performance targets, it could be because of the following:

- The change implemented may not have been the complete solution. This could be the case if the largest problem was not correctly identified and instead another problem was fixed, or multiple smaller issues need to be resolved, or no one solution can provide enough benefit to meet the requirements (the "top" problem chosen consumes the largest amount of DB time, and so it has the largest potential for improvement).

- The characteristics of the problem have changed. The changes implemented may have fixed the original problem, but a new problem affecting performance has been revealed. Sometimes the symptoms the user sees may be the same, when in fact there is a new problem in a different area. In this case, find the next bottleneck.

■ **Note** The "gotcha" about removing one bottleneck is that it may reveal a second bottleneck that adversely affects end-user performance to an even greater extent. This can happen if the original problem throttled back the throughput requests to this newly bottlenecked resource. For example, if your system has severe CPU contention and the application is tuned, you may choose to add more CPUs to increase throughput. However, if the I/O subsystem is not configured to support the increase in workload and I/O latency increases, you may find that end-user performance is worse than when CPU was the bottleneck.

To go forward, you may need to go back. Reconsider your understanding of the problem. Continue to refine the conceptual model of how the application works. Re-examine relevant statistics. Determine whether evidence was missed, and think laterally to determine what other evidence not yet examined may be relevant to the problem at hand.

Diagnostic Tools

An effective performance engineer knows what tools are available, what data they provide, and which tool to use to best resolve a particular problem. Contrary to what some may say, no single tool can possibly be the right tool for all problems. Knowing which to choose and what data each provides is a big step toward efficiently resolving the problem. Table 3-1 provides an overview of the essential tools we use frequently and how they are typically used. The ADDM, ASH, and AWR are described in more detail in the following sections.

Table 3-1. Essential Diagnostic Tools

Tool	Usage
Enterprise Manager	A graphical all-purpose tool that can be used to identify when a spike occurred, drill down to the cause, and examine ADDM recommendations. The benefit of a graphical representation of performance data is visible (pun intended). Data visualizations display any skew directly.
Automatic Database Diagnostic Monitor (ADDM)	An expert system that automatically identifies and recommends solutions for many instance-wide performance problems. Best used for longer-duration performance problems (that is, problems that are continuous or ongoing for a large proportion of the snapshot interval). The symptoms and problems are available by running the ADDM report, and through Enterprise Manager.
Active Session History (ASH)	An all-purpose tool providing data that is useful when investigating system-wide problems, shorter-duration spikes, or smaller-scoped problems (for example, for a specific user, or SQL, or a module/action).The advantage of using ASH data when compared to other diagnostic information is that the data is of a finer granularity. This allows you to look at a problem to identify how the symptoms "build up," or allows you to determine exactly which resources are involved and who is using them. The ASH data can be queried directly or accessed via a targeted ASH report.

Tool	Usage
Automatic Workload Repository (AWR)	Instance-wide summary data that is used when ADDM is not able to identify the problem in the system, and the problem is of longer duration. Also used to verify the ADDM analysis. The data can be queried directly but is most often accessed via the AWR instance report.
Statspack (SP)	Instance-wide summary data used to manually diagnose performance problems. You should use SP when you are not licensed for the Diagnostics Pack, and so can't use ADDM or AWR.
SQL trace	This traces the execution flow (resource utilization, execution plan, and waits) by SQL statement. The information can be used to examine the flow and resource utilization for a specific user, feature, or SQL statement identified as problematic.

Using and Interpreting ADDM

Why use ADDM? Simply stated, it correctly identifies the majority of instance-wide problems and their causes, and it does this automatically. Anytime you consider examining an AWR report, examine the corresponding ADDM recommendations first, because the solution may be there.

ADDM is an expert system that analyzes performance by looking at where time is spent in the database. ADDM uses AWR data to produce findings that identify where the DB time was spent in the interval, how much of a resource was used, and what was using the resource. The findings are prioritized by impact on DB time, and recommendations are prioritized by which actions will most effectively reduce DB time.

■ **Tip** Use ADDM! It's perplexing why sites that are licensed for the Diagnostics Pack (and so licensed for ADDM, ASH, and AWR) choose not to look at ADDM analysis, where the problem may already be identified, and instead perform a manual, time-consuming diagnosis. If you are averse to GUIs, ADDM reports are available in text format. Some feel that using ADDM is cheating, similar to looking at the answers for a crossword puzzle before trying to work it out yourself. This perspective is not particularly conducive to efficient problem resolution.

An ADDM report is generated by running `addmrpt.sql`. An excerpt of an ADDM report follows. This system experienced severe `cache buffers chains` contention. Diagnosing the problem would have been time-consuming and error prone; instead the problem is presented for your attention immediately.

```
                DETAILED ADDM REPORT FOR TASK 'TASK_1007' WITH ID 1007

              Analysis Period: 11-FEB-2008 from 10:00:48 to 10:30:56

              Database Version: 10.2.0.2.0

                Snapshot Range: from 271 to 272

                  Database Time: 107992 seconds

          Average Database Load: 59.7 active sessions



FINDING 1: 38% impact (40428 seconds)

Contention on buffer cache latches was consuming significant database time.

   RECOMMENDATION 1: SQL Tuning, 4.8% benefit (5182 seconds)

      ACTION: Investigate the SQL statement with SQL_ID "ayy4t6chs4tux" for

         possible performance improvements.

         RELEVANT OBJECT: SQL statement with SQL_ID ayy4t6chs4tux

         select distinct t1.col1, ts.col2…

      RATIONALE: Waiting for event "latch: cache buffers chains" in wait

         class "Concurrency" accounted for 91% of the database time spent in

         processing the SQL statement with SQL_ID " ayy4t6chs4tux".

   RECOMMENDATION 2: SQL Tuning, 2.8% benefit (3155 seconds)

      ACTION: Investigate the SQL statement with SQL_ID "sp4evavnt23s" for

         possible performance improvements.

         RELEVANT OBJECT: SQL statement with SQL_ID sp4evavnt23s

         select distinct t1.col1, ts.col2…

      RATIONALE: Waiting for event "latch: cache buffers chains" in wait
```

---

lass "Concurrency" accounted for 94% of the database time spent in

processing the SQL statement with SOL_ID " sp4evavnt23s".

<truncated>

ADDM identified and quantified the cache buffers chains latch contention in the first FINDING, and identified the multiple SQL statements contributing to the problem (only two are shown in the preceding excerpt, but there were many more, all of a similar SQL format).

Using and Interpreting the ASH Report

Active sessions are sessions that are either on the CPU or are actively waiting for an action to complete (in a non-idle wait). The time used by active foreground sessions is accumulated in the DB time statistic.

Active Session History (ASH) is a perpetually available, systemwide trace of database work. The data it contains is analogous to continuously querying and storing the results of V$SESSION (or V$SESSION_WAIT in releases before V$SESSION included wait information) while a problem is in progress—except that this data is already available without any extra effort. Using ASH enables us to go "back in time" and perform detailed analysis, without having to reproduce the problem.

Each second, data associated with all of the active sessions in the instance are sampled and associated with a TIMESTAMP (both foreground and background sessions are sampled). This history of active sessions can be queried through V$ACTIVE_SESSION_HISTORY (ASH). Prior to ASH data aging out of memory, one out of every ten ASH samples is persisted to disk. This data can be subsequently queried in DBA_HIST_ACTIVE_SESS_HISTORY.

Both ASH views have a similar structure in that they are both multidimensional fact tables; the fact is DB time, which accumulates over dimensions such as SQL_Id, EVENT#, Session Id, Instance, Service, Module, and Action. Querying ASH allows you to determine the answers to questions such as the following:

- Which events were taking the most time?

- What was a session doing?

- What does a SQL statement wait for?

For example, you can use ASH to determine which SQL statements were actively waiting for row cache locks over time, as follows:

```
break on sample_time skip 1
col name format a30
col sample_time format a30

select /*+ index(ash) */
       sample_time, name, sql_id, p1, p2, p3, count(*)
  from dba_hist_active_sess_history ash
```

```
where ash.name             = 'row cache lock'
   and ash.instance_number = &inst_id
   and ash.dbid            = &dbid
   and ash.sample_time     < to_date('&end_date','YYYY-MM-DD HH24:MI:SS')
   and ash.sample_time     > to_date('&begin_date','YYYY-MM-DD HH24:MI:SS')
   and ash.snap_id    between &bsnap_id and &esnap_id
   and ash.wait_time       = 0
group by sample_time, name, sql_id, p1, p2, p3
order by sample_time;
```

You can access ASH data without writing queries, by generating an ASH report (`ashrpt.sql`). The ASH report automatically queries data from the `DBA_HIST_ACTIVE_SESS_HISTORY` view and the `V$ACTIVE_SESSION_HISTORY` view, depending on the data needed for the specified time period (so no guessing is required as to which view contains the needed information).

The ASH report includes `Top Events`, `Load Profile`, `Top SQL`, `Top Sessions`, `Top Objects/Files/Latches`, and `Activity Over Time`, and makes it easy to identify skew in any of these dimensions. For example, it is simple to identify the top session, which accounts for the majority of the total DB time. Following are a few interesting selections from a sample RAC ASH report. The data included shows the depth and breadth of useful information summarized by this report: top event broken down by parameter, top client IDs, and top SQL broken down by event.

Top Event P1/P2/P3 Values

The `Top Events` section shows the top events waited for in the interval covered by the report, what percentage of time they were active, and what specific resources were contended for. For example, 5.18 percent of the `db file sequential read` event is specifically accounted for by one block, which is identified by the file number and block number (indicated by P1 and P2). Figure 3-1 shows an example of the `Top Events` section.

Event	% Event	P1 Value, P2 Value, P3 Value	% Activity	P1	P2	P3
log file sync	20.10	"275","0","0"	2.38	Buffer #	NOT DEFINED	NOT DEFINED
		"336","0","0"	1.81			
		"476","0","0"	1.78			
db file sequential read	5.18	"1","7785","1"	0.03	file#	block#	blocks

Figure 3-1. Top Events section from an ASH report

Top Client IDs

The Top Client IDs section shows which clients account for the majority of activity in the interval, including what program they were running. Figure 3-2 shows an example.

Client ID	% Activity	Avg Active Sessions	User	Program	Service
POE@22.222.22.222@Mozilla/4.0 (compatible; MSIE 7.0; Windo)	1.31	0.13	UserID: 23	MM	REP
RAUM@22.222.22.222@Mozilla/4.0 (compatible; MSIE 7.0; Windo)	1.12	0.11	UserID: 23	MM	REP

Figure 3-2. Top Client IDs section from an ASH report

Top SQL with Top Events

The TOP SQL section shows the top SQL for the reporting interval, the percentage of activity that the SQL was active, and a breakdown of the activity by wait event. Figure 3-3 shows an example of that section.

SQL ID	Planhash	% Activity	Event	% Event	SQL Text
8buns43hrs1c		21.14	log file sync	13.23	begin leader.rev (:1,:...
		21.14	gc current block busy	4.08	begin leader.rev (:1,:...
		21.14	gc buffer busy	1.78	begin leader.rev (:1,:...

Figure 3-3. Top SQL section from an ASH report

Using and Interpreting the AWR and Statspack Instance Reports

Both AWR and Statspack capture and persist to disk the most elemental performance measures for a system. They also provide systemwide reporting of that data. AWR has advantages over Statspack because it is integrated into the server code, and because AWR captures ASH data. AWR is also bundled with ASH and ADDM in the Diagnostics Pack, whereas Statspack is part of the server license.

The following reports ship with AWR:

AWR instance report (`awrrpt.sql`): Report for a single instance

AWR compare-period report (10g R2) (`awrddrpt.sql`): Allows you to compare to separate periods side by side in one report (for example, Monday between 10 and 11, compared to Tuesday between 10 and 11)

RAC global report (`awrgrpt.sql`): Shows a database-wide view, for RAC systems, accumulated over all instances

Global RAC compare-period report (`awrgdrpt.sql`): Is a compare-period report, database-wide for RAC systems

The Report Layout

The method for analyzing an AWR instance report and a Statspack instance report is to all intents and purposes identical. This is because AWR and Statspack capture data from the same performance data sources (that is, V$ views), and because the report formatting and layouts are very similar. Before being able to effectively use an instance report, you must orient yourself with the report layout.

The first two pages of an instance report are known as the *summary pages* (for RAC systems, a RAC-specific page is also included). The intention of the summary pages is to provide a concise overview of activity on the instance. You will note that much of the data has been normalized per second (and per transaction). This makes it easier to compare to other reports, which may not be of the exact interval or workload characteristics.

The summary pages are also used to determine a high-level description of the nature of any problem the system may encounter. The summary pages include Load Profile, Timed Events, Time Model, and OSStat. This data is used as a springboard to the related detail-sections of the report. The top of the report contains information that defines the identity and configuration of the system, including CPUs, memory usage, cache sizes, server release, and metadata about the data collection, such as the elapsed time and begin and end interval times. The remainder of the report comprises detail sections, which are intended to drill down into the specifics of a given problem. The most frequently used of these include the following (shown in the order they appear):

- Time stats: Time Model data, wait events

- SQL: Top-N SQL (ordered by CPU time, elapsed time, gets, reads, executions, parses, and so forth)

- Instance activity stats

- I/O stats: Tablespace and data file I/O

- PGA usage stats

- Enqueue activity, latch activity, latch sleeps

- Segment statistics

- Dictionary cache, row cache and library cache

- SGA memory

- init.ora parameters

Analysis Strategy

The instance summary pages are examined first to obtain a high-level view of the type of application running, what the load on the system is like, the main time-consumers, and also the elapsed and wall-clock times. Use this data to identify any atypical or outlying statistics, such as the following:

- Workload differences when compared to a "normal" workload (if you have one for comparison), using the Load Profile

- Suspiciously "high" rates of activity for any database operations, using the Load Profile

- The largest DB time usage and the CPU time used (Top Timed Events)

- Any large average wait times for wait events (Top Timed Events, drill-down to wait events, event histograms)

- Whether the activity for the majority of database time is all in the same area (for example, all I/O related, or all events all in the same wait-class)

Having a comparison report makes identifying unusual activity much easier. Comparing the problem time with a good time will help identify which of the workload characteristics have changed, as well as how the time was spent differently in one period when compared to the other. After atypical or outlying information is identified, the drill-down sections are examined to develop an in-depth understanding of the nature and cause of the problem.

■ **Tip** If both comparison periods are in the same AWR schema, use the AWR compare-period report, which displays the two periods ("bad" and "good") side by side on one screen. It also quantifies the percentage of change between the two data points.

Elapsed Time

Look at the elapsed wall-clock time for the snapshot interval. The elapsed time provides an insight as to whether the report will be reliable for resolving the problem specified: how does it compare to the duration of the problem? If the problem is characterized by a small spike (for example, 10 minutes), and yet the elapsed interval is long (for example, 2 hours), then the data in this report may not be sufficient to identify the problem. Conversely, if the problem duration is long and the elapsed time is short, the problem may not be visible. Take note of the elapsed time for the snapshot interval, because you may need it to perform some manual calculations. Also check the begin and end times for the snapshot to verify that the times correspond to the time the problem occurred.

Timed Events and Time Model

The first place to look is the timing data! (If you are not familiar with key time statistics such as DB CPU and DB time, please see the upcoming "Meaning of Key Statistics" section for definitions.) Quickly scan the Top 5 Timed Foreground Events to identify the events with the most DB time by percentage. On most systems, it is normal to see DB CPU and waits for user I/O in the top timed events (on this system, they make up 75 percent of the total DB time). The question is to determine how normal it is *for this system*, by comparing against a known baseline.

Event	Waits	Time(s)	Avg wait(ms)	%DB time	Wait Class
db file sequential read	3,152,540	20,938	7	48.31	User I/O
DB CPU				9,739	22.43
library cache pin	1,694,234	2,602	2	5.93	Concurrency
gc current block 3-way	1,342,612	1,298	1	2.92	Cluster
db file scattered read	144,353	1,111	8	2.54	User I/O

The absence of a statistic is as telling as its presence. For example, if CPU time is not in the top timed event list, and the system is clocking a lot of DB time, then the system is spending a lot of time waiting and not doing productive work.

Check whether the top events are related by type, because a set of related events may indicate one primary area of contention. For example, many I/O-related events would point to further investigation of the I/O usage and service time, whereas high CPU and user I/O-related events probably indicate that a lot of SQL is being executed.

If there is an unusual wait event that greatly outranks the others as a DB time hog, it is likely the bottleneck or a symptom of the bottleneck. For example, an unusual top timed event would be latch: session allocation. If this event was consuming 40 percent of DB time *and* there was significant wait time associated with the event, this would be a good candidate for serious investigation.

Another possibility is that sets of disjointed events may rank closely for the highest wait time. In this case, you will need to look at each one in turn, because they may or may not be related to the issue you are investigating, or to each other.

Know *what to ignore* in the Top 5 events:

- Events that *do not take up a significant portion of the DB time.* For example, library cache pin is not a significant performance contributor in this system (it accounts for only 6 percent of the total DB time).

- Events that do not take up any significant amount of *absolute time.* You need to check the absolute amount of time (that is, Time (s)) for each event to determine whether this wait is important to investigate. Events with a high %DB time may be misleading if their absolute time is small: this can happen if the snapshot interval is short or if the amount of workload on the system is small.

Confirm that the information in the top events section is consistent with the Time Model data. In this case, the top events indicate a lot of I/O wait time (in the User I/O and Cluster wait classes), and high CPU usage. A reasonable conclusion is that the system is performing a lot of SQL, and that the SQL is waiting for I/O for a great percentage of time. The average I/O wait time is 7ms, which is not large.

Statistic Name	Time (s)	% of DB Time
sql execute elapsed time	39,529.68	91.06
DB CPU	9,738.50	22.43
PL/SQL execution elapsed time	4,876.86	11.23
parse time elapsed	281.55	0.65
hard parse elapsed time	218.18	0.50
connection management call elapsed time	24.72	0.06
PL/SQL compilation elapsed time	11.62	0.03
failed parse elapsed time	0.09	0.00
DB time	43,409.98	
background elapsed time	2,635.82	
background cpu time	2,000.39	

The Time Model statistics confirm that the system is spending most of its time (90 percent) executing SQL, and the majority of that time (51 percent according to the top wait events) is spent waiting for User I/O events, with 3 percent for cluster-related block transfers.

Load Profile

Examine the Load Profile statistics to develop an understanding of the nature of the application (for example, whether it is parse intensive or I/O intensive). Also use this data to identify unusually high rates of activity, especially when compared with a baseline report.

Comparing with a known baseline helps determine whether the activity type and throughput has changed for this instance. The data is normalized Per Second (dividing by the total elapsed time), which tells you how much work per second the database is performing, and Per Transaction, which tells you how much work the database performs on average for a transaction (dividing by the total number of commits and explicit rollbacks).

Differences in the per-second times indicate that throughput has changed. This can be due to a change in the amount of work requested (for example, the number of users requesting work has increased, for executes per second), or a change in the workload mix (for example, more parsing or less sorting), or an increase in the work being performed to service the same number and type of requests.

	Per Second	Per Transaction	Per Exec	Per Call
DB Time(s):	12.1	0.2	0.01	0.01
DB CPU(s):	2.7	0.0	0.00	0.00
Redo size:	472,109.0	5,755.6		
Logical reads:	57,984.2	706.9		
Block changes:	1,975.2	24.1		
Physical reads:	1,962.8	23.9		
Physical writes:	159.1	1.9		
User calls:	965.3	11.8		
Parses:	241.6	3.0		
Hard parses:	7.7	0.1		
W/A MB processed:	193.0	2.4		
Logons:	0.8	0.0		
Executes:	1,771.8	21.6		
Rollbacks:	43.1	0.5		
Transactions:	82.0			

Comparing different statistics in the Load Profile can help determine which of the preceding conditions may apply. For example, an increase in DB time per second indicates we are either waiting more each second, or using more CPU, or both. Look at the DB CPU per second; if it has increased, we are using more CPU each second than we were previously.

■ **Tip** It may be initially confusing to think about the concept of *DB time per second*. How can you normalize time by time? My advice is to consider DB time as a measure of how much work sessions are performing (it is actually how much CPU time and how much active waiting). In that way, it makes more sense to ask, "How much extra work per second am I performing now, compared to an earlier time period?" Similarly with *CPU time per second*, it is easier to comprehend if you phrase it as follows: "How much CPU resource per second is being used in this snapshot, when compared to a baseline?"

Are the per-second execute and parse rates the same? If they are higher than the baseline, more work is being requested. If they are similar, are we using more resources to perform the same workload? Check logical and physical reads per second to see whether we are reading more.

Look at the per-transaction statistics to get an idea of whether the workload mix has changed; are we doing a similar number of parses and executes per transaction? A different transaction mix makes it hard to perform comparisons with any measure of confidence.

Examine statistics that are related to the top wait events. Is there a single consistent picture? If not, note other potential issues to investigate while looking at the top events, but don't be diverted from the top time-consumer. Are there any statistics in the Load Profile that are unusually high for this site? If so, can we put together a picture of what types of transactions or workloads may be contributing to the problem?

Sanity Check OSStat

The OS Statistics (OSStat) section can be used to compare Oracle CPU statistics with wall-clock time and also with DB time and DB CPU. Doing this enables you to determine whether there is a consistent picture of CPU utilization.

Statistic	Value
BUSY_TIME	1,413,402
IDLE_TIME	1,478,583
IOWAIT_TIME	676,805
SYS_TIME	263,369
USER_TIME	1,026,374

For illustration purposes, let's compute some CPU statistics:

% Busy: The server is at 50 percent utilization, so there is no CPU bottleneck (BUSY_TIME / (BUSY_TIME + IDLE_TIME).

USER_TIME: We see that user time makes up 73 percent of the total (USER_TIME / BUSY_TIME)

Foreground CPU usage: How much of the total CPU usage is used by Oracle foreground processes (DB CPU / BUSY_TIME)? Beware that DB CPU and BUSY_TIME are in different units, so you need to convert to the same unit: DB CPU (seconds) / BUSY_TIME (seconds) = 9,739 / 14,134 , which is ~70 percent. This means foreground Oracle processes are consuming 70 percent of the total used CPU on the system.

Compare the Oracle CPU utilization to the OS CPU utilization. Is the picture consistent? If not, which statistics may not be reliable for this problem?

Drill into Relevant Details

The purpose of gathering additional data is to help build an understanding of the characteristics of the problem, and a more detailed view of what was executing at the time the problem occurred. This requires skipping back and forth through the report to check statistics of interest. The data gathered may portray a consistent picture of one bottleneck or a series of bottlenecks.

It doesn't hurt to skim through the Wait Events and Background Wait Events sections to look for any related waits, or any anomalies in related areas. If it is relevant to do so, also cross-check the event times with any other applicable database or OS data. For example, if the events are I/O related, is the Oracle data consistent with the OS read times?

Depending on the evidence found thus far, determine whether there are any other relevant sections in the report to examine. For example, if the top events are I/O related, look at the SQL Ordered by Reads, the Tablespace I/O Stats, and File I/O Stats sections. Is the data in these sections consistent with the wait events? What other information does the drill-down data provide? Does the resource usage form a pattern?

It is also important to examine the SQL sections of the AWR report, to identify what the application was requesting of the instance at the time of the performance regression. The SQL sections also identify high-load SQL, or SQL statements that are avoidable (for example, if they are executed more times than necessary). For the system we have looked at, the SQL by Elapsed Time and by User I/O are the most relevant sections:

Executions	Elapsed/Exec(s)	%DBtime	%CPU	%IO	SOL Id	SQL Module
48,873	0.24	27.36	10.67	78.83	fudge8gkz6p42	Invoice8781

Physical Reads	Executions	Reads/Exec	%Reads	SQL Id	SQL Module
1,205,296	48,873	24.66	17.07	fudge8gkz6p42	Invoice8781

This SQL statement accounts for 78 percent of the system's I/O wait time, and 17 percent of the total reads for the system. However, the number of reads per execute is low! So tuning the SQL would not necessarily provide a huge return, although investigating whether any of the information the query accesses could be cached may reduce the I/O wait time.

Concluding Data Analysis

In summary, after you have drilled down, contended-for resources have been identified and candidate problems have been analyzed. Consider whether there is there sufficient data to build a sound theory for the cause and resolution of the problem. Ensure that no significant inconsistencies exist in the data you have gathered. If all of the evidence seems consistent, it's time to move on to formulating the theory and implementing the solution.

Meaning of Key Statistics

When looking at statistics, it is important to know what they intend to represent and what they exclude. Statistics are somewhat fallible in that they are seldom 100 percent accurate, but in most cases they do sufficiently indicate what was intended. Be sure you understand what each statistic represents and the units used (there is a big difference between microseconds and centiseconds).

(There are) lies, damn lies, and statistics

— Benjamin Disraeli

Not understanding the meaning of statistics can result in misinterpretation of the data and lead to confusion or an incorrect analysis. One such example is the well-known but little-understood buffer cache hit ratio. The manner in which the constituent statistics are incremented has changed drastically in many releases, rendering this derived statistic effectively useless, even for comparison purposes across releases.

Time-Based Statistics

Time-breakdown statistics (Time Model) make it significantly easier to determine the type of operations that are consuming resources in the database. Key statistics are as follows:

DB time: Time spent by all user processes in the database (that is,. non-idle wait time + CPU time).

DB CPU: Time spent by all user processes on the CPU, in Oracle code. On most systems, the majority of time will be spent in DB CPU, SQL execute elapsed time, or PL/SQL execution elapsed time (and possibly Java). Time spent in parse and connection management should be low, so if the levels indicate a high percentage of DB time, a problem exists in the relevant area. You can use this data to correlate with Top 5 Timed Events and Load Profile.

Database time (DB time) is an important time-based statistic: it measures the total time spent in the database by active sessions (that is, foreground user processes either actively working or actively waiting in a database call). DB time includes CPU time, I/O time, and other non-idle wait time. Because DB time represents the sum of the time that all sessions spend in database calls, it can easily exceed the elapsed wall-clock time. Two user sessions working concurrently in a database for 1 minute generates 2 minutes of DB time. DB time is not the same as user-response time, as DB time represents the time that work was performed within the database, but not network latency or middle-tier processing time.

DB time *always increases* when performance degrades, which is why it an excellent high-level performance metric for time-based problem diagnosis. For example, increases in DB time will occur in any of the following cases:

- An increase in load (either more users, more calls, or larger transactions)

- I/O performance degradation (I/O time increases and wait time increases, so DB time increases)

- Application performance degradation (wait time increases)

- CPU-bound host (foregrounds accumulate active run-queue time, wait event times are artificially inflated)

The objective of tuning an Oracle system could be stated as reducing the time that users spend in performing actions in the database, or simply reducing DB time.

■ **Note** Wait time is artificially inflated when the host is CPU bound because the wait time includes the actual time spent waiting (for example, waiting for a disk I/O), as well as the time spent by the process in the OS run-queue waiting to be rescheduled. The Oracle timer stops only when the process has been rescheduled. Therefore, when the host is CPU bound, it is important to reduce CPU utilization before addressing wait-related problems, because otherwise you may be addressing the wrong problem.

DB time and DB CPU, along with other time-model statistics, are captured at many different scopes (SQL execution, system level, and so forth). This means time-based analysis can be performed at many levels, from individual SQL to instance-wide. DB time analysis can also be performed over many dimensions: SQL ID, session ID, instance, service, module, and action. The data is available as follows:

System scope: VSYS_TIME_MODEL, VSQL (DB time is called ELAPSED_TIME in V$SQL)

Session scope: V$SESS_TIME_MODEL

All scopes in ASH: V$ACTIVE_SESSION_HISTORY and DBA_HIST_ACTIVE_SESS_HISTORY

% Activity and Average Active Sessions

ASH provides the list of sessions active in each of its samples. If we look at a time period of 10 seconds (which is also 10 ASH samples, because ASH samples each second by default) and calculate the percentage of samples that a particular session appears in ASH (that is, was sampled to be active), this provides us with the average activity of that session (% Activity). For example, if a session appeared in each of 10 consecutive samples, 10 samples / 10 seconds is a ratio of 1 (that is, an average of 100 percent active for the interval). If, however, the session appeared in only three of those ten samples, the average activity level for that session would be 33 percent.

To determine how "busy" an instance is, you can compare the total time spent by user sessions instance-wide (which is DB time from V$SYS_TIME_MODEL) and divide this statistic by the elapsed wall-clock time. This calculates the average number of active sessions during that interval (average active sessions). You can also do the same calculation database-wide (sum Δ DB time for all instances, and divide by elapsed time).

% Activity for one session = Δ session database time / Δ wall-clock (elapsed) time
Avg. active sessions = Δ instance-wide database time / Δ wall-clock (elapsed) time

ASH-Estimated DB time

You can use ASH data to estimate DB time when the actual DB time is not available—for example, if a session has exited. Because ASH samples active sessions every second, you can estimate DB time (in seconds) to be the number of ASH samples counted. For example, the following statement returns SQL IDs ordered by estimated DB time (that is, sample count), for the entire time interval residing in the ASH buffer:

```
select count(1) est_dbtime, sqlid
  from v$active_session_history
 where session_type = 'FOREGROUND'
 group by sqlid
 order by est_dbtime;
```

The estimated DB time (est_dbtime) is computed by adding the number of samples for each SQL statement. Do be aware that low sample sizes, which will occur on a mostly idle system, are less reliable to use to estimate DB time.

V$OSSTAT

V$OSSTAT is OS-related resource utilization data that the Oracle server collects. The statistics available vary by platform. You can use V$OSSTAT to determine CPU utilization (BUSY_TICKS and IDLE_TICKS), and also compare this to the host's CPU utilization statistics. Also look for high OS_CPU_WAIT_TIME, which may indicate the host is CPU bound.

V$OSSTAT statistics can be compared with the Time Model statistics, for example to determine how much of the total CPU used on the host is attributable to this instance: DB CPU / BUSY_TICKS. (The AWR and SP instance reports show this comparison; note that the units for these two statistics differ.)

Wait Classes

In 10g, each wait event (V$SYSTEM_EVENT) is classified into one of nine wait classes: Application, Commit, Concurrency, Configuration, Network, Other, System I/O, User I/O, and Idle. The class names are reasonably self-explanatory except Other, which is a catchall bucket for wait events that should not ever contribute any significant wait time.

Why are wait classes useful for diagnosis? The wait classes provide an overview of where the problem is. For example, if the top wait events are all in I/O-related wait classes (such as System I/O or User I/O), it seems reasonable to deduce that the problem is likely related to the I/O system (whether it be a higher Oracle load, or slow response due to nondatabase-related activity for shared disks).

The Optimizer

The optimizer is complex. Making modifications to optimizer parameters willy-nilly is not advisable, because the implications may be far-reaching beyond the intended scope. You must ascertain the impact (costs and benefits) to the execution and resource utilization of all important SQL statements in your application before making changes to optimizer parameters. This applies doubly for underscore (_) parameters.

Also, it becomes risky to remove these parameters after the settings have been used in a production environment, because the impact of doing so is not easily identifiable. Parameters may need to be removed to allow some classes of SQL statements to execute more efficiently, yet doing so may penalize the performance of others.

Managing Statistics

In order to make the best decision possible, the optimizer must have statistics that represent the data being accessed. However, optimizer statistics do not necessarily need to be updated regularly to be representative. There is a sweet point in the optimizer statistics-collection continuum: maintaining old statistics can be dangerous to performance, because the optimal execution plan may be different as data volumes change. Similarly, collecting statistics nightly may provide increased possibility for instability.

In addition to the optimizer becoming more complex and sophisticated over time, in recent releases of Oracle, optimizer statistics management and execution plan management have become feature rich—for example, with locking of optimizer statistics, plan stability, and SQL profiles.

Locking Statistics

It is possible to lock optimizer statistics to prevent new statistics from being gathered. This is an appropriate action to take for objects whose statistics are accurate, and whose data does not change. It is also appropriate for objects whose data volumes are highly volatile, where you wish to keep the statistics representing a specific data volume (for example, peak data).

If you are using Oracle 11g, and segments do not have their statistics locked, Oracle will automatically determine when statistics collection is needed. It does this during the Oracle scheduler window for tables without statistics, or for tables whose statistics it believes are stale. This may result in unpredictable execution plans on an unknown schedule. Alternatively, you might choose to disable automatic statistics gathering.

Execution Plan Stability and Profiles

One method to maintain the same execution plans is to leverage plan stability by using stored outlines. An *outline* is a low-level set of optimizer hints that direct the optimizer in how to construct the execution plan.

An alternative to using stored outlines is to use SQL profiles. A profile allows the optimizer to choose more-accurate plans based on the auxiliary optimizer statistics within the profile.

Summary

We hope we have demonstrated that a simple, effective performance method is feasible and attainable. A little organization, along with a rigorous and scientific approach, goes a long way to making performance planning, diagnosis, and resolution effective and less stressful. We certainly can't say the same for relying on silver bullets!

CHAPTER 4

■ ■ ■

The DBA as Designer

by Melanie Caffrey

Consider the following scenario. It is Friday, five o'clock p.m. You have plans for the evening. You are signing out and logging off, when your phone rings. That new application that was just moved into production appears to be having problems. The question posed to you is "Can you log on and see if there is something wrong with the database?" *Something wrong with the database.* How many times have you heard a question posed like that? And because production code is deemed the responsibility of the DBAs at your company, this problem now falls to you and your team.

So you log in to the new application and notice several problems right away:

- Clicking a link (presumably parameterized) presents you with the familiar hourglass icon for what seems like an eternity.

- The application allows the user to dynamically create Data Manipulation Language (DML) statements, and when you do so, with very few filters, you again find yourself staring at the hourglass icon for an interminable amount of time.

- You decide to have a look at exactly how many users are accessing this application right now and discover that it is fewer than a hundred. Some of them have active sessions that have been working for nearly 20 minutes.

In the middle of this research, you are approached by a rather panicked project manager who implores, "Can you please do something with the database to fix this?" Soon the panicked project manager is joined by several lead developers and perhaps even one rather annoyed chief information officer. All of them want to know what is wrong with production. *Because this code was tested and it was working! So what is wrong with the database?*

If you are like many DBAs at many companies, you have no idea what this application is or what it's supposed to do. Earlier that afternoon, one of the DBAs on your team was given a set of scripts to run to create this application. The DBA ran the set of scripts that created a nice resultant log file ensuring him, as well as the developers who gave him the scripts, that all objects and code were created without error. Like many DBAs, he has been told that the developers are in charge of designing and writing applications.

And if you were to ask him to look into it, he might immediately begin to increase temporary space, or create some extra indexes or redo logs, or implement that cool new initialization parameter setting he just read about on insert_your_favorite_listserve_here. Because, if he gets it right tonight—even if it's *just* for tonight—in alleviating some of the pain of the running of this application, he will be the company hero. And what could be better? It may not even occur to him to start pulling aside one or more of the lead developers leaning on the back of his chair to start asking questions about the design of this application. But it should. It could save him hours of troubleshooting time and frustration (not to mention the money it could potentially save the company).

Therefore, you decide to look into it yourself. And if you're smart, the first question you ask lead developer 1 and lead developer 2 is "Why weren't the DBAs involved in the design of this application?" After you ask this question, you'll still need to help solve the problem. However, your approach will now be (hopefully) different from that taken by your cowboy colleague illustrated earlier. You now need to try to figure out a way to introduce design improvements that are scalable and maintainable while causing minimal interruption to what is now in place in production. Good luck!

When to Get Involved in Application Design

Ideally, a DBA gets involved in application design right from the beginning. If you are not invited to an initial planning meeting for a brand new application (or even an existing one that will be overhauled), invite yourself. Trust me—it's worth the investment of your time. For as any experienced DBA knows, though the poor design in production may not be your fault (if you were never involved in its inception or implementation), it will certainly become your problem. Be proactive, not reactive. Burnout takes place quickly when you have little say in a problem you are asked (and expected) to fix. Though poor communication and lack of proper planning is a reason why many DBAs refer to developers as *duh-velopers*, there is little good that can be said about a DBA who does not make herself available to the development team for design consultation and collaboration.

In other words, if you are not helping the design effort as soon as possible, especially if you are aware that it is taking place, you are part of the problem. Given that you have enough to do in your day—what with new systems, data warehousing efforts, reorganizations, and what-have-you—spending a little time up front to alleviate the need for spending lots of time later on, sometimes late at night, under duress, seems like a small sacrifice in the long run. Putting yourself on the radar of the development team and those in charge of gathering requirements and planning project schedules, though initially may seem tedious, will save you, personally, many hours, many headaches, and hopefully a few friendships.

So how do you do that? There are several ways in which very skilled DBAs accomplish this task designed (no pun intended) to make everyone's lives easier. Personally, I have found that adhering to the following modus operandi works well for me.

DBAS AND DEVELOPERS

This chapter focuses on the relationship between DBAs and developers (and others involved in application design sessions involving the database, solely and explicitly). To keep the chapter at a manageable length while covering all I wanted to write about the importance of the DBA/developer relationship, this chapter does not discuss the (by no means less important) relationships a DBA has with other parties such as system administrators, storage administrators, network administrators, and so forth.

Be Approachable

This cannot be overstated. Developers, like DBAs, are often under huge amounts of stress and time constraints. Many developers are skilled, professional, hardworking, and capable of accomplishing great things. When they approach you for help, take them seriously, be respectful, and more important, help them. Arrogance is the key downfall I see in many DBAs. You may have worked hard to get where you are. Design concepts and planning steps may seem obvious and second nature to you. And if so, you are to be applauded. However, some DBAs tend to alienate development teams by answering "newbie" questions with answers such as "You should *know* that," thereby making the developer feel as if the question was so simple or insignificant that he has completely wasted the time and patience of the DBA he interrupted to ask for help. If you are one of these types of DBAs, prepare yourself for some long evenings and weekends, for no developer will want to come within 10 feet of you unless he is forced to. And that's a shame, for if no one is asking you for your help or opinion, then that is a bad situation for everyone involved.

The division between DBAs and developers goes back as far as the job positions of DBA and developer have been in existence. It is often most pronounced in those members of either team who have never done the other's job. Yes, it is true that the *primary* job of a DBA is to create, maintain, and tune the databases. However, many DBAs become DBAs by way of the developer-first, DBA-now progression. In other words, DBAs should be familiar with the trials and tribulations of designing and coding a system. And if you are someone who was once a developer and is now a DBA, you should assume that it is part of your job to mentor the developers, particularly when any aspect of the database comes into play. This isn't you simply being magnanimous to the developers. This is your job. It's what you get paid the big bucks for. (After all, someone mentored you once, right?) And, in the end, if done consistently, it is what will ensure you have more of your evenings, weekends, and vacations uninterrupted. What goes around comes around.

Ask for Periodic Sign-off on Design and Application Milestones

For your own sanity, you'll want to be involved in as many stages of design as possible. The more you know about the application, the more you are able to assist, opine, and change or fix easily. It isn't enough that you are around in the beginning and then again in the end, just before go-live. Milestones are to be seen as sanity-checking points in the design and development process, enabling all major players (that includes you) to agree that you are still on the same page. This is not to say that you will be writing code, per se (more on that in a moment), but simply that you see where this application is heading and are able to give the project manager the official approving nod of your head that allows everyone to keep going. Conversely, if you see a problem, then speaking about it as soon as possible can help salvage (or prevent) wasted erroneous development time and dodge any design bullets (not the magic kind, which don't exist anyway, but the deadly kind that doom systems to failure).

Attend Code Reviews

I cannot stress this suggestion enough. If you are a DBA who was once a developer, you are someone with experience. Someone who can add value to a code review. Someone with nuggets of wisdom to impart on the development team. Someone with war stories that can be provided as cautionary tales. So take this opportunity not only to see where the application is heading, and ensure that milestones are moving in the agreed-upon direction, but also to use any code review as a possible mentoring platform, and for you and other members of the DBA team to hopefully learn something new. (Yes, it is possible that developers may know a thing or two that DBAs do not. Particularly, if a DBA has not had time to keep up with all of the latest improvements in coding conventions.)

Having said that, there is no substitute for experience, and good learned behaviors and habits (no matter how obvious they may seem) should be communicated and discussed as to whether they are viable for the application at hand. Be aware that you are not shifting the responsibility completely away from the developers by providing your stamp of approval during a code review. Remember that often they really don't need your approval for their code to be implemented. Attending a code review *spreads the responsibility*. Do you see the distinction? Spreading the responsibility ensures that there is even less chance of any of you getting away with the blame game. You're all in this together.

Hold Postmortems

Even with the best planning, designing, and collaboration efforts, every once in a while problems arise. Something unexpected, in unanticipated conditions, takes place on production. And you must all look into it. Together. If you have been diligent and thoughtful about the planning and execution of your application, it should be easy enough for you to all hold *postmortems*, otherwise known as those meetings that take place after a particularly nasty production incident, that you've by now put either a short-term or long-term fix in place for, where you all look at each other and say, "How did *that* happen?" These should not be finger-pointing or blaming sessions. They should be considered brainstorming sessions just as vital as any design or application planning sessions. After all, the postmortem would not be taking place if you were truly done with design. An incident in production is proof that there was something in the design effort left unconsidered. Therefore, all the same rules for respect and professional cordiality hold just as true during a postmortem as they do during the first design brainstorming session, no matter how cranky or tired you all may be from having just been awake for the last 24 hours.

Partnership Between DBAs and Developers

If you want to have any free time (or even a life) as a DBA, it is imperative that you develop a good working relationship with the developers you will be tasked to support. It will make your life easier and their lives easier.

One of the interesting aspects about the job of a developer is that it is often a career path about growth and change leading *out*. There isn't usually an *up* that lets you stay a developer. The idea is that after you have learned and mastered good techniques for writing clear, maintainable, and scalable applications, you should desire to move on in your career. You should want to become a DBA, or technical or team lead, or a person in the upper echelons of management. But definitely now that you have mastered the art of development, you are seen as unambitious if you wish to *remain* a developer. Counterintuitive, isn't it? We don't tell engineers that once they've mastered the art of building safely structured bridges, they should no longer be doing that type of work. Nor do we tell architects that once they have a few buildings under their belt, it's time to move on to managing other architects.

However, developers who do good work are told that they should really want to do other things, do more, and move out of their comfort zone, so to speak. *Leave that development work for the young guys. Don't tell people your age if you're still doing development work.* It's funny that development work is seen as work for the younger generation. Yet it takes years of hard work to become good at it. Then once you're good at it, you should become a DBA, or consultant, or team lead of some kind, or senior manager, or CIO. But one thing is clear. You should *not* remain a developer, no matter how good you are.

One positive note to mention here is that if you are a DBA who has ever developed, and was a good developer, you are the perfect mentor for the developers you are tasked to support. So, how do you go about forging a partnership between the DBA team and the development team? Forging any partnership is truly more an art than a science. However, here are a few suggestions that can assist you in this endeavor.

Hold Brown Bag Sessions

If your goal is to get the developers to trust you and to want to include you in their design process, let alone incorporate your ideas, it behooves you to start sharing your knowledge as soon as possible. The sooner you hold whiteboard sessions about, say, how Oracle works and start helping the developers become advocates of the database you already know and love, then you've already won half the battle. Developers (usually) are starved for information and are curious by nature. Most of them *want* to do things the most maintainable and scalable way. However, left to their own inexperienced devices, they are more apt to learn the *best* way the hard way. Trial by fire. It is true that once you learn that way, you rarely forget what you've learned, but still, no one actually likes to learn that way. Being proactive about holding brown bag sessions is an invaluable investment for both your DBAs and the development team. If you share your knowledge, they are more apt to share theirs, and people who trust and like each other can work together much more efficiently, and forgive each other more readily.

Sit Near Each Other

If possible, it really helps for the DBAs and developers to be colocated. It engenders more questions, more collaboration, more impromptu brainstorming, and most important, more knowledge transfer. The more people know about, understand, and have actually put work into an application, the more people you have responsible for it. The more people responsible for it, the more likely the application is to be better designed and executed. And again, camaraderie between the DBAs and developers cannot be overestimated. The better the partnership between these two groups, the better the application, the happier the customer, and the richer the company. The better the two teams work together, the happier everyone will be in the long run.

Be Open to New Ideas

Being open to new ideas does not mean accepting every suggestion a developer has wholesale. It simply means be willing to listen. And do so, respectfully. Don't assume that because a suggestion is new, it is bad. Don't assume that your knowledge and experience immediately trumps any developer's ingenuity. Be willing to listen before you override—particularly if upon hearing a suggestion, you are not really sure of the outcome of implementing it. If you're not sure, the idea merits a discussion, at a minimum. Believe me, if you show this kind of respectful openness to the developers during a design session, you are more likely to garner respect for your ideas in return. Dismissing someone's idea when you have no actual basis in experience for doing so, can turn that person off from listening to you and can even turn them against you. This is counterproductive.

Even if an idea sounds ludicrous to you, do not say so. At least, not in those words. If you disagree with someone, you'd better be able to prove why, with some sort of example. Otherwise, you risk losing credibility. Again, this is counterproductive. So listen, quietly and respectfully. Be prepared and be helpful. Saying things like "I disagree" (full stop) is not helpful. Saying things like "I disagree and let me show you why…" is much more helpful. Prove what you say. As mentors, we often tell developers to question authority. In a design session, you are an authority. And if a developer questions your methods, she is doing the right thing. So let her know she is doing the right thing by proving what you say.

Be on the Same Side

This should seem fairly obvious, but it isn't. I was at a conference recently and had an interesting conversation with a colleague. Full disclosure here now: I currently work for Oracle Corporation. I work as a senior development manager in the Enterprise Linux group with the Unbreakable Linux Network product. Getting hired to work at Oracle was something I had long yearned for in my career. I would be working for a company whose database I truly believe in. It is a Relational Database Management System (RDBMS) I have loved for more than 12 years and feel that I can absolutely get behind. I have been speaking at Oracle user group conferences since 2000. Only since 2007 have I been an Oracle employee. Heretofore, I was always a user and customer of the Oracle product.

Come to find out, the perception of Oracle employees who attend user group conferences is that they are all salespeople to some degree. True, I do believe in the product. But I have always believed in it. I've always imparted laudatory information when discussing Oracle, and because of my non-Oracle-employee status I was never found suspicious before. I am wearing a different-colored hat these days, but I am still me. I still impart the same types of research, knowledge, and findings, and the same respect for Oracle that I always did. That hasn't changed. I haven't started gilding the lily or conveniently leaving things out just to make my employer look good. But because of the byline change on my presentation slides at this particular conference, my colleague's perception of me had changed. My credibility was now found to be suspect. I was no longer on the same side as he.

An interesting parallel can be drawn with DBAs and developers. If you ask someone whether they are a DBA or a developer, and he happens to respond one way or the other, with obvious disdain for the position he adamantly insists he does not hold ("I am a DBA! *Not* a developer."), then chances are he is not as good at what he does as he thinks he is. Without some amount of empathy and respect for those who work in the opposite position (yet complimentary position, when you really think about it), you are ensuring that both teams will suffer at least a little. Which, truly, is a rather ridiculous position to put yourself in. On the other hand, if you have been one of those DBAs or developers who have been lucky enough to work in an environment where the DBAs and developers already have mutual respect for one another, count yourself lucky indeed. You are among the minority.

With DBAs and developers, there is no reason for them to *not* be on the same side. They are both responsible for what goes into production. They are both responsible for making the customer happy. *They are both working with the same RDBMS.* So, adversarial relationships help no one and accomplish nothing. In short, if you are a DBA, learn what the developers have to go through, and encourage them to learn what you go through, all in the interest of, and with the end goal of, being on the same side.

Design-First Methodologies vs. Agile Techniques

In the early days of the field, new applications were often developed using an approach—sometimes referred to as the *waterfall* approach—in which design was done up front, and then the coding came later. More recently, developers are adopting techniques—sometimes described as *agile* techniques—that mix design and coding together. The trick is to choose the right technique for a given project.

Design-First Approach

Of the two camps, traditional vs. agile, those in the traditional camp prefer to have a solid design in place before writing a single line of code. Sometimes this is referred to as *Big Design Up Front (BDUF)* or the waterfall model. All relevant players (you, other DBAs, developers, project managers, and so forth) have come together and done, at least, the following:

- Created a complete list of system requirements

- Designed your logical entities that will store your database information

- Created an entity-relationship diagram (ERD) based on the logical entities

- Determined storage requirements

- Determined user concurrency requirements

- As a bonus, mocked up a few interface screens

In the traditional design-first camp, the argument for such an approach is that creating a good solid design before anyone begins to write code forces people to really think about the problem they are trying to solve. Designing first, before writing code, can help programmers think about how best to use that very, very, very expensive *black box* that holds the data. During design, you can discover how your entity relationships will work (or won't work, as the case may be). You can discuss potential pitfalls with chosen storage or concurrency strategies. You can decide whether an index-organized table, or even global temporary table, would be better than a heap table, for serving certain programmatic purposes, for example.

You can look carefully at the types of data you'd like to store, and therefore choose the correct datatype. Decide what the most common, frequent actions a user will perform within this new application will be. Is it mostly read? Mostly write? Evenly distributed between both actions? Will there be reporting requirements? Do these need to run concurrently alongside online transaction processing (OLTP) activity? If so, why? What compromises and negotiations can be made that will best serve both the new system and the needs of its users? As you read each question, you can see that each question potentially engenders new questions and need for more discussion. A few good design sessions can be worth their weight in gold in terms of time and money saved, and misunderstandings avoided. For those in the BDUF camp, the more questions asked up front, the better. As you can see, I am a bit of an advocate of the traditional design-up-front methodology. I like to be as prepared as possible.

Of course, the project must have, as part of its budget, money and time set aside for these planning sessions. It is amazing how many projects I have worked on where design is not even a secondary consideration, but more like a tertiary one. The unfortunate list of priorities often looks like requirements, then code, and then "tuning" (with some redesign being mixed in here, but obviously not the same as designing first). In the worst-case scenario, a few eager developers who cannot say no or push back to *the business* end up not asking enough questions, not clarifying requirements, and digging right into something they may very well have to redo. (The ubiquitous *business* explanation—as in, "We cannot change that. It is the way the business wants it," or "We must do it this way. The business requires it."—always makes me laugh.) *Cowboy coding* (unstructured, unplanned, dive-right-in hacking) is not endorsed by either BDUF or agile advocates. Whether you are in the BDUF camp or the agile camp, it's been said before that there is never time to do it right, but there is always time to do it twice. For those who prefer the design-up-front methodology, haste makes waste.

Agile Software Development

In theory, agile software development can work well if every single person involved in the application creation process is self-organized, self-disciplined, and highly collaborative with all others involved in a particular project. The various methodologies that employ agile software development are meant to promote iterations, better teamwork, collaboration, and process adaptability throughout the project life cycle. The focus is on breaking tasks into small increments with short-term planning goals in mind. These tasks don't include long-term planning, at least not directly. Each iteration employs a full software development cycle including planning, requirements gathering, analysis, design, coding, unit testing, and acceptance testing (when a working piece is demonstrated to end users). The idea is that with this approach, the project can adapt to changes in requirements quickly, thereby minimizing overall risk.

At the end of each iteration, end users (sometimes referred to as *stakeholders*) and a lead developer or team lead review progress and re-evaluate priorities. Ongoing face-to-face communication is emphasized. Working software is the primary measure of progress. Most agile teams work in a single open office space (sometimes referred to as a *bullpen*) meant to facilitate ongoing discussion and collaboration. At the beginning of the day, team members may all get together with the end users for their particular software piece and briefly report (while sometimes standing, physically, so the meetings can remain brief) what they accomplished yesterday, what they intend to work on or complete today, and any roadblocks they are experiencing. This communication is seen as necessary and helpful in uncovering potential problems. Many Internet companies (formerly referred to as *dot-coms*) employ agile techniques in order to deliver software faster.

To be fair, the characterization of agile methods being unplanned or undisciplined is misleading. Rather, it would be fairer to say that, in an adaptive to predictive continuum, agile methods fall under the adaptive side of the continuum, whereas BDUF methods fall on the predictive side of the continuum. While adaptive methods focus on adapting quickly to changing realities, they can rarely be used to describe exactly what will happen in the future. You can use such a method to report on what tasks are being completed today or next week, but only which *features* are planned for next month. Predictive methods, by comparison, focus on planning the future in as much detail as possible. These methods can usually describe in specific detail what features and tasks are planned for the entire length of the software development process.

Pros and Cons of Each Methodology

Anyone who says that the decision to choose one approach over the other is scientific and not philosophical is only fooling herself. The decision to choose one over the other has much to do with the way in which you find yourself (and your team) best able to work, how exactly you have been indoctrinated in either methodology, and last, but not least, your own personal experience in designing applications.

Do You Like Waterfalls?

The flow of the waterfall approach, explained pictorially, resembles Figure 4-1.

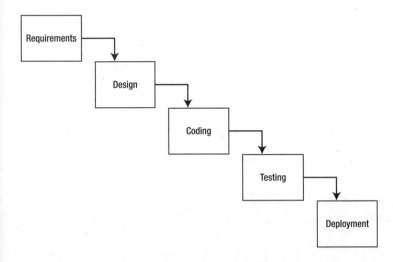

Figure 4-1. A pictorial representation of the waterfall approach

As you can see, the approach, when visualized, looks like a waterfall, starting from the top and flowing toward the bottom in one continuous direction. One phase is completed before the next phase is begun. The pros and cons of the BDUF, or waterfall, approach depend on your preferences, your experiences, and whomever you speak with who has an opinion on the matter. Table 4-1 outlines some of the pros and cons of the BDUF approach.

Table 4-1. BDUF Methodology Pros and Cons

Pro	Con
Time spent in designing is a worthwhile investment.	BDUF is poorly adaptable to changing requirements.
Less time and effort is spent fixing a bug in the early stages of a software product's life cycle.	This methodology assumes that designers are able to foresee problems without extensive prototyping and, at a minimum, some investment into implementation.
You can think through users' needs, the design, and possible problems before starting to code.	Refactoring is made difficult and time consuming, if not almost impossible.
The cheapest bug to fix is one that doesn't exist.	It is difficult to catch problems while you are still at the low-cost end of the cycle in a project; some problems first become apparent during implementation.
Measure twice, cut once.	This approach leaves little to no room for continuous testing and review.

Does Agility Equate to Flexibility?

If you take the preceding waterfall approach and revise it to resemble the way in which agility method advocates would describe it, it ends up looking similar to Figure 4-2.

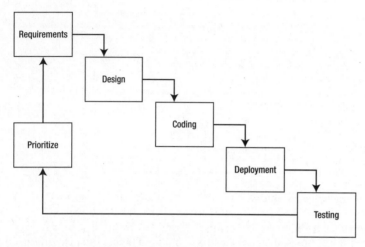

Figure 4-2. A pictorial representation of the agile approach

As you can see, this approach is iterative, cyclical. It is assumed that each software piece will be put together somewhat atomically, verified, and then revised, if necessary. Wash, rinse, repeat. As with BDUF, the pros and cons of agile methods depend on many factors, not the least of which is how large your project is, how large your team is (as in how many people will be involved: developers, DBAs, project managers, stakeholders and the like), and how big your budget is. It is also worth mentioning that this approach puts quite a bit of responsibility on the individual players and requires that they (those responsible for a particular software piece being produced) are highly motivated and self-disciplined. Table 4-2 outlines some of the pros and cons of the agile approach.

Table 4-2. Agile Methodology Pros and Cons

Pro	Con
It's very adaptable to changing requirements.	It implies that industries are not capable of communicating requirements effectively.
	Perhaps the problem is that agilists simply do not take time to elicit requirements correctly.
It provides lots of face-to-face communication and review.	Agile programmers rarely take the time to learn about their customers' core business, let alone their customers' competitors.
Customer satisfaction is emphasized.	The question "How can you help me, if you don't understand my needs and goals?" is one the customer has a right to ask of the software developer.

Pro	Con
It delivers software for customer review quickly (weeks instead of months).	It requires a highly disciplined set of individuals, that is, senior developers.
	Junior developers usually don't work well within this methodology.
Customers can often find out what they want only by working with a working system.	It puts a high degree of responsibility on the customer to assist in the Software Development Life Cycle (SDLC) process, and less accountability on the software developer.
	It increases the risk of scope creep.
Because rules can be limiting, the focus is on coding, rather than documentation.	The software industry as a whole does not have a great reputation for being great communicators or organizers.
	It is extremely difficult, if not impossible, for large groups of individuals to communicate effectively without structured documentation.

When it comes to choosing a design methodology, the answer lies somewhere in the middle between the two extremes of agile methodologies (one of which, funnily enough, is called *Extreme Programming*) and BDUF. There is really no substitute for taking the time to communicate with your customer, gather requirements as completely and thoughtfully as possible, and try to plan as much up front before actually building a system. On the other hand, some amount of iteration and refactoring will almost certainly be required. Even the best-planned systems can count on having to pad their schedules for occasional unforeseen circumstances and altered requirements. Being as organized, open to communication, and curious about your customer's business and needs can only help you to choose the best design methodology for the needs of your particular team and project.

Schema Design

Schema design, at least in my experience, is usually done much better using the BDUF design methodology. When you give yourself and all the various members of your team the ability to sit down and hold design sessions together, you can see, at a global level (as well as at a minimum), what your entities should be, how they should work together, what their datatypes and storage requirements should be, how you will enforce data integrity, and what your indexing strategies will be. And truly, schema design is just the tip of the iceberg when it comes to the myriad of things you'll want to discuss after reviewing your requirements and before starting to build your system.

Choose Your Datatypes Carefully

For those DBAs and developers who have been working for a number of years with systems that use the Oracle database, choosing the correct datatype usually comes as second nature. However, it is astounding how many developers (and a few DBAs) use strings to store everything—simply because they can. Oracle's autoconversion capabilities can be both a blessing and a curse. Merely because Oracle will autoconvert a string containing a numerical value to a number during an equality evaluation doesn't mean it is wise to store a number as a string. For example, let's look at the following code sample (run on Oracle version 11.1.0.7), starting with a table that stores identical values in two columns. The difference between the two columns is that one is declared with a number datatype, and the other with a string datatype.

```
scott%ORA11GR1> create table num_string_test
  2  (num_string varchar2(10),
  3   num_num     number);

Table created.

scott%ORA11GR1> declare
  2  begin
  3  for i in 1 .. 10046
  4  loop
  5     insert into num_string_test
  6     values (to_char(i), i);
  7  end loop;
  8  commit;
  9  end;
 10  /

PL/SQL procedure successfully completed.

scott%ORA11GR1> select count(*) from num_string_test;

  COUNT(*)
----------
     10046

scott%ORA11GR1> create index nst_num_str_idx on num_string_test(num_string);

Index created.

scott%ORA11GR1> create index nst_num_num_idx on num_string_test(num_num);

Index created.

scott%ORA11GR1> exec dbms_stats.gather_table_stats( user, 'NUM_STRING_TEST',
  2    method_opt => 'for all indexed columns', estimate_percent => 100 );

Table analyzed.

scott%ORA11GR1> set autot trace exp
scott%ORA11GR1> select *
  2      from num_string_test
  3    where num_string between 2 and 10042;

10041 rows selected.
```

```
Execution Plan
----------------------------------------------------------
Plan hash value: 3821201783

-------------------------------------------------------------------------------
|Id |Operation          |Name            |Rows  |Bytes |Cost (%CPU)|Time
-------------------------------------------------------------------------------

|  0|SELECT STATEMENT   |                |   25 |  175 |    3   (0)| 00:00:01 |

|* 1| TABLE ACCESS FULL|NUM_STRING_TEST |   25 |  175 |    3   (0)| 00:00:01 |
-------------------------------------------------------------------------------


Predicate Information (identified by operation id):
---------------------------------------------------

   1 - filter(TO_NUMBER("NUM_STRING")>=2 AND TO_NUMBER("NUM_STRING")<=10042)


scott%ORA11GR1> select *
  2     from num_string_test
  3    where num_num between 2 and 10042;

10041 rows selected.

Execution Plan
----------------------------------------------------------
Plan hash value: 3821201783

-------------------------------------------------------------------------------
|Id |Operation          |Name            |Rows  |Bytes |Cost (%CPU)|Time
-------------------------------------------------------------------------------

|  0|SELECT STATEMENT   |                |10041 |70287 |    3   (0)|00:00:01 |

|* 1| TABLE ACCESS FULL|NUM_STRING_TEST |10041 |70287 |    3   (0)|00:00:01 |
-------------------------------------------------------------------------------


Predicate Information (identified by operation id):
---------------------------------------------------

   1 - filter("NUM_NUM"<=10042 AND "NUM_NUM">=2)
```

Look carefully at the Rows component of each preceding plan. The optimizer knows that between the two NUMBER items, 2 and 10042, there are exactly 10,041 values. The optimizer also *assumes* (during plan creation time) that between the two VARCHAR2 items, there are only 25 values. Now, it is true that even if the cardinality is wrong, it won't affect what output you receive. You will still receive the correct answer as a result. However, your query plan having an incorrect assumed cardinality could impact your application's overall performance. Consider a different query against the same data, requesting an even smaller result set:

```
scott%ORA11GR1> select *
  2    from num_string_test
  3    where num_string between 2 and 42;

Execution Plan
----------------------------------------------------------
Plan hash value: 3821201783

-------------------------------------------------------------------------------
|Id |Operation           |Name           |Rows |Bytes |Cost (%CPU)|Time
-------------------------------------------------------------------------------

|  0|SELECT STATEMENT  |               |   25 |  175 |    3   (0)|00:00:01 |

|* 1| TABLE ACCESS FULL|NUM_STRING_TEST |   25 |  175 |    3   (0)| 00:00:01 |

-------------------------------------------------------------------------------


Predicate Information (identified by operation id):
---------------------------------------------------

   1 - filter(TO_NUMBER("NUM_STRING")>=2 AND TO_NUMBER("NUM_STRING")<=42)

scott%ORA11GR1> select *
  2    from num_string_test
  3    where num_num between 2 and 42;

Execution Plan
----------------------------------------------------------
Plan hash value: 1128766802

-------------------------------------------------------------------------------
|Id|Operation               |Name    |Rows  |Bytes |Cost (%CPU)
|Time     |
-------------------------------------------------------------------------------

|  0|SELECT STATEMENT        |        |   40 |  280 |    3 (0)| 00:00:01 |
```

```
| 1| TABLE ACCESS BY INDEX ROWID|NUM_STRING_TEST|   40 |  280 |    3 (0)| 00:00:01 |

|*2|  INDEX RANGE SCAN          |NST_NUM_NUM_IDX|   40 |      |    2 (0)| 00:00:01 |

----------- ------------------------------------------------------------------


Predicate Information (identified by operation id):
---------------------------------------------------

   2 - access("NUM_NUM">=2 AND "NUM_NUM"<=42)

scott%ORA11GR1>
```

Here we see a marked difference in the two plans. We are still performing a full table scan for the stringed number, but performing an index range scan for the number with a NUMBER datatype. So aside from the fact that the optimizer has to take the time to convert all strings to a number value with a TO_NUMBER function before predicate evaluation takes place, and that there is nothing stopping a user from entering *123 ½ ABC* into the num_string field, the use of that string has withheld valuable information from the optimizer.

It is true that different database parameter settings can or may influence the cost and behavior of certain or various operations. However, be aware that the effect shown in the preceding example will happen at some threshold. Similarly, storing dates and times as strings is an equally bad idea, unless you happen to enjoy having to invoke lots of TO_DATE and TO_CHAR functions merely to have date evaluation logic work properly.

Take Care in Sizing VARCHAR2 Strings

If you are using VARCHAR2(max_length_value) to store strings, those particular column values had better really take almost max_length_value. Otherwise, this is an indication that you have not properly researched the maximum length of the data you plan to store in those columns. This is the lazy approach of "this way, we will not have to worry about how large those column values get." It is better to consider the length as a constraint. A good example indicating how using the maximum length everywhere can hurt your application is that of an array fetch.

What will happen when the code prepares a query that selects 10, 20, maybe more columns that are defined as VARCHAR2(4000), for example? And they array fetch a typical amount of 100 rows. Do the math. With 20 columns all defined as VARCHAR2(4000), that comes to $20 \times 100 \times 4,000$ which equals approximately 8MB of RAM. So who should be responsible for obtaining that extra RAM (when truth be told no one should have to put in extra RAM merely to accommodate a poorly thought-out data model)? Then multiply that number by the number of connections to your application. You would be taking a sizable amount of memory for a lone query possibly executed multiple times *at the same time*.

For that matter, how about data-entry screens? If the first 20 fields on the screen each allow for 4,000 characters, that makes for one confusing (let alone, unattractive) data-entry screen. And last but not least, what will happen when users tag on a query tool (and we've all used them or seen them at one point or another) that formats each field based on database column width? The point is, think ahead and be as precise as possible. You can always expand a field if need be at a later point in time if you receive a value that is larger than any value that could have been reasonably anticipated during the design phase.

Watch Your Comparison Semantics

Using fixed-length string datatypes, such as CHAR, is helpful only if you are storing known-length values. If you store a string value of, say, 42 characters in a column defined as CHAR (100), you may be putting yourself in the position of having to use some sort of TRIM function when performing any sort of filtering or comparison logic with that data value. For example, let's look at the following code sample (run on Oracle version 11.1.0.7), starting with a table that stores identical values in two columns. The difference between the two columns is that one is declared as VARCHAR2(50), and the other is declared as CHAR(100).

```
scott%ORA11GR1> create table varchar_char_test
  2  (variable varchar2(50),
  3   fixed     char(100));

Table created.

scott%ORA11GR1> declare
  2  begin
  3     insert into varchar_char_test
  4     select object_name, object_name
  5       from all_objects;
  6  commit;
  7  end;
  8  /

PL/SQL procedure successfully completed.

scott%ORA11GR1> select variable, length(variable) vlength, fixed,
                                   length(fixed) flength
  2  from varchar_char_test
  3  where variable = 'ACL_ACE';
```

VARIABLE	VLENGTH	FIXED	FLENGTH
ACL_ACE	7	ACL_ACE	100

```
scott%ORA11GR1> select variable, fixed from varchar_char_test
  2  where fixed = 'ACL_ACE';
```

VARIABLE	FIXED
ACL_ACE	ACL_ACE

```
scott%ORA11GR1> select variable, fixed from varchar_char_test
  2  where variable = 'ACL_ACE';
```

VARIABLE	FIXED
ACL_ACE	ACL_ACE

In the preceding example queries, whether we query for fixed='ACL_ACE' or variable='ACL_ACE', the result is the same. The reason for this same result is due to Oracle's blank-padded and nonpadded comparison semantics. Oracle uses blank-padded comparison semantics only when both values in the comparison are either text literals, values returned by the USER function, or expressions of datatype CHAR or NCHAR. In the query where our predicate is fixed='ACL_ACE', the RDBMS is using blank-padded comparison semantics to resolve the comparison. Conversely, Oracle uses nonpadded comparison semantics when one or both values in the comparison are expressions of datatype VARCHAR2 or NVARCHAR2. In the query where our predicate is variable='ACL_ACE', the RDBMS is using nonpadded comparison semantics to resolve the comparison. Consider the following further code samples:

```
scott%ORA11GR1> insert into varchar_char_test values ('  ABC  ', '  ABC  ');

1 row created.

scott%ORA11GR1> commit;

Commit complete.

scott%ORA11GR1> select variable, fixed from varchar_char_test
  2  where fixed = 'ABC';

no rows selected

scott%ORA11GR1> select variable, fixed from varchar_char_test
  2  where fixed = '  ABC';

VARIABLE
--------------------------------------------------
FIXED
--------------------------------------------------------------------------------
  ABC
  ABC
```

So not only is Oracle using blank-padded comparison semantics for the CHAR datatype expression, it is using right blank-padded comparison semantics. Note that with a value that is inserted into a CHAR datatype field with left blank padding, the RDBMS required that the left blank padding be included in the comparison literal before resolving where fixed = ' ABC' correctly. Getting back to having to use TRIM functions for comparison purposes, consider the following query (run on Oracle version 11.1.0.7):

```
scott%ORA11GR1> select variable, fixed from varchar_char_test
  2  where variable  = 'ACL_ACE'
  3    and variable  = fixed;

no rows selected
```

Oracle will not use blank-padded comparison semantics in this comparison because one of the values, variable, is of datatype VARCHAR2. In this case, nonpadded comparison semantics are used. The values must be exactly equal in order for the comparison to be resolved correctly. Therefore, to have these values be compared and resolved correctly without having to change the values stored in the columns, something similar to the following could be written:

```
scott%ORA11GR1> select variable, fixed from varchar_char_test
  2  where variable  = 'ACL_ACE'
  3    and variable  = rtrim(fixed);

VARIABLE
------------------------------------------------------
FIXED
--------------------------------------------------------------------------------
ACL_ACE
ACL_ACE


scott%ORA11GR1> select variable, fixed from varchar_char_test
  2  where variable  = 'ACL_ACE'
  3    and rpad(variable, 100, ' ')  = fixed;

VARIABLE
------------------------------------------------------
FIXED
--------------------------------------------------------------------------------
ACL_ACE
ACL_ACE
```

Either way, potential performance issues (and even potential data integrity issues) arise when a query must be written such that a function, especially to perform any kind of trimming or padding actions, must be called each and every time the query is executed. These are database actions that, given proper planning during the design phase, are usually entirely avoidable.

■ **Note** Similarly, using binary large objects (BLOBs) when you should be using character large objects (CLOBs) ensures lots of unnecessary additional coding just to have a text value evaluated properly.

Don't Make the Database Guess

It cannot be overstated that choosing the correct datatype during schema design, as opposed to trying the wait-and-see approach and then "tuning" the database to change a datatype later, will save you enormous amounts of time, performance, and storage. The Oracle database is designed to recognize dates as dates, and numbers as numbers. Don't make it guess what you want. By using the correct datatypes, tell it exactly what you want. I cannot tell you how many times I have seen queries in production systems that have predicates resembling the following:

```
AND table1.object1_id1 = to_char(table2.inventory_item_id)
```

Having this type of predicate in production will only help you lose performance. Not only does a predicate like this confuse the optimizer (the estimated cardinality = values prediction will be way off), but also it can, and almost surely will, decrease data integrity. It is easy to get dirty data when you store data in a string field that should not really be stored as a string. In the preceding example, table1.object1_id1 is defined as a string. Given the type of data it stores, and because any value being compared against it via a predicate comparison in a SQL query should be converted to a character string, it is apparent that further design discussion regarding these two entities is warranted.

For instance, are these tables related in any way? If so, not only should they have their predicate comparison columns stored using the same datatype, but a foreign-key constraint, or at least some discussion regarding further normalization, is in order. Additionally, a naming convention appended with an identifier such as id, as seen in the preceding example, begs the question "Why would ID-type data be stored as a string?" Hopefully, ID-type data denotes primary-key values. And primary-key values are usually inserted using a sequence, thereby ensuring uniqueness and data integrity. Finally, if the data is inserted using an Oracle sequence, the data will be numeric and should therefore be stored in a column with a numeric datatype.

Another interesting side effect of the preceding type of predicate, one in which a type conversion such as TO_CHAR must be used against a numeric value, is that TO_CHAR(x), where x is a number, is *not deterministic*. It can give a different answer in Spain than it does in the United States (for example, some European languages use a comma rather than a period to represent the decimal point). The preceding predicate is a globalization bug just waiting to happen.

When Bigger Is Not Better

Taking the lazy approach of defining your datatypes with the maximum length possible ensures only one thing: the time required for you to complete requirements gathering and holding design sessions will be reduced. However, you will spend plenty of time trying to figure out why, for instance, now that you've created your "easy to maintain because it doesn't matter how large the string value we insert in there is because it's defined as max-length" column, you cannot index it. Think about that. That is an important issue. What is the point of storing data you cannot access easily? For example, consider the following (attempted on Oracle 11g v1, with a database block size of 8KB):

```
SQL> create table example01 (col1 varchar2(4000), col2 varchar2(4000));

Table created.

SQL> create index idx1_example01 on example01(col1);

Index created.
```

An index on one of the columns can be created. However, what if your needs require a concatenated index?

```
SQL> create index idx2_example01 on example01(col1,col2);

create index idx2_example01 on table01(col1,col2)
*
ERROR at line 1:
ORA-01450: maximum key length (6398) exceeded

SQL> show parameter db_block_size;
```

```
NAME TYPE VALUE

------------------------------------ ----------- -------

db_block_size integer 8192
```

Using an 8KB block size, I am unable to index both columns of my example01 table. I would need to double my block size to do that. If I'd simply done my homework in terms of finding out what the reasonable business expectation might be for the maximum length of data stored in both columns, chances are I would not be running into any storage-related errors when attempting to create indexes, let alone having to increase my database block size.

You must also consider queries and DML against these types of columns. Any data entry API will undoubtedly be created to allow a user to enter the maximum length value available for each column. What an ugly interface *that* will end up being. Additionally, think about the RAM requirements needed to array fetch these types of columns in queries.

What you "save" in design time, you could potentially pay for in "tuning" (which equates to occasional downed production systems while you fix the problem), additional storage requirements, and/or additional memory requirements.

> *I have many times found myself in the position of having to deal with datatypes declared at their maximum length. The downstream burden can be significant. Application testing must allow for any maximum length values. You will be forced to produce test cases where you can ensure that you can, in fact, display all 4,000 characters on a screen or report if a field being used or displayed can potentially contain 4,000 characters. Or, you'll need to document a rationale for why it is all right to truncate such a value under certain circumstances. Either way, your burden is increased.*
>
> *The irresponsible thing to do is to simply ignore the problem. Different programmers will make different choices. Some will allow for 100 characters, some for 500, others for 50, etc. And oftentimes, there is no recording or tracking of such decisions. Inevitably, at some point down the road, some poor developer finds that her particular choice has become the focal point of some problem. In reality, the blame lies with the original system designers.*
>
> *Sometimes applications will just blow up from encountering a too-large value that somehow got into the database column, but that the application was not expecting. And again, by the time this happens, the blame will probably land upon the person least responsible because the designers will have long since ridden off into the sunset.*

—Jonathan Gennick

The trouble taken to carefully design seems negligible when compared with the work, when faced with lack of proper datatype assignation, undoubtedly necessary to change or fix (or worse yet, rewrite) your system after the fact.

Heaps of Trouble

One of the most important takeaways any DBA can derive from a design session has to do with storage. You have the opportunity, during a design session, to discover not only how data will relate to each other, via say, an ERD, but also how it might best be *stored* together. Many DBAs never take advantage of more than the usual heap table and B*Tree index structures. Occasionally, I'll see a DBA using a bit-mapped index on a table with low OLTP activity and a high degree of skew. The external table gets used every once in a while, as well. Other than these few data structures, rarely do I see DBAs making full use of structures such as index-organized tables (IOTs), global temporary tables (GTTs), and clusters.

How many times have you seen a production problem solved as someone looks at a join condition and then simply adds a B*Tree index on one or more of the columns in that join condition? It is an invaluable investment of your time when you try to gather as much information as you can about how the data will be used. How will it be accessed? How often? By how many users? How will it be altered? And so forth. Reports, as every DBA knows, are of paramount interest to end users and can be a DBA's worst nightmare. If you have data that is often accessed together, meaning data stored within tables that you can reasonably assume will be joined together within a SQL query many times over, why not consider storing that data together? This is where a cluster would be an attractive option.

Some of your goals, as a DBA, are to be responsible for best utilizing storage requirements, as well as ensuring that I/O is reduced and that all caches, particularly the buffer cache, are used as efficiently as possible. Because clusters can store data from many tables together on the same block, you can immediately see an ROI by implementing this type of data structure when you discover that instead of needing to manage 75 blocks in the buffer cache to support a commonly accessed set of data using a table join, you are now managing two or three blocks. You should also, by proxy, see your I/O significantly reduced because, by using clusters, you have fewer index blocks and table blocks to retrieve and cache. You don't have to retrieve index data from multiple locations. Instead you simply retrieve index data from, say, the cluster key index (for a B*Tree cluster). You now have a decreased need for indexes on this data. And, if you've planned well, it may also be possible to obtain your actual rows of data from a single database block. Additionally, if you're using a hash cluster, you have no need for any indexes at all on this particular data, because the data is the index, and the index is the data.

For example, let's look at the following code sample (run on Oracle version 11.1.0.7) that creates a B*Tree cluster and a couple of heap tables, and then runs a query that tests the cluster's efficiency in terms of physical I/O (disk reads) and buffer cache block reads, and compares the output with that of the same query run against the heap tables.

```
scott%ORA11GR1> drop table t_tables;

Table dropped.


scott%ORA11GR1> drop table t_indexes;

Table dropped.


scott%ORA11GR1> drop table users_tables;

Table dropped.


scott%ORA11GR1> drop table users_indexes;

Table dropped.


scott%ORA11GR1> drop cluster user_items_cluster_btree;

Cluster dropped.
```

93

```
scott%ORA11GR1> drop table users_tables_heap;

Table dropped.

scott%ORA11GR1> drop table users_indexes_heap;

Table dropped.

scott%ORA11GR1> create cluster user_items_cluster_btree (
  2            table_name varchar2 (30)) size 1024;

Cluster created.

scott%ORA11GR1> create index user_items_idx
  2  on cluster user_items_cluster_btree;

Index created.

scott%ORA11GR1> create table t_tables
  2  (table_name varchar2(30), owner varchar2(30));

Table created.

scott%ORA11GR1> create table t_indexes
  2  (index_name varchar2(30), index_owner varchar2(30), table_name varchar2(30),
  3  table_owner varchar2(30));

Table created.

scott%ORA11GR1> create table users_tables
  2  (table_name varchar2(30), owner varchar2(30))
  3  cluster user_items_cluster_btree(table_name);

Table created.

scott%ORA11GR1> create table users_indexes
  2  (index_name varchar2(30), index_owner varchar2(30), table_name varchar2(30),
  3  table_owner varchar2(30))
  4  cluster user_items_cluster_btree(table_name);

Table created.
```

```
scott%ORA11GR1> create table users_tables_heap
  2  (table_name varchar2(30), owner varchar2(30));

Table created.


scott%ORA11GR1> create table users_indexes_heap
  2  (index_name varchar2(30), index_owner varchar2(30), table_name varchar2(30),
  3  table_owner varchar2(30));

Table created.


scott%ORA11GR1> create index users_tables_tablename_idx on users_tables_heap(table_name);

Index created.


scott%ORA11GR1> create index users_indexes_tablename_idx on users_indexes_heap(table_name);

Index created.
```

The two tables, t_tables and t_indexes, are populated, and then used as base tables for the populating of the subsequent cluster and heap tables so that the data remains consistent throughout the test. Data dictionary tables can be somewhat volatile, and having a consistent set of data to work with is important in order to see expected results when testing the performance of clusters vs. heap tables.

```
scott%ORA11GR1> insert into t_tables (table_name, owner)
  2  select table_name,
  3         owner
  4    from dba_tables;

2619 rows created.


scott%ORA11GR1> insert into t_indexes( index_name, index_owner,
  2                                     table_name, table_owner )
  3  select index_name,
  4         owner,
  5         table_name,
  6         table_owner
  7    from dba_indexes
  8   where (table_name, table_owner) in (
  9           select table_name, table_owner from t_tables)
 10   order by dbms_random.random;

3737 rows created.
```

Note the use of the Oracle built-in package, dbms_random, in the preceding insert action into the table t_indexes (as well as in the subsequent insert actions into the tables users_indexes and

95

users_indexes_heap). The order by dbms_random.random clause is included in order to simulate the randomness with which child records generally are inserted into any OLTP system:

```
scott%ORA11GR1> insert into users_tables (table_name, owner)
  2  select table_name,
  3         owner
  4    from t_tables;

2619 rows created.

scott%ORA11GR1> insert into users_indexes (
  2                   index_name, index_owner, table_name, table_owner )
  3  select index_name,
  4         index_owner,
  5         table_name,
  6         table_owner
  7    from t_indexes
  8   where (table_name, table_owner) in
  9         (select table_name, table_owner from users_tables)
 10   order by dbms_random.random;

3737 rows created.


scott%ORA11GR1> insert into users_tables_heap (table_name, owner)
  2  select table_name,
  3         owner
  4    from t_tables;

2619 rows created.


scott%ORA11GR1> insert into users_indexes_heap (
  2                   index_name, index_owner, table_name, table_owner )
  3  select index_name,
  4         index_owner,
  5         table_name,
  6         table_owner
  7    from t_indexes
  8   where (table_name, table_owner) in
  9         (select table_name, table_owner from users_tables_heap)
 10   order by dbms_random.random;

3737 rows created.


scott%ORA11GR1> commit;

Commit complete.
```

```
scott%ORA11GR1> analyze cluster user_items_cluster_btree compute statistics;

Cluster analyzed.

scott%ORA11GR1> exec dbms_stats.gather_table_stats( user, 'USERS_TABLES',
2    method_opt => 'for all indexed columns', estimate_percent => 100 );

Table analyzed.

scott%ORA11GR1> exec dbms_stats.gather_table_stats( user, 'USERS_INDEXES',
2    method_opt => 'for all indexed columns', estimate_percent => 100 );

Table analyzed.

scott%ORA11GR1> exec dbms_stats.gather_table_stats( user, 'USERS_TABLES_HEAP',
2    method_opt => 'for all indexed columns', estimate_percent => 100 );

Table analyzed.

scott%ORA11GR1> exec dbms_stats.gather_table_stats( user, 'USERS_INDEXES_HEAP',
2    method_opt => 'for all indexed columns', estimate_percent => 100 );

Table analyzed.


scott%ORA11GR1> alter system flush buffer_cache;

System altered.
```

Flushing the buffer cache is used in this example only to show you the maximum number of disk reads each query execution (cluster vs. heap) would do given a set of circumstances where none of the associated cluster or table blocks are already in the buffer cache.

```
scott%ORA11GR1> alter session set sql_trace=true;

Session altered.


scott%ORA11GR1> variable BIND1 varchar2(30)
scott%ORA11GR1> exec :BIND1 := 'WFS_FEATURETYPE$'

PL/SQL procedure successfully completed.


scott%ORA11GR1> select a.table_name, b.index_name /* CLUSTER_TEST */
2    from users_tables a, users_indexes b
3   where a.table_name  = b.table_name
4     and a.owner       = b.table_owner
5     and a.table_name  = :BIND1
6  order by a.table_name, b.index_name;
```

```
TABLE_NAME                       INDEX_NAME
-----------------------------    ------------------------------
WFS_FEATURETYPE$                 SYS_C004999
WFS_FEATURETYPE$                 SYS_IL0000063214C00004$$
WFS_FEATURETYPE$                 SYS_IL0000063214C00006$$
WFS_FEATURETYPE$                 SYS_IL0000063214C00015$$
WFS_FEATURETYPE$                 SYS_IL0000063214C00016$$
WFS_FEATURETYPE$                 SYS_IL0000063214C00017$$
WFS_FEATURETYPE$                 SYS_IL0000063214C00018$$
WFS_FEATURETYPE$                 SYS_IL0000063214C00019$$
WFS_FEATURETYPE$                 SYS_IL0000063214C00026$$
WFS_FEATURETYPE$                 SYS_IL0000063214C00027$$
WFS_FEATURETYPE$                 SYS_IL0000063214C00028$$
WFS_FEATURETYPE$                 SYS_IL0000063214C00029$$
WFS_FEATURETYPE$                 SYS_IL0000063214C00030$$
WFS_FEATURETYPE$                 SYS_IL0000063214C00031$$
WFS_FEATURETYPE$                 SYS_IL0000063214C00034$$
WFS_FEATURETYPE$                 SYS_IL0000063214C00035$$
WFS_FEATURETYPE$                 SYS_IL0000063214C00037$$
WFS_FEATURETYPE$                 SYS_IL0000063214C00038$$
WFS_FEATURETYPE$                 SYS_IL0000063214C00039$$
WFS_FEATURETYPE$                 UNIQUE_WFS_FT_COND

20 rows selected.


scott%ORA11GR1> select a.table_name, b.index_name /* HEAP_TEST */
  2     from users_tables_heap a, users_indexes_heap b
  3    where a.table_name  = b.table_name
  4      and a.owner       = b.table_owner
  5      and a.table_name  = :BIND1
  6    order by a.table_name, b.index_name;

TABLE_NAME                       INDEX_NAME
-----------------------------    ------------------------------
WFS_FEATURETYPE$                 SYS_C004999
WFS_FEATURETYPE$                 SYS_IL0000063214C00004$$
WFS_FEATURETYPE$                 SYS_IL0000063214C00006$$
WFS_FEATURETYPE$                 SYS_IL0000063214C00015$$
WFS_FEATURETYPE$                 SYS_IL0000063214C00016$$
WFS_FEATURETYPE$                 SYS_IL0000063214C00017$$
WFS_FEATURETYPE$                 SYS_IL0000063214C00018$$
WFS_FEATURETYPE$                 SYS_IL0000063214C00019$$
WFS_FEATURETYPE$                 SYS_IL0000063214C00026$$
WFS_FEATURETYPE$                 SYS_IL0000063214C00027$$
WFS_FEATURETYPE$                 SYS_IL0000063214C00028$$
WFS_FEATURETYPE$                 SYS_IL0000063214C00029$$
WFS_FEATURETYPE$                 SYS_IL0000063214C00030$$
WFS_FEATURETYPE$                 SYS_IL0000063214C00031$$
WFS_FEATURETYPE$                 SYS_IL0000063214C00034$$
WFS_FEATURETYPE$                 SYS_IL0000063214C00035$$
```

```
WFS_FEATURETYPE$                SYS_IL0000063214C00037$$
WFS_FEATURETYPE$                SYS_IL0000063214C00038$$
WFS_FEATURETYPE$                SYS_IL0000063214C00039$$
WFS_FEATURETYPE$                UNIQUE_WFS_FT_COND

20 rows selected.


scott%ORA11GR1> alter session set sql_trace=false;

Session altered.
```

Now a look at the TKPROF report reveals the following:

```
****************************************************************************

select a.table_name, b.index_name /* CLUSTER_TEST */
  from users_tables a, users_indexes b
 where a.table_name  = b.table_name
   and a.owner       = b.table_owner
   and a.table_name  = :BIND1
order by a.table_name, b.index_name

call     count       cpu    elapsed       disk      query    current       rows
-------  ------  --------  ----------  ---------  ---------  ----------  ----------
Parse         1      0.00        0.00          0          0           0           0
Execute       1      0.00        0.00          0          0           0           0
Fetch         3      0.00        0.00          3          5           0          20
-------  ------  --------  ----------  ---------  ---------  ----------  ----------
total         5      0.00        0.00          3          5           0          20

Misses in library cache during parse: 1
Misses in library cache during execute: 1
Optimizer mode: ALL_ROWS
Parsing user id: 81

Rows     Row Source Operation
-------  ---------------------------------------------------------
     20  SORT ORDER BY (cr=5 pr=3 pw=0 time=0 us cost=4 size=71 card=1)
     20   NESTED LOOPS  (cr=5 pr=3 pw=0 time=0 us cost=3 size=71 card=1)
      1    TABLE ACCESS CLUSTER USERS_TABLES (cr=3 pr=3 pw=0 time=0 us cost=2
             size=25 card=1)
      1     INDEX UNIQUE SCAN USER_ITEMS_IDX (cr=2 pr=2 pw=0 time=0 us
             cost=1 size=0 card=1)(object id 86282)
     20    TABLE ACCESS CLUSTER USERS_INDEXES (cr=2 pr=0 pw=0 time=0 us
             cost=1 size=46 card=1)


****************************************************************************

select a.table_name, b.index_name /* HEAP_TEST */
  from users_tables_heap a, users_indexes_heap b
```

```
  where a.table_name  = b.table_name
    and a.owner       = b.table_owner
    and a.table_name  = :BIND1
order by a.table_name, b.index_name
```

call	count	cpu	elapsed	disk	query	current	rows
Parse	1	0.00	0.00	0	0	0	0
Execute	1	0.00	0.00	0	0	0	0
Fetch	3	0.00	0.00	20	20	0	20
total	5	0.00	0.00	20	20	0	20

```
Misses in library cache during parse: 1
Misses in library cache during execute: 1
Optimizer mode: ALL_ROWS
Parsing user id: 81
```

```
Rows    Row Source Operation
-------  ---------------------------------------------------
    20   SORT ORDER BY (cr=20 pr=20 pw=0 time=0 us cost=6 size=82 card=1)
    20    NESTED LOOPS  (cr=20 pr=20 pw=0 time=0 us)
    20     NESTED LOOPS  (cr=5 pr=5 pw=0 time=0 us cost=5 size=82 card=1)
     1      TABLE ACCESS BY INDEX ROWID USERS_TABLES_HEAP (cr=3 pr=3 pw=0 time=0
            us cost=2 size=29 card=1)
     1       INDEX RANGE SCAN USERS_TABLES_TABLENAME_IDX (cr=2 pr=2 pw=0 time=0
            us cost=1 size=0 card=1)(object id 86289)
    20       INDEX RANGE SCAN USERS_INDEXES_TABLENAME_IDX (cr=2 pr=2 pw=0 time=0
            us cost=1 size=0 card=2)(object id 86290)
    20      TABLE ACCESS BY INDEX ROWID USERS_INDEXES_HEAP (cr=15 pr=15 pw=0 time=0
            us cost=3 size=53 card=1)
```

```
**************************************************************************
```

Comparing the two sets of results, we clearly see that the B*Tree cluster in this case did significantly less physical I/O and was indeed more efficient in terms of buffer cache usage. In fact, if you repeat this test multiple times, you will find that the value for the disk reads may go slightly up and/or slightly down from the value you see listed previously for the heap test, but should remain at a constant value for the cluster test.

Last but not least, if you're resolving lots of data queries by using lots of associative tables (and depending on what your ERD looks like, you may be), then using IOTs can benefit you hugely in the long run. Like clusters, your data can be physically colocated. However, unlike clusters, IOTs store data sorted by primary key, and can pack related data together, no matter the order of insertion.

Faster, Not Harder

After you've decided on your datatypes, data structures, and storage strategies, complementary types of indexing techniques are usually going to be your next consideration. Whether a system is slow is going to be 99 percent dependent on what your users deem to be *slow*. What is an acceptable response time when a user clicks a button that submits a query? Is it 5 seconds? 1 second? 500 milliseconds?

Whatever you decide, the goal should be faster access that is not overly taxing to (hard on) the system. For example, creating one single column B*Tree index for every single column included in a predicate somewhere within the application is not necessarily going to make your access faster. However, such an indexing scheme is guaranteed to create more work for your system because every DML statement executed against table values will need to execute similar DML statements against any similar column value indexes.

Therefore, your indexing strategies, like everything else involved in application design, require careful consideration. In addition to IOTs, B*Tree clusters, and hash clusters, you should really research function-based indexes (FBIs) and domain indexes to see whether they would be useful for your application's access needs. For instance, in those cases where you find you must index string values, you might consider using a function-based index that converts the string value to uppercase (if the value is stored in mixed case, that is) in order to help you provide your users with fast, case-insensitive searches. You'll also find that if you are using features such as Oracle Text, Visual Information Retrieval, Expression Filter, or Oracle Spatial (just to name a few), Oracle provides special domain indexes on unstructured datatypes. Such datatypes include those that hold data for text (like the stored WHERE clauses used for Expression Filter functionality), video, audio, image (like the ORDSYS.ORDIMAGE type used for Visual Information Retrieval), and spatial data.

FBIs can be tremendously helpful when your goal is to perform *conditional* indexing. When you want some, but not all, rows indexed, based on some condition being met, FBIs can be invaluable. For example, a situation where I recently used an FBI successfully took place as follows. Someone had placed a bitmap index in a column that had five possible values: 0, 1, 2, 3, and 4. A high preponderance of rows contained the values 1 and 3. Because of this low cardinality, someone decided to place a bitmap index on this column specifically to assist with the case where, in many filter conditions throughout the application, WHERE info_id = 3 appeared. Because this table was a high-transactional table, the frequent amount of DML performed on both the table and the bitmap index assured that performance soon slowed to a miserable crawl. As a result of a quick discussion with Tom Kyte of asktom.oracle.com fame, the bitmap index was subsequently replaced with a B*Tree index (subsequently made into an FBI) created as follows:

```
create index info_fbi on info_table(
   case when info_id = 3 then info_id else NULL end );
```

■ **Note** You will not find this solution offered in the Oracle documentation. It is Tom Kyte's clever thinking-outside-the-box solution, employing his knowledge of function-based indexes and the ways in which NULL entries are handled.

As you can see, with this type of FBI, the index remains small and indexes only those rows that match the predicate included in the index's case statement. Additionally, NULL entries are not included as index entries for this index. (Entirely NULL entries are *never* included in B*Tree indexes.) After swapping out the bitmap index for the preceding FBI, performance was greatly improved. Again, there is no substitute for careful planning regarding how, how often, and by how many users your data will be accessed.

Other Design Considerations

Just because you're the DBA doesn't mean that the database should be your *only* concern in terms of performance tuning. Although the design of a system may traditionally be left up to developers, and other system considerations may traditionally be left up to system administrators and architects, don't think that when things go wrong with any of these aspects of an application that it won't be your problem. Again, though it may not be your fault, it will certainly be your problem. So, because it can be your problem, you should have as much say as possible in all aspects of how a system is designed, built, and run.

Middle Tier vs. Database

Be careful to let developers, designers, and anyone else involved in the design of a system know on which side of the argument known as *database dependence vs. database independence* you stand. If you are wise, you stand on the side of database dependence. This is so for a myriad of reasons, including these:

- Concurrency (multiversioning, read consistency, locking, and so forth).

- Performance (database-dependent applications may perform orders of magnitude faster than database-independent applications, especially during transaction processing).

- Analytics, data integrity, built-in functions: You have so many features available to you right out of the box with your purchase of an Oracle database that it would be extremely foolish and spendthrift of you not to take as much advantage as possible of all that your Oracle database has to offer.

- Transactional modularity: When relying on an Oracle database system, using PL/SQL functions, procedures, and packages, you can modularize like business functions/actions into logical transactional units of work that can be ported to other Oracle database systems and that provide convenient code reusability.

- With support and license fees, the Oracle database is already an expensive investment for your company. Why make your company spend more than it has to simply because a few designers and developers have not taken the time to read the Oracle documentation and therefore realize that its built-in functionality will save everyone a fortune (both in time and money) in the long run, in coding, maintenance, and performance?

I also believe that companies pretty much get locked into their database platforms anyway, for reasons other than just the applications. Chasing some elusive, holy grail of database independence is likely to be as fruitful as chasing the real *holy grail would be. Basically, it'll be fruitless.*

—Jonathan Gennick

Flexibility, Security, Speed

If you ask any user to list their top three priorities for any application (that is, besides, that it give them the correct answer), they most likely would be flexibility, security, and speed. In terms of flexibility, this requirement goes back somewhat to the choice of design methodology. Now, it is true that you can save yourself and your company countless needless headaches by asking as many questions up front about the nature of the company's business and its particular needs as they pertain to the application at hand. However, it is also true that over time there will be questions you could not have anticipated. The types of questions business users ask of their database data can be infinite.

If you have not designed your database to be accommodating (as much as is possible) to users who may choose to ask questions via some other route than through the application, you have helped create a recipe for disaster. Users will use your application. However, they will almost certainly have more questions than even the best-planned application can answer. Customers' needs change over time. Occasionally, there will be a need for ad hoc SQL. If the design of your system is such that the only way to access the data is through your application, you have ensured that your database is significantly less flexible, and it will have a short-lived ability to support the needs of your users.

Data integrity, verification, and security checking performed in the application's middle tier will make your database application perform slower, be less reliable than it would be if you performed these actions at the database level, and will increase your development time drastically. It is odd that some developers feel that if they are not performing these actions in the middle tier (at the *application level*), they have somehow lost control of their application. This is naive and shortsighted. It is just as naive and shortsighted as any DBA assuming that the design of a database application is not part of a DBA's duties. Though it may not be in your HR-written job description per se, design is certainly your duty if you desire to have any life outside of work.

Keep in mind that the further from the database data any security code lives, the less secure your database data. Remember that there are others who can access the database data bypassing your application—like you and your DBA colleagues, for instance. This certainly wouldn't put the Sarbanes-Oxley auditors' minds at ease. If you cannot prove that every action on the database is auditable (which right now, only Oracle-supplied methods for auditing, or proof that someone has disabled these methods, is available for such access record-keeping), your database data is, as a result, insecure.

In terms of speed, many Java developers I have worked with love to perform constraint checking (particularly when checking for uniqueness) in the middle tier. This will never be faster than the native database code in C that already does this, right out of the box. Having to query the database over the network, check the values, and necessarily perform programmatic locks will invariably be much slower than allowing the database to perform its checks immediately upon insertion. Additionally, unless the developers are attempting to write their own database, there is no evidence anywhere that I have seen to support popular assertions that writing your own constraint-checking logic, your own sequence-generating logic, your own security checks, and, essentially, anything else that your RDBMS can perform for you automatically will do anything for you other than ensure that your customer has wasted lots of money on an RDBMS that is being severely underutilized. This application will never truly scale, never truly meet the needs of its customers, and ultimately be impossibly nightmarish to maintain. These reasons, if none others, should be your primary reasons for wanting to be involved in the design of any database application you will be tasked to support.

The Importance of Having Integrity

The importance of having integrity (in your database, that is) cannot be overstated. Assuming that the application being currently built is the only application that will ever access the current data is like creating a restaurant that serves only local customers their favorite meals. Over time, the needs of the customers will change. If it is a restaurant with delicious food, it will attract other, new customers. Those new customers may make requests such as "Do you serve dessert? Seafood? Do you have plans for extended hours on the weekend evenings?" If you are really listening to your customers and want to continue doing business with your restaurant, you will seriously consider the feasibility of all requests.

Creating a database is really no different in terms of the entrepreneurial ways in which you envision the possible uses for its data. Creating integrity within your database ensures application flexibility. Users ultimately want their data uniqueness, security, DML rules, and anything that protects the data from misuse or becoming dirty to be consistent across applications. Nothing helps you to ensure this consistency more than enforcing integrity at the database level. Referential integrity (using primary and foreign keys, for example) has additional benefits other than simply making your database available for use by multiple applications.

The cost-based optimizer is given more information about your data. If you have gathered statistics on your tables and related indices, then during query and DML execution, the cost-based optimizer is able to discover how your data tables are related to each other; it is told about the parent table to child table relationships, for example. You are able to use materialized views because Oracle will be able to rewrite a query using a materialized view after this type of information (constraint information) has been written to the data dictionary. The cost-based optimizer cannot be guaranteed to write correct and efficient access paths for you if this information is not part of your metadata. If all of the validation rules are hidden in application logic, those validation rules will need to, somehow, be replicated to any additional applications that are written to access your data.

CONSTRAINTS AND DATA WAREHOUSES

It is worth mentioning that there are those who will state that constraints should *not* be considered at certain times. Most particularly, those same people will point to a data warehouse and bemoan the fact that use of constraints can slow down the loading or updating of data. However, I would contend that constraints, especially in a data warehouse, make your retrievals infinitely faster than those retrievals would be otherwise. Having said that, then of course one has to determine where they would rather lose performance, if losing performance were inevitable. On the retrieval side of things, where retrievals are done typically hundreds of times per minute? Or on the load side of things, which is (most likely) not performed anywhere near hundreds of times per minute? In fact, the number of loads performed on most data warehouses is usually closer to no more than a handful of times per day. I would contend that a loss of performance when loading data into a data warehouse is a small price to pay when compared with the huge performance boost your users will see when constraints are used in conjunction with query results retrieval.

Invariably, something will be missed. Your data can quickly become corrupted, and your system can slow to an absolute crawl over easily avoidable issues such as your applications performing a SQL join where it is discovered that a matching primary-key value is missing. If it can happen, it most likely will happen. And again, moving this type of checking to the application only ensures that over time your application(s) will experience a significant slowdown. Having the client make a roundtrip from the client to the server each and every time the application wants to, say, verify the existence of a primary-key value before inserting a foreign-key value is like a bank teller informing a banking customer whether their minimum bank balance has been reached by manually counting each piece of currency (for instance, every dollar bill) each time the question is posed, before a fee will be incurred. It is a colossal waste of time and resources, not to mention money. *And*, even more significantly, with this method, logical corruption could easily take place.

Don't Be High Maintenance

High maintenance is a pejorative at any level. You never want your application to have this type of distinction. Inexperienced coders (or DBAs) might think it's cool to be called on to fix X, Y, or Z on an ongoing basis in the middle of the night. They might think it makes them look invaluable. But it doesn't. It makes them look incompetent. Think about it. If you buy a new car and have to take it back every week to get the door lock working properly or the brakes fixed or the steering wheel realigned, even if the technicians who do this for you correct the problem each and every time, you will not be a happy customer. Your faith in the product you have just invested your money in will be diminished. You probably will never buy another car from them again, because your perception of them will be "They are not careful."

Don't let your database applications customers think the same thing about you, your team, and/or the developers. You are all in this together. You need each other. The success or failure and the ease of (or lack thereof) database application maintenance, and therefore shelf life, of the application, reflect on all of you. If you are placing your integrity in the database, and not in the application, you are greatly assisting with maintainability. If you are using the built-in functionality available with the Oracle database, as opposed to concocting your own (inevitably inferior) homegrown solutions, you are, again, greatly assisting with maintainability. Why write in twenty lines of code what you can write in one? Less code, less bugs.

If you are performing the security checks for data access though the Oracle RDBMS, you are ten times more likely to gain and keep the trust of your customers, as well as your own peace of mind. You are also more likely to pass Sarbanes-Oxley (and other auditing outfits') security requirements. No need to rewrite, and possibly muck up, what the Oracle database already does for you easier, faster, cheaper, and, more important, with a higher degree of guaranteed correctness over time. Similarly, integrity checks performed within the database, rather than inside application logic, will perform the same across applications and provide you with invaluable data consistency and integrity that cannot be guaranteed when created programmatically outside the Oracle database.

If you must code for *database independence* with an eye to code portability, take care to code all the database components of your application in stored procedures. The API portion of your application (that is, that part of the application logic that is not specifically data driven) will be database *independent*. Your data logic should always be coded in a way that is best for the specific database you are using. When your data logic is contained within a stored procedure, it behooves you to make the best use of every Oracle feature you possibly can. Even if you later move this application to another (non-Oracle) database, it is rarely just a simple port. If it were, you would have chosen that other database to begin with.

The decision to use an Oracle database for your business and application needs is never one of capriciousness. It is an expensive database. After you've deployed an application on a particular database, it usually remains there forever. If it is moved to another database, the move is often done as part of a rework of the entire application anyway (both the API and the data layer). It is an upgrade with new features, functions, and business logic. Therefore, if your application depends on an Oracle database, it should employ every vendor-specific feature and capability it can, to ensure the highest maintainability.

The DBA as Database Evangelist

As an Oracle DBA who not only likes and appreciates the Oracle RDBMS software, but also likes and appreciates having your weekends, evenings, and vacations interrupted as little as possible, becoming your company's Oracle database evangelist should be one of your main goals. Ensuring that an application is scalable, maintainable, secure, flexible, and provides your users (foremost) with correct, dependable answers to their business queries and actions takes DBAs, designers, and developers who are proactive. When you purchase a new car, you rarely do so with the intention of figuring out a way to get around without actually driving it. So why would you do so with an Oracle database? It is amazing how many designers and developers take the *black box* approach when it comes to the Oracle database and assume that it is just a large repository. It is even more amazing how many skilled Oracle DBAs sit by and apathetically watch this happen; they negatively comment on the design process, and then wait for the inevitable production calls and e-mails that ensue after the new application is deployed. The best DBAs evangelize their chosen RDBMS.

One of my consulting projects entailed that I help to bridge the gap between DBAs and developers. Indeed, that assignment soon proved to be no small affair as the DBAs were all seasoned Oracle DBAs (averaging more than five years of experience working with various types and sizes of systems running on Oracle), and the developers were all mainly Java developers (averaging two or fewer years of experience) writing code that accessed the company's various Oracle databases. When I began this experiment, I immediately went to the DBAs in hopes that starting with people whose beloved RDBMS was close to my own heart would be easier. I found that they were decidedly biased in their opinions about the Java developers and had pretty much already made up their minds as to the efficacy of such a bridging effort as mine.

I then decided to approach the developers. I decided to take a different tact from the heretofore tried approach of my DBA colleagues, which was "You guys need to learn the database because your SQL skills <insert expletive here>." Instead I called a meeting with them and brought with me to the meeting a few Statspack reports that outlined the longest-running SQL in the past month. And I began the meeting with the following: "I need your group's help. We have long-running SQL that is impeding performance and will only get worse over time. So I thought we could put our heads together and find out the easiest way that Oracle can help you run your business actions."

Now, as you can imagine, one or two of the meeting members replied along the lines of "We can't have Oracle run our business actions. We need to have everything in the middle tier so that we have control."

And I asked, "Why? Whether you write it in the middle tier or write it in a database procedural or set-oriented language, you are still the author of it. How does writing it in a language other than Java make you lose control?"

Finally, one person replied (smiling sheepishly), "Well, we don't know that much about Oracle is the problem—and we have to write the applications."

I answered, "Fair enough. So, you don't know that much about Oracle. Did you know that much about Java when you first started learning the language? Everyone starts somewhere. So let's start with this SQL that I have in my hands and go from there."

We started small and began tuning individual SQL statements. I needed them to show me where the individual SQL statements were buried in the application code, and they needed me to help them, over time, learn about benchmarking, unit testing, and stress testing their code that accessed the database. I decreased the runtime of a query that took more than 5 minutes to just a few seconds by adding one constraint and one index on a date column. Needless to say, one of the responses to that was "Wow, I didn't know you could do that! That was so easy. I wish I had known that!" Converting some of their subroutines to packaged procedures made bind variable usage all the rage. They looked forward to seeing the lists of SQL statements on the Statspack reports decreased each time they attended a meeting. They even competed among themselves as to who would have the least number of (or none at all) SQL statements appearing on the Statspack reports. They were learning Oracle. And they were liking it— because I was showing them how certain Oracle features really did or could make *their* lives easier. And ultimately, they hadn't lost control. They were instead learning how Oracle could help them in building their applications.

I proposed that we start holding brown bag sessions. I asked, "What do you think about our meeting once a week for lunch in the main conference room to talk about Oracle? I think it would be a good idea if, each session, a different person from the group present something new that they learned regarding Oracle that week. It doesn't have to be an advanced topic, per se. Just something about Oracle that is new to *you*. Then if other members of the group are familiar with the topic being presented, they can add their own tidbits to help pad the discussion."

Inevitably, the next question was "Well, can we also hold one for Java?" You knew *that* was coming. And I replied, "Of course. Let's just choose a different day for that one." So twice a week we met for lunch, one day devoted to presentations regarding Oracle, and the other to presentations on Java. And it wasn't long before conversations turned to comparisons of different processes and how they performed in Oracle vs. when coded in Java.

A rounding out of web development processes vs. data access processes was beginning to occur. As time went on, lively debate began to take place as the developers learned more and more about Oracle. They were learning about constraints, Oracle sequences, Oracle's locking mechanisms, read consistency, analytic functions, different types of storage structures. And (at least it seemed to me) they were having fun doing so. It was a challenge for them. And they were enjoying the challenge.

Now, I'm not going to lie to you. It didn't go *completely* smoothly. I'm not going to say there weren't those standout members of the group who held religiously to their beliefs that all application processing (*all of it*) ultimately belonged in the middle tier. There were. However, as time wore on, many of the developers simply wanted to do what they did *well*. And that means they wanted to write code that performed well, and did so consistently, even with hundreds of user accesses. And they wanted to get credit for it. Learning Oracle helped them get to know their applications even better. They certainly got to know their customers' data better, which was a huge boon. And they wanted to spend less time fixing bugs and less time being called off-hours to look at a production problem.

Little by little, members of the DBA group began attending these brown bag sessions, at first sporadically, then later regularly. The only rule was this: you must be willing to listen, and listen respectfully. After that, feel free to disagree, but make sure you prove, as empirically as possible, why you disagree. The two groups reluctantly began to present to each other. But over time, many of the attendees began to realize that the two groups had quite a bit to learn from each other. I remember one of the questions asked of one of the more senior DBAs was "Why didn't you tell us about materialized views?" To which his reply was "You never asked." I later asked this same senior DBA, "How do you think the brown bags (sessions) are going?" He said, "You know, some of the developers have really stepped up. I'm liking that they are learning and using PL/SQL a lot more now." And I replied, "Yeah, I agree. So how about you? Any chance you'll start having a look at what they are doing in Java?" He just smiled like I should have known better than to ask such a question and replied, "No chance whatsoever."

I mark my success in that bridging-the-gap assignment by how much the two groups began talking to and consulting with each other. At least many of them (not all, can't win 'em all) welcomed the opportunity to learn something new from each other—*particularly* if it meant reduced on-call, dead-of-night issues. Inevitably, the two groups had quite a bit to learn from each other, and whether they did so willingly or begrudgingly, the two groups made an effort to stand in each other's shoes. But the biggest lesson learned from that assignment for me personally was, if you don't toot the horn for your chosen RDBMS (and do it in a way that sounds attractive and enticing to your target audience), who will?

Reading the Documentation and Keeping Current

As a DBA, the first on-the-job training you should be part of is ensuring that, at a minimum, both you and your team of DBAs have read the Oracle Concepts Guide. If you can convince the developers to do the same, you are way ahead of the game. Additionally, when you read the Concepts Guide, you will see that it links to virtually every other relevant piece of documentation you should review. In addition to the Oracle Concepts Guide, the following list represents a start, but by no means is an exhaustive list, for the guides and manuals you should familiarize yourself with.

- **The New Features Guide**: Whenever there are additions to or improvements in existing functionality, you can find a bite-sized description of them here. The full-length description can be found in whatever individual guide encapsulates the feature, be it related to administration or application development. This guide provides you with a quick, at-a-glance road map for new features and is extremely useful to review each time a new release of the Oracle database is made available.

- **The Performance Tuning Guide and Reference**: Because you are currently reading a book on Oracle performance tuning, the recommended reading you should be reviewing in tandem with this book is definitely the Performance Tuning Guide and Reference. Before you begin doing anything at all with an Oracle database, you should read this guide.

- **The Administrators Guide**: All of the new features specific to database administration are outlined and explained in this guide.

- **The Application Developers Guide**: I know. You are a DBA. However, if you have any hope of any database application you support being designed correctly, you'd better read this guide so when you sit in design sessions (as you surely will), you are ready to suggest to the designers and developers how best to make use of much of Oracle's built-in functionality, such as the following:

  - Designing database schemas

  - Managing data integrity

  - SQL and PL/SQL considerations

  - Implementing security

  - Indexing strategies

- **The PL/SQL Users Guide and Reference**: If you are going to suggest stored procedures and packages, you will need to know what you are talking about. Reading this guide is an invaluable starting (as well as review) point.

Knowing, Testing, and Teaching Your Software's Features

The best way to be an evangelist is through teaching your software's features. So knowing about and testing as many features available with your version and edition of the Oracle database as possible is the most surefire way to get designers and developers not only aware of, but excited about, using the Oracle database effectively in application design. Some of the more salient Oracle features and subsequent worthy discussion topics that come to mind warrant a listing of sorts. The following listing is by no means exhaustive but provides, I believe, a good starting point for Oracle features worth investigating, learning, and even evangelizing about:

- If you are designing your first data warehouse using Oracle and your team knows nothing about analytics, be the first to start testing and teaching the benefits of using this phenomenal feature.

- If people have a vague idea about but have not really used partitioning, demonstrate its impact via a test application.

- Study, test, and impart your knowledge regarding parallel processing.

- Describe the differences between, and respective benefits of, shared server and dedicated server connections.

- Dig deep into Real Application Clusters (RAC), to discern whether it is not only a viable, but potentially necessary, option for you and your system(s).

- Know the performance features and options available with the Oracle database. Get familiar with TKPROF, Autotrace, Explain Plan, Statspack, AWR, DBMS_PROFILER, and more. When you begin playing around with these tools, you will see that it not only becomes easy to make your case better for designers and developers using the Oracle database, but also vital for you to do so. With these tools at your disposal, you can readily see where your performance bottlenecks and hotspots take place. And with that knowledge in your back pocket, it becomes your duty to inform everyone else.

- Teach the developers how to look at data dictionary views. *And provide them with the access to do so.* You give away nothing and gain everything when you enlist the help of the developers in performance tuning. You make them your allies and accomplices. And more important, by doing so, you automatically spread the responsibility for the performance of any database application over a greater number of people.

- Ensure that you make yourself aware of the costs of parsing, and the advantages of using bind variables.

- Though you don't consider yourself a coder, learn why PL/SQL is the most efficient procedural programming language to access an Oracle database. Learn about the relationship between PL/SQL and dependency management tracking. Learn the difference between procedural processing and set-based processing, as well as procedural bulk processing. Learn the differences between static SQL and dynamic SQL. Learn when and why you should use an implicit cursor over an explicit cursor and vice versa.

- Instrument your code (I cannot say enough good about DBMS_APPLICATION_INFO) and encourage everyone else to do the same. Any overhead incurred in doing so is negligible and well worth its weight in gold in terms of the invaluable debugging information it can provide you.

- Know about and discuss various auditing options.

- Do *not* look for shortcuts such as special `init.ora` parameters. These types of parameters are not general panaceas and should be regarded as settings to be put in place on a case-by-case basis.

- Study Oracle's capabilities for replication, message queuing, and keeping a history of data changes (such as Workspace Manager provides you).

In short, assume that if there is a need you can think of for your application, then someone else has that same need, and chances are that the Oracle database will already provide it for you, in some way, shape, or form, directly out of the box. It is better to be the hero that brings tidings of "How our lives can all be made easier by using our Oracle database better," rather than "How I stayed up until four o'clock in the morning troubleshooting the reason why that auditing trigger we put in place didn't really work and now my family has left for vacation without me." Truly, which scenario would you choose?

Learning from Your Mistakes and Experiences

Even with the best-planned systems, every once in a while something will happen in a production system you did not anticipate. When this happens, you should find out what is different between your production system and your testing system. Is it concurrency? Read consistency? I/O? RAM? Did a query plan change? Hopefully you have put history and performance measurement recording devices in place that can help you answer these types of questions.

Triages and Postmortems

During your initial triage and postmortem, try to figure out whether anyone has immediate knowledge as to what has happened in the event of a production problem. "I added an index I thought would help." "We have changed the way our nightly stats-gathering procedures run." "We have put in place a new RMAN backup scheduled job." You get the idea.

Whatever the question may be, it is helpful to take a birds-eye look at your overall system. Statspack is an invaluable method for collecting history on the running of your system. A Statspack top SQL report can be helpful in viewing where your large SQL resource consumption is going. However, no matter whether you choose to use Statspack or some other method for gathering historical data, you should gather it. Before you *have* to use it.

After you've triaged a system to determine the difference between the way the system was running before and the way it is running now, the important thing to do is communicate to everyone involved in the design of the system what went wrong, the reasons why it went wrong, what you plan to do differently from now on so that the problem will not remain, and what everyone should keep in mind for future, similar application designs.

Constant and Iterative Knowledge Sharing

Application design is ideally a learning experience for everyone. The more complicated and sophisticated the business needs and questions, the greater the learning experience and the greater the potential for constant and iterative knowledge sharing. There is no substitute for a DBA rolling up her sleeves and sitting down with a design team to choose the best design, using the most built-in functionality, requiring the least amount of code, and hopefully resulting in the fewest numbers of production incidents. As you can see, these types of discussions don't simply begin and end with the initial database design phase. They are ongoing.

You can be a valid asset as a DBA only if you hold back nothing (in terms of knowledge) and give away everything. And if you do so, your colleagues will be a lot more willing to do the same for you. Being willing to listen, research, share, and take responsibility is the best course of action for any DBA who wants to ensure he gets the most out of his job, with the least amount of frustration, and the maximum amount of satisfaction. Good, maintainable application design begins with you.

CHAPTER 5

■ ■ ■

Running Oracle on Windows

by Niall Litchfield

You might well be wondering what this book is doing with a chapter devoted to running the Oracle database on the Microsoft Windows platform. After all, surely all serious databases run on some proprietary variety of Unix, or else on the fast-growing Linux platform. When it comes to database environments, surely the Windows environment is just a sideshow.

If you do hold such thoughts, however, then I'd say you are mistaken. To explain why, I'd like to go into a little history. In its Windows marketing material, Oracle Corporation is fond of detailing the list of firsts that it has achieved on the Windows platform. Put simply, Oracle was the first relational database available on the Windows platform with Release 7 in 1993, predating the Microsoft-developed SQL Server 6.0 offering by two years. Along the way, Oracle has released the first 64-bit database on Windows, the first with support for .Net stored procedures, and so on. Clearly Windows has historically been and continues to be a significant platform for Oracle.

For the most part, and certainly from the application developer's perspective, the choice of operating system makes absolutely no difference to the effective exploitation of the power of the Oracle database. It can, however, have a significant impact on the database administrator, who will often be interacting at the operating system level directly with the Oracle installation. This chapter, therefore, is devoted to the distinctions that administrators and operators may have to deal with.

Architecture

As everyone with a cursory understanding of computer science is aware, there are four main resources that a computer operating system manages on behalf of the applications running on it. These are:

- CPU
- Memory
- Storage
- Network

In system troubleshooting, the primary focus of this chapter, you will usually be concerned about the usage of one or more of these scarce resources. The next few sections deal therefore with the first three, network usage being the least Windows-specific area and the least likely in my experience to cause Windows-specific issues for database specialists.

CPU Resources

It is in the use of the CPU that Oracle on Windows differs most significantly from the Unix and Unix-like platforms. On every other platform, Oracle uses a process-based architecture. Whenever a new session is created—whether by the end-user, by a background process, or by an application middle tier—a new operating-system process is created. These are visible to the administrator via the process table for the Oracle process, which is exposed as the V$PROCESS dynamic performance view (in turn a view of the X$KSUPR fixed table). On Windows, although this view still exists, the mechanism is entirely different. The Windows operating system is designed, for various reasons, with a rather significant overhead for process creation, especially if shared memory needs to be available to each process. The Oracle system architecture relies heavily on shared memory and consequently, a process-based model is not appropriate on this platform. Oracle instead utilizes a multithreaded model in which each process (from an Oracle perspective) is actually an operating system thread running in the context of the oracle executable.

Using the Right Tools for the Job

Most Unix DBA staff will be familiar with drilling down from the operating system to identify a database session or sessions of interest using utilities such as top, topas, and so on. The Windows operating system does not come supplied with thread-level resource monitors, so historically it has been rather difficult to observe the database processes from the operating-system level. Instead, DBAs have tended to approach the performance story from within the database itself. Oracle does in fact supply a little-known utility with its Windows distributions, called the Oracle Administration Assistant for Windows. Figure 5-1 shows this utility, which allows you to list and kill threads within the oracle.exe process. However, it only allows you to list threads and kill them; moreover, the list is not sortable, and it is not always populated completely.

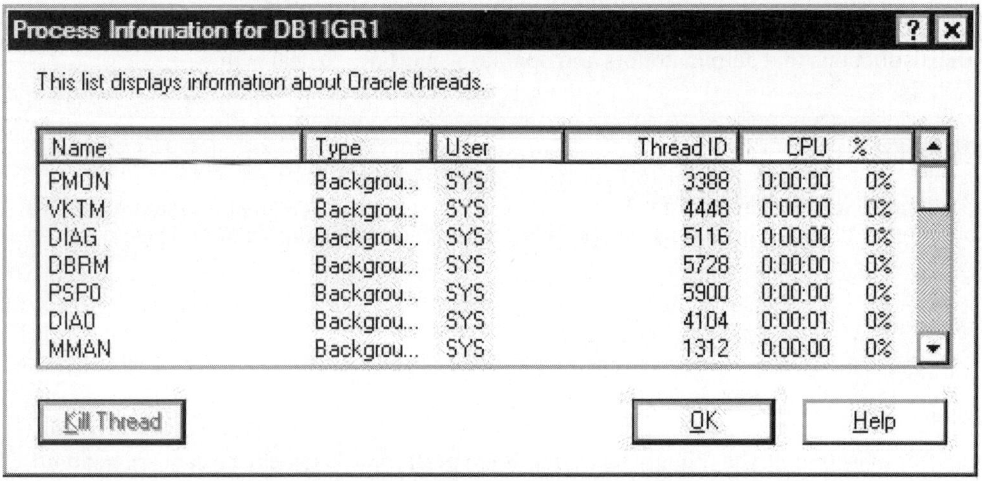

Process Information for DB11GR1

This list displays information about Oracle threads.

Name	Type	User	Thread ID	CPU	%
PMON	Backgrou...	SYS	3388	0:00:00	0%
VKTM	Backgrou...	SYS	4448	0:00:00	0%
DIAG	Backgrou...	SYS	5116	0:00:00	0%
DBRM	Backgrou...	SYS	5728	0:00:00	0%
PSP0	Backgrou...	SYS	5900	0:00:00	0%
DIA0	Backgrou...	SYS	4104	0:00:01	0%
MMAN	Backgrou...	SYS	1312	0:00:00	0%

Kill Thread   OK   Help

Figure 5-1. The Oracle Administration Assistant for Windows

Because Oracle's tool is not always reliable, and because it is often the case that the DBA will be interested in processes other than oracle.exe running on the database or application server, I recommend that a Windows DBA obtains a copy of the free tools from the sysinternals team (now owned by Microsoft). These are available from www.sysinternals.com; the particular utility we will be using is called Process Explorer (procexp.exe). Probably the best way to see the benefit of this approach is to follow along with an example.

■ **Note** Readers should take note of the way in which Process Explorer works before using it on a production system. Specifically, it dynamically loads a kernel mode driver, which fellow OakTable member Tanel Poder has reported can occasionally lead to system crashes. I have never myself seen such a crash in over a decade of using sysinternals tools.

Next, I will demonstrate how the DBA can utilize Process Explorer to drill down into the thread that is causing excessive resource consumption. We will be using Process Explorer, an idle system—in this case my laptop—and the old fashioned sqlplus.exe.

■ **Note** Incidentally, I always use the command-line version of sqlplus rather than sqlplusw.exe, since this gives me easy access to the command-line history via the up arrow and allows copy and paste via the mouse, as long as you enable quick edit mode for all your cmd.exe windows.

Setting Up the Example

We will generate a CPU load by repeatedly querying the dual table for the current time. This sort of query, incidentally, is regrettably common in modern applications, which really ought to have worked out how to tell the time before asking the database. Before you start to run the experiment you will need to set up as follows.

Open Process Explorer and locate the oracle.exe process in the pane on the left side. I use Tree View. Open two sqlplus windows, at least one of which, the monitor window, should have access to the v$process, v$session and v$sqlarea dynamic performance views.

My screen is shown in Figure 5-2. The white session is our monitoring session and is connected as sys; the black session is connected as a nonprivileged user and will be used to generate the inappropriate CPU load. For reference, my Oracle.exe process ID was 5180.

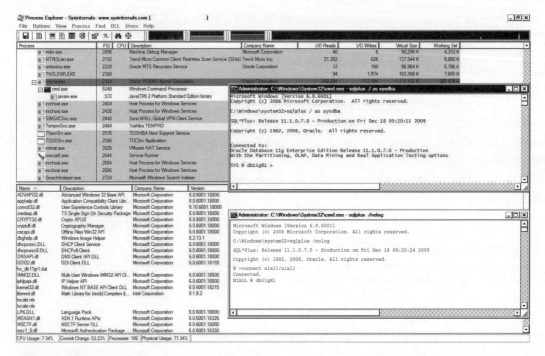

Figure 5-2. Preparation

The code we will use is as follows:

```
declare
    l_date date;
begin
    for i in 1..10000000 loop
select sysdate into l_date from dual;
    end loop;
end;
/
```

This block should be run in the black, or normal user's, `sqlplus` session. Once you start running the anonymous block you should notice an increased CPU load on the machine (likely equivalent to one processor core).

Drilling Down to a Problem Thread

Once you are running the anonymous block, you can drill down into `oracle.exe` in the Process Explorer view. As a double-check I always like to check the performance graph for the thread `procexp` has. You'll see in my case that the thread is accounting for almost 50 percent of available CPU, which is as you'd expect—this workload essentially consumes all of one CPU core, and the machine in question has two. Figure 5-3 shows this tab of the Process Monitor utility while the load is running.

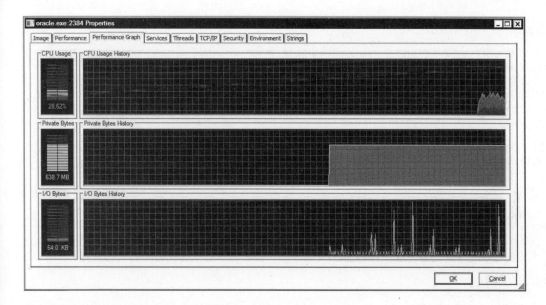

Figure 5-3. Load generation

Select the Threads tab and sort the output by CPU. Assuming an idle system, the thread corresponding to your load generation session will be top of the list. Figure 5-4 shows the sorted list as it appears on my system while running this experiment.

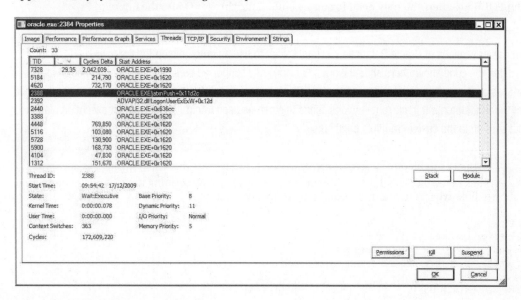

Figure 5-4. Oracle thread information

Drilling into the Thread

Note the thread ID (tid) in Figure 5-4. In the real world, of course, we would start looking for high CPU consumers if the server was being unduly stressed. DBAs from a Unix background should recognize that the process so far is the equivalent of obtaining high CPU processes from the Unix TOP or ps utilities. The next step in our troubleshooting process should be to determine what the thread in question is running. My standard query for determining what SQL statement an individual Oracle thread is running is the following:

```
select
s.sid
,     s.serial#
,     p.spid ospid
,     q.sql_text
,         s.sql_child_number
from
v$process p
,     v$session s
,     v$sqlarea q
where
p.addr = s.paddr
and     s.sql_id=q.sql_id(+)
and     p.spid = &os_process_id;
```

This query should be run from the monitoring sqlplus session (our white sqlplus window from earlier). Notice especially the last line of this query. You'll see reference to a SQL*Plus substitution variable &os_process_id. When you execute the query from SQL*Plus, you will be prompted to supply a value for that variable, you should supply the thread ID of the high CPU consumer. If you are using a tool other than SQL*Plus, then you may need to simply embed the thread ID into the query.

■ **Note** In earlier versions of Oracle Database you might want to use an outer join on the hash_value instead of the sql_id, but the code shown here should work on all currently supported versions. You need the outer join in case your session is not associated with a particular SQL statement. Finally, it always makes sense to get the child number of the SQL statement in current versions, since this can be used to pin down the exact execution plan in use by that session in the case of multiple child cursors.

In my case the thread ID I received was 620. You can see that ID at the top of the list shown earlier in Figure 5-4. A quick confirmation of the "problem" can be picked up by running the diagnostic query that I've just shown. Following is the output I obtained on my own system:

```
SYS @ db11gR1 >/
Enter value for os_process_id: 620
old  13: and     p.spid = &os_process_id
new  13: and     p.spid = 620

     SID    SERIAL# OSPID                   SQL_TEXT
---------- ---------- ------------------------ ------------------------------------
     121        31 620                     SELECT SYSDATE FROM DUAL
```

This exercise has demonstrated, I hope, that the appropriate use of third-party tools such as Process Explorer and an understanding that Oracle Database processes on Windows are implemented as operating system threads allows the traditional approach of translating operating system load into Oracle processes and then drilling down into the SQL that is the root cause of the problem to be achieved quickly and simply.

Memory

The adoption of the thread-based model for Oracle's Windows implementation of its database technology has led to one particular bottleneck, which historically has meant that Windows-based Oracle Database servers have been best suited to small and mid-range implementations. This is the restriction on 32-bit systems that means that any single userland process can only address approximately 1.7GB of memory by default. On the Windows platform this has meant that all memory used by the database server, both SGA and PGA, must fit within this limit, since it is addressed by threads of the oracle.exe process.

By contrast, on 32-bit Linux systems (that otherwise run on identical hardware), it was the SGA only that was so limited, and should an end-user process run into its address space limits because of PGA usage, only that end-user would typically be affected. There are two complementary and often confused strategies that allow 32-bit Windows databases to increase this limit somewhat.

The first is to utilize for the operating system a startup switch that changes the memory allocation model for the operating system as a whole so that 3GB of memory becomes addressable for usermode applications and 1GB is reserved for the operating system kernel (by default, the split is even at 2GB of virtual memory each). This is achieved by editing the startup file boot.ini, which is located at the root of the Windows server c: drive and adding /3 GB to the end of the line in the [operating systems] section that boots Windows; usually there is only one such line. Oracle needs no special treatment in this case and will be able to address up to approximately 2.7GB of memory once this change has been made.

■ **Note** Starting with Windows Vista, Microsoft has removed the boot.in file entirely. To change the amount of userland addressable memory on this operating system, you will need to use the new bcedit program as follows:

```
bcedit /set increaseuserva 3072
```

where 3072 is the maximum addressable memory in MB up to a 3GB limit. I have not investigated Windows Server 2008 32-bit to determine if (as seems likely) this is also the case there.

The second approach, known as Physical Address Extension (PAE), is to take advantage of changes in the Intel x86 and compatible processor range introduced with the Intel Pentium Pro range of processors. This allowed 32-bit operating systems with appropriate support to access a 36-bit address space (64GB of memory in total). Technically, this is achieved by implementing an address window, so that although there is still a 4GB address space accessible at any given stage, it is a window on a larger 64GB space. Readers with long memories may recall that this is a similar approach to the extended memory architecture introduced with the Intel 286 range of processors.

To implement PAE the DBA needs to carry out two configuration changes, one to the operating system and one within Oracle to allow Oracle to utilize the extra memory. The first is to add yet another switch to the startup command for the operating system, much as we did to allow 3GB of memory to be addressed. This switch is /PAE. When it is enabled, the operating system provides an API (known as Address Windowing Extensions) to enable programs, such as Oracle, to address the extra memory.

This second approach allows for Oracle to address very much more than 2GB of memory; however, it has some rather significant limitations. First, the memory thus addressed cannot be paged, and for this reason it is not usable by private memory areas, in particular the PGA. Second, in order to implement this functionality within the Oracle database, the DBA has to set the initialization parameter USE_INDIRECT_DATA_BUFFERS = TRUE and then needs to specify the amount of memory to use for the SGA using the old fashioned DB_BLOCK_BUFFERS parameter. This means that the dynamic memory management feature for the SGA cannot be used in conjunction with physical address extensions.

■ **Note** A very good summary of PAE on Windows , Server can be found at http://support.microsoft.com/ kb/283037.

In addition, each new Oracle session that connects—that is, each new thread of the oracle.exe process—gets an initial stack allocation of 1MB of memory. Because each new connection consumes 1MB of memory on startup, systems that use dedicated server connections and have many hundreds of connecting users will consume a significant chunk of all available memory for the process. As an example, just connecting 500 users will use almost a third of the available memory on 32-bit Windows. In order to circumvent the memory footprint of high concurrency systems, Oracle supplies a command-line utility called orastack that can be used to reduce the memory footprint of each connection. This utility works by modifying the actual Oracle executables on disk; consequently, if you choose to use this utility, you should be aware that Oracle patches may undo this workaround.

In order to use orastack you supply the name of the executable that you wish to modify and the new size in bytes to allocate for each thread. If you don't supply the second parameter you will get a display of the current settings. In the online help for orastack, Oracle suggests that 500KB is a good compromise between memory usage and stability. However there are My Oracle Support notes, for example 46001.1 (the original reference note for the Oracle Database Windows implementation), that suggest that values below 700k are prone to cause thread failure. I suggest, therefore that orastack be left well alone, not least because of the potential for instability and thread crashes, and that either a connection pooling or 64-bit solution is sought for systems that require hundreds or thousands of concurrent connections. In the event that you need to justify a move to 64-bit, or such a move is delayed, then orastack potentially could save quite considerable memory overhead as an interim measure.

Until quite recently, then, single-instance Oracle on Windows was limited to systems that required less than about 2.5GB of RAM to operate well. This meant that large database systems or systems with large numbers of connecting processes were not well suited to the Windows 32-bit platform. With the advent of widespread 64-bit computing, however, and the availability of 64-bit Oracle on 64-bit Windows (another RDBMS first for Oracle on the Windows platform, by the way) it is readily apparent that an exclusively 64-bit solution is likely to be the most appropriate choice for most Oracle databases on Windows, since this platform makes the current technical obstacles for large-scale or high-concurrency database instances on Windows a thing of the past.

Disk

By contrast to the area of addressable memory, Windows-based systems have enjoyed an historic advantage over Unix- and Linux-based systems in the area of disk I/O. Two particular facilities are of importance in designing a high-throughput system such as a database server are *asynchronous I/O* and appropriate use of caching.

Asynchronous I/O is a facility that allows a client program to issue a read or write request to the operating system for particular disk blocks and to then carry out other processing while waiting for the request to complete. This has the effect of hiding the disk latency within the execution time of other tasks. For I/O-intensive systems such as database servers, asynchronous I/O is therefore pretty much mandatory.

All modern filesystems utilize main system memory for a filesystem cache, although they will naturally give up this memory in response to client requests. In the case of an Oracle Database, however, the data blocks on which Oracle requests read/write operations typically are already cached by Oracle. As a result it is generally of no benefit to read/write performance to cache Oracle data files in the filesystem cache. Many operating systems provide the ability on some filesystems to bypass the filesystem cache entirely. Oracle has therefore provided hooks into this functionality. This facility is known as direct I/O, since Oracle is communicating directly with the files concerned.

Oracle on Windows has always done both asynchronous and direct I/O natively—that is, without the need for specialized setup. While direct I/O is available on many modern filesystems, there are a number of common filesystems in use in Unix/Linux where that is not the case. Consequently, the DBA on such systems has to determine what the supported operations on their platform are and set the controlling initialization parameters FILESYSTEMIO_OPTIONS, DISK_ASYNCH_IO, or both, appropriately. In addition, I have worked on systems where the DBA has a choice of one feature but not both. In such cases asynchronous IO should be used, but some memory may be double-cached, and under certain circumstances excessive paging may result during, for example, database backups.

■ **Note** On Windows, the parameter FILESYSTEMIO_OPTIONS has no effect and should not be set.

Management

This next section deals with some of the Windows-specific management activity that a database administrator on Windows needs to be familiar with. The general approach to system management within Windows is somewhat different from that commonly encountered on Unix systems, and as such is often unfamiliar territory for database professionals. In this section we will walk through the areas of Windows services, the Windows registry, and setting environments before finishing with a discussion of scripting using the built-in scripting environment.

The Registry

It is worth starting our review of the environment settings on Windows with a quick tour of the often misunderstood, and poorly documented, Windows registry. This is a metadata repository of information about software, hardware, users, and environments installed on a Windows server. Most documentation includes the rather stern, and often somewhat overplayed, warning that "modifying the registry directly can stop your computer from working." While it is true that the registry is designed to be manipulated programmatically, and the win32 API has a significant number of registry manipulation features, it isn't the case that modifying the registry *per se* for end-user programs is especially dangerous, other than potentially for that program itself. Conversely, it is true that the registry is designed to contain all of the information that software (in our case, Oracle) needs to operate correctly.

The registry is a hierarchical store of metadata; arranged under at least the following head keys (top levels of a hierarchy):

HKEY_CLASSES_ROOT: Contains class definitions and attributes.

HKEY_CURRENT_USER: Contains metadata about the current user's environment.

HKEY_LOCAL_MACHINE: Contains information about installed software and hardware and its current configuration.

HKEY_USERS: Contains information about local users.

For our purposes, the HKEY_LOCAL_MACHINE hierarchy is the one that we need to know more about, since it is here that information about the Oracle services, software and environment is primarily stored. The major location that we are interested in is HKEY_LOCAL_MACHINE/Software/Oracle. That is the base location for runtime Oracle-related configuration. On my VistaPC that hierarchy looks as shown in Figure 5-5.

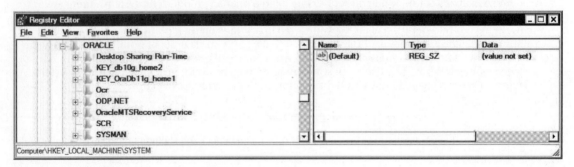

Figure 5-5. *Windows Registry hierarchy for Oracle Database software*

You'll see subkeys in Figure 5-5 for two Oracle database homes: an Oracle Database 10g Release 2 Home called OraDb10g_home1 and an Oracle Database 11g Release 1 home called OraDb11g_home1. The names of these two keys both start with KEY_. Prior to Oracle Database 10g, the Home structure was slightly different; in Oracle Database 9i and earlier, the top-level directory contained information about the current Oracle Home and there was an ALL_HOMES key as well as individual keys for each home. In addition, my system has similar hierarchies for Oracle's web support software, for the Enterprise Manager standalone software installed with each database, for the Windows .Net data provider ODP.Net, and for the Oracle Cluster Registry.

■ **Note** Many Windows systems that I see in my work as a consultant do not back up the cluster registry. You can determine its location from the registry as shown above and back it up using the ocopy utility.

We will first look at a database home (we are using the Oracle Database 11g Release 1 home here, but the entries will be similar for Oracle Database 10g as well). A screenshot of the Oracle Database registry entries appears in Figure 5-6.

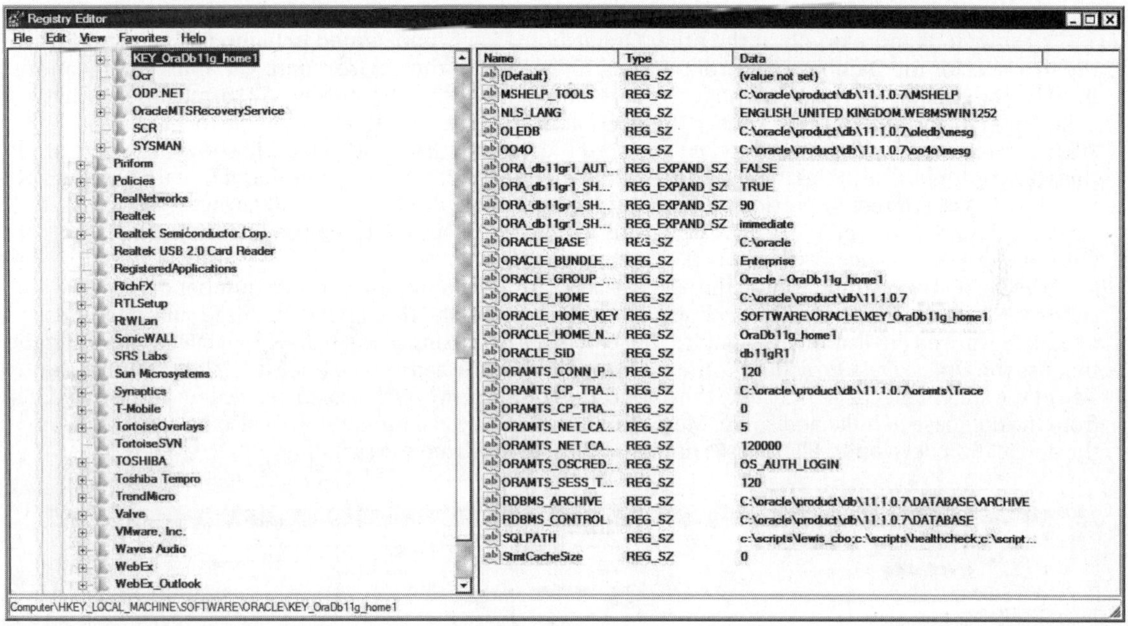

Figure 5-6. Registry settings for an Oracle Database 11g home

It is fairly obvious that the structure in Figure 5-6 contains the environment settings that on Unix would be set by sourcing the Oracle environment with the .oraenv executable file. In particular, ORACLE_HOME and ORACLE_SID are set in the registry. On servers with just a single database instance per Oracle home, this is all that needs to be done. If you run more than one database from the same Oracle home, then you will also need to set the ORACLE_SID environment variable in your scripts, or else use a valid net8 connection string. One approach that is increasingly common as disk space becomes cheaper is to run with just one database instance per ORACLE_HOME. If you have a server powerful enough to run two Oracle instances at the same time, this is the approach I recommend, both for ease of day-to-day management and for the ability to carry out maintenance (for example, database upgrades) independently.

■ **Note** In addition to ensuring that ORACLE_SID is set to the primary database running from this home, I also always use this key to set the SQLPATH environment variable used by sqlplus. This enables me to organize my script library by function, for example keeping all backup scripts together, and still execute the script simply by specifying its name in the sqlplus start command. On Windows the path separator is the semicolon (;) character.

You will also see the registry keys that control startup behavior of the Oracle database. These are the keys `ORA_SID_STARTUP`, `ORA_SID_SHUTDOWN`, `ORA_SID_STARTMODE`, and `ORA_SID_SHUTDOWN_TIMEOUT`. In versions prior to Oracle Database 10g, it is often sensible to set these directly using the Registry Editor; however; Oracle has now enhanced the command-line tool `oradim.exe` such that all necessary adjustments to these keys can be specified using the command line.

Next we look more briefly at the other Oracle home keys represented in Figure 5-6. First there are the two keys for the Database Control product. They contain the environment variables and locations used by the `emctl.pl` script to manage the correct control of the dbconsole OC4J application when called directly by the Windows service. Inspection of the `emctl.bat` executable file located in `%ORACLE_HOME%\bin` or the `dbconsole.pm` Perl script located in the same place will show the usage of these environment variables, which can, of course, also be set from the command line if scripting using `emctl` is required. In particular, if managing dbconsole directly, you will always need to set at least the `ORACLE_HOME` and `ORACLE_SID` environment variables and may, depending on the FQDN of your server, have to specify the `EMSTATE` directory as well.

Finally, it is worth mentioning the `ODP.Net` key. This key contains a variable number of subdirectories, depending on the version and components of `ODP.Net` installed. These subdirectories contain advanced environment variables that can be used to control the behavior of .Net applications that use the Oracle Data Provider. Common examples include setting the trace level, determining the size of the statement cache in use by the application or the array fetch size to be used for retrieving data from the database in bulk, and so on. Many, but not all, of these parameters can also be set in code by the application developer. Figure 5-7 shows the `ODP.Net` key from my system.

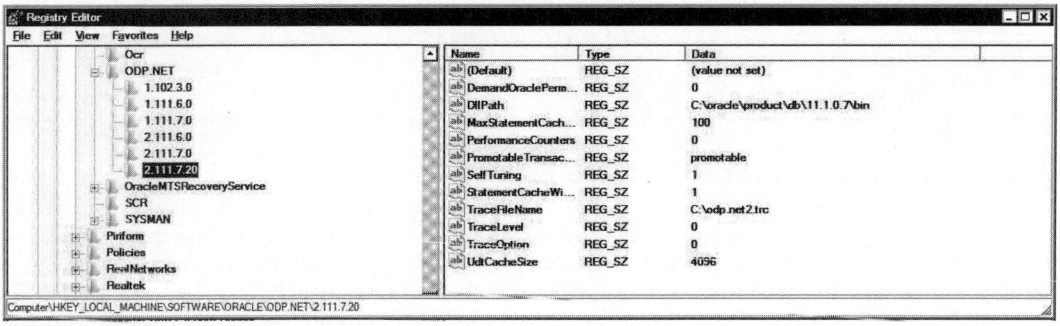

Figure 5-7. Contents of an ODP.Net registry key

Services

One of the core components of the Windows architecture is the use of *services* to provide application functionality without user input or even the requirement to log on to the server to start, stop, or interact with them. In this respect services can be thought of as the equivalent of Unix daemons. There are some significant architectural differences, however, between a Microsoft Windows service and a Unix daemon process. For example, a Windows service is always a child of the `services.exe` process, whereas a Unix daemon is nearly always an orphaned child process adopted by the `init` process. In addition, the list of services installed by Oracle often causes some confusion to people new to the Oracle database on Windows. This confusion is at least in part because the naming conventions chosen by Oracle Corporation are unhelpful and unintuitive. Before we run through the services installed by Oracle database software installs and their purposes, however, it is useful to understand the anatomy of a service.

Anatomy of a Service

A Windows service is any application that meets the following requirements:

- It runs without a user interface.

- It registers itself with the Windows service database.

- It provides certain well-known API entry points for control by the service control manager (svchost.exe).

- It provides status updates to the service control manager.

One difference between the Windows concept of a service and the concept of a Unix daemon process=is that a service is required to register itself. Another difference is that a Windows service is controlled by the operating system, whereas Unix daemons are not.

■ **Note** The registry holds the database of installed services at HKLM\System\CurrentControlSet\Services.

In addition to the mandatory attributes listed above, services can also be configured to be dependent upon one another. This is a particularly powerful feature that, if used appropriately, can greatly ease the configuration of automatic startup in a Windows environment. To use this feature requires some registry editing. First select the subkey representing the service you want to reconfigure, click Edit, and then click Add Value. Create a new value name DependOnService with a data type of REG_MULTI_SZ, and then click OK. When the data entry dialog box appears, type the name or names of the services that you prefer to start before this service, with one entry for each line, and then click OK. Figures 5.8 and 5.9 show this process in action. In this example we are making the database control service (OracleDBConsoledb11Gr1) dependent upon both the database and listener services. This means that it will not start until both of the other two services are running. In Figure 5-8 we can see the names of the two services being added to the DependOnService key.

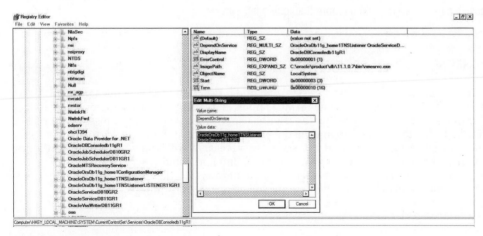

Figure 5-8. Adding service dependencies

Figure 5-9 shows the resulting dependencies in the control panel services applet.

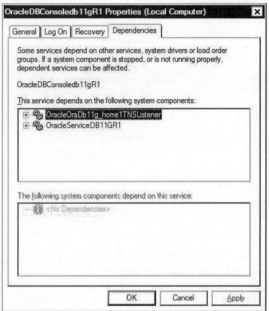

Figure 5-9. Service dependencies

■ **Note** The data type used for service dependencies is REG_MULTI_SZ , which is a string array. That type is appropriate because a service can depend on more than one other service.

Control of Services

Services can be controlled in a number of ways. The first and most common is via the services control panel Microsoft Management Console (MMC) applet (services.msc). This applet can manage both local and remote services, assuming that the user has appropriate security permissions. Services can also be controlled from the command line via the NET series of commands; in particular, net start <servicename> will start a service, and net stop <servicename> will stop it. Again, credentials to connect to a remote computer can be supplied at the command line. Finally, services may also be controlled and monitored through the Windows management interface via appropriate WQL scripts.

Oracle tends to name its services using either of the following two conventions:

Oracle<OracleHomeName><ServiceType><InstanceName>

Oracle<ServiceType><InstanceName>.

Regrettably, the main exception to these conventions is the database service itself, which simply gets the name OracleService<SID> rather than, for example, OracleDatabaseSID or OracleOraDb11g_home1DatabaseSID.

The main interface for setting properties for the database service is the oradim command-line tool. Historically this tool did not provide sufficient granularity over the control, particularly of startup. In order for an Oracle database to be started on Windows, the database service has to be started. If it isn't, the error ORA-12560 TNS Protocol error will be thrown when sqlplus attempts to connect. This is most easily rectified by ensuring that the Oracle database service starts with the operating system, by setting the startup type of the service to automatic.

In earlier versions of the software, however, setting the database service to start automatically also set the startup type of the instance to automatic (equivalent to setting the start field in oratab on Unix systems to Y). Many administrators did not want the database service to start automatically with the operating system, especially in cases where the server might only be restarted periodically for planned maintenance. In these cases it was necessary to edit the registry directly to control the startup type of the instance separately from the service. Starting with Oracle Database 10g Release 2, however, the oradim utility has been enhanced to allow the setting of the service and the instance start types separately. Consequently, there is no need to edit the registry manually to control database startup.

■ **Note** You will also get the ORA-12560 error when using IPC connections when the ORACLE_SID environment variable is incorrectly set in the command line or is not set at all in the registry. This should always be the first thing to check if you encounter problems connecting directly to the Oracle Database instance.

The database listener service is the best example of the first naming convention; for example, a listener called LSNR11G running from an Oracle Home with the default database home of OraDb11g_Home1 would get the rather unwieldy name OracleOraDb11g_Home1TNSListenerLSNR11G.

Fortunately for the fingers of DBAs everywhere, there is no need to use the cumbersome net start syntax to start the listener; the lsnrctl utility will start the listener for you just as it does in Unix. Indeed, if the listener that you wish to start does not yet have a service defined for it, the Windows implementation of lsnrctl will create the service for you.

However, the automatic service creation done by lsnrctl can have unexpected side effects if you use (as is good practice) named listeners. In the event that you make an error in the name of the listener supplied to the lsnrctl start command, the listener will, correctly, fail to start—but an operating system service will be created for it. My recommendation, therefore, is to use named listeners and to set them once and for all for automatic startup. In the event of planned maintenance, the services applet in the Control Panel can be used to start and stop them.

■ **Note** If you do create a listener service in error, or for that matter remove the Oracle software without removing the database services, the sc operating system utility can be used to remove these unwanted services.

The Database Console and Other Services

The remaining services are largely unimportant for the DBA, with the exception of the service that runs Database Console (the internal name for db control) in a non-Grid environment. For an Oracle database with an SID of db11g, this would get the name Oracledbconsoledb11g. The decision whether to run Database Control is a strategic decision for the DBA, and in many cases a political one as well. We can't fix the politics in a technical book, or often with technical arguments, but we can say that if you've chosen to use Database Control, then this service should always be set to auto start, and if you've chosen not to use it, then it should be removed (or never installed in the first place). The reason for this recommendation is simply the resource consumption of the agent and management service wrapped up in dbconsole. This can consume several hundred MB of RAM and up to 10 percent or so of available CPU cycles, depending on collection frequency and quantity.

Additional services include OracleMTSRecoveryService for integrating (specifically recovering in-doubt transactions) with the Microsoft distributed transaction coordinator OracleCSSService, which is the single instance clusterware required in Oracle Database 10g; and OracleVSSWriter, which is the integration with Microsoft volume shadow copy backups (I'd be interested in hearing from readers using this).

Finally there is a service, almost always disabled, for running operating system external procedure jobs from dbconsole, named OracleJobScheduler<SID>. In a single-instance environment, I almost always recommend running OS jobs via the O/S job scheduler so you can delete this service. In a multiple-database environment, I recommend Grid Control for OS scheduling.

Scripting

Database administrators and systems administrators both know that they have a large number of routine, repetitive tasks to perform that are subject to error, either simple typographical error or by omitting or repeating steps inadvertently. These categories of tasks are eminently suitable for scripting.

On Unix platforms such scripting is often performed by means of a shell script. Indeed, job descriptions for database administrators often list shell scripting as a required skill. The Windows platform shell (cmd.exe) is a relatively poor environment for shell scripting, largely because of its backward-compatibility with the MS-DOS PC environment common in the 1980s and 1990s.This often leads Unix administrators to consider the Windows environment as lacking in facilities to script repetitive administration tasks. There are, however, a number of technologies available to the administrator on Windows platforms that readily allow scripting of regular maintenance tasks.

Most Windows scripting should probably be carried out using an environment designed specifically for the job rather than the command line. Microsoft Windows provides a generic environment and a number of technologies that are useful for administration scripts of this nature. Specifically these are the Windows scripting host, a choice of scripting languages, and the Windows management instrumentation interface.

In general these alternative approaches require the installation or purchase of additional software on the database server itself. For now therefore we will examine using the Windows script technologies to automate an example administration task, namely monitoring and management of the database alert.log file.

While the specific task of monitoring and managing the alert log could be accomplished by use of the Oracle 10g Enterprise Manager or Grid Control products, the example I provide will illustrate most of the key techniques of Windows scripting and is also applicable to environments that choose not to manage the database via EM.

The Windows scripting host is an environment that hosts scripts to automate routine tasks. These scripts are written in a programming language that Windows script can host. The three most popular are VBScript, Jscript or Perl. The host itself comes in the form of two executables: wscript.exe runs programs in the Windows GUI; and cscript.exe is a command-line interface. For the purposes of automation I almost always use cscript. WSH Itself can run programs, access network drives, manipulate registry settings and environment variables, and so on. In addition it allows access to COM objects. Of particular interest are the FileSystem object, which allows file operations—in our example reading alert.log, and the sets of objects exposed by the management technology Windows Management Instrumentation (WMI). WMI is provided with current Windows releases and provides low-level access to the entire Windows management infrastructure and so can be used to monitor services, components, alerts and system events from a relatively simple shell, and using easy to understand scripting. In fact most of the WMI COM API is accessible via WMI Query Language, which is an SQL dialect and thus straightforward for DBA staff to pick up.

■ **Note** Those wanting to pursue Windows scripting further and also to pick up information on features such as PowerShell should visit the script center on Microsoft's Technet site at http://technet.microsoft.com/en-us/scriptcenter/default.aspx.

A typical Windows script has the following structure:

1. A declaration section for any objects or variables that are required for the script; typically this might include the WMI itself and/or the FileSystem object for working with the filesystem.

2. The main body of the script itself.

3. Any subroutines used; this is largely a matter of personal preference since such code can go in a script body, but using sensibly named and sized subroutines makes maintenance much easier.

In addition, if the script is a full-fledged WSH script, it can contain a preamble describing the script itself, detailing usage information and so on. This feature greatly aids the maintainability and clarity of the script—our alert.log monitoring script illustrates this technique.

Exercise 5-1 uses Windows Scripting Host for the task of monitoring and managing the alert log. In this exercise you'll see how to build a script that automates the process of searching the alert.log file for server errors. In addition the script rotates the alert.log file. This script is suitable therefore for scheduled execution to monitor and maintain the alert log.

Exercise 5-1: Monitoring the alert.log

A task common to all DBAs is that of monitoring and managing the alert log for the database instances they are responsible for. This is only one of a number of logs that the DBA and system administrator monitor on a regular basis. The techniques shown here will be applicable to all such file-monitoring tasks. The script is named ReadAlert.vb.wsf and is shown in the listing that follows. I have used a naming convention of <purpose>.<language>.wsf to help me distinguish between code in different languages; you may wish to use a different convention.

```
ReadAlert.vb.wsf
' Name: ReadAlert.vb.wsf


' Date: 08 Feb 2006
'

 Author: Niall Litchfield
'
' Purpose: Read the alert log of an Oracle Instance and renames at the end.
'
' Usage: Cscript.exe ReadAlert.vb.wsf /"path\to\alert.log"
<job>
<runtime>
<description>This script reads the alert log of an Oracle Instance</description>
<named
name = "log"
helpstring = "Alert.log to read"
type = "string"
required = "true"
/>
<example>Example: ReadAlert.vb.wsf
/log:"c:\oracle\10.1.0\admin\orcl\bdump\alert_orcl.log"</example>

</runtime>

<script language="VBScript">
If WScript.Arguments.Count <> 1 Then
WScript.Arguments.ShowUsage
WScript.Quit
End If
ReadAlert (Wscript.Arguments.Named.Item("log"))
RenameAlert (Wscript.Arguments.Named.Item("log"))
Sub ReadAlert(alertlog)
Dim fso, stream, line, errarray
Const ForReading = 1
' get a handle on the file system
Set fso = CreateObject("Scripting.FileSystemObject")
' try opening the file
Set stream = fso.OpenTextFile(alertlog, ForReading)
' Read the contents of the alert log
do while stream.AtEndOfStream = False
line = stream.ReadLine
if instr(1,line,"ORA-",1) = 1 then ' found error
errarray = split(line," ",2)
errcode = errArray(0)
errmsg = errArray(1)
Wscript.Echo errcode & " in Alert.log " & vbcrlf & "Further Information: " & errmsg
```

```
end if
loop
stream.Close
set stream = Nothing
set fso = Nothing
End Sub
Sub RenameAlert(alertlog)
dim fso,alert, newname
Set fso = CreateObject("Scripting.FileSystemObject")
set alert = fso.GetFile(alertlog)
newname = alertlog & "." & FormatDateTime(now(),vbLongDate)
Wscript.Echo newname
alert.Move(newname)
set alert = nothing
set fso = nothing
End Sub
</script>
</job>
```

The first thing to notice is that the file is in XML format. The script itself is enclosed in `<script>` tags and there is a preamble. The preamble is used for two things here. The first is to define the expected parameters to the script, including data types, and the second is to provide documentation so that the expected usage can be shown at runtime. Since this script is a `.wsf` file, the Windows Script environment itself is available to the script. In this example we merely enumerate the arguments received, and if an incorrect number is supplied echo the correct usage and quit the script. We then call two subroutines, the first to read the alert log and the second to rename it (so we don't check the same error twice). The arguments are supplied as named, rather than positional, arguments because of my personal preference more than anything else. The first routine creates an instance of the `FileSystemObject`, which is supplied as part of the scripting runtime libraries. This object acts as a reference to the database server filesystem. The code then opens `alert.log` using the `OpenTextFile` method of the `FileSystemObject` and reads through a line at a time checking for lines that begin with the string `ORA-`. We then use the built-in `split` function to create an array that holds the Oracle error code and the associated text. In this simplified example we merely echo the error out to stdout. In production we would likely mail the DBA using the built-in mail functionality of WMI.

The second routine grabs a reference to the alert log using the filesystem object as before and renames the file, appending a datetime to the filename. It is worth noting that the datetime used is in the system long date format. If this format contains the / character the file rename will fail, as the OS will interpret the name as a directory path.

We can execute the file directly from the command line using just the name of the script. If you've followed my naming convention the command to execute is:

```
ReadAlert.vb.wsf
```

As you can see, all that's necessary is to invoke the filename of the script. Windows detects from the extension that the file contains a WSH script, and then executes that script. Figure 5-10 shows an example execution taken from my own system.

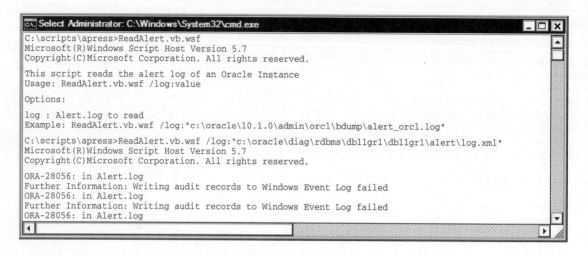

```
Select Administrator: C:\Windows\System32\cmd.exe                    _ □ ×

C:\scripts\apress>ReadAlert.vb.wsf
Microsoft(R)Windows Script Host Version 5.7
Copyright(C)Microsoft Corporation. All rights reserved.

This script reads the alert log of an Oracle Instance
Usage: ReadAlert.vb.wsf /log:value

Options:

log : Alert.log to read
Example: ReadAlert.vb.wsf /log:"c:\oracle\10.1.0\admin\orcl\bdump\alert_orcl.log"

C:\scripts\apress>ReadAlert.vb.wsf /log:"c:\oracle\diag\rdbms\db11gr1\db11gr1\alert\log.xml"
Microsoft(R)Windows Script Host Version 5.7
Copyright(C)Microsoft Corporation. All rights reserved.

ORA-28056: in Alert.log
Further Information: Writing audit records to Windows Event Log failed
ORA-28056: in Alert.log
Further Information: Writing audit records to Windows Event Log failed
ORA-28056: in Alert.log
```

Figure 5-10. Checking the alert.log

■ **Note** My code in this exercise was originally written with a text-based Oracle `alert.log` in mind. However, it can handle both XML and non-XML log files. It runs unchanged against the xml logfile in Oracle Database 11g.

In the download accompanying this book I have included a number of example scripts that will get you started with automating database management tasks using both Windows Scripting Host and traditional batch files.

Summary

This chapter has given you a whistle-stop tour of the Oracle database on Windows, in particular the implications of running 32-bit Oracle on 32-bit Windows (don't do it), the structure and logic of the registry and the services that you are likely to encounter if administering databases on Windows. I haven't covered esoteric subjects such as obtaining thread stack dumps, NTFS configuration and optimization, and so on. For the most part this is because the Oracle Database on Windows, contrary to popular opinion, really runs surprisingly well. I hope you have fun doing so,

CHAPTER 6

■ ■ ■

Managing SQL Performance

What is the first thing you think of when you see the topic "Managing SQL Performance"? Do you think of response time? Do you think of user complaints about the application running "too slow"? Do you think of AWR or ADDM reports?

As far as users are concerned, performance *is* response time. Users don't care about server and database configurations, network bandwidth, I/O rates, or query execution plans. They care about *how fast* they perceive their applications run. All that other stuff is geek speak and doesn't even blip on their radar. Regardless of whether or not all your monitoring gadgets flash green lights of perfection, if your users are complaining, you've got a problem. The truth is, the seeds of those problems very likely were planted when the code was first written.

Adopting a Performance Mindset

Managing the performance of your application SQL doesn't start when your users begin to complain. It starts before the first statement is ever written. It starts when the business tasks that your application will need to service are defined. On a time line, that starting point and the first user complaint about performance could be quite far apart. But I absolutely believe that you have to start by considering your user's experience.

If you start by thinking of how your user will experience your application, this implies that managing SQL performance is first about a mindset, not a dataset. Your mindset is, in part, related to the set of rules you've internalized. But it's also about your beliefs and feelings related to what performance is and means. Do you think managing performance is hard? Do you think managing performance is, or isn't, your responsibility? Do you think performance is something to think about later, when, or if, problems arise? Do you think managing performance is about avoiding catastrophes or about envisioning possibilities?

Sometimes your mindset is influenced by your job description. If you have not specifically been tasked with performance as a concern, you may likely ignore, or at the very least minimize, your role in ensuring optimal performance of the SQL you write. But regardless of your defined job role, I do believe that effective SQL performance management starts with your mindset. It's how you view your role and the contributions you make in regard to the performance of your code that makes the difference between an optimally performing application and a poorly performing one.

Consider the definition of the word *manage*:

1: to handle or direct with a degree of skill: as **a:** to make and keep compliant **b:** to treat with care: husband **c:** to exercise executive, administrative, and supervisory direction of
2: to work upon or try to alter for a purpose
3: to succeed in accomplishing: contrive

—Merriam-Webster Online
`www.merriam-webster.com/dictionary/manage`

This definition indicates that if you want something to be manageable, you must give it skilled attention and effort. So, first and foremost, I think managing performance is about integrating one simple principle into your mindset: *I am responsible for the performance of the code I write or maintain.* Without a conscious personal choice to accept responsibility for it, performance will *not* be manageable.

To manage performance, you first need to know how and why Oracle determines the plan operations for each query. Then you need to be able to easily and accurately capture diagnostics indicating what your application code is doing as it executes. That means learning how Oracle's cost-based optimizer works, particularly how it utilizes statistics. And it means understanding the importance of having your application well instrumented.

The statistics used by the optimizer are like fuel for your car. The quality of the fuel you put into your vehicle affects how well your car handles, how much gas mileage it gets, how often it needs maintenance, and even how long your vehicle will be serviceable. Understanding what goes in to the optimizer so that it can choose which SQL execution plan operations are best helps you know what should reasonably be expected to occur. And if you don't get the results you expect or get the performance you need, you can adjust the fuel.

After you understand what goes in to the optimizer so it can make the best plan choices, you then need to be able to capture diagnostics quickly and accurately. There are many ways to capture diagnostic data, but managing performance well requires that you be able to easily collect the metrics you need, when you need them. The best way to do this is to properly instrument your code. *Instrumentation* is just a few extra lines of code you add to your application to enable you to identify the tasks it executes (that is, SQL related to business tasks) so they are easy to find and monitor.

■ **Note** Statistics and instrumentation are not covered here, but the "Further Reading" section at the end of this chapter lists several sources for more information.

Hopefully, I've established so far that managing SQL performance starts with an attitude, a mindset. You accept responsibility for the performance of every statement you write or maintain. You build foundation knowledge about how the optimizer works and use that knowledge to feed the optimizer with quality statistics and quality code. You make your application easy to monitor by adding instrumentation that will help you get the right performance metrics when you need them. The bottom line is that your mindset is geared toward managing performance every day and not just when problems arise.

Defining and Measuring Performance

Now that we've established the mindset, let's talk about the dataset. How do you know whether the SQL you write performs *fast enough* to be acceptable? My favorite, simple definition of performance is this:

Fast now. Fast later.

—Cary Millsap

Performance is primarily related to time; how long does your SQL take to execute? But it is also related to what your SQL does; what resources must be acquired to obtain the desired result? Performance is measurable, but often the problem is measuring the right thing.

There are many ways to collect performance data. The key to managing performance efficiently is in knowing which ways provide you with the most accurate information possible with the least amount of time and effort. Then, after you get the information, you need to know how to respond to it.

Let's say you are asked to write a SQL statement to retrieve aggregate totals of customer order data. You have a system-level agreement (SLA) stating that the query must execute in 4 seconds or less 95 percent of the time. You write the query and measure how long it takes to execute by using your wristwatch's timer; the result is 3 seconds. Would you feel comfortable turning this code over to production?

I've seen this method in use—really, I have. It's a bit scary, isn't it? The measurement accuracy of your trusty timepiece is only one reason this method scares me. As I mentioned, performance is a matter of measuring time, but it's also a matter of resource use and scalability. I don't think your watch can effectively help you measure that. Although this is perhaps an extremely poor example of how performance could be measured, there are other commonly used methods that are almost as bad.

In the upcoming sections, I'll review several methods for measuring performance and how each method helps you manage, or not, your SQL's performance.

EXPLAIN PLAN

The most often used method to review the performance characteristics of a query is the EXPLAIN PLAN statement. EXPLAIN PLAN displays the series of operations Oracle performs in order to run your SQL statement. It provides information on the estimates of rows to be returned, the order of access and join methods, filter operations, and aggregations, as well as optimization information such as cost and estimated time to complete.

However, there is one main problem with relying on EXPLAIN PLAN. The output lists what is *supposed* to happen when the statement executes, not what actually does happen. In Listing 7-1, note how I execute the first statement, and then check the shared pool for the actual execution plan by using DBMS_XPLAN.DISPLAY_CURSOR. Next I execute the same statement using EXPLAIN PLAN and display the plan using DBMS_XPLAN.DISPLAY. The actual plan and the EXPLAIN PLAN do not match.

Listing 7-1. Comparing Plan Output of EXPLAIN PLAN and DBMS_XPLAN

```
SQL>variable orgid number
SQL>exec :orgid := 1;

PL/SQL procedure successfully completed.
```

133

```
SQL>set serveroutput off
SQL>SELECT AVG(BILL_SEQUENCE_ID) FROM BOM WHERE ORG_ID = :orgid ;

AVG(BILL_SEQUENCE_ID)
---------------------


1 row selected.

SQL>select * from table(dbms_xplan.display_cursor(null,null,'ALLSTATS LAST
2  +PEEKED_BINDS -ROWS'));

PLAN_TABLE_OUTPUT
---------------------------------------
SQL_ID  8xbvq97cr6zx2, child number 0
---------------------------------------
SELECT AVG(BILL_SEQUENCE_ID) FROM BOM WHERE ORG_ID = :orgid

Plan hash value: 1633877697

--------------------------------------------------------------------------------
| Id  | Operation                      | Name   |Starts | A-Rows | A-Time     | Buffers |
--------------------------------------------------------------------------------
|   0 | SELECT STATEMENT               |        |       |      1 |00:00.01    |      31 |
|   1 |  SORT AGGREGATE                |        |     1 |      1 |00:00.01    |      31 |
|   2 |   TABLE ACCESS BY INDEX ROWID  | BOM    |     1 |      0 |00:00.01    |      31 |
|*  3 |    INDEX SKIP SCAN             | BOM_N1 |     1 |      0 |00:00.01    |      31 |
--------------------------------------------------------------------------------

Peeked Binds (identified by position):
-------------------------------------

   1 - (NUMBER): 1

Predicate Information (identified by operation id):
---------------------------------------------------

   3 - access("ORG_ID"=:ORGID)
       filter("ORG_ID"=:ORGID)


26 rows selected.

SQL>
SQL>explain plan for SELECT AVG(BILL_SEQUENCE_ID) FROM BOM WHERE ORG_ID = :orgid ;

Explained.

SQL>select * from table(dbms_xplan.display) ;
```

```
PLAN_TABLE_OUTPUT
-------------------------------------------
Plan hash value: 1639627616

---------------------------------------------------------------------------
| Id  | Operation          | Name | Rows  | Bytes | Cost (%CPU)| Time     |
---------------------------------------------------------------------------
|   0 | SELECT STATEMENT   |      |     1 |     8 |  1557   (2)| 00:00:19 |
|   1 |  SORT AGGREGATE    |      |     1 |     8 |            |          |
|*  2 |   TABLE ACCESS FULL| BOM  |  607K | 4744K |  1557   (2)| 00:00:19 |
---------------------------------------------------------------------------

Predicate Information (identified by operation id):
---------------------------------------------------

   2 - filter("ORG_ID"=TO_NUMBER(:ORGID))

14 rows selected.
```

Not only are the operations shown by each display function different, but you can see how the explained version lists estimates for only Rows, Bytes, and Time. The actual data gives you a much more accurate view of what really happened. So why is the explained version so different? The reason for this difference is that EXPLAIN PLAN uses a different code path to determine the execution plan than does the optimizer. That code path treats bind variables like strings and ignores their values. On the other hand, the optimizer considers the values of bind variables and may determine a different plan choice based on those values.

If you use EXPLAIN PLAN, you may believe that the plan will use a set of operations that it does not. And if you want to be successful in managing the performance of your SQL, you need to make decisions based on actual data, not on a "best guess." The bottom line is that you can't absolutely rely on EXPLAIN PLAN to give you a clear picture of how your query is performing. So it shouldn't be your only, or primary, tool for measuring SQL performance. It can't truly measure performance. And if performance isn't measurable, it likely isn't going to be manageable.

If you can't measure it, you can't manage it.

—David Garvin

DBMS_XPLAN

In Listing 7-1, I used two functions to display execution plan output. Both functions are found in the DBMS_XPLAN supplied package. The DBMS_XPLAN package is used to format SQL execution plan output from EXPLAIN PLAN, SQL stored in the AWR, SQL from a SQL tuning set, as well as for actual cached cursors. This package makes it easy to get a detailed and nicely formatted display of execution plan information.

If you're an old-timer, like me, you may still have an old script or two that you wrote to manually format EXPLAIN PLAN output. There's no longer any need for your old scripts, because this package (available since Oracle version 9) does all the work for you. It is flexible enough to handle every display option you need and will automatically display only relevant information. For example, if your plan uses parallel execution, the display function will show you that information. But if you don't use parallel, the columns containing the data will not be included in the display. It's a fantastic utility, and you can find a lengthy description of the package and the functions it contains in the Oracle PL/SQL Packages and Types Reference for your database version.

For the examples throughout the rest of this chapter, I will use only the DBMS_XPLAN.DISPLAY_CURSOR function. This function is used to display execution plan output for any SQL loaded in the cursor cache. To use this function, you must have SELECT privilege on VSQL, VSQL_PLAN, and V$SQL_PLAN_STATISTICS. Note that these privileges are not granted by default to non-DBA users, and it may be necessary to specifically request that they be granted.

The great thing about DISPLAY_CURSOR is that you get a very nicely formatted actual execution plan with, when requested, rowsource execution statistics. As long as you can locate the SQL statement whose execution plan and statistics you wish to view in the shared pool, you can retrieve and display the execution plan data.

The way to call the function is to provide the sql_id and child_number for the SQL statement you want. The sql_id and child_number parameter values are identified in V$SQL (or V$SQLAREA or V$SQLTEXT). If you want to display the execution plan of the last statement executed in your session, you simply leave the parameters null. Listing 7-2 shows a simple example that illustrates a few key pieces of information that are output by DBMS_XPLAN.DISPLAY_CURSOR.

Listing 7-2. *Retrieving the sql_id and child_number Values for Use with DBMS_XPLAN.DISPLAY_CURSOR*

```
SQL>variable x number
SQL>exec :x := 10 ;

PL/SQL procedure successfully completed.

SQL>select /*+ GATHER_PLAN_STATISTICS KM2 */ * from dept where deptno = :x;

        DEPTNO DNAME          LOC
--------------- --------------- -------------
            10 ACCOUNTING     NEW YORK

1 row selected.

SQL>SELECT xplan.*
  2   FROM
  3     (
  4      select max(sql_id) keep
  5            (dense_rank last order by last_active_time) sql_id
  6          , max(child_number) keep
  7            (dense_rank last order by last_active_time) child_number
  8        from v$sql
  9      where upper(sql_text) like '%&1%'
 10        and upper(sql_text) not like '%FROM V$SQL WHERE UPPER(SQL_TEXT) LIKE %'
 11        ) sqlinfo,
 12      table(DBMS_XPLAN.DISPLAY_CURSOR(sqlinfo.sql_id,
sqlinfo.child_number, 'ALLSTATS LAST  +PEEKED_BINDS -ROWS')) xplan
 13  /
Enter value for 1: KM2
```

```
PLAN_TABLE_OUTPUT
--------------------------------------
SQL_ID  3h1bp5jsm6d7v, child number 0
--------------------------------------
select /*+ GATHER_PLAN_STATISTICS KM2 */ * from dept where deptno = :x

Plan hash value: 3816518310

------------------------------------------------------------------------
| Id  | Operation                  | Name          |Starts|A-Rows|A-Time   |Buffers |
------------------------------------------------------------------------
|   0 | SELECT STATEMENT           |               |      |    1|00:00.01|    2 |
|   1 |  TABLE ACCESS BY INDEX RO| DEPT            |    1|    1|00:00.01|    2 |
|*  2 |   INDEX UNIQUE SCAN        | DEPT_DEPTNO_PK |    1|    1|00:00.01|    1 |
------------------------------------------------------------------------

Peeked Binds (identified by position):
--------------------------------------

   1 - (NUMBER): 10

Predicate Information (identified by operation id):
---------------------------------------------------

   2 - access("DEPTNO"=:X)
```

To make it easy to retrieve the sql_id and child_number and execute DISPLAY_CURSOR in the future, I saved Listing 7-2's query into a script and will execute it at the SQL*Plus command line by supplying my identifying string as a command-line parameter each time I use it (for example, @pln KM2). Note also in Listing 7-2, I added KM2 as my identifying string within the hint. Adding a simple identifier like this will help you quickly locate SQL you are testing.

There are a few things to notice about the SQL I used to retrieve and display the plan:

The GATHER_PLAN_STATISTICS hint: Notice that the SQL statement used in Listing 7-2 includes the GATHER_PLAN_STATISTICS hint. Using this hint is one way to make sure that Oracle correctly gathers rowsource execution statistics during your query execution. You may also set the STATISTICS_LEVEL parameter to ALL for your session, but I find that using the hint lets me gather the rowsource data only when I need it. The rowsource execution statistics are the actual data collected when the query executed. The collected values are displayed in the A-Rows (actual rows), A-Time (actual elapsed time), and Buffers (actual logical block reads) columns in Listing 7-2. These statistics are extremely valuable in determining exactly how the execution plan performed and where you need to focus your attention to optimize the query.

The query used to retrieve the sql_id and child_number: I used the last_active_time column to order the information so that I get back only the most recent (MAX) sql_id and child_number that matches the sql_text pattern I enter. This works *almost* every time when I'm testing something, particularly if I use a unique identifier in the SQL statement I'm testing. However, if you happen to be looking for a pattern that matches more than one query text and yours wasn't the last execution, you may not get your plan, but someone else's. The more specifically you can identify your query, the more likely it is this query will give you the correct plan. If you find you have trouble, you can simply query V$SQL for a list of all SQL that matches a certain pattern. Then you can visually identify the correct statement and pass the exact sql_id and child_number into the DISPLAY_CURSOR call.

The format parameters used in the DISPLAY_CURSOR call: The DISPLAY_CURSOR call takes a third parameter named FORMAT. There are numerous options to choose for this parameter value. The default is TYPICAL, but I used a set of options that displayed the data I wanted to show for this example. The use of the ALLSTATS LAST +PEEKED_BINDS -ROWS options causes the actual rowsource execution statistics for the last execution to be displayed along with the values for bind variables used in the SQL, and leaves out the estimated rows column (E-Rows).

Extended SQL Trace Data

The Oracle database is instrumented to provide a play-by-play of exactly where your code spends its time. This feature (event 10046) can be enabled on demand by using several methods. The output is a text file that contains two basic types of information: database calls (DB calls) and operating system calls (OS calls). DB call lines begin with the tokens PARSE, EXEC, or FETCH, and each represents a single completed call to the database by the Oracle kernel. OS call lines begin with the token WAIT and represent a single completed call to the operation system by the Oracle kernel. There are also lines that begin with the token STAT that contain the execution plan data. These lines are unformatted, but equivalent to the output you'd get by using DBMS_XPLAN.DISPLAY_CURSOR to retrieve plan data from the cursor cache.

The trace data can be aggregated and summarized to provide a complete response time profile of your code's execution. That means that you can know exactly where every bit of execution time consumed by your query was used. With trace data, you can get a more complete picture of your query's response time. The STAT lines give you the rolled-up totals for the query plan and rowsource execution statistics, but you also get the detailed DB calls and any OS calls that contributed to the response time as well.

If you want the definitive tool for helping you diagnose a performance problem, extended SQL trace data gets my vote. In nearly ten years of using trace data and the response time profiles created from them, I have not encountered a performance issue that the trace data didn't reveal. I know my experience cannot speak to every possible circumstance, and I admit to hearing others speak of several issues where trace data was of little or no assistance. But in my experience, you can't beat the value of trace data when you want to manage SQL performance.

In Listing 7-3, I use extended SQL trace data to locate a problem that wasn't visible when examining only the plan data displayed using DBMS_XPLAN.DISPLAY_CURSOR.

First, the query:

```
select * from bom where item_id=11 and org_id=2;
```

I executed the query with extended SQL tracing turned on and produced a simple response time profile. The total response time was 1.00 second.

■ **Note** I used a simple Perl script to create the profile, but Method R Corporation has a software product called the Profiler that can produce response time profiles and is a phenomenal tool for this purpose. Visit http://method-r.com/software/profiler-info for more information.

Listing 7-3. A Response Time Profile Generated from Extended SQL Trace Data

Response Time Component	Duration	Pct	# Calls	Dur/Call
SQL*Net message from client	0.52s	51.9%	12151	0.000043s
CPU service	0.30s	29.8%	12155	0.000024s
unaccounted-for	0.16s	16.2%	1	0.160985s
SQL*Net message to client	0.02s	2.2%	12151	0.000002s
Total response time	1.00s	100.0%		

I then used DBMS_XPLAN.DISPLAY_CURSOR to review just the execution plan data, as shown in Listing 7-4.

Listing 7-4. Using DISPLAY_CURSOR to Display Execution Plan Data

```
--------------------------------------------------------------------------------
| Id | Operation                    | Name   | Starts | A-Rows | A-Time   | Buffers |
--------------------------------------------------------------------------------
|  0 | SELECT STATEMENT             |        |      1 |  24294 |00:00.10 |   24472 |
|  1 |  TABLE ACCESS BY INDEX ROWID | BOM    |      1 |  24294 |00:00.10 |   24472 |
|* 2 |   INDEX RANGE SCAN           | BOM_N1 |      1 |  24294 |00:00.02 |   12208 |
--------------------------------------------------------------------------------
Predicate Information (identified by operation id):
--------------------------------------------------------------------------------

   2 - access("ITEM_ID"=11 AND "ORG_ID"=2)
```

Just so you can also see how this information looks in the trace file, Listing 7-5 shows the STAT lines.

Listing 7-5. STAT Lines from the Extended SQL Trace Data

```
STAT #6 id=1 cnt=24294 pid=0 pos=1 obj=71478 op='TABLE ACCESS BY INDEX ROWID BOM
(cr=24472 pr=0 pw=0 time=100007 us cost=285 size=1481934 card=24294)'
STAT #6 id=2 cnt=24294 pid=1 pos=1 obj=71480 op='INDEX RANGE SCAN BOM_N1
(cr=12208 pr=0 pw=0 time=39970 us cost=60 size=0 card=24294)'
```

Now what? Is 1 second acceptable? Well, I expect this query to execute hundreds or thousands of times every hour, and it is not reasonable for a single execution to take a second. But if you look at the plan statistics, you'll notice that the A-Time column is showing only 1 centisecond of elapsed time consumed to access 1,252 buffers and retrieve 24,294 rows. A centisecond seems reasonable. It appears that the correct index was used because the index returned only the rowids that the parent table access step acquired and kept. But why did my response time profile's actual elapsed time of 1 second not match the time shown in the execution plan? It looks like one or the other is wrong, doesn't it?

The truth is that both of the timings are correct. The problem is that we assumed both timings measure the same thing, and they do not. To be more precise, the centisecond timing shown for the plan execution is included in the 1 second total response time. The time shown in the A-Time column represents the time it took to complete the plan operations: an index range scan and a TABLE ACCESS BY INDEX ROWID. That means there are other events that are not included in the plan execution display provided through DBMS_XPLAN.DISPLAY_CURSOR.

However, if you look at the response time profile, you can clearly see that the majority of the time was spent doing 12,151 SQL*Net message from client calls. That call indicates that the database currently isn't doing anything, but rather is waiting to be told what to do. So can you guess why all those calls are being made? It's due to the number of rows each FETCH call is limited to return in a single retrieval. In SQL*Plus, this value is set with a parameter called ARRAYSIZE. In this example, ARRAYSIZE was set to 2. That means that only 2 rows at a time are sent to the client. Because we had more than 24,000 rows to be returned, more than 12,000 network roundtrips were required to get the entire result set back to the client application.

But would we really want so many round trips to happen? What if ARRAYSIZE were set to a higher value? If ARRAYSIZE was set to 100, for example, then 100 rows per FETCH call would be retrieved and sent to the client. Therefore, given that we have approximately 24,000 total rows to be returned, it would be necessary to make about 240 calls to do so. I can now forecast how much of a response time reduction I can get if I make this change. Roughly, if only 240 SQL*Net message from client calls are made instead of more than 12,000, I can estimate the time to make those calls will reduce from 0.52 seconds (12,151 calls taking 0.000043 seconds each) to approximately 0.01 seconds (240 calls). That's simple enough, and it looks like a significant response time difference.

Listing 7-6 shows the response time profile for the same query executed after I changed the ARRAYSIZE parameter to 100.

Listing 7-6. The Response Time Profile After the ARRAYSIZE Change

Response Time Component	Duration	Pct	# Calls	Dur/Call
SQL*Net message from client	0.14s	70.1%	247	0.000549s
CPU service	0.05s	24.2%	251	0.000186s
unaccounted-for	0.01s	5.5%	1	0.010728s
SQL*Net message to client	0.00s	0.2%	247	0.000002s
Total response time	0.19s	100.0%		

That's better! My estimate was a little bit off because the duration per call was higher for this test than for the original, but I was pretty much on target with what I expected to happen. Being able to see the entire performance picture, not just one piece of it, and then accurately forecast what will happen if you make a change is the real magic of using extended SQL trace.

I could continue to experiment with ARRAYSIZE to locate the best setting, but for my purpose here, this is good enough. The point is that with just the plan execution information I reviewed by using DBMS_XPLAN.DISPLAY_CURSOR, I couldn't fully diagnose the problem. With just that portion of the total picture, I was missing a critical piece of information that I needed. After I had that information, it was a simple matter to see where my time was being used and find a way to reduce it.

So why not just use extended SQL trace all the time? Well, in some cases, it's more difficult to use it and get access to the generated trace files than it is to just grab the plan execution information quickly from the cursor cache. When tracing, you want to make sure to properly scope the trace so you capture only the data for the task you care about. Capturing extra activity that you don't care about can distort the response time profile so your task is masked within a bunch of other unimportant stuff. Also, in order to retrieve the trace file, you must have permission to access the dump file directory on your database server and then have a tool (either one you create or one you purchase) that can create a response time profile for you. Sometimes working with and around those limitations makes the use of extended SQL trace require more time and effort than some people are willing to expend.

Just remember that you have multiple tools in your performance toolbox. Use the tool that's appropriate for the task at hand. The key is to know when to use which tool. One of my favorite sayings is

"Why guess when you can know?" And because I want to know exactly where *all* my response time is going, I find using extended SQL trace invaluable. Just remember that in order to manage SQL performance well, you want to know, not just guess.

Interpreting Performance Data

After you execute your query and collect the performance data, what's next? If you can get the information but don't know how to respond to what you see, you're really no further along toward solving the problem. It's often easiest to learn by example, so I'm going to review four cases that demonstrate common problems I see over and over. I'll walk you through each example and point out how to interpret what the performance data is telling you.

Case 1: The Lack of a *Good* Index

One performance problem I run into quite frequently is caused by the absence of an index that properly covers the query predicate. There may be many indexes on the table, but none of them provide the optimal coverage for the query in question. Many times the available indexes are for only a single column, but the query predicate includes several columns. So even if the optimizer chooses to use a single-column index, a table block access will be required to retrieve the row and then apply the other filter conditions before the determination to keep the row for the result set can finally be made.

The plan execution data provides you with a clear indication of when the index being used could benefit from having additional columns. In Listing 7-7, I display only two lines, along with just their A-Rows values and the related predicate information lines, from a very long plan to point out how the index in use isn't very effective.

Listing 7-7. Excerpt of Execution Plan When a "Good" Index Does Not Exist

```
----------------------------------------------------------------
| Id  | Operation                   | Name                 | A-Rows |
----------------------------------------------------------------
|* 32 | TABLE ACCESS BY INDEX ROWID | GL_ACCOUNT_INSTANCE     |  606K|
|* 33 |   INDEX UNIQUE SCAN         | GL_ACCOUNT_INSTANCE_PK  | 3183K|


Predicate Information (identified by operation id):
---------------------------------------------------
  32 - filter(("GLI"."GL_ACCT_STAT_CD"='ACTIVE' AND
"TD"."GL_ACCT_NAME_CD"="GLI"."GL_ACCT_NAME_CD"))
  33 - access("TD"."GL_SYS_ID"="GLI"."GL_SYS_ID")
```

Notice how the index range scan shows a large number of rowids being passed to the parent table access step (more than 3.1 million), but less than 20 percent of those rows (606,000) are retained for the final result set. Now look at the Predicate Information for the parent table access step (Id = 32). Two columns have to be obtained from the row in the data block and then filtered before the row is finally accepted or rejected. If those two columns were added to the index, or if a new index with all three columns was added, 80 percent of the work currently being performed to access all the data blocks that ultimately get thrown away would be avoided. In Listing 7-8, I show the difference in the plan after the new index is created.

Listing 7-8. Excerpt of Execution Plan When a "Good" Index Does Exist

```
------------------------------------------------------------------
| Id  | Operation                   | Name                    | A-Rows |
------------------------------------------------------------------
|  32 | TABLE ACCESS BY INDEX ROWID | GL_ACCOUNT_INSTANCE     |  606K|
|* 33 |  INDEX RANGE SCAN           | GL_ACCOUNT_INSTANCE_IX5 |  606K|
------------------------------------------------------------------

Predicate Information (identified by operation id):
---------------------------------------------------
  33 - access("TD"."GL_SYS_ID"="GLI"."GL_SYS_ID" AND "GLI"."GL_ACCT_STAT_CD"='ACTIVE'
AND "TD"."GL_ACCT_NAME_CD"="GLI"."GL_ACCT_NAME_CD")
```

It was easy to see how having the filter conditions applied at the parent table access step caused more work to occur. The more often an index can provide complete coverage for the conditions in your SQL, the less work you incur to get the final result set. It may not always be possible to create an index to cover your predicates completely. However, if performance for a particular query is critical, you'll want to make sure that indexes provide the highest coverage possible.

Case 2: The Presence of Unidentified Data Skew

Query response times can vary significantly depending on the plan operations chosen by the optimizer. The optimizer depends on statistics to be able to determine the best plan choices. If the available statistics do not accurately represent your data, the optimizer's estimates for plan choice may result in operations that aren't as performance optimal as needed. A quick review of plan execution data lets you see how the optimizer's estimates stack up to the actual usage. Listing 7-9 shows the execution plan data for a query that requests only data where the object_type column contains the value 'PROCEDURE'.

Listing 7-9. Execution Plan for Query Using object_type = 'PROCEDURE'

```
----------------------------------------------------------------------------------
| Id  | Operation              | Name          |E-Rows |A-Rows |A-Time   |Buffers |
----------------------------------------------------------------------------------
|   0 | SELECT STATEMENT       |               |       |  4416 |00:00.01 |  1586 |
|   1 |  TABLE ACCESS BY INDEX R| B            | 59403 |  4416 |00:00.01 |  1586 |
|*  2 |   INDEX RANGE SCAN     | B_OBJTYPE_IDX | 59403 |  4416 |00:00.01 |   105 |
----------------------------------------------------------------------------------
Predicate Information (identified by operation id):
---------------------------------------------------
  2 - access("OBJECT_TYPE"='PROCEDURE')
```

Compare the E-Rows and A-Rows columns in Listing 7-9. It's pretty obvious that there is a significant discrepancy between the estimate and the actual values (over 13 times difference). But, the response time, of approximately 1 centisecond, wasn't a problem. If I used only EXPLAIN PLAN output, I wouldn't have noticed this difference at all and may have stopped my analysis right there.

But look at Listing 7-10 to see what happens when you use a different object_type value for the same query.

Listing 7-10. Execution Plan for Query Using object_type = 'SYNONYM'

```
--------------------------------------------------------------------------
| Id | Operation                |Name          |E-Rows |A-Rows |A-Time   |Buffers |
--------------------------------------------------------------------------
|  0 | SELECT STATEMENT         |              |       |  858K|00:18.88 |  62952 |
|  1 |  TABLE ACCESS BY INDEX R|B             | 59403 |  858K|00:18.88 |  62952 |
|* 2 |   INDEX RANGE SCAN       |B_OBJTYPE_IDX | 59403 |  858K|00:00.86 |  19441 |
--------------------------------------------------------------------------
Predicate Information (identified by operation id):
---------------------------------------------------

   2 - access("OBJECT_TYPE"='SYNONYM')
```

Ouch! This time the response time is almost 19 seconds. The plan is the same, an index range scan, but when the query returns more data than estimated, the response time is now unacceptable. You can also see that not only has the response time increased, but the buffers have increased significantly as well. This makes sense because the query retrieved more than 850,000 rows.

There's quite a difference between 1,586 buffer gets and 62,952 buffer gets for the two queries. However, there is an even more significant difference that you don't see. There is a statistic called buffer is pinned count that is viewable only if you snapshot that specific statistic name from V$SESSTAT before and after you execute your query and then diff the results. That means you won't see it when using DISPLAY_CURSOR or even in extended SQL trace data.

This statistic contains a count of buffer accesses for blocks previously pinned into the cache. The fact that those blocks are already pinned means there is less overhead to access them and requires less work on Oracle's part (particularly less latching). The main point I want to make is that the Buffers count is only part of the whole picture for an index access operation. Don't forget that more work is being done!

In this case, the buffer is pinned count value for this query is 1,655,993. That means over 1.7 million buffers were accessed to satisfy the query result. No wonder it took so long! As I said, the buffer is pinned count statistic isn't directly included in either extended SQL trace output or from the cursor cache. You have to compute it yourself for a single query execution. Although knowing about this statistic isn't critical to how you'd respond to what you see in this execution plan, I think it is important to know there is more data available that completes the picture of the work this query is doing.

If you'd like to be able to view statistics such as buffer is pinned count, capture latch statistics, and more, there are two sets of utility scripts that I use frequently to to do this: Tom Kyte's runstats package (http://asktom.oracle.com/pls/asktom/f?p=100:8:0::NO) and the Hotsos SQL Test Harness (www.hotsos.com/educ_downloads.html). Both sets of scripts are easy to install and use, and help you collect even more performance data you can use.

The bottom line in this example is that the optimizer didn't have the correct information to know that there was a skewed distribution of values in the object_type column. By default, statistics are gathered assuming that all data values are uniformly distributed. If that is not the case, statistics must be gathered specifically to capture skew. Skew is captured by the creation of a histogram and is done using the METHOD_OPT parameter when gathering object statistics as follows:

```
SQL> exec dbms_stats.gather_table_stats (user,'B',estimate_percent=>100,
method_opt=>'for columns object_type');
```

Listings 7-11 and 7-12 show how after the histogram is in place, the estimates for the two queries are accurate. Also, the plan choices are appropriate for each predicate, not to mention that the response time for the second query improves significantly.

Listing 7-11. Execution Plan for Query Using object_type = 'PROCEDURE' with Histogram in Place

```
-----------------------------------------------------------------------------
| Id  | Operation                | Name        |E-Rows |A-Rows |A-Time   |Buffers |
-----------------------------------------------------------------------------
|   0 | SELECT STATEMENT         |             |       |  4416 |00:00.01 |  1586 |
|   1 |  TABLE ACCESS BY INDEX R | B           |  4416 |  4416 |00:00.01 |  1586 |
|*  2 |   INDEX RANGE SCAN       | B_OBJTYPE_IDX | 4416 |  4416 |00:00.01 |   105 |
-----------------------------------------------------------------------------

Predicate Information (identified by operation id):
---------------------------------------------------

   2 - access("OBJECT_TYPE"='PROCEDURE')
```

Listing 7-12. Execution Plan for Query Using object_type = 'SYNONYM' with Histogram in Place

```
---------------------------------------------------------------------------------
| Id  | Operation         | Name  | E-Rows | A-Rows |  A-Time    | Buffers | Reads |
---------------------------------------------------------------------------------
|   0 | SELECT STATEMENT  |       |        |  858K  |00:00:03.49 |  49242  | 22224 |
|*  1 |  TABLE ACCESS FULL| B     |  858K  |  858K  |00:00:03.49 |  49242  | 22224 |
---------------------------------------------------------------------------------

Predicate Information (identified by operation id):
---------------------------------------------------

   1 - filter("OBJECT_TYPE"='SYNONYM')
```

Although this is a very simple example of how the presence of data skew can cause the optimizer estimates to be orders of magnitude off, the ability to compare estimated and actual values using DBMS_XPLAN.DISPLAY_CURSOR makes the issue easy to spot and correct quickly. Finding the presence of skew isn't the only time when having the estimated vs. actual comparison will pay off. But the point is that regardless of the cause, the ability to see both values at a glance makes it obvious if there is an issue at all.

Case 3: SQL That Should Be Rewritten

In some cases, you'll find that the performance problem you're reviewing can be fixed without touching the code, as you've seen in the previous examples. In my experience, however, often the best fix is to rewrite the SQL. Of course, if you can't touch the code, you'll have to find another way around, such as using stored outlines or SQL profiles. But even if you can't change the code as the final solution, you may need to modify the code in order to determine the best execution plan possible so you can save and enable it easily.

Listing 7-13 shows a seemingly simple query, but after reviewing the performance data, you'll see that rewriting it would significantly improve its performance.

Listing 7-13. *Query and Execution Plan with an Easy-to-Miss Scalability Issue*

```
SELECT  ATTR_FCTR,    ATTR_FCTR_YR,
        ATTR_FCTR_MO, PROJECT_CODE
  FROM  PRJ_ATT_FACTORS A
 WHERE  SIM_YR || SIM_MO =
        (SELECT MAX(B.SIM_YR || B.SIM_MO)
           FROM PRJ_ATT_FACTORS B
          WHERE A.PROJECT_CODE = B.PROJECT_CODE);
```

```
---------------------------------------------------------------------------
| Id  | Operation            | Name          |Starts |A-Rows |A-Time     | Buffers |
---------------------------------------------------------------------------
|   0 | SELECT STATEMENT     |               |    1  |    16 |00:00.01 |    71 |
|*  1 |  FILTER              |               |    1  |    16 |00:00.01 |    71 |
|   2 |   TABLE ACCESS FULL  | PRJ_ATT_FACTORS |  1  |    25 |00:00.01 |     8 |
|   3 |   SORT AGGREGATE     |               |    9  |     9 |00:00.01 |    63 |
|*  4 |    TABLE ACCESS FULL | PRJ_ATT_FACTORS |  9  |    25 |00:00.01 |    63 |
---------------------------------------------------------------------------

Predicate Information (identified by operation id):
---------------------------------------------------

   1 - filter("SIM_YR"||"SIM_MO"=)
   4 - filter("B"."PROJECT_CODE"=:B1)
```

This particular query has a subquery in the WHERE clause that returns the MAX year/month for a given project code. So for each row in PRJ_ATT_FACTORS, the subquery will execute as the row is filtered through the WHERE clause. That's not precisely true, because subquery caching comes into play. Subquery caching has the effect of requiring that the subquery be executed just once per distinct project code instead of once per row.

■ **Note** A wealth of information on subquery caching is available by doing a simple Google search on *Oracle subquery caching.*

Consider the ground that must be covered to obtain the final result set. My test table has 25 rows (Id = 2, A-Rows = 25). For those 25 rows, Oracle executes the MAX subquery nine times (Id = 3, Starts = 9). Because of subquery caching and because there are only nine distinct project codes in my table, it executes only nine times. After a project code is used in the subquery once, its result is retained in memory and reused, and doesn't require Oracle to issue the subquery again. But the point is that the subquery gets executed over and over again as new project codes occur.

At this point, you may be wondering why I don't just create an index on the project_code column so that instead of the subquery plan doing a full table scan, it would use the index. I could do that. But even if I create the index and it improves things, by reducing buffer gets and therefore likely time as well, the query will still be making repeated executions of the subquery. I want to find a way to avoid the repeated executions.

Also notice that the subquery is against the same table I'm accessing in the outer query. So the primary question I'd want to consider is "Can I write this query differently to avoid multiple accesses against the same table over and over?" Right now, the way the query is written, there's not much that can be done to make it scale very well. It may perform okay now, but what about when the volume of data grows? Listing 7-14 shows what happens if I double the table size to 50 rows.

Listing 7-14. Execution Plan When the Data Size (Number of Rows) in the Test Database Doubles

Id	Operation	Name	Starts	A-Rows	A-Time	Buffers
0	SELECT STATEMENT		1	32	00:00.01	127
* 1	FILTER		1	32	00:00.01	127
2	TABLE ACCESS FULL	PRJ_ATT_FACTORS	1	50	00:00.01	8
3	SORT AGGREGATE		17	17	00:00.01	119
* 4	TABLE ACCESS FULL	PRJ_ATT_FACTORS	17	50	00:00.01	119

Predicate Information (identified by operation id):

```
1 - filter("SIM_YR"||"SIM_MO"=)
4 - filter("B"."PROJECT_CODE"=:B1)
```

The number of executions of the subquery increases from 9 to 17 (check the Starts column), and the buffers accessed increases from 71 to 127. Just to give you an idea of how bad this gets as volume increases, Listing 7-15 shows this same query's plan execution data from production; the table has more than 270,000 rows.

Listing 7-15. Execution Plan from Production

Id	Operation	Name	Starts	A-Rows	A-Time	Buffers
0	SELECT STATEMENT		1	18480	04:13:58.24	52756K
* 1	FILTER		1	18480	04:13:58.24	86529
2	TABLE ACCESS FULL	PRJ_ATT_FACTORS	1	271830	00:00:01.53	3053
3	SORT AGGREGATE		142578	28843	04:13:11.10	52667K
* 4	TABLE ACCESS FULL	PRJ_ATT_FACTORS	142578	14816K	04:11:33.55	52667K

Predicate Information (identified by operation id):

```
1 - filter("SIM_YR"||"SIM_MO"=)
4 - filter("B"."PROJECT_CODE"=:B1)
```

In production, the response time for this query was more than 4 hours! So, how could I rewrite this query to eliminate the need to query the same table over and over, and do it only once? How about using an analytic function? Listing 7-16 shows the rewritten query and the new plan execution data using my test environment with a 50-row table.

Listing 7-16. Rewritten Query and Execution Plan

```
SELECT  ATTR_FCTR,     ATTR_FCTR_YR,
        ATTR_FCTR_MO, PROJECT_CODE, THE_YRMO
    FROM
        ( SELECT MAX(SIM_YR || SIM_MO)
                 OVER (PARTITION BY PROJECT_CODE) AS THE_MAX,
                 ATTR_FCTR,
                 ATTR_FCTR_YR,
                 ATTR_FCTR_MO,
                 PROJECT_CODE,
                 SIM_YR || SIM_MO AS THE_YRMO
            FROM  PRJ_ATT_FACTORS
        ) a
WHERE   a.THE_YRMO = THE_MAX ;
```

```
-------------------------------------------------------------------------------
| Id  | Operation           |Name             |Starts |A-Rows |  A-Time   |Buffers |
-------------------------------------------------------------------------------
|  0  | SELECT STATEMENT    |                 |   1   |   32  |00:00:00.01 |    7 |
|* 1  |  VIEW               |                 |   1   |   32  |00:00:00.01 |    7 |
|  2  |   WINDOW SORT       |                 |   1   |   50  |00:00:00.01 |    7 |
|  3  |    TABLE ACCESS FULL|PRJ_ATT_FACTORS  |   1   |   50  |00:00:00.01 |    7 |
-------------------------------------------------------------------------------
Predicate Information (identified by operation id):
-------------------------------------------------

   1 - filter("A"."THE_YRMO"="THE_MAX")
```

This rewritten version of the query requires only a single access on the table. Much better! Listing 7-17 shows how the rewritten query performed in production.

Listing 7-17. Rewritten Query's Production Execution Plan

```
-------------------------------------------------------------------------------
| Id  | Operation           |Name             |Starts |A-Rows |  A-Time   |Buffers |
-------------------------------------------------------------------------------
|  0  | SELECT STATEMENT    |                 |   1   | 18480 |00:00:11.47 | 1833 |
|* 1  |  VIEW               |                 |   1   | 18480 |00:00:11.47 | 1833 |
|  2  |   WINDOW SORT       |                 |   1   |271830 |00:00:09.73 | 1833 |
|  3  |    TABLE ACCESS FULL|PRJ_ATT_FACTORS  |   1   |271830 |00:00:01.59 | 1826 |
-------------------------------------------------------------------------------
Predicate Information (identified by operation id):
-------------------------------------------------

   1 - filter("A"."THE_YRMO"="THE_MAX")
```

I'd say this is a very successful optimization effort! The response time decreased from more than 4 hours to a little more than 11 seconds.

The most difficult part of this problem was determining how to rewrite the query. That part gets easier with practice, but it is important to stay on top of new coding features and syntax options that are available in the version of Oracle you are using. SQL like this has often been around for a long time, and it's easy to see the code only as it is and not think of new possibilities for how it could be written more efficiently.

Almost every SQL statement can be written in multiple ways. Just make sure that when you are considering ways to write SQL, your options aren't limited by a lack of knowledge. Sometimes overcoming *not knowing* what you can do is the biggest performance hurdle you'll have to cross.

Case 4: SQL That Unnecessarily Invokes PL/SQL

The issue of concern in this case is called *context switching*. SQL is a nonprocedural language and has a separate execution code path, often referred to as the *engine*, within the Oracle kernel. PL/SQL is a procedural language and has its own execution engine. In order for a SQL statement to call a PL/SQL code block, or a PL/SQL code block to execute a SQL statement, Oracle must switch between execution engines. This switch means extra overhead is incurred that would not otherwise be required if the switch did not happen. This "hit," even if it is very small, say 1/1000th of a second, will add up if you do it enough. For example, take a SQL statement that returns 10,000 rows. If each of those result rows has a PL/SQL function call, that would mean 10 seconds of your response time would be consumed just executing those calls (10,000 rows × 0.001 seconds). Can you really afford that extra response time consumption?

Before you jump to the conclusion that I'm making a blanket statement that PL/SQL is bad for performance and should be avoided, let me stop you. I am absolutely *not* saying that. What I want you to know is that if you have a need to execute a PL/SQL code block that provides you with a result you *cannot achieve directly through SQL*, you will pay a performance price for using it. So one thing to look for when your SQL performance is suffering is the presence of PL/SQL calls when you could get the same result another way.

The tricky part about this issue is that if you look only at the SQL execution plan data, you won't see the problem, except perhaps in terms of response time. But in your test environment where you may have only small tables to query against, even response time may not be poor enough to alert you. Listing 7-18 shows a PL/SQL function and two queries we'll use to walk through an example.

Listing 7-18. Example Queries and PL/SQL Function

```
create or replace function get_ord_tot(p_ordno IN number) return number as
   v_tot   number(13,2);
begin
   select sum(total_order_item_price)
   into v_tot
   from items
   where order_no = p_ordno;
   return v_tot;
exception
   when others then return 0;
end;
/
```

```
select cust_no, order_no, get_ord_tot(order_no)
from orders
group by cust_no, order_no;

select o.cust_no, o.order_no, sum(i.total_order_item_price)
from orders o, items i
where o.order_no = i.order_no
group by o.cust_no, o.order_no;
```

In the first query, the function GET_ORD_TOT is called to retrieve the total order amount, whereas in the second query, the same result is achieved using a table join. Listings 7-19 and 7-20 list the execution plan data for each query.

Listing 7-19. Execution Plan Data for a Query Using a PL/SQL Function

Id	Operation	Name	Starts	A-Rows	A-Time	Buffers
0	SELECT STATEMENT		1	12890	00:00:00.02	156
1	HASH GROUP BY		1	12890	00:00:00.02	156
2	TABLE ACCESS FULL	ORDERS	1	12890	00:00:00.01	156

Listing 7-20. Execution Plan Data for a Query Using a Table Join

Id	Operation	Name	Starts	A-Rows	A-Time	Buffers
0	SELECT STATEMENT		1	12890	00:00:00.10	436
1	HASH GROUP BY		1	12890	00:00:00.10	436
* 2	HASH JOIN		1	12890	00:00:00.08	436
3	TABLE ACCESS FULL	ORDERS	1	12890	00:00:00.01	156
4	VIEW	VW_GBC_5	1	12890	00:00:00.08	280
5	HASH GROUP BY		1	12890	00:00:00.08	280
6	TABLE ACCESS FULL	ITEMS	1	70975	00:00:00.01	280

```
Predicate Information (identified by operation id):
--------------------------------------------------

   2 - access("O"."ORDER_NO"="ITEM_1")
```

Compare both listings. At a glance, Listing 7-19 appears to be better in terms of overall time (A-Time) and logical I/O (Buffers). But with just a bit more scrutiny, you should notice that the first query plan doesn't contain any operations involving the ITEMS table. Huh? Did using the function call just give that data access to you for free? Obviously, it did not. What the function call did was to effectively hide the access on the ITEMS table from your view. Execution plans show only a single query's data. Queries that call PL/SQL that contains additional SQL will not be included in the execution plan data for the query you executed. The execution plan data for the second query using the table join contains everything you need, but you need more data for the first query. So if you compare just these two listings, you're really not comparing the complete picture of both executions.

To get a complete picture of each query execution for comparison, this is a case where you can benefit from collecting extended SQL trace data. Recall that with trace data you get *all* the execution data, including time spent waiting for events that don't show up in the plan data alone. So for each test, I collected trace data and created response time profiles, as shown in Listings 7-21 and 7-22.

Listing 7-21. Response Time Profile for a Query Using a PL/SQL Function

Response Time Component	Duration	Pct	# Calls	Dur/Call
CPU service	3.04s	76.3%	281	0.010826s
SQL*Net message from client	0.82s	20.7%	270	0.003050s
unaccounted-for	0.10s	2.6%	1	0.104507s
pipe get	0.02s	0.4%	1	0.015347s
SQL*Net message to client	0.00s	0.0%	270	0.000002s
Total response time	3.99s	100.0%		

Listing 7-22. Response Time Profile for a Query Using a Table Join

Response Time Component	Duration	Pct	# Calls	Dur/Call
SQL*Net message from client	0.84s	79.5%	270	0.003109s
CPU service	0.11s	10.3%	281	0.000389s
unaccounted-for	0.07s	6.9%	1	0.072339s
pipe get	0.03s	3.2%	1	0.034077s
SQL*Net message to client	0.00s	0.0%	270	0.000002s
Total response time	1.06s	100.0%		

From the two profiles in Listings 7-21 and 7-22, note in particular the total time spent executing CPU service calls. When using the PL/SQL function, 281 calls take 3.04 seconds to complete. But when using a table join, the same number of calls takes only 0.11 seconds. Also notice the difference in duration per call: 0.010826 seconds per call using the function as compared to 0.003109 seconds per call for the join. With this data, it appears pretty obvious that using the PL/SQL function has significantly greater impact than execution plan data alone seemed to indicate.

To take it one step further, Listing 7-23 shows the output from the Oracle utility tkprof I used to summarize the trace file containing the PL/SQL function. With this summarization, I can show you where the "missing" function calls and their related data are.

Listing 7-23. tkprof Output Excerpt

```
SQL ID: buy1cavrwf8ju
Plan Hash: 1902515569
SELECT SUM(TOTAL_ORDER_ITEM_PRICE)
FROM
ITEMS WHERE ORDER_NO = :B1
```

call	count	cpu	elapsed	disk	query	current	rows
Parse	1	0.00	0.00	0	0	0	0
Execute	12890	1.66	1.53	0	0	0	0
Fetch	12890	0.21	0.16	0	39124	0	12890
total	25780	1.87	1.69	0	39124	0	12890

The main query execution plan in Listing 7-19 showed only the access to the ORDERS table (12,890 rows). Using the trace data, we can look further into exactly what happened when that query executed. We can see that for each of those 12,890 rows, the query against the ITEMS table in the function was executed using the ORDER_NO as the input parameter (:B1).

Note that I'm not showing you *exactly* the amount of time accounted for by context switching. It is included in the CPU service time required to execute the function call over and over. But when you add up the overall effect of executing all those function calls plus the overhead of switching between the SQL and PL/SQL engine to do them, I think you get the picture!

I'll end by saying that the use of functions such as the one demonstrated here is most often done in the name of reusability or ease of maintenance. The argument is that if you know you'll want to use that same query against the ITEMS table in many places and if you put it in a function, you'll have only one place to make a change should one be required. I disagree with the premise of this argument that the ability to reuse or maintain application code is the first priority. PL/SQL is a procedural language extension to SQL; SQL is the core. If you've accepted the performance mindset as your own, you wouldn't choose to do anything that would degrade performance at the expense of perceived savings in maintaining that SQL. The more you code big blocks of PL/SQL that could be written in one SQL statement, you've added more code to maintain, added more complexity and opportunity for bugs, and certainly added overhead that will hit your application every day and not just during a maintenance cycle. If performance is your goal, doing everything you can in SQL directly should be your first choice.

Summary

To manage SQL performance well requires a commitment to the process. Beginning with your mindset, you accept responsibility for the performance of every SQL statement you write or maintain. A big part of fulfilling your responsibility is to keep your education up-to-date. You must know how to accurately collect and analyze performance data to move quickly and efficiently from problem diagnosis to a solution.

It's not really that hard to get the data you need. We've reviewed a couple of ways in this chapter. Regardless of the method you use to collect and review performance data, the key is to stop guessing about performance problems. Remember: *Why guess when you can know?*

You won't be able to count on every SQL performance problem you encounter being something you've seen before. There are certainly common problems that can, and do, occur. But as you grow more adept at managing SQL performance, you'll find that you no longer make the mistakes that lead to those kinds of problems in the first place. The key is to be able to pinpoint the cause of the problem quickly. If you don't know exactly how to proceed after you've identified the problem, a little bit of research should lead you to the information you need to finalize a solution.

Optimal performance doesn't just happen. Nor is it that hard to accomplish, even though many people believe it is. To achieve consistently high-performing SQL requires time, knowledge, and diligence. To do it well, you need to integrate concern for performance into your daily routine. After you've made SQL performance management part of your routine, you'll likely find that the performance issues you face will be fewer and easier to deal with when they do occur.

Further Reading

Wolfgang Breitling, "Tuning by Cardinality Feedback,"
www.centrexcc.com/Tuning%20by%20Cardinality%20Feedback.pdf

Wolfgang Breitling, "SQL Tuning with Statistics,"
www.centrexcc.com/SQL%20Tuning%20with%20Statistics.pdf

Cary Millsap, "For Developers: Making Friends with the Oracle Database,"
http://method-r.com/downloads/doc_download/10-for-developers-making-
friends-with-the-oracle-database-cary-millsap

Karen Morton, "Managing Statistics for Optimal Query Performance,"
http://method-r.com/downloads/doc_download/11-managing-statistics-for-
optimal-query-performance-karen-morton

Karen Morton, "Performance Instrumentation for PL/SQL," http://method-
r.com/downloads/doc_download/8-performance-instrumentation-for-plsql-
when-why-how-karen-morton

CHAPTER 7

∎∎∎

PL/SQL and the CBO

by Jože Senegačnik

Several years ago, I made a presentation at the Independent Oracle Users Group conference, IOUG Live 2005, with the title "The Extensible Optimizer." It's been quite a long time since that presentation, but many people, especially developers, still are not aware that the cost-based optimizer (CBO) needs some extra input whenever you use a custom PL/SQL function in the WHERE clause of a SQL statement. I have seen so many applications performing poorly because they were using PL/SQL functions in SQL statements without arming the CBO with additional knowledge about those functions. Hence this chapter, in which I will show you how to help the CBO prepare optimal execution plans when using PL/SQL functions as part of your query conditions.

Reviewing the Basics

Let's start with some basics that you need to fully understand before you can step in and provide additional information to the CBO. You may already know much of what I discuss in this section, but bear with me and review it once more. I'll keep the review short and fast.

Each SQL statement undergoes an optimization process prior to its execution. During this optimization process, the optimizer evaluates different possible access paths, join methods, and join orders. Becoming familiar with the SQL statement optimization process is important in order to understand how the CBO applies a cost to PL/SQL functions found in the WHERE clause. Later, you will see that Oracle provides the so-called extensible optimizer. The *extensible optimizer* allows you to define the selectivity and the cost of PL/SQL functions, thus enabling the optimizer to better estimate cost, and to choose an optimal execution plan.

Parsing Phase

Parsing a statement means that it is syntactically and semantically checked. At the same time, the privileges of the user issuing the statement are checked to ensure that the user is allowed to access the objects named in the SQL statement. During the parsing phase, Oracle allocates a private SQL area for the statement.

Execution Plan Preparation

The next step is preparation of an execution plan, which is the responsibility of the optimizer. The optimizer chooses either a cost-based or rule-based approach and determines the goal of optimization. (A rule-based approach is not really an option anymore, although the rule-based optimizer is still present in Oracle Database 11g.) The execution plan is a list of steps (essentially these are really function calls) that must be executed in a predefined order to successfully complete the execution of the SQL statement.

Let's walk briefly through the process of execution plan preparation. A parsed SQL statement is the input to what is called a *query transformer*. The transformer rewrites the statement when this would be advantageous for better plan generation. Most of the transformations are now cost-based, meaning that they are accepted if the cost of the transformed query is lower than the cost of the original statement.

There is also a *query plan estimator*. Its goal is to estimate the overall cost of a given plan. If statistics are available, the estimator uses them to compute the measures. Otherwise, the estimator uses default (hard-coded or predefined) values. The statistics improve the degree of accuracy of the measures. The computed measures that the CBO uses in the optimization phase are selectivity, cardinality, and cost.

Figure 7-1 is a schematic representation of the whole process of execution plan preparation.

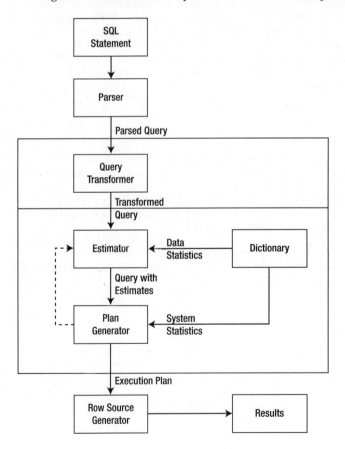

Figure 7-1. Parsing and optimizing process

Selectivity

Selectivity is the first and most important measure. It represents a fraction of rows from a row set; the row set can be a base table or a the result of a previous join or a grouping (that is, group by) operation. The estimator uses statistics to determine the selectivity of a certain predicate. A selectivity is thus tied to a query predicate, such as id = 12445, or to a combination of predicates, such as id = 12445 and 'status = 'A'.

The purpose of query predicates is to limit the scope of a query to a certain number of rows that we are interested in. Therefore, the selectivity of a predicate indicates how many rows from a row set will pass the predicate test. Selectivity lies in a value range from 0.0 to 1.0, where a selectivity of 0.0 means that no rows will be selected from a row set, and a selectivity of 1.0 means that all rows will be selected.

The estimator supposes a uniform distribution of data. This means that each value out of *n* distinct values will return the same number of rows. But in some situations, this is not true, and as a result we can face large variations in the number of rows containing a given value in a column. For such cases, we have to create a histogram. The purpose of a histogram is to help the estimator generate good selectivity estimates for columns with nonuniform data distribution. The estimator will always use a histogram when available.

There are unfortunately many cases in which DBAs and/or developers build histograms for all columns, even when some of them have uniform distribution. If a column has a uniform distribution, there is no need for a histogram. Creating unneeded histograms wastes time and may even lead to degraded performance.

When there are no statistics available, the estimator uses an internal hard-coded default value for selectivity. The predicate type governs which kind of internal defaults will be used. For example, the equality predicate is expected to return fewer rows than a range predicate. Thus, the hard-coded default for an equality predicate is lower than that for a range predicate.

Cardinality

Cardinality represents the number of rows in a row source. Remember that a row source can be a table, or it can be the result from a previous operation during the execution of a query. For example, the row source to an equality predicate could be the result of a join, or vice versa.

Analyzing a table captures the base cardinality for that table. If table statistics are not available, the estimator uses the number of extents occupied by the table from the segment header and the hard-coded default row length of 100 bytes to estimate the base cardinality.

Computed cardinality is the number of rows that are selected from a base table when predicates are applied. The computed cardinality is computed as the product of the table cardinality (base cardinality) and combined selectivity of all predicates specified in the WHERE clause. Each predicate is acting as a successive filter on the rows of the base table. The CBO assumes that there is no dependency among the predicates (this is called a *predicate independence assumption*).

The computed cardinality equals its base cardinality when there is no predicate specified. The computed cardinality for each row source (a table or result of previous operations) is visible in the execution plan. The computed cardinality thus determines how many rows will be selected and is used as a measure in the subsequent calculations of cost.

Cost

The *cost* used by the CBO represents an estimate of the number of disk I/Os and the amount of CPU and memory used in performing an operation. The cost represents *units of work* or resources used. The CBO uses disk I/O, CPU usage, and memory usage—Program Global Area (PGA) or temporary segments—as units of work for a given operation. An operation can be a full table scan, the access of rows by using an index, a join operation, the sorting of a row source, a group by operation, and many others. The cost of a query plan is the number of work units that are estimated as necessary when the statement is executed.

We can think about cost as the result of the price of the access method and the estimated cardinality of the row source. When we recall that the cardinality of a row source (that is, a table or result of previous operations) is calculated from the base cardinality of the row source and the estimated selectivity, we suddenly discover the origin for suboptimal execution plans. Both factors that are used in a cardinality computation can contribute to a plan becoming suboptimal. Incorrectly estimated selectivity and an inaccurate base cardinality of the table have same effect.

A developer, when writing the text of a SQL statement, knows the purpose of the statement and also knows what he wants to get as the result. Also the cardinality of the result set is known—or at least the developer has an idea about what that cardinality might be. Thus, comparing the estimated cardinality reported in the execution plan with the expected cardinality would be good practice for timely elimination of performance problems. When those two cardinalities differ by orders of magnitude, performance problems are almost inevitable. If the developer is expecting 10 rows to be returned, but the optimizer bases cost on returning 10,000 rows, then you are likely to have a problem.

Using the Extensible Optimizer

As you saw in the previous section, the measures of selectivity, cardinality, and cost play so important a role in execution plan preparation that you should always try to help the CBO to properly estimate them and thus prepare the optimal execution plan. And although the CBO can estimate the selectivity of predicates when regular operators are involved or when regular indexes are used, the CBO cannot do so when developers apply their own functions or create user-defined indexes. Therefore, the optimizer requires a new feature to correct this deficiency and arm developers with the ability to define selectivity and cost of execution for their user-defined functions and indexes. This feature is now available and is called the *extensible optimizer*, because it extends the standard optimizer capabilities.

To achieve this new functionality, the optimizer model was extended to allow users to create statistics collections, selectivity, and cost functions for their user-defined functions and indexes. The CBO can then apply that data to the problem of estimating query cost in order to generate execution plans that perform well.

The extensible optimizer feature allows control over the measures used by the CBO for user-defined functions and operators, and for domain indexes as well. The standard statistics that are prepared by the ANALYZE command, or with the DBMS_STATS package, support only predefined Oracle datatypes. ANALYZE and DBMS_STATS cannot generate statistics on a domain index, nor on a complex or user-defined datatype, because the database kernel doesn't know how to interpret those indexes and types.

User-Defined Statistics

The extensible optimizer feature enables you to define special statistics-collection functions used by either the DBMS_STATS package or the ANALYZE command for gathering statistics on domain indexes and columns that are defined with user-defined datatypes. Whenever a column is analyzed that is associated with a user-defined statistics collection function, that user-defined statistics collection function is called to gather statistics on the column.

User-Defined Selectivity

To improve the optimizer's selectivity estimation capabilities, the extensible optimizer feature allows definition of user-defined selectivity functions for predicates containing user-defined operators, stand-alone functions, package functions, and type methods. When the optimizer encounters such a predicate while preparing an execution plan, it calls the user-defined selectivity function and passes the entire predicate as an argument (including the relational operator, function, or type method and its arguments, the relational operator and the constant expression or bind variable). The return value (selectivity) is expressed as a percentage between 0 and 100 inclusive; values out of this range are ignored. If a user-defined selectivity function fails to return a valid value, the CBO uses heuristics to estimate the selectivity.

User-Defined Cost

The cost model has also been extended to let the developer define costs for domain indexes, index partitions, user-defined stand-alone functions, package functions, and type methods. Such costs can be defined as costs that the CBO uses by default, or they can be a result of special cost functions that the CBO calls to compute cost in order to determine an execution plan. Whenever cost information is missing, the CBO uses heuristics, but heuristics may lead to suboptimal execution plans.

The cost for a single execution of a function or domain index is defined by cost values for the following three items:

- CPU cost value is represented with the number of machine cycles executed by the function or domain index implementation. (The overhead of invoking the function is not included.) You can estimate the number of machine cycles with the package function DBMS_ODCI. ESTIMATE_CPU_UNITS.

- I/O cost value is the number of data blocks read by the function or domain index implementation.

- The NETWORK value is currently not used. It may be used in future releases, so developers are encouraged to define it. It represents the number of data blocks transmitted to the network.

Creating an Example

In the following pages, I will develop a test model for observing how the selectivity and the cost of a given function influence the preparation of an execution plan. Note that using a model to define cost and selectivity should be used only for complex cases. For the majority of cases, when you use user-defined PL/SQL functions in the WHERE clause, you need only to define the default selectivity and cost, both of which you can do by using the ASSOCIATE STATISTICS command (to be explained shortly). But let's first look at the harder way of defining selectivity and cost through implementation of a statistical type.

Creating Some Example Objects

We will first create a demo function called DEMO_FUNC1. The function really does nothing; it just returns a number with the value 0. It also implements several handy parameters that we will use later to change the selectivity and cost of the function execution.

■ **Note** This demo case is not really version dependent, and you can run it on Oracle 9i, Oracle 10g, or Oracle 11g. However, the content of the CBO trace file is highly version dependent, and therefore you can get slightly different output than is shown in this chapter.

Here is the code for our function:

```
CREATE OR REPLACE FUNCTION Demo_Func1 (
    dummy           NUMBER,
    selectivity     NUMBER,
    cpu_cost        NUMBER,
    io_cost         NUMBER,
    net_cost        NUMBER
)
    RETURN NUMBER AS
BEGIN
  RETURN 0;
END;
/
```

We must now implement the statistical type with the user-defined selectivity and cost functions. These will be called during the optimization phase by the CBO. Here is the code for our type definition, including the body:

```
CREATE OR REPLACE TYPE demo_statistics AS OBJECT (
    curnum    NUMBER,
    STATIC FUNCTION odcigetinterfaces (ifclist OUT SYS.odciobjectlist)
        RETURN NUMBER,
    STATIC FUNCTION odcistatsselectivity (
        pred            SYS.odcipredinfo,
        sel       OUT   NUMBER,
        args            SYS.odciargdesclist,
        strt            NUMBER,
        stop            NUMBER,
        dummy1          NUMBER,
        sel_input       NUMBER,
        cpu_cost        NUMBER,
        io_cost         NUMBER,
        net_cost        NUMBER,
        env             SYS.odcienv
    )
        RETURN NUMBER,
    PRAGMA RESTRICT_REFERENCES (odcistatsselectivity, WNDS, WNPS),
    STATIC FUNCTION odcistatsfunctioncost (
        func            SYS.odcifuncinfo,
        COST    OUT     SYS.odcicost,
          args          SYS.odciargdesclist,
          dummy1        NUMBER,
```

```
        sel_input    NUMBER,
        cpu_cost     NUMBER,
        io_cost      NUMBER,
        net_cost     NUMBER,
        env              SYS.odcienv
    )
      RETURN NUMBER,
      PRAGMA RESTRICT_REFERENCES (odcistatsfunctioncost, WNDS
            /*, WNPS - should be commented if we want to use
                  DBMS_OUTPUT while processing */)
);
/

CREATE OR REPLACE TYPE BODY demo_statistics IS
    STATIC FUNCTION odcigetinterfaces (ifclist OUT SYS.odciobjectlist)
        RETURN NUMBER IS
    BEGIN
        ifclist := SYS.odciobjectlist (SYS.odciobject ('SYS', 'ODCISTATS2'));
        RETURN odciconst.success;
    END odcigetinterfaces;

/* ------------------------------------------------------------------ */

    STATIC FUNCTION ODCIStatsSelectivity (
        pred             SYS.odcipredinfo,
        sel        OUT   NUMBER,
        args             SYS.odciargdesclist,
        strt             NUMBER,
        STOP             NUMBER,
        dummy1           NUMBER,
        sel_input        NUMBER,
        cpu_cost         NUMBER,
        io_cost          NUMBER,
        net_cost         NUMBER,
        env              SYS.odcienv
    )
        RETURN NUMBER IS
    BEGIN
        -- just return in function input parameter sel_input as selectivity
        sel := sel_input;
        RETURN odciconst.success;
    END;
/* ------------------------------------------------------------------ */
    STATIC FUNCTION odcistatsfunctioncost (
        func             SYS.odcifuncinfo,
        COST      OUT    SYS.odcicost,
        args             SYS.odciargdesclist,
        dummy1           NUMBER,
        sel_input        NUMBER,
        cpu_cost         NUMBER,
        io_cost          NUMBER,
```

159

```
        net_cost        NUMBER,
        env             SYS.odcienv
    )
    RETURN NUMBER IS
    fname     VARCHAR2 (30);
  BEGIN
    COST := SYS.odcicost (NULL, NULL, NULL, NULL);
    -- Get function name
    IF BITAND (func.flags, odciconst.objectfunc) > 0 THEN
        fname := UPPER(func.objectname);
    ELSE
        fname := UPPER(func.methodname);
    END IF;
    --
    -- now pass the function input parameters to the CBO in COST variable
    IF fname LIKE 'DEMO_FUNC%' THEN
        --DBMS_OUTPUT.PUT_LINE('CPU='||cpu_cost||' IO='||io_cost||
            -- 'Network='||net_cost||' Selectivity='||sel_input||'%');
        COST.CPUcost := cpu_cost;
        COST.IOcost := io_cost;
        COST.NetworkCost := net_cost;
        RETURN odciconst.success;
    ELSE
        RETURN odciconst.error;
    END IF;
  END;
END;
/
```

We need also to create the simple demo table T1:

```
create table t1 as
select object_id, 'A' status
from all_objects
where rownum <= 10000;
```

Running an Example Query

Let's run our first example query involving our demo function. We'll use the demo function in our WHERE clause. First, let's enable CBO tracing:

```
SQL> alter session set events '10053 trace name context forever, level 1';
```

Next, we'll generate an execution plan:

```
SQL> explain plan for SELECT T1.* FROM T1 T1
     WHERE demo_func1( t1.object_id, 1, 3000, 0, 0) = 1;
```

You can find the plan output in the trace file, which is produced in the user_dump_dest directory. The detailed contents of the trace file are highly version dependent. On my system, the plan came out as follows. Notice in particular the bold lines. These indicate how little useful information the CBO had to work with. (They also indicate opportunities for improvement!)

```
...
***************************************
BASE STATISTICAL INFORMATION
***********************
Table Stats::
  Table: T1  Alias: T1
    #Rows: 10000  #Blks:  16  AvgRowLen:  9.00
***************************************
SINGLE TABLE ACCESS PATH
  No statistics type defined for function DEMO_FUNC1
  No default cost defined for function DEMO_FUNC1
  No statistics type defined for function DEMO_FUNC1
  No default selectivity defined for function DEMO_FUNC1
  Table: T1  Alias: T1
    Card: Original: 10000  Rounded: 100  Computed: 100.00  Non Adjusted: 100.00
  Access Path: TableScan
    Cost:  13.03  Resp: 13.03  Degree: 0
      Cost_io: 5.00  Cost_cpu: 32115943
      Resp_io: 5.00  Resp_cpu: 32115943
  Best:: AccessPath: TableScan
         Cost: 13.03  Degree: 1  Resp: 13.03  Card: 100.00  Bytes: 0
...
Final - All Rows Plan:  Best join order: 1
  Cost: 13.0290  Degree: 1  Card: 100.0000  Bytes: 500
  Resc: 13.0290  Resc_io: 5.0000  Resc_cpu: 32115943
  Resp: 13.0290  Resp_io: 5.0000  Resc_cpu: 32115943
...
-----------------------------------+---------------------------------+
| Id | Operation          | Name   | Rows | Bytes | Cost | Time       |
-----------------------------------+---------------------------------+
| 0  | SELECT STATEMENT   |        |      |       |  13  |            |
| 1  |  TABLE ACCESS FULL | T1     | 100  | 500   |  13  | 00:00:01   |
-----------------------------------+---------------------------------+
Predicate Information:
----------------------
1 - filter("DEMO_FUNC1"("T1"."OBJECT_ID",1,3000,0,0)=1)
...
```

From this excerpt, we can see how the CBO reports that there are no statistics types defined for function DEMO_FUNC1. Neither default cost nor default selectivity are defined for DEMO_FUNC1. Therefore, the CBO uses a default selectivity of 1 percent (0.01), and also a default cost of 3,000 CPU units. The default I/O cost is 0.

How do we know these default numbers? The value for default selectivity is quite obvious: the base table cardinality is 10,000 rows, and the estimated cardinality of the result set is 100. We will determine the default CPU cost later. Table 7-1 lists the defaults used when the CBO knows nothing about the user-defined function.

Table 7-1. CBO Defaults for User-Defined Functions in a WHERE Clause

Default for	Value
Selectivity	1% (0.01)
CPU cost	3,000
I/O cost	0
Network cost	0

Giving the CBO Better Information

Now we will associate our statistics type with our DEMO_FUNC1. In order for a statistic type to act as an interface for user-defined functions, it must be somehow bound to a database object such as a column, stand-alone function, object type, index, index type, or package. Such an association is created with the ASSOCIATE STATISTICS command, as follows:

```
SQL> ASSOCIATE STATISTICS WITH FUNCTIONS Demo_Func1 USING demo_statistics;
Statistics associated.
```

Now we should rerun our SQL statement, and the CBO's report will be quite different. The following section goes into the details of how and why that is.

Understanding How It Works

Now that you've seen an example, it's time to go deeper into the underlying mechanism. How exactly does the CBO invoke user-defined selectivity and cost functions? What goes on "under the hood?" Let's answer those questions.

As we've discussed earlier, the optimizer determines three measures during the optimization phase: selectivity, cardinality and cost. When we associate a statistical type with a user-defined datatype or index type, the CBO calls the user-defined cost and selectivity functions at certain points from the optimization process. Following is an excerpt from the CBO trace file, produced by event 10053, where we can see how and when these calls are performed. To save space and make this section more readable, the details about the function call parameters are omitted. A full listing from the same process, showing all details, is available as part of the example download for this book. (You can find this code in the Source Code/Download area of the Apress website at www.apress.com.)

```
QUERY
SELECT T1.* FROM T1 WHERE demo_func1( t1.object_id, 1, 3000, 1, 0) = 1;

****************************
SYSTEM STATISTICS INFORMATION
****************************
  Using WORKLOAD Stats
  CPUSPEED: 1000 millions instructions/sec
```

```
    SREADTIM: 4 milliseconds
    MREADTIM: 8 millisecons
    MBRC: 8.000000 blocks
    MAXTHR: 1000000 bytes/sec
    SLAVETHR: -1 bytes/sec
**************************************
BASE STATISTICAL INFORMATION
***********************
Table Stats::
  Table: T1  Alias: T1
    #Rows: 10000  #Blks:  16  AvgRowLen:  9.00
***************************************
SINGLE TABLE ACCESS PATH
  Calling user-defined function cost function...
    predicate: "HS2006"."DEMO_FUNC1"("T1"."OBJECT_ID",1,3000,0,0)
...
  HS2006.DEMO_STATISTICS.ODCIStatsFunctionCost returned:
    CPUCost     : 3000
    IOCost      : 0
    NetworkCost : 0
  Calling user-defined selectivity function...
    predicate: "HS2006"."DEMO_FUNC1"("T1"."OBJECT_ID",1,3000,0,0)=1
...
  HS2006.DEMO_STATISTICS.ODCIStatsSelectivity returned selectivity: 1.00000000%
...
  Table: T1  Alias: T1
    Card: Original: 10000  Rounded: 100  Computed: 100.00  Non Adjusted: 100.00
  Access Path: TableScan
    Cost:  13.03  Resp: 13.03  Degree: 0
      Cost_io: 5.00  Cost_cpu: 32115943
      Resp_io: 5.00  Resp_cpu: 32115943
  Best:: AccessPath: TableScan
        Cost: 13.03  Degree: 1  Resp: 13.03  Card: 100.00  Bytes: 0
...
Final - All Rows Plan:  Best join order: 1
  Cost: 13.0290  Degree: 1  Card: 100.0000  Bytes: 500
  Resc: 13.0290  Resc_io: 5.0000  Resc_cpu: 32115943
  Resp: 13.0290  Resp_io: 5.0000  Resc_cpu: 32115943
...
```

Id	Operation	Name	Rows	Bytes	Cost	Time
0	SELECT STATEMENT				13	
1	TABLE ACCESS FULL	T1	100	500	13	00:00:01

```
Predicate Information:
----------------------
1 - filter("DEMO_FUNC1"("T1"."OBJECT_ID",1,3000,0,0)=1)
```

As you can see from this excerpt, the CPU cost is the same as in the previous case (32115943) when the CBO used default (hard-coded) values. (See the earlier section "Running an Example Query.") We can see that the CBO converts the CPU cost to the same unit as I/O cost. The conversion formula, determined by Wolfgang Breitling, member of OakTable.net, is as follows:

Cost = CPU-RSC / (1,000 × CPUSPEED × SREADTIM)

The variables have the following meanings:

CPU-RSC: CPU cost

CPUSPEED: CPU speed from system statistics

SREADTIM: Single-block read time from system statistics

When we insert actual numbers in the preceding case, we get the following result:

Cost = 32,115,943 / (1,000 × 1,000 × 4) = 8.028986, or rounded to 8.029

There is also the question of how the CBO determines the original I/O cost when system statistics are present. The formula determined by Wolfgang Breitling is the following:

I/O Cost = 1 + ceil (number_of_blocks / MBRC) × (MREADTIM / SREADTIM)

The MBRC, MREADTIM, and SREADTIM values are part of the system statistics stored in the `SYS.AUX_STATS$` table. The variables have the following meanings:

Number_of_blocks: Number of database blocks occupied by the table

MBRC: Average number of blocks read in one multiblock I/O operation

MREADTIM: Average time for a multiblock read operation (in milliseconds)

SREADTIM: Average time for a single-block read operation (in milliseconds)

Again, if we check the I/O cost by applying the preceding formula and we input the right values, we get the following:

I/O Cost = 1 + ceil [(16/8) × (8/4)] = 1 + ceil (2 × 2) = 1 + 4 = 5

Thus, the overall cost of execution is 5 + 8.029 = 13.03. The results would be quite different without the system statistics that switch on the new cost model introduced in Oracle 9i.

Indicating Default Selectivity and Default Cost

The statistics type is one of the possible ways for telling the CBO the "truth" about the selectivity and the cost of a function's execution during SQL statement processing. Unfortunately, developing a statistics type is very time-consuming. Fortunately, we have a shortcut of simply specifying default selectivity and cost values.

■ **Note** Most of the time, it should be enough to associate default selectivity and default cost with given functions used in the WHERE clause. Generally, you should find that you need to create a statistics type only for a relatively few, unusual cases.

Specifying Defaults (Syntax)

Default selectivity is expressed as a percentage between 0 percent and 100 percent. The default cost is defined as the combined CPU, I/O, *and* network cost. The latter is currently ignored by the CBO. The syntax for defining default selectivity and/or default cost is the following:

```
SQL> ASSOCIATE STATISTICS WITH FUNCTIONS
  2  func1 DEFAULT SELECTIVITY 12, DEFAULT COST (312722, 5, 0);
```

This association defines in this particular case default selectivity of 12 percent (0.12), a default CPU cost of 312,722, an I/O cost of 5, and a network cost of 0.

Determining a Default Cost

In order to correctly determine CPU and I/O cost, we can trace the execution of a function or package. Then we can use tkprof output figures to determine the CPU time and number of I/O operations. When we figure out the required CPU time per execution, we can use the DBMS_ODCI.ESTIMATE_CPU_UNITS function to convert the CPU time per execution to the approximate number of CPU instructions. The returned number is defined as thousands of instructions. In the following case, we will calculate the CPU cost for a function that always executes in 0.002 seconds:

```
SQL> variable a number
SQL> begin :a := 1000*DBMS_ODCI.ESTIMATE_CPU_UNITS(0.002);end;
  2  /

PL/SQL procedure successfully completed.

SQL> print a;

         A
----------
312722,323
```

Breaking the Association

When we want to break the association between the statistics type and the function or we want to "remove" the default cost or selectivity for the function, we can use the DISASSOCIATE STATISTICS FROM command. To disassociate a statistics type from our DEMO_FUNC1, you should run the following:

```
SQL> DISASSOCIATE STATISTICS FROM FUNCTIONS Demo_Func1;

Statistics disassociated
```

Influencing the Execution Plans

Now we should look how the properly defined selectivity or cost of a function may change the execution of a SQL statement that is invoking that function as part of a predicate. First we will create some additional objects so we can prepare more-complex queries:

```
create table t2 as select * from t1;

insert into t2 select * from t2;

insert into t2 select * from t2;

commit;

analyze table t2 compute statistics;

create table t3 as select * from t1 where rownum <= 5000;

analyze table t3 compute statistics;

create index t1_i1 on t1(object_id) compute statistics;

create index t2_i1 on t2(object_id) compute statistics;

create index t3_i1 on t3(object_id) compute statistics;
```

■ **Note** Don't forget to associate statistics with DEMO_FUNC1 again if you ran the previous test.

We have associated our DEMO_FUNC1 with our demo_statistics type, and we can observe what happens when we change the CPU or I/O cost or the selectivity. Here we use the statistics type purely because it was prepared so that we can simply define the selectivity or cost of execution as the function's parameter. We could do this also by associating/disassociating default selectivity and cost.

Example 1: Influence of the Increased Cost

Let's now start our next experiment. We begin by looking at the execution for our SQL statement:

```
SQL> EXPLAIN PLAN FOR
    SELECT T1.*, T2.*, t3.*
    FROM T1 T1, T2 T2, t3 t3
    WHERE T1.object_id = T2.object_id
    AND   T1.object_id = t3.object_id
    AND   T1.object_id BETWEEN 1000 AND 2000
    AND Demo_Func1(T2.object_id,1,3000,0,0)=0;
```

Explained.

```
SQL> select * from table(dbms_xplan.display);
```

```
--------------------------------------------------------------------------------
| Id  | Operation                    | Name  | Rows  | Bytes | Cost (%CPU)|
--------------------------------------------------------------------------------
|   0 | SELECT STATEMENT             |       |    27 |   378 |    35  (20)|
|*  1 |  HASH JOIN                   |       |    27 |   378 |    35  (20)|
|*  2 |   HASH JOIN                  |       |    29 |   290 |    30  (20)|
|*  3 |    TABLE ACCESS FULL         | T2    |    29 |   145 |    25  (24)|
|   4 |    TABLE ACCESS BY INDEX ROWID| T1   |   721 |  3605 |     5   (0)|
|*  5 |     INDEX RANGE SCAN         | T1_I1 |   721 |       |     3   (0)|
|*  6 |   TABLE ACCESS FULL          | T3    |   680 |  2720 |     4   (0)|
--------------------------------------------------------------------------------
```

Predicate Information (identified by operation id):

```
   1 - access("T1"."OBJECT_ID"="T3"."OBJECT_ID")
   2 - access("T1"."OBJECT_ID"="T2"."OBJECT_ID")
   3 - filter("T2"."OBJECT_ID"<=2000 AND "T2"."OBJECT_ID">=1000 AND
            "DEMO_FUNC1"("T2"."OBJECT_ID",1,3000,0,0)=0)
   5 - access("T1"."OBJECT_ID">=1000 AND "T1"."OBJECT_ID"<=2000)
   6 - filter("T3"."OBJECT_ID"<=2000 AND "T3"."OBJECT_ID">=1000)
```

In this case, we have used the default selectivity, CPU, and I/O cost (selectivity of 1 percent, CPU cost of 3,000, IO cost of 0, and network cost of 0). Table T2 on which we apply our DEMO_FUNC1 is accessed by a full table scan. Let's see what happens if we increase the CPU cost by 100 times (300,000):

```
EXPLAIN PLAN FOR
SELECT T1.*, T2.*, t3.* FROM T1 T1, T2 T2, t3 t3
WHERE T1.object_id = T2.object_id
AND    T1.object_id = t3.object_id
AND    T1.object_id BETWEEN 1000 AND 2000
AND Demo_Func1(T2.object_id,1,300000,0,0)=0;
```

```
--------------------------------------------------------------------------------
| Id  | Operation                     | Name  | Rows  | Bytes | Cost (%CPU)|
--------------------------------------------------------------------------------
|   0 | SELECT STATEMENT              |       |    27 |   378 |   264  (83)|
|*  1 |  HASH JOIN                    |       |    27 |   378 |   264  (83)|
|*  2 |   HASH JOIN                   |       |    29 |   290 |   259  (84)|
|   3 |    TABLE ACCESS BY INDEX ROWID| T2    |    29 |   145 |   254  (86)|
|*  4 |     INDEX RANGE SCAN          | T2_I1 |    29 |       |   224  (97)|
|   5 |    TABLE ACCESS BY INDEX ROWID| T1    |   721 |  3605 |     5   (0)|
|*  6 |     INDEX RANGE SCAN          | T1_I1 |   721 |       |     3   (0)|
|*  7 |   TABLE ACCESS FULL           | T3    |   680 |  2720 |     4   (0)|
--------------------------------------------------------------------------------
```

```
Predicate Information (identified by operation id):
--------------------------------------------------

   1 - access("T1"."OBJECT_ID"="T3"."OBJECT_ID")
   2 - access("T1"."OBJECT_ID"="T2"."OBJECT_ID")
   4 - access("T2"."OBJECT_ID">=1000 AND "T2"."OBJECT_ID"<=2000)
       filter("DEMO_FUNC1"("T2"."OBJECT_ID",1,300000,0,0)=0)
   6 - access("T1"."OBJECT_ID">=1000 AND "T1"."OBJECT_ID"<=2000)
   7 - filter("T3"."OBJECT_ID"<=2000 AND "T3"."OBJECT_ID">=1000)
```

The execution plan has changed, and the T2 table is now accessed by the index rowid. What happened? The CBO first performs an index range scan operation ("T2"."OBJECT_ID">=1000 AND "T2"."OBJECT_ID"<=2000) and afterward applies our DEMO_FUNC1. The cost of the index range scan plus the cost of executing DEMO_FUNC1 on 29 rows that are estimated to be returned from the index range scan operation is less than the cost of a full table scan.

What we can also observe is that the overall cost of the execution increased from 35 to 264 because of the increased CPU cost of the executing function. Why? We find a detailed answer in the CBO trace file:

```
...
Table: T2 Alias: T2
Card: Original: 40000 Rounded: 29 Computed: 28.84 Non Adjusted: 28.84
Access Path: TableScan
Cost: 377.25 Resp: 377.25 Degree: 0
Cost_io: 19.00 Cost_cpu: 1432995574
Resp_io: 19.00 Resp_cpu: 1432995574
...
Access Path: index (RangeScan)
Index: T2_I1
resc_io: 37.00 resc_cpu: 845223
ix_sel: 0.072096 ix_sel_with_filters: 7.2096e-004
Cost: 253.55 Resp: 253.55 Degree: 1
Best:: AccessPath: IndexRange Index: T2_I1
Cost: 253.55 Degree: 1 Resp: 253.55 Card: 28.84 Bytes: 0
...
```

It is obvious that the cost of a full table scan on table T2 is 377.25 while the index range scan costs only 253.55. Therefore, the CBO decides to use the execution plan with the lower cost.

From this very simple example, we can conclude how important it is to properly define the selectivity or cost of a function. Therefore, we have to define at least the default selectivity and cost for functions when using predicates in the SQL statement.

Example 2: Influence on the Order of Operations with Default Statistics

Statistics can influence not only the choice of operations to perform, but also the order in which they are performed. Let's create a copy of the DEMO_FUNC1 function, which will be DEMO_FUNC2:

```
CREATE OR REPLACE FUNCTION Demo_Func2 (
    dummy           NUMBER,
```

```
  selectivity    NUMBER,
  cpu_cost       NUMBER,
  io_cost        NUMBER,
  net_cost       NUMBER
)
  RETURN NUMBER AS
BEGIN
  RETURN 0;
END;
/
```

We can associate this function with the same statistics type demo_statistics because it can be used for all functions with the name DEMO_FUNC%.

```
SQL> ASSOCIATE STATISTICS WITH FUNCTIONS Demo_Func2 USING demo_statistics;
```

Now we will examine how the selectivity and cost influence the order of function execution. In the output from the DBMS_XPLAN package, we can observe the order of execution in the section labeled Predicate Information. The CBO first executes the function that is more selective or has lower cost. If there is no difference in the cost, or no statistics are associated with a function, the order of execution is the same as the order in which the functions are listed in the WHERE clause.

To begin our example, let's first disassociate statistics from the functions:

```
SQL> DISASSOCIATE STATISTICS FROM FUNCTIONS Demo_Func1, Demo_func2;
Statistics disassociated.
```

Next, we generate a query plan and display the results using dbms_xplan.display:

```
SQL> explain plan for
  2  SELECT * FROM T1
  3  WHERE Demo_Func2(object_id,10,5000,0,0)=0
  4* AND   Demo_Func1(object_id,10,5000,0,0)=0;

Explained.

SQL> select * from table(dbms_xplan.display);
```

```
--------------------------------------------------------------------------
| Id  | Operation          | Name | Rows  | Bytes | Cost (%CPU)| Time     |
--------------------------------------------------------------------------
|   0 | SELECT STATEMENT   |      |     1 |     5 |    13  (62)| 00:00:01 |
|*  1 |  TABLE ACCESS FULL | T1   |     1 |     5 |    13  (62)| 00:00:01 |
--------------------------------------------------------------------------

Predicate Information (identified by operation id):
---------------------------------------------------
   1 - filter("DEMO_FUNC2"("OBJECT_ID",10,5000,0,0)=0 AND
              "DEMO_FUNC1"("OBJECT_ID",10,5000,0,0)=0)
```

Now let's change the order of functions in the WHERE clause:

```
SQL> explain plan for
  2  SELECT * FROM T1
  3  WHERE Demo_Func1(object_id,10,5000,0,0)=0
  4  AND   Demo_Func2(object_id,10,5000,0,0)=0;

Explained.

SQL> select * from table(dbms_xplan.display);
```

```
---------------------------------------------------------------------------
| Id | Operation         | Name | Rows | Bytes | Cost (%CPU)| Time     |
---------------------------------------------------------------------------
|  0 | SELECT STATEMENT  |      |    1 |     5 |   13  (62)| 00:00:01 |
|* 1 | TABLE ACCESS FULL | T1   |    1 |     5 |   13  (62)| 00:00:01 |
---------------------------------------------------------------------------

Predicate Information (identified by operation id):
---------------------------------------------------
   1 - filter("DEMO_FUNC1"("OBJECT_ID",10,5000,0,0)=0 AND
              "DEMO_FUNC2"("OBJECT_ID",10,5000,0,0)=0)
```

We can see that the order of execution is the same as the order of the functions in the WHERE clause.

Example 3: Influence on the Order of Operations

Our next experiment will use different selectivities and costs. This time, we will associate the statistics type created with our two demo functions:

```
SQL> ASSOCIATE STATISTICS WITH FUNCTIONS
          Demo_Func1, Demo_Func2 USING demo_statistics;

Statistics associated.
```

Next, we generate and review an execution plan for a given set of selectivity and cost values. The following example shows the plan. You can see that the first function to be executed is the one having the lower cost:

```
SQL> explain plan for
  2  SELECT * FROM T1
  3  WHERE Demo_Func1(object_id,10,10000,0,0)=0
  4  AND   Demo_Func2(object_id,10,5000,0,0)=0;

Explained.

SQL> select * from table(dbms_xplan.display);
```

```
-------------------------------------------------------------
| Id | Operation          | Name | Rows  | Bytes | Cost (%CPU)|
-------------------------------------------------------------
|  0 | SELECT STATEMENT   |      |   100 |   500 |   21  (77)|
|* 1 |  TABLE ACCESS FULL | T1   |   100 |   500 |   21  (77)|
-------------------------------------------------------------
```

Predicate Information (identified by operation id):

```
   1 - filter("DEMO_FUNC2"("OBJECT_ID",10,5000,0,0)=0 AND
               "DEMO_FUNC1"("OBJECT_ID",10,10000,0,0)=0)
```

The proper order of the execution is very important in order to achieve the optimal execution plan. Therefore, execution of functions that are very costly in terms of CPU usage or that perform a lot of I/O should be postponed as much as possible in order to be executed on the smallest possible set of rows.

In the next case, we will specify the same cost for both functions, but the selectivities will be different:

```
SQL> explain plan for
  2  SELECT * FROM T1
  3  WHERE Demo_Func1(object_id,20,5000,0,0) = 0
  4  AND   Demo_Func2(object_id,10,5000,0,0) = 0;

Explained.

SQL> select * from table(dbms_xplan.display);
```

```
-------------------------------------------------------------
| Id | Operation          | Name | Rows  | Bytes | Cost (%CPU)|
-------------------------------------------------------------
|  0 | SELECT STATEMENT   |      |   200 |  1000 |   19  (74)|
|* 1 |  TABLE ACCESS FULL | T1   |   200 |  1000 |   19  (74)|
-------------------------------------------------------------
```

Predicate Information (identified by operation id):

```
   1 - filter("DEMO_FUNC2"("OBJECT_ID",10,5000,0,0)=0 AND
               "DEMO_FUNC1"("OBJECT_ID",20,5000,0,0)=0)
```

This time, the CBO first executes the function that selects fewer rows in order to limit as much as possible the number of rows that will need to pass through all filter conditions. Here again the CBO makes a smart decision to narrow down the number of rows as much as possible in the first step of execution by executing the function with lower selectivity, which results in having a smaller number of rows pass through this filter.

Summary

From the simple examples shown in this chapter, we can conclude that defining selectivity and cost for user-defined functions, whether written in PL/SQL or perhaps in other language, is very important when those functions are used in query predicates. Without knowing details of selectivity and cost, the CBO can only make guesses that are usually far from what you would expect and hope for. I have encountered many such cases over the past years in which the CBO was preparing suboptimal plans just because selectivity and cost information was not available. For all these cases, a simple default selectivity and cost definition helped so much that afterward the execution plans were quite different and were performing significantly better.

CHAPTER 8

■ ■ ■

Understanding Performance Optimization Methods

by Charles Hooper and Randolf Geist

The range of performance-related information captured by default in an Oracle Relational Database Management System (RDBMS) is astounding, and the breadth and depth of that detail continues to grow with each release of the Oracle database product. As needed, the database administrator is able to enable greater precision with more tightly focused information capture to investigate a specific problem, isolate the cause, and develop a plan that either directly addresses the problem within the database instance, or sufficiently describes the problem for the application development team.

For many other database platforms, one of the few options for improving performance is to blindly fix problems through the addition of hardware. In contrast, the performance-related information captured by an Oracle instance permits focused analysis of the specific performance issue that is impacting time-critical business activities. The vast list of performance-related information—including system-level and session-level statistics, system-level and session-level wait events, various performance views including V$LOCK and V$SYS_TIME_MODEL, Statspack, and Automatic Workload Repository (AWR) reports, EXPLAIN PLANs and DBMS_XPLANs, 10046 traces with and without tkprof analysis, 10053 cost-based optimizer traces, block-level dumps and systemstate dumps, and much more—potentially creates situations in which the database administrator is overwhelmed by all of the options when trying to select a suitable starting point for performance analysis.

To make good use of what Oracle Database has to offer, you must do the following:

1. Understand the options available.

2. Apply a decision-making process to help in choosing the correct option for a given problem.

This and the next chapter address these two items. This chapter is about the *understanding* part. We walk you through a number of common optimization methods, discussing pros and cons, and laying the groundwork for making the right decisions. Chapter 10, which follows next, provides a decision-making process that we believe will help you apply the right method to the right problem.

■ **Note** Most of the methods described in this chapter may be used without purchasing additional-cost items, such as a Diagnostics Pack or Tuning Pack license.

Blindly Changing Parameters

Oracle has several initialization parameters, some of which are hidden, that control memory utilization, execution plan costing, latch spin behavior, maximum I/O size for multiblock reads from disk, and so forth. (All hidden parameters begin with an underscore character and should not be changed without authorization from Oracle support.) It is easy to fall into a pattern of blindly changing the initialization parameters without identifying the actual source of the problem that the initialization parameter changes are expected to magically correct. The approach of blindly changing the initialization parameters without understanding the scope or purpose of the parameters nor the source of the problem is apparently encouraged by various Oracle books, official-looking web pages, and web discussion threads. The following quote from a discussion thread illustrates the fundamental problem from making blind changes:

> *Any suggestion please, actually I have been playing with it [PGA_AGGREGATE_TARGET], setting it to 1GB, 2GB, 25GB, 2500GB, but the performance is the same...how can I maximize my 16GB RAM?*

This quote is from a DBA who attempted to use the blindly changing parameters approach for an optimization method, in response to a Statspack report showing enq: TX - row lock contention as the highest wait for the time period of the report. The DBA set the PGA_AGGREGATE_TARGET to a value that exceeded the total memory in the server by a factor of 156.25 to address a problem likely caused by a second session attempting to modify a row that was modified by another session without a subsequent commit. Changing the wrong parameter probably will not help resolve performance problems and might just lead to new performance problems.

Blindly changing initialization parameters may be exciting, but perhaps for the wrong reasons. We do not recommend this approach.

Monitoring and Reacting to the BCHR

The concept of using the buffer cache hit ratio (BCHR) as a "barometer" for determining how well the database instance is performing has been around since at least the mid 1990s (plus or minus a decade). The motivation for using this ratio as a reference is founded on the principle that it takes 1,000 times (or 10 times or 100 times or 10,000 times) longer to fetch a block from disk than from the server's RAM. The suggestions for the use of the BCHR statistic are typically one of the following:

- If the buffer cache hit ratio falls below *x* percent, increase the DB_CACHE_SIZE parameter, increase the DB_BLOCK_BUFFERS parameter, move objects to the KEEP buffer pool, and so forth.

- If the buffer cache hit ratio increases or decreases significantly, something in the system has changed, and the problem should be investigated.

The following are some questions that might be raised regarding the buffer cache hit ratio:

- What is the correct formula for calculating the buffer cache hit ratio? The *Oracle Database Performance Tuning Guide 11g Release 2 (11.2)* book from the official Oracle documentation indicates that the following statistics from V$SYSSTAT should be used for calculating the ratio: physical reads cache, consistent gets from cache, and db block gets from cache. Many other sources, however, suggest using a formula such as (logical reads - physical reads)/logical reads. Still others suggest the use of one of the following formulas: 1 - (physical reads)/(consistent gets + db block gets), (logical reads)/(logical reads + physical reads), 1 - (physical reads - physical reads direct - physical reads direct (lob))/(consistent gets + db block gets), or 1 - (physical reads - (physical reads direct + physical reads direct (lob)))/(db block gets + consistent gets - (physical reads direct + physical reads direct (lob))).

- If the buffer cache hit ratio for a selected time period is 100 percent, is that a good indication, a bad indication, or an unknown indicator?

- If the buffer cache hit ratio is typically 90 percent, yet for a selected time period it approaches 100 percent, is that a good indication, a bad indication, or an unknown indicator?

- If the buffer cache hit ratio is typically 90 percent, yet for a selected time period it approaches 80 percent, is that a good indication, a bad indication, or an unknown indicator?

- If the buffer cache hit ratio is typically 98 percent, and for a selected time period it remains at 98 percent, is that a good indication, a bad indication, or an unknown indicator?

It is perhaps easy to state that an increasing buffer cache hit ratio is good, while a decreasing buffer cache hit ratio is bad, but is that a correct analysis? A poorly constructed SQL statement, or one with an inefficient execution plan, may repeatedly access the same index and table blocks, creating hot blocks, which remain in the buffer cache. Repeated accesses of the same blocks artificially inflates the BCHR, giving the appearance that the database instance is performing better than expected, when in fact the performance is much worse than expected because of the inefficient execution of the SQL statements.

A decrease in the BCHR may indicate that a more efficient execution plan was selected for one or several SQL statements, or a less efficient plan was selected for a SQL statement that now performs full table scans on large tables rather than using an index that would provide more-direct access to the small number of rows needed from the table.

No change in the BCHR might indicate that the database instance is performing exactly as well as it had in the past. Or it could indicate that a very inefficient SQL statement had repeatedly read the same blocks in the buffer cache, which increased the BCHR, while at the same time another very inefficient SQL statement had switched to a plan that read many blocks from disk during a full table scan, which decreased the BCHR. In such a case, the effects of the two problems may cancel each other out, resulting in no apparent change of the BCHR.

If the BCHR appears to be too low in the database instance, a solution is available. Several years ago, Jonathan Lewis and Connor McDonald each developed a script that is able to set the BCHR to a specified value. The scripts might prove to be helpful, if for no other reason than to see why the BCHR should largely be ignored.

With the preceding description in mind, a quick demonstration on Oracle 11.1.0.7 follows with the default NOWORKLOAD system statistics, an 8KB block size Automatic Segment Space Management (ASSM) tablespace, and DB_FILE_MULTIBLOCK_READ_COUNT left unset to permit Oracle to autotune the parameter. This demonstration shows why a higher value for the BCHR might not be better than a lower value, and why arbitrarily adjusting parameters to use available indexes might not improve performance.

The 100 million rows created by the following script are inserted in a cyclic ascending sequence followed by a descending sequence with numbers between 0 and 10,000 (to simulate a data capture during a quality inspection of multiple engine cylinder walls, with 32 inspection points along the x coordinate axis for each cylinder wall). An index is then created on the table, followed by statistics collection on the table and its index without the generation of histograms.

```
SQL> CREATE TABLE T1 (
  2    ID NUMBER,
  3    DESCRIPTION VARCHAR2(80));

SQL> INSERT INTO T1
  2  SELECT
  3    CEIL(ABS(SIN(ROWNUM/9.9999)*10000)),
  4    'This is the long description for this number '||
         TO_CHAR(CEIL(ABS(SIN(ROWNUM/9.9999)*10000)))
  5  FROM
  6    (SELECT
  7      ROWNUM RN
  8    FROM
  9      DUAL
 10    CONNECT BY
 11      LEVEL<=10000),
 12    (SELECT
 13      ROWNUM RN
 14    FROM
 15      DUAL
 16    CONNECT BY
 17      LEVEL<=10000);

SQL> COMMIT;

SQL> CREATE INDEX IND_T1 ON T1(ID);

SQL> EXEC DBMS_STATS.GATHER_TABLE_STATS(OWNNAME=>USER,TABNAME=>'T1',
        CASCADE=>TRUE, METHOD_OPT=>'FOR ALL COLUMNS SIZE 1')

SQL> ANALYZE INDEX IND_T1 VALIDATE STRUCTURE;
```

With the tablespace using ASSM AUTOALLOCATE extent management, the extents were allocated in sizes ranging from 64KB to 64MB, as indicated by the following:

```
SQL> SELECT
  2    SEGMENT_NAME SEGMENT,
  3    COUNT(*) EXTENTS,
  4    BYTES/1024 EXT_SIZE_KB,
  5    (COUNT(*) * BYTES)/1048576 TOTAL_MB
  6  FROM
  7    DBA_EXTENTS
```

```
 8  WHERE
 9    OWNER=USER
10    AND SEGMENT_NAME IN ('IND_T1','T1')
11  GROUP BY
12    SEGMENT_NAME,
13    BYTES
14  ORDER BY
15    SEGMENT_NAME,
16    BYTES;
```

SEGMENT	EXTENTS	EXT_SIZE_KB	TOTAL_MB
IND_T1	16	64	1
IND_T1	63	1,024	63
IND_T1	120	8,192	960
IND_T1	10	65,536	640
T1	16	64	1
T1	63	1,024	63
T1	120	8,192	960
T1	1	15,360	15
T1	1	22,528	22
T1	1	63,488	62
T1	82	65,536	5,248

The preceding output indicates that in a best-case scenario, the first 16 multiblock reads of this table during a full table scan will be limited to 8 blocks per multiblock read (assuming an 8KB block size) because of the 64KB extent size for the first 16 extents. While only the contents of the extents up to the high watermark for the table will be accessed during a full table scan, roughly 6.22GB were allocated to the table's extents.

There is an ANALYZE command near the end of the preceding example. Analyzing the index to validate its structure added a row into the INDEX_STATS view showing the following values (DBA_INDEXES reported that the clustering factor of the index was estimated at a value of 101,149,320, which is greater than the number of rows in the table):

```
SQL> SELECT
 2    HEIGHT,
 3    BLOCKS,
 4    LF_BLKS,
 5    LF_ROWS,
 6    DISTINCT_KEYS,
 7    MOST_REPEATED_KEY,
 8    PCT_USED
 9  FROM
10    INDEX_STATS
11  WHERE
12    NAME='IND_T1';
```

HEIGHT	BLOCKS	LF_BLKS	LF_ROWS	DISTINCT_KEYS	MOST_REPEATED_KEY	PCT_USED
3	212,992	208,854	100,000,000	10,000	900,324	90

With the table created, the following example displays the execution plan for the query without executing the SQL statement, and with the OPTIMIZER_INDEX_COST_ADJ parameter set to the default value of 100:

```
SQL> SET AUTOTRACE TRACEONLY EXPLAIN
SQL> ALTER SESSION SET OPTIMIZER_INDEX_COST_ADJ=100;

SQL> SELECT
  2    ID,
  3    DESCRIPTION
  4  FROM
  5    T1
  6  WHERE
  7    ID BETWEEN 1 AND 400;

Execution Plan
----------------------------------------------------------
Plan hash value: 3617692013
```

Id	Operation	Name	Rows	Bytes	Cost (%CPU)	Time
0	SELECT STATEMENT		4000K	202M	221K (1)	00:44:17
* 1	TABLE ACCESS FULL	T1	4000K	202M	221K (1)	00:44:17

```
Predicate Information (identified by operation id):
---------------------------------------------------

   1 - filter("ID"<=400 AND "ID">=1)
```

This shows that the Oracle optimizer elected to perform a full table scan with a calculated cost of about 221,000 even though an index is present on the ID column and the query will select approximately 2.5 percent of the rows in the table (the index was likely not selected because of its clustering factor).

To convince Oracle to use the index by reducing the associated calculated cost, we can set the OPTIMIZER_INDEX_COST_ADJ parameter to 5 at the session level. If system statistics have been collected and the MBRC system statistic value is greater than 8, the optimizer may not switch to an index range scan.

```
SQL> ALTER SESSION SET OPTIMIZER_INDEX_COST_ADJ=5;

SQL> SELECT
  2    ID,
  3    DESCRIPTION
  4  FROM
  5    T1
  6  WHERE
  7    ID BETWEEN 1 AND 400;

Execution Plan
----------------------------------------------------------
Plan hash value: 634656657
```

```
---------------------------------------------------------------------
| Id |Operation                   | Name   | Rows  | Bytes | Cost (%CPU)| Time       |
---------------------------------------------------------------------
|   0|SELECT STATEMENT            |        | 4000K |  202M |  202K  (1)| 00:40:34 |
|   1| TABLE ACCESS BY INDEX ROWID| T1     | 4000K |  202M |  202K  (1)| 00:40:34 |
|*  2|  INDEX RANGE SCAN          | IND_T1 | 4072K |       |   427  (1)| 00:00:06 |
---------------------------------------------------------------------

Predicate Information (identified by operation id):
-------------------------------------------------

   2 - access("ID">=1 AND "ID"<=400)
```

The preceding output shows that the Oracle optimizer selected to perform an index range scan using the index, with a calculated cost of about 202,000, because of the adjusted cost for the index access (at 5 percent of its original calculated cost). This resulted in a lower calculated cost for the plan and thus the selection of the new plan. With the KEEP buffer pool cache size set to 6GB, the database instance automatically restricted the default buffer pool cache (used by the table T1 and its index) to approximately 1.3GB, as indicated by the __DB_CACHE_SIZE parameter's value of 1,375,731,712.

■ **Note** Blindly changing the OPTIMIZER_INDEX_COST_ADJ parameter to force index access paths where the optimizer would otherwise use full table scans is not a recommended performance-tuning approach. The parameter change is global, meaning that the change may improve the performance of some queries while potentially introducing crippling performance problems for other queries.

To test the performance of the two execution plans, we will perform the following operations: the SQL*Plus fetch size is set to 100 rows (to reduce the number of round-trips), the output of the fetched rows to the screen is disabled (to eliminate client-side delays caused by formatting and scrolling the output onscreen), execution timing is enabled, and the buffer cache is flushed twice to force physical reads from disk (to simulate querying an infrequently accessed table). First, we test the execution plan with the full table scan:

```
SQL> SET ARRAYSIZE 100
SQL> SET AUTOTRACE TRACEONLY STATISTICS
SQL> SET TIMING ON
SQL> ALTER SYSTEM FLUSH BUFFER_CACHE;
SQL> ALTER SYSTEM FLUSH BUFFER_CACHE;

SQL> ALTER SESSION SET OPTIMIZER_INDEX_COST_ADJ=100;

SQL> SELECT
  2    ID,
  3    DESCRIPTION
  4  FROM
  5    T1
  6  WHERE
  7    ID BETWEEN 1 AND 400;
```

```
2547158 rows selected.

Elapsed: 00:00:35.38

Statistics
----------------------------------------------------
          0  recursive calls
          0  db block gets
     838497  consistent gets
     813234  physical reads
          0  redo size
  138445496  bytes sent via SQL*Net to client
     280540  bytes received via SQL*Net from client
      25473  SQL*Net roundtrips to/from client
          0  sorts (memory)
          0  sorts (disk)
    2547158  rows processed
```

The plan using the full table scan required 838,497 consistent block gets, with 813,234 out of the 838,497 blocks actually read from disk, and the remaining blocks satisfied by existing blocks already in Oracle's buffer cache. The full table scan allowed Oracle to return 2,547,158 of the 100,000,000 rows (2.55 percent) in 35.38 seconds. Using the formula from the 11g Performance Tuning Guide, the buffer cache hit ratio for this execution plan is about 3.01 percent.

Now, we repeat the test with the OPTIMIZER_INDEX_COST_ADJ parameter set to 5 so that the Oracle optimizer would switch to the index access plan:

```
SQL> ALTER SYSTEM FLUSH BUFFER_CACHE;
SQL> ALTER SYSTEM FLUSH BUFFER_CACHE;
SQL> ALTER SESSION SET OPTIMIZER_INDEX_COST_ADJ=5;

SQL> SELECT
  2    ID,
  3    DESCRIPTION
  4  FROM
  5    T1
  6  WHERE
  7    ID BETWEEN 1 AND 400;

2547158 rows selected.

Elapsed: 01:38:07.11

Statistics
-------------------------------------------------------------
          0  recursive calls
          0  db block gets
    2573650  consistent gets
    2374287  physical reads
          0  redo size
  148633730  bytes sent via SQL*Net to client
```

```
 280540  bytes received via SQL*Net from client
  25473  SQL*Net roundtrips to/from client
      0  sorts (memory)
      0  sorts (disk)
2547158  rows processed
```

The execution plan using the index access required 2,374,287 blocks from disk, with 2,573,650 in-memory consistent gets (which required the 2,374,287 blocks from disk) requiring approximately 1 hour and 38 minutes. Using the formula from the 11g Performance Tuning Guide, the BCHR for this execution plan is about 7.75 percent. With the larger BCHR, the SQL statement required approximately 166 times as long to complete.

Changing the WHERE clause in the original SQL statement to ID BETWEEN 1 AND 10 caused 63,662 rows to be retrieved (0.06 percent of the total rows). The plan using the full table scan with the modified WHERE clause completed in roughly 34.61 seconds (with 813,876 consistent gets and 813,234 physical block reads), while the plan using the index access required 2 minutes and 40.16 seconds (with 64,425 consistent gets and 63,789 physical block reads). This performance result suggests that very small percentages of a table may be obtained more efficiently by a full table scan than by an index range scan when the only available index has a very high clustering factor.

The disk throughput during the full table scan ranged from 200MB to 300MB per second because of the 1MB multiblock read size, while the disk throughput during the index range scan never exceeded 5MB per second because of the exclusive use of single-block reads. The final example, which returned 0.06 percent of the rows in the table, would dramatically negatively impact the overall buffer cache hit ratio because 12.75 times as many blocks were retrieved from disk during the faster full table scan. Without flushing the buffer cache between executions to simulate a rarely accessed table, the execution time for the final test decreases to 34.88 seconds and 0.32 seconds, respectively. The time difference when blocks are cached in Oracle's buffer cache demonstrates one reason why the execution time for the same SQL statement with the same plan may at times execute very slowly, and at other times very quickly. Increasing the default buffer pool size from roughly 1.3GB to roughly 6.6GB and re-executing the original SQL statement decreased the time for the full table scan to 31.68 seconds, and the index range scan decreased to 32 minutes and 40.27 seconds. Competition for space in the buffer cache memory could also explain why some queries execute quickly at times and significantly slower at other times.

While testing Oracle 11.2.0.1 with direct I/O disabled and asynchronous I/O disabled (specified with an unset FILESYSTEMIO_OPTIONS parameter), and using the original buffer cache settings (8000MB SGA_TARGET and 6GB DB_KEEP_CACHE_SIZE) and the original WHERE clause, the execution plan using the full table scan completed in 11.82 seconds (a decrease from 42.45 seconds observed in that Oracle release). The execution plan using the index access path completed in 19.23 seconds (a decrease from 1 hour, 16 minutes, and 46 seconds observed in that Oracle release) because of the effects of file caching at the operating system level.

This change in performance is not necessarily dependent on the Oracle release. Oracle 11.1.0.6 on the same server returned the result using the full table scan access path in 13.43 seconds, and the query result using the index access path in 22.59 seconds with an unset FILESYSTEMIO_OPTIONS parameter. The potential performance side effects from relying on the availability of extra memory for operating system file caching may not be obvious until the solution is put into production, when the systemwide memory utilization may increase sufficiently so that little extra memory is available for the operating system file cache. Additional competition for server CPU time is a second potential side effect. Relying on I/O buffered by the operating system may explain why, in some cases, a solution executes quickly in a test environment but slowly in production.

What conclusions may be drawn from the preceding information? Even when retrieving 0.06 percent (or some other small number) of the rows in a table, a full table scan may complete faster than an index range scan when a large number of blocks need to be read from disk for both access paths. The OPTIMIZER_INDEX_COST_ADJ parameter indicates the percentage of the index access cost to retain, and it is not a magic parameter that may be adjusted without considering potential problems. A higher buffer cache hit ratio does not necessarily indicate better performance—it may actually be a sign of less-efficient plans. Finally, the first two performance-monitoring and optimization methods do not appear to be terribly reliable, or at the least do not offer repeatable improvements.

Monitoring Delta Values of System/Session Stats

Several views in an Oracle database show statistics at the systemwide level and the session level. These views typically show the accumulated values since the database was last brought online. For the statistics to add value for analysis, there must be two samplings of the statistics with a known duration of time between the samplings. The difference between the ending values and the starting values is commonly known as the *delta values*.

Likely the most commonly accessed systemwide views showing statistics are the V$SYSSTAT view and its related session-level view V$SESSTAT. Views such as V$SESS_IO show a subset of the statistics found in V$SESSTAT, primarily including logical and physical block reads and block changes. Statistics in the V$SYSSTAT view typically fall into one or two categories, or classes, of statistics from the following list (the number appearing in parentheses is the numeric representation of the class): user (1), redo (2), enqueue (4), cache (8), OS (16), RAC (32), SQL (64), and debug (128). If a statistic falls into multiple classes, the value assigned to the CLASS column is the sum of the values associated with each class type (BITAND(CLASS,1)>0 locates all of those statistics belonging to the user class as well as those that belong to both the user class and the RAC class). The statistics indicating elapsed time (DB time, parse time cpu, parse time elapsed, redo synch time, redo write time, and so forth) are indicated in centiseconds, meaning that the indicated times need to be divided by 100 to obtain the elapsed seconds.

V$SYS_TIME_MODEL, introduced in Oracle 10.1, and its associated session-level view V$SESS_TIME_MODEL show the amount of time and CPU usage at the system level and session level, respectively, that were utilized for tasks such as hard parsing, sequence maintenance, PL/SQL execution, and so forth. The time indicated must be divided by 1,000,000 to obtain the elapsed seconds. To be properly understood, the statistics in these views should be manually rearranged in a tree structure similar to the following:

```
SQL> SELECT
  2    VALUE,
  3    STAT_NAME
  4  FROM
  5    V$SYS_TIME_MODEL;

          VALUE  STAT_NAME
--------------  --------------------------------------------------
   284,815,279  background elapsed time
    34,678,994    background cpu time
12,702,393,076  DB time
 7,800,938,927    DB CPU
       674,299    connection management call elapsed time
        97,139    sequence load elapsed time
12,757,866,016    sql execute elapsed time
   595,228,023    parse time elapsed
   582,948,813      hard parse elapsed time
```

```
      1,248,232         hard parse (sharing criteria) elapsed time
         45,602          hard parse (bind mismatch) elapsed time
    521,883,138       failed parse elapsed time
              0          failed parse (out of shared memory) elapsed time
 11,037,668,116     PL/SQL execution elapsed time
              0       inbound PL/SQL rpc elapsed time
      5,633,722       PL/SQL compilation elapsed time
              0       Java execution elapsed time
```

From the preceding, it is apparent that 522 of the 595 seconds spent parsing SQL statements resulted in a parse error, which is roughly 4 percent of the elapsed time spent executing SQL statements.

V$OSSTAT shows, from the operating system's perspective, the activity of the server's CPUs since the server was last booted. The statistics prefixed with AVG_ show the statistics totals divided by the number of CPUs in the server. Some statistics, such as LOAD, OS_CPU_WAIT_TIME, NICE_TIME, and IOWAIT_TIME may not display on all platforms. The statistics in Oracle 10.1 actually have a _TICKS suffix rather than a _TIME suffix. Note that the following statistics were not properly constrained to the time period containing the 1 hour of intense activity. On average, the server appears to be mostly idle, with only the RSRC_MGR_CPU_WAIT_TIME statistic suggesting that there was a period of significant competition for CPU time:

```
SQL> SELECT
  2    VALUE,
  3    STAT_NAME
  4  FROM
  5    V$OSSTAT;

        VALUE STAT_NAME
------------- ----------------------
            8 NUM_CPUS
   74,407,427 IDLE_TIME
    2,245,241 BUSY_TIME
    1,908,037 USER_TIME
      339,400 SYS_TIME
    9,298,148 AVG_IDLE_TIME
      277,841 AVG_BUSY_TIME
      235,767 AVG_USER_TIME
       39,641 AVG_SYS_TIME
       14,087 RSRC_MGR_CPU_WAIT_TIME
12,874,489,856 PHYSICAL_MEMORY_BYTES
```

Various views are present in the database that may not be queried without an Enterprise Edition license and a license for the Diagnostics Pack, with usage statistics for those features, as well as no-cost features, identified in the view DBA_FEATURE_USAGE_STATISTICS. Most of the views requiring the additional-cost license are prefixed with either DBA_HIST_ or DBA_ADVISOR_, including DBA_HIST_ACTIVE_SESS_HISTORY, DBA_HIST_SYSSTAT, DBA_HIST_SYSTEM_EVENT, DBA_HIST_SYS_TIME_MODEL, DBA_ADVISOR_FINDINGS, DBA_ADVISOR_RATIONALE, and DBA_ADVISOR_RECOMMENDATIONS.

Statistics alone likely do not provide enough detail for a root cause analysis to determine why session activity is slower than expected when there is an abundance of available CPU time, but the statistics are one component of a useful performance-monitoring method. The Time Model statistics provide a good indication of where time was spent. The time-based statistics suggest similar information, while the non-time-based statistics provide a context for those statistics. The delta values of system statistics are helpful, but additional information is usually required for a root cause analysis.

Monitoring File Activity

File access activity is exposed through a number of system views, including V$SYSSTAT/V$SESSTAT, V$FILESTAT, V$TEMPSTAT, V$SESSMETRIC, V$SEGSTAT, and V$IOSTAT_FUNCTION. V$SYSSTAT and V$SESSTAT provide statistics that help determine file activity, including physical reads, physical writes, physical read bytes, physical write bytes, redo size, redo write time, consistent changes, user I/O wait time, user commits, and user rollbacks. Although V$SYSSTAT and V$SESSTAT provide helpful information at the systemwide and individual session level, those views do not address the question of which mount point/drive or file is experiencing slow performance. The following example shows the majority of the systemwide statistics from the V$SYSSTAT view that are helpful for monitoring file-related activity:

```
SQL> SELECT
  2     NAME,VALUE
  3  FROM
  4     V$SYSSTAT
  5  WHERE
  6     NAME IN ('physical reads', 'physical writes', 'physical read bytes',
  7              'physical write bytes', 'redo size', 'redo write time',
  8              'consistent changes', 'user I/O wait time', 'user commits',
  9              'user rollbacks', 'sorts (memory)', 'sorts (disk)',
 10              'workarea executions - optimal', 'workarea executions - onepass',
 11              'workarea executions - multipass');
```

NAME	VALUE
user commits	10,485
user rollbacks	588
user I/O wait time	744,647
physical reads	12,559,322
physical read bytes	102,885,965,824
consistent changes	13,133
physical writes	2,202,309
physical write bytes	18,041,315,328
redo size	8,697,933,420
redo write time	20,041
workarea executions - optimal	5,096
workarea executions - onepass	2
workarea executions - multipass	0
sorts (memory)	136,714
sorts (disk)	1

Using the preceding statistics, it is possible to determine that a total of 12,559,322 blocks were read from disk for a total of 95.8GB, but it is unclear whether these blocks were read one block at a time with 12.5 million read requests, or all were read using 1MB multiblock reads. 8.1GB of redo was written to disk in 200.41 seconds, indicating that the redo was written at an average write speed of 41.4MB per second, and most of that redo writing was likely the result of the 10,485 commits and 588 rollbacks (there are, of course, a couple of other sources of redo generation). The consistent changes statistic indicates the number of times undo/rollback entries were applied to database blocks in order to obtain a consistent read of blocks. There was only a single sort to disk, and most of the work area executions were completed in memory.

V$FILESTAT and V$TEMPSTAT provide access to the statistics needed to monitor file activity for an individual file. For instance, the following SQL statement retrieves the access characteristics of data files 6 and 7 since the last opening of the database:

```
SQL> SELECT
  2    FILE#, PHYRDS, PHYWRTS, PHYBLKRD, PHYBLKWRT, SINGLEBLKRDS,
  3    READTIM, WRITETIM, SINGLEBLKRDTIM, AVGIOTIM, LSTIOTIM,
  4    MINIOTIM, MAXIORTM,  MAXIOWTM
  5  FROM
  6    V$FILESTAT
  7  WHERE
  8    FILE# IN (6,7);
```

FILE#	PHYRDS	PHYWRTS	PHYBLKRD	PHYBLKWRT	SINGLEBLKRDS	READTIM
6	111	91	111	91	18	422

WRITETIM	SINGLEBLKRDTIM	AVGIOTIM	LSTIOTIM	MINIOTIM	MAXIORTM	MAXIOWTM
2	34	0	1	0	12	2

FILE#	PHYRDS	PHYWRTS	PHYBLKRD	PHYBLKWRT	SINGLEBLKRDS	READTIM
7	2650662	966000	12335315	1831293	79154	8553311

WRITETIM	SINGLEBLKRDTIM	AVGIOTIM	LSTIOTIM	MINIOTIM	MAXIORTM	MAXIOWTM
6493094	48587	0	1	0	69	145

The scale of the time intervals (columns with names containing TIM or TM) is centiseconds, while the scale of the columns containing BLK is blocks. V$TEMPSTAT provides similar access statistics for the temp tablespaces. Using the preceding statistics, it is clear that absolute file 7 experienced much more activity than file 6. For file 6, all of the reads and writes were performed one block at a time (PHYBLKRD / PHYRDS), even though the SINGLEBLKRDS statistic showed that there were only 18 single-block reads. (Single-block reads performed by direct path are not included in the SINGLEBLKRDS statistic but are included in the PHYBLKRD statistic. Such direct-path single-block reads might occur during database opening when the DBWR process, the LGWR process, and the session executing the ALTER DATABASE OPEN command read the data file header block, and when the CKPT process performs a checkpoint.) The total read time for the file was 4.22 seconds, with an average read time of 38ms, and the longest read time of 120ms. In contrast, file 7 has had some multiblock reads with an average of 4.8 blocks per read ((12335315-79154)/(2650662-79154)) and an average read time of 32ms. The average read times for these files are longer than what should be expected, and may indicate a problem of disk contention caused by processing within multiple sessions.

File 7 may be one of several data files used by a tablespace (to determine the data files used by a tablespace, query V$DATAFILE), and objects within a single tablespace may have extents located in one or more of the data files. File-level statistics need to be interpreted in the context of the segment-level statistics, because the extents might span several data files of a tablespace. Nevertheless, the statistics provide an indication of whether a particular set of files were involved in the majority of I/O. With the assumption that the tablespace that uses absolute file 7 has only a single data file (or the extents are evenly scattered among the data files), a query such as the following might locate those objects with a large percentage of the physical block reads in file 7 (more than a million physical block reads—which was the first of several numbers tested):

```
SQL> SELECT /*+ ORDERED */
  2     DO.OWNER,
  3     DO.OBJECT_NAME,
  4     DO.OBJECT_TYPE,
  5     SS.VALUE
  6  FROM
  7     V$DATAFILE D,
  8     V$SEGMENT_STATISTICS SS,
  9     DBA_OBJECTS DO
 10  WHERE
 11     D.FILE#=7
 12     AND D.TS#=SS.TS#
 13     AND SS.STATISTIC_NAME='physical reads'
 14     AND SS.VALUE>1000000
 15     AND SS.OBJ#=DO.DATA_OBJECT_ID
 16     AND SS.DATAOBJ#=DO.DATA_OBJECT_ID;

OWNER       OBJECT OBJECT_TYPE        VALUE
---------- ------ ----------- --------------
TESTUSER    T1     TABLE         11,166,201
```

V$SEGSTAT provides access to the logical and physical activity of a segment (table, index, partition, and so forth) and the number of buffer busy waits much like V$SEGMENT_STATISTICS, but accesses to the V$SEGSTAT view are less resource intensive. To retrieve the remaining statistics for the table T1, you can query V$SEGSTAT:

```
SQL> SELECT
  2     DO.OBJECT_NAME,
  3     SS.STATISTIC_NAME,
  4     SS.VALUE
  5  FROM
  6     DBA_OBJECTS DO,
  7     V$SEGSTAT SS
  8  WHERE
  9     DO.OWNER='TESTUSER'
 10     AND DO.OBJECT_NAME='T1'
 11     AND DO.OBJECT_ID=SS.OBJ#
 12     AND DO.DATA_OBJECT_ID=SS.DATAOBJ#
 13  ORDER BY
 14     DO.OBJECT_NAME,
 15     SS.STATISTIC_NAME;

OBJECT STATISTIC_NAME                           VALUE
------ -------------------------------- ----------------
T1     ITL waits                                     0
T1     buffer busy waits                             0
T1     db block changes                      5,205,072
```

T1	gc buffer busy	0
T1	gc cr blocks received	0
T1	gc current blocks received	0
T1	logical reads	18,642,240
T1	physical reads	11,166,201
T1	physical reads direct	0
T1	physical writes	1,620,384
T1	physical writes direct	0
T1	row lock waits	0
T1	segment scans	13
T1	space allocated	6,698,303,488
T1	space used	5,860,972,542

If the tablespace uses a single data file, by comparing the output of the preceding SQL statement that accessed V$SEGSTAT with the output of the preceding query that accessed V$FILESTAT, access to the table T1 is responsible for approximately 90.5 percent of the physical block reads and 88.5 percent of the physical block writes in the tablespace.

An additional step in the investigation may involve the examination of the blocks from data file 7 remaining in the buffer cache for the table T1. The view V$BH provides details about the specific blocks located in the buffer cache and the status of those blocks. The STATUS column indicates one of seven modes (free—not currently in use, xcur—exclusive mode, scur—shared current mode, cr—consistent read mode, read—in the process of being read from disk, mrec—in media recovery mode, and irec—in instance recovery mode). The DIRTY column indicates whether the block had been modified since being read from disk, for each data block in the buffer cache. Although only one current mode version of a block may exist in the buffer cache, multiple consistent read versions of an individual block may exist. X$BH, which is accessible only to the SYS user (unless a view is built that references X$BH), is one of the base tables of V$BH, and provides a TCH column for each block in the buffer cache that indicates the number of times a specific version of a block was accessed from the buffer cache. The following query indicates the number of blocks in the buffer cache (per data file and status) that belong to table T1:

```
SQL> SELECT
  2    DO.OBJECT_NAME, BH.FILE#, BH.STATUS, COUNT(*) BLOCKS
  3  FROM
  4    DBA_OBJECTS DO, V$BH BH
  5  WHERE
  6    DO.DATA_OBJECT_ID = BH.OBJD
  7    AND DO.OWNER='TESTUSER'
  8    AND DO.OBJECT_NAME IN ('T1')
  9  GROUP BY
 10    DO.OBJECT_NAME, BH.FILE#, BH.STATUS
 11  ORDER BY
 12    COUNT(*) DESC;

OBJECT  FILE# STATUS      BLOCKS
------  ----- ----------  --------
T1          7 read            23
T1          7 cr            4112
T1          7 free         38895
T1          7 xcur         80968
```

The preceding output indicates that 23 blocks for the table T1 were in the process of being read into the buffer cache, 4,112 consistent read copies of various blocks for the table were in the buffer cache, 38,895 blocks that had been used for buffering blocks for the table T1 were at the time of the capture available for reuse by other objects' blocks, and 80,968 blocks were in exclusive mode (the current mode version of the data blocks). Grouping on FILE# and BLOCK# may also prove to be helpful when examining a range of blocks belonging to the object—in this case, the first couple of blocks including the segment header block. For example:

FILE#	BLOCK#	STATUS	CNT
7	1289609	xcur	1
7	1289610	cr	1
7	1289610	xcur	1
7	1289611	cr	207
7	1289611	xcur	1
7	1289612	cr	4
7	1289612	xcur	1
7	1289613	cr	4
7	1289613	xcur	1
7	1289614	cr	4
7	1289614	xcur	1

The preceding output shows that most of the blocks in the selected block range had a single xcur version and four consistent read copies, except for block 1289611 (the segment header block), which at the time had 207 consistent read copies in the buffer cache. The _DB_BLOCK_MAX_CR_DBA hidden parameter defaults to a value of 6 in recent releases, and should have limited the number of consistent read copies to no more than six per block. Thus Oracle may have encountered a special condition, such as many sessions attempting to simultaneously insert into the table, causing the table to rapidly increase in size. In this case, many sessions may have needed to apply undo to block 1289611 to produce a version of the block that showed only committed changes in the block as of a specific system change number (SCN) required by the session.

With the preceding information, a possible investigation should follow to determine whether the relatively high activity for the table T1 is expected. If it is not expected, the execution plans that reference this table should be examined.

If the query of V$SYSSTAT showed that there were a greater number of sorts to disk, and that the number continued to steadily increase, it would be beneficial to check V$SESSTAT to determine the sessions responsible for the increasing number of sorts to disk. Also helpful is a check of the V$TEMPSEG_USAGE view, which provides details related to in-process temp tablespace usage. Here's an example of a query to check that view:

```
SQL> SELECT /*+ ORDERED */
  2    TU.USERNAME, S.SID, S.SERIAL#, S.SQL_ID, S.SQL_ADDRESS, TU.SEGTYPE,
  3    TU.EXTENTS, TU.BLOCKS, SQL.SQL_TEXT
  4  FROM
  5    V$TEMPSEG_USAGE TU, V$SESSION S, V$SQL SQL
  6  WHERE
  7    TU.SESSION_ADDR=S.SADDR
  8    AND TU.SESSION_NUM=S.SERIAL#
  9    AND S.SQL_ID=SQL.SQL_ID
 10    AND S.SQL_ADDRESS=SQL.ADDRESS;
```

```
USERNAME   SID  SERIAL# SQL_ID        SQL_ADDRESS       SEGTYPE EXTENTS   BLOCKS
--------   ----- -------- ------------- ----------------- ------- ------- ----------
TESTUSER   165   2171 7pqxpw71fkjvj 000000027DB50320 SORT       370    47360

SQL_TEXT
--------------- -------------------------------------------------------
SELECT * FROM T1,T2 WHERE T1.ID<=100 AND T2.ID<=1000 ORDER BY T1.ID
```

The preceding query is using roughly 370MB of temp space based on the default 1MB extent size specified for the temp tablespace. Considering that a predicate is probably missing from the WHERE clause, seeing a DBMS_XPLAN for the query might be helpful. For example:

```
-----------------------------------------------------------------------------------
| Id |Operation                    | Name   | Rows  | Bytes | Cost (%CPU)| Time     |
-----------------------------------------------------------------------------------
|  0|SELECT STATEMENT              |        |       |       | 119G(100)|          |
|  1| MERGE JOIN CARTESIAN         |        | 6552G | 643T|  119G  (3)|999:59:59 |
|  2|  TABLE ACCESS BY INDEX ROWID| T1     | 1005K|  50M| 1006K  (1)| 00:07:10 |
|* 3|   INDEX RANGE SCAN           | IND_T1 | 1005K|      |  2293  (9)| 00:00:01 |
|  4|  BUFFER SORT                 |        | 6516K| 341M|  119G  (3)|999:59:59 |
|* 5|   TABLE ACCESS FULL          | T2     | 6516K| 341M|  118K  (3)| 00:00:51 |
-----------------------------------------------------------------------------------

Predicate Information (identified by operation id):
---------------------------------------------------
   3 - access("T1"."ID"<=100)
   5 - filter("T2"."ID"<=1000)

Note
-----
   - dynamic sampling used for this statement
```

Notice the MERGE JOIN CARTESIAN on line 1 in the preceding plan with the extremely large number of rows expected to be generated by that operation.

Returning again to the characteristics of physical data file access performance. To be useful, the delta values of the statistics need to be considered, rather than the accumulated values since the database was last opened. SYS.DBMS_SYSTEM.KCFRMS is an undocumented procedure that resets the max and min wait time columns in V$FILESTAT, but the procedure may execute slowly when many sessions are connected to the database instance. Monitoring file access offers significant drill-down capability, but a lot of the critical information (the why and how much) needed to correct specific performance problems directly affecting end users is simply not visible.

Oracle 10.1 introduced the V$FILE_HISTOGRAM view, which indicates the number of physical block reads (single-block reads, which are captured in the db file sequential read wait event) that completed within several time ranges. Unlike the other views, which indicate the total and/or average wait times, the V$FILE_HISTOGRAM view permits examining whether many quickly completed file accesses have offset several extremely long duration file accesses. This might result in an acceptable average performance for the period (displayed in V$SYSTEM_EVENT, for instance), while the actual performance experienced by end users was unacceptable because of the several extremely long waits for block reads. A long sequence of very slow I/O requests might be an indication of an I/O subsystem that is near its I/O capacity limit, suggesting that pushing the I/O subsystem further with an increased load could result in much more significant performance issues. The V$FILE_HISTOGRAM view also provides evidence of the number of single-block read requests that were satisfied by the memory buffer in the SAN or by the operating system's file cache; block reads that completed in less than 4ms are typically an indication of a read from some form of cache memory. Statistics are collected in this view when the STATISTICS_LEVEL is set to either TYPICAL or ALL. The TIMED_STATISTICS parameter defaults to TRUE when the STATISTICS_LEVEL parameter is set to either TYPICAL or ALL. The TIMED_STATISTICS parameter must be set to TRUE for most performance-monitoring activities.

A SQL statement to retrieve the number of physical single-block reads that completed in each time range follows, with partial query output limited because of space constraints. Ideally, the output of the entire SQL statement should be executed and examined:

```
SQL> SELECT
  2      FILE# FI,
  3      MAX(DECODE(SINGLEBLKRDTIM_MILLI,1,SINGLEBLKRDS,0)) MILLI1,
  4      MAX(DECODE(SINGLEBLKRDTIM_MILLI,2,SINGLEBLKRDS,0)) MILLI2,
  5      MAX(DECODE(SINGLEBLKRDTIM_MILLI,4,SINGLEBLKRDS,0)) MILLI4,
  6      MAX(DECODE(SINGLEBLKRDTIM_MILLI,8,SINGLEBLKRDS,0)) MILLI8,
  7      MAX(DECODE(SINGLEBLKRDTIM_MILLI,16,SINGLEBLKRDS,0)) MILLI16,
  8      MAX(DECODE(SINGLEBLKRDTIM_MILLI,32,SINGLEBLKRDS,0)) MILLI32,
  9      MAX(DECODE(SINGLEBLKRDTIM_MILLI,64,SINGLEBLKRDS,0)) MILLI64,
 10      MAX(DECODE(SINGLEBLKRDTIM_MILLI,128,SINGLEBLKRDS,0)) MILLI128,
 11      MAX(DECODE(SINGLEBLKRDTIM_MILLI,256,SINGLEBLKRDS,0)) MILLI256,
 12      MAX(DECODE(SINGLEBLKRDTIM_MILLI,512,SINGLEBLKRDS,0)) MILLI512,
 13      MAX(DECODE(SINGLEBLKRDTIM_MILLI,1024,SINGLEBLKRDS,0)) MILLI1024,
 14      MAX(DECODE(SINGLEBLKRDTIM_MILLI,2048,SINGLEBLKRDS,0)) MILLI2048
 15  FROM
 16      V$FILE_HISTOGRAM
 17  GROUP BY
 18      FILE#
 19  ORDER BY
 20      FILE#;
```

FI	MILLI1	MILLI2	MILLI4	MILLI8	MILLI16	MILLI32	MILLI64	MILLI128	MILLI256
1	9,191	93	382	1,154	1,461	1,200	353	28	1
2	156	9	17	51	60	42	12	0	0
3	5,408	76	176	445	556	650	286	47	9
4	10,699	1	12	7	8	4	0	0	0
5	0	0	0	0	0	4	0	0	0
6	0	0	0	4	0	0	0	0	0
7	135,330	1,139	1,739	2,497	1,668	1,794	930	130	3
8	0	0	0	1	3	1	0	0	0
9	0	0	0	0	3	1	0	0	0

Monitoring the Delta Values of System/Session Waits

When a session is not actively executing code on the server's CPUs (including processing SQL statements, waiting for memory accesses to complete, parsing SQL statements, and spinning while attempting to acquire latches), the session accumulates time in one of several wait events. (The session may motivate kernel mode CPU usage, such as when the operating system waits for a disk I/O request to complete, while the session accumulates wait time in a wait event.) The number of named wait events has gradually increased since the days of Oracle 7, when there were just over 100 wait events—to 887 in Oracle 10.2.0.4, 995 in Oracle 11.1.0.7, and 1,118 in 11.2.0.1.

The wait events starting with the 10.1 release are logically grouped into several wait classes that include Administrative, Application, Commit, Concurrency, Configuration, Idle, Network, Other, System I/O, and User I/O. When examining systemwide wait events, the majority of the waits in the Idle wait class may be ignored, although waits in that wait class are sometimes extremely important when examining session-level activity (answering the question of how much of the elapsed time is not caused by the database instance waiting on the availability of resources, which include concurrency waiting for a lock, concurrency/contention waiting for a latch, completion of disk I/O requests, and server CPU time). The wait events visible in most of the views indicate the accumulated total since the database was opened, or accumulated at the session level since the session connected. For this reason, it is necessary to capture the starting values at a specific time, wait for a while, collect the ending values of the wait events, and then subtract the first statistic values from the second.

V$SYSTEM_EVENT is a view that provides systemwide wait events since the last opening of the database. Consider the following SQL statement accessing data from multiple queries of V$SYSTEM_EVENT (stored in the table DATALOG.SYSTEM_EVENT), captured by using a slightly more advanced technique than that shown in the upcoming "Sampling Performance with Low Overhead" section. (See the script MonitoringWaitsExtColl.sql for a simplified version of the data capture to a temp table.) The following SQL statement shows the delta values of wait events between 2 p.m. and 2:04 p.m. The AVERAGE column is calculated for just the delta time period.

```
SQL> SELECT
  2    SE2.EVENT,
  3    SE2.TOTAL_WAITS-SE1.TOTAL_WAITS WAITS,
  4    SE2.TOTAL_TIMEOUTS-SE1.TOTAL_TIMEOUTS TIME_OUTS,
  5    (SE2.TIME_WAITED-SE1.TIME_WAITED)/100 SECONDS,
  6    ROUND((SE2.TIME_WAITED-SE1.TIME_WAITED)
  7      /(SE2.TOTAL_WAITS-SE1.TOTAL_WAITS)/100,6) AVERAGE
  8  FROM
  9    DATALOG.SYSTEM_EVENT SE1,
 10    DATALOG.SYSTEM_EVENT SE2
 11  WHERE
 12    SE1.CHECK_DATE=TO_DATE('08/03/2009 14:00','MM/DD/YYYY HH24:MI')
 13    AND SE2.CHECK_DATE=TO_DATE('08/03/2009 14:04','MM/DD/YYYY HH24:MI')
 14    AND SUBSTR(SE1.EVENT,1,5) NOT IN ('DIAG ','jobq ','rdbms','Space',
                                        'SQL*N','Strea')
 15    AND SE1.EVENT NOT LIKE 'wait for unread%'
 16    AND SE1.EVENT NOT LIKE '%timer'
 17    AND SE2.EVENT=SE1.EVENT
 18    AND (SE2.TIME_WAITED-SE1.TIME_WAITED)>0
 19  ORDER BY
 20    (SE2.TIME_WAITED-SE1.TIME_WAITED) DESC;
```

EVENT	WAITS	TIME_OUTS	SECONDS	AVERAGE
enq: TX - row lock contention	13	11	36.71	2.823846
db file parallel write	1,459	0	3.07	0.002104
log file parallel write	342	0	2.04	0.005965
control file sequential read	1,390	0	0.27	0.000194
control file parallel write	92	0	0.11	0.001196

```
log file sync                     60          0      0.10  0.001667
db file sequential read            7          0      0.07  0.010000
os thread startup                  2          0      0.02  0.010000
buffer busy waits                265          0      0.01  0.000038
```

From the preceding, it appears that there were 13 individual waits (TOTAL_WAITS column in V$SYSTEM_EVENT) due to an enqueue, specifically a TX - row lock contention issue. The delta value for the TIME_OUTS column (TOTAL_TIMEOUTS column in V$SYSTEM_EVENT) is 11, nearly the same as the number of waits on this event for the time period. In this case, the value for the TIME_OUTS column is important—the time-out for this wait event is 3 seconds. This implies that a single session might have accounted for 12 of the waits (plus the 11 time_outs), which would suggest that the session could have waited a continuous 36 seconds, with a second session starting to wait on the same wait event. A lot may happen in 4 minutes, and it could be that thousands of sessions were connected to the instance, and one session briefly attempted to modify a row that was already modified but not committed by another session. The log file sync wait event indicates that 60 commits or rollbacks occurred in this time interval. The other wait events are very short in duration, so there probably is little need to investigate this time period. The delta values for the systemwide wait events between 2:04 p.m. and 2:05 p.m. are listed here:

```
EVENT                          WAITS  TIME_OUTS  SECONDS  AVERAGE
------------------------------ -----  ---------  -------  --------
enq: TX - row lock contention     55         46   150.53  2.736909
db file parallel write           565          0     1.52  0.002690
log file parallel write           84          0     0.36  0.004286
control file parallel write       27          0     0.32  0.011852
log file sync                     47          0     0.30  0.006383
control file sequential read   1,318          0     0.20  0.000152
db file sequential read           12          0     0.05  0.004167
buffer busy waits                 59          0     0.01  0.000169
os thread startup                  1          0     0.01  0.010000
```

For a time period one-quarter as long as the previous period, there are 4.23 times as many waits on the enq: TX - row lock contention wait event, 4.18 times as many time-outs, and the total duration of the wait event is 4.1 times as long. The average wait time and number of waits for the other events are not too significant, although the log file sync wait shows 47 commits or rollbacks in the 1-minute time period. (This might not be important, but it might suggest that either there was not a lot of activity in the system, or very long pauses appeared between commits.) Combining the calculated delta values from V$SESSION_EVENT and joining with V$SESSION, the sessions contributing to the systemwide wait events previously listed may be determined. You can generate a result such as the following list. (Note that creating this output will require a logging table similar to that found in the script MonitoringWaitsExtColl.sql.)

```
SID USER   PROGRAM       EVENT                          WAITS  SECONDS  AVERAGE
--- -----  ------------  ------------------------------ -----  -------  --------
285 user1  receiveqs.exe enq: TX - row lock contention     24    68.09  2.837083
323 user2  bclabr.exe    enq: TX - row lock contention     12    32.66  2.721667
222 user2  bclabr.exe    enq: TX - row lock contention      8    23.99  2.998750
164 user3  rcvent.exe    enq: TX - row lock contention      8    19.77  2.471250
260 user2  bclabr.exe    enq: TX - row lock contention      3     6.02  2.006667
187 user2  bclabr.exe    log file sync                      7     0.17  0.024286
184 user1  hyperextend.exe control file sequential read 1,210     0.13  0.000107
298 dbsnmp emagent.exe   control file sequential read      85     0.06  0.000706
299 dbsnmp emagent.exe   log file sync                      3     0.05  0.016667
```

```
298 dbsnmp   emagent.exe      db file sequential read      28   0.03  0.001071
164 user3    rcvent.exe       db file sequential read       3   0.02  0.006667
195 user4    symbol8146.exe   log file sync                26   0.02  0.000769
164 user3    rcvent.exe       log file sync                15   0.01  0.000667
222 user2    bclabr.exe       db file sequential read       2   0.01  0.005000
222 user2    bclabr.exe       log file sync                13   0.01  0.000769
260 user2    bclabr.exe       db file sequential read       1   0.01  0.010000
260 user2    bclabr.exe       log file sync                 8   0.01  0.001250
265 user5    glbsch.exe       log file sync                 6   0.01  0.001667
285 user1    receiveqs.exe    log file sync                23   0.01  0.000435
294 user1    receiveqs.exe    log file sync                17   0.01  0.000588
310 sysman   oms              log file sync                17   0.01  0.000588
```

From the preceding output, for this 1-minute (actually 69-second) time period, five sessions were contributing to the enq: TX - row lock contention wait event. The first session listed had been waiting in the wait event for almost the full duration of the time period. The second session listed had been waiting in the wait event nearly half of the time, and considering that the average wait time is close to the 3-second time-out for the wait event, had possibly experienced one continuous wait lasting 32.66 seconds. The contributors to the other wait events are also visible from the delta values captured from V$SESSION_EVENT. Considering that sessions were actively waiting on an enqueue wait, checking V$SESSION_WAIT joined to V$SESSION in order to determine the instantaneous waits as of that moment might prove helpful. (Recent releases of Oracle include many of the columns of interest in the V$SESSION view. Note that displaying the SQL_ID column is a better choice than the SQL_HASH_VALUE column with more-recent releases of Oracle.) Note that creating this output will require a logging table similar to that found in the script MonitoringWaitsExtColl.sql. See the upcoming section "Investigating Enqueue Waits" for the SQL statement used to generate the data for the following output.

```
Time      SID STATE    S.W  SQL_HASH     OBJ  FILE   BLOCK  ROW
--------  --- -------  ---  ----------   -----  ----  -------  ---
14:04:06  285 WAITING    0  424447188   12388     4  1046809   21
14:04:35  285 WAITING   28  424447188   12388     4  1046809   21
14:04:36  285 WAITING    0  424447188   12659     4  1428494    3
14:05:08  285 WAITING   27  424447188   12659     4  1428494    3

14:04:09  323 WAITING    0 3356061964   12388     4  1478818   15
14:04:35  323 WAITING   25 3356061964   12388     4  1478818   15

14:04:16  164 WAITING    0 2276257234   12638     4   178024    0
14:04:35  164 WAITING   19 2276257234   12638     4   178024    0

14:04:42  222 WAITING    0 1428055991      -1     0        0    0
14:05:08  222 WAITING   25 1428055991      -1     0        0    0
```

The preceding output shows the history for four of the five sessions accumulating time in the enq: TX - row lock contention wait event, showing the first time in the time period that the waiting started, and the last time that wait was found for the session. Something apparently happened at 14:04:35 that allowed sessions 285, 323, and 164 to stop waiting on this event. Something again happened around 14:04:36 that caused session 285 to start waiting on a different object, which possibly caused session 222 to start waiting a couple of seconds later. The numbers in the OBJ (ROW_WAIT_OBJ# from V$SESSION), FILE (ROW_WAIT_FILE#), BLOCK (ROW_WAIT_BLOCK#), and ROW (ROW_WAIT_ROW#) columns could be used to determine the exact row in the database that was the point of contention in the object. The ROW column

193

is 0 for session 164, while all of the data is missing for session 222, which probably has significance that will be revealed in a later investigation. The following SQL statement will retrieve the object that first caused session 285 to wait in this time period, followed by a SQL statement using the OWNER and OBJECT_NAME from the first SQL statement to retrieve the exact row that was the point of contention:

```
SQL> SELECT
  2    OWNER, OBJECT_NAME, OBJECT_TYPE
  3  FROM
  4    DBA_OBJECTS
  5  WHERE
  6    OBJECT_ID = 12388;

SQL> SELECT
  2    *
  3  FROM
  4    owner.object_name
  5  WHERE
  6    ROWID = DBMS_ROWID.ROWID_CREATE(1, 12388, 4, 1046809, 21);
```

Exploring the information captured from V$LOCK for the delta period would also prove helpful in this case, in order to not only determine what the sessions were waiting for, but also the source of the wait. The following SQL statement shows currently blocked sessions as well as the blocking sessions:

```
SQL> SELECT
  2    S.SID, S.USERNAME, S.PROGRAM, S.SQL_HASH_VALUE SQL_HASH, L.TYPE, L.LMODE LM,
  3    L.REQUEST RQ, DECODE(L.BLOCK,1,'Blocker','Blocked') BLOCK, L.ID1, L.ID2
  4  FROM
  5    V$LOCK L, V$SESSION S
  6  WHERE
  7    L.SID=S.SID
  8    AND (L.ID1, L.ID2, L.TYPE) IN
  9    (SELECT
 10      ID1, ID2, TYPE
 11    FROM
 12      V$LOCK
 13    WHERE
 14      REQUEST > 0);
```

The following output shows historical information captured by the preceding SQL statement for the time period under investigation:

Time	SID	PROGRAM	SQL_HASH	TYPE	LM	RQ	BLOCK	ID1	ID2
14:04:06	265	GLBSCH.EXE	0	TX	6	0	**Blocker**	327715	1153495
14:04:06	285	RECEIVEQS.EXE	424447188	TX	0	6	Blocked	327715	1153495
...									
14:04:34	265	GLBSCH.EXE	0	TX	6	0	**Blocker**	327715	1153495
14:04:34	285	RECEIVEQS.EXE	424447188	TX	0	6	Blocked	327715	1153495
14:04:34	323	BCLABR.EXE	3356061964	TX	0	6	Blocked	327715	1153495
14:04:34	285	RECEIVEQS.EXE	424447188	TX	6	0	**Blocker**	131077	1266115
14:04:34	164	RCVENT.EXE	2276257234	TX	0	4	Blocked	131077	1266115

```
14:04:35 285 RECEIVEQS.EXE            0 TX    6  0 Blocker 131077 1266115
14:04:35 164 RCVENT.EXE      2276257234 TX    0  4 Blocked 131077 1266115
14:04:36 265 GLBSCH.EXE      1230988610 TX    6  0 Blocker 524321 1149877
14:04:36 285 RECEIVEQS.EXE    424447188 TX    0  6 Blocked 524321 1149877
...
14:04:42 265 GLBSCH.EXE      1230988610 TX    6  0 Blocker 524321 1149877
14:04:42 285 RECEIVEQS.EXE    424447188 TX    0  6 Blocked 524321 1149877
14:04:42 285 RECEIVEQS.EXE    424447188 TX    6  0 Blocker 655392 1148950
14:04:42 222 BCLABR.EXE      1428055991 TX    0  4 Blocked 655392 1148950
```

The preceding output provides insight into what happened in the database instance. Session 265 (GLBSCH.EXE) frequently, but not always, appeared as the blocker (entries with the same ID1 and ID2 values are related Blocker and Blocked entries). At 14:04:34, session 265 (GLBSCH.EXE) held a mode 6 lock on a row (or multiple rows) that prevented session 285 (RECEIVEQS.EXE) from obtaining a mode 6 lock on the row indicated by V$SESSION in the previous output (12388, 4, 1046809, 21), and prevented session 323 from obtaining a mode 6 lock on the row indicated by V$SESSION in the previous output (12388, 4, 1478818, 15). Session 323 was also blocked by session 265. While session 285 was blocked by session 265, it already held a mode 6 lock on a row (or multiple rows), which prevented session 164 from obtaining a mode 4 lock on the row. In this case, session 164 was attempting to insert a row with the same primary-key value as had already been inserted but not committed by session 285. An investigation of the SQL statements executed by the sessions revealed that the contention between session 285 and 164 was due to the ERP system to which the programs belong not using sequences to generate sequential numbers for a primary key, but instead relying on a nearly platform-independent SELECT MAX(TRANSACTION_ID)+1 SQL statement to determine the next sequential number for the primary-key column.

Oracle 10.1 introduced the V$EVENT_HISTOGRAM view, which indicates the number of wait events that completed within several time ranges, increasing in duration by powers of 2 from 2^0 (1ms or less) to at least 2^{22} (4,194,304ms). In contrast to the total and/or average wait times presented in other views, such as V$SYSTEM_EVENT, the V$EVENT_HISTOGRAM view provides a method to quickly determine whether important performance information was lost because of the aggregating or averaging of the wait event elapsed times. The times reported in views such as V$SYSTEM_EVENT may hide the fact that many very short duration wait times (such as disk reads that were satisfied by SAN caches) may offset several very long duration wait times, yielding an otherwise satisfactory average wait time. In such a case, the significance of the several very long duration waits that directly impacted end users may be lost in the averages for the sampling delta time period.

Following is a SQL statement to retrieve information from the view in a collapsed cross-tab format for a wait event starting with db file. The output of the following statement is not from the time period of the preceding performance investigation.

```
SQL> SELECT
  2    EVENT,
  3    MAX(DECODE(WAIT_TIME_MILLI,1,WAIT_COUNT,0)) MILLI1,
  4    MAX(DECODE(WAIT_TIME_MILLI,2,WAIT_COUNT,0)) MILLI2,
  5    MAX(DECODE(WAIT_TIME_MILLI,4,WAIT_COUNT,0)) MILLI4,
  6    MAX(DECODE(WAIT_TIME_MILLI,8,WAIT_COUNT,0)) MILLI8,
  7    MAX(DECODE(WAIT_TIME_MILLI,16,WAIT_COUNT,0)) MILLI16
  8  FROM
  9    V$EVENT_HISTOGRAM
 10  WHERE
 11    EVENT LIKE 'db file%'
 12  GROUP BY
 13    EVENT
 14  ORDER BY
```

```
 15    EVENT;

EVENT                          MILLI1       MILLI2      MILLI4      MILLI8     MILLI16
-------------------------  ----------   ----------  ----------  ----------  ----------
db file parallel read               5            6           5          20          85
db file parallel write         70,453        5,346       3,496       2,892       3,702
db file scattered read         30,361        4,488       4,509       1,748       1,871
db file sequential read     2,930,609        9,906      13,896      20,235      15,285
db file single write               16            0           0           0           0
```

If one of the top wait events for the period had been buffer busy waits (and/or the associated read by other session wait introduced in Oracle 10.1), an investigation of the delta values from the V$WAITSTAT view would reveal the type of blocks involved in the waits for the period. Starting with Oracle 10.1, the P3 parameter of a buffer busy waits wait event in V$SESSION_WAIT (and V$SESSION) indicates the block class (data block, sort block, undo header, and so forth), while on earlier releases the P3 parameter indicates the reason code for the wait. ROW_WAIT_OBJ#, ROW_WAIT_FILE#, and ROW_WAIT_BLOCK# from V$SESSION may be used to locate the specific object and block responsible for the buffer busy waits wait events.

The V$SESSION_WAIT view shows in-process wait events for sessions. The columns in the V$SESSION_WAIT view as well as its equivalent columns in V$SESSION cannot be correctly interpreted without first checking the STATE column. A session is waiting in a wait event only if the STATE column indicates WAITING. When the session is waiting in a wait event, the WAIT_TIME column shows a value of 0, and the SECONDS_IN_WAIT column indicates the number of seconds the session has waited so far. Note that the SECONDS_IN_WAIT column is updated only approximately every 3 seconds. If the STATE column shows Waited Known Time, the WAIT_TIME column indicates the duration in centiseconds of the last wait event (you must divide by 100 to arrive at seconds). The SECONDS_IN_WAIT column indicates the number of seconds since the last wait started in seconds, indicating that the session is currently *not* waiting and has been active on the CPU for SECONDS_IN_WAIT - (WAIT_TIME / 100) seconds. If the STATE column contains Waited Unknown Time or Waited Short Time, the WAIT_TIME column is meaningless. Note that Waited Unknown Time likely indicates that the TIMED_STATISTICS initialization parameter is set to FALSE.

Oracle 11.1 adds the column WAIT_TIME_MICRO, which provides much greater accuracy than the SECONDS_IN_WAIT column, but the column values must be divided by 1,000,000 to scale the column values to seconds. This column indicates the current duration of an in-process wait and the duration of the previous wait when the session is active on the CPU. Also added in 11.1.0.6 is the column TIME_SINCE_LAST_WAIT_MICRO, which indicates the approximate amount of time the session has been active on the CPU since the last wait ended. This column is essentially a greater-precision version of the formula SECONDS_IN_WAIT - (WAIT_TIME / 100), which utilizes two columns that are deprecated as of Oracle 11.1.

Monitoring CPU Utilization

CPU saturation may lead to latch contention, long-duration log file waits (log file sync, log file parallel write), cluster-related waits, increased duration of single-block and multiblock reads, and significant increases in server response time. Server CPU usage may be a result of processing within the Oracle database instance, a result of other non-Oracle database related processes, or a result of operating system activity (typically captured in kernel CPU time).

There are various views within the Oracle database, and various operating system commands that retrieve CPU utilization statistics. Multitasking-capable operating systems automatically share available CPU time among the various processes and process threads running on the server, typically based on a process/thread priority and the willingness of a process to yield CPU time. As the CPU utilization continues to increase above 80 percent, processes needing to run on the CPU increasingly queue while waiting for CPU time. (See the queuing theory analysis in *Forecasting Oracle Performance* by Craig Shallahamer, Apress, 2007.)

Metalink Doc ID 164768.1, "Diagnosing High CPU Utilization," describes various methods to quickly check CPU utilization at the operating system level on Unix/Linux as well as the basics of finding excessive CPU utilization in the database instance. Metalink Doc ID 301137.1 describes a set of logging scripts named *OS Watcher* for the Unix and Linux platforms that logs the output of the ps, top, mpstat, iostat, netstat, traceroute, and vmstat utilities on scheduled time intervals. Metalink Doc ID 433472.1 describes a similar OS Watcher script for the Windows platform that queries the Windows performance data by using the LOGMAN Windows utility. The Oracle OTN website offers the *Oracle Cluster Health Monitor* tool, previously known as the *Instantaneous Problem Detection tool,* or IPD/OS (www.oracle.com/technology/products/database/clustering/ipd_download_homepage.html). This tool captures a variety of information from nodes participating in a Real Application Clusters (RAC) configuration, storing information about network I/O rates, file I/O rates, CPU usage, CPU run queue, and available memory, with information captured as frequently as once a second typically with a 24-hour rolling history.

CPU Load Generators

Before examining CPU utilization, let's look at ways to place a load on your CPU. This section presents some scripts to generate artificial CPU loads for 10-minute intervals. The scripts use a loop that repeatedly adds 0.000001 to a variable. On an eight-CPU server, for instance, it might be necessary to execute one of the scripts eight times simultaneously to fully consume all available CPU capacity.

Following is the Windows version of the CPU load generator. It is written as a Windows Script Host script named CPULoad.vbs:

```
Dim i
Dim STime

STime = Now

Do While DateDiff("n", STime, Now) < 10
  i = i + 0.000001
Loop
```

You can execute the script as follows:

```
start cscript CPULoad.vbs
```

Next is the Unix/Linux CPU load generator, written as a Bash script named CPULoad.sh. The +%s syntax used in the script may not be supported on all platforms.

```
#!/bin/bash
i=0
STime=`date +%s`

while [ `date +%s` -lt $(($STime+$((600)))) ]; do
  i=i+0.000001
done
```

Be sure to first adjust permissions to make the script executable. Then you can execute it as follows:

```
sh CPULoad.sh
```

Finally, we have a database instance CPU load generator that uses an anonymous PL/SQL block that is saved in a file named CPULoad.sql:

```
DECLARE
  i NUMBER := 0;
  STime DATE := SYSDATE;
BEGIN
  WHILE (SYSDATE - STime) < 0.006945 LOOP
    i := i + 0.000001;
  END LOOP;
END;
/
```

Invoke CPULoad.sql as follows:

```
sqlplus MyUser/MyUserPassword@MyDB @CPULoad.sql
```

Determining the CPU Run Queue

The underlying mechanics of the CPU run queue vary by operating system. For example, on Windows a single run queue is shared by all CPUs in the server. This approach tends to spread the existing CPU load evenly across all CPUs as it allows processes and process threads to run on a different CPU during each time slice. However, this approach also means that the cache memory built into CPUs tends to be a bit less useful than it would be if the same processes always executed on the same CPU. Linux kernel versions prior to 2.6 also maintained a single run queue. With the 2.6 Linux kernel, each CPU has a separate run queue. An independent run queue potentially permits a process to continue running on the same CPU, but an unfortunate side effect of this approach may occur when two or more critical background processes (such as LGWR and DBWR) must compete for CPU time on a CPU that is heavily loaded with other process activity. With the 2.6 Linux kernel, the process scheduler potentially rebalances processes set to run on a particular CPU, switching processes to less-utilized CPUs every 200ms, and artificially increases the priority of I/O-intensive processes while artificially decreasing the priority of CPU-intensive processes.

Viewing the run queue on Windows is possible with a simple Windows Script Host script that queries the Win32_PerfRawData_PerfOS_System WMI view, or by viewing the statistic in the Windows Performance Monitor. Viewing the user mode and system (kernel) time per Oracle instance is possible by querying the Win32_Process WMI view. The following WSH script queries both of the WMI views on the local server (or a remote server by specifying a server name rather than a period), retrieving the run queue, and then for each database instance the number of CPU seconds of user mode and system mode time consumed in the time interval. The information is output to the screen, and also to a text file using an ADO stream object.

```
Dim intInstance, intOldCSPerSec, intOldProcesses, intOldThreads
Dim strSQL, strSQL2, strOut, strComputer, sglUMTime(20), sglKMTime(20)
Dim sglWorkingSet(20), sglPageFileUsage(20), sglOUMTime(20), sglOKMTime(20)
Dim sglOldWorkingSet(20), sglOldPageFileUsage(20), objWMIService
Dim colItems, objItem, adsFile
```

```
Set adsFile = CreateObject("ADODB.Stream")
adsFile.Type = 2
adsFile.Charset = "iso-8859-1"
adsFile.Open

strSQL - "SELECT * FROM Win32_PerfRawData_PerfOS_System"
strSQL2 = "SELECT * FROM Win32_Process Where Name like 'Oracle%'"

strComputer = "."   ' the . indicates the local computer
Set objWMIService = GetObject("winmgmts:{impersonationLevel=impersonate}!\\" _
    & strComputer & "\root\CIMV2")

intOldCSPerSec = 0
For intInstance = 1 to 20
    sglOUMTime(intInstance) = 0
    sglOKMTime(intInstance) = 0
    sglOldWorkingSet(intInstance) = 0
    sglOldPageFileUsage(intInstance) = 0
Next

For i = 1 to 20
  Set colItems = objWMIService.ExecQuery(strSQL,"WQL",48)

  For Each objItem in colItems
    strOut = Now() & "  Processes: " & objItem.Processes
    strOut = strOut & "  Threads: " & objItem.Threads
    strOut = strOut & "  C. Switches: " & objItem.ContextSwitchesPersec _
                                        - intOldCSPerSec
    strOut = strOut & "  Q. Length: " & objItem.ProcessorQueueLength

    'Write to screen
    Wscript.Echo strOut

    'Write to log file
    adsFile.WriteText(strOut & vbCrLf)

    intOldCSPerSec = objItem.ContextSwitchesPersec
    intOldProcesses = objItem.Processes
    intOldThreads = objItem.Threads
  Next

  Set colItems = Nothing
  Set colItems = objWMIService.ExecQuery(strSQL2,"WQL",48)

  intInstance = 0
  For Each objItem in colItems
    intInstance = intInstance + 1
    sglUMTime(intInstance) = Round(objItem.UserModeTime/10000000, 2)
    sglKMTime(intInstance) = Round(objItem.KernelModeTime/10000000, 2)
    sglWorkingSet(intInstance) = Round(objItem.WorkingSetSize/1048576, 2)
    sglPageFileUsage(intInstance) = Round(objItem.PageFileUsage/1048576, 2)
```

199

```
        strOut = "Instance: " & objItem.CommandLine & vbCrLf
        strOut = strOut & " User Time: " & Round(sglUMTime(intInstance) _
                                        - sglOUMTime(intInstance),2) & "S"
        strOut = strOut & " Sys  Time: " & Round(sglKMTime(intInstance) _
                                        - sglOKMTime(intInstance),2) & "S"
        strOut = strOut & " Memory: " & sglWorkingSet(intInstance) & "MB"
        strOut = strOut & " Page File: " & sglPageFileUsage(intInstance) & _
                                        "MB" & vbCrLf

        'Write to screen
        Wscript.Echo strOut

        'Write to log file
        adsFile.WriteText(strOut & vbCrLf)

        sglOUMTime(intInstance) = Round(objItem.UserModeTime/10000000, 2)
        sglOKMTime(intInstance) = Round(objItem.KernelModeTime/10000000, 2)
        sglOldWorkingSet(intInstance) = Round(objItem.WorkingSetSize/1048576, 2)
        sglOldPageFileUsage(intInstance) = Round(objItem.PageFileUsage/1048576, 2)
    Next

    'Wait one second before sampling again
    Wscript.Sleep 1 * 1000
Next

adsFile.SaveToFile "C:\CPU Status.txt", 2
adsFile.close
```

Sample output from a server with eight CPUs looks like this:

```
7/18/2009 7:38:31 PM  Processes: 96  Threads: 903  C. Switches: 6075  Q. Length: 14
Instance: c:\oracle\product\10.2.0\db_1\bin\ORACLE.EXE OR10
 User Time: 0.31S Sys  Time: 0.75S  Memory:  760.25MB  Page File: 7.97MB
Instance: c:\oracle\product\11.1.0\db_1\bin\ORACLE.EXE OR11
 User Time: 2.73S Sys  Time: 0S     Memory: 1128.68MB  Page File: 7.98MB

7/18/2009 7:38:33 PM  Processes: 97  Threads: 904  C. Switches: 4335  Q. Length: 16
Instance: c:\oracle\product\10.2.0\db_1\bin\ORACLE.EXE OR10
 User Time: 0.24S Sys  Time: 0.86S  Memory:  760.25MB  Page File: 7.97MB
Instance: c:\oracle\product\11.1.0\db_1\bin\ORACLE.EXE OR11
 User Time: 2.74S Sys  Time: 0S     Memory: 1128.68MB  Page File: 7.98MB

7/18/2009 7:38:34 PM  Processes: 95  Threads: 905  C. Switches: 5815  Q. Length: 17
Instance: c:\oracle\product\10.2.0\db_1\bin\ORACLE.EXE OR10
 User Time: 0.22S Sys  Time: 0.84S  Memory:  760.25MB  Page File: 7.97MB
Instance: c:\oracle\product\11.1.0\db_1\bin\ORACLE.EXE OR11
 User Time: 2.78S Sys  Time: 0S     Memory: 1128.68MB  Page File: 7.98MB
```

The preceding output shows that the run queue length on the server gradually increased to the point where it is just beyond twice the CPU count of the server, which indicates that all CPUs were saturated at the moment the WMI query executed. This CPU saturation will noticeably affect performance, especially in online transaction processing (OLTP) environments, and should be investigated. The instance OR10 is using between three and four times as much system mode time as user mode time, and should be investigated. The combined total user and system time is roughly 3.84 CPU seconds of a possible 8 CPU seconds; this difference should be investigated to determine the other sources of the CPU consumption.

Unix and Linux provide run queue and CPU utilization information with the sar command. With the -q 60 5 parameters, the runq-sz column in the following output indicates the average run queue length every 60 seconds with five sampling iterations:

```
sar -q 60 5

03:58:27 PM   runq-sz  plist-sz  ldavg-1  ldavg-5  ldavg-15
03:59:27 PM        42       332    39.21    20.83      8.81
04:00:27 PM        48       348    47.13    26.40     11.47
04:01:27 PM        57       361    52.45    31.67     14.21
04:02:27 PM        45       416    59.42    37.36     17.25
04:03:27 PM        26       338    57.97    41.22     19.85
Average:           44       359    51.24    31.50     14.32
```

Determining CPU Utilization

The V$SYSSTAT and V$SESSTAT views contain a couple of statistics related to CPU consumption: CPU used by this session (class user), CPU used when call started (class debug), recursive cpu usage (class user), parse time cpu (class SQL), as well as a couple of others added in more-recent releases of Oracle. Table 8-1 shows the CPU utilization and logical reads from V$SESSTAT for a session executing a long-running query that required a hard parse on 11.1.0.7. This table provides an indication of the lack of read consistency offered by the V$SESSTAT view, and the point in query execution at which the various statistics are updated.

Table 8-1. Session-Level Statistics During Query Execution on Oracle 11.1.0.7

Statistic	0	1 min	2 min	5 min	5:35 min
CPU used by this session	0	47	47	47	33,473
CPU used when call started	0	0	0	0	33,473
consistent gets	52	23,336,696	46,998,419	117,494,756	131,022,925
consistent gets - examination	7	6,798,235	13,699,304	34,197,105	38,148,347
consistent gets from cache	52	23,336,702	46,998,483	117,494,762	131,022,925
consistent gets from cache (fastpath)	43	10,920,233	24,918,074	62,698,903	71,067,945

Statistic	0	1 min	2 min	5 min	5:35 min
no work - consistent read gets	37	16,434,001	33,088,076	82,770,661	92,286,554
parse time cpu	0	47	47	47	47
recursive cpu usage	0	47	47	47	47

When a query is executed, the CPU used by this session statistic is updated after parsing completes and only again after the first fetch call completes. The CPU used when call started statistic is not updated until the first fetch completes. The various consistent gets statistics continue to accumulate in near real-time. Because of the lack of read consistency of the V$SESSTAT view, Table 8-1 shows slight inconsistencies between the consistent gets and the consistent gets from cache statistics until the query execution completes. VSYS_TIME_MODEL, VSESS_TIME_MODEL, and V$OSSTAT continue to update CPU statistics in near real-time, as does the view V$SQL for the SQL statement being executed.

Table 8-2 shows statistics from V$OSSTAT and V$SYS_TIME_MODEL during an 8-minute and 35-second time period where the server's eight CPUs were completely saturated with running processes. Without proper time scoping (capturing the starting values in this case), the CPUs appear to be only 65 percent utilized, but by capturing the starting values, it is possible to determine that the IDLE_TIME statistic remained unchanged in the capture period while the BUSY_TIME statistic continued to increase. The database instance accounted for 1,558.17 seconds ((DB CPU + background cpu time) / 1,000,000) of the 4,120 possible CPU seconds in the time interval, indicating that the database instance was competing for CPU time with other processes (other database instances or non-Oracle processes) running on the same server.

Table 8-2. CPU Usage from V$OSSTAT and V$SYS_TIME_MODEL on Oracle 11.1.0.7

Statistic	Start	3:10 min	8:35 min
V$OSSTAT IDLE_TIME	618,910	618,910	618,910
V$OSSTAT BUSY_TIME	736,579	887,228	1,145,735
V$OSSTAT USER_TIME	732,544	883,032	1,128,963
V$OSSTAT SYS_TIME	4,044	4,205	16,781
V$OSSTAT RSRC_MGR_CPU_WAIT_TIME	589	2,934	14,086
V$SYS_TIME_MODEL DB CPU	4,653,899,814	5,231,337,516	6,211,850,598
V$SYS_TIME_MODEL background cpu time	3,666,019	3,806,420	3,884,421

Sampling Performance with Low Overhead

When trying to determine whether, in fact, a performance problem exists within the database instance prior to reports of problems from end users (or other members of the IT staff), it is important to select a method for sampling database performance statistics that is nonintrusive, requires few database server resources, and offers a quick method of determining whether a more thorough analysis might be required. Such sampling methods might involve capturing delta values for wait events (V$SYSTEM_EVENT, V$SESSION_EVENT), capturing delta values for system statistics (V$SYSSTAT, V$SESSTAT), capturing operating system performance statistics by using various resources (V$OSSTAT, sar, vmstat, iostat, netstat, and so forth to determine CPU utilization, CPU run queue length, memory utilization, I/O statistics, network utilization levels, and so forth), capturing deltas that indicate how sessions in the Oracle instance are spending time (V$SYS_TIME_MODEL), or reviewing existing Statspack reports or AWR reports (with an appropriate Enterprise Edition license and Diagnostics Pack license).

Capturing Some Statistics

Capturing delta values for a short duration, and not values since the database was last opened, is a requirement when attempting to understand current problems. To capture this data with a minimal impact on system performance, temporary holding tables must be created or the performance data must be exported to another application, such as Microsoft Excel. (Using global temp tables is efficient, but these types of tables may limit the ability to perform historical analysis.)

Following is a temporary holding tables creation script, with an owner of DATALOG:

```
SQL> CREATE GLOBAL TEMPORARY TABLE
  2    DATALOG.TS_SYSTEM_EVENT ON COMMIT DELETE ROWS AS
  3  SELECT
  4    EVENT,
  5    TOTAL_WAITS,
  6    TOTAL_TIMEOUTS,
  7    TIME_WAITED,
  8    TIME_WAITED_MICRO
  9  FROM
 10    V$SYSTEM_EVENT
 11  WHERE
 12    0=1;

SQL> CREATE GLOBAL TEMPORARY TABLE
  2    DATALOG.TE_SYSTEM_EVENT ON COMMIT DELETE ROWS AS
  3  SELECT
  4    EVENT,
  5    TOTAL_WAITS,
  6    TOTAL_TIMEOUTS,
  7    TIME_WAITED,
  8    TIME_WAITED_MICRO
  9  FROM
 10    V$SYSTEM_EVENT
 11  WHERE
 12    0=1;
```

```
SQL> CREATE GLOBAL TEMPORARY TABLE
  2    DATALOG.TS_OSSTAT ON COMMIT DELETE ROWS AS
  3  SELECT
  4    STAT_NAME,
  5    VALUE
  6  FROM
  7    V$OSSTAT
  8  WHERE
  9    0=1;

SQL> CREATE GLOBAL TEMPORARY TABLE
  2    DATALOG.TE_OSSTAT ON COMMIT DELETE ROWS AS
  3  SELECT
  4    STAT_NAME,
  5    VALUE
  6  FROM
  7    V$OSSTAT
  8  WHERE
  9    0=1;

SQL> CREATE GLOBAL TEMPORARY TABLE
  2    DATALOG.TS_SYS_TIME_MODEL ON COMMIT DELETE ROWS AS
  3  SELECT
  4    STAT_NAME,
  5    VALUE
  6  FROM
  7    V$SYS_TIME_MODEL
  8  WHERE
  9    0=1;

SQL> CREATE GLOBAL TEMPORARY TABLE
  2    DATALOG.TE_SYS_TIME_MODEL ON COMMIT DELETE ROWS AS
  3  SELECT
  4    STAT_NAME,
  5    VALUE
  6  FROM
  7    V$SYS_TIME_MODEL
  8  WHERE
  9    0=1;

SQL> CREATE GLOBAL TEMPORARY TABLE
  2    DATALOG.TS_SYSSTAT ON COMMIT DELETE ROWS AS
  3  SELECT
  4    NAME,
  5    VALUE
  6  FROM
  7    V$SYSSTAT
  8  WHERE
  9    0=1;
```

```
SQL> CREATE GLOBAL TEMPORARY TABLE
  2    DATALOG.TE_SYSSTAT ON COMMIT DELETE ROWS AS
  3  SELECT
  4    NAME,
  5    VALUE
  6  FROM
  7    V$SYSSTAT
  8  WHERE
  9    0=1;
```

When it is time to sample the delta values of the statistics, the following code will be executed, which collects the starting statistics values, waits 10 minutes, collects the ending statistics values, and then outputs the delta values. Note that an outer join is used between the table containing the ending statistics values and the table containing the starting statistics values. This outer join is not needed for some of the queries but is included for the sake of consistency when comparing statistics from the various performance views. A commit is executed at the start of the script to clear previous values from the temporary tables (existing rows are deleted from the global temp tables when commits are executed).

Following is our data-collection script and output script. It allows you to specify capture duration in seconds:

```
SQL> COMMIT;

SQL> DEFINE CAPTURE_SECONDS=600

SQL> INSERT INTO
  2    DATALOG.TS_SYSTEM_EVENT
  3  SELECT
  4    EVENT,
  5    TOTAL_WAITS,
  6    TOTAL_TIMEOUTS,
  7    TIME_WAITED,
  8    TIME_WAITED_MICRO
  9  FROM
 10    V$SYSTEM_EVENT;

SQL> INSERT INTO
  2    DATALOG.TS_OSSTAT
  3  SELECT
  4    STAT_NAME,
  5    VALUE
  6  FROM
  7    V$OSSTAT;

SQL> INSERT INTO
  2    DATALOG.TS_SYS_TIME_MODEL
  3  SELECT
  4    STAT_NAME,
  5    VALUE
  6  FROM
  7    V$SYS_TIME_MODEL;
```

```
SQL> INSERT INTO
  2     DATALOG.TS_SYSSTAT
  3  SELECT
  4     NAME,
  5     VALUE
  6  FROM
  7     V$SYSSTAT;

SQL> EXEC DBMS_LOCK.SLEEP(&&CAPTURE_SECONDS);

SQL> INSERT INTO
  2     DATALOG.TE_SYSTEM_EVENT
  3  SELECT
  4     EVENT,
  5     TOTAL_WAITS,
  6     TOTAL_TIMEOUTS,
  7     TIME_WAITED,
  8     TIME_WAITED_MICRO
  9  FROM
 10     V$SYSTEM_EVENT;

SQL> INSERT INTO
  2     DATALOG.TE_OSSTAT
  3  SELECT
  4     STAT_NAME,
  5     VALUE
  6  FROM
  7     V$OSSTAT;

SQL> INSERT INTO
  2     DATALOG.TE_SYS_TIME_MODEL
  3  SELECT
  4     STAT_NAME,
  5     VALUE
  6  FROM
  7     V$SYS_TIME_MODEL;

SQL> INSERT INTO
  2     DATALOG.TE_SYSSTAT
  3  SELECT
  4     NAME,
  5     VALUE
  6  FROM
  7     V$SYSSTAT;


SQL> SPOOL quickcheck.txt

SQL> SET PAGESIZE 200
SQL> COL WAIT_CLASS FORMAT A15 TRU
SQL> COL DELTA FORMAT 9999999990
SQL> COL DELTA_SEC FORMAT 99999990.00
SQL> COL WAIT_PERCENT FORMAT 990.00
```

```
/* Ranked wait time by wait class, including CPU used - note that the 'CPU used
     by this session' statistic is not posted until in-process queries complete */
SQL> SELECT
  2    WAIT_CLASS,
  3    DELTA,
  4    DELTA_SEC,
  5    ROUND(RATIO_TO_REPORT(DELTA) OVER () * 100,2) WAIT_PERCENT
  6  FROM
  7    (SELECT
  8      EN.WAIT_CLASS,
  9      SUM(TE.TIME_WAITED-NVL(TS.TIME_WAITED,0)) DELTA,
 10      SUM(ROUND((TE.TIME_WAITED-NVL(TS.TIME_WAITED,0))
                     / &&CAPTURE_SECONDS,2)) DELTA_SEC
 11    FROM
 12      DATALOG.TE_SYSTEM_EVENT TE,
 13      DATALOG.TS_SYSTEM_EVENT TS,
 14      V$EVENT_NAME EN
 15    WHERE
 16      TE.EVENT=TS.EVENT(+)
 17      AND TE.TIME_WAITED-NVL(TS.TIME_WAITED,0)>0
 18      AND TE.EVENT=EN.NAME
 19      AND EN.WAIT_CLASS<>'Idle'
 20    GROUP BY
 21      EN.WAIT_CLASS
 22    UNION ALL
 23    SELECT
 24      'CPU' WAIT_CLASS,
 25      ROUND(SUM((TE.VALUE-NVL(TS.VALUE,0))/10000),0) DELTA,
 26      ROUND(SUM((TE.VALUE-NVL(TS.VALUE,0))/10000)
                     / &&CAPTURE_SECONDS,2) DELTA_SEC
 27    FROM
 28      DATALOG.TE_SYS_TIME_MODEL TE,
 29      DATALOG.TS_SYS_TIME_MODEL TS
 30    WHERE
 31      TE.STAT_NAME IN ('DB CPU', 'background cpu time')
 32      AND TE.STAT_NAME=TS.STAT_NAME(+) )
 33  ORDER BY
 34    WAIT_CLASS;

SQL> COL EVENT FORMAT A30 TRU

/* Wait time by wait event name */
SQL> SELECT
  2    TE.EVENT,
  3    TE.TOTAL_WAITS-NVL(TS.TOTAL_WAITS,0) WAITS,
  4    TE.TOTAL_TIMEOUTS-NVL(TS.TOTAL_TIMEOUTS,0) T_OUTS,
  5    TE.TIME_WAITED-NVL(TS.TIME_WAITED,0) DELTA,
  6    ROUND((TE.TIME_WAITED-NVL(TS.TIME_WAITED,0))
                     / &&CAPTURE_SECONDS,2) DELTA_SEC
  7  FROM
```

```
   8    DATALOG.TE_SYSTEM_EVENT TE,
   9    DATALOG.TS_SYSTEM_EVENT TS
  10  WHERE
  11    TE.EVENT=TS.EVENT(+)
  12    AND TE.TIME_WAITED-NVL(TS.TIME_WAITED,0)>0
  13  ORDER BY
  14    TE.EVENT;

SQL> COL STAT_NAME FORMAT A25 TRU

/* Operating system statistics */
SQL> SELECT
   2    TE.STAT_NAME,
   3    TE.VALUE END_VALUE,
   4    TE.VALUE-NVL(TS.VALUE,0) DELTA,
   5    ROUND((TE.VALUE-NVL(TS.VALUE,0))
                     / &&CAPTURE_SECONDS,2) DELTA_SEC
   6  FROM
   7    DATALOG.TE_OSSTAT TE,
   8    DATALOG.TS_OSSTAT TS
   9  WHERE
  10    TE.STAT_NAME=TS.STAT_NAME(+)
  11  ORDER BY
  12    TE.STAT_NAME;

SQL> COL STAT_NAME FORMAT A50 TRU

/* CPU time and elapsed time for Oracle activities */
SQL> SELECT
   2    TE.STAT_NAME,
   3    TE.VALUE-NVL(TS.VALUE,0) DELTA,
   4    ROUND((TE.VALUE-NVL(TS.VALUE,0))/ &&CAPTURE_SECONDS,2) DELTA_SEC
   5  FROM
   6    DATALOG.TE_SYS_TIME_MODEL TE,
   7    DATALOG.TS_SYS_TIME_MODEL TS
   8  WHERE
   9    TE.STAT_NAME=TS.STAT_NAME(+)
  10  ORDER BY
  11    TE.STAT_NAME;

SQL> COL NAME FORMAT A50 TRU

/* System level statistics */
SQL> SELECT
   2    TE.NAME,
   3    TE.VALUE-NVL(TS.VALUE,0) DELTA,
   4    ROUND((TE.VALUE-NVL(TS.VALUE,0))/ &&CAPTURE_SECONDS,2) DELTA_SEC
   5  FROM
   6    DATALOG.TE_SYSSTAT TE,
   7    DATALOG.TS_SYSSTAT TS
   8  WHERE
   9    TE.NAME=TS.NAME(+)
```

```
10    AND TE.VALUE-NVL(TS.VALUE,0)<>0
11  ORDER BY
12    TE.NAME;
```

SQL> SPOOL OFF

The goal of the preceding code is to quickly determine whether there are CPU overconsumption issues, file I/O issues, or concurrency issues within the sampled time period. A logical series of questions, as well as what might be examined while reviewing the output contained in the quickcheck.txt file follows.

Decision Tree for Quickly Interpreting the Statistics

This decision tree helps determine whether a problem exists in the database instance that requires further investigation. Is there a CPU overconsumption issue? (CPU utilization should be below 90 percent, and run queue per CPU should be two or less.) Note that if the server has, for instance, ten CPUs, there are ten CPU seconds for every second of the data-collection period. This calculation of available CPU time must be considered when determining the severity of CPU consumption issues. Here is the calculation to make:

$$V\$OSSTAT.STAT\_NAME(\text{``}BUSY\_TIME\text{''})/(V\$OSSTAT.STAT\_NAME(\text{``}BUSY\_TIME\text{''}) + \\ V\$OSSTAT.STAT\_NAME(\text{``}IDLE\_TIME\text{''}))*100$$

And following is a SQL statement to make this calculation by using the captured statistics:

```
SQL> SELECT
 2    BUSY_TIME/(BUSY_TIME+IDLE_TIME)*100 PERCENT_BUSY
 3  FROM
 4    (SELECT
 5      MAX(DECODE(TE.STAT_NAME,'BUSY_TIME',
                    TE.VALUE-NVL(TS.VALUE,0),NULL)) BUSY_TIME,
 6      MAX(DECODE(TE.STAT_NAME,'IDLE_TIME',
                    TE.VALUE-NVL(TS.VALUE,0),NULL)) IDLE_TIME
 7    FROM
 8      DATALOG.TE_OSSTAT TE,
 9      DATALOG.TS_OSSTAT TS
10    WHERE
11      TE.STAT_NAME=TS.STAT_NAME(+)
12      AND TE.STAT_NAME IN ('BUSY_TIME','IDLE_TIME'));
```

(Also check the run queue. See the earlier "Determining the CPU Run Queue" section.)

If the preceding statistics comparison indicates that the server is experiencing CPU overconsumption issues, further comparison of the captured statistics will help determine the source of the CPU consumption. Here is the calculation to determine whether the largest percentage of CPU time is caused by user mode (program/process) or system mode (operating system kernel) processing:

$$V\$OSSTAT.STAT\_NAME(\text{``}USER\_TIME\text{''})/(V\$OSSTAT.STAT\_NAME(\text{``}USER\_TIME\text{''}) + \\ V\$OSSTAT.STAT\_NAME(\text{``}SYS\_TIME\text{''}))$$

Is the CPU consumption a result of processing within the Oracle instance, or is some other process running on the server consuming CPU time? Note that the statistic V$SYSSTAT.NAME("CPU used by this session") does not account for any query that started executing but has not yet completed, so that statistic will not be used. Here is the calculation to determine the percentage of total server CPU usage during the time period that is a result of processing within your database instance:

```
((V$SYS_TIME_MODEL("DB CPU") + V$SYS_TIME_MODEL("background cpu time")) /
                        V$OSSTAT.STAT_NAME("BUSY_TIME"))/100
```

The following is a SQL statement to perform this calculation by using the captured statistics:

```
SQL> SELECT
  2     ROUND(S.VALUE/O.VALUE/100,2) ORACLE_CPU_PERCENT
  3  FROM
  4     (SELECT
  5        SUM(TE.VALUE-NVL(TS.VALUE,0)) VALUE
  6     FROM
  7        DATALOG.TE_SYS_TIME_MODEL TE,
  8        DATALOG.TS_SYS_TIME_MODEL TS
  9     WHERE
 10        TE.STAT_NAME IN ('DB CPU', 'background cpu time')
 11        AND TE.STAT_NAME=TS.STAT_NAME(+) ) S,
 12     (SELECT
 13        TE.VALUE-NVL(TS.VALUE,0) VALUE
 14     FROM
 15        DATALOG.TE_OSSTAT TE,
 16        DATALOG.TS_OSSTAT TS
 17     WHERE
 18        TE.STAT_NAME='BUSY_TIME'
 19        AND TE.STAT_NAME=TS.STAT_NAME(+) ) O;
```

If the majority of the CPU consumption during the capture period was caused by the database instance, determine whether the user calls (user activity) or Oracle background processes are responsible for the largest percentage of CPU consumption in the database instance. Here is the calculation to determine the percentage of CPU time consumed by user calls within the database instance:

```
V$SYS_TIME_MODEL.STAT_NAME("DB CPU")/(V$SYS_TIME_MODEL.STAT_NAME("DB CPU")
                        + V$SYS_TIME_MODEL.STAT_NAME("background CPU time"))*100
```

Determine whether a significant percentage of the CPU consumption within the database instance is due to parsing of SQL statements or other activities. Here is the calculation to determine the parse CPU time as a percentage of the CPU usage for user calls:

```
((V$SYSSTAT.NAME("parse time cpu")*10000)/V$SYS_TIME_MODEL.STAT_NAME("DB CPU"))*100
```

If the CPU time used for parsing is a large percentage of the total CPU used by user calls, investigate whether hard parsing is a problem within the database instance. Although Oracle does not record the CPU time consumed just by hard parses, Oracle 10.1 and later do report the elapsed time required for hard parsing. The hard-parse elapsed time statistic includes both CPU time and wait event time. Here is the calculation to determine the hard-parse elapsed time as a percentage of the CPU usage for user calls:

```
V$SYS_TIME_MODEL.STAT_NAME("hard parse elapsed time") /
    V$SYS_TIME_MODEL.STAT_NAME("DB CPU")
```

If a significant percentage of the CPU time consumed by user calls is not the result of parsing, investigate other sources of CPU usage. Contributors to recursive CPU usage include execution of anonymous PL/SQL blocks, execution of PL/SQL procedures and functions, execution of triggers, and space management calls. Contributors to the other CPU category include excessive logical I/O (consistent gets and db block gets), completely in-memory work area executions (workarea executions - optimal), excessive numbers of rows retrieved by full table scans (table scan rows gotten), excessive latch spins while attempting to acquire a latch, implicit data type conversions, and so forth. Here are the calculations to determine recursive CPU time and other CPU time:

```
RECURSIVE = V$SYSSTAT("recursive cpu usage")
OTHER =     V$SYSSTAT("CPU used by this session") –
            (V$SYSSTAT("recursive cpu usage") + V$SYSSTAT("parse time cpu"))
```

If it is determined that a significant portion of the server's CPU usage is not the result of processing within the database instance, check other processes running on the server. On a computer running Windows XP Pro or later, or Windows Server 2003 or later, write the currently running tasks, CPU consumption, memory consumption, and status for the local computer (denoted by the period character) or a remote computer to a log file (for older versions of Windows, download pslist from Microsoft's website) with the following command:

```
TASKLIST /S . /V /FO TABLE > C:\Running_Processes.txt
```

On Unix/Linux use either the ps or top commands to display CPU utilization by process.

If it is determined that SYSTEM (kernel mode) CPU time is significant compared to USER mode CPU time, check the operating-system-level contributors to SYSTEM (kernel mode) CPU time. CPU time reported as SYSTEM time by the database instance is commonly referred to as *kernel mode CPU time*, which is accumulated while the operating system performs calls on behalf of user mode processes. Tasks requiring kernel mode CPU time include network I/O, disk I/O (especially with buffered file systems), timer calls (typically gettimeofday calls), memory access requests, memory management, process creation/termination, and so forth. Use operating system utilities (sar, top, netstat, iostat, WMI calls) to determine overall I/O and process creation rates. Use operating system utilities to determine the process consuming the greatest amount of kernel mode CPU time. Consider capturing stack traces for processes currently consuming a significant portion of the systemwide kernel mode CPU time in order to determine the exact kernel calls executed (see Metalink Doc ID 436797.1, which shows usage of strace). SYSTEMTAP (sourceware.org/systemtap/) on the Linux platform provides a toolset for monitoring system (kernel mode) activity. Consider using a statistic data aggregator tool such as OS Watcher (available from Metalink), LTOM (see Metalink Doc ID 352363.1), or Oracle Cluster Health Monitor (available from Oracle's OTN site). See the description of the various operating system utilities in the "Tuning Oracle Database" topic of the *Oracle Database Administrator's Reference for Linux and UNIX-Based Operating Systems* book in the Oracle documentation. On Solaris the command prstat -m -s cpu may be used to list the kernel mode and user mode time consumed by each process (developers.sun.com/solaris/articles/prstat.html).

■ **Note** Oracle release 11.1 introduced a new timer implementation that reduces the kernel mode CPU time for gettimeofday calls, making the parameter value STATISTICS_LEVEL=ALL less likely to consume excessive kernel CPU time (see Metalink Doc ID 436797.1, and Table 10-1 in the next chapter shows a significant improvement with STATISTICS_LEVEL=ALL on the Windows 64-bit platform running Oracle 11.1.0.7 compared to Oracle 10.2.0.4). Using HugePages/Large Page Support, if supported, helps reduce kernel CPU time needed to manage memory, as memory will be managed in either 2MB or 4MB contiguous blocks rather than the typical 4KB contiguous blocks.

Is there an issue with significant wait time on wait events, and is the wait time concentrated in one or two wait classes (Concurrency, User I/O, and so forth)? If that is the case, capture delta values of session-level wait events (V$SESSION_EVENT) to determine the sessions that contributed the most significant portion of each wait event. The *Oracle Database Performance Tuning Guide for 11g* book from the Oracle documentation library contains a helpful trouble resolution procedure for many of the most common wait event types. If the wait time is present mostly in one or two sessions, remotely enable a 10046 trace for the sessions to determine the contributing causes for the wait time. If, for instance, the most significant wait times are for enqueue-type wait events (enqueue, enq: TM - contention, enq: TX - row lock contention, enq: HW - contention, and so forth), see the upcoming section, "Investigating Enqueue Waits." If the wait time is spread among several sessions, collect a Statspack or AWR report to determine the next troubleshooting step.

Creating Statspack or AWR Reports

Statspack reports and AWR reports provide a substantial amount of information, typically showing the total and average statistics, and wait events between a beginning time period and an ending time period. Because the statistics are averaged across the time interval, it is important to carefully select the start time and duration of the statistics capture; a capture lasting three days is likely worthless, and a capture lasting 2 minutes might have accuracy issues if most SQL statements do not fully start and complete in the capture period. Statspack reports may be captured at various levels, including 5, 6, 7, and 10. So much information is potentially captured by a Statspack report that it might be difficult to sort through 70+ pages of data in the report to determine whether a performance problem actually exists in the database instance. A full discussion of Statspack report contents might require a full chapter or a complete book.

The following commands create a level 7 Statspack capture, wait 10 minutes using DBMS_LOCK.SLEEP, and then collect a second level 7 Statspack capture. For this method to work, the SYS user must grant the PERFSTAT user execute permissions on the DBMS_LOCK package. The use of DBMS_LOCK could cause the PL/SQL lock timer wait event to appear in the top five waits, which could push an otherwise important wait event from that top 5 ranking.

```
SQL> CONNECT PERFSTAT/PerfPassword
SQL> EXEC STATSPACK.SNAP(i_snap_level=>7)
SQL> EXEC DBMS_LOCK.SLEEP(600)
SQL> EXEC STATSPACK.SNAP(i_snap_level=>7)
```

As an alternative to using DBMS_LOCK, forcing the SQL*Plus process to sleep may be accomplished with a call to a batch file that uses a sleep command. On the Windows platform, a script such as the following may be created and saved as C:\sleep.vbs:

```
Const lngSleepSecondsDefault = 600
Dim lngSleepSeconds
Dim objScriptArguments
Dim strArgument

Set objScriptArguments = WScript.Arguments

If objScriptArguments.Count = 0 then
  lngSleepSeconds = lngSleepSecondsDefault
Else
  For Each strArgument in objScriptArguments
    If IsNumeric(strArgument) Then
      lngSleepSeconds = cLng(strArgument)
      Exit For
    End If
  Next
  If lngSleepSeconds <= 0 Then
    lngSleepSeconds = lngSleepSecondsDefault
  End If
End If

WScript.Sleep lngSleepSeconds * 1000
```

A similar script may be developed for the Unix/Linux platform that uses the sleep command, or the sleep command may be called directly by the SQL*Plus HOST call. The modified script to collect two Statspack snaps with a 10-minute delay between the snaps follows:

```
SQL> CONNECT PERFSTAT/PerfPassword
SQL> EXEC STATSPACK.SNAP(i_snap_level=>7)
SQL> HOST C:\SLEEP.VBS 600
SQL> EXEC STATSPACK.SNAP(i_snap_level=>7)
```

Generating a Statspack report from two Statspack snaps is as simple as executing the spreport.sql script found in the rdbms/admin directory of the Oracle home. The following SQL*Plus command executes the script that generates a Statspack report:

```
SQL> @?/rdbms/admin/spreport.sql
```

AWR reports may be generated by using the automatically generated AWR snapshots with the following command:

```
SQL> @?/rdbms/admin/awrrpt.sql
```

Statspack reports capture a significant amount of detail, combining the statistics captures of most of the other monitoring methods into a single report. Statspack reports operate at the systemwide level, which may make it a bit difficult to locate problems impacting a single session. See Metalink Doc ID 94224.1, "FAQ—Statspack Complete Reference"; Metalink Doc ID 394937.1, "Statistics Package (STATSPACK) Guide"; or the Statspack-related entries on Jonathan Lewis's blog (jonathanlewis.wordpress.com/category/statspack/) for additional information about Statspack reports.

Statspack reports captured at level 6 or greater capture the execution plans for SQL statements that meet the criteria for inclusion in Statspack reports. This facilitates examination of plan changes from one snapshot to another. Metalink Doc ID 209197.1 explains how to output the captured execution plans for SQL statements using the sprepsql.sql script found in the rdbms/admin directory of the Oracle home using the OLD_HASH_VALUE for the SQL statement. Another method is available using the DBMS_XPLAN.DISPLAY function, as the following demonstrates (TYPICAL -PREDICATE -NOTE are passed in as the third parameter of DBMS_XPLAN.DISPLAY to omit the predicate output that is not captured by Statspack and AWR, and to eliminate the note indicating that the plan table was an old version).

```
SQL> SELECT
  2    SQL_ID,
  3    COUNT(DISTINCT PLAN_HASH_VALUE) C
  4  FROM
  5    PERFSTAT.STATS$SQL_PLAN_USAGE
  6  GROUP BY
  7    SQL_ID
  8  HAVING
  9    COUNT(DISTINCT PLAN_HASH_VALUE)>1;

SQL_ID          C
-------------- --
0fr8zhn4ymu3v  2
0h6b2sajwb74n  2
1gu8t96d0bdmu  2
39m4sx9k63ba2  2
4b57myt9mpz37  3
52tr7ay85qwn0  5
...


SQL> SET LINESIZE 150
SQL> SET PAGESIZE 10000
SQL> SPOOL C:\StatspackPlan.txt

SQL> SELECT /*+ ORDERED */
  2    T.*
  3  FROM
  4    (SELECT DISTINCT
  5       PLAN_HASH_VALUE
  6     FROM
  7       PERFSTAT.STATS$SQL_PLAN_USAGE
  8     WHERE
  9       SQL_ID='0fr8zhn4ymu3v'
 10     ORDER BY
 11       PLAN_HASH_VALUE) SPU,
 12    TABLE(DBMS_XPLAN.DISPLAY(
 13      'PERFSTAT.STATS$SQL_PLAN',
 14      NULL,
 15      'TYPICAL -PREDICATE -NOTE',
 16      'PLAN_HASH_VALUE='||SPU.PLAN_HASH_VALUE)) T;
```

```
SQL> SPOOL OFF
```

```
-----------------------------------------------------------------------
| Id |Operation                |Name      |Rows |Bytes|Cost (%CPU)| Time    |
-----------------------------------------------------------------------
|* 0 |SELECT STATEMENT         |          |     |     |  2 (100)|         |
|* 1 | TABLE ACCESS BY INDEX ROWID|OPQTYPE$ |   1 |  27 |  2   (0)| 00:00:01 |
|* 2 |  INDEX RANGE SCAN       |I_OPQTYPE1|   1 |     |  1   (0)| 00:00:01 |
-----------------------------------------------------------------------
```

```
-----------------------------------------------------
| Id  | Operation             | Name      | Cost |
-----------------------------------------------------
|*  0 | SELECT STATEMENT      |           |      |
|*  1 |  SORT ORDER BY        |           |   0  |
|*  2 |   TABLE ACCESS CLUSTER| OPQTYPE$  |      |
|*  3 |    INDEX UNIQUE SCAN   | I_OBJ#    |      |
-----------------------------------------------------
```

Monitoring the Delta Values for SQL Statements

A variety of views in an Oracle RDBMS provide statistics for SQL statements that may provide helpful information for performance-monitoring tasks. The V$SQLAREA view groups the statistics for all related child cursors together for cursors in the library cache. Although this grouping simplifies some tasks, accessing the view is potentially resource intensive because of the increased demand for the library cache latch. Statistics are maintained for the number of consistent gets, blocks read from disk, parse calls, executions, fetches, sorts, memory utilization, loads, invalidations, and several other statistics. Since Oracle release 9.2, the view has also exposed the elapsed time and CPU utilization. This view is updated every 1 to 5 seconds.

The V$SQL view provides similar information without grouping all child cursors together, which not only makes accessing this view less resource intensive, but also allows viewing statistics for the various child cursors in the event that the execution plan for a SQL statement changed because of statistics gathering, sessions executing with different optimizer parameters, bind variable definition/value length changes, or adaptive cursor sharing. This view is updated every 1 to 5 seconds.

The V$SQLSTATS view was introduced with Oracle 10.2 as a more efficient method for reviewing cursor statistics, with the SQL_ID and PLAN_HASH_VALUE columns acting as primary-key columns. Statistics for cursors may remain in this view after the cursor itself ages out of the library cache. This view is updated every 1 to 5 seconds.

The V$SESSION_LONGOPS view provides status updates for operations that have been active for at least 6 seconds, providing the SID and SERIAL# of the session responsible for the execution, the elapsed time of the operation, an estimate of the number of remaining seconds, and line of the execution plan that is currently executing.

Oracle 11.1 introduced the V$SQL_MONITOR view, which requires a license for the Tuning Pack to query this view. SQL statements executed with parallel execution enabled, and those SQL statements consuming at least 5 seconds of CPU time or I/O time are monitored automatically. Otherwise, monitoring may be enabled by using a /*+ MONITOR */ hint. Statistics in the V$SQL_MONITOR view are typically updated once a second, and typically remain in the view for at least a minute after the SQL execution completes.

A script to create logging tables for SQL execution statistics follows, along with a script to capture the SQL statistic delta values over a 10-minute time period and output the statistics for those SQL statements with at least 10 seconds of elapsed execution time:

```
SQL> CREATE GLOBAL TEMPORARY TABLE
  2    DATALOG.TS_SQLSTATS ON COMMIT DELETE ROWS AS
  3  SELECT
  4    SQL_ID, PLAN_HASH_VALUE, LAST_ACTIVE_TIME, CPU_TIME, ELAPSED_TIME,
  5    AVG_HARD_PARSE_TIME, APPLICATION_WAIT_TIME, CONCURRENCY_WAIT_TIME,
  6    CLUSTER_WAIT_TIME, USER_IO_WAIT_TIME, PLSQL_EXEC_TIME, JAVA_EXEC_TIME,
  7    PARSE_CALLS, LOADS, VERSION_COUNT, INVALIDATIONS, EXECUTIONS, FETCHES,
  8    ROWS_PROCESSED, BUFFER_GETS, DISK_READS, DIRECT_WRITES, SORTS, SHARABLE_MEM,
  9    TOTAL_SHARABLE_MEM
 10  FROM
 11    V$SQLSTATS
 12  WHERE
 13    0=1;

SQL> CREATE GLOBAL TEMPORARY TABLE
  2    DATALOG.TE_SQLSTATS ON COMMIT DELETE ROWS AS
  3  SELECT
  4    SQL_ID, PLAN_HASH_VALUE, LAST_ACTIVE_TIME, CPU_TIME, ELAPSED_TIME,
  5    AVG_HARD_PARSE_TIME, APPLICATION_WAIT_TIME, CONCURRENCY_WAIT_TIME,
  6    CLUSTER_WAIT_TIME, USER_IO_WAIT_TIME, PLSQL_EXEC_TIME, JAVA_EXEC_TIME,
  7    PARSE_CALLS, LOADS, VERSION_COUNT, INVALIDATIONS, EXECUTIONS, FETCHES,
  8    ROWS_PROCESSED, BUFFER_GETS, DISK_READS, DIRECT_WRITES, SORTS, SHARABLE_MEM,
  9    TOTAL_SHARABLE_MEM
 10  FROM
 11    V$SQLSTATS
 12  WHERE
 13    0=1;

SQL> COMMIT;

SQL> DEFINE CAPTURE_SECONDS=600

SQL> INSERT INTO
  2    DATALOG.TS_SQLSTATS
  3  SELECT
  4    SQL_ID, PLAN_HASH_VALUE, LAST_ACTIVE_TIME, CPU_TIME, ELAPSED_TIME,
  5    AVG_HARD_PARSE_TIME, APPLICATION_WAIT_TIME, CONCURRENCY_WAIT_TIME,
  6    CLUSTER_WAIT_TIME, USER_IO_WAIT_TIME, PLSQL_EXEC_TIME, JAVA_EXEC_TIME,
  7    PARSE_CALLS, LOADS, VERSION_COUNT, INVALIDATIONS, EXECUTIONS, FETCHES,
  8    ROWS_PROCESSED, BUFFER_GETS, DISK_READS, DIRECT_WRITES, SORTS, SHARABLE_MEM,
  9    TOTAL_SHARABLE_MEM
 10  FROM
 11    V$SQLSTATS;

SQL> EXEC DBMS_LOCK.SLEEP(&&CAPTURE_SECONDS);
```

```
SQL> INSERT INTO
  2    DATALOG.TE_SQLSTATS
  3  SELECT
  4    SQL_ID, PLAN_HASH_VALUE, LAST_ACTIVE_TIME, CPU_TIME, ELAPSED_TIME,
  5    AVG_HARD_PARSE_TIME, APPLICATION_WAIT_TIME, CONCURRENCY_WAIT_TIME,
  6    CLUSTER_WAIT_TIMF, USER_IO_WAIT_TIME, PLSQL_EXEC_TIME, JAVA_EXEC_TIME,
  7    PARSE_CALLS, LOADS, VERSION_COUNT, INVALIDATIONS, EXECUTIONS, FETCHES,
  8    ROWS_PROCESSED, BUFFER_GETS, DISK_READS, DIRECT_WRITES, SORTS, SHARABLE_MEM,
  9    TOTAL_SHARABLE_MEM
 10  FROM
 11    V$SQLSTATS;

SQL> COLUMN CPU_S FORMAT 9,990.00
SQL> COLUMN ELA_S FORMAT 9,990.00
SQL> COLUMN APP_S FORMAT 9,990.00
SQL> COLUMN CON_S FORMAT 9,990.00
SQL> COLUMN CLU_S FORMAT 9,990.00
SQL> COLUMN USR_S FORMAT 9,990.00

SQL> SET LINESIZE 180
SQL> SET PAGESIZE 200
SQL> SPOOL SQLSTATS.TXT

SQL> SELECT
  2    TE.SQL_ID, TE.PLAN_HASH_VALUE PHV,
  3    (TE.CPU_TIME-NVL(TS.CPU_TIME,0))/1000000 CPU_S,
  4    (TE.ELAPSED_TIME-NVL(TS.ELAPSED_TIME,0))/1000000 ELA_S,
  5    TE.PARSE_CALLS-NVL(TS.PARSE_CALLS,0) PAR_C,
  6    TE.EXECUTIONS-NVL(TS.EXECUTIONS,0) EXEC,
  7    (TE.APPLICATION_WAIT_TIME-NVL(TS.APPLICATION_WAIT_TIME,0))/1000000 APP_S,
  8    (TE.CONCURRENCY_WAIT_TIME-NVL(TS.CONCURRENCY_WAIT_TIME,0))/1000000 CON_S,
  9    (TE.CLUSTER_WAIT_TIME-NVL(TS.CLUSTER_WAIT_TIME,0))/1000000 CLU_S,
 10    (TE.USER_IO_WAIT_TIME-NVL(TS.USER_IO_WAIT_TIME,0))/1000000 USR_S
 11  FROM
 12    DATALOG.TS_SQLSTATS TS,
 13    DATALOG.TE_SQLSTATS TE
 14  WHERE
 15    TE.SQL_ID=TS.SQL_ID(+)
 16    AND TE.PLAN_HASH_VALUE=TS.PLAN_HASH_VALUE(+)
 17    AND (TE.ELAPSED_TIME-NVL(TS.ELAPSED_TIME,0))>=10000000
 18  ORDER BY
 19    (TE.ELAPSED_TIME-NVL(TS.ELAPSED_TIME,0)) DESC;

SQL> SPOOL OFF
```

SQL_ID	PHV	CPU_S	ELA_S	PAR_C	EXEC	APP_S	CON_S	CLU_S	USR_S
4q9qq5mta9t07	1584794551	230.32	236.57	2893	2893	0.00	0.00	0.00	0.00
cnbgwf9x3mcqj	85458804	47.17	51.98	2893	2893	0.00	0.00	0.00	0.00
9bz3rn13xf68a	3894554182	28.04	30.30	3039	3039	0.00	0.00	0.00	0.00
0pb8dqzx301b4	1082151180	10.42	10.42	0	21533	0.00	0.00	0.00	0.00

The statistics for the first SQL statement show that it consumed nearly 4 minutes of CPU time in the 10-minute time period with less than 0.01 seconds lost in any of the wait event categories. What is the cause of the potentially excessive CPU time? Each of the 2,893 executions of the SQL statement required either a hard parse or a soft parse. While parsing is potentially time-consuming and CPU intensive, more information is required to determine the source of the CPU consumption. In the event that the plan for a SQL statement changed during the 10-minute capture period, the PLAN_HASH_VALUE is not used to restrict the output for the following query:

```
SQL> SELECT
  2    TE.SQL_ID,
  3    TE.PLAN_HASH_VALUE PHV,
  4    TE.EXECUTIONS-NVL(TS.EXECUTIONS,0) EXECUTIONS,
  5    TE.FETCHES-NVL(TS.FETCHES,0) FETCHES,
  6    TE.ROWS_PROCESSED-NVL(TS.ROWS_PROCESSED,0) ROW_PRO,
  7    TE.BUFFER_GETS-NVL(TS.BUFFER_GETS,0) BUFFER_GETS,
  8    TE.DISK_READS-NVL(TE.DISK_READS,0) DISK_READS
  9  FROM
 10    DATALOG.TS_SQLSTATS TS,
 11    DATALOG.TE_SQLSTATS TE
 12  WHERE
 13    TE.SQL_ID=TS.SQL_ID(+)
 14    AND TE.PLAN_HASH_VALUE=TS.PLAN_HASH_VALUE(+)
 15    AND TE.SQL_ID IN
           ('4q9qq5mta9t07','cnbgwf9x3mcqj','9bz3rn13xf68a','0pb8dqzx301b4')
 16  ORDER BY
 17    TE.BUFFER_GETS DESC;
```

SQL_ID	PHV	EXECUTIONS	FETCHES	ROW_PRO	BUFFER_GETS	DISK_READS
4q9qq5mta9t07	1584794551	2,893	2,893	9,703	21,355,893	0
cnbgwf9x3mcqj	85458804	2,893	2,893	16,459	4,755,669	0
9bz3rn13xf68a	3894554182	3,039	3,039	10,265	1,061,466	0
0pb8dqzx301b4	1082151180	21,533	0	21,533	130,799	0

The SQL statement with SQL_ID 4q9qq5mta9t07 was executed 2,893 times, there were the same number of fetches as execution calls, and on average each fetch retrieved 3.35 rows. The likely source of the CPU consumption for the SQL statement is the 21.36 million consistent gets, with an average of 2,201 consistent gets per row fetched. Examining the SQL statement and plan might help determine whether the significant number of consistent gets per row fetched is expected. V$SQL may be queried using the SQL_ID and PLAN_HASH_VALUE to determine the SQL statement, all child cursors numbers (CHILD_NUMBER), and the user initially parsing the SQL statement. Statspack, by default, uses the following thresholds to determine whether a SQL statement will be included in a Statspack report (these values may provide a starting point for analysis when scaled to the capture time interval and expected activity in the database instance): 10,000 BUFFER_GETS, 1,000 DISK_READS, 100 EXECUTIONS, 1,000 PARSE_CALLS, 1,048,576 bytes of SHARABLE_MEM, and 20 for the value of VERSION_COUNT.

Examining Execution Plans and Plan Statistics

Oracle databases provide a variety of views that may be used to monitor plans for SQL statements and the statistics associated with those plans, typically with separate plans and statistics for each child cursor.

V$SQL_PLAN indicates the execution plan for SQL statements with cost, cardinality, byte estimates, partition ranges, access predicates, and filter predicates—essentially all of the information that is output when a typical execution plan is displayed. This view was introduced in Oracle 9.0.1 and enhanced in Oracle 9.2 to also include access predicates and filter predicates.

V$SQL_SHARED_CURSOR indicates the reason why multiple child cursors for the same SQL statement were generated (statistics collection, optimizer environment change, multiple objects with the same name in different schemas, and so forth).

V$SQL_PLAN_STATISTICS indicates actual execution statistics for a SQL statement child cursor, such as showing the number of SQL statement executions, the number of executions of an operation in a plan (STARTS), the actual number of rows generated by an operation in a plan (OUTPUT_ROWS), the number of buffer gets and blocks read from disk, and the elapsed time for all executions, as well as for the statistics from just the last execution when the STATISTICS_LEVEL is set to ALL or the GATHER_PLAN_STATISTICS hint is specified in the SQL statement.

V$SQL_WORKAREA_ACTIVE provides an estimate of memory utilization statistics for an operation in a plan to complete a sort, group by, hash join, bitmap create/merge, and for buffering. Estimates are provided indicating the amount of memory required for an optimal (in-memory) execution as well as a one-pass (temp tablespace) execution. Counts of total executions, optimal executions, one-pass executions, and multipass executions are maintained, as well as an indication of how the last execution completed.

V$SQL_PLAN_STATISTICS_ALL combines the output of V$SQL_PLAN_STATISTICS and V$SQL_WORKAREA_ACTIVE to eliminate the need for manually specifying an inefficient outer join between the two views when the plan operations need to be examined with the work area execution statistics.

Oracle 9.2 introduced DBMS_XPLAN.DISPLAY, which outputs a formatted version of the PLAN_TABLE for explained SQL statements (EXPLAIN PLAN FOR …). Oracle 10.1 introduced the function DBMS_XPLAN.DISPLAY_CURSOR to output the execution plan for either the last SQL statement executed, or a SQL statement identified by SQL_ID and CHILD_NUMBER. A third parameter of the function controls the level of detail provided in the plan.

Tanel Poder created a script that produces an output similar to DBMS_XPLAN.DISPLAY_CURSOR and works with Oracle 9.0.1 (blog.tanelpoder.com/2009/05/26/scripts-for-showing-execution-plans-via-plain-sql-and-also-in-oracle-9i/). Alberto Dell'Era wrote a utility script, simply named xplan, that lists optimizer parameters in effect during the creation of an execution plan, information from V$SQL (CPU time, elapsed time, consistent gets, physical block reads, and so forth), execution plan statistics, tables accessed by the plan with the table statistics, and indexes accessed along with the statistics for these indexes (www.adellera.it/blog/2009/08/07/xplan-20/). Metalink Doc IDs 215187.1 and 235530.1 describe SQLTXPLAIN, which generates HTML reports that include a wide range of information such as table statistics, stored outlines, execution plans for child cursors, and initialization parameters (note that the default configuration accesses the SQL Tuning Advisor, which requires an Enterprise Edition license and a license for the Oracle Tuning Pack).

Execution plans generated for SQL statements containing bind variables may not be reliable, especially when bind peeking and histograms are involved. DBMS_XPLAN.DISPLAY_CURSOR with NULL specified for the first two parameters displays the actual execution plan used for the last SQL statement submitted to the database instance. Sample execution plans generated by DBMS_XPLAN follow using the dataset created by this script:

```
SQL> CREATE TABLE T3 AS
  2  SELECT
  3     ROWNUM C1,
  4     LPAD('A',100,'A') C2
  5  FROM
  6     DUAL
  7  CONNECT BY
  8     LEVEL<=10000;

SQL> CREATE TABLE T4 AS
  2  SELECT
  3     ROWNUM C1,
  4     LPAD('A',100,'A') C2
  5  FROM
  6     DUAL
  7  CONNECT BY
  8     LEVEL<=10000;

SQL> CREATE INDEX IND_T4 ON T4(C1);

SQL> EXEC DBMS_STATS.GATHER_TABLE_STATS(OWNNAME=>USER,TABNAME=>'T3',CASCADE=>TRUE)
SQL> EXEC DBMS_STATS.GATHER_TABLE_STATS(OWNNAME=>USER,TABNAME=>'T4',CASCADE=>TRUE)

SQL> ALTER SYSTEM FLUSH BUFFER_CACHE;

SQL> ALTER SESSION SET STATISTICS_LEVEL='ALL';

SQL> VARIABLE N1 NUMBER
SQL> VARIABLE N2 NUMBER
SQL> EXEC :N1:=1
SQL> EXEC :N2:=100

SQL> SELECT
  2     T3.C1,
  3     T4.C2
  4  FROM
  5     T3,
  6     T4
  7  WHERE
  8     T3.C1 BETWEEN :N1 AND :N2
  9     AND T3.C1=T4.C1;
```

Following is an execution of DBMS_XPLAN.DISPLAY_CURSOR. In the example, we pass the string 'TYPICAL' as the third parameter:

```
SQL> SELECT * FROM TABLE(DBMS_XPLAN.DISPLAY_CURSOR(NULL,NULL,'TYPICAL'));

SQL_ID  41rcjcqgz38z2, child number 0
-----------------------------------
SELECT    T3.C1,    T4.C2 FROM    T3,    T4 WHERE    T3.C1 BETWEEN :N1
AND :N2    AND T3.C1=T4.C1

Plan hash value: 1980773432
```

Id	Operation	Name	Rows	Bytes	Cost (%CPU)	Time
0	SELECT STATEMENT				52 (100)	
* 1	FILTER					
* 2	HASH JOIN		99	10692	52 (2)	00:00:01
* 3	TABLE ACCESS FULL	T3	100	400	47 (0)	00:00:01
4	TABLE ACCESS BY INDEX ROWID	T4	100	10400	4 (0)	00:00:01
* 5	INDEX RANGE SCAN	IND_T4	100		2 (0)	00:00:01

```
Predicate Information (identified by operation id):
---------------------------------------------------
   1 - filter(:N1<=:N2)
   2 - access("T3"."C1"="T4"."C1")
   3 - filter(("T3"."C1"<=:N2 AND "T3"."C1">=:N1))
   5 - access("T4"."C1">=:N1 AND "T4"."C1"<=:N2)
```

And the following is another execution of DBMS_XPLAN.DISPLAY_CURSOR. This time we pass the string 'ALLSTATS LAST' as the third parameter:

```
SQL> ALTER SYSTEM FLUSH BUFFER_CACHE;

SQL> EXEC :N2:=10000

SQL> SELECT
  2    T3.C1,
  3    T4.C2
  4  FROM
  5    T3,
  6    T4
  7  WHERE
  8    T3.C1 BETWEEN :N1 AND :N2
  9    AND T3.C1=T4.C1;

SQL> SELECT * FROM TABLE(DBMS_XPLAN.DISPLAY_CURSOR(NULL,NULL,'ALLSTATS LAST'));
```

```
Plan hash value: 1980773432
-------------------------------------------------------------------------
| Id  | Operation                     | Name   | Starts | E-Rows | A-Rows |
-------------------------------------------------------------------------
|   0 | SELECT STATEMENT              |        |      1 |        |  10000 |
|*  1 |  FILTER                       |        |      1 |        |  10000 |
|*  2 |   HASH JOIN                   |        |      1 |     99 |  10000 |
|*  3 |    TABLE ACCESS FULL          | T3     |      1 |    100 |  10000 |
|   4 |    TABLE ACCESS BY INDEX ROWID| T4     |      1 |    100 |  10000 |
|*  5 |     INDEX RANGE SCAN          | IND_T4 |      1 |    100 |  10000 |
-------------------------------------------------------------------------


----------------------------------------------------------------------
|  A-Time    | Buffers | Reads |  OMem |  1Mem | Used-Mem |
----------------------------------------------------------------------
|00:00:00.07 |    1666 |   355 |       |       |          |
|00:00:00.07 |    1666 |   355 |       |       |          |
|00:00:00.07 |    1666 |   355 | 1517K | 1517K | 1882K (0)|
|00:00:00.07 |     158 |   155 |       |       |          |
|00:00:00.01 |    1508 |   200 |       |       |          |
|00:00:00.01 |     687 |    32 |       |       |          |
----------------------------------------------------------------------


Predicate Information (identified by operation id):
--------------------------------------------------------
   1 - filter(:N1<=:N2)
   2 - access("T3"."C1"="T4"."C1")
   3 - filter(("T3"."C1"<=:N2 AND "T3"."C1">=:N1))
   5 - access("T4"."C1">=:N1 AND "T4"."C1"<=:N2)
```

The first of the preceding plans displays the estimated row cardinalities (the number of rows expected to be returned by the operation), as well as the estimated number of bytes to be returned. The final two columns show a calculated cost for that operation of the plan, including all child operations, and the estimated execution time. The Predicate Information section of the execution plan shows the conditions applied to indexes and joins during access (the access entries), as well as the restrictions applied to the table data to filter out unwanted data as specified by the conditions in the WHERE clause (the filter entries) and automatically generated predicates added by the optimizer. Filter predicates may appear for plan lines showing index accesses when the leading column(s) of a composite index are not specified in the WHERE clause (resulting in an index skip scan operation in the plan); when intermediate columns of an index are omitted from the WHERE clause, for instance, specifying access criteria for columns 1, 2, and 4 of a composite index, but not column 3, which prevents column 4 from being used as restriction criteria during the access operation; and when a range comparison (less than, greater than, between, and so forth) is used on a composite index's column, those restrictions placed on columns in the index definition after the column with the range operation may not be examined during the access operation. The filter predicate entries are also able to reveal potentially time-consuming implicit datatype conversions in joining and filtering predicates.

The second of the preceding plans displays the estimated row cardinalities as well as the actual number of rows returned. This execution plan indicates that the optimizer predicted that tables T3 and T4 would each return 100 rows (possibly due to bind variable peeking during a previous hard parse) when in fact 10,000 rows were returned from each table to enter as input into the hash join. This could lead to performance problems that might be addressed automatically with Oracle 11g's adaptive cursor-sharing feature. The Starts column indicates the number of times that operation in the plan was executed, which in the preceding cases is 1. The A-Time column lists the actual execution time for the SQL statement in the first row of the plan, with approximate times for the remaining plan rows when the GATHER_PLAN_STATISTICS hint is used, or the actual execution time when the STATISTICS_LEVEL parameter is set to ALL. The Buffers column indicates the number of logical reads (typically consistent gets) performed during the operation plus the number of logical reads at child operations. The Reads column indicates the number of physical blocks read from disk at the operation plus the number of physical blocks read from disk by child operations. The HASH JOIN operation includes 1,517KB in the OMEM column (estimated memory needed for an optimal execution), 1,517KB in the 1MEM column (estimated memory needed for a one-pass operation) and 1,882KB in the Used-Mem column (actual amount of memory used during the last execution).

Flushing the buffer cache and forcing a nested loop operation between the tables by using an index hint produces a plan similar to the following, which highlights one of the potential problems when reviewing cardinality estimates that appear in explain plans. The displayed estimated rows returned for operations 5 and 6 are shown as 1 because that is the number of rows Oracle estimated would be retrieved per nested loop iteration of the inner row source, with the number of iterations determined by the number of rows of the outer driving table (the actual value is displayed in the Starts column when reviewing the actual statistics, as shown here).

Id	Operation	Name	Starts	E-Rows	A-Rows
0	SELECT STATEMENT		1		10000
* 1	FILTER		1		10000
2	NESTED LOOPS		1		10000
3	NESTED LOOPS		1	99	10000
* 4	TABLE ACCESS FULL	T3	1	100	10000
* 5	INDEX RANGE SCAN	IND_T4	10000	1	10000
6	TABLE ACCESS BY INDEX ROWID	T4	10000	1	10000

A-Time	Buffers	Reads
00:00:00.03	876	355
00:00:00.03	876	355
00:00:00.03	876	355
00:00:00.03	623	187
00:00:00.01	257	155
00:00:00.03	366	32
00:00:00.01	253	168

```
Predicate Information (identified by operation id):
---------------------------------------------------
   1 - filter(:N1<=:N2)
   4 - filter(("T3"."C1"<=:N2 AND "T3"."C1">=:N1))
   5 - access("T3"."C1"="T4"."C1")
       filter(("T4"."C1"<=:N2 AND "T4"."C1">=:N1))
```

Although scanning the SQL statements in the library cache may lead to excessive latching in a busy database instance, the following script will display the execution plans for all SQL statements with at least 10 child cursors and the reason for the multiple child cursors.

```
SQL> SPOOL HighChildCountPlans.txt
SQL> SET HEADING OFF
SQL> SET ARRAYSIZE 1000
SQL> SET LINESIZE 150
SQL> SET PAGESIZE 2000

SQL> SELECT /*+ LEADING(S) */
  2    T.PLAN_TABLE_OUTPUT
  3  FROM
  4    (SELECT
  5      SQL_ID, CHILD_NUMBER,
  6      COUNT(*) OVER (PARTITION BY SQL_ID) C
  7    FROM
  8      V$SQL
  9    ORDER BY
 10      SQL_ID, CHILD_NUMBER) S,
 11    TABLE(DBMS_XPLAN.DISPLAY_CURSOR(S.SQL_ID,S.CHILD_NUMBER,'TYPICAL')) T
 12  WHERE
 13    S.C>=10;

SQL> SPOOL OFF
SQL> SPOOL HighChildCountReason.txt
SQL> DESC V$SQL_SHARED_CURSOR
SQL> SET LINESIZE 200
SQL> SET HEADING ON
SQL> BREAK ON SQL_ID SKIP 1

SQL> SELECT /*+ LEADING(S) */
  2    SSC.*
  3  FROM
  4    (SELECT
  5      SQL_ID, CHILD_NUMBER,
  6      COUNT(*) OVER (PARTITION BY SQL_ID) C
  7    FROM
  8      V$SQL
  9    ORDER BY
 10      SQL_ID, CHILD_NUMBER) S,
 11    V$SQL_SHARED_CURSOR SSC
 12  WHERE
 13    S.C>=10
 14    AND S.SQL_ID=SSC.SQL_ID
 15    AND S.CHILD_NUMBER=SSC.CHILD_NUMBER;

SQL> SPOOL OFF
```

Partial output from the preceding script captured in the file HighChildCountPlans.txt follows:

```
SQL_ID  f6rs5tka838kp, child number 0
-------------------------------------
SELECT T3.C1, T4.C2 FROM T3, T4 WHERE T3.C1 BETWEEN :N1 AND :N2 AND T3.C1=T4.C1

Plan hash value: 1980173432

-------------------------------------------------------------------------------
| Id |Operation                   | Name  | Rows | Bytes | Cost (%CPU)| Time     |
-------------------------------------------------------------------------------
|   0|SELECT STATEMENT            |       |      |       |  51 (100)|          |
|*  1| FILTER                     |       |      |       |          |          |
|*  2|  HASH JOIN                 |       |    1 |   108 |  51   (2)| 00:00:01 |
|*  3|   TABLE ACCESS FULL        | T3    |    2 |     8 |  47   (0)| 00:00:01 |
|   4|   TABLE ACCESS BY INDEX ROWID| T4  |    2 |   208 |   3   (0)| 00:00:01 |
|*  5|    INDEX RANGE SCAN        | IND_T4|    2 |       |   2   (0)| 00:00:01 |
-------------------------------------------------------------------------------

Predicate Information (identified by operation id):
---------------------------------------------------

   1 - filter(:N1<=:N2)
   2 - access("T3"."C1"="T4"."C1")
   3 - filter(("T3"."C1"<=:N2 AND "T3"."C1">=:N1))
   5 - access("T4"."C1">=:N1 AND "T4"."C1"<=:N2)


SQL_ID  f6rs5tka838kp, child number 1
-------------------------------------
SELECT T3.C1, T4.C2 FROM T3, T4 WHERE T3.C1 BETWEEN :N1 AND :N2 AND T3.C1=T4.C1

Plan hash value: 1686232353

-----------------------------------------------------------------------------
| Id | Operation          | Name | Rows  | Bytes | Cost (%CPU)| Time     |
-----------------------------------------------------------------------------
|   0 | SELECT STATEMENT   |      |       |       |  95 (100)|          |
|*  1 |  FILTER            |      |       |       |          |          |
|*  2 |   HASH JOIN        |      | 10000 | 1054K |  95   (2)| 00:00:02 |
|*  3 |    TABLE ACCESS FULL| T3  | 10000 | 40000 |  47   (0)| 00:00:01 |
|*  4 |    TABLE ACCESS FULL| T4  | 10000 | 1015K |  47   (0)| 00:00:01 |
-----------------------------------------------------------------------------

Predicate Information (identified by operation id):
---------------------------------------------------

   1 - filter(:N1<=:N2)
   2 - access("T3"."C1"="T4"."C1")
   3 - filter(("T3"."C1">=:N1 AND "T3"."C1"<=:N2))
   4 - filter(("T4"."C1">=:N1 AND "T4"."C1"<=:N2))
```

```
SQL_ID  f6rs5tka838kp, child number 2
---------------------------------------
SELECT T3.C1, T4.C2 FROM T3, T4 WHERE T3.C1 BETWEEN :N1 AND :N2 AND T3.C1=T4.C1

Plan hash value: 1980773432


------------------------------------------------------------------------------------
| Id |Operation                    | Name  | Rows | Bytes | Cost (%CPU)| Time     |
------------------------------------------------------------------------------------
|   0|SELECT STATEMENT             |       |      |       | 52 (100)|            |
|*  1| FILTER                      |       |      |       |         |            |
|*  2|  HASH JOIN                  |       |  99  | 10692 | 52   (2)| 00:00:01   |
|*  3|   TABLE ACCESS FULL         | T3    | 100  |  400  | 47   (0)| 00:00:01   |
|   4|   TABLE ACCESS BY INDEX ROWID| T4   | 100  | 10400 |  4   (0)| 00:00:01   |
|*  5|    INDEX RANGE SCAN         | IND_T4| 100  |       |  2   (0)| 00:00:01   |
------------------------------------------------------------------------------------

Predicate Information (identified by operation id):
---------------------------------------------------
   1 - filter(:N1<=:N2)
   2 - access("T3"."C1"="T4"."C1")
   3 - filter(("T3"."C1"<=:N2 AND "T3"."C1">=:N1))
   5 - access("T4"."C1">=:N1 AND "T4"."C1"<=:N2)
...
```

The following is partial output from the preceding script that was captured in the file HighChildCountReason.txt:

```
CHILD_NUMBER USOOSLFEBPISTABDLTRIIRLIOEMUTNFAITDLDBPCSCPTMBMROPMFLPLAFLRLH
------------ --------------------------------------------------------------
           0 NNNNNNNNNNNNNNNNNNNNNNNNNNNNNNNNNNNNNNNNNNNNNNNNNNNNYNNNNNNNN
           1 NNNNNNNNNNNNNNNNNNYNNNNNNNNNNNNNNNNNNNNNNNNNNNNNNNNNNNNNNNNNN
           2 NNNNNNNNNNNNNNNNNNNYNNNNNNNNNNNNNNNNNNNNNNNNNNNNNNNNNNNNNNNNN
           3 NNYNNNNNNNNNNNNNNNNNNNNNNNNNNNNNNNNNNNNNNNNNNNYNNNNNNNNNNNNNN
           4 NNNNNNNNNNNNNNNNNNNYNNNNNNNNNNNNNNNNNNNNNNNNNNNNNNNNNNNNNNNNN
...
```

As reported, child cursor 0 was marked with LOAD_OPTIMIZER_STATS set to Y (IS_SHAREABLE in V$SQL is set to N for this child cursor, indicating that it will no longer be used); child cursors 1, 2, and 4 were created because of ROW_LEVEL_SEC_MISMATCH (an indication of adaptive cursor sharing); and child cursor 3 was created because of OPTIMIZER_MISMATCH and OPTIMIZER_MODE_MISMATCH. In V$SQL, IS_BIND_SENSITIVE (bind peeking was used to generate the execution plan, and the execution plan selected depends on the peeked bind values) and IS_BIND_AWARE (cursor is using adaptive cursor sharing) are specified as Y for child cursors 1, 2, and 4, while only IS_BIND_SENSITIVE was set for child cursor 0. Child cursor 3 was created with session-altered values for OPTIMIZER_FEATURES_ENABLE and OPTIMIZER_INDEX_COST_ADJ. The IS_BIND_SENSITIVE and IS_BIND_AWARE columns were introduced in Oracle 11.1. For more information, see Metalink Doc ID 296377.1.

Examining Optimizer Parameters Affecting Plans

V$SQL_OPTIMIZER_ENV shows the optimizer parameters that influenced the decisions made by the cost-based optimizer when an execution plan was developed for a child cursor. The view may be joined to V$SQL by using the columns HASH_VALUE (or in 10.1 and above, SQL_ID) and CHILD_ADDRESS. The following output shows the contents of V$SQL_OPTIMIZER_ENV for child cursor 3 from the previous section, which indicated that the child cursor was created because of an OPTIMIZER_MISMATCH and OPTIMIZER_MODE_MISMATCH condition.

```
SQL> SELECT
  2    CHILD_NUMBER CN,
  3    NAME,
  4    VALUE,
  5    ISDEFAULT DEF
  6  FROM
  7    V$SQL_OPTIMIZER_ENV
  8  WHERE
  9    SQL_ID='f6rs5tka838kp'
 10    AND CHILD_NUMBER=3
 11  ORDER BY
 12    NAME;
```

CN	NAME	VALUE	DEF
3	_pga_max_size	368640 KB	NO
3	active_instance_count	1	YES
3	bitmap_merge_area_size	1048576	YES
3	cell_offload_compaction	ADAPTIVE	YES
3	cell_offload_plan_display	AUTO	YES
3	cell_offload_processing	true	YES
3	cpu_count	8	YES
3	cursor_sharing	exact	YES
3	db_file_multiblock_read_count	128	YES
3	hash_area_size	131072	YES
3	is_recur_flags	0	YES
3	optimizer_capture_sql_plan_baseline	false	YES
3	optimizer_dynamic_sampling	1	NO
3	optimizer_features_enable	**9.2.0**	NO
3	optimizer_index_caching	0	YES
3	optimizer_index_cost_adj	**20**	NO
3	optimizer_mode	**choose**	NO
3	optimizer_secure_view_merging	true	YES
3	optimizer_use_invisible_indexes	false	YES
3	optimizer_use_pending_statistics	false	YES
3	optimizer_use_sql_plan_baselines	true	YES
3	parallel_ddl_mode	enabled	YES

```
3 parallel_degree                   0              YES
3 parallel_dml_mode                 disabled       YES
3 parallel_execution_enabled        true           YES
3 parallel_query_default_dop        0              YES
3 parallel_query_mode               enabled        YES
3 parallel_threads_per_cpu          2              YES
3 pga_aggregate_target              1843200 KB     YES
3 query_rewrite_enabled             false          NO
3 query_rewrite_integrity           enforced       YES
3 result_cache_mode                 MANUAL         YES
3 skip_unusable_indexes             false          NO
3 sort_area_retained_size           0              YES
3 sort_area_size                    65536          YES
3 star_transformation_enabled       false          YES
3 statistics_level                  typical        YES
3 transaction_isolation_level       read_commited  YES
3 workarea_size_policy              auto           YES
```

The V$SYS_OPTIMIZER_ENV view indicates the systemwide default cost-based optimizer parameters that are inherited by sessions as connections are made to the database instance. The V$SES_OPTIMIZER_ENV view indicates the session-level cost-based optimizer parameters used when parsing SQL statements. Comparing V$SYS_OPTIMIZER_ENV to V$SES_OPTIMIZER_ENV for each session permits an easy method to determine session-modified parameters that may impact the query optimizer, potentially resulting in excessive numbers of child cursors for the same SQL statement.

Setting Oracle event 10132 at the session level or system level causes execution plans, and the optimizer parameters influencing those execution plans, to be written to a trace file during every hard parse. For example:

```
SQL> ALTER SESSION SET TRACEFILE_IDENTIFIER = 'sql_hard_parse_plans';
SQL> ALTER SESSION SET EVENTS '10132 TRACE NAME CONTEXT FOREVER, LEVEL 1';

SQL> VARIABLE N1 NUMBER
SQL> VARIABLE N2 NUMBER

SQL> EXEC :N1 := 1
SQL> EXEC :N2 := 100

SQL> SELECT
  2    T3.C1, T4.C2
  3  FROM
  4    T3, T4
  5  WHERE
  6    T3.C1 BETWEEN :N1 AND :N2
  7    AND T3.C1=T4.C1;

SQL> ALTER SESSION SET EVENTS '10132 TRACE NAME CONTEXT OFF';
```

Partial trace file output follows:

```
============
Plan Table
============

---------------------------------------------------+------------------------------------+
| Id| Operation                     | Name   | Rows  | Bytes | Cost  | Time      |
---------------------------------------------------+------------------------------------+
|  0 | SELECT STATEMENT              |        |       |       |  52   |           |
|  1 |  FILTER                       |        |       |       |       |           |
|  2 |   HASH JOIN                   |        |   99  |  10K  |  52   | 00:00:01  |
|  3 |    TABLE ACCESS FULL          | T3     |  100  |  400  |  47   | 00:00:01  |
|  4 |    TABLE ACCESS BY INDEX ROWID| T4     |  100  |  10K  |   4   | 00:00:01  |
|  5 |     INDEX RANGE SCAN          | IND_T4 |  100  |       |   2   | 00:00:01  |
---------------------------------------------------+------------------------------------+
Predicate Information:
----------------------

1 - filter(:N1<=:N2)
2 - access("T3"."C1"="T4"."C1")
3 - filter(("T3"."C1"<=:N2 AND "T3"."C1">=:N1))
5 - access("T4"."C1">=:N1 AND "T4"."C1"<=:N2)


Content of other_xml column
===========================
   db_version     : 11.2.0.1
   parse_schema   : TESTUSER
   plan_hash      : 1980773432
   plan_hash_2    : 178662651
Peeked Binds
============
  Bind variable information
    position=1
    datatype(code)=2
    datatype(string)=NUMBER
    precision=0
    scale=0
    max length=22
    value=1
  Bind variable information
    position=2
    datatype(code)=2
    datatype(string)=NUMBER
    precision=0
    scale=0
    max length=22
    value=100
  Outline Data:
  /*+
    BEGIN_OUTLINE_DATA
      IGNORE_OPTIM_EMBEDDED_HINTS
      OPTIMIZER_FEATURES_ENABLE('11.2.0.1')
```

```
      DB_VERSION('11.2.0.1')
      ALL_ROWS
      OUTLINE_LEAF(@"SEL$1")
      FULL(@"SEL$1" "T3"@"SEL$1")
      INDEX_RS_ASC(@"SEL$1" "T4"@"SEL$1" ("T4"."C1"))
      LEADING(@"SEL$1" "T3"@"SEL$1" "T4"@"SEL$1")
      USE_HASH(@"SEL$1" "T4"@"SEL$1")
    END_OUTLINE_DATA
  */

Optimizer state dump:
Compilation Environment Dump
optimizer_mode_hinted                 = false
optimizer_features_hinted             = 0.0.0
parallel_execution_enabled            = true
parallel_query_forced_dop             = 0
parallel_dml_forced_dop               = 0
parallel_ddl_forced_degree            = 0
parallel_ddl_forced_instances         = 0
_query_rewrite_fudge                  = 90
optimizer_features_enable             = 11.2.0.1
...
```

Table and index statistics, as well as system (CPU) statistics, are also considered by the cost-based optimizer when generating execution plans. The cost-based optimizer decisions may be viewed by generating a 10053 trace during a hard parse.

Generating 10053 Cost-Based Optimizer Traces

When you need to gain a deeper understanding of why a particular execution plan was created by the cost-based optimizer, 10053 cost-based optimizer traces provide access to the cost-based decisions made by the optimizer during the development of the execution plan. 10053 traces are especially helpful because of the wealth of information provided during a hard parse when SQL statements exhibit slower-than-expected performance, or an optimizer-related bug is suspected, and the officially supported tools for reviewing the execution plans (such as EXPLAIN PLAN) do not provide sufficient information to determine the rationale for the execution plan.

The contents of 10053 trace files are undocumented and potentially change with each release and patch set version of Oracle. With the 10.2 release, various changes and additions have been made to the 10053 trace file that make such trace files even more helpful than in previous releases. 10053 trace files are organized in several sections, and this portion of the chapter describes the most helpful sections of the 10053 trace files. The accompanying script 10053OptimizerTrace.sql may be used to reproduce most of the aspects highlighted in this section.

Activating and Deactivating the Optimizer Trace

The cost-based optimizer trace may be activated by using the following SQL statement to set event 10053:

```
SQL> ALTER SESSION SET EVENTS '10053 trace name context forever, level 1';
```

Only those SQL statements requiring a hard parse, which are executed after the preceding command, will be included in the corresponding trace file. In general, it is advisable to set a unique trace identifier name, which becomes part of the trace filename, before activating the 10053 trace to help locate the generated trace file in the server's udump (or trace) directory. Setting the trace identifier name is accomplished with the following SQL statement:

```
SQL> ALTER SESSION SET TRACEFILE_IDENTIFIER = '<string_to_identify_the_trace_file>';
```

Disabling the 10053 optimizer trace is accomplished with the following command:

```
SQL> ALTER SESSION SET EVENTS '10053 trace name context off';
```

Query Blocks

Starting with Oracle 10.1, the 10053 trace files contain a section titled Query Block Signature, which lists each of the query blocks (inline views, subqueries, and so forth) found in the SQL statement. The Query Block Signature section lists the tables and aliases that are part of the query block (the nbfros and the corresponding fro(N)). Queries containing nonmergeable views will contain multiple query blocks, and the trace file will consist of separate sections, each optimizing a query block and a final section that combines the nonmergeable query blocks.

Query blocks may be named by using the qb_name hint starting with Oracle 10.1. Without a hinted query block name, Oracle will generate a standardized name similar to SEL$1, MISC$2 for each query block. These query block names may then be used in the extended 10g hint syntax to indicate a specific query block to which the hint applies. Furthermore, because of the automatic transformations applied to the SQL statements during optimization, the arrangement of the query blocks may change, making it difficult to correctly apply hints to query blocks using Oracle-generated (nonhinted) query block names. The following output shows two query blocks that were identified in a 10053 trace file:

```
---------------------
QUERY BLOCK SIGNATURE
---------------------
  signature (): qb_name=SEL$1 nbfros=1 flg=0
    fro(0): flg=5 objn=0 hint_alias="from$_subquery$_001"@"SEL$1"

Registered qb: SEL$2 0x81e57e4 (PARSER)
---------------------
QUERY BLOCK SIGNATURE
---------------------
  signature (): qb_name=SEL$2 nbfros=1 flg=0
    fro(0): flg=4 objn=75329 hint_alias="TEST_SORT"@"SEL$2"
```

Peeked Bind Variables

A very helpful section of the optimizer trace file shows the bind variables' values that were examined when optimizing the statement, thus allowing the SQL statement to be optimized as if constants were specified in the SQL statement rather than bind variables with default selectivity estimates. Unfortunately, this section does not show the bind variable names as used in the SQL statement. Instead, the sequential position of the bind variable is listed, so it is necessary to match the sequential order of the bind variables as listed in the SQL statement with those in this section of the trace file. The following output shows the peeked bind variables section from a 10053 trace file:

```
*****************************************
Peeked values of the binds in SQL statement
*****************************************
----- Bind Info (kkscoacd) -----
 Bind#0
  oacdty=01 mxl=32(06) mxlc=00 mal=00 scl=00 pre=00
  oacflg=10 fl2=0100 frm=01 csi=178 siz=32 off=0
  kxsbbbfp=08212f24  bln=32  avl=06  flg=09
  value="SELECT"
 Bind#1
  oacdty=02 mxl=22(02) mxlc=00 mal=00 scl=00 pre=00
  oacflg=10 fl2=0100 frm=00 csi=00 siz=24 off=0
  kxsbbbfp=08212f14  bln=22  avl=02  flg=09
  value=51
```

This section is helpful in two ways. First, it obviously shows the actual values used to optimize the statement, which is often crucial in understanding the decisions of the optimizer, in particular if range comparisons or skewed data with histograms are involved. Starting with release 10.1, the "out-of-range" predicates for equal comparisons may also play an important role. Note that certain bind variable data types are not shown in a human readable format. An example is the group of TIMESTAMP data types. Values from that family are displayed as follows:

```
Bind#1
  oacdty=180 mxl=11(11) mxlc=00 mal=00 scl=06 pre=00
  oacflg=01 fl2=206001 frm=00 csi=06 siz=0 off=8
  kxsbbbfp=08f786e4  bln=11  avl=11  flg=01
  value=
Dump of memory from 0x08F786E4 to 0x08F786EF
8F786E0          16096D78 02011701 0040AEEB      [xm........@.]
```

Other datatypes whose values are not shown in this section include those based on NCHAR and NVARCHAR (National Character Set). For those datatypes, the VALUE will simply be shown as a blank, and no raw dump will be included. However, the Peeked Binds subsection of the PLAN_TABLE section (available starting with release 10.2) toward the end of the trace file will show these values based on the National Character Set.

Second, the *peeked values* section shows the actual bind variable datatype specified by the application. The bind variable datatype is listed after dty= prior to Oracle 10.1, and listed after oacdty= starting with Oracle 10.1. The Oracle OCI documentation contains a list of all datatype constants, and the information may also be found in Metalink Doc IDs 67701.1 and 154170.1. The bind variable descriptions may be very important when trying to understand why obviously available indexes were apparently ignored by the optimizer. In particular, starting with release 9.2 of the Oracle JDBC driver, Java objects that contain a date and time portion (for example, java.util.Date or java.sql.Timestamp) were bound by default to a bind variable data type of TIMESTAMP, which effectively eliminates the usage of any normal indexes created on DATE type columns in the database, because the optimizer implicitly forces a conversion of the DATE column values to TIMESTAMP values for the comparison. Refer to the JDBC FAQ on the OTN website for more information. Up to release 10.2 of the Oracle JDBC driver version, a workaround is available that does not require application or database datatype changes (for example, convert DATE to TIMESTAMP): set the oracle.jdbc.V8Compatible property to TRUE. This setting will bind Java objects to bind variables of DATE datatype. Note that setting this property to TRUE has some other effects—for example, database DATEs will be mapped to java.sql.Timestamp rather than to java.sql.Date. Starting with the 11.1 release of the JDBC driver, this property is not supported because connectivity to pre-9.2 releases is no longer supported.

Optimizer Parameters Used

Another helpful section of the trace file lists parameters that are relevant to the optimizer decision process. This section lists many more parameters than those listed in the V$SQL_OPTIMIZER_ENV view and its session and instance counterparts, V$SES_OPTIMIZER_ENV and V$SYS_OPTIMIZER_ENV, respectively. Even with the additional parameters included in the 10053 trace file, the list does not include all of the parameters that may be relevant to the optimizer and are found in the fixed tables X$KSPPI and X$KSPPSV, which are accessible to only the SYS user. Starting with Oracle 10.1, the parameters included in the trace file are divided into two sections that show parameters with altered values (at the instance or session level) and parameters with values that are the default for the specific Oracle release.

Oracle 10.2 also introduced a related section titled PARAMETERS IN OPT_PARAM HINT in the trace file, which shows any parameters altered through the OPT_PARAM hint. This hint became officially documented in the 11.1 documentation, even though Metalink Doc ID 377333.1 indicates that the hint also should have been included in the 10.2 documentation. The Oracle 11.2 SQL language reference documentation states that the OPT_PARAM hint is valid for only five parameters, but the optimizer is apparently able to display other parameters modified by an OPT_PARAM hint, including the undocumented parameters (those parameters beginning with an underscore, only change the undocumented parameters under the guidance of Oracle support), in the PARAMETERS IN OPT_PARAM HINT section of the trace file. For the OPT_PARAM hint, the parameter name should be enclosed in single quotes, and string value parameters should also be specified in single quotes.

The list of parameters is helpful for two reasons. First, the list indicates exactly which settings were used to optimize the SQL statement, which might provide a clue why different performance results were obtained due to the altered parameters. Second, the parameter output may be helpful following a database upgrade, allowing a comparison of the new default values to those from the previous release. Such a comparison helps illustrate the degree to which the new default parameters contribute to significant performance problems after an upgrade.

Transformations

Another quite interesting section of the trace file covers the transformations applied to the input SQL statement. The query optimizer attempts to perform various transformations before actually starting to optimize the SQL statement. Starting with Oracle 10.1, this approach has been greatly extended to include a new section in the trace file titled CBQT (cost-based query transformation). Prior to Oracle 10.1, the query transformations were applied based on a heuristic approach without any costing involved, which meant a strict order for transformation: first, perform any transformations that apply according to the rules, and second, optimize the resulting transformed statement.

Starting with Oracle 10.1 there is a "feedback" loop between the transformation and optimization phases, making the whole optimization phase much more complex (which also means that a hard parse on 10.1 may take significantly longer than in previous releases because of the number of transformations tried and costed). The "feedback" loop means that starting with Oracle 10.1, transformations may be rejected because of costing calculations performed, whereas those same transformations were applied unconditionally in previous releases. For example, in Oracle 9i, subqueries are always unnested if it is logically possible to perform the unnest operation without changing the meaning of the SQL statement, whereas in Oracle 10g, costs are calculated for both forms of the SQL statement, with the lowest cost determining whether the subquery will be transformed. This difference in behavior might lead to different execution plans than in previous releases, potentially resulting in significantly changed performance (a decrease in performance is possible).

Several types of query transformations are available to the cost-based optimizer. For instance, a trace file from Oracle 11.1.0.7 reports the following list of attempted query transformations:

```
CBQT - cost-based query transformation

CSE - common subexpression elimination

JPPD - join predicate push-down

OJPPD - old-style (non-cost-based) JPPD

FPD - filter push-down

PM - predicate move-around

CVM - complex view merging

SVM - simple view merging

SPJ - select-project-join

SJC - set join conversion

SU - subquery unnesting

OBYE - order by elimination

ST - star transformation

JE - join elimination
```

Finally, this section shows additional predicates generated by the optimizer through transitive closure or database constraints (check constraints, foreign-key constraints). It is often amazing how different a SQL statement might appear after transformations have been applied. For instance, the following SQL statement (see the script 10053QueryTransformation.sql, which creates the T7 and T8 tables and generates a 10053 trace file for each query) might be transformed from this:

```
SELECT
  C1, SUBSTR(C2,1,20) C2
FROM
  T7
WHERE
  EXISTS (
    SELECT
      1
    FROM
      T8
    WHERE
      T8.C1=T7.C1);
```

...into the following:

```
SELECT
  "T7"."C1" "C1", SUBSTR("T7"."C2",1,20) "C2"
FROM
  "TESTUSER"."T8" "T8", "TESTUSER"."T7" "T7"
WHERE
  "T8"."C1"="T7"."C1";
```

A similar query using IN syntax such as the following, with a nearly useless WHERE clause in the subquery, might be transformed from this:

```
SELECT
  C1, SUBSTR(C2,1,20) C2
FROM
  T7
WHERE
  C1 IN (
    SELECT
      T8.C1
    FROM
      T8
    WHERE
      T8.C1=T8.C1);
```

...into the following on Oracle 10.2.0.4:

```
SELECT
  "T7"."C1" "C1", SUBSTR("T7"."C2",1,20) "C2"
FROM
  "TESTUSER"."T8" "T8","TESTUSER"."T7" "T7"
WHERE
  "T8"."C1" IS NOT NULL
  AND "T7"."C1"="T8"."C1";
```

Oracle 10.2.0.4 removed the T8.C1=T8.C1 predicate from the subquery during optimization and transformation, replacing it with T8.C1 IS NOT NULL. Oracle 11.1.0.7 generated the T8.C1 IS NOT NULL predicate, did not include the changed predicate in the modified SQL statement written to the trace file, but did show the modified predicate in the plan output's access predicates. Looking at the transformed statement might help in understanding why the optimizer came up with a particular execution plan.

System Statistics

Oracle releases 9.0.1 and greater support system statistics (also known as *CPU Costing*) to take into account CPU performance and I/O performance in optimizer cost calculations. Prior to Oracle 10.1, the optimizer used the system statistics cost only if the statistics were collected, whereas on Oracle 10.1 the optimizer will use default NOWORKLOAD system statistics in cost calculations until server-specific statistics are collected with DBMS_STATS. Starting with release 10.2, the system statistics used to optimize a SQL statement will be shown in the 10053 trace file. Note that this section will be included in the trace file even when system statistics have not been gathered (thus NOWORKLOAD system statistics exist) and the

235

OPTIMIZER_FEATURES_ENABLE parameter is set to a value less than 10.1. In such a case, the optimizer will set the calculated CPU costing values to 0 as the code paths for the earlier Oracle releases are not aware of the various NOWORKLOAD statistics maintained in SYS.AUX_STATS$, which causes the optimizer to switch back to the I/O cost model used in earlier releases. The following output from a 10053 trace file indicates that default NOWORKLOAD system statistics are used during query optimization:

```
----------------------------
SYSTEM STATISTICS INFORMATION
----------------------------
  Using NOWORKLOAD Stats
  CPUSPEEDNW: 430 millions instructions/sec (default is 100)
  IOTFRSPEED: 4096 bytes per millisecond (default is 4096)
  IOSEEKTIM: 10 milliseconds (default is 10)
  MBRC: -1 blocks (default is 8)
```

Base Statistical Information

This section of the trace file lists the object statistics that will be used to optimize the SQL statement. Although this section of the trace file basically simply echoes what is available from the corresponding dictionary views DBA_TAB_STATISTICS, DBA_TAB_COL_STATISTICS, and so forth, this section can be very helpful when partitioning is involved and you need to understand which level of statistics have been used for a specific object. If the partition key(s) are specified through bind variables for a SQL statement, an EXPLAIN PLAN output for the SQL statement and the actual execution plan might differ significantly. This difference is due to bind variable peeking not being performed during an EXPLAIN PLAN, while by default bind variable peeking will be used by the optimizer during an actual execution of the statement to determine the partitions and their corresponding statistics. The EXPLAIN PLAN output might be based on global statistics, while the actual execution plan might be based on partition-level statistics in the case that partition pruning to a single partition is possible. In both cases, the PSTART and PSTOP indicators show KEY, but the calculations will be based on different sets of statistics. Note that starting with release 11.1, there is an oddity in this section, such that the column statistics are no longer shown, only table-level and index statistics are available in this section.

The following output is an example of this section from a 10053 trace file that shows a bug in the 10.2.0.4 patch set when pruning to a single list subpartition and using composite range-list partitioning:

```
***************************************
BASE STATISTICAL INFORMATION
***********************
Table Stats::
 Table: PARTITION_TEST Alias:PARTITION_TEST(making adjustments for partition skews)
  ORIGINAL VALUES::    #Rows: 0  #Blks:  1  AvgRowLen:  0.00
  SUBPARTITIONS::
  PRUNED: 1
  ANALYZED: 1  UNANALYZED: 0
  Partition [2]  (NOT ANALYZED)
    #Rows: 0  #Blks:  58593632  AvgRowLen:  1025.00
    #Rows: 0  #Blks:  1  AvgRowLen:  0.00
***************************************
```

```
SINGLE TABLE ACCESS PATH
-------------------------------------------
BEGIN Single Table Cardinality Estimation
-------------------------------------------
Column (#1): X_PKEY(NUMBER)  Part#: 2
  AvgLen: 22.00 NDV: 0 Nulls: 0 Density: 0.0000e+000 Min: 0 Max: 0
Column (#1): X_PKEY(NUMBER)
  AvgLen: 22.00 NDV: 0 Nulls: 0 Density: 0.0000e+000 Min: 0 Max: 0
Column (#2): X_SLICE(VARCHAR2)  Part#: 2
  AvgLen: 20.00 NDV: 0 Nulls: 0 Density: 0.0000e+000 Min: 0 Max: 0
Column (#2): X_SLICE(VARCHAR2)
  AvgLen: 20.00 NDV: 0 Nulls: 0 Density: 0.0000e+000 Min: 0 Max: 0
Table: PARTITION_TEST  Alias: PARTITION_TEST
  Card: Original: 0  Rounded: 1  Computed: 0.00  Non Adjusted: 0.00
-------------------------------------------
END   Single Table Cardinality Estimation
-------------------------------------------
Access Path: TableScan
  Cost:  2.00  Resp: 2.00  Degree: 0
    Cost_io: 2.00  Cost_cpu: 7121
    Resp_io: 2.00  Resp_cpu: 7121
Best:: AccessPath: TableScan
      Cost: 2.00  Degree: 1  Resp: 2.00  Card: 0.00  Bytes: 0
```

For the preceding example, statistics on all levels (subpartition, partition, and global/composite level) had been gathered, but a bug in the 10.2.0.4 patch set attempted to prune to a single list subpartition without reasonable column and row statistics. This bug was introduced by a feature added to Oracle 10.2.0.4 that permits the optimizer to use subpartition statistics when pruning to a single subpartition. Unfortunately, as Oracle 10.2.0.3 and below use partition-level statistics and not subpartition statistics, such statistics may have been omitted from the statistics-gathering job. When using 10.2.0.4 or later while range-list composite partitioning is in use, it might be necessary to adjust the statistics-gathering strategy to gather subpartition-level statistics to support the optimizer when pruning to a single list subpartition (provided the mentioned bug has been fixed by applying the corresponding one-off patch for bug 7210921).

The following output is from the same test case captured in an Oracle 11.1.0.7 10053 trace file:

```
*************************************
BASE STATISTICAL INFORMATION
***********************
Table Stats::
 Table: PARTITION_TEST Alias:PARTITION_TEST(making adjustments for partition skews)
  ORIGINAL VALUES::    #Rows: 10 #Blks:  1 AvgRowLen:  10.00
  SUBPARTITIONS::
  PRUNED: 1
  ANALYZED: 1  UNANALYZED: 0
  Partition [3]
    #Rows: 10  #Blks:  1  AvgRowLen:  10.00
    #Rows: 10  #Blks:  1  AvgRowLen:  10.00
Access path analysis for PARTITION_TEST
*************************************
```

```
SINGLE TABLE ACCESS PATH
  Single Table Cardinality Estimation for PARTITION_TEST[PARTITION_TEST]

  Table: PARTITION_TEST  Alias: PARTITION_TEST
    Card: Original: 10.000000  Rounded: 10  Computed: 10.00  Non Adjusted: 10.00
  Access Path: TableScan
    Cost:  2.00  Resp: 2.00  Degree: 0
      Cost_io: 2.00  Cost_cpu: 8081
      Resp_io: 2.00  Resp_cpu: 8081
  Best:: AccessPath: TableScan
         Cost: 2.00  Degree: 1  Resp: 2.00  Card: 10.00  Bytes: 0


***************************************
```

Unfortunately, the column statistics are missing from the preceding trace, but at least the correct cardinality estimate of 10 rows may be seen, along with the fact the optimizer pruned to the correct single list subpartition.

Dynamic Sampling

If dynamic sampling was used during a hard parse of a SQL statement, a note will appear in the DBMS_XPLAN.DISPLAY output for the SQL statement indicating that dynamic sampling had been used, but no additional information is provided. The note is based on the contents of the OTHER_XML column of the PLAN_TABLE, where an entry will appear stating dynamic_sampling: yes. The 10053 trace file reveals more detail about the dynamic sampling performed. This section shows the actual query generated to run the dynamic sampling along with the results obtained:

```
SINGLE TABLE ACCESS PATH
  -----------------------------------------
  BEGIN Single Table Cardinality Estimation
  -----------------------------------------
*** 2009-03-15 12:42:21.246
** Performing dynamic sampling initial checks. **
** Dynamic sampling initial checks returning TRUE (level = 2).
** Dynamic sampling updated table stats.: blocks=2
*** 2009-03-15 12:42:21.246
** Generated dynamic sampling query:
   query text :
SELECT /* OPT_DYN_SAMP */ /*+ ALL_ROWS IGNORE_WHERE_CLAUSE NO_PARALLEL(SAMPLESUB)
   opt_param('parallel_execution_enabled', 'false') NO_PARALLEL_INDEX(SAMPLESUB)
   NO_SQL_TUNE */ NVL(SUM(C1),0), NVL(SUM(C2),0) FROM (SELECT
   /*+ NO_PARALLEL("TEST_BIND_EXPL_DYN") FULL("TEST_BIND_EXPL_DYN")
   NO_PARALLEL_INDEX("TEST_BIND_EXPL_DYN") */ 1 AS C1, 1 AS C2 FROM
   "TEST_BIND_EXPL_DYN" "TEST_BIND_EXPL_DYN") SAMPLESUB
*** 2009-03-15 12:42:21.246
** Executed dynamic sampling query:
   level : 2
   sample pct. : 100.000000
   actual sample size : 100
   filtered sample card. : 100
```

```
    orig. card. : 164
    block cnt. table stat. : 2
    block cnt. for sampling: 2
    max. sample block cnt. : 64
    sample block cnt. : 2
    min. sel. est. : -1.00000000
** Using dynamic sampling card. : 100
** Dynamic sampling updated table card.
  Column (#4): OBJECT_ID(NUMBER)  NO STATISTICS (using defaults)
    AvgLen: 13.00 NDV: 3 Nulls: 0 Density: 0.32
  Table: TEST_BIND_EXPL_DYN  Alias: TEST_BIND_EXPL_DYN
    Card: Original: 100  Rounded: 1  Computed: 1.00  Non Adjusted: 1.00
  -----------------------------------------
  END   Single Table Cardinality Estimation
  -----------------------------------------
Access Path: TableScan
    Cost:  2.00  Resp: 2.00  Degree: 0
      Cost_io: 2.00  Cost_cpu: 50423
      Resp_io: 2.00  Resp_cpu: 50423
Best:: AccessPath: TableScan
        Cost: 2.00  Degree: 1  Resp: 2.00  Card: 1.00  Bytes: 0
```

In particular, the following details will be shown:

> level: The dynamic sampling level applied.

> sample pct.: The calculated sample percentage based on the level and the total number of blocks of the segment.

> actual sample size: The number of rows sampled.

> filtered sample card.: The filtered cardinality.

> orig. card.: The original cardinality based on the (possibly) missing statistics. This can be quite interesting when dealing with expressions or correlated column values and dynamic sampling levels greater than 2. With dynamic sampling level 3 or greater, the dynamic sampling will also be used when statistics have been gathered.

> block cnt. table stat.: The number of blocks according to the statistics.

> block cnt. for sampling: The number of blocks to be used for sampling, according to the calculation.

> max. sample block cnt.: The maximum number of blocks to sample according to the dynamic sampling level.

> sample block cnt.: The actual number of blocks used for sampling.

> min. sel. est.: The minimum selectivity estimate based on information available before the dynamic sampling took place.

Dynamic sampling may be used by the optimizer for various purposes:

- If there are no object statistics available, it may be used to provide the number of table blocks for the cost calculation, which obviously are taken from the segment size information. Note that in this case, any existing index leaf block statistics of indexes on the table will also be replaced by the corresponding index segment block statistic for this optimization (not persistent for later SQL statement optimizations).

- Additionally, dynamic sampling may be used for both selectivity and cardinality estimates as well as basic column-level statistics, in particular the number of distinct values (NDV) and the number of NULLs in case a column of the table is used as a join predicate. These basic column statistics are crucial for the join selectivity and cardinality calculations and therefore help the optimizer to come up with reasonable join-related estimates. Note that at present (up to version 11.2.0.1), only a single join predicate gets its basic column statistics estimated. Any further columns of a multicolumn join won't be estimated and therefore will use default column statistics for the join selectivity and cardinality estimates. This means that correlated columns used for joins cannot be detected by dynamic sampling. In order to address this potential issue, see the "Performance Optimization Issues" section in Chapter 10.

- If the table has statistics, then usually only the selectivity estimate obtained via dynamic sampling will be used (and only if a filter predicate has been supplied—otherwise, no dynamic sampling will take place in this case). The cardinality will be obtained from the existing statistics.

- If the table does not have any statistics, the cardinality from the dynamic sampling will be used, and dynamic sampling will be performed even without a filter predicate supplied. To force the optimizer to use the cardinality and table (and implicitly index) blocks estimate obtained from dynamic sampling even if the table has statistics, use the hint DYNAMIC_SAMPLING_EST_CDN (table_or_alias_name). See the following 10053 trace excerpts for the different usages of dynamic sampling:

```
Table Blocks:
Number of blocks:
** Dynamic sampling updated table stats.: blocks=12

Additional evaluation of a suitable index (index matches single table access predicates):
** Dynamic sampling index access candidate : IDX_OPT_10053_TRACE2

Basic Column Statistics:
    ndv C3 : 50
        scaled : 50.00
    nulls C4 : 0
        scaled : 0.00
    min. sel. est. : 0.00010000
** Dynamic sampling col. stats.:
  Column (#1): ID(NUMBER)  Part#: 0
    AvgLen: 22.00 NDV: 50 Nulls: 0 Density: 0.02
```

```
** Using dynamic sampling NULLs estimates.
** Using dynamic sampling NDV estimates.
   Scaled NDVs using cardinality = 50.

Table Cardinality:
Cardinality estimate:
** Using dynamic sampling card. : 1000

Table Selectivity:
Selectivity estimate:
** Using single table dynamic sel. est. : 0.00600000

Index Selectivity:
     index IDX_OPT_10053_TRACE2 selectivity est.: 0.10000000
```

Single Table Access Path

In the Single Table Access Path section of a 10053 trace file, the optimizer calculates the cardinality estimates (expected number of rows) for each table involved in the query block, and the best access path to acquire the rows with the assumption that only constant filter predicates will be used and all join conditions will be ignored. The cardinality estimates are required for the different join orders tried, because any of the tables might be selected as the initial table of a join, or a join method may be selected that does not apply any join conditions while acquiring the rows from the tables as is the case with sort/merge and hash joins.

Starting with release 10.2, the cost of acquiring the estimated number of rows will be displayed with statistics for both the I/O cost and CPU cost; previous releases display the final combined I/O and CPU cost only when system statistics are enabled. The following shows the Single Table Access Path section of a 10053 trace file:

```
SINGLE TABLE ACCESS PATH
  Single Table Cardinality Estimation for XYZ[XYZ]

  Table: XYZ  Alias: XYZ
    Card:Original:10000.000000  Rounded:421  Computed:421.05  Non Adjusted:421.05
  Access Path: TableScan
    Cost:  33.89  Resp: 33.89  Degree: 0
      Cost_io: 33.00  Cost_cpu: 5273886
      Resp_io: 33.00  Resp_cpu: 5273886
  Best:: AccessPath: TableScan
        Cost: 33.89  Degree: 1  Resp: 33.89  Card: 421.05  Bytes: 0
```

This section is extremely helpful with pinpointing wrong cardinality and/or cost estimate problems. Parallel execution calculated costs are also displayed in this section of 10053 trace files. Remember, however, that the cardinality estimates in this section consider each table individually and do not take into account any join conditions, so the resulting cardinality estimates when performing the join operations might be totally different.

General Plans

The General Plans section of a 10053 trace file covers all of the different join orders attempted with the various tables and intermediate result sets. Note that Oracle will join only one other table or intermediate result set at a time to an existing table or result set. Three join methods are available to the optimizer: nested loop, sort/merge, and hash join. One particularly interesting piece of information output in this section of a 10053 trace is the join cardinality and selectivity calculations, which are reported as part of the NL Join (nested loop join method) calculations. The join cardinality and selectivity calculations are an important component of a 10053 trace file, which likely explains why the NL Join calculations are always included in a 10053 trace file, even when a specific join type is specified by using a USE_MERGE or USE_HASH hint. The following output shows the nested loop join cost calculations for full table scan access paths as well as index access paths:

```
NL Join
  Outer table: Card: 10.00  Cost: 22022.71  Resp: 22022.71  Degree: 1  Bytes: 4
  Inner table: JOIN_TABLE  Alias: B
  Access Path: TableScan
    NL Join:  Cost: 2224681.61  Resp: 2224681.61  Degree: 0
      Cost_io: 2209379.00  Cost_cpu: 89056581507
      Resp_io: 2209379.00  Resp_cpu: 89056581507
  Access Path: index (UniqueScan)
    Index: JOIN_TABLE_PK
    resc_io: 3.00  resc_cpu: 23434
    ix_sel: 1.0000e-007  ix_sel_with_filters: 1.0000e-007
    NL Join: Cost: 22052.75  Resp: 22052.75  Degree: 1
      Cost_io: 21908.00  Cost_cpu: 842415850
      Resp_io: 21908.00  Resp_cpu: 842415850
  Access Path: index (AllEqUnique)
    Index: JOIN_TABLE_PK
    resc_io: 3.00  resc_cpu: 23434
    ix_sel: 1.0000e-007  ix_sel_with_filters: 1.0000e-007
    NL Join: Cost: 22052.75  Resp: 22052.75  Degree: 1
      Cost_io: 21908.00  Cost_cpu: 842415850
      Resp_io: 21908.00  Resp_cpu: 842415850
  Best NL cost: 22052.75
        resc: 22052.75 resc_io: 21908.00 resc_cpu: 842415850
        resp: 22052.75 resp_io: 21908.00 resp_cpu: 842415850
Join Card:  10.00 = outer (10.00) * inner (10000000.00) * sel (1.0000e-007)
Join Card - Rounded: 10 Computed: 10.00
```

It is important to understand that although the optimizer trace reveals a lot of information, it is never complete. The trace file does not reveal how the optimizer arrived at the join selectivity calculated, although Oracle 10.1 and above perform a sanity check for multicolumn join conditions that shows the calculation of the revised join selectivity. The following output shows the nested loop cost calculations from a 10053 trace in which a sanity check is applied to correct the selectivity calculation for a table named SALES_HASH:

```
NL Join
  Outer table: Card: 150.15  Cost: 2.02  Resp: 2.02  Degree: 1  Bytes: 13
  Inner table: PARTITION_TEST  Alias: A
  Access Path: TableScan
    NL Join:  Cost: 59.97  Resp: 59.97  Degree: 1
```

```
     Cost_io: 56.67  Cost_cpu: 16175534
      Resp_io: 56.67  Resp_cpu: 16175534
  Best NL cost: 59.97
          resc: 59.97 resc_io: 56.67 resc_cpu: 16175534
          resp: 59.97 resp_io: 56.67 resp_cpu: 16175534
Using multi-column join key sanity check for table SALES_HASH
Revised join sel:1.0000e-003 = 6.6225e-006 * (1/1000.00) * (1/6.6225e-006)
Join Card:   151.65 = outer (150.15) * inner (1010.00) * sel (1.0000e-003)
Join Card - Rounded: 152 Computed: 151.65
```

Plan Table

Starting with release 10.2, the 10053 optimizer trace file contains a final Plan Table section that includes the resulting execution plan including the predicates applied, with a display format that is very close to that provided by the DBMS_XPLAN.DISPLAY functions with TYPICAL as the format parameter. Prior to release 10.2, when the execution plan was included in optimizer trace files, it would not appear in the now-standard, highly formatted DBMS_XPLAN format, but instead as a rough plan outline.

Starting with release 10.2, the optimizer trace file also includes the contents of the OTHER_XML column, which contains other information that is potentially very helpful (this column is found in V$SQL_PLAN and the conventional PLAN_TABLE). This XML information covers various details about the execution plan, including the following:

- The database version that parsed the statement
- The parsing schema
- Dynamic sampling usage
- The PLAN_HASH_VALUE
- The peeked bind values used to optimize the statement (which basically echoes the peeked binds shown in the Peeked Bind Variables section of the trace file). Note that bind values of the NCHAR or NVARCHAR datatype will be shown here but not in the Peeked Binds section at the beginning of the trace file. Bind values of the TIMESTAMP datatype will not be shown here either.
- The complete set of hints that may be used to force this execution plan using outlines or SQL profiles.

Note that the latter two sets of information may also be obtained by using the DBMS_XPLAN.DISPLAY_CURSOR function, supplying the (undocumented) format options PEEKED_BINDS and OUTLINE. For example:

```
============
Plan Table
============
-------------------------------------------------+-----------------------------------------+
| Id | Operation        | Name              | Rows | Bytes | Cost | Time     |
-------------------------------------------------+-----------------------------------------+
| 0  | SELECT STATEMENT |                   |      |       |   2  |          |
| 1  |  TABLE ACCESS FULL | TEST_BIND_EXPL_DYN|   1 |  128  |   2  | 00:00:01 |
-------------------------------------------------+-----------------------------------------+
```

```
Predicate Information:
----------------------
1 - filter("OBJECT_ID"=:B1)

Content of other_xml column
===========================
  db_version    : 10.2.0.4
  parse_schema  : CBO_TEST
  dynamic_sampling: yes
  plan_hash     : 2114186118
Peeked Binds
============
  Bind variable information
    position=1
    datatype(code)=2
    datatype(string)=NUMBER
    precision=0
    scale=0
    max length=22
    value=5
  Outline Data:
  /*+
    BEGIN_OUTLINE_DATA
      IGNORE_OPTIM_EMBEDDED_HINTS
      OPTIMIZER_FEATURES_ENABLE('10.2.0.4')
      OPT_PARAM('query_rewrite_enabled' 'false')
      ALL_ROWS
      OUTLINE_LEAF(@"SEL$1")
      FULL(@"SEL$1" "TEST_BIND_EXPL_DYN"@"SEL$1")
    END_OUTLINE_DATA
  */
```

Query Block Registry

This section of the 10053 trace file, available starting with release 10.2, is included at the end of the trace file and shows the different query blocks that have been identified and how these potentially have been transformed. This means that some of the initial query blocks might have been replaced by others, or have been merged into a new query block. The following is an example of two initial query blocks (PARSER) that have been merged into a new one by a view merge transformation (FINAL).

```
Query Block Registry:
*********************
SEL$1 0x1af166e0 (PARSER)
  SEL$4A78348A 0x1af166e0 (VIEW MERGE SEL$1; SEL$E112F6F0) [FINAL]
SEL$E112F6F0 0x1af0ca2c (PARSER)
  SEL$4A78348A 0x1af166e0 (VIEW MERGE SEL$1; SEL$E112F6F0) [FINAL]
```

The Query Block Registry section may omit some of the query blocks when a complex SQL statement is optimized. The trace file will indicate the omission of query blocks with the inclusion of ... at the end of the Query Block Registry section.

Hints

If a SQL statement included any hints, the 10053 optimizer trace file will contain a section called Dumping Hints that lists all hints in their "parsed" form and some further attributes. Note that although hints might be invalid or malformed (for instance, because of a nonexisting alias or a simple typo), those hints will be displayed in this section without an error indicator (err=0 might be displayed even when the hint is invalid). The used indicator might be more helpful because invalid or malformed hints that could not be applied will show up identified with used=0. Here is an example of that section:

```
Dumping Hints
=============
  atom_hint=(@=21A2A390 err=0 resol=1 used=0 token=1018 org=1 lvl=3
             txt=OPT_ESTIMATE (TABLE "A" SCALE_ROWS=0.000010 ) )
  atom_hint=(@=21A2EC38 err=0 resol=1 used=1 token=1018 org=1 lvl=3
             txt=OPT_ESTIMATE (TABLE "A" SCALE_ROWS=0.000010 ) )
```

Note that the DYNAMIC_SAMPLING hint in releases 10.2, 11.1, and 11.2 seems to cause the following output, even when the hint is correctly specified and used. This appears to be more of an odd behavior than a feature:

```
Dumping Hints
=============
  atom_hint=(@=1C387418 err=5 resol=1 used=1 token=832 org=1 lvl=2
             txt=DYNAMIC_SAMPLING ())
********** WARNING: SOME HINTS HAVE ERRORS *********
```

Note that the warning message indicates that some hints had errors. In this particular case, the trace file incorrectly reported the previous hint error when the DYNAMIC_SAMPLING hint was correctly specified in the SQL statement and was implemented by the optimizer during query optimization.

The Query

Of course, the most crucial information should also be contained in the 10053 trace file: the actual query text that was optimized. Depending on the release version of Oracle, the actual query text is displayed at the beginning of the trace file, or at the bottom, or in both locations (starting with release 10.2). Here is an example of how a query's text appears in the trace file:

```
******* UNPARSED QUERY IS *******
SELECT "A"."X_PKEY" "X_PKEY","A"."X_SLICE" "X_SLICE","A"."DATA1" "DATA1",
       "B"."INVOICE_NO" "INVOICE_NO","B"."SALE_YEAR" "SALE_YEAR",
       "B"."SALE_MONTH" "SALE_MONTH","B"."SALE_DAY" "SALE_DAY",
       VALUE(KOKBF$) "PLAN_TABLE_OUTPUT"
 FROM "CBO_TEST"."PARTITION_TEST" "A","CBO_TEST"."SALES_HASH" "B",
      TABLE("SYS"."DBMS_XPLAN"."DISPLAY"()) "KOKBF$"
 WHERE "A"."DATA1"="B"."SALE_DAY" AND "A"."X_PKEY"="B"."INVOICE_NO"
   AND "A"."X_PKEY">=0 AND "A"."X_PKEY"<=150 AND "B"."INVOICE_NO"<=150
   AND "B"."INVOICE_NO">=0 AND "A"."DATA1"=TO_NUMBER(VALUE(KOKBF$))
kkoqbc-subheap (delete addr=08E7C590, in-use=31536, alloc=0)
kkoqbc-end
          : call(in-use=48104, alloc=0), compile(in-use=44600, alloc=0)
```

```
apadrv-end: call(in-use=48104, alloc=0), compile(in-use=45244, alloc=0)

sql_id=332wa51fnz145.
Current SQL statement for this session:
explain plan for select * from partition_test a, sales_hash b,
                               table(dbms_xplan.display) c
where a.x_pkey = b.invoice_no
and a.x_pkey >= 0 and a.x_pkey <= 150
and a.data1 = b.sale_day
and to_number(c.plan_table_output) = a.data1
```

Generating 10046 Extended Traces

Extended 10046 SQL traces, enabled by setting event 10046, or through the use of procedures in the packages DBMS_SUPPORT, DBMS_MONITOR, DBMS_SYSTEM, or SQL*Plus's ORADEBUG, provide a wealth of performance information specific to an individual session. 10046 extended traces may be enabled at level 4 (bind variables), 8 (wait events), or 12 (bind variables and wait events). Such trace files help determine CPU consumption, recursive SQL statement executions (those SQL statements executed by triggers, PL/SQL functions, the cost-based optimizer, and for purposes of space management), reasons for delays other than CPU consumption, actual execution plans, bind variables submitted to SQL statements, and as a method of mapping the progressive execution of application processes to a timeline.

The level of detail provided in 10046 extended trace files varies by Oracle database release, with more-recent releases providing significantly enhanced output. The resulting trace file located in the udump directory on the server (trace directory starting with release 11.1) may be analyzed with tkprof (see Metalink Doc ID 41634.1), TRCANLZR (see Metalink Doc ID 224270.1), TVD$XTAT (see *Troubleshooting Oracle Performance* by Christian Antognini, Apress, 2008), ESQLTRCPROF (see *Secrets of the Oracle Database* by Norbert Debes, Apress, 2009), the Hotsos Profiler (Method R), OraSRP (www.oracledba.ru/orasrp/), one of several other 10046 extended trace file analyzers, or by manually reviewing the contents of the files. Providing tkprof with an insert=statfile.sql parameter causes tkprof to generate a file named statfile.sql that includes generated insert statements, allowing the permanent storage of the tkprof output in the database. Providing tkprof with a record=sqlfile.txt parameter causes tkprof to record all user-executed SQL statements (dep=0) found in the 10046 trace file to a log file name sqlfile.txt.

When the SESSION_CACHED_CURSORS parameter is set to a value greater than 0, the STAT lines for a SQL statement may not be written to the trace file starting with the fourth execution of the SQL statement by the session. After the third execution of the same SQL statement, Oracle will hold the cursor open in the cached cursors for the session. Setting the SESSION_CACHED_CURSORS parameter to 0 at the session level eliminates this problem at the expense of additional resource consumption due to soft parses when the session repeatedly executes the same SQL statement without holding the cursor open in the application code.

Prior to the introduction of a new default setting in Oracle 11.1 (FIRST_EXECUTION, which is discussed later in this chapter), STAT lines were written to trace files only when cursors closed, which might necessitate the closing of the application, or execution of another simple SQL statement, such as SELECT SYSDATE FROM DUAL, before attempting to disable an extended 10046 trace for the session.

Brief Summary of a Raw 10046 Extended Trace File's Contents

Oracle's 10046 extended trace files contain a large number of keywords that help determine what operations a session is performing, and the delays present while performing those operations. The following are many of the useful keywords found in 10046 extended trace files:

len: Number of characters in the SQL statement.

dep: Indicates the application/trigger depth at which the SQL statement was executed. dep=0 indicates that it was executed by the client application. dep=1 indicates that the SQL statement was executed by a trigger, the Oracle optimizer, or a space management call. dep=2 usually indicates that the SQL statement was called from a trigger but also may appear in situations where a hard parse is required during space management activities. dep=3 usually indicates that the SQL statement was called from a trigger that was called from a trigger. (Hard parses during space management activities or hard parses of SQL statements in triggers could also generate dep=3 calls.)

oct: Identifies the Oracle command type, which is related to the V$SESSION.COMMAND column and the V$SQL.COMMAND_TYPE column. Common command type values include: 1 = create table, 2 = insert, 3 = select, 6 = update, 7 = delete, and 9 = create index. See the "Command Column of V$SESSION and Corresponding Commands" table in the Oracle Reference documentation (Table 8-2 in the *Oracle Database Reference 11g Release 2* book) for a complete list of command types.

hv: Identifies the SQL hash value of the SQL statement in the various SQL-related views (VSQL, VSQL_PLAN, V$SQL_PLAN_STATISTICS, V$SQL_OPTIMIZER_ENV, V$SQL_SHARED_CURSOR, and so forth). Use with the SQL address found in the ad= statistic.

ad: Identifies the SQL address of the SQL statement in the various SQL-related views. Use with the SQL hash value found in the hv= statistic or the sqlid.

sqlid: Output in Oracle 11.1 and above trace files that identifies the SQL_ID found in various views in Oracle 10.1 and above.

tim: Timestamp measured in 1/1,000,000 of a second (some Unix platforms cheat through a bit-shifting function, where the divisor is actually 2^{20}, or 1,048,576). The tim statistic may be used to track the progress in the 10046 trace file by taking the delta value of the most recent tim, subtracting the first tim, and dividing the result by 1,000,000 to arrive at the number of seconds into the trace file. Some platforms, such as Oracle 10.2 on Windows, use a 32-bit value (even on 64-bit Windows) for the tim statistic, which causes the statistic to wrap around zero roughly once every 71 minutes and 35 seconds.

c: CPU time. The amount of CPU resources required at that point in the execution. On 8.1.7.4 and earlier releases, divide by 100 to obtain the number of seconds. For releases after 8.1.7.4, divide by 1,000,000 to obtain the number of seconds.

e: Elapsed time. The number of seconds as measured by a high-precision clock at that point in the execution. This may be significantly different from CPU seconds. On 8.1.7.4 and earlier releases, divide by 100 to obtain the number of seconds. For releases after 8.1.7.4, divide by 1,000,000 to obtain the number of seconds.

p: Physical blocks read from disk, which may be read one block at a time or as part of a multiblock read.

cr: Consistent reads of blocks, possibly requiring the application of undo blocks so that a block may be rolled back to a specific SCN number (the specific SCN is partially based on the isolation level set for the session). The cr statistic in a trace file relates to the consistent gets statistic in V$SYSSTAT and V$SESSTAT.

cu: Current mode reads of blocks, which contain committed and uncommitted data. Blocks of this type are often required as block contents are modified through inserts, updates, and deletes. The cu statistic in a trace file relates to the db block gets statistic in V$SYSSTAT and V$SESSTAT.

mis: Number of library cache misses at that stage of execution for the SQL statement. When a 10046 trace is first enabled for a session, previously hard-parsed SQL statements may need to be reparsed on the next access, which may then provide misleading information about the frequency of hard parses within the session.

r: Number of rows returned by the call.

og: Optimizer goal—1 = ALL_ROWS, 2 = FIRST_ROWS (and FIRST_ROWS_n), 3 = RULE, 4 = CHOOSE.

XCTEND rlbk=0: Indicates that the client issued a COMMIT, and if this is followed by rd_only=1, it indicates that no information changed in the database as a result of the COMMIT. rlbk=1 indicates that the session performed a ROLLBACK, rather than a COMMIT.

ela: Elapsed time in 1/100 of a second for releases 8.1.7.4 and earlier, and in 1/1,000,000 of a second for releases after 8.1.7.4.

p1: The meaning of this statistic depends on the wait event; see V$EVENT_NAME.PARAMETER1. On Oracle 10.1 and above, the actual meaning of the p1 parameter from V$EVENT_NAME.PARAMETER1 appears in the trace file, rather than the identifier p1.

p2: The meaning of this statistic depends on the wait event; see V$EVENT_NAME.PARAMETER2. On Oracle 10.1 and above, the actual meaning of the p2 parameter from V$EVENT_NAME.PARAMETER2 appears in the trace file, rather than the identifier p2.

p3: The meaning of this statistic depends on the wait event; see V$EVENT_NAME.PARAMETER3. On Oracle 10.1 and above, the actual meaning of the p3 parameter from V$EVENT_NAME.PARAMETER3 appears in the trace file, rather than the identifier p3.

STAT lines: The row source execution plan.

1. id: Line identifier in the execution plan, used to identify child operations.

2. cnt: Number of rows returned or processed.

3. pid: Parent operation line identifier, used to determine indentation of the plan based on the indentation of the parent operation line identifier.

4. obj: Object ID of the object referenced at the stage of the plan. When the object name does not appear on a STAT line (or on a WAIT line), query DBA_OBJECTS for a matching value in the OBJECT_ID column to locate the owner, object name, and object type (and in some cases the subobject name).

See *Optimizing Oracle Performance* or Metalink Doc ID 39817.1 for descriptions of additional keywords found in 10046 extended trace files.

Enabling a 10046 Extended Trace

The 10046 extended traces may be enabled in several ways for sessions, depending on the following: the Oracle database release, whether application source code may be modified, and the point at which tracing must be initiated.

Logon Trigger That Enables 10046 Tracing on Logon for a Program

A logon trigger may be created to permit starting a 10046 extended trace for a session connecting from a specific application, as shown in the following code sample. Such a trigger may help when troubleshooting situations in which an entire execution of an application must be captured. This situation might arise when troubleshooting the execution of an automated process, or when it is suspected that session-level optimizer parameters are modified at logon, or when a subset of the users experience problems with an application while other users do not, and so forth. Logon triggers must be created when connected as the SYS user or a user with the ADMINISTER DATABASE TRIGGER system privilege.

```
CREATE OR REPLACE TRIGGER LOGON_CAPTURE_10046 AFTER LOGON ON DATABASE
DECLARE
  SHOULD_EXECUTE INTEGER;
  TRACEFILE VARCHAR2(150);
BEGIN
  SELECT DECODE(SUBSTR(UPPER(PROGRAM),1,5),'MYAPP',1,0) INTO SHOULD_EXECUTE
    FROM V$SESSION WHERE SID=(SELECT SID FROM V$MYSTAT WHERE ROWNUM=1);
  IF SHOULD_EXECUTE > 0 THEN
    TRACEFILE := 'ALTER SESSION SET TRACEFILE_IDENTIFIER =
      '''||USER||TO_CHAR(SYSDATE,'YYMMDDHH24MI')||'''';
    EXECUTE IMMEDIATE TRACEFILE;
    EXECUTE IMMEDIATE 'ALTER SESSION SET MAX_DUMP_FILE_SIZE=UNLIMITED';
    EXECUTE IMMEDIATE 'ALTER SESSION SET TIMED_STATISTICS=TRUE';
```

```
    EXECUTE IMMEDIATE 'ALTER SESSION SET EVENTS ''10046 TRACE NAME CONTEXT FOREVER,
        LEVEL 12''';
  END IF;
END;
/
```

The preceding logon trigger will do the following:

- Enable a 10046 trace at level 12 for a session in which the first five characters of the PROGRAM column for the session are MYAPP.

- Use the DECODE syntax, allowing for a simple modification to permit extending the trigger to enable a 10046 trace when sessions are created from several different programs.

- Assign a portion of the trace filename as the username and current date/time.

- Permit the trace file to grow without limit.

- Enable timed statistics so that timing information will be included in wait events and execution plans. Setting the TIMED_STATISTICS parameter to TRUE is critical for many performance-monitoring activities.

Enabling 10046 Tracing—Application Source Code May Be Modified

When it is possible to modify an application's source code, a SQL statement like one of the following two statements may be added to the source code to enable a 10046 trace for a specific section of code. The second method actually executes a PL/SQL procedure, so the custom code that must be added to the application source code may be more involved than that required for the first method. These statements may also be executed at the SQL*Plus command prompt to enable a 10046 trace for a set of SQL statements.

```
SQL> ALTER SESSION SET EVENTS '10046 TRACE NAME CONTEXT FOREVER, LEVEL 12';
  -or-
SQL> EXEC DBMS_SESSION.SESSION_TRACE_ENABLE(WAITS=>TRUE,BINDS=>TRUE)
```

Oracle 11.1 and later support a third parameter for DBMS_SESSION.SESSION_TRACE_ENABLE that controls when the STAT (row source execution plan) lines are written to the trace file. The default value for the new parameter is NULL, which outputs the STAT lines after the first execution, rather than when the cursor is closed. The possible values for this third parameter include NEVER (do not write the STAT lines), FIRST_EXECUTION (write the STAT lines only after the first execution when the cursor is held open and repeatedly re-executed), and ALL_EXECUTIONS (write the STAT lines after each execution when the cursor is repeatedly re-executed, for instance, with different bind variable values). Setting the parameter to ALL_EXECUTIONS causes the STAT lines to be written to the trace file even when the SQL statement resides in the session's cursor cache. The 11g syntax to output the STAT lines after each execution follows:

```
SQL> EXEC DBMS_SESSION.SESSION_TRACE_ENABLE(WAITS=>TRUE,BINDS=>TRUE,
                                PLAN_STAT=>'ALL_EXECUTIONS')
```

The ALTER SESSION method for enabling a 10046 extended trace does not change the values shown in the SQL_TRACE, SQL_TRACE_WAITS, and SQL_TRACE_BINDS columns in V$SESSION, while DBMS_SESSION's SESSION_TRACE_ENABLE does change those columns to indicate the type of trace enabled for the session. Compare the query results with each other in the following example:

```
SQL> ALTER SESSION SET EVENTS '10046 TRACE NAME CONTEXT FOREVER, LEVEL 12';

SQL> SELECT
  2    SQL_TRACE, SQL_TRACE_WAITS, SQL_TRACE_BINDS
  3  FROM
  4    V$SESSION
  5  WHERE
  6    SID=(SELECT SID FROM V$MYSTAT WHERE ROWNUM=1);

SQL_TRACE SQL_TRACE_WAITS SQL_TRACE_BINDS
--------- --------------- ---------------
DISABLED  FALSE           FALSE


SQL> EXEC DBMS_SESSION.SESSION_TRACE_ENABLE(WAITS=>TRUE, BINDS=>TRUE)

SQL> SELECT
  2    SQL_TRACE, SQL_TRACE_WAITS, SQL_TRACE_BINDS
  3  FROM
  4    V$SESSION
  5  WHERE
  6    SID=(SELECT SID FROM V$MYSTAT WHERE ROWNUM=1);

SQL_TRACE SQL_TRACE_WAITS SQL_TRACE_BINDS
--------- --------------- ---------------
ENABLED   TRUE            TRUE
```

Enabling 10046 Tracing—Application Source Code Cannot Be Modified

To remotely enable a trace for another session, the SID and SERIAL# for the other session must be determined. The following SQL statement lists all user sessions by username, computer, and application program:

```
SQL> SELECT
  2    SID, SERIAL#, USERNAME, PROGRAM, MACHINE
  3  FROM
  4    V$SESSION
  5  WHERE
  6    USERNAME IS NOT NULL
  7  ORDER BY
  8    USERNAME, MACHINE, PROGRAM;
```

With the SID and SERIAL# from the output of the preceding SQL statement, enabling a 10046 trace may be accomplished by using one of several methods. Examples follow. Replace the SID and SERIAL# in the following commands with the SID and SERIAL# returned by the preceding SQL statement:

```
SQL> EXEC SYS.DBMS_SYSTEM.SET_EV(SID, SERIAL# ,10046 ,12, '')
  -or-
SQL> EXEC SYS.DBMS_SUPPORT.START_TRACE_IN_SESSION(SID, SERIAL#,
                                    WAITS=>TRUE, BINDS=>TRUE)
  -or-
SQL> EXEC DBMS_MONITOR.SESSION_TRACE_ENABLE(SESSION_ID=>SID,SERIAL_NUM=>SERIAL#,
                                    WAITS=>TRUE, BINDS=>TRUE)
  -or-
SQL> EXEC SYS.DBMS_SYSTEM.SET_SQL_TRACE_IN_SESSION(SID,SERIAL#,TRUE)
```

The SYS.DBMS_SYSTEM.SET_EV method is unsupported, but works fine with older releases of Oracle, where the other methods do not exist. DBMS_SUPPORT is a package that first appeared in Oracle 8.0.6 (the package may be installed in Oracle 7.2 or later) and typically must be manually installed by running the script dbmssupp.sql, found in the rdbms/admin directory of the Oracle home. DBMS_MONITOR is a package that first appeared in Oracle 10.1.

The trace files will be created in the directory indicated by the USER_DUMP_DEST initialization parameter (typically a directory named udump prior to Oracle 11.1, and a directory named trace starting with Oracle 11.1). Oracle 11.1 and later support a fifth parameter for the DBMS_MONITOR.START_TRACE_IN_SESSION procedure, which controls the frequency at which the STAT lines are output to the trace file. The possible parameter values are identical to those of the DBMS_SESSION.SESSION_TRACE_ENABLE procedure. An example of enabling a 10046 extended trace follows:

```
SQL> SELECT
  2    SID, SERIAL#, SQL_TRACE, SQL_TRACE_WAITS, SQL_TRACE_BINDS
  3  FROM
  4    V$SESSION
  5  WHERE
  6    SID=(SELECT SID FROM V$MYSTAT WHERE ROWNUM=1);

     SID    SERIAL# SQL_TRACE SQL_TRACE_WAITS SQL_TRACE_BINDS
---------- ---------- --------- --------------- ---------------
     170     46206 DISABLED  FALSE           FALSE


SQL> EXEC SYS.DBMS_SYSTEM.SET_EV(170, 46206, 10046, 12, '');

SQL> SELECT
  2    SID, SERIAL#, SQL_TRACE, SQL_TRACE_WAITS, SQL_TRACE_BINDS
  3  FROM
  4    V$SESSION
  5  WHERE
  6    SID=(SELECT SID FROM V$MYSTAT WHERE ROWNUM=1);

     SID    SERIAL# SQL_TRACE SQL_TRACE_WAITS SQL_TRACE_BINDS
---------- ---------- --------- --------------- ---------------
     170     46206 ENABLED   TRUE            TRUE
```

Disabling 10046 Tracing

The method used to disable the capturing of session activity to a trace file depends on the method used to enable the trace. The different methods follow:

```
SQL> ALTER SESSION SET EVENTS '10046 TRACE NAME CONTEXT OFF';
  -or-
SQL> EXEC DBMS_SESSION.SESSION_TRACE_DISABLE
  -or-
SQL> EXEC SYS.DBMS_SYSTEM.SET_EV(SID, SERIAL#, 10046, 0, '')
  -or-
SQL> EXEC SYS.DBMS_SUPPORT.STOP_TRACE_IN_SESSION(SID, SERIAL#)
  -or-
SQL> EXEC DBMS_MONITOR.SESSION_TRACE_DISABLE(SESSION_ID=>SID, SERIAL_NUM=>SERIAL#)
  -or-
SQL> EXEC SYS.DBMS_SYSTEM.SET_SQL_TRACE_IN_SESSION(SID, SERIAL#, FALSE)
```

Sample Trace File Analysis with Oracle 11.1.0.7

The following script creates two tables with 10,000 rows each and an index on one of the tables. Statistics are gathered for the tables and index, the buffer cache is flushed to force physical reads, the fetch array size is set to the SQL*Plus default of 15, and output of the rows returned by the SQL statements is disabled (to reduce client-side formatting and scrolling delays). Finally, two bind variables are defined, the SQL statement is executed, the second bind variable value is changed to the maximum value contained in column C1, the fetch array size is set to 100, and then the SQL statement is executed a second time.

```
SQL> CREATE TABLE T3 AS
  2  SELECT
  3    ROWNUM C1,
  4    LPAD('A',100,'A') C2
  5  FROM
  6    DUAL
  7  CONNECT BY
  8    LEVEL<=10000;

SQL> CREATE TABLE T4 AS
  2  SELECT
  3    ROWNUM C1,
  4    LPAD('A',100,'A') C2
  5  FROM
  6    DUAL
  7  CONNECT BY
  8    LEVEL<=10000;

SQL> CREATE INDEX IND_T4 ON T4(C1);

SQL> EXEC DBMS_STATS.GATHER_TABLE_STATS(OWNNAME=>USER,TABNAME=>'T3',CASCADE=>TRUE)
SQL> EXEC DBMS_STATS.GATHER_TABLE_STATS(OWNNAME=>USER,TABNAME=>'T4',CASCADE=>TRUE)
```

```
SQL> ALTER SYSTEM FLUSH BUFFER_CACHE;
SQL> ALTER SYSTEM FLUSH BUFFER_CACHE;
SQL> SET ARRAYSIZE 15
SQL> SET AUTOTRACE TRACEONLY STATISTICS

SQL> VARIABLE N1 NUMBER
SQL> VARIABLE N2 NUMBER

SQL> EXEC :N1 := 1
SQL> EXEC :N2 := 2

SQL> EXEC DBMS_SESSION.SESSION_TRACE_ENABLE(WAITS=>TRUE, BINDS=>TRUE,
                                     PLAN_STAT=>'ALL_EXECUTIONS')

SQL> SELECT
  2     T3.C1, T4.C2
  3  FROM
  4     T3, T4
  5  WHERE
  6     T3.C1 BETWEEN :N1 AND :N2
  7     AND T3.C1=T4.C1;

SQL> EXEC :N2 := 10000
SQL> SET ARRAYSIZE 100

SQL> SELECT
  2     T3.C1, T4.C2
  3  FROM
  4     T3, T4
  5  WHERE
  6     T3.C1 BETWEEN :N1 AND :N2
  7     AND T3.C1=T4.C1;

SQL> SELECT SYSDATE FROM DUAL;

SQL> EXEC DBMS_SESSION.SESSION_TRACE_DISABLE;
```

Passing the trace file through tkprof provides a quick analysis, but a lot of useful information is missing from the tkprof output, and in this case what is left is a little misleading. For example:

```
*****************************************************************************
SELECT
  T3.C1, T4.C2
FROM
  T3, T4
WHERE
  T3.C1 BETWEEN :N1 AND :N2
  AND T3.C1=T4.C1
```

call	count	cpu	elapsed	disk	query	current	rows
Parse	2	0.00	0.00	0	0	0	0
Execute	2	0.00	0.00	0	0	0	0
Fetch	103	0.00	0.09	312	579	0	10002
total	107	0.00	0.09	312	579	0	10002

```
Misses in library cache during parse: 0
Optimizer mode: ALL_ROWS
Parsing user id: 56

Rows    Row Source Operation
-------  -------------------------------------------------------
     2   FILTER  (cr=163 pr=158 pw=0 time=0 us)
     2    HASH JOIN  (cr=163 pr=158 pw=0 time=0 us cost=51 size=108 card=1)
     2     TABLE ACCESS FULL T3 (cr=158 pr=155 pw=0 time=0 us cost=47 size=8
                    card=2)
     2     TABLE ACCESS BY INDEX ROWID T4 (cr=5 pr=3 pw=0 time=0 us cost=3 size=208
                    card=2)
     2      INDEX RANGE SCAN IND_T4 (cr=3 pr=2 pw=0 time=0 us cost=2 size=0
                    card=2)(object id 66389)
```

```
Elapsed times include waiting on following events:
  Event waited on                         Times   Max. Wait  Total Waited
  ----------------------------------------  Waited  ----------  ------------
  SQL*Net message to client                 103       0.00        0.00
  db file sequential read                     5       0.01        0.01
  db file scattered read                     34       0.02        0.10
  SQL*Net message from client               103       0.00        0.03
****************************************************************************
```

The summary of the parses, executes, and fetches show that there were two parses and executes, with 103 fetches requiring 0.09 seconds to retrieve 10,002 rows. 312 blocks were read from disk, with 579 consistent block gets. In the preceding output, the Row Source Operation execution plan shows the details only for the first execution of the SQL statement, which is a potential problem highlighted by this example. With the first and second bind variables set to a small number, the use of the index range scan on the IND_T4 index is a good choice. However, when the second bind variable is set to the maximum value for column C1, a full table scan is more appropriate. Oracle 11.1 introduced a feature called *adaptive cursor sharing* that potentially alters the execution plan through the generation of additional child cursors when the re-execution of a cursor will potentially result in an inefficient execution plan. (This may not happen on the first execution with the changed bind variables.) Here is a shortened version of the raw 10046 extended trace:

```
=====================
PARSING IN CURSOR #2 len=87 dep=0 uid=56 oct=3 lid=56 tim=682839239833
                hv=2202874380 ad='2731260d0' sqlid='5f2624a1nuchc'
SELECT
  T3.C1, T4.C2
FROM
  T3, T4
```

```
WHERE
  T3.C1 BETWEEN :N1 AND :N2
  AND T3.C1=T4.C1
END OF STMT
PARSE #2:c=0,e=0,p=0,cr=0,cu=0,mis=0,r=0,dep=0,og=1,plh=487071653,tim=682839239833
BINDS #2:
 Bind#0
  oacdty=02 mxl=22(22) mxlc=00 mal=00 scl=00 pre=00
  oacflg=03 fl2=1000000 frm=00 csi=00 siz=48 off=0
  kxsbbbfp=1e6b6118  bln=22  avl=02  flg=05
  value=1
 Bind#1
  oacdty=02 mxl=22(22) mxlc=00 mal=00 scl=00 pre=00
  oacflg=03 fl2=1000000 frm=00 csi=00 siz=0 off=24
  kxsbbbfp=1e6b6130  bln=22  avl=02  flg=01
  value=2
```

Both bind variables passed in have oacdty specified as 02, indicating that the bind variables are in fact defined as numbers. The first bind variable has a value of 1, and the second has a value of 2. Following is a continuation of the 10046 extended trace file that includes the execution of the SQL statements and several wait events related to the execution of that SQL statement:

```
EXEC #2:c=0,e=0,p=0,cr=0,cu=0,mis=0,r=0,dep=0,og=1,plh=2205292220,tim=682839239833
WAIT #2: nam='SQL*Net message to client' ela= 2 driver id=1413697536 #bytes=1 p3=0
          obj#=12522 tim=682839244040
WAIT #2: nam='db file sequential read' ela= 11350 file#=7 block#=1347114 blocks=1
          obj#=66387 tim=682839255613
WAIT #2: nam='db file scattered read' ela= 9005 file#=7 block#=1347115 blocks=5
          obj#=66387 tim=682839264715
WAIT #2: nam='db file scattered read' ela= 1086 file#=7 block#=1347120 blocks=8
          obj#=66387 tim=682839266002
...
WAIT #2: nam='db file scattered read' ela= 1076 file#=7 block#=2171040 blocks=8
          obj#=66387 tim=682839306943
WAIT #2: nam='db file scattered read' ela= 10721 file#=7 block#=2031746 blocks=36
          obj#=66387 tim=682839317836
WAIT #2: nam='db file sequential read' ela= 5765 file#=7 block#=2031923 blocks=1
          obj#=66389 tim=682839323835
WAIT #2: nam='db file sequential read' ela= 358 file#=7 block#=2031924 blocks=1
          obj#=66389 tim=682839324247
WAIT #2: nam='db file sequential read' ela= 274 file#=7 block#=2171059 blocks=1
          obj#=66388 tim=682839324571
```

The preceding shows a series of wait events related to reading multiple blocks at a time (db file scattered read wait event) as well as reading individual blocks (db file sequential read wait event) for three objects (66387 is the table T3, 66389 is the index on table T4, and 66388 is the table T4). The db file scattered read wait events show a maximum of 8 blocks (64KB) being requested initially, and then the number of blocks read in a single request jumped to 36. The objects were created in an ASSM AUTOALLOCATE tablespace, where roughly the first 16 extents are created at 64KB and then the extent size increased to 1MB. The maximum number of blocks that may be read in a single multiblock read is limited by the extent size, intermediate blocks already residing in the buffer cache, the DB_FILE_MULTIBLOCK_READ_COUNT parameter, and the operating system.

There is a wide variation in the read times, with the first single-block read requiring 0.011 seconds (11ms), and the last requiring 0.000274 seconds (0.274ms). The first single-block read at 11ms is at the top end of what is considered a reasonable amount of time for a single-block read from a hard drive. The final single-block read, at 0.274ms, is quite likely an impossibly low time for a single-block read, which probably indicates that the requested block was already in the cache built into the drive, in the cache built into the RAID controller (or SAN), or in a cache provided by the operating system. (A 7,200 RPM drive rotates once every 8.3ms, while a 15,000 RPM drive rotates once every 4.0ms, so in theory this time might be possible if the hard drive head did not need to be repositioned over a different track and the two blocks were physically close on disk.) The final multiblock read of 36 blocks completed in slightly less time than the initial single-block read. The following is a continuation of the 10046 trace file that includes the fetch calls, wait events related to sending the query results to the client computer, and the row source execution plan for the SQL statement:

```
FETCH #2:c=0,e=59406,p=158,cr=161,cu=0,mis=0,r=1,dep=0,og=1,plh=2205292220,
        tim=682839299239
WAIT #2: nam='SQL*Net message from client' ela= 271 driver id=1413697536 #bytes=1
        p3=0 obj#=66388 tim=682839324942
WAIT #2: nam='SQL*Net message to client' ela= 3 driver id=1413697536 #bytes=1 p3=0
        obj#=66388 tim=682839324989
FETCH #2:c=0,e=0,p=0,cr=2,cu=0,mis=0,r=1,dep=0,og=1,plh=2205292220,tim=682839299239
STAT #2 id=1 cnt=2 pid=0 pos=1 obj=0 op='FILTER  (cr=163 pr=158 pw=0 time=0 us)'
STAT #2 id=2 cnt=2 pid=1 pos=1 obj=0 op='HASH JOIN  (cr=163 pr=158 pw=0
        time=0 us cost=51 size=108 card=1)'
STAT #2 id=3 cnt=2 pid=2 pos=1 obj=66387 op='TABLE ACCESS FULL T3 (cr=158 pr=155
        pw=0 time=0 us cost=47 size=8 card=2)'
STAT #2 id=4 cnt=2 pid=2 pos=2 obj=66388 op='TABLE ACCESS BY INDEX ROWID T4 (cr=5
        pr=3 pw=0 time=0 us cost=3 size=208 card=2)'
STAT #2 id=5 cnt=2 pid=4 pos=1 obj=66389 op='INDEX RANGE SCAN IND_T4 (cr=3 pr=2
        pw=0 time=0 us cost=2 size=0 card=2)'
WAIT #2: nam='SQL*Net message from client' ela= 474 driver id=1413697536 #bytes=1
        p3=0 obj#=66388 tim=682839325611
CLOSE #2:c=0,e=0,dep=0,type=0,tim=682839330481
```

SQL*Plus performed two fetches, each retrieving a single row, even though the fetch array size was specified as 15. This is a typical behavior of SQL*Plus during the initial fetch call regardless of the ARRAYSIZE setting. The plan showed that a full table scan was performed on the table T3 and an index range scan on table T4 using the index IND_T4. This matched the row source operation output produced by SQL*Plus. Starting with release Oracle 11.1, a line is output in the trace file to show that cursor 2 closed. The following is a continuation of the 10046 extended trace file, which shows the second execution of the SQL statement with the modified bind variable values:

```
=======================
PARSING IN CURSOR #2 len=87 dep=0 uid=56 oct=3 lid=56 tim=682839330481 hv=2202874380
        ad='2731260d0' sqlid='5f2624a1nuchc'
SELECT
  T3.C1, T4.C2
FROM
  T3, T4
WHERE
```

```
   T3.C1 BETWEEN :N1 AND :N2
   AND T3.C1=T4.C1
END OF STMT
PARSE #2:c=0,e=0,p=0,cr=0,cu=0,mis=0,r=0,dep=0,og=1,plh=487071653,tim=682839330481
BINDS #2:
 Bind#0
  oacdty=02 mxl=22(22) mxlc=00 mal=00 scl=00 pre=00
  oacflg=03 fl2=1000000 frm=00 csi=00 siz=48 off=0
  kxsbbbfp=1e6b5d00  bln=22  avl=02  flg=05
  value=1
 Bind#1
  oacdty=02 mxl=22(22) mxlc=00 mal=00 scl=00 pre=00
  oacflg=03 fl2=1000000 frm=00 csi=00 siz=0 off=24
  kxsbbbfp=1e6b5d18  bln=22  avl=02  flg=01
  value=10000
EXEC #2:c=0,e=0,p=0,cr=0,cu=0,mis=0,r=0,dep=0,og=1,plh=487071653,tim=682839330481
WAIT #2: nam='SQL*Net message to client' ela= 2 driver id=1413697536 #bytes=1 p3=0
         obj#=66388 tim=682839337060
WAIT #2: nam='db file sequential read' ela= 332 file#=7 block#=2171058 blocks=1
         obj#=66388 tim=682839340021
FETCH #2:c=0,e=0,p=1,cr=162,cu=0,mis=0,r=1,dep=0,og=1,plh=487071653,tim=682839330481
WAIT #2: nam='SQL*Net message from client' ela= 255 driver id=1413697536 #bytes=1
         p3=0 obj#=66388 tim=682839340738
WAIT #2: nam='SQL*Net message to client' ela= 2 driver id=1413697536 #bytes=1 p3=0
         obj#=66388 tim=682839340782
WAIT #2: nam='db file scattered read' ela= 1018 file#=7 block#=2171060 blocks=4
         obj#=66388 tim=682839341872
FETCH #2:c=0,e=0,p=4,cr=2,cu=0,mis=0,r=100,dep=0,og=1,plh=487071653,tim=682839330481
```

In the preceding output, the reading of obj #66388 (table T4) had to be broken into a read request for a single block, and a multiblock read of four blocks because block 2171059 was already in the buffer cache as a result of the previous execution of the SQL statement, and there were only four blocks remaining to be read in the 64KB extent. The first fetch retrieved a single row, while the second fetch obeyed the fetch array size, which was adjusted to 100 in the script. The following is a continuation of the 10046 extended trace file, which shows the final fetch call and the row source execution plan:

```
FETCH #2:c=0,e=0,p=0,cr=3,cu=0,mis=0,r=100,dep=0,og=1,plh=487071653,
         tim=682839424040
WAIT #2: nam='SQL*Net message from client' ela= 276 driver id=1413697536 #bytes=1
         p3=0 obj#=66388 tim=682839436092
WAIT #2: nam='SQL*Net message to client' ela= 2 driver id=1413697536 #bytes=1 p3=0
         obj#=66388 tim=682839436129
FETCH #2:c=0,e=0,p=0,cr=2,cu=0,mis=0,r=99,dep=0,og=1,plh=487071653,tim=682839424040
STAT #2 id=1 cnt=10000 pid=0 pos=1 obj=0 op='FILTER  (cr=416 pr=154 pw=0 time=0 us)'
STAT #2 id=2 cnt=10000 pid=1 pos=1 obj=0 op='HASH JOIN  (cr=416 pr=154 pw=0
         time=0 us cost=95 size=1080000 card=10000)'
STAT #2 id=3 cnt=10000 pid=2 pos=1 obj=66387 op='TABLE ACCESS FULL T3 (cr=158 pr=0
         pw=0 time=0 us cost=47 size=40000 card=10000)'
STAT #2 id=4 cnt=10000 pid=2 pos=2 obj=66388 op='TABLE ACCESS FULL T4 (cr=258
         pr=154 pw=0 time=0 us cost=47 size=1040000 card=10000)'
```

```
WAIT #2: nam='SQL*Net message from client' ela= 985 driver id=1413697536 #bytes=1
         p3=0 obj#=66388 tim=682839437395
CLOSE #2:c=0,e=0,dep=0,type=1,tim=682839424040

======================
```

The final fetch retrieved 99 rows as a result of the first fetch retrieving a single row. The STAT lines indicate that the plan for the second execution of the SQL statement used two full table scans, rather than a full table scan of the table T3 and an index range scan on table T4 using the index IND_T4, as indicated in the tkprof output. The views V$SQL_CS_STATISTICS, V$SQL_CS_SELECTIVITY, and V$SQL_CS_HISTOGRAM provide information related to adaptive cursor sharing. The sqlid from the parse calls in the trace file provides sufficient information for investigation of the child cursors. Output from two of those views for this SQL statement is as follows:

```
SQL> SELECT
  2    CHILD_NUMBER, EXECUTIONS, ROWS_PROCESSED, BUFFER_GETS, BIND_SET_HASH_VALUE
  3  FROM
  4    V$SQL_CS_STATISTICS
  5  WHERE
  6    SQL_ID='5f2624a1nuchc'
  7  ORDER BY
  8    CHILD_NUMBER;
```

CHILD_NUMBER	EXECUTIONS	ROWS_PROCESSED	BUFFER_GETS	BIND_SET_HASH_VALUE
0	1	24	163	2702357211
1	1	24	163	2702357211
2	1	100000	416	982654583

```
SQL> SELECT
  2    CHILD_NUMBER, PREDICATE, RANGE_ID, LOW, HIGH
  3  FROM
  4    V$SQL_CS_SELECTIVITY
  5  WHERE
  6    SQL_ID='5f2624a1nuchc'
  7  ORDER BY
  8    CHILD_NUMBER, PREDICATE DESC;
```

CHILD_NUMBER	PREDICATE	RANGE_ID	LOW	HIGH
1	>=N1	0	0.900000	1.100000
1	>=N1	0	0.900000	1.100000
1	<=N2	0	0.000180	0.000220
1	<=N2	0	0.000180	0.000220
2	>=N1	0	0.900000	1.100000
2	>=N1	0	0.900000	1.100000
2	<=N2	0	0.900000	1.100000
2	<=N2	0	0.900000	1.100000

The view V$SQL_CS_STATISTICS indicates the number of rows processed, as well as the number of consistent gets for the execution when the child execution plan was generated because of adaptive cursor sharing. The view V$SQL_CS_SELECTIVITY indicates the selectivity range of the supplied predicates (the bind variable values) that will help the optimizer determine the most appropriate execution plan during a future execution of the SQL statement with similar supplied bind variable values.

The AdaptiveCursorBindTest.sql script demonstrates adaptive cursor sharing in Oracle 11.1.0.6 and above by submitting roughly 10,000 different bind variable combinations for the preceding SQL statement, which used the tables T3 and T4. During testing with Oracle 11.1.0.7 and 11.2.0.1, 67 child cursors numbered 0 through 66 were created for the SQL statement, with all 67 of the child cursors remaining in the library cache after the script completed, but only three of the child cursors were identified with IS_SHAREABLE set to Y in the V$SQL view. During testing with Oracle 11.1.0.6, 2,385 child cursors numbered 0 through 1025 (CHILD_NUMBERs 63 and 300 through 332 each showed two entries in V$SQL during another test run when 1,057 child cursors remained in the library cache) were created for the SQL statement—but only seven of the child cursors were identified with IS_SHAREABLE set to Y in the V$SQL view. (Other test runs resulted in different child cursor counts, and typically one child cursor identified as shareable. The excessive child cursor count problem is a known bug that was corrected in Oracle 11.1.0.7.)

Examining Server Stack Traces

A variety of methods are available, partially dependent on the operating system, to see the current state of the database instance during performance-monitoring exercises when other methods fail to produce meaningful results. The methods include triggering trace file output on error, SQL*Plus's dumps generated by ORADEBUG (and ALTER SYSTEM/SESSION), and operating system utilities to capture the current execution stack for an Oracle process. Julian Dyke's website (www.juliandyke.com) documents most of the ALTER SYSTEM/SESSION commands and their equivalent ORADEBUG syntax used to write trace information. Tanel Poder's blog (blog.tanelpoder.com) documents operating system utilities that may be used to retrieve stack traces for Oracle processes.

Generating a Trace File on Error

When an error message is returned to the client application, it is not always possible to determine the exact cause of the error message. Oracle's ERRORSTACK level 3 trace dump and PROCESSSTATE trace dump output all open cursors for the session with bind variable values. Such traces are one of the few methods that allow another session's bind variable values to be viewed. Oracle 10.1 introduced a CURSORDUMP trace dump, which at level 4 outputs all of the SQL statements in the library cache to a trace file.

Oracle is able to automatically generate trace files when a particular error message, such as ORA-01722 Invalid Number, is returned to the client application. To enable this feature including the error stack (level 0), function call stack (level 1—the execution stack for the process), process state (level 2), and context area (level 3), execute the following in the session (note that 1722 refers to the ORA-01722 error):

```
SQL> ALTER SESSION SET EVENTS '1722 TRACE NAME ERRORSTACK LEVEL 3';
```

Exercise caution when generating ERRORSTACK traces for another session because the other session may be terminated by the instance after a couple minutes if the session is executing a long-running query. Should this happen, a message similar to the following may appear in the alert log:

```
Process 0x000000026C70CA10 appears to be hung while dumping
Current time = 5460109, process death time = 5398099 interval = 60000
Attempting to kill process 0x000000026C70CA10 with OS pid = 4808
OSD kill succeeded for process 000000026C70CA10
```

Initiating a Trace with SQL*Plus ORADEBUG

The SQL*Plus ORADEBUG command may be used by users with the SYSDBA role (such as the user SYS). The SQL*Plus ORADEBUG command must be attached to an Oracle process, either the process for the current SQL*Plus session, or another session's process to obtain information about the session's activity or the systemwide activity. The following SQL statement retrieves the PID and SPID values, either of which may be used to attach to another session's process:

```
SQL> SET PAGESIZE 1000
SQL> COLUMN USERNAME FORMAT A15
SQL> COLUMN PROGRAM FORMAT A20
SQL> COLUMN PID FORMAT 99990

SQL> SELECT
  2    P.PID, P.SPID, S.USERNAME, S.PROGRAM
  3  FROM
  4    V$PROCESS P, V$SESSION S
  5  WHERE
  6    P.ADDR=S.PADDR
  7  ORDER BY
  8    S.USERNAME, P.PROGRAM;

  PID SPID          USERNAME         PROGRAM
----- ------------  ---------------  ------------------
   14 3424          HOOPER           sqlplus.exe
   17 864           SYS              sqlplus.exe
   15 3536          SYSADM           Vm.exe
   10 4208                           ORACLE.EXE (CJQ0)
    7 1532                           ORACLE.EXE (CKPT)
...
```

To attach to the session for the username HOOPER, execute one of the following in SQL*Plus:

```
SQL> ORADEBUG SETORAPID 14
  -or-
SQL> ORADEBUG SETOSPID 3424
```

To attach to the session of the username SYS, the current session, execute the following in SQL*Plus:

```
SQL> ORADEBUG SETMYPID
```

When connected to an Oracle instance running on a Windows server, where there is a single Oracle process per database instance with multiple process threads, SQL*Plus will output the following when ORADEBUG SETOSPID 3424 is executed:

```
Oracle pid: 14, Windows thread id: 3424, image: ORACLE.EXE (SHAD)
```

The ORADEBUG SETORAPID 14 command executed in Oracle 11.2.0.1 running on Linux will output the following:

```
Oracle pid: 14, Unix process pid: 3424, image: oracle (TNS V1-V3)
```

A couple of other ORADEBUG commands are helpful when dumping information. The following sets an unlimited maximum trace file size for the attached process:

```
SQL> ORADEBUG UNLIMIT
```

The following closes the trace file for the attached process:

```
SQL> ORADEBUG CLOSE_TRACE
```

The following displays the trace filename for the attached process (the column TRACEFILE in the view V$PROCESS starting with Oracle 11.1 also shows the trace filename):

```
SQL> ORADEBUG TRACEFILE_NAME
```

To display a list of commands for ORADEBUG, use the following command:

```
SQL> ORADEBUG HELP
```

Listing Events Set in Another Session

In the SQL*Plus session for the username HOOPER (PID 14, SPID 3424), events 10053 (cost-based optimizer), 10046 (extended SQL trace), 10032 (sort statistics), and 10033 (sort intermediate run statistics) can be enabled via the following code:

```
SQL> ALTER SESSION SET EVENTS '10053 trace name context forever, level 1';
SQL> ALTER SESSION SET EVENTS '10046 trace name context forever, level 12';
SQL> ALTER SESSION SET EVENTS '10032 trace name context forever, level 1';
SQL> ALTER SESSION SET EVENTS '10033 trace name context forever, level 1';
```

In the session connected as the SYS user, attach to the process for the username HOOPER by using one of the following two methods (use the PID or SPID values returned by the query of V$PROCESS and V$SESSION):

```
SQL> ORADEBUG SETORAPID 14
  -or-
SQL> ORADEBUG SETOSPID 3424

Windows thread id: 3424, image: ORACLE.EXE (SHAD)
```

To write the events enabled for the other session to that session's trace file on Oracle 9.0.1 through 10.2.0.5, execute the following. (Note: A value of 1 following the keyword EVENTS indicates the session group's event settings should be written, 2 indicates the process group's event settings, and 4 indicates instance-wide events).

```
SQL> ORADEBUG DUMP EVENTS 1
```

The following information was written to the trace file for the other session:

```
Received ORADEBUG command 'DUMP EVENTS 1' from process Windows thread id: 864,
    image:
Dump event group for level SESSION
TC Addr Evt#(b10) Action    TR Addr    Arm     Life
F4FA338 10033       1        f4fa3c8 0 0
        TR Name              TR level   TR address      TR arm     TR life   TR type
        CONTEXT                         1 0          -1         2          0
F4F0EA0 10032       1        f288cd0 0 0
        TR Name              TR level   TR address      TR arm     TR life   TR type
        CONTEXT                         1 0          -1         2          0
F4F0D48 10046       1        f4f0dd8 0 0
        TR Name              TR level   TR address      TR arm     TR life   TR type
        CONTEXT                         12 0         -1         2          0
F4F0BF0 10053       1        f4f0c80 0 0
        TR Name              TR level   TR address      TR arm     TR life   TR type
        CONTEXT                         1 0          -1         2          0
```

The bold items in the preceding output indicate the trace file event and enabled level for the event. Oracle 11.1 and above do not support the EVENTS keyword. However, Oracle 10g and 11g support an equivalent syntax that outputs directly to the SQL*Plus window.

Issue the ORADEBUG EVENTDUMP command to dump output directly to your window. The session keyword is case sensitive, and the keywords process and system may also be used, which refer to the process group's event settings, and the instance-wide event settings, respectively. Here's an example:

```
SQL> ORADEBUG EVENTDUMP session
```

The output from Oracle 10.2.0.4 appears as follows:

```
10033 trace name CONTEXT level 1, forever
10053 trace name CONTEXT level 1, forever
10046 trace name CONTEXT level 12, forever
10032 trace name CONTEXT level 1, forever
```

The output from Oracle 11.2.0.1 and 11.1.0.7 appears as follows:

```
10033 trace name context forever, level 1
10032 trace name context forever, level 1
sql_trace level=12
trace [RDBMS.SQL_OPTIMIZER]
trace [RDBMS.SQL_Transform]
trace [RDBMS.SQL_MVRW]
trace [RDBMS.SQL_VMerge]
```

```
trace [RDBMS.SQL_Virtual]
trace [RDBMS.SQL_APA]
trace [RDBMS.SQL_Costing]
trace [RDBMS.SQL_Parallel_Optimization]
trace [RDBMS.SQL_Plan_Management]
```

Notice that the output from 11.2.0.1 and 11.1.0.7 show descriptive names rather than event numbers for the 10046 trace (sql_trace level=12) and the 10053 trace (trace [RDBMS.SQL_OPTIMIZER]).

HANGANALYZE Dump

HANGANALYZE dumps drill into the specific processes in the database instance that are blocked by another session (an enqueue-type wait, for instance), processes that are spinning because of a problem in the database instance (such as an internal deadlock on pins or latches), and other situations involving severe performance problems. A level 3 HANGANALYZE dump with a level 2 SYSTEMSTATE dump are typically sufficient for analysis. Unlike SYSTEMSTATE dumps, HANGANALYZE dumps use internal kernel calls to identify specific sessions of interest, identifying the waiting sessions and blocking sessions. See Metalink Doc ID 215858.1 "Interpreting HANGANALYZE Trace Files to Diagnose Hanging and Performance Problems" for additional detail about HANGANALYZE dumps.

A couple of sections from a level 3 HANGANALYZE dump follow:

```
SQL> ORADEBUG HANGANALYZE 3

Chains most likely to have caused the hang:
 [a] Chain 1 Signature: 'SQL*Net message from client'<=
                                              'enq: TX - row lock contention'
    Chain 1 Signature Hash: 0x38c48850
 [b] Chain 2 Signature: 'SQL*Net message from client'<=
                                              'enq: TX - row lock contention'
    Chain 2 Signature Hash: 0x38c48850
 [c] Chain 3 Signature: <not in a wait>
    Chain 3 Signature Hash: 0x673a0128


------------------------------------------------------------------------- Chain 1:
-------------------------------------------------------------------------
    Oracle session identified by:
    {
                instance: 1 (or112.or112)
                   os id: 7924
              process id: 28, oracle@airforce-5.test.org (TNS V1-V3)
              session id: 316
        session serial #: 167
    }
    is waiting for 'enq: TX - row lock contention' with wait info:
    {
                      p1: 'name|mode'=0x54580004
                      p2: 'usn<<16 | slot'=0x90000
                      p3: 'sequence'=0x831
            time in wait: 3 min 19 sec
           timeout after: never
```

```
              wait id: 25
             blocking: 0 sessions
          current sql: INSERT INTO T5 VALUES(20)
          short stack: ksedsts()+461<-ksdxfstk()+32<-ksdxcb()+1782<- ...
         wait history:
           * time between current wait and wait #1: 0.000397 sec
             1.      event: 'SQL*Net message from client'
                time waited: 6.521500 sec
                    wait id: 24             p1: 'driver id'=0x62657100
                                            p2: '#bytes'=0x1
           * time between wait #1 and #2: 0.000002 sec
             2.      event: 'SQL*Net message to client'
                time waited: 0.000001 sec
                    wait id: 23             p1: 'driver id'=0x62657100
                                            p2: '#bytes'=0x1
           * time between wait #2 and #3: 0.000032 sec
             3.      event: 'SQL*Net message from client'
                time waited: 0.000025 sec
                    wait id: 22             p1: 'driver id'=0x62657100
                                            p2: '#bytes'=0x1
     }
     and is blocked by
 => Oracle session identified by:
     {
                instance: 1 (or112.or112)
                  os id: 7854
              process id: 26, oracle@airforce-5.test.org (TNS V1-V3)
              session id: 159
         session serial #: 1033
     }
     which is waiting for 'SQL*Net message from client' with wait info:
     {
                       p1: 'driver id'=0x62657100
                       p2: '#bytes'=0x1
             time in wait: 4 min 4 sec
            timeout after: never
                  wait id: 51
                 blocking: 2 sessions
              current sql: <none>
              short stack: ksedsts()+461<-ksdxfstk()+32<-ksdxcb()+1782<- ...
             wait history:
               * time between current wait and wait #1: 0.000006 sec
                 1.      event: 'SQL*Net message to client'
                    time waited: 0.000002 sec
                        wait id: 50             p1: 'driver id'=0x62657100
                                                p2: '#bytes'=0x1
               * time between wait #1 and #2: 0.000154 sec
                 2.      event: 'db file sequential read'
                    time waited: 0.008198 sec
                        wait id: 49             p1: 'file#'=0x7
                                                p2: 'block#'=0x244238
```

```
                                                  p3: 'blocks'=0x1
             * time between wait #2 and #3: 0.000028 sec
             3.         event: 'db file sequential read'
                  time waited: 0.019260 sec
                       wait id: 48          p1: 'file#'=0x7
                                            p2: 'block#'=0x244239
                                            p3: 'blocks'=0x1
      }
      …
```

HEAPDUMP Dumps

HEAPDUMP dumps provide a method to determine the contents of various memory regions in the database instance including the SGA, PGA, large pool, Java pool, and so forth. The level specified for the HEAPDUMP determines which memory region is dumped and whether recursion is used to find the five largest subheaps. Adding 268435456 (10000000 in hexadecimal) to the level number causes Oracle to break out the five largest subheaps, while adding 536870912 (20000000 in hexadecimal) to the level number causes Oracle to break out the top five sub-subheaps of the top five subheaps. Requesting the top five break out eliminates some of the manual work that would have had to be performed during a problem analysis. HEAPDUMPs are helpful when troubleshooting ORA-4030 (PGA) and ORA-4031 (shared pool) errors.

■ **Note** In the HEAPDUMP output, Chunk identifies the memory address, sz= lists the memory size in bytes, the next column lists the type of memory chunk, and the final column lists the reason for allocation.

Java Pool Memory Allocation

The Java pool memory holds the shared portion of each Java class used per session, and in a shared server configuration the Java pool also maintains the Java state per session (a portion of the UGA). Exercise caution when writing the Java pool contents to a trace file because the shared pool latch is held while creating the dump file.

The following commands instruct SQL*Plus's ORADEBUG to connect to the process for the current session, remove the maximum trace file size limitation, specify a portion of the trace filename to help the DBA locate the trace file, write a description of the Java pool contents to the trace file, and then close the trace file. A portion of the trace file follows the commands:

```
SQL> ORADEBUG SETMYPID
SQL> ORADEBUG UNLIMIT
SQL> ALTER SESSION SET TRACEFILE_IDENTIFIER='JAVA_POOL';
SQL> ORADEBUG DUMP HEAPDUMP 128
SQL> ORADEBUG CLOSE_TRACE

HEAP DUMP heap name="java pool"  desc=0000000011891E10
  extent sz=0x1040 alt=216 het=32767 rec=9 flg=-126 opc=0
  parent=0000000000000000 owner=0000000000000000 nex=0000000000000000 xsz=0x0
```

```
      heap=0000000000000000
 fl2=0x20, nex=0000000000000000
 ds for latch 1:
 ds for latch 2:
 reserved granule count 1 (granule size 67108864)
RESERVED FXTENTS
  0x60000000
Counted elements on list: 1
```

Large Pool Memory Allocation

The large pool memory is used by parallel execution (parallel query) for parallel execution message buffers, Recovery Manager for disk I/O buffers when I/O slaves are used, shared server allocation of the User Global Area (UGA), and Oracle XA (X/Open Distributed Transaction Processing Architecture). The large pool does not maintain a least recently used list, and the instance does not attempt to age infrequently used objects out of the large pool. Exercise caution when writing the large pool contents to a trace file, because the shared pool latch is held while creating the dump file.

The following commands instruct ORADEBUG to connect to the process for the current session, remove the maximum trace file size limitation, specify a portion of the trace filename to help the DBA locate the trace file, write a description of the large pool contents to the trace file, and then close the trace file. A portion of the trace file follows:

```
SQL> ORADEBUG SETMYPID
SQL> ORADEBUG UNLIMIT
SQL> ALTER SESSION SET TRACEFILE_IDENTIFIER='LARGE_POOL';
SQL> ORADEBUG DUMP HEAPDUMP 32
SQL> ORADEBUG CLOSE_TRACE

HEAP DUMP heap name="large pool"  desc=0000000006F12550
 extent sz=0xfe0 alt=216 het=32767 rec=9 flg=-126 opc=0
 parent=0000000000000000 owner=0000000000000000 nex=0000000000000000 xsz=0x41ae0
         heap=0000000000000000
 fl2=0x20, nex=0000000000000000
 ds for latch 1:
 ds for latch 2: 0x117f15a0
 reserved granule count 0 (granule size 67108864)
 *****************************************************
HEAP DUMP heap name="large pool"  desc=00000000117F15A0
 extent sz=0xfe0 alt=216 het=32767 rec=9 flg=-126 opc=0
 parent=0000000000000000 owner=0000000000000000 nex=0000000000000000 xsz=0x4000000
         heap=0000000000000000
 fl2=0x20, nex=0000000000000000
 latch set 2 of 2
 durations disabled for this heap
 reserved granules for root 0 (granule size 67108864)
EXTENT 0 addr=00000000CC000000
  Chunk    0cc000058 sz= 66032680    free      "              "
  Chunk    0cfef9480 sz=   269024    freeable  "PX msg pool   "
  Chunk    0cff3af60 sz=   269024    freeable  "PX msg pool   "
  Chunk    0cff7ca40 sz=   269024    freeable  "PX msg pool   "
```

```
  Chunk        0cffbe520 sz=    269024    freeable  "PX msg pool      "
Total heap size    = 67108776
FREE LISTS:
 Bucket 0 size=8216
 Bucket 1 size=16408
 Bucket 2 size=32792
 Bucket 3 size=65560
 Bucket 4 size=131096
 Bucket 5 size=262168
 Bucket 6 size=524312
 Bucket 7 size=1048600
 Bucket 8 size=2097176
 Bucket 9 size=4194328
  Chunk        0cc000058 sz= 66032680     free       "                "
Total free space   = 66032680
UNPINNED RECREATABLE CHUNKS (lru first):
SEPARATOR
Unpinned space     =        0  rcr=0 trn=0
PERMANENT CHUNKS:
Permanent space    =        0
```

PGA and UGA Memory Allocation

PGA/UGA dumps are useful when troubleshooting ORA-4030 out of process memory when trying to allocate %s bytes errors that may be an indication of a PGA memory leak in a session causing the memory used by the process to continue increasing in size. Multiple HEAPDUMPs may be required when troubleshooting ORA-4030 errors.

The following commands instruct ORADEBUG to connect to the process for the current session, remove the maximum trace file size limitation, specify a portion of the trace filename to help the DBA locate the trace file, write a description of the PGA and UGA contents to the trace file, and then close the trace file. A portion of the trace file follows:

```
SQL> ORADEBUG SETMYPID
SQL> ORADEBUG UNLIMIT
SQL> ALTER SESSION SET TRACEFILE_IDENTIFIER='PGA_UGA';
SQL> ORADEBUG DUMP HEAPDUMP 5
SQL> ORADEBUG CLOSE_TRACE

HEAP DUMP heap name="session heap"  desc=000000001F675968
 extent sz=0xff80 alt=32767 het=32767 rec=0 flg=2 opc=3
 parent=000000001ABB1C90 owner=000000026CACD920 nex=0000000000000000 xsz=0x1e278
        heap=0000000000000000
 fl2=0x60, nex=0000000000000000
EXTENT 0 addr=0000000020530080
  Chunk        020530090 sz=     22088    free       "                "
  Chunk        0205356d8 sz=       432    freeable  "kqdAlloc        "
  Chunk        020535888 sz=      4160    freeable  "koh-kghu sessi  "
               ds=000000001CC0F660
  Chunk        0205368c8 sz=        72    free       "                "
  Chunk        020536910 sz=       416    freeable  "kgsc ht segs    "
```

```
   Chunk        020536ab0 sz=        832    freeable   "kxsc:kkspsc0-2 "
   Chunk        020536df0 sz=        432    freeable   "kqdAlloc       "
   Chunk        020536fa0 sz=        976    freeable   "kgsc:kxsc      "
   Chunk        020537370 sz=      35984    free       "               "
EXTENT 1 addr=000000001F150080
   Chunk        01f150090 sz=      60736    free       "               "
...

HEAP DUMP heap name="pga heap"  desc=000000001ABAC570
 extent sz=0x20c0 alt=184 het=32767 rec=0 flg=2 opc=2
 parent=0000000000000000 owner=0000000000000000 nex=0000000000000000 xsz=0x1fff0
         heap=0000000000000000
fl2=0x60, nex=0000000000000000
EXTENT 0 addr=000000001DC60010
   Chunk        01dc60020 sz=      32544    free       "               "
   Chunk        01dc67f40 sz=      32832    freeable   "kgh stack      "
   Chunk        01dc6ff80 sz=      65664    freeable   "XVMsubheap     "
                ds=000000001F53E550
EXTENT 1 addr=000000001DB60010
   Chunk        01db60020 sz=       1048    free       "               "
   Chunk        01db60438 sz=       4224    freeable   "Alloc environm "
                ds=000000001F4D3B10
...

HEAP DUMP heap name="top call heap"  desc=000000001ABB1A70
 extent sz=0x20c0 alt=200 het=32767 rec=0 flg=3 opc=3
 parent=0000000000000000 owner=0000000000000000 nex=0000000000000000 xsz=0xfff8
         heap=0000000000000000
 fl2=0x60, nex=0000000000000000
EXTENT 0 addr=000000001F130008
   Chunk        01f130018 sz=      65512    free       "               "
...

HEAP DUMP heap name="top uga heap"  desc=000000001ABB1C90
 extent sz=0xffc0 alt=200 het=32767 rec=0 flg=2 opc=3
 parent=0000000000000000 owner=0000000000000000 nex=0000000000000000 xsz=0x1fff8
         heap=0000000000000000
 fl2=0x60, nex=0000000000000000
EXTENT 0 addr=0000000020530008
   Chunk        020530018 sz=         80    free       "               "
   Chunk        020530068 sz=      65432    freeable   "session heap   "
                ds=000000001F675968
```

Shared Pool Memory Allocation

Generating traces showing shared pool memory allocation is not recommended during periods of heavy instance activity as the HEAPDUMP will hold the shared pool latches until the dump competes. Holding the shared pool latches for a long time will affect performance and may cause the instance to freeze if the shared pool is large. Tanel Poder's website offers a HEAPDUMP analyzer script that will help locate useful information found in such dumps (www.tanelpoder.com/files/scripts/heapdump_analyzer). Adding the number 536870912 to the normal level 2 for shared pool dumps causes the database instance to output the top five sub-subheaps.

The following commands instruct ORADEBUG to connect to the process for the current session, remove the maximum trace file size limitation, specify a portion of the trace filename to help the DBA locate the trace file, write a description of the shared pool contents identifying the top five sub-subheaps to the trace file, and then close the trace file. A portion of the trace file follows:

```
SQL> ORADEBUG SETMYPID
SQL> ORADEBUG UNLIMIT
SQL> ALTER SESSION SET TRACEFILE_IDENTIFIER='SGA_TOP_5';
SQL> ORADEBUG DUMP HEAPDUMP 536870914
SQL> ORADEBUG CLOSE_TRACE


KGH Latch Directory Information
ldir state: 2  last allocated slot: 114
Slot [  1] Latch: 0000000006F1C9F0  Index: 2  Flags:  3  State: 2
           next:  0000000000000000
Slot [  2] Latch: 000000026CD444B0  Index: 1  Flags:  3  State: 2
           next:  0000000000000000
Slot [  3] Latch: 000000026CD44590  Index: 2  Flags:  3  State: 2
           next:  0000000000000000
Slot [  4] Latch: 0000000006F1CDB0  Index: 1  Flags:  3  State: 2
           next:  0000000000000000
…
HEAP DUMP heap name="sga heap(1,0)"  desc=0000000011730A20
 extent sz=0xfe0 alt=216 het=32767 rec=9 flg=-126 opc=0
 parent=0000000000000000 owner=0000000000000000 nex=0000000000000000 xsz=0x4000000
         heap=0000000000000000
 fl2=0x20, nex=0000000000000000
 latch set 1 of 2
 durations enabled for this heap
 reserved granules for root 0 (granule size 67108864)
EXTENT 0 addr=0000000264000000
  Chunk        264000058 sz=        48  R-freeable  "reserved stoppe"
  Chunk        264000088 sz=  3358536  R-free      "              "
  Chunk        264333fd0 sz=        48  R-freeable  "reserved stoppe"
  Chunk        264334000 sz= 63750144    perm       "perm          "  alo=18851360
EXTENT 1 addr=0000000278000000
  Chunk        278000058 sz=        48  R-freeable  "reserved stoppe"
  Chunk        278000088 sz=  3358536  R-free      "              "
  Chunk        278333fd0 sz=        48  R-freeable  "reserved stoppe"
  Chunk        278334000 sz= 63741648    perm       "perm          "  alo=63741648
  Chunk        27bffded0 sz=      8496    free       "              "
Total heap size    =134217552
FREE LISTS:
 Bucket 0 size=32
 Bucket 1 size=40
 Bucket 2 size=48
…
UNPINNED RECREATABLE CHUNKS (lru first):
  Chunk        273faa8a0 sz=        56    recreate  "fixed allocatio"
               latch=0000000006F28C00
```

```
Chunk         273e75048 sz=       448    recreate  "KGL handles      "
              latch=0000000000000000
Chunk         0d7fffba8 sz=      1112    recreate  "PCursor          "
              latch=0000000000000000
Chunk         273f4ab00 sz=        88    recreate  "fixed allocatio"
              latch=0000000268FA9D18
Chunk         273e4cd58 sz=      1072    recreate  "KQR PO           "
              latch=0000000268FA9D18
Chunk         273e4c928 sz=      1072    recreate  "KQR PO           "
              latch=0000000268FA9D18
Chunk         273f4af40 sz=        56    recreate  "fixed allocatio"
              latch=0000000268FA9698
Chunk         273f4aef8 sz=        72    recreate  "fixed allocatio"
              latch=0000000006F270A0
Chunk         273e49a10 sz=        56    recreate  "fixed allocatio"
              latch=0000000268FA9018
...
Permanent space     =     38824
FIVE LARGEST SUB HEAPS for heap name="PLS SGA hp"    desc=0000000277FECBC0
*******************************************************
*******************************************************
*******************************************************

HEAP DUMP heap name="sga heap(2,2)"  desc=000000001173D2F8
 extent sz=0xfe0 alt=216 het=32767 rec=9 flg=-126 opc=0
 parent=0000000000000000 owner=0000000000000000 nex=0000000000000000 xsz=0x4000000
        heap=0000000000000000
 fl2=0x20, nex=0000000000000000
 latch set 2 of 2
 durations enabled for this heap
 reserved granules for root 0 (granule size 67108864)
EXTENT 0 addr=00000000D0000000
  Chunk         0d0000058 sz=        48 R-freeable  "reserved stoppe"
  Chunk         0d0000088 sz=   3358536 R-free       "                "
  Chunk         0d0333fd0 sz=        48 R-freeable  "reserved stoppe"
  Chunk         0d0334000 sz=  53898368 free         "                "
  Chunk         0d369ac80 sz=      4096 freeable    "Cursor Stats    "
              ds=00000002647E3150
...
Total heap size     = 67108776
FREE LISTS:
 Bucket 0 size=32
 Bucket 1 size=40
 Bucket 2 size=48
 Bucket 3 size=56
 Bucket 4 size=64
...
FIVE LARGEST SUB HEAPS for heap name="Cursor Stats"    desc=00000002647E3150
*******************************************************
SUBHEAP 2: desc=00000002647E2FB0
*******************************************************
HEAP DUMP heap name="Cursor Stats"  desc=00000002647E2FB0
```

```
extent sz=0xfe8 alt=32767 het=32767 rec=9 flg=2 opc=0
parent=0000000006F10BF0 owner=0000000000000000 nex=0000000000000000 xsz=0xfe8
      heap=0000000000000000
fl2=0x26, nex=0000000000000000
EXTENT 0 addr=00000000D36C67E0
  Chunk        0d36c67f0 sz=      1696     free       "              "
  Chunk        0d36c6e90 sz=        72     freeable  "kks pstat     "
```

Process State Dump

Process state dumps provide a lot of detailed information about the history of a process, such as the last ten wait events and some of the recent SQL statements executed by the session that uses the process. The following example shows how to initiate a process state dump by using the ORADEBUG command from within SQL*Plus:

SQL> ORADEBUG SETORAPID 25

Oracle pid: 25, Unix process pid: 5143, image: oracle (TNS V1-V3)

SQL> ORADEBUG DUMP PROCESSSTATE 10

```
    client details:
      O/S info: user: oracle, term: pts/2, ospid: 5143
      machine: airforce-5.test.org program: sqlplus@airforce-5.test.org (TNS V1-V3)
      application name: sqlplus@airforce-5.test.org (TNS V1-V3),
                         hash value=473927202
    Current Wait Stack:
      Not in wait; last wait ended 0.000475 sec ago
    Wait State:
      fixed_waits=0 flags=0x21 boundary=(nil)/-1
    Session Wait History:
        elapsed time of 0.000497 sec since last wait
     0: waited for 'SQL*Net message from client'
        driver id=0x62657100, #bytes=0x1, =0x0
        wait_id=213 seq_num=214 snap_id=1
        wait times: snap=36.256320 sec, exc=36.256320 sec, total=36.256320 sec
        wait times: max=infinite
        wait counts: calls=0 os=0
        occurred after 0.000005 sec of elapsed time
     1: waited for 'SQL*Net message to client'
        driver id=0x62657100, #bytes=0x1, =0x0
        wait_id=212 seq_num=213 snap_id=1
        wait times: snap=0.000003 sec, exc=0.000003 sec, total=0.000003 sec
        wait times: max=infinite
        wait counts: calls=0 os=0
        occurred after 0.000106 sec of elapsed time
...
      SO: 0x25aea0cf0, type: 74, owner: 0x250928cb0, flag: INIT/-/-/0x00 if: 0x3
                 c: 0x3
```

```
proc=0x25077ce30, name=LIBRARY OBJECT LOCK, file=kgl.h LINE:8348, pg=0

LibraryObjectLock:  Address=5aea0cf0 Handle=5a6d7130 Mode=N CanBeBrokenCount=1
  Incarnation=1 ExecutionCount=0

  User=50928cb0 Session=50928cb0 ReferenceCount=1 Flags=CNB/[0001]
    SavepointNum=4aa70f89
LibraryHandle:  Address=5a6d7130 Hash=c73552cd LockMode=N PinMode=0
                LoadLockMode=0
  Status=VALD
  ObjectName:  Name=        ALTER SESSION SET
                            TRACEFILE_IDENTIFIER='PROCESS_STATE_10'

    FullHashValue=a9458398a45d9f926c25487bc73552cd Namespace=SQL AREA(00)
      Type=CURSOR(00) Identifier=3342160589 OwnerIdn=186
  Statistics:  InvalidationCount=0 ExecutionCount=0 LoadCount=1 ActiveLocks=2
    TotalLockCount=2 TotalPinCount=1
  Counters:  BrokenCount=1 RevocablePointer=1 KeepDependency=0 KeepHandle=0
    BucketInUse=1 HandleInUse=1
  Concurrency:  DependencyMutex=5a6d71e0(0, 0, 0, 0)
                Mutex=5a6d7258(0, 9, 0, 0)
  Flags=RON/PIN/TIM/PN0/DBN/[10012841]
  WaitersLists:
    Lock=5a6d71c0[5a6d71c0,5a6d71c0]
    Pin=5a6d71d0[5a6d71a0,5a6d71a0]
  Timestamp:  Current=09-08-2009 22:14:16
  LibraryObject:  Address=42538700 HeapMask=0000-0001-0001 Flags=EXS[0000]
    Flags2=[0000] PublicFlags=[0000]
  NamespaceDump:
    Parent Cursor:  sql_id=6s9a8gg3manqd parent=0x2425387e8 maxchild=0
                    plk=y ppn=n
```

SHORT_STACK Dump

A SHORT_STACK dump shows the process stack for the attached process, output directly to the SQL*Plus screen. It may be necessary to execute the SHORT_STACK dump multiple times to determine the status of the process through the use of the process stack traces. With the help of Metalink Doc ID 175982.1 "ORA-600 Lookup Error Categories," it is possible to decode portions of the SHORT_STACK output to determine the session's current status. Initiate a SHORT_STACK dump for a process after connecting to the process as demonstrated here:

SQL> ORADEBUG SETORAPID 26

```
Oracle pid: 26, Windows thread id: 836, image: ORACLE.EXE (SHAD)
```

SQL> ORADEBUG SHORT_STACK

When a Windows session is sitting idle, a SHORT_STACK dump for that session's process might look like the following, with the thread creation at the end of the output and the current processing located toward the start of the output. (This output helps determine the portion of the SHORT_STACK output that may be ignored during later ORADEBUG SHORT_STACK dumps.)

```
<-ksedsts()+334<-ksdxfstk()+42<-ksdxcb()+1861<-ssthreadsrgruncallback()+559<-Or
cleOradebugThreadStart()+965<-0000000076CCBE3D<-0000000076ED6A51<-0000000076EF6
5A<-000007FEFC7DF231<-000007FEFC7E16A8<-000007FEFDFA21A9<-00000000003D407C<-000
0000003CEF92<-0000000008CB35E3<-0000000008CB69C1<-0000000008BB7B3E<-__PGOSF159_
pikndf2()+1068<-opitsk()+1207<-opiino()+1140<-opiodr()+1324<-opidrv()+810<-sou2
()+52<-opimai_real()+151<-opimai()+96<-OracleThreadStart()+704<-0000000076CCBE3
<-0000000076ED6A51
```

The following is an example of a SHORT_STACK dump, which shows a session executing a query that resulted in a disk read. The data block was brought into the buffer cache so a row in that block that was needed deep in the query's execution plan (inside an in-line view containing a GROUP BY clause) could be examined as a result of an index lookup:

```
<-ksedsts()+334<-ksdxfstk()+42<-ksdxcb()+1861<-ssthreadsrgruncallback()+559<-Ora
cleOradebugThreadStart()+965<-0000000076CCBE3D<-0000000076ED6A51<-0000000076EF70
5A<-0000000076CDC1B8<-skgfrwat()+150<-ksfdwtio()+321<-ksfdbio()+2193<-kcfprd()+1
222<-kcbzib()+18747<-kcb_prefetch()+298<-ktrprefetch()+85<-kdstlps()+678<-qerpfP
refetch()+342<-qerpfRealFetch()+614<-qerpfFetch()+82<-qertbFetchByRowID()+629<-q
ersoProcessULS()+208<-qersoFetch()+4477<-qerjotFetch()+393<-qerjoFetch()+815<-qe
rjotFetch()+621<-qerjotFetch()+621<-qerjoFetch()+815<-qerflFetch()+177<-qerjoFet
ch()+815<-qerjoFetch()+815<-qerflFetch()+177<-qerjoFetch()+815<-qerjoFetch()+815
<-qerflFetch()+177<-qerjoFetch()+815<-qerjoFetch()+815<-qerflFetch()+177<-qerjoF
etch()+815<-qerjoFetch()+815<-qerflFetch()+177<-qerjoFetch()+815<-qerghFetch()+4
887<-qervwFetch()+174<-opifch2()+3630<-kpoal8()+3236<-opiodr()+1324<-ttcpip()+46
31<-opitsk()+2103<-opiino()+1140<-opiodr()+1324<-opidrv()+810<-sou2o()+52<-opima
i_real()+151<-opimai()+96<-OracleThreadStart()+704<-0000000076CCBE3D<-0000000076
ED6A51
```

Reading the stack dump from the bottom up (with a couple of items skipped), you have the following: OracleThreadStart (the creation of the session's process/thread) ▶ opi (Oracle server functions—top of the server stack) ▶ ttc (two-task common layer) ▶ opiodr (communication) ▶ kpoal8 (support for programmatic operations) ▶ opifch (Oracle server functions—top of the server stack) ▶ qervw (view row source) ▶ qergh (group by no-sort, hash) ▶ qerjo (row source join) ▶ qerfl (filter row source) ▶ qerjo (row source join) ▶ qerfl (filter row source) ▶ qerjo (row source join) ▶ qerfl (filter row source) ▶ qerjo (row source join) ▶ qerfl (filter row source) ▶ qerjo (row source join) ▶ qerso (sort row source) ▶ qertb (table row source) ▶ qerpf (query execution row source prefetch) ▶ kds (retrieving or updating a row) ▶ ktc (kernel transaction read consistency) ▶ kcb (manages buffer cache operations) ▶ kcf (manages operations on the control files) ▶ ksf (various kernel operations, such disk I/O).

Tanel Poder's blog (blog.tanelpoder.com) offers scripts named OS_EXPLAIN and OStackProf that simplify the decoding of stack traces.

SYSTEMSTATE Dump

SYSTEMSTATE dumps are performed using nonread consistent techniques, meaning that the data output at the end of a long duration dump may not have existed in its current state when the dump was initiated. It may require a long time to output the dump when a large number of users are connected, and the data contained in the dump may be excessive when attempting to address a system hang—in such a case, a HANGANALYZE dump may prove to be a better choice. SYSTEMSTATE dumps captured at level 2 are helpful when used in conjunction with a level 3 HANGANALYZE dump. To also include a short stack output in the trace file, set event 10998 or add 256 to the SYSTEMSTATE dump level.

The following commands instruct ORADEBUG to connect to the process for the current session, remove the maximum trace file size limitation, specify a portion of the trace filename to help the DBA locate the trace file, write a level 2 SYSTEMSTATE dump to the trace file (without including a short stack dump), and then close the trace file:

```
SQL> ORADEBUG SETMYPID
SQL> ORADEBUG UNLIMIT
SQL> ALTER SESSION SET TRACEFILE_IDENTIFIER='SYSTEMSTATE';
SQL> ORADEBUG DUMP SYSTEMSTATE 2
SQL> ORADEBUG CLOSE_TRACE
```

See Metalink Doc ID 423153.1, "Understanding and Reading Systemstates," for examples of using SYSTEMSTATE dumps to troubleshoot various waits including enqueues, rowcache locks, library cache pins/mutexes, library cache locks, and latch free.

Operating-System-Generated Stack Traces

Use great caution when generating stack traces by using operating system utilities with production database instances. Doing so might crash either the session or the instance because of the need of some operating system utilities to temporarily pause the execution of the process so that the process's current stack can be read. It may be necessary to capture many (up to 100) stack traces to determine the current status of the process.

Solaris (and FreeBSD) provides the DTrace utility and the pstack utility to perform stack traces at the operating system level. The pstack utility on Linux differs from that on other Unix platforms because it is a wrapper script around the GNU Project Debugger (GDB), which must pause the execution of the process to retrieve the process's stack trace. A search of the Internet indicates that several groups are in the process of creating a Linux-based version of the DTrace utility (www.crisp.demon.co.uk offers one such version, but it may not be ready for use in a production environment).

See Tanel Poder's blog (blog.tanelpoder.com) for his dstackprof script and various demonstrations of performance diagnostics using operating system stack traces. Additionally, the Linux SYSTEMTAP utility (sourceware.org/systemtap/) provides a toolset for tracing kernel mode activity.

Reviewing the Enterprise Manager ADDM Findings

The Automated Database Diagnostic Monitor (ADDM) is a feature built into Oracle releases 10.1 and above that attempts to identify the root cause of performance problems and offer one or more suggestions to address the root cause of the problems identified. ADDM is executed during each AWR collection, which happens once an hour by default.

ADDM uses the statistics collected for the AWR reports as a basis for problem detection. From the statistics, ADDM attempts to identify a wide variety of problems including excessive parsing; lock contention issues; redo log problems (size and archiving); buffer busy waits; SQL statements contributing to CPU utilization and each class of wait event; PL/SQL causing an excessive system load; I/O problems such as excessive block reads, slower than expected read time (controlled by ADDM's parameter DBIO_EXPECTED, which defaults to 10ms, and is specified in microseconds); SGA,

PGA, and buffer cache sizes; and RAC performance (interconnect performance and hot blocks). Because ADDM works with historical data collected by AWR, one of the advantages of ADDM is its ability to troubleshoot problems after the performance issue disappears, which may allow the DBA to implement a correction before the performance issue recurs. The ADDM findings are ranked by an estimate of the performance issue's effect on the systemwide DB time statistic.

The accuracy of the recommendations may vary greatly based on the selected snapshot range. With database instances that experience variable workloads, one ADDM report may indicate that there was excessive utilization of the page file (suggesting that the server was exceeding the available system RAM), and another ADDM report using AWR snapshots collected a couple of hours earlier may suggest adding more memory to the SGA_TARGET parameter to reduce the number of physical block reads (suggesting that the server was not using enough of the available system RAM). Before blindly implementing changes, compare the ADDM reports from multiple AWR snapshots. Suggestions offered by ADDM reports include executing the SQL Tuning Advisor for high-load SQL statements (those with a large number of logical I/Os and/or physical I/Os), executing the Segment Advisor for hot objects, using bind variables to reduce the number of hard parses, moving objects to ASSM tablespaces, changing physical hardware such as the number of CPUs and disk layout, and changing initialization parameters.

To use ADDM, the user must be granted the ADVISOR and SELECT_CATALOG_ROLE, as well as EXECUTE on DBMS_WORKLOAD_REPOSITORY. The easiest way to create an ADDM report is with the Enterprise Manager Database Control, which allows creating a report for a time interval that ends before the next AWR report is scheduled to be captured with just a couple of clicks of the mouse. To generate an ADDM report from the SQL*Plus command line, enter the following and follow the prompts:

```
SQL> @?/rdbms/admin/addmrpt.sql
```

Typical ADDM report findings might include the following:

```
Summary of Findings
-------------------
    Description              Active Sessions       Recommendations
                             Percent of Activity
    --------------------     -------------------   ---------------
1   Virtual Memory Paging    5.45 | 100.00         1
2   I/O Throughput           5.45 | 100.00         4
3   Top SQL by DB Time       2.86 |  52.41         2
4   Top SQL By I/O           1.89 |  34.70         1
5   Top Segments by I/O      1.88 |  34.49         1
6   CPU Usage                0.94 |  17.29         1
7   Hard Parse               0.16 |   2.95         0


Finding 1: Virtual Memory Paging
Impact is 5.45 active sessions, 100% of total activity.
--------------------------------------------------------
Significant virtual memory paging was detected on the host operating system.

    Recommendation 1: Host Configuration
    Estimated benefit is 5.45 active sessions, 100% of total activity.
    ----------------------------------------------------------------
    Action
        Host operating system was experiencing significant paging but no
```

```
particular root cause could be detected. Investigate processes that do
not belong to this instance running on the host that are consuming
significant amount of virtual memory. Also consider adding more physical
memory to the host.
```

The preceding message indicates that ADDM found that the server was making extensive utilization of the swap file, which might indicate that the server has insufficient RAM installed. ADDM made the recommendation to look at the other, non-Oracle processes, and to consider adding more RAM to the server. The ADDM report continues next with finding number two, an I/O throughput warning with a suggested corrective action:

```
Finding 2: I/O Throughput
Impact is 5.45 active sessions, 100% of total activity.
-------------------------------------------------------
The throughput of the I/O subsystem was significantly lower than expected.

    Recommendation 1: Host Configuration
    Estimated benefit is 5.45 active sessions, 100% of total activity.
    ------------------------------------------------------------------
    Action
        Consider increasing the throughput of the I/O subsystem. Oracle's
        recommended solution is to stripe all data file using the SAME
        methodology. You might also need to increase the number of disks for
        better performance. Alternatively, consider using Oracle's Automatic
        Storage Management solution.
    Rationale
        During the analysis period, the average data files' I/O throughput was
        2.7 M per second for reads and 2 M per second for writes. The average
        response time for single block reads was 30 milliseconds.
```

The preceding message appeared in part because of the average response time for a single-block read exceeding the 10ms default. The relatively low average read speed of 2.7MB per second might be directly related to an excessive number of random I/Os in different parts of the disks due to a significant number of single-block read requests. Moving the data files to a RAID 10 array with many drive spindles may reduce the random I/O time by reducing the number of track-to-track movements of the hard drive heads, but it might be worthwhile to verify that a change in the hard drive arrays will improve performance sufficiently to justify the cost and downtime required to implement the recommendation. The ADDM report continues next with finding number three, the SQL statements contributing to the greatest percentage of the DB time statistic for the time period of the report:

```
Finding 3: Top SQL by DB Time
Impact is 2.86 active sessions, 52.41% of total activity.
---------------------------------------------------------
SQL statements consuming significant database time were found.

    Recommendation 1: SQL Tuning
    Estimated benefit is 1.9 active sessions, 34.89% of total activity.
    ------------------------------------------------------------------
    Action
        Run SQL Tuning Advisor on the SQL statement with SQL_ID "fqc4vp7f1gc3c"
        Related Object
```

```
SQL statement with SQL_ID fqc4vp7f1gc3c.
SELECT
ID,
DESCRIPTION
FROM
T1
WHERE
ID BETWEEN 1 AND 400
```

ADDM identified a couple of the high-load SQL statements, with one of those SQL statements shown in the preceding output. ADDM recommended running the SQL Tuning Advisor for this SQL statement to help improve performance by finding a more efficient execution plan, which may involve adding an index or adding hints when creating a SQL profile for the SQL statement. Findings 4 (Top SQL by I/O), 5 (Top Segments by I/O), and 6 (CPU Usage) are omitted as the findings identified the same SQL statement and table T1 as had been identified in finding 3. The ADDM report continues next with finding 7, the impact of hard parsing on overall performance:

```
Finding 7: Hard Parse
Impact is .16 active sessions, 2.95% of total activity.
----------------------------------------------------------
Hard parsing of SQL statements was consuming significant database time.
Hard parses due to cursor environment mismatch were not consuming significant
  database time.
Hard parsing SQL statements that encountered parse errors was not consuming
  significant database time.
Hard parses due to literal usage and cursor invalidation were not consuming
  significant database time.
The SGA was adequately sized.
```

ADDM apparently checked the delta values from the V$SYS_TIME_MODEL view and the ending values from the V$SGA_TARGET_ADVICE view to determine most, if not all, of the items in finding 7. An ADDM report using an ending snapshot captured an hour earlier suggested the following for finding 7, which is in sharp contrast to the memory shortage condition and the advice that the SGA was properly sized:

```
Finding 7: Undersized SGA
Impact is .06 active sessions, 1.79% of total activity.
----------------------------------------------------------
The SGA was inadequately sized, causing additional I/O or hard parses.
The value of parameter "sga_target" was "8000 M" during the analysis period.

   Recommendation 1: Database Configuration
   Estimated benefit is .06 active sessions, 1.62% of total activity.
   ----------------------------------------------------------------
   Action
      Increase the size of the SGA by setting the parameter "sga_target" to
      9000 M.

   Symptoms That Led to the Finding:
   ----------------------------------
      Wait class "User I/O" was consuming significant database time.
      Impact is 1.08 active sessions, 30.25% of total activity.
```

ADDM is enabled by default. Accessing ADDM information requires an Enterprise Edition of Oracle as well as a license for the Diagnostics Pack, and potentially a license for the Tuning Pack. If a license for the Diagnostics Pack is not available for the database, it is possible to disable ADDM and AWR logging. Starting with Oracle release 11.1.0.6, the CONTROL_MANAGEMENT_PACK_ACCESS parameter may be set to DIAGNOSTIC+TUNING (the default), DIAGNOSTIC, or NONE. Setting the parameter to NONE disables ADDM for the database. To disable ADDM in prior releases, see Metalink Doc ID 436386.1.

Examining Network Packets

Network packet-capture utilities, such as tcpdump and Wireshark/Ethereal provide insight into the performance problems that might occur in the network connection between the server and client, as well as network configuration problems on the client and server computers. A partial Wireshark packet capture follows, in which a client computer submitted a SQL statement to be executed by the database instance:

```
No.    Time           Source      Destination Protocol          Info
 1 17:35:37.710542 client-ip   server-ip   TNS      Request, Data (6), Data
 2 17:35:37.710975 server-ip   client-ip   TNS      Response, Data (6), Data
 3 17:35:37.711041 client-ip   server-ip   TNS      Request, Data (6), Data
 4 17:35:37.711215 server-ip   client-ip   TNS      Response, Data (6), Data
 5 17:35:37.712464 client-ip   server-ip   TNS      Request, Data (6), Data
 6 17:35:37.712686 server-ip   client-ip   TNS      Response, Data (6), Data
 7 17:35:37.712726 client-ip   server-ip   TNS      Request, Data (6), Data
 8 17:35:37.713044 server-ip   client-ip   TNS      Response, Data (6), Data
 9 17:35:37.897954 client-ip   server-ip   TCP      1447 > 1521 [ACK] Seq=279
                            Ack=970 Win=64934 [TCP CHECKSUM INCORRECT] Len=0
```

The TCP CHECKSUM INCORRECT message may indicate a signal-quality problem on the network connection causing corrupt packets, but in this case the message is caused by a network card driver's performance optimization that offloads the TCP checksum calculation from the client's CPU to the network card's CPU. The detail of the first packet sent by the client follows, with the data section showing the SQL statement sent by SQL*Plus in clear text. (When the extra-cost Oracle Advanced Security Option is enabled, the data section of the packet will appear as a scrambled sequence of characters rather than clear text.)

```
Frame  1 (184 bytes on wire, 184 bytes captured)
Ethernet II, Src: Intel_b0:dd:31 (00:11:11:b0:dd:31),
             Dst: Intel_b0:cc:62 (00:0e:0c:b0:cc:62)
Internet Protocol, Src: 192.30.176.183 (192.30.176.183),
                   Dst: 192.30.176.45 (192.30.176.45)
Transmission Control Protocol, Src Port: 3285 (3285),
                               Dst Port: 1521 (1521), Seq: 0, Ack: 0, Len: 130
Transparent Network Substrate Protocol
    Packet Length: 130
    Packet Checksum: 0x0000
    Packet Type: Data (6)
    Reserved Byte: 00
    Header Checksum: 0x0000
    Data
```

```
        Data Flag: 0x0000
        Data (120 bytes)

0000  03 4a 90 01 00 00 00 01 00 00 00 00 01 49 00 00 00    .J..........I...
0010  00 00 00 00 00 01 01 00 00 00 00 00 00 00 00 00       ................
0020  00 00 00 00 00 00 00 00 00 00 49 0a 53 45 4c 45       ..........I.SELE
0030  43 54 20 50 41 52 53 45 5f 44 49 53 4b 2c 45 58       CT PARSE_DISK,EX
0040  45 5f 44 49 53 4b 2c 46 45 54 43 48 5f 44 49 53       E_DISK,FETCH_DIS
0050  4b 20 46 52 4f 4d 20 54 4b 50 52 4f 46 5f 54 41       K FROM TKPROF_TA
0060  42 4c 45 20 57 48 45 52 45 20 52 4f 57 4e 55 4d       BLE WHERE ROWNUM
0070  3c 3d 34 30 02 00 00 00                               <=40....
```

Patterns like the following in Wireshark, or another packet-capture utility, suggest the presence of a high-latency connection between the client and server:

```
No  Time        Source     Dest.       Protocol  Info
40  10.296875   server-ip  client-ip   TNS       Response, Data (6), Data
41  10.625000   server-ip  client-ip   TNS       Response, Data (6), Data
42  10.953125   server-ip  client-ip   TNS       Response, Data (6), Data
43  11.250000   server-ip  client-ip   TNS       Response, Data (6), Data
44  11.562500   server-ip  client-ip   TNS       Response, Data (6), Data
45  11.875000   server-ip  client-ip   TNS       Response, Data (6), Data
46  12.203125   server-ip  client-ip   TNS       Response, Data (6), Data
47  12.531250   server-ip  client-ip   TNS       Response, Data (6), Data
48  12.843750   server-ip  client-ip   TNS       Response, Data (6), Data
49  13.140625   server-ip  client-ip   TNS       Response, Data (6), Data
50  13.406250   server-ip  client-ip   TNS       Response, Data (6), Data
51  13.687500   server-ip  client-ip   TNS       Response, Data (6), Data
52  13.984375   server-ip  client-ip   TNS       Response, Data (6), Data
53  14.281250   server-ip  client-ip   TNS       Response, Data (6), Data
54  14.578125   server-ip  client-ip   TNS       Response, Data (6), Data
55  14.859375   server-ip  client-ip   TNS       Response, Data (6), Data
56  15.156250   server-ip  client-ip   TNS       Response, Data (6), Data
57  15.468750   server-ip  client-ip   TNS       Response, Data (6), Data
58  15.781250   server-ip  client-ip   TNS       Response, Data (6), Data
```

The preceding output has a repeating, consistent pattern of an approximate 0.30-second (300ms) delay between each packet received from the server by the client. The delay, although not as long as would be expected through a satellite link where 1- to 2-second delays would be more common, indicate a potential problem source for chatty database applications that retrieve few rows per fetch call, and send many database platform-independent SQL statements to the database instance rather than a single complex database platform-dependent SQL statement that accomplishes the same task.

Patterns like the following in Wireshark, or another packet-capture utility, suggest that either the network connection between the server and client is faulty (bad wiring, failing switch, failing router, electromagnetic interference), the network card in the server or client is faulty, or a similar problem is present:

```
No    Time        Source     Dest.       Protocol  Info
1312  15.420056   client-ip  server-ip   TNS       Request, Data (6), Data
1313  15.484834   server-ip  client-ip   TCP       [TCP Previous segment lost]
                                                    [TCP segment of a reassembled PDU]
```

```
1314  15.484937  client-ip  server-ip  TCP   [TCP Dup ACK 1312#1] 59325 > ncube-lm
                                              [ACK] Seq=6637 Ack=187880 Win=4280
                                              Len=0 SLE=188416 SRE=188445
1315  15.722792  server-ip  client-ip  TCP   [TCP Retransmission]
                                              [TCP segment of a reassembled PDU]
1316  15.722908  client-ip  server-ip  TCP   59325 > ncube-lm [ACK] Seq=6637
                                              Ack=188445 Win=4139 Len=0
1317  15.728453  client-ip  server-ip  TNS   Request, Data (6), Data
1318  16.014293  client-ip  server-ip  TNS   [TCP Retransmission]
                                              Request, Data (6), Data
1319  16.019287  server-ip  client-ip  TCP   [TCP segment of a reassembled PDU]
1320  16.024773  server-ip  client-ip  TCP   [TCP Dup ACK 1319#1] ncube-lm > 59325
                                              [ACK]
                                              Seq=188981 Ack=6658 Win=259 Len=0
                                              SLE=6637 SRE=6658
1321  16.217053  client-ip  server-ip  TCP   59325 > ncube-lm [ACK] Seq=6658
                                              Ack=188981
                                              Win=4420 Len=0
1322  16.219773  server-ip  client-ip  TNS   Response, Data (6), Data
1323  16.230122  client-ip  server-ip  TNS   Request, Data (6), Data
1324  16.237361  server-ip  client-ip  TCP   [TCP segment of a reassembled PDU]
1325  16.239679  server-ip  client-ip  TNS   Response, Data (6), Data
1326  16.239730  client-ip  server-ip  TCP   59325 > ncube-lm [ACK] Seq=6679
                                              Ack=189641 Win=4255 Len=0
1327  16.249971  client-ip  server-ip  TNS   Request, Data (6), Data
1328  16.265952  server-ip  client-ip  TCP   [TCP segment of a reassembled PDU]
1329  16.267749  server-ip  client-ip  TNS   Response, Data (6), Data
```

Here there are occasional delays of just over 0.2 seconds, usually accompanied by TCP retransmissions, lost segments, and duplicate ACKs.

Patterns like the following in Wireshark, or another packet-capture utility, suggest that a server administrator or network administrator had implemented the TcpAckFrequency advice found in the document titled "Performance Tuning Guidelines for Windows Server 2003" on Microsoft's website (http://download.microsoft.com/download/2/8/0/2800a518-7ac6-4aac-bd85-74d2c52e1ec6/tuning.doc):

```
No   Time       Source     Dest.      Protocol  Info
12   1.487036   server-ip  client-ip  TNS   Response, Data (6), Data
13   1.487149   server-ip  client-ip  TCP   [TCP segment of a reassembled PDU]
14   1.487194   server-ip  client-ip  TNS   Response, Data (6), Data
15   1.487322   server-ip  client-ip  TCP   [TCP segment of a reassembled PDU]
16   1.487369   server-ip  client-ip  TNS   Response, Data (6), Data
17   1.674851   client-ip  server-ip  TCP   49196 > ncube-lm [ACK] Seq=197 Ack=12414
18   1.675434   server-ip  client-ip  TCP   [TCP segment of a reassembled PDU]
19   1.675518   server-ip  client-ip  TNS   Response, Data (6), Data
20   1.675578   server-ip  client-ip  TCP   [TCP segment of a reassembled PDU]
21   1.675661   server-ip  client-ip  TNS   Response, Data (6), Data
22   1.675763   server-ip  client-ip  TCP   [TCP segment of a reassembled PDU]
23   1.675809   server-ip  client-ip  TNS   Response, Data (6), Data
24   1.675935   server-ip  client-ip  TCP   [TCP segment of a reassembled PDU]
25   1.675982   server-ip  client-ip  TNS   Response, Data (6), Data
26   1.676108   server-ip  client-ip  TCP   [TCP segment of a reassembled PDU]
```

```
27   1.676155   server-ip   client-ip   TNS   Response, Data (6), Data
28   1.676281   server-ip   client-ip   TCP   [TCP segment of a reassembled PDU]
29   1.676328   server-ip   client-ip   TNS   Response, Data (6), Data
30   1.877692   client-ip   server-ip   TCP   49196 > ncube-lm [ACK] Seq=197 Ack=24480
31   1.878241   server-ip   client-ip   TCP   [TCP segment of a reassembled PDU]
32   1.878336   server-ip   client-ip   TNS   Response, Data (6), Data
33   1.878382   server-ip   client-ip   TCP   [TCP segment of a reassembled PDU]
34   1.878465   server-ip   client-ip   TNS   Response, Data (6), Data
35   1.878580   server-ip   client-ip   TCP   [TCP segment of a reassembled PDU]
36   1.878624   server-ip   client-ip   TNS   Response, Data (6), Data
37   1.878757   server-ip   client-ip   TCP   [TCP segment of a reassembled PDU]
38   1.878800   server-ip   client-ip   TNS   Response, Data (6), Data
39   1.878915   server-ip   client-ip   TCP   [TCP segment of a reassembled PDU]
40   1.878961   server-ip   client-ip   TNS   Response, Data (6), Data
41   1.879088   server-ip   client-ip   TCP   [TCP segment of a reassembled PDU]
42   1.879134   server-ip   client-ip   TNS   Response, Data (6), Data
43   2.080452   client-ip   server-ip   TCP   49196 > ncube-lm [ACK] Seq=197 Ack=36546
44   2.081029   server-ip   client-ip   TCP   [TCP segment of a reassembled PDU]
45   2.081117   server-ip   client-ip   TNS   Response, Data (6), Data
46   2.283257   client-ip   server-ip   TCP   49196 > ncube-lm [ACK] Seq=197 Ack=38336
47   2.469999   client-ip   server-ip   TNS   Request, Data (6), Data
```

In this output, there are several delays of approximately 0.2 seconds between the packet sent by the server and the ACK packet sent by the client, as well as several other packets that were tightly grouped together and all transmitted within the span of 1ms. In this case, the output indicates that either the TcpAckFrequency parameter in the Windows Registry was modified for the computer indicated as client-ip, or that a general Nagle and delayed ACK problem is present (the 0.2-second delay between some of the packets without retransmits is the identifying characteristic). This pattern seems to occur most frequently when a client retrieves more than 10,000 bytes (five default SDU sizes) of data from the server in a single fetch call. A 10046 extended trace might show the preceding packet-capture behavior as follows (because of space constraints, nonessential entries such as driver id were removed from the trace file lines):

```
WAIT #2: nam='SQL*Net message from client' ela= 346881 tim=21065510174
WAIT #2: nam='SQL*Net message to client' ela= 2 tim=21065510620
WAIT #2: nam='SQL*Net more data to client' ela= 40 tim=21065510898
WAIT #2: nam='SQL*Net more data to client' ela= 31 tim=21065511056
WAIT #2: nam='SQL*Net more data to client' ela= 31 tim=21065511204
WAIT #2: nam='SQL*Net more data to client' ela= 31 tim=21065511384
WAIT #2: nam='SQL*Net more data to client' ela= 31 tim=21065511621
WAIT #2: nam='SQL*Net more data to client' ela= 197058 tim=21065708888
WAIT #2: nam='SQL*Net more data to client' ela= 33 tim=21065709193
WAIT #2: nam='SQL*Net more data to client' ela= 61 tim=21065709389
WAIT #2: nam='SQL*Net more data to client' ela= 31 tim=21065709591
WAIT #2: nam='SQL*Net more data to client' ela= 31 tim=21065709771
WAIT #2: nam='SQL*Net more data to client' ela= 32 tim=21065709905
WAIT #2: nam='SQL*Net more data to client' ela= 201558 #bytes=1997 tim=21065911573
WAIT #2: nam='SQL*Net more data to client' ela= 32 #bytes=1999 tim=21065911826
WAIT #2: nam='SQL*Net more data to client' ela= 34 #bytes=2004 tim=21065912013
WAIT #2: nam='SQL*Net more data to client' ela= 48 #bytes=2006 tim=21065912285
WAIT #2: nam='SQL*Net more data to client' ela= 32 #bytes=1989 tim=21065912444
FETCH #2:c=31201,e=402003,p=0,cr=0,cu=0,mis=0,r=1000,dep=0,og=1,tim=21065912612
```

The additional elapsed time associated with the ACK delay contributed to the elapsed time of the fetch call. Without examining the raw trace file with the help of the network packet capture, the exact source of the problem would be difficult to determine. This problem is not limited to database connectivity. As a comparison, transmitting a 132MB file from a file server over a gigabit network to a client normally requires roughly 3 seconds. With the presence of the preceding ACK delay, the same transfer requires roughly 45 minutes.

Examining Client-Side Traces

Client-side trace options are available from a variety of sources including Oracle's SQL*Net (see Metalink Doc IDs 779226.1, 219968.1, and 395525.1); Windows client tracing (see Metalink Doc ID 216912.1) using ODBC, Oracle Provider for OLE DB, Oracle Objects for OLE (OO4O), Oracle Data Provider for .NET (ODP.NET), and Oracle Service for Microsoft Transaction Server (ORAMTS); client-side file- and registry-monitoring utilities on the Windows platform including Process Monitor (Sysinternals/Microsoft), FileMon (Sysinternals/Microsoft), and RegMon (Sysinternals/Microsoft); and window message monitoring on the Windows platform with Spy++ (Microsoft).

In general, client-side traces help verify that a client-side application is behaving properly when executing. However, client-side traces also help identify communication problems between the client and server, help to pinpoint protocol errors, as well as identify syntax errors in the SQL statements submitted by the client application.

SQL*Net Tracing

Several parameters in the sqlnet.ora file control whether logging is enabled for the client, server, or listener, as well as the level of detail and location of the log files. The following are entries in a sqlnet.ora file on a Windows client, enabling a level 16 (SUPPORT level) log, with the resulting log files written to the C:\TRACEFILES directory:

```
TRACE_LEVEL_CLIENT = 16
TRACE_DIRECTORY_CLIENT=C:\TRACEFILES
TRACE_UNIQUE_CLIENT = ON
TRACE_TIMESTAMP_CLIENT = ON
```

A partial SQL*Net trace file follows, showing a SQL statement submitted by the client that resulted in an ORA-02005 error returned from the database instance:

```
[12-AUG-2009 16:39:06:896] niogrc: entry
[12-AUG-2009 16:39:06:896] nsdo: entry
[12-AUG-2009 16:39:06:896] nsdo: cid=0, opcode=84, *bl=0,
                           *what=1, uflgs=0x20, cflgs=0x3
[12-AUG-2009 16:39:06:896] snsbitts_ts: entry
[12-AUG-2009 16:39:06:896] snsbitts_ts: acquired the bit
[12-AUG-2009 16:39:06:896] snsbitts_ts: normal exit
[12-AUG-2009 16:39:06:896] nsdo: rank=64, nsctxrnk=0
[12-AUG-2009 16:39:06:896] snsbitcl_ts: entry
[12-AUG-2009 16:39:06:896] snsbitcl_ts: normal exit
[12-AUG-2009 16:39:06:896] nsdo: nsctx: state=8, flg=0x400d, mvd=0
[12-AUG-2009 16:39:06:896] nsdo: gtn=127, gtc=127, ptn=10, ptc=2011
[12-AUG-2009 16:39:06:896] nsdofls: entry
```

```
[12-AUG-2009 16:39:06:896] nsdofls: DATA flags: 0x0
[12-AUG-2009 16:39:06:896] nsdofls: sending NSPTDA packet
[12-AUG-2009 16:39:06:896] nspsend: entry
[12-AUG-2009 16:39:06:896] nspsend: plen=177, type=6
[12-AUG-2009 16:39:06:896] nttwr: entry
[12-AUG-2009 16:39:06:896] nttwr: socket 308 had bytes written=177
[12-AUG-2009 16:39:06:896] nttwr: exit
[12-AUG-2009 16:39:06:896] nspsend: packet dump
[12-AUG-2009 16:39:06:896] nspsend: 00 B1 00 00 06 00 00 00  |........|
[12-AUG-2009 16:39:06:896] nspsend: 00 00 03 4A FE 01 00 00  |...J....|
[12-AUG-2009 16:39:06:896] nspsend: 00 03 00 00 00 78 14 FD  |.....x..|
[12-AUG-2009 16:39:06:896] nspsend: 02 63 00 00 00 00 00 00  |.c......|
[12-AUG-2009 16:39:06:896] nspsend: 00 00 00 00 00 48 D8 12  |.....H..|
[12-AUG-2009 16:39:06:896] nspsend: 00 01 00 00 00 00 00 00  |........|
[12-AUG-2009 16:39:06:896] nspsend: 00 00 00 00 00 00 00 00  |........|
[12-AUG-2009 16:39:06:896] nspsend: 00 00 00 00 00 00 00 00  |........|
[12-AUG-2009 16:39:06:896] nspsend: 00 00 00 00 00 00 00 00  |........|
[12-AUG-2009 16:39:06:896] nspsend: 00 63 53 45 4C 45 43 54  |.cSELECT|
[12-AUG-2009 16:39:06:896] nspsend: 20 42 49 54 53 20 46 52  |.BITS.FR|
[12-AUG-2009 16:39:06:896] nspsend: 4F 4D 20 50 41 52 54 5F  |OM.PART_|
[12-AUG-2009 16:39:06:896] nspsend: 4D 46 47 5F 42 49 4E 41  |MFG_BINA|
[12-AUG-2009 16:39:06:896] nspsend: 52 59 20 20 77 68 65 72  |RY..wher|
[12-AUG-2009 16:39:06:896] nspsend: 65 20 54 59 50 45 20 3D  |e.TYPE.=|
[12-AUG-2009 16:39:06:896] nspsend: 20 3A 31 20 20 20 20 20  |.:1.....|
[12-AUG-2009 16:39:06:896] nspsend: 20 20 61 6E 64 20 50 41  |..and.PA|
[12-AUG-2009 16:39:06:896] nspsend: 52 54 5F 49 44 20 3D 20  |RT_ID.=.|
[12-AUG-2009 16:39:06:896] nspsend: 3A 32 20 20 20 20 20 20  |:2......|
[12-AUG-2009 16:39:06:896] nspsend: 20 20 20 20 20 20 20 20  |........|
[12-AUG-2009 16:39:06:896] nspsend: 20 20 20 20 20 20 20 20  |........|
[12-AUG-2009 16:39:06:896] nspsend: 20 20 20 20 20 02 00 00  |........|
[12-AUG-2009 16:39:06:896] nspsend: 00                       |.       |
[12-AUG-2009 16:39:06:896] nspsend: 177 bytes to transport
[12-AUG-2009 16:39:06:896] nspsend: normal exit
[12-AUG-2009 16:39:06:896] nsdofls: exit (0)
[12-AUG-2009 16:39:06:896] snsbitts_ts: entry
[12-AUG-2009 16:39:06:896] snsbitts_ts: acquired the bit
[12-AUG-2009 16:39:06:896] snsbitts_ts: normal exit
[12-AUG-2009 16:39:06:896] nsdo: nsctxrnk=0
[12-AUG-2009 16:39:06:896] snsbitcl_ts: entry
[12-AUG-2009 16:39:06:896] snsbitcl_ts: normal exit
[12-AUG-2009 16:39:06:896] nsdo: normal exit
...
[12-AUG-2009 16:39:06:928] nsdo: switching to application buffer
[12-AUG-2009 16:39:06:928] nsrdr: entry
[12-AUG-2009 16:39:06:928] nsrdr: recving a packet
[12-AUG-2009 16:39:06:928] nsprecv: entry
[12-AUG-2009 16:39:06:928] nsprecv: reading from transport...
[12-AUG-2009 16:39:06:928] nttrd: entry
[12-AUG-2009 16:39:06:928] nttrd: socket 308 had bytes read=96
[12-AUG-2009 16:39:06:928] nttrd: exit
[12-AUG-2009 16:39:06:928] nsprecv: 96 bytes from transport
```

```
[12-AUG-2009 16:39:06:928] nsprecv: tlen=96, plen=96, type=6
[12-AUG-2009 16:39:06:928] nsprecv: packet dump
[12-AUG-2009 16:39:06:928] nsprecv: 00 60 00 00 06 00 00 00   |.`......|
[12-AUG-2009 16:39:06:928] nsprecv: 00 00 08 4B 00 4B 4F 52   |...K.KOR|
[12-AUG-2009 16:39:06:928] nsprecv: 41 2D 30 32 30 30 35 3A   |A-02005:|
[12-AUG-2009 16:39:06:928] nsprecv: 20 69 6D 70 6C 69 63 69   |.implici|
[12-AUG-2009 16:39:06:928] nsprecv: 74 20 28 2D 31 29 20 6C   |t.(-1).l|
[12-AUG-2009 16:39:06:928] nsprecv: 65 6E 67 74 68 20 6E 6F   |ength.no|
[12-AUG-2009 16:39:06:928] nsprecv: 74 20 76 61 6C 69 64 20   |t.valid.|
[12-AUG-2009 16:39:06:928] nsprecv: 66 6F 72 20 74 68 69 73   |for.this|
[12-AUG-2009 16:39:06:928] nsprecv: 20 62 69 6E 64 20 6F 72   |.bind.or|
[12-AUG-2009 16:39:06:928] nsprecv: 20 64 65 66 69 6E 65 20   |.define.|
[12-AUG-2009 16:39:06:928] nsprecv: 64 61 74 61 74 79 70 65   |datatype|
[12-AUG-2009 16:39:06:928] nsprecv: 0A 09 05 00 00 00 FD 01   |........|
[12-AUG-2009 16:39:06:928] nsprecv: normal exit
[12-AUG-2009 16:39:06:928] nsrdr: got NSPTDA packet
[12-AUG-2009 16:39:06:928] nsrdr: NSPTDA flags: 0x0
[12-AUG-2009 16:39:06:928] nsrdr: normal exit
[12-AUG-2009 16:39:06:928] snsbitts_ts: entry
[12-AUG-2009 16:39:06:928] snsbitts_ts: acquired the bit
[12-AUG-2009 16:39:06:928] snsbitts_ts: normal exit
[12-AUG-2009 16:39:06:928] snsbitcl_ts: entry
[12-AUG-2009 16:39:06:928] snsbitcl_ts: normal exit
[12-AUG-2009 16:39:06:928] nsdo: *what=1, *bl=2001
```

Process Monitor Tracing

Process Monitor, available as a free download from Microsoft's website, time-synchronizes Windows Registry accesses with local and remote file accesses, allowing generated log files to be manually time sequenced with SQL*Net traces, network packet traces, and 10046 extended SQL traces. Process Monitor traces help to determine activity of the client computer when the database instance reports that the database session was waiting in the SQL*Net message from client wait event.

Following is an example of a Process Monitor log file:

```
Seq  Time of Day       Process Name PID  Operation     Path       Result       Detail
7934 1:16:48.3778617 ORDENT.EXE    1040 RegOpenKey    HKLM\Software\Business Objects
     \Suite 11.0\Crystal Reports NAME NOT FOUND  Desired Access: All Access
7942 1:16:48.3782891 ORDENT.EXE    1040 QueryOpen     C:\WINDOWS\system32\msimtf.dll
     SUCCESS  CreationTime: 8/4/2004 8:00:00 AM,
     LastAccessTime: 8/27/2008 1:16:47 PM, LastWriteTime: 4/14/2008 5:42:00 AM,
     ChangeTime: 7/11/2008 8:56:32 AM, AllocationSize: 159,744, EndOfFile: 159,232,
     FileAttributes: A
7945 1:16:48.3785250 ORDENT.EXE    1040 CreateFile    C:\WINDOWS\system32\msimtf.dll
     SUCCESS  Desired Access: Execute/Traverse, Synchronize, Disposition: Open,
     Options: Synchronous IO Non-Alert, Non-Directory File, Attributes: n/a,
     ShareMode: Read, Delete, AllocationSize: n/a, OpenResult: Opened
7947 1:16:48.3787125 ORDENT.EXE    1040 QueryStdFile  C:\WINDOWS\system32\msimtf.dll
     SUCCESS  AllocationSize: 159,744, EndOfFile: 159,232, NumberOfLinks: 1,
     DeletePending: False, Directory: False
7952 1:16:48.3789142 ORDENT.EXE    1040 CloseFile     C:\WINDOWS\system32\msimtf.dll
```

SUCCESS

Spy++ Tracing

Microsoft's Spy++ utility (`msdn.microsoft.com/en-us/library/aa264396(VS.60).aspx`), typically distributed with Microsoft's programming environments, allows wiretapping a window's message queue to determine messages received from other windows (or the operating system), as well as those messages sent to other windows (or the operating system). The following log file shows messages sent by and received from the Java-based version of Enterprise Manager when a node in Enterprise Manager was expanded:

```
006003BC S WM_ACTIVATEAPP fActive:True dwThreadID:00000000 [wParam:00000001
           lParam:00000000]
006003BC R WM_ACTIVATEAPP lResult:00000000
016902B8 S WM_NCACTIVATE fActive:True [wParam:00000001 lParam:00000000]
016902B8 S .WM_GETTEXT cchTextMax:510 lpszText:0357EF20 [wParam:000001FE
              lParam:0357EF20]
016902B8 R .WM_GETTEXT cchCopied:33 lpszText:0357EF20
              ("Oracle Enterprise Manager Console") [lResult:00000021]
016902B8 R WM_NCACTIVATE lResult:00000001
016902B8 S WM_ACTIVATE fActive:WA_CLICKACTIVE fMinimized:False hwnd:(null)
              [wParam:00000002 lParam:00000000]
016902B8 R WM_ACTIVATE lResult:00000000
000C0522 S WM_SETCURSOR hwnd:000C0522 nHittest:HTCLIENT wMouseMsg:WM_LBUTTONDOWN
              [wParam:000C0522 lParam:02010001]
000C0522 R WM_SETCURSOR fHaltProcessing:False [lResult:00000000]
000C0522 S message:0xC38E [Registered:"SunAwtComponent"] wParam:00000000
              lParam:00000000
000C0522 R message:0xC38E [Registered:"SunAwtComponent"] lResult:00000001
000C0522 S WM_NCHITTEST xPos:231 yPos:782 [wParam:00000000 lParam:030E00E7]
000C0522 R WM_NCHITTEST nHittest:HTCLIENT [lResult:00000001]
000C0522 S message:0xC38E [Registered:"SunAwtComponent"] wParam:00000000
              lParam:00000000
000C0522 R message:0xC38E [Registered:"SunAwtComponent"] lResult:00000001
000C0522 P WM_LBUTTONDOWN fwKeys:MK_LBUTTON xPos:129 yPos:167
              [wParam:00000001 lParam:00A70081 time:59:00:05.765]
000C0522 S message:0x8007 [User-defined:WM_USER+31751] wParam:0363F94C
              lParam:00000000
```

Although no performance issues are identified in this brief capture, it is possible to examine some of the types of messages that appear in a Spy++ message log in response to end-user activity. See the "Problem After Upgrading the ERP Version" sample investigation in Chapter 10 for a demonstration of Spy++ message logging playing a significant role in a performance problem investigation.

Investigating Enqueue Waits

When investigating enqueue-type waits (enqueue - in releases prior to Oracle 10.1, enq: TM - contention, enq: TX - row lock contention, enq: HW - contention, and so forth in Oracle 10.1 and above), consider querying V$SESSION_WAIT while the wait is occurring. (Note that the columns of interest in this view are accessible from V$SESSION beginning with the 10.1 release of Oracle.) Through this query, you can determine the in-process waits (EVENT column), the duration of the current/last wait (SECONDS_IN_WAIT, WAIT_TIME), and the detail associated with the waits (P1, P2, P3 columns).

Query V$LOCK to determine the other session causing the enqueue wait (ID1, ID2, and BLOCK columns). Query V$SESSION to determine the object, data block, and possibly row causing the enqueue (ROW_WAIT_OBJ#, ROW_WAIT_FILE#, ROW_WAIT_BLOCK#, ROW_WAIT_ROW#) as well as the last SQL statement executed by the session (SQL_ID with SQL_CHILD_NUMBER, or SQL_ADDRESS and SQL_HASH_VALUE and SQL_CHILD_NUMBER).

The following setup demonstrates how enqueue waits may happen in an Oracle RDBMS. This example creates two tables with a foreign-key relationship between the tables, and uses three sessions to show the effects of missing indexes on foreign-key columns and potential primary-key violations:

```
SQL> CREATE TABLE T5(C1 NUMBER(10) PRIMARY KEY);

SQL> INSERT INTO T5 VALUES(1);
SQL> INSERT INTO T5 VALUES(2);
SQL> INSERT INTO T5 VALUES(3);
SQL> INSERT INTO T5 VALUES(4);
SQL> COMMIT;

SQL> CREATE TABLE T6(
  2     C1 NUMBER(10) PRIMARY KEY,
  3     C2 NUMBER(10),
  4     CONSTRAINT FK_T5_C1 FOREIGN KEY(C2) REFERENCES T5(C1) ENABLE);

SQL> INSERT INTO T6 VALUES(1,1);
SQL> INSERT INTO T6 VALUES(2,2);
SQL> INSERT INTO T6 VALUES(3,3);
SQL> INSERT INTO T6 VALUES(4,4);
SQL> COMMIT;
```

In the following script, session 1 (SID 177) inserts a new row in the parent and child tables without a commit:

```
SQL> INSERT INTO T5 VALUES(10);
SQL> INSERT INTO T6 VALUES(10,10);
```

In the following script, session 2 (SID 154) inserts a new row into the parent and child tables, deletes a child row for a committed record, and then attempts to change the primary-key value of the associated row in the parent table:

```
SQL> INSERT INTO T5 VALUES(20);
SQL> INSERT INTO T6 VALUES(20,20);
SQL> DELETE FROM T6 WHERE C1=4;
SQL> UPDATE T5 SET C1=30 WHERE C1=4;
{session 2 hangs}
```

Session 3 (SID 155), not able to see the uncommitted row inserted by session 2, attempts to insert a row with the same primary-key value:

```
SQL> INSERT INTO T5 VALUES(20);
{session 3 hangs}
```

The following SQL statement retrieves either the current and/or the most recent wait events for the sessions. Because of space limitations, the USERNAME, PROGRAM, SQL_ID, SQL_ADDRESS, SQL_HASH_VALUE, and SQL_CHILD_NUMBER columns are not displayed. The omitted columns have limited value for this test case, but will prove to be helpful when attempting to troubleshoot problems in a production environment.

```
SQL> SELECT /*+ ORDERED */
  2     S.SID, S.USERNAME, S.PROGRAM, S.STATUS, SW.EVENT, SW.WAIT_TIME WT, SW.STATE,
  3     SW.SECONDS_IN_WAIT S_I_W, S.SQL_ID, S.SQL_ADDRESS, S.SQL_HASH_VALUE,
  4     S.SQL_CHILD_NUMBER, S.ROW_WAIT_OBJ# OBJ#, S.ROW_WAIT_FILE# FILE#,
  5     S.ROW_WAIT_BLOCK# BLOCK#, S.ROW_WAIT_ROW# ROW#, SW.P1, SW.P2, SW.P3
  6  FROM
  7     V$SESSION_WAIT SW, V$SESSION S
  8  WHERE
  9     S.USERNAME IS NOT NULL
 10     AND SW.SID=S.SID
 11     AND SW.EVENT NOT LIKE '%SQL*Net%'
 12     AND SW.EVENT NOT IN ('Streams AQ: waiting for messages in the queue',
 13                          'wait for unread message on broadcast channel');
```

SID	EVENT	WT	STATE	S_I_W	OBJ#	FILE#	BLOCK#	ROW#	P1	P2	P3
154	enq: TM - contention	0	WAITING	51	-1	0	0	0	1414332421	67165	0
155	enq: TM - contention	0	WAITING	33	-1	0	0	0	1414332419	67165	0

The STATE column effectively determines how the results from the query should be interpreted. If the STATE is indicated as WAITING, the session is currently in the wait event and the SECONDS_IN_WAIT column indicates, with a precision of about 3 seconds, how long the session has waited on the most recent wait event. The SQL_ID or HASH_VALUE may be used to see the most recent SQL statement executed by the session by querying V$SQL. (Oracle 10.1 and above also offer the PREV_SQL_ID and related columns in V$SESSION so that the previous SQL statement may also be determined.)

Two of the common enqueue lock types include TX and TM:

- TX enqueues may be caused by the following:

  - One session modifying a row without a commit followed by another session attempting to modify the same row

  - Potential primary-key/unique-key violations in which two sessions attempt to insert or modify rows to have the same primary- or unique-key value

  - Insufficient space in the block to add another ITL slot

  - Waiting for an index block split completion

  - Multiple sessions attempting to modify the rows covered by a single bitmap index fragment

- TM enqueues are transaction resource locks that most frequently occur due to missing foreign-key indexes.

Enqueue locks occur in various modes ranging from 1 to 6:

- Mode 1 is known as a NULL lock, indicating that no session holds the resource (SELECT statement).

- Mode 2 is a row shared S(SS) lock indicating read access to a compound resource (SELECT FOR UPDATE, LOCK ROW SHARE).

- Mode 3 is a row exclusive X(SX) lock indicating write access to a compound resource (INSERT, UPDATE, DELETE, LOCK ROW EXCLUSIVE).

- Mode 4 is a share (S) lock indicating that one or more sessions are reading (LOCK SHARE, CREATE INDEX).

- Mode 5 is a share row exclusive X(SSX) lock that is a combination of read access for one part of a compound resource and write access to another part of a compound resource (LOCK SHARE ROW EXCLUSIVE).

- Mode 6 is an exclusive (X) lock indicating that the session is writing (INSERT, UPDATE TABLE, LOCK EXCLUSIVE, ALTER TABLE, DROP TABLE, DROP INDEX, TRUNCATE TABLE).

The output of the SQL statement that queried V$SESSION_WAIT and V$SESSION listed waits for enq: TM - contention, an indication of a TM enqueue. V$LOCK may be checked to determine the blocking session (recent releases of Oracle include the BLOCKING_SESSION column in V$SESSION). The USERNAME, PROGRAM, SQL_ADDRESS, SQL_HASH_VALUE, SQL_CHILD_NUMBER, ROW_WAIT_OBJ#, ROW_WAIT_FILE#, ROW_WAIT_BLOCK#, and ROW_WAIT_ROW# columns are not displayed in the following output. The omitted columns have limited value for this test case (some of the columns are displayed by the SQL statement that accessed $SESSION_WAIT and V$SESSION), but will prove to be helpful when attempting to troubleshoot problems in a production environment. The following SQL statement is used to identify blocked sessions and the blocker sessions, the lock types, and the last SQL statement executed by the sessions:

```
SQL> SELECT
  2    S.SID, S.USERNAME, S.PROGRAM, S.SQL_ID, S.SQL_ADDRESS, S.SQL_HASH_VALUE,
  3    S.SQL_CHILD_NUMBER CN, S.ROW_WAIT_OBJ#, S.ROW_WAIT_FILE#, S.ROW_WAIT_BLOCK#,
  4    S.ROW_WAIT_ROW#, L.LMODE, L.REQUEST, L.ID1, L.ID2, L.TYPE, L.BLOCK
  5  FROM
  6    V$LOCK L,
  7    V$SESSION S
  8  WHERE
  9    (L.ID1, L.ID2, L.TYPE) IN
 10      (SELECT
 11         ID1, ID2, TYPE
 12       FROM
 13         V$LOCK
 14       WHERE
 15         REQUEST > 0)
 16    AND L.SID=S.SID;
```

SID	SQL_ID	CN	LMODE	REQUEST	ID1	ID2	TY	BLOCK
177			3	0	67165	0	TM	1
154	0sm4pxpb5ybd0	0	3	5	67165	0	TM	1
155	873s5kmm4fkfa	0	0	3	67165	0	TM	0

The preceding output is interesting in that SID 177 (session 1) was holding a mode 3 lock on object 67165 (T6). The SQL_ID for session 1 is NULL, which would make it difficult to determine the SQL statement that caused the initial enqueue. SID 154 (session 2) was holding a mode 3 lock on the same object, and was attempting to acquire a mode 5 lock on the same object. SID 155 (session 3), which should be waiting on a potential primary-key violation in an enq: TX - row lock contention wait event, if not for the activity of session 1, was instead attempting to acquire a mode 3 lock on object 67165 (session 3 on Oracle 10.2.0.4 attempted to acquire a mode 2 lock). Session 1 was blocking session 2, which was blocking session 3. The SQL_ID for session 2 did not indicate the SQL statement that caused the blocking of session 3. Instead it indicated the SQL statement that caused it to start waiting on the enq: TM - contention wait event. When session 1 eventually committed, the transaction for session 2 (SID 154) or session 3 (SID 155) automatically rolled back because of a deadlock. (Oracle 10.2.0.4 did not force a rollback due to a deadlock; instead session 3 remained hanging on a different enqueue wait event.) On Oracle 11.1.0.7 and 11.2.0.1, the following deadlock graph was written to a trace file when session 1 issued a COMMIT command:

```
Deadlock graph:
                        ---------Blocker(s)--------  ---------Waiter(s)---------
Resource Name           process session holds waits  process session holds waits
TM-0001065d-00000000       40      155     SX           25      154     SX  SSX
TX-0009000b-00000db5       25      154     X            40      155          S

session 155: DID 0001-0028-00000032  session 154: DID 0001-0019-00000E6E
session 154: DID 0001-0019-00000E6E  session 155: DID 0001-0028-00000032

Rows waited on:
  Session 155: no row
  Session 154: no row
```

After session 1 committed on Oracle 10.2.0.4, the output of the two SQL statements appeared as follows:

```
SID EVENT              WT STATE    S_I_W OBJ# FILE# BLOCK# ROW#          P1       P2 P3
--- ----------------- -- -------  ----- ---- ----- ------- ---- ----------- ------- --
155 enq: TX - row lock  0 WAITING   117   -1     7 1466532    0 1415053316 2228265 25
        contention


SID SQL_ID          CN LMODE REQUEST     ID1 ID2 TY BLOCK
--- -------------- -- ----- -------  ------- --- -- -----
154                      6       0  2228265  25 TX     1
155 873s5kmm4fkfa  0      0       4  2228265  25 TX     0
```

Since the OBJ# column indicated -1 rather than an actual object ID, the FILE# and BLOCK# columns may be used to locate the object causing session 3 to wait in the enq: TX - row lock contention wait. (Caution: The first query is potentially very inefficient in large databases.)

```
SQL> SELECT
  2    DE.OWNER,
  3    DE.SEGMENT_NAME,
  4    DE.SEGMENT_TYPE,
  5    DE.TABLESPACE_NAME
  6  FROM
```

```
  7    DBA_EXTENTS DE
  8  WHERE
  9    DE.FILE_ID = 7
 10    AND 1466532 BETWEEN BLOCK_ID AND BLOCK_ID+BLOCKS-1;

OWNER     SEGMENT_NAME SEGMENT_TYPE TABLESPACE_NAME
--------  ------------ ------------ ----------------
TESTUSER SYS_C0011456 INDEX         USERS

SQL> SELECT
  2    TABLE_NAME
  3  FROM
  4    DBA_INDEXES
  5  WHERE
  6    OWNER = 'TESTUSER'
  7    AND INDEX_NAME = 'SYS_C0011456';

TABLE_NAME
----------

T5
```

The primary-key index on table T5 is the object causing session 3 to wait in the enq: TX - row lock contention wait, because of a potential primary-key violation if session 2 issues a commit.

For additional information, see Metalink Doc ID 62354.1, "TX Transaction Locks—Example Wait Scenarios"; Doc ID 33453.1, "Referential Integrity and Locking"; and Doc ID 102925.1, "Tracing Sessions: Waiting on an Enqueue." Kyle Hailey published a helpful presentation on the topic of enqueue waits (www.perfvision.com/papers/09_enqueues.ppt).

Summary

This has been a long chapter. We've introduced you to many methods for evaluating and optimizing performance. As you might imagine, the trick is to make the right choice at any given time. When you face a performance problem, how do you choose the method to apply? Our next chapter addresses that very question, helping you to pick the right method at the right time for the right result.

The script files listed in Table 8-3 include the test cases and example scripts presented in this chapter.

Table 8-3. Files for Chapter 8

Filename	Description
10053OptimizerTrace.sql	A test case to reproduce most of the aspects mentioned in the "Generating 10053 Cost-Based Optimizer Traces" section of the chapter. Creates the partitioned table T_OPT_10053_TRACE1 and the unpartitioned table T_OPT_10053_TRACE2.
10053QueryTransformation.sql	Creates the sample tables T7 and T8 and then demonstrates capturing a 10053 trace file for two simple SQL statements that will likely be transformed by the cost-based optimizer.

Filename	Description
AdaptiveCursorBindTest.sql	Demonstrates generation of additional child cursors due to adaptive cursor sharing in Oracle 11g. Uses the tables created by the scripts in the section "Sample Trace File Analysis with Oracle 11.1.0.7."
BCHRSampleTable.sql	Creates the sample table T1 and index with 100,000,000 rows. Used in the section "Monitoring and Reacting to the BCHR."
BCHRTestQueries.sql	Script used to test the performance of forced index access through the adjustment of the OPTIMIZER_INDEX_COST_ADJ parameter to a low value when accessing an infrequently used table having a high clustering factor value for the primary-key index. The script helps demonstrate why a higher BCHR does not always translate into better performance. Used in the section "Monitoring and Reacting to the BCHR."
BufferCacheBlocks.sql	Lists the number of blocks in the buffer cache for the table T9, and the number and mode of the blocks.
BufferCacheCRCopyGen.sql	Script that when executed simultaneously by 100 sessions causes a large number of consistent read copies of the segment header block and various other blocks.
BufferCacheTable.sql	Creates the sample table T9 used by the scripts BufferCacheCRCopyGen.sql and BufferCacheBlocks.sql.
CPULoad.sh	Unix/Linux Bash script that places a load on the server's CPUs to simulate CPU consumption from another database instance or non-Oracle background process running on the server. Used in the section "CPU Load Generators."
CPULoad.sql	Anonymous PL/SQL block that places a load on the server's CPUs to simulate CPU consumption within the database instance. Used in the section "CPU Load Generators."
CPULoad.vbs	VBS script that places a load on the server's CPUs to simulate CPU consumption from another database instance or a non-Oracle background process running on the server. Used in the section "CPU Load Generators."
CPURunQueue.vbs	VBS script that uses Windows Management Instrumentation (WMI) to retrieve the number of processes and threads, and processor queue length, as well as the delta value of the content switches for the previous second. For each Oracle instance running on the server, displays the instance name, user mode time, kernel mode time, and memory consumption. Capable of querying local and remote servers. Used in the section "Determining the CPU Run Queue."

Filename	Description
ExamineOptimizerParam.sql	Script that retrieves the optimizer parameters considered when CHILD_NUMBER 3 for SQL_ID f6rs5tka8j8kp was created. Also demonstrates using event 10132 to write a trace file containing the optimizer parameters, peeked bind variables, and execution plan during every hard parse.
ExecutionPlansCreateTable.sql	Creates the sample tables T3 and T4 and the index IND_T4 with 10,000 rows each. Used in the section "Examining Execution Plans and Plan Statistics."
ExecutionPlansQueries.sql	Script used to demonstrate retrieving execution plans for the last SQL statement with DBMS_XPLAN using TYPICAL and ALLSTATS LAST format parameters. Used in the section "Examining Execution Plans and Plan Statistics."
Extend10046Adaptive.sql	Investigates the adaptive cursor sharing views V$SQL_CS_STATISTICS and V$SQL_CS_SELECTIVITY for a SQL statement. Used in the section "Sample Trace File Analysis with Oracle 11.1.0.7."
Extend10046LogonTrigger.sql	Script creates a logon trigger to enable a 10046 extended trace when a session connects to the database using an application with MYAPP as the first five characters of the application's EXE name.
Extend10046Queries.sql	Queries used to generate output in the 10046 trace file. Used in the section "Sample Trace File Analysis with Oracle 11.1.0.7."
Extend10046Table.sql	Creates the sample tables T3 and T4 and the index IND_T4 with 10,000 rows each. Used in the section "Sample Trace File Analysis with Oracle 11.1.0.7."
HighChildCountPlans.sql	For cursors with more than 10 child cursors, retrieves the execution plans for the child cursors using DBMS_XPLAN and the reason for the generation of the child cursor. Used in the section "Examining Execution Plans and Plan Statistics."
HintList11.1.0.7.txt	List of SQL hints available on Oracle 11.1.0.7.
HintList11.2.0.1.txt	List of SQL hints available on Oracle 11.2.0.1.
InvestigateEnqueueQueries.sql	Queries used to investigate the enqueue waits. Used in the section "Investigating Enqueue Waits."
InvestigateEnqueueSesAct.sql	Data Manipulation Language (DML) activity for the three sessions involved in the enqueue waits. Used in the section "Investigating Enqueue Waits."

Filename	Description
InvestigateEnqueueTable.sql	Creates the sample tables T5 and T6 without a foreign-key index on table T6. Used in the section "Investigating Enqueue Waits."
LowOverheadDataCollect.sql	Script used to collect and report the delta values of various statistics and wait events to permit a quick analysis of system performance. Used in the section "Sampling Performance with Low Overhead."
LowOverheadInsPercBusy.sql	Script calculates the percentage of used CPU at the operating system level that was consumed by the database instance. Used in the section "Sampling Performance with Low Overhead."
LowOverheadPercentBusy.sql	Script calculates the percentage of available CPU time at the operating system level that was used in the sampling period. Used in the section "Sampling Performance with Low Overhead."
LowOverheadProcessList.bat	Windows 2008 Server/Windows Vista/Windows 7 script that outputs the computer's process list to a text file. Used in the section "Sampling Performance with Low Overhead."
LowOverheadTable.sql	Creates the temporary tables used in the section "Sampling Performance with Low Overhead."
MonitoringFileActivity.sql	SQL statements used in the section "Monitoring File Activity."
MonitoringSQLDataCollect.sql	Script used to collect and report the statistic delta values for SQL statements in the library cache, where the elapsed time for the SQL statement exceeds 10 seconds. Used in the section "Monitoring the Delta Values for SQL Statements."
MonitoringSQLInvestigate.sql	Script further investigates the four SQL statements found to consume at least 10 seconds of elapsed time. Used in the section "Monitoring the Delta Values for SQL Statements."
MonitoringSQLTable.sql	Creates the temporary tables used in the section "Monitoring the Delta Values for SQL Statements."
MonitoringWaits.sql	SQL statements used in the section "Monitoring the Delta Values of System/Session Waits."
MonitoringWaitsExtColl.sql	SQL statements that create a sample logging table for time-based wait event analysis, insert into the table, and select the delta values from the table. Ideally, the capture would occur when an event, such as a blocking lock, is detected as well as capturing on a scheduled time interval. This script creates only one of several tables that would be required to reproduce the test case in the "Monitoring the

Filename	Description
	Delta Values of System/Session Waits" section.
OradebugPGAMemoryFill.sql	This script allocates a large portion of memory to the PGA by performing a bulk collect of the rows from the sample table T1. Executing the script using several sessions may cause the memory limit specified by the PGA_AGGREGATE_TARGET to be exceeded, which may force other SQL statements executing in the instance to switch from optimal (in-memory) executions to one-pass or multipass executions (demonstrating another cause for a query to execute quickly at times and slowly at other times).
OradebugProcessList.sql	Lists the PID, SPID, USERNAME, and PROGRAM needed to attach to a session's process using SQL*Plus's ORADEBUG.
SampleInvestigationUpg.sql	The four-page SQL statement from the "Problem after Upgrading the Oracle Release Version" sample investigation in chapter 10.
Sleep.vbs	VBS script that may be called from a SQL*Plus script to pause the execution of a script for a specified number of seconds without using DBMS_LOCK. Used in the section "Creating Statspack or AWR Reports."
StatspackPlans.sql	SQL statements that output the execution plans for Statspack snapshots captured at level 6 or greater. Uses DBMS_XPLAN. Used in the section "Creating Statspack or AWR Reports."
StatspackSnap.sql	Captures a starting Statspack snapshot, waits 10 minutes using the OS command sleep, and then captures a second Statspack snapshot.

CHAPTER 9

■ ■ ■

Choosing a Performance Optimization Method

by Randolf Geist and Charles Hooper

Because there are many performance-monitoring methods, selecting the most appropriate methods that lead to a successful optimization strategy may prove to be a difficult task. This chapter begins by providing recommended starting points for performance monitoring when performance problems are reported to the DBA. Next, this chapter demonstrates the usage of several performance-monitoring methods while troubleshooting three types of performance problems, switching between the various monitoring methods as necessary. Finally, this chapter describes several common performance optimization issues, the most appropriate method to attack those issues, and several strategy guidelines that affect the course of the optimization method.

Decision Tree for Performance Monitoring

To find a starting point for performance monitoring, first determine why optimization is required. Are any end users reporting slower-than-expected performance, or have IT members indicated the existence of potential CPU, I/O, or network load problems? If users have reported problems, are the problem reports specific to a single job function, or are problems reported by people performing various job functions in different departments? Are the performance problems concentrated during a specific time of day, or are they present regardless of the time? Have any changes been implemented in the application recently, or has the same application version been in use for years? Has the performance of the application recently declined, or has it always been below expected levels? Was the release version of Oracle Database used by the application changed, or have any Oracle patches been applied? Have any Oracle parameters changed? Has the server configuration changed? Have any mid-tier application servers changed? If managed network switches are in use, are those switches reporting problems with network links (for example, CRC errors, 10Mb half-duplex speeds, lost links, or broadcast storms), or are the users connected by a high-latency WAN line? Have end users reported general slowness of their computers, or is the slowness specific to the database application? With answers to as many of the preceding questions as possible, you can determine the starting point of the optimization process.

Performance Problems Not Yet Reported

If performance problems have not yet surfaced, but the DBA wants to check the server resource usage to determine whether further investigation is required, an efficient, low-impact method should be used to examine performance. In this case, suggestions include the use of the "Sampling Performance with Low Overhead" method from Chapter 9, review of scheduled Statspack reports, review of AWR reports (if licensed to use this feature), review of ADDM reports (if licensed to use this feature), or review of Enterprise Manager's performance metrics (if licensed to use this feature).

Problems Reported by End Users

If end users have reported performance problems, a more focused approach should be employed to isolate the problems. The method of attack is dependent on several variables that help determine the problems' scope.

Specific to a Single User or Job Function

If a performance problem is specific to a single user or job function, has existed for a long time, appears only during specific times of the day/week/month, *and is specific to a single SQL statement*, the scope of the problem is well defined. In such a case, a targeted method should be used with SQL statement scope. Suggestions for attacking the problem include enabling a 10046 extended trace at level 8 or 12, enabled just before the SQL statement is executed. The trace file should be compared with a trace file generated by another session. Watch for signs of contention between sessions or resource shortages on the server. Examine the possibility of significant physical reads for rarely utilized procedures, and session-level parameters that result in poor execution plans. Other suggestions include monitoring the delta values associated with the SQL statement by periodically querying V$SQL or V$SQLSTATS, or by using DBMS_XPLAN to examine the SQL statement's plan, specifying ALLSTATS LAST as the format parameter (this will require either the addition of a GATHER_PLAN_STATISTICS hint in the SQL statement or STATISTICS_LEVEL to be set to ALL for the session).

If a performance problem is specific to a single user or job function, has existed for a long time, appears only during specific times of the day/week/month, and *appears only in a particular procedure* in an application module, a targeted method with procedure scope should be utilized. A 10046 extended trace at level 8 or 12, enabled just before the procedure starts, provides significant detail specific to the procedure's activity. Compare the trace file with a trace file generated by another session. Watch for signs of contention between sessions or resource shortages on the server. Examine the possibility of significant physical reads for rarely utilized procedures, and session-level parameters that result in poor execution plans.

If the scope of the performance problem is all activity within a particular application module, consider using a targeted method with module-level scope, such as a 10046 extended trace enabled by a logon trigger. Compare the trace file with one generated by another session. Watch for signs of contention between sessions or resource shortages on the server. Examine the possibility of significant physical reads for rarely utilized modules, and session-level parameters that result in poor execution plans. If Unix/Linux is used for the database server's operating system, consider using LTOM (see Metalink Doc ID 352363.1).

If the scope of the performance problem is all database applications for a single user, use a method that targets that specific user. Suggestions include a 10046 extended trace at level 8 or 12, enabled in a logon trigger. Compare the trace files with those generated by another user's session. Check client and server configuration files (such as tnsnames.ora, sqlnet.ora, protocol.ora, and listener.ora) for inappropriate settings. Compare files with those used by other computers. Check for the possibility that the client computer is setting session-level parameters that result in poor execution plans. If Unix/Linux is used for the database server's operating system, consider using LTOM (see Metalink Doc ID 352363.1).

If the performance problem is not necessarily database specific but is present in all applications using the network, use a method that targets the network connection between the client and the server(s). Suggestions include checking intermediate network switches between the client and the server, comparing network packet captures of the problematic client with those collected from another client, checking for failing hardware, and checking for DNS problems.

If the performance problem is not necessarily limited to database or network performance, but instead all activities on a client's computer, use a method that targets the specific client computer. Suggestions include examining scheduled tasks on the client computer, looking for compatibility issues between the various running tasks, and checking for client CPU and/or disk saturation. On a Windows client, consider using Process Explorer (Sysinternals/Microsoft), Windows Task Manager, Windows Performance Monitor, Vista/Windows 7 Resource Monitor, or WMI queries. On Unix/Linux clients, consider using `sar`, `top`, `vmstat`, `iostat`, `netstat`, or a similar utility. Metalink's OS Watcher may also prove helpful.

If the performance problem only recently appeared, determine what changed recently: initialization parameter change, server upgrade, Oracle release version change, client upgrade, network upgrade, installation of other applications, failing hardware, number of users, data volume, and so forth. Focus on what changed, as well as the potential benefits and negatives of the change.

Not Specific to a Single User or Job Function

With problems that impact many users, start with performance-monitoring methods that provide a macro view of the performance problem. Suggestions include Statspack reports, AWR reports (with appropriate license), ADDM reports (with appropriate license), or Enterprise Manager Database Control/Grid Control performance monitoring (with appropriate license). As problems are identified, locate specific sessions experiencing those performance problems, and then follow the suggestions in the preceding section, "Specific to a Single User or Job Function." Determine what, if anything, changed recently: initialization parameter change, server upgrade, Oracle release version change, client upgrade, network upgrade, installation of other applications, failing hardware, number of users, data volume. If it is determined that one or more items have changed, focus on what changed and on the potential benefits and negatives of the change. Are any users not experiencing problems? Then investigate why those users are not experiencing problems.

Problems Reported by IT Staff

If IT staff have reported performance problems, the problem report might be a little less focused on specific application-level problems, and more focused on a system-level performance problem from the point of view of the server(s), storage, and network hardware. In such a case, it might be necessary to start with the hardware performance metrics and work back to specific application actions that resulted in the identified performance problems.

If an IT staff member noticed hardware-related performance problems, start at the server level with operating system utilities, such as `sar`, `top`, `vmstat`, `iostat`, `netstat`, or a similar utility on the Unix/Linux platform; on the Windows platform, consider using `netstat/nbtstat`, Task Manager, Windows Performance Monitor, Windows 2008 Resource Monitor, or WMI queries. Determine whether there is a performance problem that is caused by a process related to the Oracle instance, or some other process on the computer. In the case of performance problems caused by Oracle-related processes, consider drilling into the Oracle process activity by using the operating system process identifier (PID) to search V$PROCESS for a matching PID, and then join to V$SESSION on V$PROCESS.ADDR=V$SESSION.PADDR. Follow the "Problems Reported by End Users" portion of this decision tree to continue troubleshooting. If the problem cannot be isolated to a small number of Oracle-related processes, use a macro scope-monitoring method, such as Statspack, AWR reports, or Enterprise Manager's performance-monitoring features.

If an IT staff member noticed application-related performance problems, identify whether the problem is specific to just the application, a specific application module, a specific function in the module, a specific username, or a specific client computer. Have any changes been made to optimizer parameters, server configuration, network configuration, client configuration, Oracle release version, application version, data volume, or number of users? Follow the "Problems Reported by End Users" portion of this decision tree to continue troubleshooting after the problem is isolated to user actions.

Sample Investigations

Keep in mind the description of various performance-monitoring methods from the preceding chapter. We now want to show examples of implementing some of those methods. The following subsections show the implementation of several of the methods while troubleshooting three types of problems, showing how you can use these methods to identify and potentially solve performance problems found in the wild.

Quick Checkup

A member of the IT group reported that a potential problem exists with an application that accesses the Oracle database server. The application is requiring much more time to complete than normal. The specific application function that is suspected to be problematic is executed sporadically by different users throughout the day, and is reported to be requiring several minutes to complete when it should complete in a couple of seconds. For this potential problem, the script from Chapter 9's "Sampling Performance with Low Overhead" section is executed with a 180-second capture duration. Following are the results:

```
/* Ranked wait time by wait class, including CPU used */
WAIT_CLASS           DELTA    DELTA_SEC WAIT_PERCENT
---------------  -----------  ---------- ------------
CPU                    16824       93.47        99.95
System I/O                 8        0.05         0.05
```

The preceding results show that 99.95 percent of the apparent wait time (from the end-user point of view) for the database instance was due to CPU utilization. This particular server has eight CPUs, and the preceding code indicates that the server used 93.47 centiseconds (0.935 seconds) of CPU time per second of a possible 8 CPU seconds. The overall CPU consumption for the database instance is 11.69 percent of the total available CPU time, as an average for the 3-minute time interval. The true wait events, all in the wait class System I/O, totaled an insignificant amount of time in the 3-minute time period. On average, the database instance is not experiencing a problem. At this point, you must determine whether to continue investigating, or report back to the member of the IT group that no problems were found. The output of the "Sampling Performance with Low Overhead" script continues here:

```
/* Wait time by wait event name */
EVENT                            WAITS      T_OUTS       DELTA    DELTA_SEC
-------------------------------  --------   ---------   --------  ----------
PL/SQL lock timer                    1          1       18001      100.01
SQL*Net message from client        369          0      159768      887.60
Streams AQ: qmn coordinator id      12          6       16801       93.34
Streams AQ: qmn slave idle wai       6          0       16801       93.34
Streams AQ: waiting for messag      36         36       18025      100.14
control file parallel write         60          0           1        0.01
control file sequential read        60          0           1        0.01
db file parallel write              19          0           6        0.03
jobq slave wait                     60         57       18027      100.15
pmon timer                          60         60       18064      100.36
rdbms ipc message                  591        573      144155      800.86
wait for unread message on bro     178        178       18048      100.27
```

The PL/SQL lock timer wait event was caused by the statistic collection script's call to DBMS_LOCK.SLEEP, and because only a single wait was recorded, it is not the case that the application function used DBMS_LOCK.SLEEP to intentionally delay execution. The SQL*Net message from client wait seems to indicate that only about nine sessions on average were connected. However, that wait event is updated for a session only when the next call is received from the session, so that wait event may be misleading at the system level. The remaining wait events are insignificant. Again, you must determine whether to continue investigating or to report back to the member of the IT group that no problems were found. The output of the "Sampling Performance with Low Overhead" script continues here:

```
/* Operating system statistics */
STAT_NAME               END_VALUE       DELTA   DELTA_SEC
----------------------  ----------   ---------  ----------
AVG_BUSY_TIME               94628        2205       12.25
AVG_IDLE_TIME             1309160       15784       87.69
AVG_SYS_TIME            1.1529E+19        1949       10.83
AVG_USER_TIME               25661         250        1.39
BUSY_TIME                  761617       17705       98.36
IDLE_TIME                10477951      126340      701.89
NUM_CPUS                        8           0        0.00
RSRC_MGR_CPU_WAIT_TIME          0           0        0.00
SYS_TIME                   552294       15653       86.96
USER_TIME                  209323        2052       11.40
```

The AVG_BUSY_TIME and AVG_IDLE_TIME statistics basically confirm that on average the server's CPUs (for all processes and operating system activities) were 12.25 percent busy (one of eight CPUs) as was determined earlier. The RSRC_MGR_CPU_WAIT_TIME statistic indicates that Oracle processes were not waiting for the CPU to become available, so there probably is not a problem with CPU contention. Nearly 87 percent of the CPU time was consumed by operating system kernel code, which is very high and likely indicates a problem. The output of the "Sampling Performance with Low Overhead" script continues:

```
/* CPU time and elapsed time for Oracle activities */
STAT_NAME                                             DELTA     DELTA_SEC
-------------------------------------------------- ----------- ------------
DB CPU                                              168173412   934296.73
DB time                                             168254862   934749.23
Java execution elapsed time                                 0        0.00
PL/SQL compilation elapsed time                          577        3.21
PL/SQL execution elapsed time                          27365      152.03
RMAN cpu time (backup/restore)                             0        0.00
background cpu time                                     67181      373.23
background elapsed time                                120861      671.45
connection management call elapsed time                 1089        6.05
failed parse (out of shared memory) elapsed time           0        0.00
failed parse elapsed time                                  0        0.00
hard parse (bind mismatch) elapsed time                    0        0.00
hard parse (sharing criteria) elapsed time                 0        0.00
hard parse elapsed time                                 4789       26.61
inbound PL/SQL rpc elapsed time                            0        0.00
parse time elapsed                                      8223       45.68
repeated bind elapsed time                                22        0.12
sequence load elapsed time                                 0        0.00
sql execute elapsed time                            168236887   934649.37
```

Scaling this to seconds by dividing the DELTA_SEC column by 1,000,000 and reorganizing the statistics into a tree form to show the statistics' hierarchy, the following reveals the breakdown of where the database instance consumed time:

```
0.0007 background elapsed time
0.0004    background cpu time
0.9347 DB time
0.9343    DB CPU
0.0000    connection management call elapsed time
0.0000    sequence load elapsed time
0.9346    sql execute elapsed time
0.0000    parse time elapsed
0.0000      hard parse elapsed time
0.0000        hard parse (sharing criteria) elapsed time
0.0000          hard parse (bind mismatch) elapsed time
0.0000      failed parse elapsed time
0.0000        failed parse (out of shared memory) elapsed time
0.0002    PL/SQL execution elapsed time
0.0000    inbound PL/SQL rpc elapsed time
0.0000    PL/SQL compilation elapsed time
0.0000    Java execution elapsed time
```

The Oracle background processes did not present a CPU consumption problem, so the foreground process section of the tree is examined. The DB time statistic is an accumulation of CPU time used by the foreground processes (the user sessions) and the wait events for the foreground processes. The DB CPU statistic is a large portion of the DB time statistic as was found in the preceding Ranked wait time by wait class, including CPU used section. Most of the DB time statistic is accounted for by the sql execute elapsed time statistic, which is the amount of time spent performing executes and fetches of SQL statements. In an optimal environment, a large percentage of the DB time should be accumulated in the sql execute elapsed time statistic, but the general goal should be to minimize the DB time statistic because it indicates how long all of the connected sessions have waited for their requests from the database instance. Again, you must determine whether to continue investigating or to report back to the member of the IT group that no problems were found. The output of the "Sampling Performance with Low Overhead" script continues:

```
/* System level statistics */
NAME                                               DELTA      DELTA_SEC
-------------------------------------------------- ---------- ------------
CPU used by this session                                    7         0.04
CPU used when call started                                  9         0.05
CR blocks created                                           6         0.03
Cached Commit SCN referenced                          1143224      6351.24
DB time                                                 72723       404.02
DBWR checkpoint buffers written                            25         0.14
DBWR transaction table writes                               7         0.04
DBWR undo block writes                                     12         0.07
IMU CR rollbacks                                            6         0.03
IMU Flushes                                                42         0.23
IMU commits                                                18         0.10
IMU undo allocation size                                75912       421.73
SQL*Net roundtrips to/from client                         365         2.03
background timeouts                                       573         3.18
buffer is not pinned count                            5354420     29746.78
buffer is pinned count                                6152582     34181.01
bytes received via SQL*Net from client                  36033       200.18
bytes sent via SQL*Net to client                       327369      1818.72
calls to get snapshot scn: kcmgss                        1015         5.64
calls to kcmgas                                            27         0.15
calls to kcmgcs                                             1         0.01
commit cleanouts                                           30         0.17
commit cleanouts successfully completed                    30         0.17
consistent changes                                         38         0.21
consistent gets                                       7851751     43620.84
consistent gets - examination                         4893946     27188.59
consistent gets from cache                            7851751     43620.84
cursor authentications                                      1         0.01
data blocks consistent reads - undo records applie          6         0.03
db block changes                                          188         1.04
db block gets                                             162         0.90
db block gets from cache                                  162         0.90
deferred (CURRENT) block cleanout applications             23         0.13
enqueue conversions                                        36         0.20
enqueue releases                                         1576         8.76
enqueue requests                                         1584         8.80
execute count                                             581         3.23
free buffer requested                                      18         0.10
immediate (CURRENT) block cleanout applications             6         0.03
```

index crx upgrade (positioned)	463	2.57
index fast full scans (full)	3	0.02
index fetch by key	1656292	9201.62
index scans kdiixs1	1677833	9321.29
logons cumulative	4	0.02
messages received	37	0.21
messages sent	37	0.21
no work - consistent read gets	2957175	16428.75
opened cursors cumulative	145	0.81
parse count (hard)	5	0.03
parse count (total)	148	0.82
parse time cpu	1	0.01
parse time elapsed	2	0.01
physical read total IO requests	60	0.33
physical read total bytes	983040	5461.33
physical write IO requests	19	0.11
physical write bytes	204800	1137.78
physical write total IO requests	163	0.91
physical write total bytes	2201600	12231.11
physical write total multi block requests	23	0.13
physical writes	25	0.14
physical writes from cache	25	0.14
physical writes non checkpoint	6	0.03
recursive calls	2067	11.48
recursive cpu usage	1	0.01
redo blocks written	60	0.33
redo entries	49	0.27
redo size	22336	124.09
redo synch writes	9	0.05
redo wastage	7316	40.64
redo writes	24	0.13
rollbacks only - consistent read gets	6	0.03
rows fetched via callback	1656253	9201.41
session cursor cache count	54	0.30
session cursor cache hits	53	0.29
session logical reads	7851911	43621.73
session pga memory	4855960	26977.56
session pga memory max	31725720	176254.00
session uga memory	###########	71586840.84
session uga memory max	3645328	20251.82
shared hash latch upgrades - no wait	466	2.59
sorts (memory)	108	0.60
sorts (rows)	10507	58.37
switch current to new buffer	3	0.02
table fetch by rowid	4086754	22704.19
table scan blocks gotten	352	1.96
table scan rows gotten	8623	47.91
table scans (short tables)	69	0.38
undo change vector size	7548	41.93
user calls	418	2.32
user commits	18	0.10

```
workarea executions - optimal                          63        0.35
workarea memory allocated                            1074        5.97
```

Page 7–10 of the *Oracle Database Performance Tuning Guide 11g Release 1* book states that the buffer cache hit ratio may be determined by using the following formula, using the statistics from V$SYSSTAT:

```
1 - (('physical reads cache') / ('consistent gets from cache' +
                                 'db block gets from cache'))
```

Because the buffer cache hit ratio was advocated as a valid performance-tuning metric by various sources over the years, it will be used here to determine whether continued investigation is required:

```
buffer cache hit ratio = 1 - (0 / (7851751 + 162)) = 1 - 0 = 1 = 100%
```

You must determine whether to continue investigating or to report back to the member of the IT group that no problems were found. Is a 100 percent buffer cache hit ratio a good indication or a bad indication? The statistic CPU used by this session indicates that on average the CPU consumption is 0.0004 CPU seconds for each of the 180 seconds in the sampling period, but that statistic value is significantly less than the average 0.9343 seconds of CPU time per second suggested by the DB CPU statistic from V$SYS_TIME_MODEL. This is a sign of a potential problem, or at least of a query that needed more than 3 minutes to complete. Note the number of consistent gets per second, all of which were apparently processed by a single CPU based on the previously mentioned statistics. The next step might be one of the following:

- Examine the delta values for the V$SESS_TIME_MODEL view to locate a session with high values for the DB CPU statistic. After a session is found, examine V$SESSION.SQL_ID and V$SESSION.SQL_CHILD_NUMBER to determine the SQL statement being executed by the session.

- Use an operating system tool, such as ps on Unix /Linux to find a process that is consuming a lot of CPU time. On Windows, use a WMI call to locate the process identifier of the Oracle database instance, and then use a second WMI call to locate the specific thread causing excessive CPU consumption. After the Unix process or Windows thread is determined, join V$PROCESS to V$SESSION on V$SESSION.PADDR=V$PROCESS.ADDR, and then locate the SQL statement being executed by the session.

- Examine the delta values of BUFFER_GETS, CPU_TIME, and ELAPSED_TIME in V$SQL to locate the SQL statement with the greatest change in the delta values. This investigation may result in an increased number of latch: library cache waits in the instance. The V$SESSION_LONGOPS view may also provide additional helpful information.

- Consider capturing multiple Statspack or AWR reports with 10- to 15-minute time intervals. If a SQL statement appears in the Statspack/AWR report indicating much more CPU time consumed than there were seconds in the time interval, and parallel query was not used by the SQL statement, the SQL statement is a likely contributor to the problem. Such a query likely started in another time interval and completed in the time interval under investigation.

Problem After Upgrading the Oracle Release Version

This sample investigation uses several methods from Chapter 9 to resolve a performance problem that resulted after a release version upgrade of the Oracle database product. Monitoring methods utilized include those outlined in the Chapter 9 sections "Examining Execution Plans and Plan Statistics," "Examining Optimizer Parameters Affecting Plans," Generating 10053 Cost-Based Optimizer Traces," and "Generating 10046 Extended Traces."

Shortly after upgrading from Oracle Database 8.1.7.3 on a 32-bit platform to Oracle Database 10.2.0.2 (or a more recent release, such as 11.2.0.1) on a 64-bit platform, a query containing an inline view that had previously completed in 10 seconds now requires in excess of an hour on the more-powerful 64-bit server. Because this problem is isolated to a specific SQL statement, gathering an hour-long Statspack or AWR report would likely prove to be mostly a wasted effort, with specific problem areas lost in the averages of an hour-long report that covered all sessions in the database instance. A more direct approach would include examining the explain plan (more specifically, a DBMS_XPLAN, if available on the Oracle release in use). EXPLAIN PLANs on Oracle 10.1 and above automatically output plans by using DBMS_XPLAN, but the plan's output may not always show the actual execution plan that will be used.

The following code uses a SQL*Plus feature that permits determining the expected execution plan without actually executing the SQL statement:

```
SQL> SET AUTOTRACE TRACEONLY EXPLAIN

SQL> SELECT
  1     TOP_LEVEL_PART_ID, REQ.PURC_PART_ID, REQ.TOTAL_QTY,
  2     REQ.TOTAL_QTY*TPPD.INCREASE "Increase",
  3     REQ.R1_PART_ID, REQ.R2_PART_ID, REQ.R3_PART_ID,
  4     REQ.R4_PART_ID, REQ.R5_PART_ID, REQ.R6_PART_ID,
  5     REQ.R1_CALC_QTY, REQ.R2_CALC_QTY, REQ.R3_CALC_QTY,
  6     REQ.R4_CALC_QTY, REQ.R5_CALC_QTY, REQ.R6_CALC_QTY
  7   FROM
...
```

The remainder of the four-page SQL statement is available in the script library (SampleInvestigationUpg.sql) for this chapter, available on the Apress website at www.apress.com.

The following shows the output of the preceding commands. Note that the Bytes, Cost, and Time columns were removed from the output because of space constraints:

```
-----------------------------------------------------------------------------
|Id |Operation                              | Name       | Rows |
-----------------------------------------------------------------------------
|0  |SELECT STATEMENT                       |            |      |
|1  | VIEW                                  |            |    1 |
|2  |  HASH UNIQUE                          |            |    1 |
|3  |   NESTED LOOPS OUTER                  |            |    1 |
|4  |    FILTER                             |            |      |
|5  |     NESTED LOOPS OUTER                |            |    1 |
|6  |      NESTED LOOPS OUTER               |            |    1 |
|7  |       NESTED LOOPS OUTER              |            |    1 |
|8  |        FILTER                         |            |      |
|9  |         NESTED LOOPS OUTER            |            |    1 |
|10 |          FILTER                       |            |      |
```

|11	NESTED LOOPS OUTER		1
|12	NESTED LOOPS OUTER		1
|13	NESTED LOOPS OUTER		1
|14	NESTED LOOPS OUTER		1
|15	FILTER		
|16	NESTED LOOPS OUTER		1
|17	FILTER		
|18	NESTED LOOPS OUTER		1
|19	NESTED LOOPS		1
|20	NESTED LOOPS		1
|21	MERGE JOIN CARTESIAN		1
|22	TABLE ACCESS FULL	TEMP_PART_PRICE_DATE| 1
|23	BUFFER SORT		6895
|24	TABLE ACCESS FULL	CUSTOMER_ORDER	6895
|25	TABLE ACCESS BY INDEX ROWID	CUST_ORDER_LINE	1
|26	INDEX RANGE SCAN	SYS_C007880	38
|27	TABLE ACCESS BY INDEX ROWID	REQUIREMENT	1
|28	INDEX RANGE SCAN	X_REQUIREMENT_5	1
|29	TABLE ACCESS BY INDEX ROWID	REQUIREMENT	1
|30	INDEX RANGE SCAN	SYS_C008088	1
|31	TABLE ACCESS BY INDEX ROWID	REQUIREMENT	1
|32	INDEX RANGE SCAN	SYS_C008088	1
|33	TABLE ACCESS BY INDEX ROWID	PART	1
|34	INDEX UNIQUE SCAN	SYS_C007999	1
|35	TABLE ACCESS BY INDEX ROWID	PART	1
|36	INDEX UNIQUE SCAN	SYS_C007999	1
|37	TABLE ACCESS BY INDEX ROWID	PART	1
|38	INDEX UNIQUE SCAN	SYS_C007999	1
|39	TABLE ACCESS BY INDEX ROWID	REQUIREMENT	1
|40	INDEX RANGE SCAN	SYS_C008088	1
|41	TABLE ACCESS BY INDEX ROWID	REQUIREMENT	1
|42	INDEX RANGE SCAN	SYS_C008088	1
|43	TABLE ACCESS BY INDEX ROWID	PART	1
|44	INDEX UNIQUE SCAN	SYS_C007999	1
|45	TABLE ACCESS BY INDEX ROWID	PART	1
|46	INDEX UNIQUE SCAN	SYS_C007999	1
|47	TABLE ACCESS BY INDEX ROWID	REQUIREMENT	1
|48	INDEX RANGE SCAN	SYS_C008088	1
|49	TABLE ACCESS BY INDEX ROWID	PART	1
|50	INDEX UNIQUE SCAN	SYS_C007999	1

The plan shows that the Oracle optimizer attempted to use a Cartesian merge join (MERGE JOIN CARTESIAN) to drive into the complex inline view, specifically targeting the CUSTOMER_ORDER table by using the one row Oracle expects to find in the TEMP_PART_PRICE_DATE table (228 rows are actually in the table at the time of the execution). A Cartesian merge join was used because the two tables share no WHERE clause columns in common. The developer of this SQL statement expected Oracle to retrieve the rows from the CUST_ORDER_LINE inline view and then drive from those rows into the REQUIREMENT R table, as had happened with Oracle 8.1.7.3. If the estimated number of rows displayed in the preceding plan were close (with one row in the TEMP_PART_PRICE_DATE table), this plan might be efficient. The join order of the preceding plan changed a bit on Oracle 11.1.0.7 to a Cartesian join

307

between the TEMP_PART_PRICE_DATE and REQUIREMENT tables, followed by nested loop outer joins of PART » CUST_ORDER_LINE » CUSTOMER_ORDER and then a repeating pattern of nested loop outer joins with the REQUIREMENT and PART tables. As a result, the query on 11.1.0.7 completed in roughly 7 minutes and 34 seconds on the same server.

DBMS_XPLAN is able to retrieve the actual number of rows returned by each step in the execution plan if the statistics level is set to ALL (or a /*+ GATHER_PLAN_STATISTICS */ hint is provided in the query to gather execution statistics) when the SQL statement is executed. However, it would be helpful in this case to also have access to the wait event detail if a large number of blocks need to be read from disk, or an excessive amount of temp space is required for the various steps in the execution plan, or other problems occur. Rather than using DBMS_XPLAN, a 10046 extended trace at level 8 or 12 is enabled prior to executing the query, and then the resulting trace file is processed using tkprof or another utility for parsing the trace file. With the file moved from the server to a client computer and renamed, the trace file is processed with tkprof. (Note: The trace was generated on a server with a slightly faster CPU, running Oracle 10.2.0.4 with STATISTICS_LEVEL set to ALL at the session level, and portions of the Row Source Operation output were trimmed to save space.)

```
C:\>TKPROF C:\CARTESIAN.TRC C:\CARTESIAN.TXT
```

The tkprof summary for the SQL file follows:

```
call     count       cpu     elapsed      disk       query    current         rows
-------  ------  --------  ----------  --------  ----------  ---------  -----------
Parse         1      0.00        0.00         0           0          0            0
Execute       1      0.00        0.00         0           0          0            0
Fetch         8   2857.12     2858.98       286   128958761          0          739
-------  ------  --------  ----------  --------  ----------  ---------  -----------
total        10   2857.12     2858.98       286   128958761          0          739

Misses in library cache during parse: 0
Optimizer mode: ALL_ROWS
Parsing user id: 46

Elapsed times include waiting on following events:
  Event waited on                             Times   Max. Wait  Total Waited
  ------------------------------------------  Waited  ----------  ------------
  SQL*Net message to client                        8        0.00          0.00
  db file sequential read                        241        0.03          0.43
  db file scattered read                          14        0.01          0.04
  SQL*Net more data to client                     16        0.00          0.00
  SQL*Net message from client                      8        0.50          0.53
```

The preceding output indicates that no time was lost during the parse or execute calls, that the plan for the SQL statement was already present in the library cache, and that the SQL statement was optimized with the ALL_ROWS optimizer mode (indicating that Oracle attempted to optimize the SQL statement so that all rows of the SQL statement would be retrieved as quickly as possible, rather than optimizing so that just the first couple of rows would be retrieved as quickly as possible). The interesting statistics are present in the fetch line. The 739 rows were retrieved in eight fetches, indicating that the array fetch size was at least 93 rows. The client did not fetch a single row at a time, which might cause some of the long query execution time if the client were connected over a high-latency network connection (a satellite link with a 1000ms ping time would likely require approximately 14 minutes to transfer the rows, one row at a time). The elapsed time for the query is reported as 2,859 seconds, with

2,857 seconds of CPU time. Why so many CPU seconds? The query statistic shows that there were nearly 129 million consistent gets where data blocks were read from memory, with 286 blocks physically read from disk. Each consistent get requires CPU time while the 8KB block is read from memory and undo is potentially applied to the block so that it is consistent as of the time that the query started (also potentially determined by the default isolation level). Examining the wait events, 0.47 seconds were lost due to reading blocks from disk, and 0.53 seconds were lost waiting for the next request from the client, indicating that the remaining time was spent on the CPU. The Oracle 10.2.0.4 trace file did not output the STAT lines for this SQL statement, resulting in the exclusion of the Row Source Operation section from the tkprof output.

By generating a 10053 trace during a hard parse of the SQL statement, a significant clue regarding the plan produced by the Oracle optimizer is found in the 10053 trace file for the query. When the statistics were last collected for the TEMP_PART_PRICE table, no rows were present in the table because the application that executes the SQL statement truncates the table on exit:

```
BASE STATISTICAL INFORMATION
***********************
Table Stats::
  Table: TEMP_PART_PRICE_DATE  Alias: TPPD
    #Rows: 0  #Blks:  1  AvgRowLen:  0.00
Index Stats::
  Index: SYS_C008418  Col#: 1
    LVLS: 0  #LB: 0  #DK: 0  LB/K: 0.00  DB/K: 0.00  CLUF: 0.00
```

The issues uncovered as the cause of the performance problem include the following:

- The optimizer's expected order of execution for the SQL statement did not result in a Cartesian join between a table with 0 rows and a table with 6,895 rows, which would have produced 0 rows ($0 \times 6,895$), but between a table with 228 rows and a table with 6,872 rows, which produced 1,566,816 rows. This miscalculation due to incorrect statistics caused the step in the plan with ID 5 to produce 14 million rows.

- The statistics for the table, although recently collected, are incorrect as of the time the query executed because of the application truncating the table on exit.

- The STATISTICS_LEVEL is set to ALL at the session level, which tends to increase the time required for queries to complete. (This parameter was changed at the session level to allow DBMS_XPLAN to retrieve the actual execution statistics from the previous execution by passing in 'ALLSTATS LAST' as the format parameter).

With the issues identified, there are several possible fixes for the SQL statement:

- Add an /*+ ORDERED */ hint immediately following the initial SELECT keyword. (Alternatively, use a /*+ LEADING */ hint with the first couple of table aliases specified. The LEADING hint offers a little more flexibility as the cardinality changes over time, and eliminates the need to reformat the SQL statement.) This hint will force the Oracle optimizer to process the outermost view and table in the order in which those objects are listed in the SQL statement. This change significantly improved the performance of the query from 66 minutes and 44 seconds to 6.44 seconds (Oracle 11.1.0.7 execution time was 0.54 seconds). The resulting execution plan for the inline view did not match the developer's expected plan, likely due in part to the number of tables in the query. The expected plan would have driven from the inline view containing the CUST_ORDER_LINE table into the

REQUIREMENT R table, and then to PART P, REQUIREMENT R2, PART P2, and so forth. To achieve this execution plan, the order of the inline view and tables must be changed to match the expected join order, and then another /*+ ORDERED */ hint added to the SQL statement immediately following the SELECT keyword that joins those tables. The end result with the two ORDERED hints is an execution time of 2.65 seconds (Oracle 11.1.0.7 execution time was 0.29 seconds). This solution corrects a single SQL statement without addressing the root cause of the poor initial execution plan—the incorrect statistics for the TEMP_PART_PRICE table.

- Add an /*+ OPTIMIZER_FEATURES_ENABLE('9.2.0') */ hint immediately following the initial SELECT keyword. This hint sets the OPTIMIZER_FEATURES_HINTED and _OPTIMIZER_UNDO_COST_CHANGE parameters to 9.2.0 while leaving the OPTIMIZER_FEATURES_ENABLE parameter unchanged (other optimizer parameters are also changed temporarily). The end result with the OPTIMIZER_FEATURES_ENABLE hint is an execution time of 6.87 seconds (Oracle 11.1.0.7 execution time was 1.26 seconds). This solution corrects a single SQL statement without addressing the root cause of the poor initial execution plan—the incorrect statistics for the TEMP_PART_PRICE table.

- Add a /*+ CARDINALITY(TPPD 200) */ hint immediately following the initial SELECT keyword. This hint artificially sets the cardinality (expected number of rows) for the table aliased as TPPD to 200 rows rather than the 0 rows indicated by the table's statistics. The end result with the CARDINALITY hint is an execution time of 4.71 seconds (Oracle 11.1.0.7 execution time was 2.26 seconds). This solution addresses the root cause of the poor execution plan (incorrect statistics), but only for a single SQL statement. Although the CARDINALITY hint is listed in the V$SQL_HINT view of Oracle 11.2.0.1, the CARDINALITY hint is undocumented and may become deprecated in a future Oracle release. Once deprecated, the hint may be removed from the list of hints recognized by the future version of the query optimizer, causing the SQL statement to again perform poorly.

- Add an /*+ OPT_ESTIMATE(TABLE, TPPD, ROWS=200) */ hint immediately following the initial SELECT keyword. This hint artificially sets the cardinality (expected number of rows) for the table aliased as TPPD to 200 rows rather than the 0 rows indicated by the table's statistics. The end result with the OPT_ESTIMATE hint is an execution time of 4.71 seconds (essentially the same as the CARDINALITY hint, Oracle 11.1.0.7 execution time was 2.23 seconds). This solution addresses the root cause of the poor execution plan (incorrect statistics), but only for a single SQL statement. OPT_ESTIMATE hints, although undocumented, are used by SQL profiles in Oracle 10.1 and above, and are thus less likely to become deprecated. The OPT_ESTIMATE hint achieved the same performance improvement as the CARDINALITY hint, and should be selected over the CARDINALITY hint because of the potential future deprecation of the CARDINALITY hint. (Although not included in this sample investigation, a DYNAMIC_SAMPLING hint added to the SQL statement is another approach that should allow the query optimizer to automatically discover and address the incorrect statistics for the TEMP_PART_PRICE table. However, adding this hint may increase the parse time for the SQL statement.)

- Artificially set the statistics for the TEMP_PART_PRICE_DATE table with this command: EXEC DBMS_STATS.SET_TABLE_STATS(OWNNAME=>USER, TABNAME=>'TEMP_PART_PRICE_DATE', NUMROWS=>200, NUMBLKS=>15, NO_INVALIDATE=>FALSE);. The end result of artificially setting the table statistics with the DBMS_STATS procedure is an execution time of 4.71 seconds (essentially the same as the OPT_ESTIMATE hint). This solution addresses the root cause of the poor execution plan (incorrect statistics) for all SQL statements accessing the table, but the default automated stale statistics collection task in Oracle 10.1 and above may reset the statistics, on a nightly basis, for this table to 0 rows and 1 block. After the statistics for the table are set, the DBMS_STATS.LOCK_TABLE_STATISTICS procedure may be used with this table to prevent the nightly stale statistics collection from resetting the statistics.

The tkprof output for the SQL statement with the artificial table statistics set, running Oracle 10.2.0.4 with STATISTICS_LEVEL set to ALL at the session level, follows:

```
TKPROF C:\NOCARTESIAN.TRC C:\NOCARTESIAN.TXT

call     count      cpu    elapsed      disk      query    current       rows
-------  ------  -------  ---------  --------  ---------  ---------  ---------
Parse         1     1.18       1.21         7         14          0          0
Execute       1     0.00       0.00         0          0          0          0
Fetch         9     3.55       3.55         0      68098          0        738
-------  ------  -------  ---------  --------  ---------  ---------  ---------
total        11     4.74       4.76         7      68112          0        738

Misses in library cache during parse: 1
Optimizer mode: ALL_ROWS
Parsing user id: 46

Elapsed times include waiting on following events:
  Event waited on                          Times    Max. Wait  Total Waited
  ----------------------------------------  Waited  ----------  ------------
  SQL*Net message to client                     9        0.00          0.00
  SQL*Net message from client                   9        0.00          0.00
  SQL*Net more data to client                  12        0.00          0.00
```

The output shows that the number of consistent gets dropped from 128,958,761 to 68,098 (ignoring the 14 consistent gets during the hard parse), the CPU time dropped from 2,857.12 seconds to 3.55 seconds (ignoring the 1.18 seconds for the hard parse), and as a minor improvement the 0.47 seconds for the blocks to be read from disk disappeared because the table and index blocks are now cached. 1.21 seconds were lost because of a hard parse of the SQL statement. The following shows the trimmed output of a DBMS_XPLAN for the query with the format parameter set to 'ALLSTATS LAST' so that the actual number of rows returned by each stage of the plan may be determined:

```
-----------------------------------------------------------------------------
| Id |Operation                          | Name             |A-Rows |
-----------------------------------------------------------------------------
|  1|  NESTED LOOPS                       |                  |   739 |
|  2|   NESTED LOOPS OUTER                |                  |  3224 |
|  3|    NESTED LOOPS OUTER               |                  |  3224 |
|  4|     NESTED LOOPS OUTER              |                  |  3224 |
```

```
|   5|        NESTED LOOPS OUTER                    |                      | 3224 |
|   6|         NESTED LOOPS OUTER                   |                      | 3224 |
|   7|          NESTED LOOPS OUTER                  |                      | 3224 |
|*  8|           HASH JOIN                          |                      | 3224 |
|   9|            VIEW                              |                      |  288 |
|  10|             HASH UNIQUE                      |                      |  288 |
|* 11|              HASH JOIN                       |                      | 4853 |
|* 12|               TABLE ACCESS FULL              | CUSTOMER_ORDER       | 6872 |
|* 13|               TABLE ACCESS FULL              | CUST_ORDER_LINE      | 4857 |
|* 14|            FILTER                            |                      | 31826|
|* 15|             HASH JOIN RIGHT OUTER            |                      | 31826|
|  16|              TABLE ACCESS BY INDEX ROWID     | REQUIREMENT          | 30970|
|* 17|               INDEX RANGE SCAN               | X_REQUIREMENT_5      | 30970|
|* 18|              FILTER                          |                      | 31826|
|* 19|               HASH JOIN RIGHT OUTER          |                      | 31826|
|  20|                TABLE ACCESS BY INDEX ROWID   | REQUIREMENT          | 30970|
|* 21|                 INDEX RANGE SCAN             | X_REQUIREMENT_5      | 30970|
|* 22|                FILTER                        |                      | 31826|
|* 23|                 HASH JOIN RIGHT OUTER        |                      | 31826|
|  24|                  TABLE ACCESS BY INDEX ROWID | REQUIREMENT          | 30970|
|* 25|                   INDEX RANGE SCAN           | X_REQUIREMENT_5      | 30970|
|* 26|                  FILTER                      |                      | 31811|
|* 27|                   HASH JOIN RIGHT OUTER      |                      | 31815|
|  28|                    TABLE ACCESS BY INDEX ROWID| REQUIREMENT         | 30970|
|* 29|                     INDEX RANGE SCAN         | X_REQUIREMENT_5      | 30970|
|* 30|                    FILTER                    |                      | 31556|
|* 31|                     HASH JOIN OUTER          |                      | 31627|
|  32|                      TABLE ACCESS BY INDEX ROWID| REQUIREMENT      | 28673|
|* 33|                       INDEX RANGE SCAN       | X_REQUIREMENT_5      | 28673|
|  34|                      TABLE ACCESS BY INDEX ROWID| REQUIREMENT      | 30970|
|* 35|                       INDEX RANGE SCAN       | X_REQUIREMENT_5      | 30970|
|* 36|            TABLE ACCESS BY INDEX ROWID       | PART                 | 1690 |
|* 37|             INDEX UNIQUE SCAN                | SYS_C007999          | 3224 |
|* 38|            TABLE ACCESS BY INDEX ROWID       | PART                 | 1020 |
|* 39|             INDEX UNIQUE SCAN                | SYS_C007999          | 1940 |
|* 40|            TABLE ACCESS BY INDEX ROWID       | PART                 |  255 |
|* 41|             INDEX UNIQUE SCAN                | SYS_C007999          | 1046 |
|* 42|            TABLE ACCESS BY INDEX ROWID       | PART                 |   26 |
|* 43|             INDEX UNIQUE SCAN                | SYS_C007999          |  261 |
|* 44|            TABLE ACCESS BY INDEX ROWID       | PART                 |    8 |
|* 45|             INDEX UNIQUE SCAN                | SYS_C007999          |   27 |
|* 46|            TABLE ACCESS BY INDEX ROWID       | PART                 |    0 |
|* 47|             INDEX UNIQUE SCAN                | SYS_C007999          |    8 |
|* 48|           TABLE ACCESS BY INDEX ROWID        | TEMP_PART_PRICE_DATE |  739 |
|* 49|            INDEX UNIQUE SCAN                 | SYS_C008418          |  739 |
---------------------------------------------------------------------------------------
```

Table 9-1 shows the test results for the various solutions listed earlier, both with and without blocks precached in the KEEP buffer pool. Examining Table 9-1 for this particular SQL statement, there is a definite performance penalty on Oracle 10.2.0.4 when the statistics level is changed from TYPICAL to ALL. On Oracle 11.1.0.7, the performance penalty still exists for the change in statistics level, but the penalty is much less severe. In this experiment, the solution with the two ORDERED hints offered the most dramatic improvement in performance.

Table 9-1. Summary of Performance with Physical Reads (and Without Physical Reads)

Query Modification	10.2 TYPICAL	10.2 ALL	11.1 TYPICAL	11.1 ALL
Original query	6:56.73	1:06:44.31	5:35.58	7:34.21
Single ORDERED hint	14.86 (0.48)	20.60 (6.44)	15.56 (0.45)	15.50 (0.54)
Two ORDERED hints	14.39 (0.28)	16.36 (2.65)	16.73 (0.23)	17.11 (0.29)
OPTIMIZER_FEATURES_ENABLE	14.86 (1.06)	21.35 (6.87)	15.80 (1.15)	15.31 (1.26)
CARDINALITY	15.22 (1.42)	18.23 (4.71)	16.81 (2.13)	17.23 (2.26)
OPT_ESTIMATE	15.08 (1.43)	18.14 (4.71)	16.39 (2.13)	17.05 (2.23)
DBMS_STATS	17.12 (1.43)	20.23 (4.71)	16.41 (2.13)	17.23 (2.26)

Problem After Upgrading the ERP Version

This sample investigation uses several methods from Chapter 9 to find a resolution for a performance problem that resulted after an application change. Monitoring methods utilized include those described in the Chapter 9 sections "Generating 10046 Extended Traces," "Examining Network Packets," and "Examining Client-Side Traces."

New versions of software packages are primarily intended to introduce new features while also eliminating bugs from prior versions. The later release might be built using a different development environment, might target a wider range of database platforms, might introduce support for a wider range of end-user languages, and might target faster or more-capable client computers. When encountering application functionality that takes two, ten, or a hundred times longer to complete than in the previous version, is it sufficient to just assume that the software is working as designed, or should the performance issue be investigated? Accepting poor performance should not be the first option. Determining that poor performance was introduced in a new version of an application may be difficult to accomplish. Gathering 10046 traces at level 12 for time-critical application features, as well as Statspack or AWR reports, prior to an application upgrade permits before and after performance comparisons.

For this particular investigation, a 10046 trace at level 12 is enabled just before the start of a slower-than-expected application feature started executing. The slower-than-expected feature is the opening and saving of a customer order, a task that might be performed by a single user 50 to 200 times a day.

Prior to the ERP upgrade, opening a large customer order required roughly 8.5 seconds, while saving the same large customer order might require roughly 14 seconds. The equivalent operations on the new version required roughly 18.25 seconds and 62 seconds, respectively. The 10046 extended trace indicated that the elapsed time of the parse, execute, and fetch calls totaled 1.99 seconds when opening a large customer order. Because the 1.99-second total is a small portion of the 18.25 seconds required for this function to complete, additional investigation is needed to determine where the remaining 16.26 seconds were lost. Once again, a 10046 trace at level 12 was enabled on the server, as well as a Wireshark network packet capture and Process Monitor file/registry capture on the client side. The additional logging permits time referencing of the server-side activity with that of the client side. An unfortunate side effect of the additional logging is an increased impact of the performance-monitoring activity on the duration of the customer order open, resulting in a new customer order open time of roughly 38.5 seconds. A summary of the 10046 trace file contents follows:

```
Total for Trace File:
|PARSEs   3115|CPU S  0.078125|CLOCK S  0.087701|ROWs     0|PHY RD BLKs  0
             |CON RD BLKs (Mem)      0|CUR RD BLKs (Mem)  0|SHARED POOL MISs  1|
|EXECs    5088|CPU S  1.125000|CLOCK S  1.117020|ROWs     1|PHY RD BLKs  0
             |CON RD BLKs (Mem)      1|CUR RD BLKs (Mem)  5|SHARED POOL MISs  0|
|FETCHs   9081|CPU S  0.609375|CLOCK S  0.786847|ROWs  2274|PHY RD BLKs  2
             |CON RD BLKs (Mem)  47846|CUR RD BLKs (Mem)  0|SHARED POOL MISs  0|


Wait Event Summary:
SQL*Net message to client       0.017635  On Client/Network
                    Min Wait: 0.000001  Avg Wait: 0.000001  Max Wait: 0.000016
SQL*Net message from client    36.687106  On Client/Network
                    Min Wait: 0.000121  Avg Wait: 0.003430  Max Wait: 0.104871
SQL*Net more data from client   0.000093  On Client/Network
                    Min Wait: 0.000007  Avg Wait: 0.000013  Max Wait: 0.000020
SQL*Net more data to client     0.000539  On Client/Network
                    Min Wait: 0.000016  Avg Wait: 0.000026  Max Wait: 0.000049
latch: library cache            0.000239  On DB Server
                    Min Wait: 0.000020  Avg Wait: 0.000040  Max Wait: 0.000060
db file sequential read         0.026275  On DB Server
                    Min Wait: 0.000356  Avg Wait: 0.013138  Max Wait: 0.025919
log file sync                   0.000590  On DB Server
                    Min Wait: 0.000295  Avg Wait: 0.000295  Max Wait: 0.000295
```

The SQL statement consuming the greatest percentage of server-side time has the following statistics (this is a very long SQL statement, so the SQL statement is not displayed here):

```
Similar SQL Statements in Group: 1
First Reference: Cursor 4   Ver 5   Parse at 0.425167
|PARSEs      1|CPU S  0.000000|CLOCK S  0.000189|ROWs     0|PHY RD BLKs  0
             |CON RD BLKs (Mem)      0|CUR RD BLKs (Mem)  0|SHARED POOL MISs  0|
|EXECs     990|CPU S  0.578125|CLOCK S  0.516969|ROWs     0|PHY RD BLKs  0
             |CON RD BLKs (Mem)      0|CUR RD BLKs (Mem)  0|SHARED POOL MISs  0|
|FETCHs   1979|CPU S  0.343750|CLOCK S  0.422574|ROWs     0|PHY RD BLKs  0
             |CON RD BLKs (Mem)  27706|CUR RD BLKs (Mem)  0|SHARED POOL MISs  0|
  CPU S 50.86%  CLOCK S 47.19%
   *    0.646431 seconds of time related to client/network events
|          ++++++++++||          ++++++++++|
```

The statistics indicate that the SQL statement was executed 990 times (once for every order line), 1,979 fetch calls were made by the application, and 0 rows were returned. The average execution time is reasonably quick. Another interesting SQL statement has these statistics:

```
Similar SQL Statements in Group: 990
First Reference: Cursor 14   Ver 1    Parse at 0.572967
|PARSEs  990|CPU S  0.062500|CLOCK S  0.018927|ROWs       0|PHY RD BLKs  0
            |CON RD BLKs (Mem)      0|CUR RD BLKs (Mem)  0|SHARED POOL MISs  0|
|EXECs      0|CPU S  0.000000|CLOCK S  0.000000|ROWs       0|PHY RD BLKs  0
            |CON RD BLKs (Mem)      0|CUR RD BLKs (Mem)  0|SHARED POOL MISs  0|
|FETCHs     0|CPU S  0.000000|CLOCK S  0.000000|ROWs       0|PHY RD BLKs  0
            |CON RD BLKs (Mem)      0|CUR RD BLKs (Mem)  0|SHARED POOL MISs  0|
   CPU S 3.45%  CLOCK S 0.95%
 *   28.751060 seconds of time related to client/network events

select tax_exempt from cust_address where customer_id = :1 and addr_no = :2;
```

The preceding SQL statement was submitted to the database to be parsed 990 times (once for every order line), but the SQL statement was never actually executed. At most, this SQL statement would need to be executed a single time per customer order, because the columns in the WHERE clause are associated with the table containing the order header information, rather than the line detail information. This fact might point to a bug in the ERP system or a situation caused by over-modularization of program functionality. What is interesting about this SQL statement is not the execution time, but the accumulated 28.75 seconds in the SQL*Net message from client wait event. Based on the wait time in this wait event, it appears that the ERP module performs significant client-side processing after this SQL statement is sent to the database to be parsed, and that the accumulated wait after this SQL statement is sent accounts for roughly 75 percent of the new total execution time with all logging enabled. With the Wireshark network packet log file time sequenced with the Process Monitor file/registry log file using a known common zero point, it is possible to determine what happened outside the database instance during this delay.

```
8.438075 seconds, client sends the SQL statement just prior to the SQL of interest
8.438693 seconds, server's response to the SQL statement is received at the client
8.439098 seconds, client sends the SQL statement identified above
8.439493 seconds, server's response to the parse call is received at the client
(processing at the client)
8.477592 seconds, client sends the bind values to start loading line 2 of the order
8.481907 seconds, server's response to the new bind variables is received at
                  the client
8.482367 seconds, client sends the bind values to another SQL statement for line 2
8.483012 seconds, server's response to the new bind variables is received at
                  the client
...
```

From the preceding code, you can see that the typical round-trip time from the client, over the network to the server, up through the server's network stack to the Oracle instance for processing, back down through the server's network stack, and over the network and back to the client is roughly 0.000618 seconds. A delay of 0.000618 seconds for this round-trip time is reasonable for a low-latency gigabit switched LAN. At least in the packets captured during the time interval, there were no duplicate ACKs reported, no retransmits, and no 0.2-second delays that might be a sign of a mismatch of the ACK sending frequency on the two sides of the network connection. With this in mind, the network link and server's network stack might be eliminated as the source of the vast majority of the SQL*Net message from client wait time. The 0.038099-second gap between the network activity at time interval 8.439493 and time interval 8.477592 is the time interval that should be examined. If this delay happens for the next 989 lines in the order, the accumulated wait time for the client will be roughly 37.7 seconds, which is remarkably close to the elapsed 38.5 seconds for the customer order open time with all logging enabled.

The Process Monitor log for this time interval is the key to understanding the delay. If repeating patterns of activity lasting roughly 0.030 to 0.039 seconds are found in the Process Monitor log, the source of the delay might be determined. The start and end times of the activity might be used to time-synchronize the log to that of the Wireshark log so that a common zero point for both logs may be identified. With the start time set to the calculated zero point, the pattern appears as follows:

```
1.493 seconds, close a file named sql.ini
(apparent processing at the database server or in memory on client)
1.498 seconds, access the HKLM\Control Panel\International branch of the
             Windows registry
1.498 through 1.500 seconds, access a file named win.ini
1.500 through 1.501 seconds, access the International branch of the
             Windows registry
1.501 through 1.502 seconds, access a file named win.ini
(process above repeated several times)
1.518 through 1.519 seconds, access the International branch of the
             Windows registry
1.519 through 1.521 seconds, access a file named win.ini
(apparent processing at the database server or in memory on client)
1.531 seconds, attempt to read two registry keys related to Crystal Reports 11
1.533 through 1.534 seconds, access the International branch of the
             Windows registry
1.534 through 1.535 seconds, access a file named win.ini
(the process above repeated many times)
```

Analysis of this pattern indicates that for each customer order line read from the database, the ERP module updates 10 onscreen fields, and for each of the 10 onscreen fields, the file named win.ini is accessed twice (32-bit and 64-bit applications should not need to access this file) and 21 Windows Registry lookups are performed to read various entries in the branch HKCU\Control Panel\International as well as those entries related to Crystal Reports 11 (not installed on the client computer). The client-side activity during the customer order open contributed to most of the document open time, and the accumulated time for the preceding activity is very close to the 0.038-second delay found in the Wireshark log, so further analysis might prove helpful.

Microsoft's Spy++ utility permits digging deeper into the application performance issues, essentially providing a wiretap into the application message queues (which allow one window object to communicate with another) of various window objects within an application. The Spy++ logs for the ERP module show interesting behavior that likely contributed to the performance problems with that module when opening and saving large customer orders:

```
001D04BC S .....WM_GETTEXTLENGTH wParam:00000000 lParam:00000000
001D04BC R .....WM_GETTEXTLENGTH cch:5 [lResult:00000005]
001D04BC S .....WM_GETTEXT cchTextMax:6 lpszText:0012C794 [wParam:00000006
             lParam:0012C794]
001D04BC R .....WM_GETTEXT cchCopied:5 lpszText:0012C794 ("12459")
             [lResult:00000005]
```

```
001405A6 S .....message:0x0415 [User-defined:WM_USER+21] wParam:00000000
                   lParam:00000000
001405A6 R .....message:0x0415 [User-defined:WM_USER+21] lResult:00000001
...
001405A6 R .....message:0x0428 [User-defined:WM_USER+40] lResult:00000000
001D04BC S .....WM_GETTEXTLENGTH wParam:00000000 lParam:00000000
001D04BC R .....WM_GETTEXTLENGTH cch:5 [lResult:00000005]
001D04BC S .....WM_GETTEXT cchTextMax:6 lpszText:0012C794 [wParam:00000006
                   lParam:0012C794]
001D04BC R .....WM_GETTEXT cchCopied:5 lpszText:0012C794 ("12459")
                   [lResult:00000005]
001405A6 S .....message:0x0415 [User-defined:WM_USER+21] wParam:00000000
                   lParam:00000000
001405A6 R .....message:0x0415 [User-defined:WM_USER+21] lResult:00000001
001405A6 S .....message:0x0428 [User-defined:WM_USER+40] wParam:00000000
                   lParam:0012D018
001405A6 R .....message:0x0428 [User-defined:WM_USER+40] lResult:00000001
00160624 S .....message:0x0431 [User-defined:WM_USER+49] wParam:00000000
                   lParam:00000008
00160624 R .....message:0x0431 [User-defined:WM_USER+49] lResult:00000000
001D04BC S .....WM_GETTEXTLENGTH wParam:00000000 lParam:00000000
001D04BC R .....WM_GETTEXTLENGTH cch:5 [lResult:00000005]
001D04BC S .....WM_GETTEXT cchTextMax:6 lpszText:0012C794 [wParam:00000006
                   lParam:0012C794]
001D04BC R .....WM_GETTEXT cchCopied:5 lpszText:0012C794 ("12459")
                   [lResult:00000005]
...
```

The preceding partial log shows a repeating pattern in the messages sent among the various windows and subwindows in the ERP module while opening a customer order. The ERP module window repeatedly sent a message to a text field, first requesting the length of the field's data, and then requesting the field's data. Although a single execution of the WM_GETTEXTLENGTH and WM_GETTEXT messages complete very quickly, sending those messages thousands of times (rather than sending the messages once and storing the result in a variable) is an unnecessary waste of CPU resources on the client computer.

Based on the Spy++ logs, the module also updates several onscreen text fields for every customer order line read, providing accumulated order totals through the last order line read. The following message sequence is required for the update of a single onscreen field. Note the presence of the $ and . in the text sent to the field, which is likely the end result of the registry scans identified earlier in the HKLM\Control Panel\International branch of the Windows Registry, as these characters vary based on the regional settings of the operating system. The Spy++ log continues here:

```
001A0BD2 S .....WM_SETTEXT lpsz:0012D04C ("$24,228.00") [wParam:00000000
                   lParam:0012D04C]
00F10540 S ......WM_CTLCOLORSTATIC hdcStatic:04010B13 hwndStatic:001A0BD2
                    [wParam:04010B13 lParam:001A0BD2]
00F10540 R ......WM_CTLCOLORSTATIC hBrush:25101E78 [lResult:25101E78]
00F10540 S ......WM_CTLCOLORSTATIC hdcStatic:04010B13 hwndStatic:001A0BD2
                    [wParam:04010B13 lParam:001A0BD2]
00F10540 R ......WM_CTLCOLORSTATIC hBrush:25101E78 [lResult:25101E78]
00F10540 S ......WM_CTLCOLORSTATIC hdcStatic:04010B13 hwndStatic:001A0BD2
```

```
                        [wParam:04010B13 lParam:001A0BD2]
00F10540 R ......WM_CTLCOLORSTATIC hBrush:25101E78 [lResult:25101E78]
00F10540 S ......WM_CTLCOLORSTATIC hdcStatic:04010B13 hwndStatic:001A0BD2
                        [wParam:04010B13 lParam:001A0BD2]
00F10540 R ......WM_CTLCOLORSTATIC hBrush:25101E78 [lResult:25101E78]
001A0BD2 R .....WM_SETTEXT fSuccess:True [lResult:00000001]
001A0BD2 S .....WM_PAINT hdc:00000000 [wParam:00000000 lParam:00000000]
001A0BD2 S ......WM_ERASEBKGND hdc:04010B13 [wParam:04010B13 lParam:00000000]
00F10540 S .......WM_CTLCOLORSTATIC hdcStatic:04010B13 hwndStatic:001A0BD2
                        [wParam:04010B13 lParam:001A0BD2]
00F10540 R .......WM_CTLCOLORSTATIC hBrush:25101E78 [lResult:25101E78]
001A0BD2 R ......WM_ERASEBKGND fErased:True [lResult:00000001]
00F10540 S .....WM_CTLCOLORSTATIC hdcStatic:17010A56 hwndStatic:001A0BD2
                        [wParam:17010A56 lParam:001A0BD2]
00F10540 R ......WM_CTLCOLORSTATIC hBrush:25101E78 [lResult:25101E78]
00F10540 S .....WM_CTLCOLORSTATIC hdcStatic:17010A56 hwndStatic:001A0BD2
                        [wParam:17010A56 lParam:001A0BD2]
00F10540 R ......WM_CTLCOLORSTATIC hBrush:25101E78 [lResult:25101E78]
00F10540 S .....WM_CTLCOLORSTATIC hdcStatic:04010B13 hwndStatic:001A0BD2
                        [wParam:04010B13 lParam:001A0BD2]
00F10540 R ......WM_CTLCOLORSTATIC hBrush:25101E78 [lResult:25101E78]
00F10540 S .....WM_CTLCOLORSTATIC hdcStatic:04010B13 hwndStatic:001A0BD2
                        [wParam:04010B13 lParam:001A0BD2]
00F10540 R ......WM_CTLCOLORSTATIC hBrush:25101E78 [lResult:25101E78]
00F10540 S .....WM_CTLCOLORSTATIC hdcStatic:17010A56 hwndStatic:001A0BD2
                        [wParam:17010A56 lParam:001A0BD2]
00F10540 R .....WM_CTLCOLORSTATIC hBrush:25101E78 [lResult:25101E78]
00F10540 S .....WM_CTLCOLORSTATIC hdcStatic:04010B13 hwndStatic:001A0BD2
                        [wParam:04010B13 lParam:001A0BD2]
00F10540 R ......WM_CTLCOLORSTATIC hBrush:25101E78 [lResult:25101E78]
00F10540 S ......WM_CTLCOLORSTATIC hdcStatic:17010A56 hwndStatic:001A0BD2
                        [wParam:17010A56 lParam:001A0BD2]
00F10540 R ......WM_CTLCOLORSTATIC hBrush:25101E78 [lResult:25101E78]
00F10540 S ......WM_CTLCOLORSTATIC hdcStatic:04010B13 hwndStatic:001A0BD2
                        [wParam:04010B13 lParam:001A0BD2]
00F10540 R ......WM_CTLCOLORSTATIC hBrush:25101E78 [lResult:25101E78]
001A0BD2 R .....WM_PAINT lResult:00000001
```

Immediately after the preceding onscreen field updated, something a bit strange appeared in the Spy++ logs. For each customer order line, the ERP module updated a hidden window to have a caption of "Effective Exchange Rates For *order ID*" (this window is used to view currency conversions between foreign and native currencies). The module then populated several fields within that window, apparently in anticipation that someone would decide to adjust the currency exchange rate between the customer order currency and the native currency (even if the order is already in the native currency). This unnecessary work involves an extra 190 window messages per order line, and likely is a contributor to the client-side performance issue when opening an order. The Spy++ log continues here:

```
001F0B80 S .....message:0x4069 [User-defined:WM_USER+15465] wParam:00000000
```

```
                lParam:00000000
001F0B80 S ......WM_GETTEXT cchTextMax:100 lpszText:0012C0B4
                [wParam:00000064 lParam:0012C0B4]
001F0B80 R ......WM_GETTEXT cchCopied:10 lpszText:0012C0B4 ("$24,228.00")
                [lResult:0000000A]
00230C9A S ......message:0x4077 [User-defined:WM_USER+15479] wParam:00000000
                lParam:00000000
00150C9E S .......message:0x4077 [User-defined:WM_USER+15479]
                wParam:00000000 lParam:00000000
00230C9A S ........WM_SETTEXT lpsz:020EC7C8 ("Effective Exchange Rates For 12459")
                [wParam:00000000 lParam:020EC7C8]
00230C9A S ........WM_GETTEXT cchTextMax:510 lpszText:0012AE34
                [wParam:000001FE lParam:0012AE34]
00230C9A R ........WM_GETTEXT cchCopied:34 lpszText:0012AE34
                ("Effective Exchange Rates For 12459") [lResult:00000022]
00230C9A R ........WM_SETTEXT fSuccess:True [lResult:00000001]
00140D74 R .......message:0x0431 [User-defined:WM_USER+49] lResult:00000000
00130DA4 S ........WM_GETTEXT cchTextMax:180 lpszText:0012ACEC
                [wParam:000000B4 lParam:0012ACEC]
00130DA4 R ........WM_GETTEXT cchCopied:10 lpszText:0012ACEC ("$21,536.00")
                [lResult:0000000A]
00130DA4 S ........WM_GETTEXT cchTextMax:180 lpszText:0012ACEC
                [wParam:000000B4 lParam:0012ACEC]
00130DA4 R ........WM_GETTEXT cchCopied:10 lpszText:0012ACEC ("$21,536.00")
                [lResult:0000000A]
00130DA4 S ........WM_SETTEXT lpsz:0012B634 ("$21,536.00") [wParam:00000000
                lParam:0012B634]
00230C9A S .........WM_COMMAND wNotifyCode:EN_UPDATE wID:4105 hwndCtl:00130DA4
                [wParam:04001009 lParam:00130DA4]
00230C9A R .........WM_COMMAND lResult:00000000
00230C9A S .........WM_COMMAND wNotifyCode:EN_CHANGE wID:4105 hwndCtl:00130DA4
                [wParam:03001009 lParam:00130DA4]
00230C9A R .........WM_COMMAND lResult:00000000
00130DA4 R ........WM_SETTEXT fSuccess:True [lResult:00000001]
...
```

With the cause of the slow client-side performance issue isolated for the application developers, the Spy++ logs are examined to determine the cause of the 62-second save time for large orders. When the ERP module performed a save operation, the log showed that immediately after the save operation completed, an exact duplicate of the order open process executed. Thus the actual save process time was roughly 44 of the 62 seconds. During the save, a grid-type window in the ERP module repeatedly scrolled as each order line was processed. The Spy++ logs show thousands of messages similar to the following:

```
00030808 S ..message:0x0428 [User-defined:WM_USER+40] wParam:00000000
            lParam:0012DC38
00030808 R ..message:0x0428 [User-defined:WM_USER+40] lResult:00000000
00030808 S ..message:0x0439 [User-defined:WM_USER+57] wParam:000080B3
            lParam:00000000
00030808 R ..message:0x0439 [User-defined:WM_USER+57] lResult:00000000
00030808 S ..message:0x0415 [User-defined:WM_USER+21] wParam:00000000
            lParam:00000000
```

```
00030808 R ..message:0x0415 [User-defined:WM_USER+21] lResult:0000000E
00030808 S ..message:0x0428 [User-defined:WM_USER+40] wParam:00000000
              lParam:0012DC38
00030808 R ..message:0x0428 [User-defined:WM_USER+40] lResult:00000000
...
00030808 S .WM_GETFONT wParam:00000000 lParam:00000000
00030808 R .WM_GETFONT hfont:040A2DB1 ("MS Sans Serif" 8pt) [lResult:040A2DB1]
00030808 S .WM_GETFONT wParam:00000000 lParam:00000000
00030808 R .WM_GETFONT hfont:040A2DB1 ("MS Sans Serif" 8pt) [lResult:040A2DB1]
000216C6 S .message:0x0431 [User-defined:WM_USER+49] wParam:00000000 lParam:00000001
000216C6 R .message:0x0431 [User-defined:WM_USER+49] lResult:00000000
00030808 S .message:0x0434 [User-defined:WM_USER+52] wParam:0000004E lParam:00000000
00030808 R .message:0x0434 [User-defined:WM_USER+52] lResult:0000004E
00030808 S .message:0x0427 [User-defined:WM_USER+39] wParam:0000004E lParam:00000000
00030808 R .message:0x0427 [User-defined:WM_USER+39] lResult:000216BC
000216BC S .message:0x042B [User-defined:WM_USER+43] wParam:00000000 lParam:00000000
000216BC R .message:0x042B [User-defined:WM_USER+43] lResult:0000005A
00030808 S .WM_GETFONT wParam:00000000 lParam:00000000
00030808 R .WM_GETFONT hfont:040A2DB1 ("MS Sans Serif" 8pt) [lResult:040A2DB1]
00030808 S .WM_GETFONT wParam:00000000 lParam:00000000
00030808 R .WM_GETFONT hfont:040A2DB1 ("MS Sans Serif" 8pt) [lResult:040A2DB1].
```

Spy++ showed that the window with the handle 00030808 was the grid-type control that scrolled during the save operation. A Windows best programming practice introduced in the mid 1990s recommended disabling the repainting of window objects that must be updated repeatedly in a loop, and then forcing a repaint of the object after the loop ends. Whether or not window objects are repainted is controlled by the WM_SETREDRAW message, which may be sent to a window object by using the SendMessage or PostMessage Windows API calls. Although it is not possible to fix all of the performance issues with this ERP module without direct access to the source code, you can rename the unnecessarily accessed win.ini file and then send messages into the ERP module's window objects to permit executing performance tests that may provide the developers additional incentive to fix the client-side performance issue. Each performance test was repeated twice on a client computer, with the results displayed here:

```
                                                      Seconds
Normal Open                                           18.30, 18.26
No win.ini                                            17.48, 17.96
Disable repainting of on-screen fields               16.21, 16.31
No win.ini/Disable repainting of fields              15.99, 15.67
No win.ini/Disable repainting of fields and grid     16.14, 15.70

Normal Save                                           62.12, 61.87
No win.ini                                            60.92, 60.73
Disable repainting of on-screen fields               59.74, 59.87
No win.ini/Disable repainting of fields              58.99, 58.98
No win.ini/Disable repainting of fields and grid     17.38, 16.85
```

This shows that by just avoiding some of the unnecessary work performed client-side, the save time decreased by about 44.25 seconds (the actual save component of the time decreased from 44 seconds to 1.15 seconds), allowing the new save operation to complete faster than the original open time.

Performance Optimization Issues

Performance problems arrive from many sources, including faulty or insufficient hardware resources, inefficient SQL, contention between multiple sessions, and problems with the shared pool. The following sections in this chapter describe various performance issues and the systematic optimization methods to address those issues. (These methods were described earlier in Chapter 9.) We've chosen four examples to look at:

Inefficient SQL: This section begins a look into one of the most common performance-optimization problems that a DBA faces, that of specific SQL statements that do not perform well. We begin by collecting data, verifying the problem, and determining whether the problem lies in the parse phase or the execution phase.

Parse performance issues: Assuming the problem lies in the parsing phase, we look at some ways to further narrow and then resolve the problem.

High execution time or fetch time issues: Often the problem with a poorly performing SQL statement is that it takes a long time to execute, to find and fetch the rows that it needs to return. In this section, we delve into this common trouble area, again looking at ways to apply methods from Chapter 9 toward finding a solution.

Shared pool abuse: We end the chapter by looking at a class of problems resulting from poor management of the shared pool. We look at some possible solutions and at some guidelines for investigating root causes.

Inefficient SQL

If a particular SQL statement or a group of SQL statements have been identified that perform poorly while other SQL statements perform well, or a session runs slowly with most of the time spent on the execution of a particular SQL statement, then inefficient SQL processing has likely been identified. The inefficient SQL statement might have been identified by running custom tests or benchmarks, eventually triggered by end-user complaints, Statspack/AWR/ADDM reports that showed the SQL as part of the Top SQL or bottleneck categories, or an apparent hang where a lot of CPU time and/or I/O resources were consumed. Inefficient SQL statements might appear after structural changes to a schema (caused by an application upgrade, for example), changes to the object or system statistics, changes to the data volume (typically an increase, but possibly also a decrease), changes to the application logic (for example, caused by an application upgrade), or a database upgrade (particularly noteworthy is the upgrade from a previous release to Oracle 10.1 or later because of the various changes to the optimizer and statistics management introduced in Oracle 10.1).

Verify the Inefficiency

Your next steps should include a verification step to ensure that the root cause of the issue has been identified, and that the inefficient SQL identified is actually the cause of the performance problems. This step is crucial because there is a risk of attacking the wrong SQL statement, in the process wasting significant time and effort with little or no benefit. The verification exercise ideally consists of the following steps:

1. Clearly describe the problem, including the following:

    a. How the problem was identified (for example, end-user complaints, order system hanging)

    b. The severity of the problem (for example, orders cannot be processed)

    c. A description of the steps required to reproduce the issue

    d. Clear distinction between what *is* working and what *is not* working (for example, the order entry form is hanging, whereas the invoice processing is working fine)

    e. The expected or acceptable behavior

    f. What has been done so far to rectify the issue (for example, object statistics have been checked, but no anomalies were identified)

2. Generate an isolated test case that reproduces the issue at will and has the following characteristics:

    a. Covers the inefficient SQL identified

    b. Is as generic as possible, allowing you to easily transfer the identified issue to Oracle Support if required

    c. Shows evidence that the statement identified is inefficient (for example, the SQL*Plus timing facility reports that the statement takes 306 seconds to complete instead of expected subsecond execution time)

Collect Additional Data

After a SQL statement is positively verified to be the root cause of the performance problem, the next step requires collection of additional data about the inefficient SQL statement. Ideally, if it is possible to create an isolated test case, execute the test case with an extended SQL trace enabled (see the "Generating 10046 Extended Traces" section in Chapter 9). Special considerations are required if a shared server configuration is in use. In this case, the execution might be spread across several trace files, because multiple shared servers might have been involved in the execution. Oracle 10.1 and later provide the trcsess utility to merge multiple trace files into one. If it was not possible to create an isolated test case, it might be necessary to generate an extended SQL trace for a user session that is affected by the execution of the inefficient SQL. In the event that it is not possible to execute an isolated test case, which is the preferred method for most situations, you should perform the following verifications.

Verify That the Trace File Covers Only One Test

Verify that the trace file covers only the recent test by checking the timestamps in the trace file. You can use the various timestamp information written into the trace file. In the following 10046 extended trace file, you can see the explicit timestamps starting with *** written at the beginning of the trace and from time to time by Oracle into the trace file. You can also use the tim= information, which is expressed in microseconds in recent releases. Here you can see that between the timestamp with value 672319555990 (672319.555990 seconds) and the timestamp with value 672627452347 (672627.452347 seconds), there is a difference of 308 seconds, which corresponds quite exactly to the 5 minutes 8 seconds difference seen in the other timestamp information:

```
WAIT #1: nam='db file scattered read' ela= 1082 file#=8 block#=7401 blocks=8
          obj#=63838 tim=672319552388
WAIT #1: nam='db file scattered read' ela= 1044 file#=8 block#=7409 blocks=8
          obj#=63838 tim=672319555990
*** 2009-10-29 09:26:33.492
WAIT #1: nam='db file scattered read' ela= 1068 file#=8 block#=7417 blocks=8
          obj#=63838 tim=672319559701
WAIT #1: nam='db file scattered read' ela= 1057 file#=8 block#=7425 blocks=8
          obj#=63838 tim=672319563333
WAIT #1: nam='db file scattered read' ela= 1075 file#=8 block#=7433 blocks=8
          obj#=63838 tim=672319566948
...
PARSE #4:c=0,e=242,p=0,cr=0,cu=0,mis=0,r=0,dep=0,og=0,tim=672327440086
EXEC #4:c=0,e=140,p=0,cr=0,cu=0,mis=0,r=0,dep=0,og=0,tim=672327440338
*** 2009-10-29 09:31:41.385
WAIT #2: nam='SQL*Net message to client' ela= 3 driver id=1413697536 #bytes=1 p3=0
          obj#=63838 tim=672627452347
WAIT #2: nam='SQL*Net message from client' ela= 754 driver id=1413697536 #bytes=1
          p3=0 obj#=63838 tim=672627453214
=====================
PARSING IN CURSOR #1 len=66 dep=0 uid=61 oct=3 lid=61 tim=672627453448
          hv=2693617790 ad='1c1aa024'
select
        count(*)
from
        test_table t
END OF STMT
PARSE #1:c=0,e=120,p=0,cr=0,cu=0,mis=0,r=0,dep=0,og=1,tim=672627453439
EXEC #1:c=0,e=94,p=0,cr=0,cu=0,mis=0,r=0,dep=0,og=1,tim=672627453678
```

If you identify such old contents from previous traces, delete any lines that belong to an unrelated test case.

Verify That the Trace File Is Complete

Verify that the trace file is complete, which means that the trace was not started or stopped during the execution of the SQL statement. One way to identify such a situation is to compare the elapsed time that each of the wait events contributed to the call with the tim= statistic following the wait events. In the following example, the sum of the wait events' elapsed time exceeds the elapsed time of the call following the wait events. You can also see that recent releases of Oracle add a "synthetic" parse call to the trace in case the trace has been started after the parse call of the corresponding cursor. The important point is that the FETCH call following the WAIT events accounts for only 5 microseconds, but the preceding WAIT events show a greater elapsed time. You can also observe that the timestamps in bold indicate an elapsed time of at least 2.7 seconds (258930.403020 − 258927.694079 = 2.708941 seconds).

```
*** ACTION NAME:() 2009-11-01 18:14:15.879
*** MODULE NAME:(SQL*Plus) 2009-11-01 18:14:15.879
*** SERVICE NAME:(orcl) 2009-11-01 18:14:15.879
*** SESSION ID:(141.39) 2009-11-01 18:14:15.879
WAIT #2: nam='db file scattered read' ela= 1075 file#=8 block#=4361 blocks=8
        obj#=63838 tim=258927694079
WAIT #2: nam='db file scattered read' ela= 1029 file#=8 block#=4369 blocks=8
        obj#=63838 tim=258927706619
WAIT #2: nam='db file scattered read' ela= 990 file#=8 block#=4377 blocks=8
        obj#=63838 tim=258927708124
WAIT #2: nam='db file scattered read' ela= 1574 file#=8 block#=4385 blocks=8
        obj#=63838 tim=258927710190
...
WAIT #2: nam='db file scattered read' ela= 975 file#=8 block#=14121 blocks=8
        obj#=63838 tim=258930395799
WAIT #2: nam='db file scattered read' ela= 973 file#=8 block#=14129 blocks=8
        obj#=63838 tim=258930397602
WAIT #2: nam='db file scattered read' ela= 976 file#=8 block#=14137 blocks=8
        obj#=63838 tim=258930399398
WAIT #2: nam='db file scattered read' ela= 975 file#=8 block#=14145 blocks=8
        obj#=63838 tim=258930401215
WAIT #2: nam='db file scattered read' ela= 982 file#=8 block#=14153 blocks=8
        obj#=63838 tim=258930403020
WAIT #2: nam='SQL*Net message from client' ela= 22584 driver id=1413697536 #bytes=1
        p3=0 obj#=63838 tim=258930430318
=====================
PARSING IN CURSOR #2 len=61 dep=0 uid=61 oct=3 lid=61 tim=258930430407
        hv=3954673823 ad='1884c73c'
select count(*)
from test_table
where id < 0
END OF STMT
FETCH #2:c=0,e=5,p=0,cr=0,cu=0,mis=0,r=0,dep=0,og=0,tim=258930430401
WAIT #2: nam='SQL*Net message to client' ela= 3 driver id=1413697536 #bytes=1
        p3=0 obj#=63838 tim=258930430514
```

Here is another trace of the same SQL statement, but this time the trace is complete. Notice in particular that the FETCH call following the WAITs shows an elapsed time that corresponds to the elapsed time of the preceding WAIT events:

```
*** ACTION NAME:() 2009-11-01 18:27:39.106
*** MODULE NAME:(SQL*Plus) 2009-11-01 18:27:39.106
*** SERVICE NAME:(orcl) 2009-11-01 18:27:39.106
*** SESSION ID:(142.146) 2009-11-01 18:27:39.106
=====================
PARSING IN CURSOR #1 len=47 dep=0 uid=61 oct=47 lid=61 tim=259730855081
        hv=774405238 ad='188423b8'
BEGIN dbms_monitor.session_trace_enable; END;
```

```
END OF STMT
EXEC #1:c=0,e=201,p=0,cr=0,cu=0,mis=1,r=1,dep=0,og=1,tim=259730855076
WAIT #1: nam='SQL*Net message to client' ela= 5 driver id=1413697536 #bytes=1
        p3=0 obj#=10209 tim=259730857244
WAIT #1: nam='SQL*Net message from client' ela- 4649 driver id=1413697536
        #bytes=1 p3=0 obj#=10209 tim=259730861998
=====================
PARSING IN CURSOR #2 len=61 dep=0 uid=61 oct=3 lid=61 tim=259730863743
        hv=3954673823 ad='1884c73c'
select count(*)
from test_table
where id < 0
END OF STMT
PARSE #2:c=0,e=1340,p=0,cr=0,cu=0,mis=1,r=0,dep=0,og=1,tim=259730863738
EXEC #2:c=0,e=79,p=0,cr=0,cu=0,mis=0,r=0,dep=0,og=1,tim=259730864468
WAIT #2: nam='SQL*Net message to client' ela= 4 driver id=1413697536 #bytes=1
        p3=0 obj#=10209 tim=259730864578
WAIT #2: nam='db file sequential read' ela= 13143 file#=8 block#=9 blocks=1
        obj#=63838 tim=259730877964
WAIT #2: nam='db file scattered read' ela= 1014 file#=8 block#=10 blocks=8
        obj#=63838 tim=259730879232
WAIT #2: nam='db file scattered read' ela= 970 file#=8 block#=18 blocks=8
        obj#=63838 tim=259730880719
...
WAIT #2: nam='db file scattered read' ela= 988 file#=8 block#=14177 blocks=8
        obj#=63838 tim=259734569280
WAIT #2: nam='db file scattered read' ela= 978 file#=8 block#=14185 blocks=8
        obj#=63838 tim=259734571360
WAIT #2: nam='db file scattered read' ela= 989 file#=8 block#=14193 blocks=8
        obj#=63838 tim=259734573625
WAIT #2: nam='db file sequential read' ela= 297 file#=8 block#=14201 blocks=1
        obj#=63838 tim=259734574937
FETCH #2:c=1682419,e=3710464,p=13681,cr=13693,cu=0,mis=0,r=1,dep=0,og=1,
        tim=259734575144
WAIT #2: nam='SQL*Net message from client' ela= 620 driver id=1413697536 #bytes=1
        p3=0 obj#=63838 tim=259734575977
FETCH #2:c=0,e=5,p=0,cr=0,cu=0,mis=0,r=0,dep=0,og=0,tim=259734576068
WAIT #2: nam='SQL*Net message to client' ela= 3 driver id=1413697536 #bytes=1
        p3=0 obj#=63838 tim=259734576124
```

Verify That the Issue Is a Database Issue

A final step is to verify that the issue resides within the Oracle RDBMS and is not a client issue (network/connectivity issue, slow fetch, no array fetch processing, and so forth). To that end, check the generated trace file for WAIT events reported between calls (usually FETCH calls). The following example shows that between each fetch call, the database waits 2 seconds for the client:

```
=====================
PARSING IN CURSOR #1 len=43 dep=1 uid=61 oct=3 lid=61 tim=2456420409 hv=3841442455
ad='1c123120'
SELECT * FROM TEST_TABLE T
```

```
END OF STMT
PARSE #1:c=50072,e=643835,p=160,cr=177,cu=0,mis=1,r=0,dep=1,og=1,tim=2456420399
EXEC #1:c=0,e=40,p=0,cr=0,cu=0,mis=0,r=0,dep=1,og=1,tim=2456420550
WAIT #1: nam='db file scattered read' ela= 6354 file#=8 block#=10 blocks=8
        obj#=63838 tim=2456427157
FETCH #1:c=0,e=6702,p=8,cr=4,cu=0,mis=0,r=1,dep=1,og=1,tim=2456427340
WAIT #1: nam='SQL*Net message from client' ela= 1994072 driver id=1413697536
        #bytes=1 p3=0 obj#=63838 tim=2458421685
FETCH #1:c=0,e=50,p=0,cr=1,cu=0,mis=0,r=1,dep=1,og=1,tim=2458421903
WAIT #1: nam='SQL*Net message from client' ela= 2002550 driver id=1413697536
        #bytes=1 p3=0 obj#=63838 tim=2460424569
FETCH #1:c=0,e=49,p=0,cr=1,cu=0,mis=0,r=1,dep=1,og=1,tim=2460424800
WAIT #1: nam='SQL*Net message from client' ela= 2002526 driver id=1413697536
        #bytes=1 p3=0 obj#=63838 tim=2462427444
FETCH #1:c=0,e=49,p=0,cr=1,cu=0,mis=0,r=1,dep=1,og=1,tim=2462427656
```

This may also be checked by comparing the elapsed time reported in a tkprof output for the statement to the time waited on the SQL*Net message from client wait event. (An extended SQL trace must be enabled with wait events to see the WAIT lines in the trace file.) The following example shows that the majority of the time was waited on the SQL*Net message from client wait event:

```
SELECT *
FROM
 TEST_TABLE T

call     count       cpu   elapsed       disk      query    current       rows
------- ------  -------- ---------- ---------- ---------- ---------- ----------
Parse        1      0.00      0.03          1          1          0          0
Execute      1      0.00      0.00          0          0          0          0
Fetch       12      0.00      0.00          8         15          0         12
------- ------  -------- ---------- ---------- ---------- ---------- ----------
total       14      0.00      0.04          9         16          0         12

Misses in library cache during parse: 1
Optimizer mode: ALL_ROWS
Parsing user id: 61      (recursive depth: 1)

Rows     Row Source Operation
-------  ---------------------------------------------------
     12  TABLE ACCESS FULL TEST_TABLE (cr=15 pr=8 pw=0 time=6692 us)

Elapsed times include waiting on following events:
  Event waited on                          Times   Max. Wait  Total Waited
  ----------------------------------------  Waited  ----------  ------------
  db file scattered read                        1        0.00          0.00
  SQL*Net message from client                  12        2.01         22.02
********************************************************************************
```

Also, the elapsed time reported in the tkprof output for the statement ideally should be close to the wait time measured at the application/end-user level, which will confirm that the SQL being traced is the source of the performance problem.

For an in-depth discussion of how to interpret extended SQL trace files, we recommend that you read *Optimizing Oracle Performance* by Cary Millsap and Jeff Holt (O'Reilly Media, 2003).

Determine Whether It Is a Parse or Execution Problem

After it has been determined that the identified SQL statement is the problematic SQL statement, tkprof output may be used to distinguish between statements that spend most of their time in execute/fetch phases and those that spend most of their time in the parse phase. If the statement spends most of its elapsed time in the parse phase, continue with the "Parse Performance Issues" section that follows. If the statement spends most of its elapsed time in the execute/fetch phase, continue with the upcoming "High Execution Time or Fetch Time Issues" section.

It is important to obtain the execution plan for the SQL statement. The preferred method to do so in 10.1 and later is through the use of the provided DBMS_XPLAN.DISPLAY_CURSOR function, ideally in conjunction with the STATISTICS_LEVEL parameter set to ALL at the session level for the execution of the statement. (See the section "Examining Execution Plans and Plan Statistics" in Chapter 9 for a detailed description of how to do this.) For Oracle releases prior to 10.1, Tanel Poder's XM.SQL, XMS.SQL, or XMSH.SQL scripts (http://blog.tanelpoder.com/2009/05/26/scripts-for-showing-execution-plans-via-plain-sql-and-also-in-oracle-9i/) or Alberto Dell'Era's XPLAN.SQL (www.adellera.it/scripts_etcetera/xplan/index.html) may be used to obtain a similar output. The crucial point here is that all these tools obtain the actual execution plan from the library cache rather than an EXPLAIN PLAN output, which might be different from the actual execution plan used to execute the SQL statement. Oracle also provides the SQLTXPLAIN tool on Metalink that can gather extended information about a SQL statement (see Doc ID 215187.1 for more information). However, this tool is based on EXPLAIN PLAN and therefore might report incorrect information about the execution plans.

For further diagnosis, it is also helpful to consult historic information contained in Statspack or AWR reports about the SQL statement identified. Note that the Statspack level captured must be at least level 6 to collect historic SQL execution plans. Either the SPREPSQL.SQL or AWRSQRPT.SQL scripts may be used to obtain historic information about a particular SQL statement. The SQL statement must be identified by OLD_HASH_VALUE or SQL_ID in order to run these reports. By reviewing historic execution plans, it might be possible to detect changes to the execution plan that happened in the past and possibly retrieve a good-performing version of the SQL statement along with its execution plan. This review process might allow for a comparison of the bad and the good execution plan.

The sources of inefficient SQL are numerous. Those sources include performing an unnecessary amount of work in the SQL statement (such as retrieving 10,000 rows when only the first row is needed by the application), as well as the optimizer selecting an inappropriate access path for the data retrieval, which might result from a variety of sources, including the following:

- Missing or incorrect statistics

- Missing NOT NULL or other check constraints for columns

- Missing foreign-key constraints for columns

- Missing join conditions

- Automatic query transformations performed by the optimizer (which might remove a join or add additional predicates to the WHERE clause)

- Joining a large number of tables

- Using poor query form (mixing ANSI join syntax with Oracle-specific join syntax, placing scalar queries in column positions of other queries, using multiple layers of statically defined views)

Inefficient processing of data is another contributor to performance problems. Inefficient processing includes the following:

- Performing row-by-row (otherwise known as slow-by-slow) operations in PL/SQL as well as in application code

- Performing an excessive number of commits (for instance, using the autocommit feature in some programming environments)

- Performing an insufficient number of commits (changing a row and executing the commit for that row long after the row must be updated by other sessions)

- Performing Data Definition Language (DDL) calls on tables and other objects while sessions are attempting to use those objects, or creating/dropping tables in procedural code rather than reusing suitable global temporary tables or permanent tables (abusing techniques from non-Oracle database environments)

- Treating the Oracle database as if it were a different database platform, such as Microsoft SQL Server (such as using a custom-developed sequence generator routine in place of an Oracle SEQUENCE object)

The potential symptoms of inefficient SQL include the following:

- Excessive physical I/O, which leads to session waits on I/O, which leads to delays that are visible in various wait events

- Excessive logical I/O, which leads to excessive CPU usage and contention on latches and data block buffers

- Excessive CPU usage (see Chapter 9 for a detailed discussion)

- Excessive temp space usage, direct path read and write

- Excessive number of consistent gets (for example, applying a significant amount of undo to provide read consistency)

- Excessive undo generation

- Excessive redo generation

- Excessive waits for log writer completion (due to excessive COMMITs)

- Excessive PGA memory usage (for example, due to inappropriate PL/SQL bulk processing)

Parse Performance Issues

This section covers some of the common causes of excessive parse time and possible solutions. It is important to note that parsing of a statement does not necessarily need to be performed as part of a PARSE call, but can also be triggered by an EXEC call, if the cursor has been invalidated since the initial parse. This means that you might have "parse" performance issues although you don't see many PARSE calls in the trace file. The relevant statistics are shown by tkprof as Misses in library cache during parse and Misses in library cache during execute. The number of times shown there represents the number of times the statement required a full parse, including an optimization phase, whereas the remaining "soft" PARSE calls (see the Parse statistic in the tkprof output) are less resource intensive. Ideally, an application can avoid both "soft" and "hard" parses by parsing a cursor once and keeping it open as long as required for further executions of the same cursor. Provided that the cursor doesn't get invalidated, this will parse the cursor only once but execute as many times as required.

Majority of Parse Time Spent on the CPU

If the majority of parse time is spent on the CPU and/or a large number of consistent gets occur during the parse step according to the trace file analyzer, then check for one of the following causes:

- The SQL statement is parsed many times. Excessive parsing of a SQL statement, either "soft" or "hard" parsing, will increase CPU usage and potentially lead to contention in the shared pool. The following tkprof output shows a statement that had to be parsed at each execution (Misses in library cache during execute: 2384), although the application (PL/SQL in this case) attempted to parse the statement only once and keep the cursor open for further executions (PARSE count = 1):

```
SELECT *
FROM
 HARD_PARSE_TEST


call     count      cpu    elapsed     disk        query      current        rows
-------  ------  -------- ----------  ---------  ----------  -----------  ----------
Parse        1     0.02       0.04        0           0            0           0
Execute   2384   442.18     902.85        0           0            0           0
Fetch     2384     1.61       2.90        0        9534            0      238300
-------  ------  -------- ----------  ---------  ----------  -----------  ----------
total     4769   443.81     905.80        0        9534            0      238300

Misses in library cache during parse: 1
Misses in library cache during execute: 2384
Optimizer mode: ALL_ROWS
Parsing user id: 61      (recursive depth: 1)


Rows     Row Source Operation
-------  --------------------------------------------------------
      0  TABLE ACCESS FULL HARD_PARSE_TEST (cr=0 pr=0 pw=0 time=6 us)

Elapsed times include waiting on following events:
  Event waited on                             Times     Max. Wait  Total Waited
  -------------------------------------------- Waited   ----------  ------------
  latch: row cache objects                     7891        0.06         6.81
  cursor: pin S                                 191        0.02         0.60
  cursor: pin S wait on X                       310        0.03         4.22
  latch: shared pool                            270        0.02         0.22
  latch: library cache                          539        0.12         2.67
  latch: library cache lock                     125        0.03         0.16
  latch free                                     57        0.00         0.03
  kksfbc child completion                         4        0.06         0.23
```

- Dynamic sampling is used, possibly set with a high level, attempting to sample a large fraction of an object. This may be verified by checking the DBMS_XPLAN notes section and the 10053 optimizer trace (see the "Examining Execution Plans and Plan Statistics" as well as the "Generating 10053 Cost-Based Optimizer Traces" sections of Chapter 9). You can also find evidence of the recursive queries executed by Oracle in the extended SQL trace file by checking for SQL statements that include the comment /* OPT_DYN_SAMP */.

If dynamic sampling is responsible for most of the parse time, check whether a lower level of dynamic sampling might be sufficient to analyze less data, or look for alternatives such as stored outlines or SQL profiles, which may be used to lock down the execution plan. The following tkprof output shows a statement that spends most of its time during the PARSE call, caused by dynamic sampling. The actual execution required only a fraction of the parse time:

```
select  /*+ dynamic_sampling(t 10) */
        count(*)
from
        dynamic_sampling_test_table t
where
        val1 = 25

call     count       cpu    elapsed       disk      query    current       rows
------- ------  -------- ---------- ---------- ---------- ---------- ----------
Parse        1      0.59       1.98      10005      10015          0          0
Execute      1      0.00       0.00          0          0          0          0
Fetch        2      0.00       0.00          0          3          0          1
------- ------  -------- ---------- ---------- ---------- ---------- ----------
total        4      0.59       1.98      10005      10018          0          1

Misses in library cache during parse: 1
Optimizer mode: ALL_ROWS
Parsing user id: 61

Rows     Row Source Operation
-------  ---------------------------------------------------------
      1  SORT AGGREGATE (cr=3 pr=0 pw=0 time=289 us)
    200   INDEX RANGE SCAN IDX_DYNAMIC_SAMPLING_TEST (cr=3 pr=0 pw=0 time=837 us)
                                    (object id 63769)


Elapsed times include waiting on following events:
  Event waited on                            Times    Max. Wait  Total Waited
  ----------------------------------------  Waited   ----------  ------------
  db file sequential read                        2        0.00          0.00
  SQL*Net message to client                      2        0.00          0.00
  SQL*Net message from client                    2        0.04          0.04
```

- The query uses many IN list parameters or OR statements. In some releases of Oracle, this might lead to excessive parse times. It might be possible to avoid having the query optimizer perform a concatenation rewrite by using the NO_EXPAND hint, which allows the optimizer in recent Oracle releases to use the IN-LIST ITERATOR operation instead. This operation might still be inefficient in terms of execution but requires significantly less parse time. A problem similar to that described in Metalink Doc ID 744664.1—"High Parse Time and Memory Usage for Query with Complex OR Predicates or IN-Lists After Upgrade to 10.2 or 11.1," might also contribute to performance problems.

- At least one of the tables used in the query has a very large number of partitions (for example, more than 1,000 / 10,000 partitions). In general, this will increase the parse time because the optimizer potentially has to process the partition-level statistics of many partitions. Some older releases of Oracle may hit a bug that causes excessive CPU and memory usage (Bug 2785102).

Majority of Parse Time Spent on Wait Events

If the majority of parse time is spent in wait events, contention for resources (for example, waits for library cache locks/pins or latches) should be investigated, in addition to identifying issues with client connectivity and very long SQL statements that need to be transmitted to the database instance.

If SQL*Net more data from client wait events are encountered in the trace file immediately before the PARSE line, there might an issue with the client attempting to transfer a lengthy SQL statement to the database instance. Check the client network connectivity. Possible workarounds include usage of PL/SQL REF CURSORs to avoid the transfer of the large SQL text from the client to the server.

High Execution Time or Fetch Time Issues

Your trace file analyzer output will often show that most of the time consumed by a poorly executing SQL statement is spent in the execution and/or fetch phases. When that's the case, there are many potential root problems. The following subsections detail different paths of investigation you should consider.

General Optimizer Settings and Object Statistics

Optimizer settings and object statistics can play a significant role in whether SQL performs well or poorly. Following are some general areas that you can investigate if you suspect that settings or statistics are the problem:

Representative object statistics: The estimates of the cost-based optimizer (CBO) are based on the object (table/index) statistics along with other information. If these statistics are not representative, the calculations performed might yield inaccurate selectivity and cardinality estimates, possibly leading to bad execution plans. This may be checked by comparing the estimated number of rows to the actual number of rows returned by execution plan operations. The simplest way to perform this comparison is the execution of the SQL statement with STATISTICS_LEVEL set to ALL (available as of release 9.2) and obtaining the Row Source execution statistics with DBMS_XPLAN.DISPLAY_CURSOR (available starting with release 10.1), XMSH.SQL by Tanel Poder, or XPLAN.SQL by Alberto Dell'Era. See the "Examining Execution Plans and Plan Statistics" section of Chapter 9.

Inadequate statistics: The statistics have been gathered with too low of a sample size and therefore are not representative. Check the SAMPLE_SIZE column from the object's statistics, and compare it to the NUM_ROWS column. If the sample size is too low, consider regathering the statistics with a larger sample size. Note that the resulting change in statistics will potentially impact many SQL statements and might result in worse performance for some of those SQL statements.

Determine whether the index statistics have not been refreshed—for example, the CASCADE option of DBMS_STATS.GATHER_TABLE_STATS was set to the value of FALSE. (FALSE was the default prior to the 10.1 release. In 10.1, the default changed to DBMS_STATS.AUTO_CASCADE.) Incorrect index statistics might have a significant impact on execution plans, so consider regathering the index statistics.

Outdated statistics: If the tables were last analyzed a long time ago and have undergone significant data changes since the statistics were gathered, consider refreshing the statistics. Starting with release 10.1, the default statistics-gathering job when enabled should take care of objects that have undergone significant changes (more than 10 percent changes or a truncate). However, it might still be necessary to manually gather statistics if data has been modified by bulk processing that is then used immediately after the bulk modification.

Manually modified statistics: Check for USER_STATS=YES in the corresponding dictionary views (or the SQLTXPLAIN report). Verify why statistics were manually set by using the DBMS_STATS.SET_*_STATS procedures, and regather statistics if necessary.

Usage of rule-based optimizer (RBO): In previous releases of Oracle (pre-10.1), the RBO might be used instead of the cost-based optimizer (CBO) when no statistics have been gathered on the objects involved in the query and the OPTIMIZER_MODE is set to the default value of CHOOSE. More-recent releases also exhibit the same behavior when the OPTIMIZER_MODE is changed from the default ALL_ROWS to CHOOSE. The RBO might also be forced by using the RULE hint for particular SQL statements or in general by setting the OPTIMIZER_MODE to RULE. Although the RBO might yield deterministic and stable performance for typical OLTP-like queries, the CBO should be used with recent releases of Oracle to take advantage of descending indexes (added in Oracle 8i), function-based indexes, hash joins, bitmap indexes, and various other features. Using certain features such as ANSI-style joins, partitioned tables/indexes, star joins, index skip scans, and hints might cause an automatic switch to the CBO optimizer. Note that switching from the RBO to the CBO at the instance level (by modifying the OPTIMIZER_MODE parameter or by gathering statistics on objects that previously had no statistics) may have a significant impact on all SQL statements optimized, and therefore requires thorough preparation and testing efforts. Note that the RBO is not supported as of the 10.1 release of Oracle.

Histogram Issues

If your object statistics include histograms, they can as easily be part of the problem as part of the solution. Following are some things to check:

- Histograms might be missing on columns with skewed data. Starting with release 10.1, histograms might be created on columns that do not benefit from them (default SIZE AUTO option). In addition, the histograms might have been created with a too-small bucket size, resulting in height-balanced histograms rather than frequency histograms. Consider adding histograms to columns containing skewed data, removing histograms from columns where the histograms seem to be questionable, or re-creating histograms by using a larger number of buckets (the maximum number of buckets is 254) to create frequency histograms instead of height-balanced histograms.

- Check column data. Only columns containing character data that differs within the first 32 bytes, and columns containing numeric data with a precision less than 15, will benefit from a histogram; this is a limitation of histograms. Remove histograms from columns that do not meet the preceding criteria to avoid situations where the optimizer is led to believe that only a single value is present in a column based on the apparent single value contained in the histogram.

- Check data skew. If the number of distinct values is large, the maximum number of buckets (254) might not be sufficient to detect the data skew or popular values. In such a case, the histogram should be removed, or another method to support the optimizer should be considered (for example hints), or a histogram should be manually created that reflects the most popular values of the column data (using DBMS_STATS.SET_COLUMN_STATS).

Common Parameters Influencing Optimizer

Initialization parameters represent another avenue of exploration. Some parameters have a great deal of influence on the cost-based optimizer's behavior. For example, the following parameters and settings will tend to influence the cost-based optimizer to favor full table scans, hash joins, and sort-merge joins:

OPTIMIZER_INDEX_COST_ADJ: This parameter influences all index costs calculated by the optimizer. The default value is 100, with values larger than 100 scaling index access costs up, thus favoring full table scans and hash joins or sort-merge joins.

DB_FILE_MULTIBLOCK_READ_COUNT (DBFMBRC): High values for DBFMBRC decrease the cost of full table scans (and fast full index scans) with system statistics disabled or with NOWORKLOAD system statistics.

System statistics (on 9.2 or later): Unrepresentative or manually modified system statistics (query the current values from SYS.AUX_STATS$ or retrieve via DBMS_STATS.GET_SYSTEM_STATS) might cause similar effects to poorly selected values for OPTIMIZER_INDEX_COST_ADJ and DB_FILE_MULTIBLOCK_READ_COUNT. In particular, a small ratio for MREADTIM/SREADTIM or a high value for the MBRC settings may indicate inappropriate values for system statistics. With NOWORKLOAD system statistics, the MREADTIM and SREADTIM are derived from the values for DB_BLOCK_SIZE, IOTFRSPEED, and IOSEEKTIM.

Conversely, if you wish to favor index scans and nested loop joins, you can look at setting your instance parameters along the following lines:

OPTIMIZER_INDEX_COST_ADJ: This parameter influences all index costs calculated by the optimizer. The default value is 100, with values below 100 scaling index access costs down, thus favoring index accesses and nested loop joins.

DB_FILE_MULTIBLOCK_READ_COUNT (DBFMBRC): Lower values for DBFMBRC with system statistics disabled or with NOWORKLOAD system statistics causes the optimizer to increasingly favor index access paths.

OPTIMIZER_INDEX_CACHING: This parameter influences the cost of the access to the inner table of nested loop joins and in-list iterator operations. The default value is 0. Large values decrease the cost of these operations, thus favoring index scans and nested loop joins.

System statistics (on 9.2 or later): Unrepresentative or manually modified system statistics might cause similar effects to poorly selected values for OPTIMIZER_INDEX_COST_ADJ, OPTIMIZER_INDEX_CACHING, and DB_FILE_MULTIBLOCK_READ_COUNT. In particular, a large ratio for MREADTIM/SREADTIM or a low value for the MBRC settings may indicate inappropriate values for system statistics.

Statement and Physical Design Issues

How you structure your database and your SQL statements can also help avoid performance problems. Database design issues such as constraints, or the lack thereof, do matter. Similarly, changing the way that you express a query problem in SQL can also make a notable difference on performance. Following are some things to think about and investigate:

Missing constraints: Adding appropriate constraints not only maintains data integrity but also may provide additional information to the optimizer. Additional predicates may be derived by the optimizer from check constraints and unique constraints, helping the optimizer find more-efficient access paths, such as a unique access operation, where it might have otherwise required a range scan operation. Foreign keys also allow the optimizer in recent releases of Oracle (starting with release 10.2) to eliminate tables completely from joins if the table is referenced only in the join conditions (join elimination feature).

Restructure SQL: If a rewrite of the SQL statement is possible, determine whether a more efficient form of the SQL statement may be constructed. Using analytic functions to avoid self-joins, converting nested subqueries into joins, and evaluating the usage of common subquery expression (CSE, also known as the WITH clause) may help the optimizer derive better cardinality estimates and/or a more efficient access path to the data. This may permit the optimizer to leverage transformations that could not be applied to the original form of the query.

Missing join predicates: Although sometimes a Cartesian product (cross join) is intended in a SQL statement and sometimes the optimizer correctly identifies that using a cross join is the most efficient execution method, always check the join predicates when a MERGE JOIN CARTESIAN operation exists in the execution plan. Every table in the FROM clause should have at least one join predicate applied that links the table to another table. Missing predicates are sometimes difficult to identify in complex statements using the traditional Oracle SQL join syntax, which locates both the filter and join predicates in the WHERE clause. Rewriting the SQL statement by using ANSI SQL join syntax, thus isolating the join conditions, may help identify missing join predicates. This process may be tedious when a query is complex, but the exercise might yield a better understanding of the SQL statement's purpose and necessary join conditions. Note that in some releases of Oracle, rewriting the same query by using ANSI join syntax might lead to different execution plans than those obtained with traditional Oracle join syntax, so test the rewritten SQL statement thoroughly. After the missing join predicates are determined, those join predicates should be added to the original SQL statement.

Unusual predicates: In Oracle releases prior to 9.2, repeated filter predicates (for example, COL = X AND COL = X AND COL = X) or spurious join predicates (A.JOIN_COL = A.JOIN_COL) in WHERE clauses lead to underestimated selectivity calculations. Incorrect selectivity estimates lead to incorrect cardinality estimates and often result in the optimizer choosing the wrong join order and/or wrong access methods. This issue might cause the optimizer, for example, to select a nested loop join by using an index, when a hash join with a full table scan would be more appropriate.

Fine-grained access control (FGAC), virtual private database (VPD), row-level security (RLS): Using FGAC might lead to performance issues if the resulting query's additional predicates may be used to further restrict data volumes through index access paths, but appropriate indexes do not exist. The additional generated predicates may also result in calculated row cardinality changes that then result in the optimizer selecting an unexpected execution plan. Detecting issues introduced by FGAC may be tricky because the predicates automatically added to the WHERE clause are not made visible, which means that the final SQL statement generated with the FGAC predicates added will not show the FGAC predicates in the V$SQL view. The original query might perform well without the

FGAC predicates applied, but for performance optimization, the actual query executed is needed in order to analyze the performance problem. There are several ways to identify the predicates applied by FGAC:

- Check the ACCESS and FILTER predicate section of the execution plan. Although the query text associated with the execution plan does not show the additional FGAC predicates, the additional predicates should appear in the Predicate Information section of the execution plan when DBMS_XPLAN is used to display execution plans.

- Use V$VPD_POLICY. The FGAC predicates applied to SQL statements currently in the library cache are visible in the V$VPD_POLICY view.

- Enable event 10730. Diagnostic event 10730 may be enabled, which will write additional information about the virtual private database (VPD) activity to the trace file when a 10046 SQL trace is also enabled.

Oracle bug 5195882, "Queries in FGAC Using Full Table Scan Instead of Index Access," may also present a problem in Oracle releases prior to 10.2.0.3. A possible workaround for the bug is to set OPTIMIZER_SECURE_VIEW_MERGING = FALSE.

Query uses many IN list parameters or OR statements: Some releases of Oracle might choose a full table scan operation with large IN / OR lists rather than expanding the list into separate query blocks (concatenation transformation), each using an index access path. Depending on the data distribution and data volume, the concatenated access path using indexes may be more efficient. A concatenation transformation may be specified for a SQL statement by supplying a USE_CONCAT hint. See Metalink Doc ID 17214.1 for more information.

Data Access Issues

The access path selected by the optimizer is crucial to the performance of the SQL execution. If a predicate of a query identifies only a few rows from a table, an index access might be beneficial. Likewise, if a predicate identifies many rows from a table, a full table scan might be more efficient. Following are some often fruitful avenues of investigation:

Compare the cardinality estimates with the actual cardinality: Bad cardinality estimates of the optimizer often lead to suboptimal execution plans. Therefore, it is crucial to identify whether the cardinality estimates are close to the actual cardinalities. The simplest way to perform this check is to follow the steps in the "Examining Execution Plans and Plan Statistics" section of Chapter 9 to obtain output from DBMS_XPLAN.DISPLAY_CURSOR, or use one of the other methods in that section to obtain the actual execution plan along with Row Source Execution statistics. These statistics are generated when the parameter STATISTICS_LEVEL is set to ALL (preferably at the session level) or when using the GATHER_PLAN_STATISTICS hint. With the Row Source Execution statistics gathered, it is possible to compare the A-ROWS information (actual number of rows) to the E-ROWS information (estimated number of rows). If there are significant differences in the values, a bad cardinality estimate is present for the execution plan. Some of the most common reasons for bad cardinality/selectivity estimates are as follows :

- Outdated or unrepresentative statistics: See the preceding discussion about representative statistics.

- Bind variable peeking: Sometimes sharing an execution plan because of bind variable usage might lead to inefficient future executions of the SQL statement. This may happen when the bind variable values used to parse the SQL statement lead to significantly different selectivity/cardinality estimates than those values submitted during later executions. This applies in particular to columns with skewed data distributions, and in cases where the passed-in bind variable values are significantly outside the recorded low and high values for the columns (the optimizer scales the selectivity accordingly if the predicate values are outside the range of known column values). It might help to remove histograms on the affected columns as a damage-limitation measure when there is skewed column data distribution (keep in mind, however, that doing so might affect other queries negatively). Applying application logic to prevent plans from being shared inappropriately is another approach when it is possible to determine that a plan should not be shared. This might be accomplished by artificially introducing two copies of a SQL statement that differ only by an embedded comment. Oracle 11.1 introduced the adaptive cursor-sharing feature, which attempts to detect inefficient sharing of execution plans and automatically generates additional child cursors for the same SQL statement, potentially with different execution plans.

Correlated column values: If a SQL statement attempts to filter on related columns (ZIP code and city, for instance), the optimizer assumes that each predicate is completely independent of the other (each predicate thus impacts the calculated selectivity), but the two predicates are correlated and therefore do not actually reduce the result set to the degree estimated by the optimizer. A couple of methods to address the problem include the following:

- Use extended statistics. Oracle 11.1 introduced extended statistics, which collect statistics across multiple columns. With extended statistics, the optimizer is able to detect correlated column values and arrive at a more reasonable selectivity calculation.

- Use dynamic sampling. Dynamic sampling statistics are automatically applied to selectivity and cardinality estimates when two or more predicates reference a single table, if session or cursor level dynamic sampling is enabled at level four or greater. For finer control you can also use table level dynamic sampling. Note that dynamic sampling might increase the time required to parse the statement, and changes at either the session or system-wide level might negatively impact other statements.

- Use the SQL Tuning Advisor, which is available starting with release 10.1 to generate a SQL profile that corrects the bad selectivity estimates. (Use of this feature requires an additional-cost license.)

- Use hints to obtain the desired execution plan and lock the plan by using an outline (see Metalink Doc IDs 604022.1 and 144194.1) or a SQL profile, or use SQL Plan Management (SPM), which is available starting with release 11.1.

- If the column values are not skewed, it might be helpful to generate an index on the correlated columns. More-recent releases of Oracle (10.2.0.4 and later) may utilize the number of distinct keys from the index during selectivity calculations when an equality comparison is applied to all columns included in the index.

- If it is not possible to modify or rewrite the SQL statement, manually modifying the underlying table and index statistics may help the optimizer obtain better selectivity/cardinality estimates. Wolfgang Breitling's website (www.centrexcc.com) contains several articles that describe tuning through the modification of statistics.

Optimizer Not Using (Correct) Index

Sometimes a SQL statement will perform poorly from not using an index or not using a correct index. If there's no suitable index, the optimizer will likely use a full table scan. Sometimes too, the optimizer will choose a different index than you think is reasonable. If the optimizer is not using an index or is choosing what you believe to be the wrong index, then investigate the following:

- Check that a suitable index exists. A suitable index should include as many as possible of the filter predicates as leading columns of a composite index. If such an index does not exist, the optimizer (starting with release 9.0.1) may choose to use an INDEX SKIP SCAN operation with an index, which effectively runs an index range scan operation per distinct value of the skipped columns. As such, this operation is sensible only if the number of distinct values of the skipped columns is low. Otherwise, this operation tends to be inefficient. Note that any column that is included in the index definition after a skipped column, or after a column that was used in an inequality comparison, cannot be used to reduce the number of index leaf blocks scanned. This condition may be seen when examining the Predicate Information section of the execution plan. Columns that cannot be used to access the index blocks directly will appear as an additional FILTER predicate that is applied to the index.

- Check the selectivity/cardinality estimates. See the preceding discussion about selectivity/cardinality issues.

- Check the clustering factor of the index. When accessing a table through an index access path, most elapsed time (and thus the optimizer's calculated cost) is caused by the random access to each of the table rows identified by the index. If the table data is ordered similarly to an index, the calculated cost will be significantly lower than that of a randomly scattered single-row index access to the table, because the same table block read from disk may be used to satisfy multiple contiguous single-table-row requests from the index. When the table rows are randomly scattered when examined in the order of the index, every row referenced by the index potentially requires a different table block to be read from disk. The ordered relation between the index and the table data is represented by the clustering factor statistic. A low clustering factor (close to the number of blocks in the table) represents an index that is sorted similar to the table data; a high clustering factor value (close to the number of rows in the table) represents an index whose sort order is significantly different from that of the table and therefore potentially requires a lot of blocks to be read from disk while accessing the same number of rows. There is not much that can be done to decrease a bad clustering factor other than changing the order in which the rows are physically stored in the table, but obviously this will only decrease (improve) the clustering factor for a single index, while potentially increasing the clustering factor for the remaining indexes. Different indexes very likely will have a different sort order. It is possible to add more columns to an existing index to try to reduce the number of randomly ordered table rows accessed (note that adding an additional column to an index may further increase the clustering factor). Another option is to consider changing the heap-organized table into an index-organized table (IOT), but the effectiveness of this approach may depend on the number and size of the columns as well as the requirement for secondary indexes on the IOT, because secondary indexes tend to become less efficient over time as the table data is modified. Indexes with a high clustering factor will have a comparatively high calculated cost for `TABLE ACCESS BY INDEX ROWID` operations, and therefore the optimizer might choose a full table scan access path or a different index.

- Check for implicit datatype conversions and usage of functions in the `WHERE` clause. Any datatype conversion or usage of functions in the `WHERE` clause may prevent the optimizer from using an index that exists on the function's referenced columns, and this will influence the optimizer's selectivity/cardinality estimates. Avoid implicit data conversions through the use of explicit conversion functions (if possible and applicable, apply the function on a literal rather than a table's column) to document the conversion properly. If necessary, function-based indexes may be created on expressions that include columns referenced by functions.

- Check the `OPTIMIZER_INDEX_COST_ADJ` and `OPTIMIZER_INDEX_CACHING` parameters for nondefault values. Lowering index access costs by using these two parameters may lead to inappropriate index usage, in particular if the calculated reduced costs of multiple access paths using different indexes end up with the same reduced calculated cost. Rather than using `OPTIMIZER_INDEX_COST_ADJ` to decrease index access costs, it is recommended to alter the system statistics to increase the cost of full table scan operations to correctly reflect the performance characteristics of the server hardware. Modifying system statistics helps to limit the number of cases where multiple indexes end up with the same cost after applying the cost reductions. In certain cases, the `OPTIMIZER_INDEX_CACHING` parameter might still be appropriate even when using system statistics, in particular if the optimizer underestimates the caching effect of nested loop joins or in-list operators.

- Check whether there are any hints added to the query that prevent index usage— for example, `NO_INDEX` and `FULL`. Remove those hints that are inappropriate.

- Check hints for spelling or semantic errors in cases where the hints are apparently ignored by the optimizer.

- Check the advice offered by the SQL Access Advisor for the SQL statement (with the appropriate license for this feature) to determine possible improvements offered by enhanced index usage and other structural changes such as adding materialized views.

Pagination (Top N) Queries

Retrieving only a small number of rows from a larger result set is typical of a `Top N` type query. Web applications (such as Search results in the Google or Amazon.com sites) typically need to show only the first rows of a larger result set; queries implemented by those types of applications are typically pagination type queries. The result set usually needs to be ordered by a deterministic criteria, and the optimizer must be aware that only the first `N` rows are needed, which may be achieved in one of several ways:

- Use the `FIRST_ROWS(N)` hint. The `FIRST_ROWS(N)` hint, where `N` represents the number of rows expected to be processed, will change the way the optimizer works out the execution plan, potentially increasing the chance that an index access path will be used to avoid a sort operation.

- Modify the `OPTIMIZER_MODE`. The `OPTIMIZER_MODE` parameter may be set to `FIRST_ROWS_1`, `FIRST_ROWS_10`, `FIRST_ROWS_100`, or `FIRST_ROWS_1000` to instruct the optimizer to optimize SQL statements to retrieve the first 1, 10, 100, or 1,000 rows as quickly as possible. This parameter value has a similar effect to the `FIRST_ROWS(N)` hint, but affects all SQL statements parsed either within the session or on a systemwide level, rather than for just a single SQL statement. In most cases, it is not recommended to use the deprecated `FIRST_ROWS` optimizer mode because that mode has built-in heuristics that often lead to bad execution plans. (In Oracle releases prior to 10.1 the optimizer always uses an available index to avoid a sort and tries to avoid full table scan operations when joining multiple row sources by favoring nested loop joins, rather than calculating the cost of both approaches. The `FIRST_ROWS` optimizer mode in more recent releases is still susceptible to inefficient execution plans.)

- Add a `ROWNUM` restriction to the `WHERE` clause: The `FIRST_ROWS(N)` optimization may also be specified by adding a `ROWNUM <= N` predicate to the `WHERE` clause of the SQL statement. The original SQL statement must be wrapped inside an inline view that includes the SQL statement's `ORDER BY` clause (when a deterministic order is required), and the `ROWNUM` predicate must be specified outside that inline view:

```
SELECT
       *
FROM
       (
         SELECT   ...
         FROM     ...
         ORDER BY ...
       )
WHERE
       ROWNUM <= N;
```

Processing Large Result Sets

If it is known that a query will process a large amount of data or return a large result set, verify the following:

The query is reasonable: Is it really necessary to process the large result set, and in particular is it really desirable to return a large result set to the client?

The query uses an efficient access path: Processing a large amount of data is usually accomplished most efficiently when using full table scan operations.

In order to speed up a query that must process a large amount of data, consider one of the following approaches:

- Make sure that the `OPTIMIZER_MODE` is set to `ALL_ROWS`.

- Increase the PGA memory available for processing by either increasing the `PGA_AGGREGATE_TARGET`, or switching to manual work-area size management (`WORKAREA_SIZE_POLICY = MANUAL`) with a large `SORT_AREA_SIZE` and `HASH_AREA_SIZE` setting.

- Oracle offers in the Enterprise Edition various parallel execution features including parallel query and parallel DML/DDL execution. Determine whether parallel execution will improve performance.

- Consider using materialized views for pre-aggregation of data. Oracle's Enterprise Edition is able to use materialized views that statically store query results in the database, potentially improving performance when the optimizer transparently rewrites join and summary queries to use already prepared materialized views when obtaining the result set.

- If it is necessary to transfer a large amount of data to the client, consider increasing the fetch array size from the default value used by the program that submits the query. The ARRAYSIZE setting in SQL*Plus controls the fetch array size in that program, but the method for specifying the fetch array size depends on the client environment—for instance, Java using Java Database Connectivity (JDBC), Oracle Call Interface (OCI), Microsoft's ActiveX Data Objects (ADO), and so forth.

Join Issues

Joins are a common cause of poorly performing SQL. A large part of the optimizer's work lies in optimizing joins, in making them perform at the least possible cost. Sometimes the optimizer needs a little help. Following are some possible problems to look at:

- Inefficient join order caused by the optimizer selecting the wrong starting row source: It is crucial for joins to use a join order that starts with the tables/row sources (in the case of nonmergeable views) that produce the least number of rows, possibly after applying filter predicates, which ideally produces a single-row row source. If the single-table access path estimates are incorrect (see the section "Generating 10053 Cost-Based Optimizer Traces" in Chapter 9 to determine how to obtain the single-table access estimates for all tables involved), then the optimizer might start the join with the wrong table/row source, causing the joins to process more rows than expected. When an underestimate of cardinality is encountered, check the object statistics and predicates applied. In particular, when using functions in predicates, the default of 1 percent or 5 percent selectivity depending on the comparison method (equality or inequality comparisons such as ranges, respectively) is used by the optimizer, which might be significantly different from the actual selectivity of the function.

- General inefficient join order: Estimating the correct join selectivity/cardinality is one of the biggest challenges to the optimizer. If the join selectivity/cardinality estimate is wrong, the effects of the miscalculation will echo through the remaining plan. This potentially leads to an inefficient overall join order used by the optimizer, which then results in more rows being processed than necessary. The objective here is to eliminate rows as early as possible.

- Multicolumn joins: When joining tables on multiple columns, the optimizer might significantly underestimate the resulting join cardinality if the join columns are correlated. If the number of distinct values of the combined join columns is less than the multiplied number of distinct values for each individual column (for example, 20 distinct values in COL1 and 10 distinct values in COL2, but only 30 distinct values for COL1, COL2 instead of $20 \times 10 = 200$), then you have identified correlated column values. Recent releases of Oracle will try to apply sanity checks to multicolumn joins. You can help by having a unique index on the join columns on one side of the join, in which case Oracle will use the number of distinct keys from this index for the join cardinality estimate. Oracle 10.1 also added further multicolumn join sanity checks that use the number of rows from the row sources involved as join cardinality if the estimated selectivity is below a certain limit. Oracle 11.1 adds further options to address the correlated column issue by the new multicolumn extended statistics.

- Check the statistics and the predicates applied: Expressions and functions in join predicates will use the default 1 percent or 5 percent selectivity, as already described. It might be possible to generate a function-based index if function expressions in the join predicates cannot be avoided, which will allow the optimizer to use the column statistics from the hidden column that is generated for the function-based index. When adding a function-based index, statistics must be regathered on the table to obtain statistics for the new hidden column by using FOR ALL HIDDEN COLUMNS (or FOR ALL COLUMNS to collect updated statistics on all of the table's columns) as the METHOD_OPT parameter in the DBMS_STATS call. Starting with release 11.1, it is possible to generate extended statistics on expressions, or use a virtual column instead.

- Check for histograms on the join columns: Histograms may influence the join selectivity/cardinality estimates significantly, and not always for the better. If a histogram does not exist for columns used in a join, a histogram (ideally frequency based) may be created on the join columns. If a histogram already exists, it might be beneficial to remove the histogram, keeping in mind that doing so may affect other queries. Automatic histogram generation is controlled by the METHOD_OPT parameter of DBMS_STATS. Note that starting with release 10.1, the default METHOD_OPT value is FOR ALL COLUMNS SIZE AUTO, which might generate histograms on columns that do not improve the join selectivity/cardinality estimates.

Parallel Processing Issues

When using the parallel execution feature of Oracle Enterprise Edition, some of the following issues might be encountered:

- Parallel execution does not use the requested degree of parallelism: It is important to understand how the parallel degree of the parallel execution is determined. If there are not enough parallel servers available, Oracle may execute the statement with a reduced parallel degree unless the parameter PARALLEL_MIN_PERCENT is used to define a threshold for the reduction. It might be necessary to increase the PARALLEL_MAX_SERVERS parameter or reduce the requested degree, in particular if multiple queries using parallel executions are processed concurrently. The PARALLEL_ADAPTIVE_MULTI_USER parameter might help when concurrent parallel executions are processed, which will automatically reduce the parallel degree of an operation. Note that Oracle 11.2 introduced the automatic parallel degree (AUTO DOP) feature, which handles the degree of parallelism differently (controlled by the new parameters PARALLEL_DEGREE_POLICY and PARALLEL_MIN_TIME_THRESHOLD). The session and systemwide statistics in V$SESSTAT, V$MYSTAT, and V$SYSSTAT may be checked to determine the number of parallel executions that have been downgraded by examining the delta values for the following statistics:

```
NAME
---------------------------------------------
Parallel operations not downgraded
Parallel operations downgraded to serial
Parallel operations downgraded 75 to 99 pct
Parallel operations downgraded 50 to 75 pct
Parallel operations downgraded 25 to 50 pct
Parallel operations downgraded 1 to 25 pct
```

- Furthermore, the V$PX_SESSION dynamic performance view indicates the actual degree and requested degree of parallelism for currently running parallel executions. Note that a parallel execution may actually require more parallel slaves than the degree requested, and therefore might be downgraded to a lower degree of parallelism. A parallel execution may consist of multiple parallel slave sets—for example, an execution in parallel that performs a full table scan with an aggregation or sort. An aggregation or sort usually also requires two parallel slave sets, resulting in twice the number of slaves specified for the requested parallel degree.

- A query runs in parallel, but was intended to be executed serially: In some cases, a query actually runs in parallel when it should not. Some of the reasons include the following:

  1. A PARALLEL hint has been used to request the costing of a particular parallel degree, which then adjusted the cost of the parallel execution so that the cost was lower than other access methods.

  2. The session was forced to use parallel execution:
     ALTER SESSION FORCE PARALLEL QUERY | DML | DDL

  3. Some of the objects involved in the query have a default parallel degree greater than 1 defined. Note that both tables and indexes must be checked. Typically, the modification of an index's parallel degree may be caused by index rebuilds that were executed in parallel to speed up the rebuild. Rebuilding an index in parallel automatically sets the parallel degree of the index to a value greater than 1.

Shared Pool Abuse

Every SQL statement submitted to an Oracle database instance must be parsed before the SQL statement may be executed. SQL statement parses are considered to be soft parses if the SQL statement already exists in a shareable and compatible form in the library cache. To be considered compatible, the following must all be true:

- The optimizer environment that existed during the initial hard parse (visible in the view V$SQL_OPTIMIZER_ENV) must match that of the session (visible in the view V$SES_OPTIMIZER_ENV) submitting the SQL statement to the database instance.

- The objects referenced in the SQL statement must resolve to the same owner and object names as those referenced when the SQL statement was hard parsed, and the parsing user must be authorized to access those objects.

- When bind variables are used in the SQL statement, the bind variables must be defined as the same datatype, and bind variables on character columns must have the same approximate data length (organized in ranges of 0–32 bytes, 33–128 bytes, 129–2,000 bytes, and 2,001–4,000 bytes).

- When bind variables are used in the presence of adaptive cursor sharing (a feature added in release 11.1), the supplied bind variables must be expected to produce roughly the same row source selectivity values.

- When literals (constants) are used in the SQL statement, the literals are identical to those in the previously parsed version. If literals differ, the hashed value for the SQL statement will differ, and therefore the SQL statement is not the same, unless the literals are automatically replaced with bind variables by setting the CURSOR_SHARING parameter to either FORCE or SIMILAR.

Soft parses (recorded as a library cache hit) are potentially expensive operations because they involve syntax and security checking, as well as obtaining the library cache latch (held while scanning child cursors in releases prior to 11.1—a mutex replaces the library cache latch starting with release 11.1). Hard parses (recorded as a library cache miss) are more expensive than soft parses, because the parse process also includes a SQL optimization stage (optimal execution plan produced), a SQL row source generation stage (query plan/row source tree produced), and then a stage that adds the parsed SQL statement to the library cache. A hard parse might require obtaining and then releasing the shared pool and library cache latches multiple times (possibly 20 to 30 times) to parse the SQL statement and add it to the library cache.

Resolving Shared Pool Abuse

The number of hard and soft parses should be minimized. In many cases, reducing the number of parse calls may be accomplished only through modification of the application source code, but the Oracle RDBMS also offers features that may be used to reduce the impact of application code problems causing excessive hard and/or soft parses. Methods to reduce the number of hard and/or soft parses include the following:

- Modify the application code to utilize bind variables rather than literals. Not all literals should necessarily be replaced with bind variables. Those literals that do not change from one execution to the next should not be replaced (a literal that always has the value of 10, for instance), and those literals whose values have a significant impact on the number of rows returned (a column with skewed data) also should not be replaced with bind variables. Changing the application to make better use of bind variables will help reduce the number of hard parses.

- Modify the application code to keep cursors open, pass in new bind variables, and re-execute the SQL statement as needed. This change will help reduce the number of soft parses.

- Set the SESSION_CACHED_CURSORS parameter to a reasonable value. This parameter controls the number of cursors for each session that will be held open after the client application explicitly closes the cursor. A SQL statement must be executed at least three times to be added to the session cursor cache. Setting the SESSION_CACHED_CURSORS parameter to a reasonable value will help reduce the number of soft parses if the same SQL statement is repeatedly executed by the same session. A properly set value for this parameter is almost as effective as rewriting the application code to hold the cursors open in the client application.

- Set the CURSOR_SHARING parameter to either FORCE or SIMILAR, thus changing the parameter from the default value of EXACT. This parameter causes literal values to be automatically replaced with bind variables. Since the parameter's introduction with release 8.1, various bug reports have surfaced associated with this parameter, ranging from poor execution performance to data accuracy errors to ORA-07445 errors during a parse of simple SQL statements. Before changing this parameter from its default value, research the known bugs, limitations, and potential problems for the specific Oracle release in use. Also check for potential problems caused by the universal replacement of literals with bind variables in the presence of columns with histograms when bind variable peeking is enabled.

- Increase the size of the shared pool to allow more of the hard-parsed SQL statements to remain in the shared pool. This will reduce the need for sessions to hard-parse the same SQL statement because of the SQL statement being forced out of the library cache to make room for other SQL statements. Even with a large shared pool size, SQL statements that properly use bind variables could still be forced out of the library cache because of applications submitting large numbers of SQL statements with literals, so increasing the size of the shared pool will not necessarily decrease the number of hard parses.

General Guidelines for Investigating Shared Pool Abuse

The Oracle RDBMS offers a variety of counters, CPU consumption statistics, and elapsed time statistics that are useful for investigating shared pool abuse. Oracle release 11.1 offers the following statistics in V$SYSSTAT (instance level) and V$SESSTAT (session level) for identifying shared pool abuse: DB time, CPU used by this session, parse time cpu, parse time elapsed, parse count (total), parse count (hard), parse count (failures), parse count (describe), session cursor cache count, and session cursor cache hits. (The statistic parse count (describe) is not present prior to release 11.1, and DB time is not present prior to release 10.1.) Release 10.1 introduced various time model statistics to provide a better view into the impact of parsing activity with the views V$SYS_TIME_MODEL (instance level) and V$SESS_TIME_MODEL (session level). The views offer the following statistics, which are helpful for investigating shared pool abuse: DB time, DB CPU, parse time elapsed, hard parse elapsed time, failed parse elapsed time, failed parse (out of shared memory) elapsed time, hard parse (sharing criteria) elapsed time, hard parse (bind mismatch) elapsed time, and repeated bind elapsed time.

   If there appears to be a hard-parse problem, determine the contributors to the hard-parse elapsed time. Compare the V$SYS_TIME_MODEL.STAT_NAME("hard parse elapsed time") statistic with its substatistic hard parse (sharing criteria) elapsed time and its substatistic hard parse (bind mismatch) elapsed time to determine whether SQL statements are being hard parsed because of passed-in bind variables. Examine V$SQL to find cursors with many child cursors and then check V$SQL_SHARED_CURSOR for those SQL statements with several child cursors to determine what caused the generation of the multiple child cursors.

If there appears to be a parse problem, but not a hard-parse problem, excessive soft parses might be a problem. Soft-parse problems potentially indicate application design problems in which cursors for the same set of SQL statements are repeatedly opened and closed, possibly due to application coding standards that stress modularization of application logic into black-box style function calls that are repeatedly called in an application loop. If the initialization parameter SESSION_CACHED_CURSORS is adjusted so that it is set appropriately, the performance issues related to excessive soft parsing of the same SQL statements by the same session may be significantly reduced (see Metalink Doc ID 32895.1, "SQL Parsing Flow Diagram" to better understand the steps involved in parsing SQL statements). Compare the value of this parameter to the number of cursors reported as actually cached for the session by examining the statistic session cursor cache count and the number of accesses of those cached cursors in the statistic session cursor cache hits from the view V$SESSTAT for each session. A SQL statement must be executed at least three times by the session before it becomes eligible for inclusion in the session's cached cursors.

If a session is found that is spending an excessive number of seconds parsing based on the delta value of the statistic V$SESSTAT.NAME("parse time cpu")/100, enable a 10046 trace at level 12 for the session for a couple of minutes and process the resulting trace file (located in the udump directory on the server) by using tkprof with the parameter sort=prsela,fchela,exeela, or manually review the raw trace file by using a text editor to locate large values for the c= or e= entry on the lines beginning with PARSE #.

CHAPTER 10

■ ■ ■

Managing the Very Large Database

by Tim Gorman

I'm often asked what size database can be called a VLDB. *Is it this many gigabytes, or that many terabytes? Best definition I've heard is that* VLDB *means* bigger than you're comfortable managing.

—Cary Millsap

Everything is magnified in VLDB. There are no *minor issues.*

—Abdul Ebadi

Some years ago, I taught a class on administering databases for data warehouses on Oracle entitled "Scaling to Infinity: Partitioning Data Warehouses on Oracle." I still teach it, and I find it enormously enjoyable because it encompasses topics that I love: how to build very large databases (VLDBs) and how to build them so that loading and querying is almost effortless and natural, no matter how large they become. Moreover, with my good friend Gary Dodge as mentor and primary author, over the years I've co-authored two well-regarded but now-obsolete books on data warehousing on Oracle. All of this came as a result of years of building, designing, and managing very large Oracle databases, and I have to say that I couldn't imagine any job being more challenging and more fun.

With this background, I wish I could say that the "ruling junta" of the Oak Table Network (and you know who you are) asked me to write this chapter about very large databases because of my past authoring experience and my experience teaching. But, in real life, things just are never that simple.

The difference between fact and fiction? In fiction, everything has to make sense.

—Tom Clancy

The true reason is downright embarrassing and possibly even professionally damning. Conversing around the virtual Oak Table (that is, our e-mail forum) one evening, I told a story—a true story, and a recent one to boot—about how I came to drop an index on a 45-terabyte (TB) table in a live production data warehouse. The index, all 20,000+ partitions of it, was about 15TB. I thought I had tested, but missed one detail, and with 25 years of experience in the IT industry—more than 15 years of which was as an Oracle DBA—I learned yet another important lesson. It goes to prove that we are never past the learning phase in this profession.

Look, listen, and learn, for an original mistake is as rare as an original idea.

—Gene Fosnight

In the most deeply sympathetic manner imaginable, upon hearing that story, the Oak Table junta nominated me to write a chapter in this book about that mishap. Okay, okay, they weren't all that sympathetic—it was more of a leering grin. Still, that is how I came to be here. If anyone asks, just say it's because I'm an expert on the topic. But you and I both know that being an *expert* is really the aggregation of lessons learned from mistakes—that, and being an hour further ahead in the documentation than others.

Experience is what you get soon after you need it.

—Unknown

That is indeed how experience is gained, but expertise can be gained by listening to those with experience. The purpose of this chapter is to transfer some of the lessons learned along the way, so you are not starting out from ground level on this remarkable journey. Among the topics include some important mindsets for the design and implementation of any very large database, specifically the "physical" design of the database components and the storage subsystem underlying the database. We'll discuss the crucial role that table- and index-partitioning plays in scaling a database toward infinity, as well as the role that the EXCHANGE PARTITION operation plays in making large-scale data loading fast and efficient. Very important, we'll discuss how these basic implementation decisions impact everyday tasks such as backups and (hopefully infrequent) tasks such as database recovery. After all, loading data into a database quickly enough to make use of it is only part of the problem. It is also important that we can protect that data in a dangerous, uncertain, and ever-moving world.

Designing (or Retrofitting) a VLDB

No matter where you stand right now, whether it is at the beginning of a green-field project to build a huge new application based on a very large database, or whether you are managing an environment whose requirements have shifted so that now things are growing faster than originally planned, it is important to recognize the actual constraints on database growth.

The technical constraints are not immediately obvious. They aren't directly tied to CPU capacity or primary memory on the server(s), although that varies by platform. If your database servers use Windows or Linux, the CPU and memory capacity of a single server is generally somewhat constrained, topping out at a few dozen CPUs or *cores*, and you'll almost certainly have to scale outward by using Oracle Real Application Clusters (RAC) and lashing multiple servers together. However, if your database servers use one of the proprietary Unix platforms, individual servers on these platforms can scale to hundreds of CPU and/or cores, as well as hundreds or thousands of gigabytes of RAM. On these platforms, there is less need to consider lashing together individual servers using Oracle RAC, but the possibility still exists.

Still, whether you scale up by choosing larger servers, or scale out by using RAC, or both, resources such as CPU and RAM capacity are not technical constraints to very large databases. The decision depends on what you can afford. So, talk to your server vendor, who will be happy to recommend a good starting-off point for a server or server(s), and will undoubtedly chart out a growth path for expansion if the initial server purchases are underconfigured or overwhelmed by the workload.

Neither is storage a technical constraint. There are storage-area network (SAN) products that offer petabytes of redundant and easily managed storage. Take your pick, determine your budget, and any amount of storage becomes available. Again, talk to your vendor, start with an expandable framework, and plan to grow.

Instead, for a very large database, the technical constraints consist of the following:

- Limits hard-coded within Oracle

- Backup media throughput, affecting the speed of backups and restores

- Incremental financial costs due to growth (Yes, we do live in the real world.)

In summary, we need to know our limits and design to work within them. We need to understand how we can protect the data, because we do not want to outgrow our ability to recover from failures (please refer back to Cary Millsap's comment at the beginning of the chapter). And, we have to do it without bankrupting those for whom we work.

So, because there are so few remaining limitations within the Oracle RDBMS, we'll discuss them last, toward the end of the chapter. And because the other two technical constraints are so closely related to one another and their solutions are so closely entwined, we'll tackle them first by using an imaginary scenario that is quickly becoming real.

Infinity Is So Imprecise...

The word *infinity* generally turns technical people off. It is most often associated with the hyperbole from someone who is selling something. A person who cites the word *infinity* either lacks the knowledge to use more-precise terms, or is too lazy to try. Instead, let's use the extreme concept of *infinity* to clarify scalability problems seen in everyday database systems. Whether in philosophy, politics, or computers, nothing clarifies an issue like considering the extreme case. In this case, we will discuss the optimal management of very large databases on Oracle. And, instead of citing infinity, let's put a finite number out there.

As an example, around 2004, someone on the ORACLE-L e-mail forum (an e-mail thread that can be viewed at http://mail-archive.com/oracle-l@fatcity.com/msg18775.html) mentioned a conundrum he was considering, a proposal for a data warehouse for the scientific analysis of astronomical data, gathered from instruments both earth-based and in orbit. For an IT professional, the most interesting aspect of this proposal was the amount of data involved, because the instruments were expected to generate about 50TB of data every day. That is an average of 660 megabytes (MB) to be loaded every second of every day. Minute after minute. Hour after hour. Day after day. Month after month. A relentless tide of data to be loaded. And after it is loaded, then what?

Capacity is one problem, as retaining data loaded at that rate for seven years would result in about 127,850TB of data, or just under 125 petabytes (PB). Figuring conservatively that indexes might add another 50 percent of volume on top of the data volume (even though in numerous situations indexes exceed data in volume), and if we add another 50 percent to that figure, then we are looking at 191,775TB, or 187PB. Hard-disk storage costs are constantly decreasing, but even so, an initial purchase of about 30PB of storage and continuing at a rate of 30PB per year can add up to some fairly prohibitive numbers, easily stretching into tens or hundreds of millions of dollars.

Throughput is the other problem. So far, we've discussed only the loading of the data. To support an average sustained data load rate of 660 megabytes per second (MBps) of data, the current state of the art is hard disks that have maximum throughput of 150–200 MBps. Obviously, we're right at the trembling edge of sustainable throughput with this storage technology, and extremely careful planning would be necessary for this throughput rate to be feasibly supported over a long period of time. Clearly, RAID-0 (also known as *striping*) is necessary to permit the workload (that is, 660MBps) to be distributed across multiple devices, each capable of (at most) 150–200 MBps. But is 660MBps really the workload to be supported?

If you know how modern relational databases work, you know that we've only scratched the surface in considering the raw volume to be loaded. The purpose of a database is to support queries and additional modifications to the data, not just simply to load raw data, so obviously we still have not yet considered the full life cycle of processing of loaded data from the standpoint of I/O accounting:

- Data inserted into tables in the database (that is, writing 660MBps or so)

- Optionally, database recovery records generated (also known as redo or journaling records) for loaded data (that is, writing another 500–660MBps or so, perhaps reading yet another 500–MBps during archival)

- Optionally, transaction recovery records generated (also known as undo or rollback records) for loaded data (that is, another 30MBps, perhaps)

- Indexes built on newly inserted data (that is, writing another 330MBps or so)

- Optionally, database recovery records generated (redo or journaling records) for indexes built (that is, writing another 200–330MBps, perhaps reading yet another 200--330MBps during archival)

- Optionally, transaction recovery records generated (undo or rollback records) for indexes built (that is, writing another 330MBps or so)

- Data and indexes analyzed to gather statistics for use by the cost-based optimizer (that is, reading another 330MBps for tables, reading another 150MBps for indexes)

- End-user query activity—very heavy utilization over the first year (that is, pure guessing, reading another 660MBps)

- End-user query activity—moderate utilization over the second and third years (that is, pure guessing, reading another 60MBps)

- End-user query activity—light utilization over the fourth through seventh years (that is, pure guessing, reading another 6MBps)

- Backups of data to backup media (that is, reading another 660MBps for tables, reading another 330MBps for indexes)

- Weekly or monthly or quarterly backups, over the course of seven years

- Removal of data after it has aged seven years (that is, writing another 660MBps for tables, writing another 330MBps for indexes)

- Optionally, database recovery records generated (redo or journaling records) for removed data and index entries (that is, writing another 990MBps, reading another 990MBps during archival)

- Optionally, transaction recovery records generated (undo or rollback records) for removed data and index entries (that is, writing another 990MBps)

Remember, even though these activities are sequential for any particular row of data, from a systemwide perspective they are all happening at once, during the same second in time. Minute after minute. Hour after hour. Day after day. Month after month. A relentless tide of data, washing back and forth like the waves on a beach, except picture in your mind tsunamis, not just waves suitable for surfing and wading.

So, if you add up all these estimates of the throughput demands on I/O resulting from the activities listed, the original stated workload of 660Mbps of data balloons to a more realistic workload of almost 10 gigabytes per second (GBps)! Minute after minute. Hour after hour. Day after day. Month after month.

This is a 15:1 ratio—for every byte of data loaded, we can prove that 15 bytes or more will be read or written, at a minimum, during the lifetime of the data. So, after we consider the full range of activities involving I/O performed with relational database systems, the true problem is actually that of supporting I/O throughput of 10GBps using storage devices that can sustain maximum throughput of 150–200MBps.

Infinity isn't just numbers that exceed the imagination. Anybody can imagine 50TB a day. Infinity is anything that is beyond your grasp. This theoretical example is still apparently years beyond our grasp with standard storage options. But what can we do to improve this situation? Even with new storage options such as Exadata, which is already promising to meet the storage throughput requirements illustrated here, does it make sense to simply rely on sheer processing and storage power to save the day? Or, can we push the requirements back down, reduce the requirements, to meet the state of the art as it improves to meet us?

Pushing the horizon of infinity further has to be accomplished step by step. If the entire task is considered in its entirety only, it might well be impossible. But if you take the big problem, break it down into chunks, and attack each chunk, you can achieve success in the face of the most extreme requirements. You can reach 50TB a day.

In fact, it is already here. In mid-2009, I was contracted to begin implementation of a data warehouse that was expected to reach a size of 9PB after 12 months. A little basic math shows that as loading approximately 25TB per day. The scope of the project was later scaled way back, and the data volumes hacked to a fraction of that total, but the mission and the data to support it is still out there, waiting to be loaded and exploited.

The future is now. And obscenely large Oracle databases are up and running right this minute, and more are being built. Here is how they become feasible.

Partitioning

Scalability toward infinity starts with partitioning, plain and simple. You'll need to decide which of your tables (and their associated indexes and large object, or LOB, segments) will become huge in size, and then partition them so they become a large number of manageable objects.

Consider, as an analogy, the term *calculus*, which in Latin literally means *small stones*. The essential method of calculus is to take complex problems, such as calculating the area enclosed by a curving line or the volume enclosed by a curving surface, and break the problem into smaller, easily derived shapes (such as squares), which at a certain granularity is indistinguishable from a curve. The use of partitioning in a very large database on Oracle represents a method of operation not much different, except the emphasis is on managing the small chunks.

■ **Note** This chapter does not explain the basic concepts of partitioning. Please consult the standard Oracle documentation in the *Oracle Database Concepts* manual for any version since Oracle 8 version 8.0.

Partitioning literally permits subsets of a table or index to be managed as an independent object, while permitting the whole collection of partitions to be viewed and managed by the application as a whole. Quite clearly, the important concept here is *divide and conquer*. Rather than allow everything to grow into a single large unmanageable glob, break the glob into many smaller, more-manageable chunks.

Oracle has supported table and index partitioning since Oracle 8 version 8.0 was introduced in 1997. Since then, various additional partitioning features have been released, but they have been incremental improvements rather than revolutionary change:

- (1997) Oracle 8 v 8.0
  - Range partitioning (includes ADD, DROP, RENAME, TRUNCATE, MODIFY, MOVE, SPLIT, and EXCHANGE partition operations)
  - Partition pruning during data searches
- (1999) Oracle 8i v 8.1
  - Hash partitioning
  - Composite range/hash subpartitioning
  - Merge partition operation added
- (2002) Oracle 9i v 9.2
  - List partitioning
  - Composite range/list subpartitioning
  - UPDATE GLOBAL INDEXES clause added
- (2004) Oracle 10g v 10.1
  - Hash- and list-partitioned global indexes
- (2005) Oracle 10g v 10.2
  - Limit on partitions and subpartitions increased from 65,535 to 4 billion
- (2007) Oracle 11g v 11.1
  - Composite range-range, list-range, list-list, and list-hash partitioning
  - Interval, reference, and system partitioning added
  - Enhanced partition-change tracking for change data capture
- (2009) Oracle 11g v 11.2
  - Virtual columns as primary keys for reference-partitioned tables
  - System-managed indexes for list-partitioned tables

Obviously, this is an abbreviated list of milestones showing only high-level functionality. For a more complete list, please reference the Oracle New Features Guide with each version. But, from the perspective of performance scalability, the most important partitioning feature is hidden in the very first set of features introduced way back in the beginning—the exchange partition and partition pruning.

Let's discuss the power of the exchange partition operation first.

Everything Is a Segment

Prior to Oracle 8, tables and indexes were stored as individual *segments* within a tablespace. Segments are composed of extents, and extents are composed of blocks, with blocks being the smallest unit of space actually managed by the database. One could manipulate the number of blocks within an extent according to whether the table or index was large or small, to make extent management easier. One could also manipulate the number of extents within a segment, to make space management within a tablespace easier. One could also spread a tablespace across multiple data files, to try to distribute I/O load across volumes or to allow a segment or tablespace to be larger than any particular storage device or volume. But there was no way to effectively manage a segment that grew huge.

In Oracle 8 and beyond, partitions are themselves *segments*, and they can be stored and managed independently of one another. In Oracle 8i and beyond, subpartitions are themselves segments, to be stored and managed independently of one another. But from a user's perspective, these partitions and subpartitions are invisible and do not change the user's logical viewpoint of the table. They are simply physical implementation mechanisms within a table or an index. What the user sees is the table or index, whether it is an individual segment or a collection of segments.

The EXCHANGE PARTITION operation makes this physical implementation of partitions and subpartitions as segments quite clear. In the original EXCHANGE PARTITION operation in Oracle 8 v 8.0, an individual partition could be "exchanged" with a nonpartitioned table. This sounds confusing at first, until you remember that everything is a segment. The partition is a segment. The nonpartitioned table is a segment. The EXCHANGE PARTITION operation is merely changing the identity of the partition to become that of a nonpartitioned table, and then changing the identity of the nonpartitioned table to become that of a segment.

This magic is performed entirely within the Oracle data dictionary. The identities of the segments themselves do not change. Nor does any of the data within the segments get moved. Instead, the identity of segment A (formerly a partition) is changed from SEGMENT_TYPE = 'TABLE PARTITION' to 'TABLE', and the identity of segment B (formerly a nonpartitioned table) is changed from SEGMENT_TYPE = 'TABLE' to 'TABLE PARTITION'. As long as both the partition and the table have the same *logical shape* (that is, the same columns, data types, scalability, precision, data-integrity constraints such as NULL/NOT-NULL, and so forth), this kind of identity switching is valid.

The EXCHANGE PARTITION operation is thus a very clever mechanism, but does not seem more useful than a simple parlor trick in database management. After all, what possible benefit does it have? In fact, partition exchange is the most important single feature in partition management. By using it, data warehouse databases can achieve infinite scalability and availability. When it is not used, it is utterly impossible for an Oracle database supporting a data warehouse to achieve anything approaching infinity.

Data Manipulation with Partitioning

Awareness of the power of the EXCHANGE PARTITION operation is the key to optimizing data manipulation, and ultimately this operation facilitates a very large database. It is not enough to simply break large segments into hundreds or thousands of smaller segments, and then leave things at that. How does that help? Let's walk through a couple of scenarios in large-scale data manipulation, and hopefully that will demonstrate the point.

Deleting or Updating Millions of Rows

These things happen. You have a fact table that has more than 150 columns in it. You build a SQL*Loader control file to load data into a weekly partitioned table. Life is good; pretty soon you've got a billion rows in your table. Then, the "busy season" hits, and you add another 3 billion rows in just a few months. Pretty soon, someone realizes that the format of the data feed was changed inadvertently over that period of time, and several columns were transposed, switched on one another.

What to do?

When this happened on a project I worked on in 1998, we were running Oracle 8 v 8.0.5.2. Parallel UPDATE commands had just been introduced, and using those was our first inclination. Run an UPDATE statement against this 4-billion-row table, and switch those transposed columns back to the way they ought to be. We had a good-sized 32 CPU Sun E6500, pretty good hardware for the time. So, we should be able to drive an UPDATE with parallelism of 64, 96, or 128 for an emergency like this, right?

It quickly became obvious that we were going nowhere with that approach. Redo generation went through the roof, causing the UPDATEs to bottleneck on "log file sync" waits as the LGWR was overwhelmed. Moreover, while this huge UPDATE statement was running, we had to monitor the rollback segments to which each of the parallel worker processes attached themselves, and constantly add more space. Our update was going nowhere. So we took a different approach.

For each of the affected weekly partitions, we ran a highly parallel, unrecoverable (nologging) CREATE TABLE … AS SELECT statement. The SELECT portion of the command fixed the transposed columns only for those rows where the error existed, using conditional DECODE logic. It selected only the rows in a particular partition by explicitly naming the partition in the FROM clause; there was no need for a WHERE clause.

Because the command was running in parallel, Oracle was also using a direct-path mechanism for inserting the rows into the new table. A direct-path load does most of its work within the memory address space of the session, and bypasses the SGA. In other words, instead of manipulating buffers in the Oracle buffer cache, a direct-path insert will format database blocks within the process's own memory. When it comes time to write these filled database blocks to disk, a process running a direct-path insert will write directly to the data file, into a temporary segment, instead of the table itself. When the direct-path insert completes, the temporary segment is reidentified as a data segment and is appended to the table.

This method of loading also affects transaction management. Because a direct-path insert operation is not manipulating buffers in the Oracle buffer cache and is inserting directly into a temporary segment, there is no need to generate rollback or undo information. When a direct-path insert operation fails, the temporary segment that was being inserted into is simply dropped. Because of these efficiencies (that is, no contention in the SGA, no rollback/undo generated), a direct-path insert operation is the fastest way to load large volumes of data into an Oracle database.

However, a direct-path operation demands exclusive access to the object being loaded, because it is not cooperating with other database sessions via the SGA. If there are any indexes on a table being loaded, they are marked unusable and need to be rebuilt, because direct-path operations do not maintain indexes like conventional SQL operations. So, a direct-path load is not something that you can do on a live production table that is being accessed by live production users. So, in many ways, a direct-path load is extremely helpful, but it comes with the cost that it can be used only under certain conditions.

In addition to not generating rollback or undo, a direct-path insert operation can also be instructed not to generate redo for an operation. Again, this is possible because the direct-path insert operation is not manipulating buffers in the Oracle buffer cache. So, the UNRECOVERABLE clause (renamed to a NOLOGGING clause in later versions) is an instruction to a direct-path insert operation not to generate any redo for the loading of rows into the table. This reduces possible contention even further by relieving the workload of the LGWR process in the database, but the obvious downside is that, without redo, the normal database recovery process cannot perform recovery. So, if media failure or corruption occurs to the tables loaded via direct-path insert operations, there is a good chance the data could be lost. Often, people consider that a good trade-off for having a faster load, assuming that they are able to load the data over again. Another excellent strategy is to schedule an Oracle Recovery Manager (RMAN) incremental backup immediately after the direct-path insert operation completes, which will make the just-loaded rows recoverable.

One further point: since Oracle 9i, table compression has been a feature available only with direct-path insert operations. So, using a direct-path insert also ensures that you can take advantage of table compression, which reduces the amount of space table data consumes, thus saving both I/O operations as well as storage. So, in order to use table compression, you need to use direct-path insert operations. In order to use direct-path insert operations, you ought to use the exchange partition data load technique. So, there is a chain of dependencies in these features.

But, let's compare the two operations:

- A parallel UPDATE statement generates insane volumes of rollback/undo as part of normal processing, generates equally insane volumes of redo as part of normal processing, requires searches for the rows to manipulate prior to manipulating them, and performs all work within the Oracle buffer cache, requiring each parallel worker process to latch/lock buffers after they're retrieved, before manipulating them.

- A parallel unrecoverable/nologging CREATE TABLE … AS SELECT operation, using parallel direct-path sessions, has no contention with other sessions in the database nor between its own parallel worker processes. It does not generate rollback/undo or redo, except for the Data Definition Language (DDL) commands involved with extent allocation.

Clearly, one of these options is going to correct the transposed columns within a partition faster. As it turns out, the CREATE TABLE … AS SELECT operations completed within 10–15 minutes per partition, while the massively parallel UPDATE commands did not complete at all, to my recollection.

So, after the CREATE TABLE … AS SELECT command completed, it was a simple matter to create indexes on the newly created table that matched the LOCAL partitioned indexes on the big table, and then run the ANALYZE command (remember this was v 8.0.5) on the table and indexes. After these additional tasks were complete, it was another simple matter to run the ALTER TABLE … EXCHANGE PARTITION command to switch the identity of the newly created table with the partition that was its original source.

So, in the end, we were able to complete the correction of several billion rows in the latter half of an afternoon. We had about 25 weekly partitions to correct, and each was rebuilt in a matter of 10–15 minutes, indexed (another couple minutes), analyzed (another few minutes), and then exchanged into the live production table.

The beauty of this method was that users querying the live production table were not interrupted—the exchange partition operation does not interrupt queries. Queries that were already "in flight" when the exchange partition operation was started continued to run, and would continue to access the segment that was a partition when the query began. The fact that the segment that was formerly a partition was now a stand-alone table makes no difference, as long as it is not dropped following the exchange. So, in-flight queries were not affected. Obviously, queries started after the exchange partition took place saw only the segment that was switched into place, and never saw the segment that was the previous partition.

A further beauty of this method was that a rollback of the operation was so easy. If we had made a mistake in correcting the previous mistake, we could easily put the "old" partitions back into place by running an exchange partition operation again.

The basic lesson from this is that *the fastest mass update is actually an insert.* When you have a partitioned table, you can use an insert command to perform an update operation.

How would this scenario been different if the goal was to delete millions of rows rather than updating millions of rows? Not much different, because we would use the CREATE TABLE … AS SELECT command to select the rows that wouldn't be deleted, and then index, analyze, and exchange partition just as described. All of the conditions would be similar—a parallel DELETE command is just as inefficient as a parallel UPDATE for the same reasons. So, the basic lesson cited in the previous paragraph should be amended just a bit, to read *the fastest mass update or delete is actually an insert.*

Loading Millions of Rows

The scenario described in the previous section shows the basic five-step method of loading data into a partitioned table using the exchange partition:

1. Create a "temporary" table that will later be switched with a target partition in the partitioned target table.

2. Load the temporary table using the fastest methods appropriate for the situation (for example, direct-path insert).

3. Gather cost-based optimizer statistics on the just-loaded temporary table.

4. Create indexes on the just-loaded temporary table to match the LOCAL partitioned indexes on the partitioned target table, if any.

5. Exchange the target partition in the target table with the just-loaded temporary table.

The UPDATE scenario in the previous section performed steps 1 and 2 in a single operation by using CREATE TABLE … AS SELECT, but the basic principle remains the same. If your application demands that large volumes of rows be inserted (that is, data loading in a data warehouse), this basic five-step algorithm is the fastest way to accomplish this task, with the added benefit of not affecting queries running against the target partitioned table.

Faster loads using direct-path inserts, less transactional overhead of rollback/undo and redo being generated, and minimal contention with other database sessions. More wheat, less chaff; more signal, less noise. There just isn't any faster way to manipulate large volumes of data within the database.

Partition Pruning

Undoubtedly, the biggest advantage of partitioning is *pruning*, where the Oracle optimizer is enabled to decide which partitions to scan within a table or index, and which to ignore completely. This is accomplished two ways: explicitly and implicitly.

Explicit partition pruning occurs when the name of the partition or subpartition is specified in the FROM clause:

```
select count(*) from order_lines partition (p20091215);
select count(*) from order_lines subpartition (p20091215_sp0053);
```

The first query will scan only rows in the partition P20091215, containing rows from December 15, 2009. The second query will scan rows only for order type 53 for Dec. 15, 2009, an even smaller set of data. This form of partition pruning is not often used embedded within application code—at least, it shouldn't be! Instead, it is most often used during some type of maintenance operation, such as a data migration, troubleshooting data corruption, and the like.

Implicit partition pruning is far more commonly used, and it involves the Oracle cost-based optimizer being aware of the structure of the partitioned table and indexes while it parses the WHERE clause of the SQL statement in order to construct an execution plan. For example, suppose we have a table ORDER_LINES, which is range partitioned by day on the column ORDER_DATE and list subpartitioned on the column LINE_TYPE. The Oracle optimizer is capable of looking at the following SQL statement:

```
select count(*) from order_lines
where order_date >= '2009-12-15'
and order_date < '2009-12-16';
```

...and constructing an execution plan that will scan only the partition P20091215, which contains the order lines for order date Dec. 15, 2009. Likewise, the optimizer can look at the following SQL statement:

```
select count(*) from order_lines where order_type = 53;
```

...and construct an execution plan that will scan all of the orders of type 53 throughout all of the partitions of the ORDER_LINES table, regardless of the ORDER_DATE value, if that is what is desired. And finally, for the best-case scenario of partition pruning, the Oracle optimizer can look at the following SQL statement:

```
select count(*) from order_lines
where order_date >= '2009-12-15' and order_date < '2009-12-16'
and order_type = 53;
```

...and construct an execution plan that prunes the ORDER_DATE partitions down to the single-range partition containing data for Dec. 15, 2009, and then also prune the list subpartitions down to the subpartition within that partition of type 53, in order to triangulate directly to the subpartition named P20091215_SP0053. And this is just the starting point for the execution of the query, after having the optimizer prune away all of the partitions and subpartitions that the query simply would never need to scan because of the logic of the query. It is a powerful and simple mechanism.

However, there are pitfalls. Just as with indexes, the optimizer can "miss" a pruning opportunity because the partition key column (that is, ORDER_DATE) or subpartition key column (ORDER_TYPE) is contained in a function or expression. A very common problem arises because of a matter of programming style in dealing with the time component of the DATE datatype. Many people like to use the TRUNC() function to truncate the time component of the DATE datatype, resulting in a query like this:

```
select count(*) from order_lines where trunc(order_date) = '2009-12-15';
```

While logically correct in that this query will accurately count all of the rows where the ORDER_DATE belongs to the day Dec. 15, 2009, the optimizer will not create an execution plan that involves pruning to that partition, because the expression TRUNC(ORDER_DATE) is different from the simple column name ORDER_DATE, which is the partition key column. Unlike indexes, there are no function-based partition keys or expression-based partition keys, so programmers must alter their style of programming and leave the partition key and subpartition key columns free of expressions. Some situations in which this occurs are particularly subtle. Consider the following SQL statement:

```
select count(*) from order_lines where order_type = '53';
```

Although there is no explicit function or expression around the subpartition key column ORDER_TYPE, the Oracle optimizer is faced with the task of performing an implicit datatype conversion. That is, the text string 53 is being compared to the numeric column ORDER_TYPE. When this happens, the Oracle optimizer does not fail the SQL statement with an error message stating that a text string cannot be compared to a numeric column. Instead, it performs the implicit conversion itself. It can either wrap a TO_NUMBER() function around the text string value of 53, or it can wrap a TO_CHAR() function around the numeric column ORDER_TYPE. In most of these situations, especially those situations as simple as this, the Oracle optimizer is smart enough to realize that implicitly wrapping the TO_NUMBER() function around the text string 53 is safe and will not cause a conversion error. But please realize that the safest option for the Oracle optimizer is to wrap the TO_CHAR() function around the numeric column, because there is never a possibility of a conversion error when converting any data type to a text string. So, in more-complex situations, perhaps where bind variables are involved, the optimizer may choose to perform the conversion this way, and thus turn off pruning as a result.

The solution, as with any programming language, is to never rely on implicit conversion, and perform all conversions explicitly.

Partition Configuration

Partition pruning and subpartition pruning are the features that offer the greatest benefits when breaking huge tables and indexes into smaller chunks, by ensuring performance scalability in a very large database no matter how large it becomes. As you can see from these brief examples, these benefits come only from choosing columns that are frequently used as search criteria, so that the mechanism of pruning is used naturally. So, in order to realize the benefits of pruning, the following decisions must be made:

1. Which column(s) will be partition keys?

2. What partitioning scheme (that is, range, list, or hash) to use?

    1. What "granularity" of range partitioning to use? How many hash or list partitions should be created?

3. If range partitioning in Oracle 10 g R2 or earlier, or if range or list partitioning in Oracle 11g R1 or later, whether to subpartition as well?

    a. Which column(s) will be subpartition keys?

    b. What subpartitioning scheme to use?

    c. What granularity of range subpartitioning to use? How many hash or list subpartitions should each partition have?

At the same time, the use of the EXCHANGE PARTITION mass data-loading technique enables many of the other important features such as direct-path insert operations, table compression, nologging, and others. So we need to configure partitioning to enable pruning during queries, but we also need to configure partitioning to optimize mass data loading, mass data migration, and mass data purging, if any of these operations will become necessary.

Partition configuration is something to be considered individually for each table, based on how it is loaded, how it is accessed by the application, and finally how it will be purged. Of course, for any application, there are bound to be similarities between tables that aid in answering these questions, but never forget that there may be exceptions, so don't create a template and apply it indiscriminately.

For many very large databases, most large tables are effectively range partitioned by time, especially databases supporting business intelligence or data warehousing applications. This is because these types of applications generally consist of data that is inserted and then can be modified for a period of time afterward. After a certain period of time (hours, days, weeks, or months), data is considered read-only. For these types of applications, it is also common to specify dates or times as search criteria, providing a perfect use-case for pruning. Further, there is frequently a need to maintain a *rolling window* of data, perhaps only the past 3 months, or the past 13 months, or 25 months, and so forth. Again, this provides an almost perfect use-case for range partitioning by time, because operations such as DROP PARTITION or TRUNCATE PARTITION can be used to purge data that is no longer necessary.

It would not make much sense to list partitions by time, because list partitioning deals only with individual data values and does not include the concept of adjacent data values. So, in order to specify a partition containing a day's worth of data by using a DATE column, we would have to list all 86,400 possible seconds in each day. That isn't feasible, and even if we found a way around that problem, we'd still be faced with the inability to relate a list partition for one day to a list partition for the next day, or grouping into weeks, months, quarters, or years. Each method of partitioning is best suited to different types of data and the search operators used upon them:

-   Range partitioning uses a finite to infinite list of data values, searched using equivalence operators (that is, =) and range operators (>, >=, <, <=, BETWEEN, LIKE, and so forth).

-   List partitioning uses a finite list of identified data values plus DEFAULT for everything else, searched using equivalence operators only.

-   Hash partitioning uses an infinite list of data values, searched using equivalence operators only.

So, as an example, let's assume we have a table named ORDER_LINES that we would like to partition because it will grow to a huge size, and we would like to keep this data around for seven years, after which it is important (for legal reasons) that we purge the data out of the system as soon as possible. Let's assume that this ORDER_LINES table has about thirty columns, four of which are

DATE datatypes, so we're going to have to choose among these four DATE columns to decide which will be our RANGE partition key. What is the best way to do this?

Let's further assume that the four DATE columns are ORDER_DATE, PAYMENT_DATE, SHIPMENT_DATE, and LAST_UPDATED_DATE. It is important to be able to identify how these four columns are used, and to which communities of users they are of interest. A column such as LAST_UPDATED_DATE might be of interest to security auditors and application administrators, but few others. A column such as ORDER_DATE (indicating the date that the order was placed) is likely to be of interest to a wide audience of application users. PAYMENT_DATE and SHIPMENT_DATE are each of interest to a somewhat narrower group of users, perhaps the financial accounting team and the production team, respectively.

So in many cases, the choice of a partition-key column distills down to this question: whose perspective is most important, whose queries deserve most to be optimized by pruning? It almost becomes a political battle, facilitated and guided by the IT team but decided by the application owners. We are looking for a column that is frequently used as search criteria, but that might also have a relationship to how data is loaded and how data is to be purged. Similar criteria are used in searching for columns to use as subpartition keys. Here, we are also looking for columns that are frequently used as search criteria in SQL statements.

For the granularity of range partitioning, the best bet is to try to ensure the best use of pruning during queries. There is little benefit to deciding in favor of monthly range partitions if end users frequently query for a day's worth of data, or even a few hours or minutes of data. In that situation, when end users query for a few hours of data, it makes the most sense to partition down to hourly ranges. Likewise, on tables where end-users never query for less than whole months, it does not make sense to partition daily or hourly. Look for the lowest granularity of access, loading, and purging, and partition to that granularity.

Information Life Cycle Management

All this effort has been devoted to partitioning, to making large objects into constellations of smaller objects. Are pruning and the exchange partition data-loading technique the only benefits?

One other benefit of partitioning that has not been explored here is the ability to place partitions, even subpartitions, into different tablespaces. Generally, when placing tables and indexes into tablespaces, we think in terms of schemas and the growth characteristics of the table or index in question, and create a tablespace named APPDATA_LARGE or APPINDEX_SMALL, and place the table or index into the tablespace we feel appropriate.

But what about the importance of time?

In general, when data is newly inserted, it is very busy. It is first created, and it is probably requeried multiple times soon after it is inserted. Perhaps it is even modified soon after it is inserted. Certainly new data is queried numerous times, either for use in a form or a report, but also while gathering statistics for the Oracle cost-based optimizer.

However, generally as time goes on, data is modified less and less frequently, and even the query activity lessens. At some point, data modifications cease altogether, and the data becomes essentially read-only, and it is read infrequently at that. Finally, there comes a point where the data is no longer useful even for querying, so it is purged.

If all of this sounds like the description of a biological life form, it should, because it is. Just as in life, data has a life cycle. Just as in life, not all data has the exact same life cycle, but the basic principles are the same. When data is relatively new, it is written to and read from. Later, if it is written to at all, it is an infrequent event, but it might still be read frequently. Finally, at some point, the data is not even read frequently, and later still not at all, and then can be removed.

Figure 10-1 shows a fairly common data life cycle.

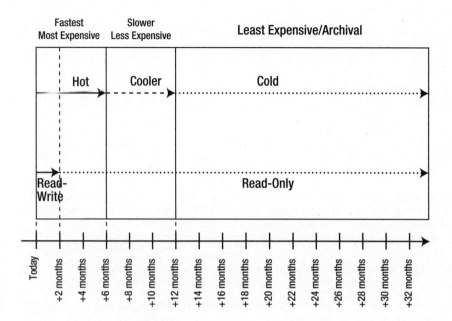

Figure 10-1. Data life cycle

In Figure 10-1, we see three *tiers* of storage in use:

- The fastest and most expensive storage, intended to optimize I/Os per second (IOPS), also known as *hot* data

- Slower and less-expensive storage, intended to provide reasonable read performance (*cooler* data)

- The least expensive archival storage, intended to provide storage for infrequently read data (*cold* data)

We also see another continuum, showing that data can be set to read-only after it has been in the database two months, implying that it can be changed only during the first two months of its life cycle.

Notice that the size of tier 1 (that is, the fastest and most expensive) and tier 2 (slower, less expensive) storage is likely to remain relatively static as time passes. In fact, unless the rate at which data is loaded changes, only tier 3 (least expensive, archival) storage will increase in size.

In this manner, we can control the costs of the most volatile resource in a very large database, storage. We can assure those who are paying for the application infrastructure that we will not locate "idle" data on expensive storage, and that the only type of storage that will increase in size will be the least expensive. Placing data onto the storage according to its access patterns is *right-sizing* the storage to the way that data is being used.

But information lifecycle management (ILM) of this sort is simply not possible in an Oracle database unless you plan for it. You must range partition tables by time, and you must locate those partitions in tablespaces, which themselves are designed to store data from a given point in time.

Let's go back to the example of the ORDER_LINES table, which is range partitioned on ORDER_DATE by day, and list subpartitioned on ORDER_TYPE. We can place all of the partitions for this table into a single huge tablespace, but that would not permit us to use tiered storage, as shown in Figure 10-1.

But let's consider creating tablespaces to hold a month's worth of ORDER_LINES partitions and their index partitions. So, we might consider having tablespaces with names such as ORDLINE_200909, ORDLINE_200910, ORDLINE_200911, and so on. Each of these monthly tablespaces would hold all of the table and index partitions for that month.

Now, with time-variant tablespaces, we can create a new tablespace on tier 1 storage, initially in read-write status. After two months, we change the tablespace from read-write to read-only status. After six months, we move that tablespace from tier 1 to tier 2 storage. Then, after 12 months, we move that tablespace from tier 2 to tier 3 storage, and after seven years, we drop that tablespace and all the partitions with it.

The key here is that the tablespace must be in read-only status before we can consider moving it. If we cannot set the tablespace to read-only, the whole concept of ILM falls apart, because it is not feasible to move tablespaces and data files around when the tablespace is available in read-write status.

There are two major methods to migrate tablespaces from one tier of storage to another:

- Using RMAN to first copy the data files in the tablespace to the new location, and then switch the identity of the data files from the old location to the new location

- Creating the new tablespace in the new location, using CREATE TABLE … AS SELECT to copy the data from the existing partitions to the new tables, and then using the exchange partition technique to switch the old partitions with the new tables in the new tablespace

Each of these two techniques has its advantages and its disadvantages. The advantage of the RMAN technique is simplicity and no need to take another backup of the moved tablespaces. The advantage of the copy/exchange technique is the opportunity to compress a previously uncompressed partition during the copy phase.

Tiered storage is not easy to achieve, because you have to design it in almost from the beginning. But if you view the very large tables and indexes in your very large database as having a life cycle, then provisioning the storage for a very large database resembles less of an unpredictable bottomless black hole and more of a predictable factory assembly line.

Backup Optimization and Guaranteed Recovery

We've discussed how partitioning enables queries to scale, enables mass data loads to scale, and even enables storage to scale. But there is another common day-to-day activity that absolutely needs to scale, or else the entire enterprise is in danger of collapsing.

Recovery is "job one" for a database administrator.

—Tim Gorman

The ability to recover from any failure and recover back to the point-in-time of the failure is the most convincing argument in favor of a database management system (DBMS) such as Oracle. There is no doubt that data can be retrieved faster from a simple flat file. As a database administrator, I don't know how many times I have had to listen to programmers, managers, and sales people bash the Oracle database as a bloated, overpriced, resource-gobbling, underperforming virus. I cannot argue any of those points, except *underperforming.*

For enterprise computing, it really doesn't matter if some other form of database is faster or less expensive or requires less expertise to manage. What matters is that the data is available for use. Performance means nothing if the data disappears. How much money you've spent means nothing if the data disappears. No database management software is better at protecting data than Oracle.

But even so, there are limits. If Oracle is called upon to restore and recover all or part of a 5PB database in the event of a failure, can we claim success if the recovery takes so long that the business dies while we are doing so? Or, even worse, if obtaining backups takes so long that we simply cannot restore and recover at all? Failures happen, and invariably they happen when we're most vulnerable to them.

Since the 1980s, Oracle has permitted *hot backups*, or backups taken while the database is up and fully available. So, for more than 20 years, it has never been necessary to set aside a special time to take backups and to complete all backups within that time window. Database administrators have always had 24 hours a day, 7 days a week to use as windows in which to take database backups.

But the problem is one of volume. There are throughput limitations on backup media, and there are resource limitations on backup processes. If you have a 5PB database, just how feasible would it be to back it up every single night? Most systems administrators are happy to achieve throughput rates of 500–1,000GB per hour on backups, but at that rate it would take 5,000–10,000 hours (200–400 days) to back up a 5PB database. Ask your system administrator what it would take to double or quadruple the rate of backups, and then realize that such radical improvements would simply reduce the time to complete a backup from 200–400 days to only 50–80 days, a meaningless victory at best. What is needed is not an incremental change, but a radical change, and partitioning for ILM provides just that radical change, in the form of incremental backups and read-only tablespaces. Why do we take frequent backups? To capture and protect recent changes to the data.

In an Oracle database, where do recent changes occur? Within read-write tablespaces. Tablespaces that are set to read-only status have, by definition, not changed. Is there is a need to back them up frequently? The answer is no. Is there a need to back them up more than once after they are set to read-only? The answer is probably, because nobody can convincingly guarantee the integrity and availability of a single set of backups.

So, look again at Figure 10-1, and note the dividing line between read-write and read-only. Clearly, the majority of the volume of a database that is configured for ILM is read-only and needs to be backed up only infrequently, perhaps once or twice per year, if not less frequently, depending on how much you trust your backup media. It is only the read-write portion of the database, along with the archived redo log files, that need to be backed up frequently, on a daily or weekly basis.

At this point, it is worth mentioning the importance of the CROSSCHECK command in RMAN. Tape handling has grown more complicated, and the huge volumes of tapes to be stored and retrieved makes the retrieval of infrequently accessed volumes quite questionable. The RMAN recovery catalog has a record of a backup set piece, and it has the name of that piece on backup media, but does the backup media manager subsystem still have that piece available? The CROSSCHECK commands in RMAN should be run at least once per full backup cycle to ensure that the RMAN recovery catalog holds only valid information about the availability of backup set pieces on media. For example, sometimes retention policies set within the backup media management software cause an older tape to be reused, without RMAN knowing. The CROSSCHECK command walks through all of the backup sets in the RMAN recovery catalog and asks the backup media manager to "touch" each one of them. It is also wise to use the CROSSCHECK command before any RESTORE or RECOVER operation in RMAN, to make sure that the restore commands are compiled from valid information. Database recovery is invariably done in a rush, with a great deal of tension and pressure, and knowing that RMAN will not abort because of a preventable error helps everyone's blood pressure stay within normal ranges.

So, fine-tuning the read-write portion of the database is crucial for scaling the most important capability of the very large database: recovery. It is most certainly possible to protect even the largest of very large Oracle databases against any type of failure, but again, this demands up-front planning and design. Luckily, this planning and design coincides precisely with the goals of ILM, and Oracle provides the toolkit for this in the features of partitioning, read-only tablespaces, and incremental backups by Oracle RMAN.

So, hopefully now the true advantage of partitioning becomes clearer. Breaking large objects into smaller ones, just for the sake of doing so, does not provide much benefit. However, the way in which those smaller objects are managed, how they are stored, according to a life cycle, makes all the difference in the world.

Further Notes on Storage

When attending a social function, it is generally risky to discuss topics such as politics, religion, and sex. Lots of people thrive on risk; many people can't live without the thrill. In the world of Oracle database administrators, many topics are similarly risky because they provoke responses similar to those found when discussing politics, religion, or sex, and sometimes all three together.

The question: Which should be used, file systems, "raw" devices, or Automated Space Management (ASM)?

Here are some things to consider, and you can decide which are most important to your requirements:

- Raw devices are undeniably the optimal form of storage for Oracle database files from a performance perspective, because of the lack of redundant memory caching, access to kernelized asynchronous I/O, and the more direct access to data.

- File systems are undeniably the optimal form of storage for Oracle database files from a manageability perspective, because of decades of familiarity and ease of access using OS utilities as well as Oracle utilities, as well as the ability to change file attributes (that is, size) easily and quickly.

- Raw devices are generally the most difficult form of storage for Oracle DBAs to manage because these devices are managed by system administrators and because they typically cannot be created, renamed, extended, shrunk, or dropped on an on-demand basis.

- Most of the recent advances in file system technology (asynchronous I/O, direct or unbuffered I/O, clustered file systems, and so forth) have to do with dismantling the internal services of file systems and making them seem more like raw devices.

Oracle ASM provides all of the performance advantages of raw devices mentioned in the preceding list, with most of the ease of manageability of a file system mentioned, without any of the disadvantages mentioned. Lots of people are suspicious of Oracle ASM because they feel it is too new, unfamiliar, and buggy. But I have worked with Oracle ASM in some of the most extreme database environments I have ever experienced, and it nicely complements the best features of the Oracle database without limitations.

In the world of very large databases, removing limitations and enabling all of the features available is vital. Try ASM, if you haven't already. There is a learning curve, but you'll be glad you invested the effort.

Limits of Which to Be Aware

Back in the beginning of the chapter, I briefly mentioned that Oracle has some limits of which to be aware. There aren't many, but they can still stop you dead in your tracks, especially if you are using partitioning and ILM.

Database Block Size

In a VLDB environment, choose the largest database block size supported by your platform. Most platforms have a maximum DB_BLOCK_SIZE value of 16,384 bytes (16 kilobytes), some have a maximum size of 32,768 bytes (32KB). The most common database block size used by Oracle databases is 8,192 bytes (8KB), and that is more than sufficient for many very large databases. However, there are numerous limits based on database block size, so it worthwhile to choose wisely:

- Maximum size of an extent in a segment (4 billion database blocks for dictionary-managed tablespaces, 2 billion database blocks for locally managed tablespaces)

- Maximum control file size (20,000 database blocks)

- Maximum data file size (4 million database blocks for SMALLFILE tablespaces, 4 billion database blocks for BIGFILE tablespaces)

- Maximum database size (65,533 times the maximum data file sizes cited earlier)

Choosing a block size is not the seeming life-or-death choice it used to be, especially since Oracle 9i, when tablespaces could have their own block sizes. But in the world of the very large database, with so many limitations tied to block size, it is worth giving some additional thought at the outset.

Number of Files in a Database

As recently as Oracle 11g R2, the limit on the number of data files in a database is 65,533. This may seem like an unattainable number of data files, and for the vast majority of Oracle databases on the planet it is certainly more than sufficient, but we're in the rarified stratosphere of very large databases, and this limit is certainly not unattainable. In particular, the principles of ILM with the creation of time-variant tablespaces or at least tablespaces created for each milestone in the data life cycle might cause a very large database to approach this limit. If you have automated the task of monitoring space in such a way that additional data files are added to tablespaces approaching a threshold of *full*, it is very likely that a database with 4,000 or 5,000 tablespaces can approach this limit.

Consider also that Oracle still has a maximum of 65,533 tablespaces. That fact is closely related to the data file limit, something that makes sense if you stop and think about the fact that each tablespace must have at least one data file. So, an Oracle database that will grow into the hundreds or thousands of terabytes can easily have hundreds or thousands of tablespaces, and if we manage space the way smaller databases are managed, we can approach these limits.

So, here are two bits of advice for the planning and designing of the very large database:

- Be sure to take advantage of data file autoextension.

    - Choose a standard maximum size for all data files, whose limit is usually bound by the database block size for the tablespace. It is not necessary to preallocate this maximum size for all data files, as Oracle can automatically extend data files. Especially if you are using Oracle ASM, please consider data file and temp file autoextension before adding more data files and temp files.

- Consider using BIGFILE tablespaces.

    - Starting with Oracle 10g, Oracle provides the concept of BIGFILE tablespaces, which are tablespaces that are permitted one and only one data file. This single data file is capable of growing to 4 billion database blocks, whereas the data files of traditional (SMALLFILE) tablespaces can grow to only 4 million database blocks.

These are not strict admonitions, of course. There aren't any *thou shalt* proclamations here. Mostly this is because not every form of storage permits the use of data file autoextension, such as raw devices.

The fact that Oracle ASM accommodates data file autoextension and BIGFILE tablespaces very naturally should be another argument in favor of it, and away from the older conventional wisdom of favoring file systems or raw devices.

Storage That Can Migrate

Very few ideas in information technology are truly new. Many new concepts are just updated reissues of technology perfected decades ago, rediscovered by a new generation. One such concept is hierarchical storage management (HSM), which is storage that automatically and transparently moves storage volumes from high-cost to low-cost storage, and back again, in order to utilize the high-cost storage only on demand.

There have been various implementations of HSM over the years, but most commonly HSM is implemented as a limited amount of high-end storage presented to the system as a *cache*. All of the volumes in the HSM are available at all times, but if a volume is not used for a prespecified period of time, most of the volume (except for a small header element) is *migrated* transparently off to lower-cost storage. When the volume is accessed by the application again, the HSM migrates the requested portions of the volume back to the higher-cost storage cache. While this migration is happening, the application waits. So, from the perspective of the application, in this case an Oracle database, the volumes on HSM can be used as data files, but at times accessing these data files comes with a long delay upon first access.

HSM technology is well-suited to very large Oracle databases, especially those databases that have a well-defined ILM strategy making use of tiered storage. HSM volumes are often ideal as tier 3, or archival-class, storage for infrequently used data. And, as long as the HSM volumes are always available to the Oracle database instance, it is possible to mount them as Oracle data files.

There is a subtle problem, however, involving the Oracle data dictionary views DBA_EXTENTS and DBA_FREE_SPACE. These views are accessed frequently, both by database administrators, as well as monitoring utilities such as Oracle Enterprise Manager. If you look at the definitions of these views, they consist of two UNIONed subqueries, one subquery against the dictionary-managed tablespace information (that is, SYS.UET$ for used dictionary-managed extents and SYS.FET$ for free dictionary-managed extents), and the other subquery on the locally managed tablespace information (that is, SYS.X$KTFBUE for used locally managed extents and SYS.X$KTFBFE for free locally managed extents).

Now, the information in SYS.UET$ and SYS.FET$ tables is always easily queried, because they are located within the SYSTEM tablespace. But the information presented via the SYS.X$KTFBUE and SYS.X$KTFBFE views actually resides on the data files themselves—hence the name *locally managed tablespaces*. This decentralization of used- and free-extent information is generally good for performance scalability, but it is queries against the DBA_EXTENTS and DBA_FREE_SPACE view that suffer from this decentralized information. It simply takes more time to accumulate all this information, especially as the number of data files increases. This is not a performance problem for database applications, but it can be a performance problem for monitoring utilities that periodically or frequently query these views.

HSM volumes make the problem of accessing the DBA_EXTENTS and DBA_FREE_SPACE views even worse. If even a few data files on HSM volumes have been migrated to lower-cost storage, any query on DBA_EXTENTS and DBA_FREE_SPACE will recall them, just to read the extent information. If you have a regularly scheduled job in Oracle Enterprise Manager to check space utilization, it is possible that this simple innocuous task can bring the HSM storage array to its knees, and frustrate the database administrator who cannot monitor space utilization in a timely manner.

So, if you are building a very large database, and you are planning on using tiered storage as part of your ILM strategy, and you are considering using HSM volumes as your tier 3 storage, and your very large Oracle database is created with a locally managed SYSTEM tablespace (the default setting), then you are in trouble.

An Oracle database with a locally managed SYSTEM tablespace cannot have any dictionary-managed tablespaces. An Oracle database with a dictionary-managed SYSTEM tablespace can accommodate both locally managed as well as dictionary-managed tablespaces. And, as it turns out, tablespaces created on (or migrated to) HSM volumes had better be dictionary managed, so as not to run into the file-open latency problem every time the DBA_EXTENTS and DBA_FREE_SPACE views are queried.

Parameter READ_ONLY_OPEN_DELAYED

Normally, when an Oracle database is opened, the Oracle background processes attempt to "touch" each of the data files in the database, to ensure that they are available. When using HSM storage, this method of doing things can take an inordinately long time, because "touching" the headers of each data file on HSM storage can take a long time, as those files are recalled and migrated back to cache.

The parameter READ_ONLY_OPEN_DELAYED changes this behavior at instance startup. Data files belonging to tablespaces that are read-only are only touched when they are accessed, not when the database is opened. So, as the number of data files grows larger, and as the number of read-only tablespaces increases, you can keep the time needed to restart the database instance to a minimum by setting this parameter to TRUE, especially if you have read-only tablespaces based on migrateable HSM storage.

Summary

The world of the very large database is demanding. It is important to keep in mind where limitations exist, and try to address them from the outset. This chapter has laid out most, if not all, of the relevant limitations within the Oracle RDBMS as of this writing.

But the features and capabilities of the RDBMS software do not represent the biggest potential limitation. Instead, a very large database must be designed from the outset to accommodate the entire life cycle of the data. Most often, a data life cycle is based on time and aging, but sometimes different types of applications will yield a data life cycle based on other criteria. Know the criteria that separates data when it is newly created, when it can become read-only, and when it can be moved to different tiers of storage, before it is finally purged. Everything dies, including data—it is just a matter of bothering to look far enough to understand that life cycle.

CHAPTER 11

■ ■ ■

Statistics

by Jonathan Lewis

In principle, there are only a few things you have to get right to create an efficient application: get the data in the right place, create high-precision access paths for the important user functions, and make sure that you don't introduce mechanisms that waste resources or cause contention between competing processes.

Ultimately, an application is just a set of SQL statements controlled by layers of application code. If you can make the SQL run efficiently and don't make the application code do in 100 steps something that should have been done in a couple of SQL statements, you're probably going to build a good application.

But even when you design a good data structure, create a perfect indexing strategy, and get the right balance between the application code and the SQL, you may still face an important problem. You will find that some SQL statements that clearly should run efficiently will fail to do so—and there are two possible reasons for this:

- The optimizer may literally be unable to produce a certain execution plan that seems to be an obvious choice to the human eye.

- The plan you want is technically available, but the statistics used by the optimizer make it look inappropriate.

In this chapter, I address the importance of statistics—highlighting a few of the problems, explaining why they appear, and suggesting strategies for working around them. Before looking at statistics, though, I'd like to start with a couple of warnings.

It Can't Be Done!

I often hear people claiming they've found a bug in Oracle because it won't do what they want. In general, you need to be cautious about such claims. Yet occasionally they are true (or close to true—just because Oracle can't do something, it's not necessarily a bug), and this can lead to a huge waste of personal time. Imagine, for example, that you've just written a piece of code that should obviously use a really elegant and efficient execution path, and the optimizer doesn't find it. After 30 minutes or so of checking input values and bind variable types, experimenting with hints, and so on, what should you do?

1. Call it an Oracle bug and rewrite the SQL to do the same job in a completely different way?

2. Keep struggling with hints and statistics until you finally give up and fall back on option 1?

Time is an important commodity. If you give up too soon and rewrite the statement, you may spend a lot *more* time writing and testing the new statement, introducing extra complexity (and future risk of error) to the code. If you get too wrapped up in solving the original execution path problem, you may waste a huge amount of time investigating a problem that can't be fixed. I can't give you a sensible guideline on how much time to spend on a problem before putting it to one side, but if you want a couple of hints, consider the following:

- Remember that the time you spend investigating is time spent improving your problem-solving skills (providing you work methodically and write up your conclusions), so it is a good investment.

- The more complex the query, the more risk there may be in trying to rewrite it—so complex queries deserve more time, and simpler queries deserve less time before you try rewriting them.

As far as investigating is concerned, there are two strategies I follow. First, can I take a complex query, identify where it's probably going wrong, and strip it down to a much simpler example? Second, if I see some odd behavior on my current version of Oracle (and can reproduce it), does the same behavior appear on the previous and next versions of Oracle? Here are a couple of examples I've addressed recently that demonstrate what I mean.

■ **Note** In my previous book, *Cost-Based Oracle Fundamentals* (Apress, 2005), I provided a detailed description of my working environment and complete scripts (in the downloads). This chapter is much less formal and doesn't include so much detail nor are there any downloadable scripts. However, as a guideline, most examples were created and tested on Oracle 10.2.0.3, and then re-executed against 9.2.0.8 and 11.1.0.6.

Where I mention gathering stats, I generally use `dbms_stats.gather_table_stats()` with `cascade` set to `true` to collect index stats, `method_opt` set to `for all columns size 1` to avoid histograms, and `estimate_percent` set to `100` because the tests usually involve small tables. I also tend to disable *CPU costing* (also known as *system statistics*) simply to ensure that my test cases are more likely to be repeatable.

Subquery Anomaly

At a user group meeting, I was approached by someone who had a problem with a fairly complex query running under Oracle 11g. The query included a couple of views (one nonmergeable), a couple of subqueries, and a `UNION`; and the optimizer had decided that the cardinality of the nonmergeable view was 1 (when 40 million would have been a better estimate).

The DBA had tracked this problem down to a filter subquery operating as the last step of the nonmergeable view, and had found a line in the 10053 trace file reading `Final adjusted join cardinality: 1, sq. fil. factor: 4.9915e+08`. This was obviously relevant. (How else do you get from 40 million rows down to 1, apart from dividing by something close to 40 million?) But where did that magic number come from, and what could he do about it?

It's probably fairly well known by now that Oracle often uses 1 percent or 5 percent as a scaling factor for *unknown selectivity*, and that both these factors appear frequently in calculations involving subqueries. However, that's a long way from 49,915,000, so I was curious and volunteered to take a look at the trace file.

The file size was 12MB, and the plan was 70 lines—so not a simple task at first sight. But plenty of clues made it possible to simplify the problem. We had reason to believe that the critical issue probably related to a subquery, operating as a filter subquery, and operating at the end of a no-merge view. I noticed one significant number when looking at the subquery in isolation. Here's the most significant (but camouflaged) text of the critical WHERE clause:

```
1 = (select nvl(max(tableX.flag),1) from tableX where tableX.id = main_table.id)
```

Tracking down the information the optimizer had about tableX, I found the following:

```
SINGLE TABLE ACCESS PATH
-------------------------------------------
BEGIN Single Table Cardinality Estimation
-------------------------------------------
Column (#1): ID(NUMBER)
  AvgLen: 7.00 NDV: 4991490 Nulls: 0 Density: 2.0034e-07
     Min: 1501376845 Max: 1630612660
  Histogram: HtBal #Bkts: 254  UncompBkts: 254  EndPtVals: 255
Table: TABLEX  Alias: TABLEX
  Card: Original: 3621333248  Rounded: 726  Computed: 725.50  Non Adjusted: 725.50
-------------------------------------------
END   Single Table Cardinality Estimation
-------------------------------------------
```

Notice the coincidence: we have a *subquery filter selectivity* of 4.9915e + 08, and we have a column with a *number of distinct values* of 4.99149e + 06 which, allowing for a factor of 100 (1 percent for a subquery, perhaps), is a pretty good match. This was enough to make me think it was worth creating a little model (using 11.1.0.6), as follows:

```
create table t1
as
with generator as (
        select   --+ materialize
                 rownum          id
        from     all_objects
        where    rownum <= 3000
)
select
        mod(rownum,733)          id1,
        rownum                   id2,
        mod(rownum,11)           n1,
        lpad(rownum,10,'0')      small_vc,
        rpad('x',100)            padding
from
        generator       v1,
        generator       v2
where
        rownum <= 100000
```

```
;

alter table t1 add constraint t1_pk primary key(id1, id2);

create table t2
as
with generator as (
        select    --+ materialize
                  rownum            id
        from      all_objects
        where     rownum <= 3000
)
select
        mod(rownum,735)           id1,
        trunc((rownum-1)/735)     id2,
        mod(rownum,11)            n1,
        lpad(rownum,10,'0')       small_vc,
        rpad('x',100)             padding
from
        generator        v1,
        generator        v2
where
        rownum <= 100000
;

alter table t2 add constraint t2_pk primary key(id1, id2);

-- gather statistics on the tables

alter session set events '10053 trace name context forever';

select
        *
from
        t1
where
        1 = (
                select
                        nvl(max(n1),1)
                from
                        t2
                where
                        t2.id1 = t1.id1
        )
;
```

I've rigged the data so that the query returns no rows, but it does take a few seconds to complete. The thing I wanted to see was the 10053 trace file to check whether it reported a large sq. fil. factor. Sure enough, I found the line Final adjusted join cardinality: 1, sq. fil. factor: 73300.000000, which, you'll notice, is 100 times the number of distinct values of t1.id1 (the factor of 100—or, inversely, 1 percent—suggests that the optimizer is treating the subquery correlated to t1.id1 as a function(t1.id1) = constant), and the execution plan (from a call to explain plan, and omitting the Predicate section) looked like this:

```
--------------------------------------------------------------------
| Id | Operation                     | Name  | Rows  | Bytes | Cost |
--------------------------------------------------------------------
|   0 | SELECT STATEMENT             |       |     1 |   123 |  102K|
|*  1 |  FILTER                      |       |       |       |      |
|   2 |   TABLE ACCESS FULL          | T1    |  100K |   11M |  273 |
|   3 |   SORT AGGREGATE             |       |     1 |     7 |      |
|   4 |    TABLE ACCESS BY INDEX ROWID| T2   |   136 |   952 |  139 |
|*  5 |     INDEX RANGE SCAN         | T2_PK |   136 |       |    2 |
--------------------------------------------------------------------
```

Note, particularly, the final cardinality of the SELECT statement: it's just 1. The way the algorithm is working at present, the result for queries like this is always going to be 1, and a cardinality of 1 often results in the optimizer doing something totally inappropriate for the next step of the plan.

■ **Note** I don't often resort to generating a 10053 trace when investigating a performance problem. It's very much the last resort when the (runtime) execution plan doesn't give me enough clues to work out what's gone wrong. If you do decide to enable event 10053, remember that you get the trace file dumped only when a statement is optimized (or *hard parsed*, to use the popular terminology).

Of course, there's no sensible way that the optimizer could work out the correct cardinality after a subquery like this. Depending on the business, the subquery might eliminate nearly all the data or hardly any of the data. However, what it's supposed to be doing is probably the typical "guess" for a predicate of function(columnX) = constant, which uses a 1 percent selectivity (change the equality to *greater than* or *less than* and you'd see that 1 percent change to 5 percent). Unfortunately, a bug seems to have been introduced in 10g—perhaps as a side effect of a bug fix applied to 9i.

Having reached this point, of course, I was in a position to raise a service request (SR) with Oracle Corp. That wouldn't necessarily result in a quick fix, but at least there's a chance of a patch appearing eventually.

With the script in hand, though, I could also run a few other tests for related problems, possible workarounds, and version dependencies. I said that I wondered whether this was a bug introduced by a fix to 9i. Here's the execution plan for the same test on 9i (9.2.0.8):

```
--------------------------------------------------------------------
| Id | Operation                     | Name  | Rows  | Bytes | Cost |
--------------------------------------------------------------------
|   0 | SELECT STATEMENT             |       |  1000 |  120K |  139K|
|*  1 |  FILTER                      |       |       |       |      |
|   2 |   TABLE ACCESS FULL          | T1    |  1000 |  120K |  273 |
|   3 |   SORT AGGREGATE             |       |     1 |     7 |      |
|   4 |    TABLE ACCESS BY INDEX ROWID| T2   |   136 |   952 |  139 |
|*  5 |     INDEX RANGE SCAN         | T2_PK |   136 |       |    2 |
--------------------------------------------------------------------
```

Note how the final cardinality is 1 percent of 100,000 (the number of rows in t1). Note also, though, that the 1 percent has been applied prematurely in the plan (it's been given as the number of rows selected from the table (line 2) *before* the filter subquery has been applied), and this introduces a threat that I've described in some detail on my blog at
http://jonathanlewis.wordpress.com/2006/11/08/subquery-selectivity/.

Interestingly, by playing around a little with the test script, I found an option that might be a viable workaround for some variants of the query, and might even be a most appropriate optimization anyway. When running the test on 10g (10.2.0.3) or 11g and adding a /*+ push_subq */ hint to the subquery (which is a bit silly in this particular example, because there is no earlier point in the plan that the subquery could run), the 1 percent selectivity reappears with the following plan:

```
---------------------------------------------------------------------------
| Id  | Operation                     | Name  | Rows  | Bytes | Cost  |
---------------------------------------------------------------------------
|   0 | SELECT STATEMENT              |       | 1000  | 120K  |  412  |
|*  1 |  TABLE ACCESS FULL            | T1    | 1000  | 120K  |  273  |
|   2 |   SORT AGGREGATE              |       |    1  |    7  |       |
|   3 |    TABLE ACCESS BY INDEX ROWID| T2    |  136  |  952  |  139  |
|*  4 |     INDEX RANGE SCAN          | T2_PK |  136  |       |    2  |
---------------------------------------------------------------------------
```

In the changes to the code from 9i to 10g to deal with the error of applying the subquery filter factor too early, Oracle Corp. seem to have left a special case where the wrong filter factor is applied when it's applied late.

And then, with yet another simple variation, I got yet another result. When I removed the nvl() function from max(n1), the optimizer was suddenly able to unnest the subquery to produce the following plan:

```
------------------------------------------------------------------
| Id  | Operation              | Name    | Rows  | Bytes | Cost  |
------------------------------------------------------------------
|   0 | SELECT STATEMENT       |         | 1097  | 159K  |  710  |
|*  1 |  HASH JOIN             |         | 1097  | 159K  |  710  |
|   2 |   VIEW                 | VW_SQ_1 |    8  |  208  |  435  |
|*  3 |    FILTER              |         |       |       |       |
|   4 |     HASH GROUP BY      |         |    8  |   88  |  435  |
|   5 |      TABLE ACCESS FULL | T2      | 100K  | 1074K |  269  |
|   6 |   TABLE ACCESS FULL    | T1      | 100K  |  11M  |  273  |
------------------------------------------------------------------
```

Be careful with code changes like this, though. Getting rid of nvl() changed the meaning of the query quite dramatically—with an effect similar to turning an outer join into an inner join. Unless I had a constraint in place to ensure that every value of id1 in t1 had at least one matching row in t2, removing nvl() would cause the loss of some of the required data.

Partition Elimination

In the previous example, you saw how stripping a production problem to the bare minimum enables us to identify the basic cause, prepare a test case, and help find a workaround to the problem. Sometimes we get the chance to work from the opposite direction and discover that a feature isn't going to work in the current release before we've spent lots of time developing real production code. Consider the following investigation into possible threats related to partition elimination for a system based on Oracle 10g. Here's a simple creation script and query:

```
create table pt_range (
        id      not null,
        grp,
        small_vc,
        padding
)
nologging
partition by range(id) (
        partition p200 values less than (200),
        partition p400 values less than (400),
        partition p600 values less than (600)
)
as
select
        round(rownum/20,2)              id,
        trunc(rownum/50)                grp,
        to_char(trunc(rownum/20))       small_vc,
        rpad('x',100)                   padding
from
        all_objects
where
        rownum < 12000
;

alter table pt_range add constraint pt_pk primary key (id) using index local;

-- gather stats at this point

select max(id) from pt_range;
```

It is obvious to the human eye that the best way for Oracle to execute this query is to start at the top partition and work downward until it finds a partition with some data in it, and then find the maximum value in that partition. But what does the execution plan look like? This is what I got in 10.2.0.3:

Id	Operation	Name	Rows	Bytes	Cost	Pstart	Pstop
0	SELECT STATEMENT		1	5	2		
1	SORT AGGREGATE		1	5			
2	PARTITION RANGE ALL		11999	59995	2	1	3
3	INDEX FULL SCAN (MIN/MAX)	PT_PK	11999	59995	2	1	3

The optimizer has been fairly clever—using an index full scan (min/max) because it "knows" that the highest value in an index is at the right-hand edge—but it says it's going to start from the bottom partition (pstart = 1) and work upward (pstop = 3) to the top partition (and, just in case you haven't noticed it in the manuals, a partitioned table in 10g can have a little over 1 million partitions).

As soon as you see this example, you're bound to ask yourself a few questions because most of the work your users do will probably be with "more recent" partitions, which means that you might want to ensure that, if possible, their queries start at the top partition and work backward, stopping as soon as possible. So is it possible for the optimizer to create a plan that visits partitions in descending order? And if it is, will Oracle be able to stop the descent early? And how do we know that the preceding plan didn't visit the partitions in reverse order at runtime execution anyway?

■ **Note** The execution path index full scan (min/max) doesn't do a full scan of the index, and the very large row counts that appear with it are misleading. The (min/max) tag tells you that Oracle is going to jump straight to the smallest or largest relevant value in the index without scanning any extra leaf blocks.

Let's answer that last question first. There are various ways we could check what's going on with partition elimination, but if you search the message file ($ORACLE_HOME/rdbms/mesg/oraus.msg, if you're running under Unix), you'll find event 10128 described as follows:

```
10128, 00000, "Dump Partition Pruning Information"
// *Cause:
// *Action:  set this event only under the supervision of Oracle development
//
//   LEVEL       ACTION
//-------------------------------------------------------------------------
//   0x0001      dump pruning decriptor for each partitioned object
//   0x0002      dump partition iterators
//   0x0004      dump optimizer decisions about partition-wise join
//   0x0008      dump rowid range scan pruning information
```

So rerun my test, but set event 10128 at level 2 to see what that tells us—and the query will crash:

```
SQL> alter session set events '10128 trace name context forever, level 2';

Session altered.

SQL> select max(id) from pt_range;
select max(id) from pt_range
                    *
ERROR at line 1:
ORA-00604: error occurred at recursive SQL level 1
ORA-00942: table or view does not exist
```

This is a little surprising, but enable event 10046 and try again and you discover that Oracle is trying to insert some data into a table called kkpap_pruning. After a little experimentation, you can work out a suitable definition for the table and create it with the following SQL:

```
create table kkpap_pruning
        partitioning_flag       number,
        iterator                varchar2(32),
```

```
        partition_level        varchar2(32),
        order_pt               varchar2(12),
        call_time              varchar2(12),
        part#                  number,
        subp#                  number,
        abs#                   number
)
;
```

After this table exists, the 10128 event trace at level 2 succeeds, and you can see that your query really did visit every single partition starting from the bottom and working upward (you'll see a couple of example trace files a bit later). So the next question is, can we make Oracle walk through the partitions in descending order? Well, we have an index on the Id column, and if anything is going to make Oracle visit the partitions in reverse order, here's a query that surely will: select id from pt_range order by id desc;. Here's the execution plan (dumped from v$sql_plan by setting event 10132, but with the Time column deleted) and the partitioning information from the 10128 trace:

```
-------------------------------------------------+---------------------+-------------+
| Id| Operation                   | Name  | Rows | Bytes | Cost |Pstart|Pstop |
-------------------------------------------------+---------------------+-------------+
| 0 | SELECT STATEMENT            |       |      |       | 28   |      |      |
| 1 |   PARTITION RANGE ALL       |       | 12K  | 59K   | 28   | 3    | 1    |
| 2 |    INDEX FULL SCAN DESCENDING| PT_PK | 12K  | 59K   | 28   | 3    | 1    |
-------------------------------------------------+---------------------+-------------+
```

```
Partition Iterator Information:
  partition level = PARTITION
  call time = RUN
  order = DESCENDING
  Partition iterator for level 1:
   iterator = RANGE [0, 2]
   index = 2
  current partition: part# = 2, subp# = 1048576, abs# = 2
  current partition: part# = 1, subp# = 1048576, abs# = 1
  current partition: part# = 0, subp# = 1048576, abs# = 0
```

Notice how the plan claims that we are visiting the partitions in descending order (we start at partition 3 and stop at partition 1). When we check the partition iterator information, we can see that the order is explicitly given as DESCENDING, and then each partition has been listed as it was visited, and we see that the list is in descending order. (It's funny how Oracle can't decide whether to start counting from zero or one sometimes. I vaguely remember coming across a bug in a very early version of partitioning, where one partition got "lost" when you ran a query because of this difference of opinion between two Oracle programmers.)

We still have one more detail to pursue: can Oracle stop short when visiting partitions in descending order? The answer is yes, and here's a rather clunky but effective piece of code, with its execution plan and trace, to find the maximum value of id using the minimum effort:

```
select
        id
from
        (
```

```
            select  id
            from    pt_range
            order by
                    id desc
        )
where
        rownum = 1
;
```

```
---------------------------------------------+--------------------+--------------+
| Id | Operation                   | Name   | Rows | Bytes | Cost |Pstart| Pstop |
---------------------------------------------+--------------------+--------------+
|  0 | SELECT STATEMENT            |        |      |       |   2  |      |       |
|  1 |  COUNT STOPKEY              |        |      |       |      |      |       |
|  2 |   PARTITION RANGE ALL       |        |   1  |   13  |   2  |  3   |   1   |
|  3 |    VIEW                     |        |   1  |   13  |   2  |      |       |
|  4 |     INDEX FULL SCAN DESCENDING | PT_PK | 12K |   59K |   2  |  3   |   1   |
---------------------------------------------+--------------------+--------------+
```

```
Partition Iterator Information:
  partition level = PARTITION
  call time = RUN
  order = DESCENDING
  Partition iterator for level 1:
   iterator = RANGE [0, 2]
   index = 2
  current partition: part# = 2, subp# = 1048576, abs# = 2
```

The coding strategy is pretty horrid for such a simple query but, until the optimizer gets a little more "special case" code, it's the sort of thing you just have to do. Of course, you'll keep the test case and rerun it for each version of Oracle as you upgrade because one day the simple select max() might do what you want, and you will be able to stop using messy (possibly complicated) workarounds.

You'll notice that the execution plan still says that we will (or may have to) visit every single partition in descending order—after all, the top partitions could be empty. But at runtime, we see that the partition iterator information tells us that we visited only the top partition.

Lack of Knowledge

So we can run into problems with the optimizer because there are bugs, and because there are restrictions on what it can do. But quite often we come across a problem that isn't a bug or restriction; it's just the optimizer picking the wrong execution plan because the information it has won't allow it to see the right plan. This may be because the query is inherently difficult, or it may simply be that the available statistics are misleading. In this section, you will look at the first of those problems, starting with a simple (catch) question: how many people in the world have more than the average number of legs?

A common response I get to this question is a suspicious frown as people try to work out where the catch is, followed (usually) by the answer "not very many." The correct answer is "almost all of them." Most people are born with two legs; a few unfortunate people will have lost a leg or even both, or been

born with one or more missing. Therefore, the average number of legs is just slightly less than two because of a few rare cases that don't conform to the standard, so most people have more than average.

People are easily fooled (sometimes into giving the right answer) when they're thinking about the results they expect from a query because they apply background knowledge and prejudices. The machine has no knowledge; it can only apply arithmetic.

■ **Note** Quick quiz: What's the difference between the mean, the median, and the mode (without looking it up on Wikipedia)? This is a question to separate the statisticians from the rest of the human race. Informally, the *mean* is the sum of all values divided by the number of values; the *median* is the middle value (such that 50 percent of the data points have a higher value, and 50 percent a lower); and the *mode* is the most commonly occurring value. Generally, the *average* is interpreted as the *mean*, but sometimes people say *average* while visualizing the mode or median.

Take another example: how many people in your company earn more than the average salary? If everyone earns about the same amount, and there are no particularly high-paid or low-paid workers, it's quite possible that the answer matches the default human response of "about half." But if you have even a small number of outliers, the figure could be a long way from 50 percent. Include a handful of highly paid executives, and they drag the average (mean) wage up a little bit, and suddenly nearly everyone is earning less than average. Include a group of low-paid office cleaners who drag the average (mean) wage down a little bit, and suddenly nearly everyone is earning more than average.

So what does Oracle do when presented with a complex query that starts by selecting all the employees earning more than the average salary and then goes on to join seven other tables? Ideally, Oracle should run the first part of the query before trying to work how to run the second part of the query, but the optimizer doesn't work like that at present (even though dynamic sampling is a step in that direction). So what does it do? It "guesses" that the answer is 5 percent of the employees.

If this type of guess causes you problems, you may find some cases where your front-end code should break one query into two. Run the calculation of average salary first, and then feed that value into a simpler query to get the employees earning more than that value. But not all problems of this type have such a simple solution.

Here's another, harder, example: how many of your customers placed orders for at least four different products since the start of the month? Imagine putting that into a complex query:

```
select
        ...
from
        ...
        customers       cus,
        ...
where
        4 < (
                select
                        count(distinct(orl.product_id))
                from
                        orders          ord,
                        order_lines     orl
```

```
        where
                ord.id_cust       = cus.id
        and     ord.date_placed   >= trunc(sysdate,'MM')
        and     orl.ord_id        = ord.id
        )
and
        ...
;
```

It doesn't matter how much information you give me about number of customers, number of orders, number of order lines, number of days you've traded, number of days since the start of month, number of products ever appearing in order lines, average number of order lines per order, average number of orders per customer, average number of orders per day, or average number of order-lines per product. There is no way I can estimate how many customers I have to report unless I run part of the query before deciding what to do next. So what does Oracle do? Again it guesses 5 percent. This might be a perfect estimate, it might be adequate, or it might be a total disaster. And if you want to report the customers who ordered exactly four products, the guess is 1 percent. (Pause for thought: According to Oracle, 5 percent ordered more than four products, 1 percent ordered exactly four products, and 5 percent ordered fewer than four products—so the optimizer has just lost 89 percent of your customers somewhere!) In fact, as you saw in the earlier part of this chapter, I've discovered what seems to be a bug in this type of query, which means you may find that Oracle's estimate of customers is just one, but the 1 percent and 5 percent reappear if you "push" the subquery up the parse tree with the push_subq hint.

This problem is much harder to fix, of course, than the previous example. You don't need just one value; you need a list of customer IDs, and you need to know how big it is. There are strategies to deal with this type of problem, of course. In this case, perhaps, you would put the customers table with its subquery into an inline view with the no_merge hint and then use a cardinality hint on the inline view to give the optimizer the right idea about the number of customers it would return. Every complex case requires its own special treatment, but a few generic strategies tend to keep reappearing.

There are simpler examples in which derived statistics or partial results need to be created before the optimizer can handle the more complex types of queries, and Oracle has introduced features to help. The obvious examples come from *dependent columns*, for which there are two strategies: dynamic sampling from 9i onward, and extended statistics in 11g.

Imagine you run a parcel delivery service, with the marketing slogan that any parcel not delivered within 48 hours will be delivered free. As part of the quality control process, you have a query that lists all the parcels you've picked up in the last 24 hours that have not yet been delivered. For the sake of getting some easy numbers into the arithmetic, let's assume that you've been delivering 1,000 parcels per day for the last three years (call it 1,000 days). The query you run will look something like this:

```
select
        ...
from
        ...
        parcels     pcl,
        ...
where
        pcl.pickup_date >= sysdate - 1
and     pcl.delivery_status = 'In-transit'
and
        ...
;
```

From the optimizer's perspective, the statistics tell it that the date range you want is one day out of 1,000, and that the status you want identifies one parcel in 1,000. When the optimizer combines predicates, it does so by multiplying their individual selectivities—which means its estimate for this query is one parcel in a million (1,000 × 1,000), and this could easily lead to an unsuitable execution path for the report.

The problem is that the optimizer bases its arithmetic on the assumption that all predicates are independent. But think about the business: Most of the parcels that are still in transit are probably the parcels that were picked up in the last 24 hours. Most of the parcels picked up in the last 24 hours are probably still in transit. Our predicates are not independent; they're almost asking the same question in two different ways at the same time.

This problem, however, is a little different from the previous examples. There is a degree of simplicity to it that makes it seem that we (or Oracle Corp.) ought to be able to do something about it. The problem is somehow more static than the subquery problems, because the difficulty is contained within a single table. And Oracle does, indeed, give us a couple of possible strategies to address this type of problem. In 9i, we have *dynamic sampling*. We can tell Oracle to check the data from a few blocks to measure the effects of the combined predicate. In 11g, we can create *extended statistics*—in this case, numbers about the combination of the two columns. So let's build a test dataset and see what happens:

```
create table parcels
nologging                    -- adjust as necessary
as
with generator as (
        select  --+ materialize
                rownum          id
        from    all_objects
        where   rownum <= 3000
)
select
        rownum                                          id,
        sysdate - trunc((1000000 - rownum)/1000,2)      pickup_date,
        case
                when rownum > 999000
                        then 'In-transit'
                        else 'Delivered'
        end                                             delivery_status,
        lpad(rownum,10)                                 small_vc,
        lpad('x',150)                                   padding
from
        generator       v1,
        generator       v2
where
        rownum <= 1000000
;
```

I've created a dataset of 1,000,000 rows with a pickup date ranging over the previous 1,000 days (with ten pickups every 864 seconds). The last thousand rows have a pickup date in the last 24 hours and a status of In-transit; the previous 999,000 rows have a status of Delivered. In this case, I collected statistics that included a histogram on the status column, because there were only two values with an extreme difference in the number of appearances of the values. The query we want to run—and get a reasonable cardinality for—is just this:

```
select
        *
from
        parcels         pcl
where
        pcl.pickup_date       >= sysdate - 1
and     pcl.delivery_status = 'In-transit'
;
```

With the statistics I have, Oracle's cardinality estimate is just one row: one parcel in 1,000 matches the first predicate, one parcel in 1,000 matches the second predicate, so one parcel in 1,000,000 matches the combination. So let's see the effect of dynamic sampling. A quick check of user_tables tells me that there are 26,300 blocks in this table; if I use the hint /*+ dynamic_sampling(pcl, 4) */, this will sample approximately 256 blocks—roughly 1 percent of the table. Here's the resulting execution plan running on 10.2.0.3; the plan is always a full tablescan because there are no indexes, but it's the cardinality (Rows) estimate that matters:

```
---------------------------------------------------------
| Id | Operation         | Name    | Rows | Bytes | Cost |
---------------------------------------------------------
|  0 | SELECT STATEMENT  |         |    1 |   184 | 3996 |
|* 1 |   TABLE ACCESS FULL| PARCELS |    1 |   184 | 3996 |
---------------------------------------------------------
```

Sampling at 1 percent didn't help; we still have an estimated cardinality of 1. And as we step through the different levels of sampling, Table 11-1 indicates what we see. (I've added the approximate number of blocks sampled by each level. I'll describe what the Test(b) column is about in a moment.)

Table 11-1. Cardinality Estimates at Different Sampling Levels (10.2.0.3)

Level	Sample Size	Cardinality	Test (b)
1	32	1	675
2	64	15,220	462
3	128	1	1,004
4	256	1	1,101
5	512	1,971	1,292
6	1,024	1	840
7	2,048	964	1,023

Level	Sample Size	Cardinality	Test (b)
8	4,096	228	966
9	8,192	834	1,054
10	Whole table	1,000	1,000

I happen to have picked an example in which dynamic sampling really doesn't behave gracefully. In fact, I picked two extremes and then combined them. The critical data I need to sample (the pickup date) is in order, and the skewed data (the delivery status) is physically separated into two very discrete physical locations in the table. So even at fairly large sample sizes, the sample failed to pick up a representative set of data.

You may be particularly surprised by the extreme error for level 6, where the sample size was up to 1,024 blocks. In fact, in every case with the cardinality greater than 1 the notes from the execution plan reported dynamic sampling used for this statement, but this report didn't appear for all other levels. This merited a little extra investigation, so I reran the test with events 10053 and 10046 enabled to see more of what was happening, and this is what I got (with some editing):

```
** Dynamic sampling initial checks returning TRUE (level = 6).
...
** Executed dynamic sampling query:
    level : 6
    sample pct. : 3.887221
    actual sample size : 39520
    filtered sample card. : 0
    orig. card. : 1000000
    block cnt. table stat. : 26317
    block cnt. for sampling: 26317
    max. sample block cnt. : 1024
    sample block cnt. : 1023
    min. sel. est. : 0.00000099
** Not using dynamic sampling for single table sel. or cardinality.
```

So the optimizer tried dynamic sampling, sampled 1,023 blocks, and then decided that the sample should be ignored because it didn't find any rows that matched the critical predicate. And if you want to know how much work went into that sample, here's the output from tkprof applied to the sampling query:

```
call     count       cpu    elapsed       disk      query    current       rows
-------  ------  --------  ---------  ---------  ---------  ---------  ----------
Parse         1      0.00       0.00          0          0          0           0
Execute       1      0.00       0.00          0          0          0           0
Fetch         1      0.84       8.12      21126       1063          0           1
-------  ------  --------  ---------  ---------  ---------  ---------  ----------
total         3      0.84       8.12      21126       1063          0           1
```

It took 8 seconds to sample the table. And if you look at the numbers, we've reported 21,126 physical reads for 1,063 buffer gets. You may find that when your sample gets above something like 1 percent of a table, the optimizer may decide to do multiblock reads and read far more than the number of blocks indicated by the sample size. Of that 21,126 physical reads, my session reported 19,857 as prefetched blocks aged out before use.

Just to demonstrate the problems introduced by the ordering and positioning of the data, I recreated the data set, but "sorted" it into a random order. In Table 11-1 the column headed Test (b) shows you the optimizer's estimated cardinality at different sample sizes with this randomized ordering. Sadly, of course, the particular combination of date ordering and status in my original model is the one that tends to appear in real data systems, and dynamic sampling may not help.

Because dynamic sampling has not worked particularly well in this case, let's look to 11g and extended statistics. The problem we have is the combination of the date and status predicate, so we will define a *column group* on the table, which allows us to collect some statistics about the combination:

```
begin
        dbms_output.put_line(
                dbms_stats.create_extended_stats(
                        ownname          => user,
                        tabname          => 'PARCELS',
                        extension        => '(pickup_date, delivery_status)'
                )
        );
end;
/
```

The name of the function is misleading. We haven't—at this point—created any statistics; we have simply declared something that is effectively a definition for a virtual column. The function will return a name for the virtual column (in this case it happened to be SYS_STUFL_WNT5TOFU#C60$6L3XHE2), so we still have to collect statistics, perhaps with a call to dbms_stats.gather_table_stats using a method_opt of for all hidden columns size 254, or even for columns SYS_STUFL_WNT5TOFU#C60$6L3XHE2 size 254.

Unfortunately, we've found the weak spot in this promising feature as well. When we check the execution plan, we find that the estimated cardinality is still 1, even when we create a histogram of 254 buckets. The problem is that column group statistics can't deal with ranges; they can deal only with simple equality. If I had asked about delivery_status = 'In-transit' and pickup_date = date'2009-07-01' (sysdate was the middle of July when I wrote this chapter, so adjust as necessary), the optimizer would have correctly estimated 10 rows based on the num_distinct from the extended stats. After changing our query to use simple equality and then checking the 10053 trace file, we can even see the optimizer in action in the single table access path workings:

```
  Column (#6):
    NewDensity:0.000010, OldDensity:0.000010
        BktCnt:254, PopBktCnt:0, PopValCnt:0, NDV:99998
  ColGroup (#1, VC) SYS_STUFL_WNT5TOFU#C60$6L3XHE2
    Col#: 2 3    CorStregth: 2.00
  ColGroup Usage:: PredCnt: 2  Matches Full:
    Using density: 0.000010 of col #6 as selectivity of unpopular value pred #0
    Partial:  Sel: 0.0000
```

Column 6 (in our five-column table) is that "virtual column" SYS_STUFL_WNT5TOFU#C60$6L3XHE2, and as you can see, the optimizer has recognized that it has a WHERE clause using both columns, and has used the gathered statistics. But there is no such usage in the trace for the query with the range scan—and if you think about it, how could there be?

So in some real-life situations, we can know more about the data than the optimizer, because we understand the meaning of the data. Sometimes features can help the optimizer to "see" the traps that we know are hidden in the queries—and I particularly like the benefits you can get from extended statistics and virtual columns in 11g. However, as you have just seen, in other cases, even the latest features can't help the optimizer estimate the correct volume of data.

Problems with Statistics

Even when the optimizer can estimate the volume of data reasonably accurately, that still may not be enough. As you saw in the previous section, the patterns in the data distribution made it impossible for dynamic sampling (in its current implementation) to produce a good estimate of volume. The pattern of data distribution can cause further problems even if the optimizer is able to work out exactly how much data it has to collect. The fundamental calculations that the optimizer uses are based on two questions: How much data? and Where is it? Even if the optimizer resolves the *how much* question well, it may still choose the wrong execution path if it answers the *where* question badly. And it's easy to imagine scenarios of the *where* question causing the problem—especially when you consider that for many businesses, the recent past is very important.

Think of an order-processing system that has been taking 1,000 orders per day for the last three years (my convenient million-row table again). This time, though, we'll make it easy for the optimizer to work out the volume of data we want reported by asking for all orders placed in the last 24 hours (that is, since sysdate – 1), an easy and "obvious" 1,000 rows. Imagine we have an orders table, a structure something like the following (with real data, rather than one large "padding" column):

```
create table orders (
        date_placed     date        not null,
        order_id        number(8),
        time_stamp      timestamp,
        id_owner        number(2),
        padding         varchar2(168)
)
tablespace test_8k_assm
;

create index ord_placed on orders(date_placed);
```

With this structure, we would expect to see roughly 38 rows per block, so we could reasonably expect the data for the last 24 hours to be in the last 26 blocks (1,000/38). We can always model data entry with a simple PL/SQL loop, to check our estimates. When we do, counting through a sequence number to insert a row every 86.4 seconds for 1,000 days, we find that our assumptions are fairly accurate, and the optimizer even agrees with us, because when asked for one day's worth of data, it produces the following execution plan:

```
---------------------------------------------------------------------
| Id  | Operation                    | Name       | Rows | Bytes | Cost |
---------------------------------------------------------------------
|   0 | SELECT STATEMENT             |            |    1 |    13 |   32 |
|   1 |  SORT AGGREGATE              |            |    1 |    13 |      |
|   2 |   TABLE ACCESS BY INDEX ROWID| ORDERS     | 1001 | 13013 |   32 |
|*  3 |    INDEX RANGE SCAN          | ORD_PLACED | 1001 |       |    5 |
---------------------------------------------------------------------
```

Predicate Information (identified by operation id):
----
   3 - access("DATE_PLACED">=SYSDATE@!-1)

As you can see, the optimizer correctly predicts 1,000 rows and (interpreting the Cost column) thinks the table data will be spread across roughly 27 blocks (32 – 5).

But this first attempt at modeling data input probably isn't sufficiently realistic. The drawback to a single loop is that it doesn't model concurrency properly, and several problems can appear as the level of concurrency increases. So let's build a better model and see what happens. Instead of a single loop to insert the data, I'll run 20 loops concurrently. I'll still use the sequence generator and arithmetic to create rows that seem to have been entered every 86.4 seconds, but I'll adjust the PL/SQL code so the loops themselves have a random pause after each insertion. As a result, the execution plan changes to this:

```
-----------------------------------------------------------
| Id  | Operation        | Name   | Rows  | Bytes | Cost  |
-----------------------------------------------------------
|   0 | SELECT STATEMENT |        |     1 |    13 |   647 |
|   1 |  SORT AGGREGATE  |        |     1 |    13 |       |
|*  2 |   TABLE ACCESS FULL| ORDERS | 1015 | 13195 |   647 |
-----------------------------------------------------------
```

Predicate Information (identified by operation id):
----
   2 - filter("DATE_PLACED">=SYSDATE@!-1)

The optimizer has chosen a tablescan because the cost of the indexed access path would have been 893 (a fact we can check by adding a hint to the SQL and checking the resulting plan). Roughly speaking, Oracle thinks our 1,000 rows are scattered across 890 table blocks, rather than being grouped in the 26 that we know they're in. This has happened because we have used an Oracle feature that attempts to address a concurrency problem.

You'll notice that I created the table in a tablespace called test_8k_assm—a name suggesting that the tablespace is using a block size of 8KB and automatic segment space management (ASSM). My table is using bitmap technology to find free space, and (roughly speaking) this has the effect of allowing a process to pick one of 16 possible table blocks as the target when it wants to insert a new row.

I have 20 processes inserting sequential values, but the insertion point is moving randomly back and forth across a few blocks. This has the effect of scattering my 1,000 rows randomly across a small patch of the table. Unfortunately, the algorithm used by Oracle when gathering index stats can't tell the difference between data that is scattered across a few blocks (as ours is) and data that is scattered randomly across the entire table. (For the technical enthusiast, the clustering_factor for this index was about 28,000 when the data was loaded by a single process, and about 870,000 when loaded by 20 concurrent processes.)

In my case, I was able to "solve" the problem easily. Before I started the test, I had set the parameter db_file_multiblock_read_count to 128 (a value that I still see appearing frequently even in OLTP systems), and you're not supposed to set this parameter in 10g. When I removed the parameter from my parameter file (which had the effect of switching the _db_file_optimizer_read_count to the default of 8), the tablescan became much more expensive and the (still expensive) indexed access path reappeared.

A more appropriate solution would have been to tell the optimizer that this was a good index, and that the data was fairly well clustered by adjusting the value of the clustering_factor with a call to dbms_stats.set_index_stats(), one of the procedures supplied by Oracle for dealing with statistical problems.

■ **Note** I often get the impression that clustering_factor is the single commonest cause of inappropriate execution plans, although the "no-correlation" effect for combined predicates, and the limitations (and bugs) in the subquery algorithms do appear rather often. When I'm feeling pessimistic, I sometimes think that the only reason the optimizer gets the right plan is because the overestimate of cost due to the clustering_factor has been cancelled by the underestimate on cardinality due to the other two effects.

Timing

There is one final problem that I see quite commonly with statistics, and it's best described through a few examples.

Multinationals

Imagine that client X is an international bank. This client has offices around the world, with four major hubs of activity: London, New York, Tokyo, and Sydney. At 10 p.m., Oracle's automatic stats-collection job starts up and runs for a couple of hours.

There are two problems with this strategy. The job runs once per day, but there are four daily cycles going on around the world, so there should be some sort of cycle to statistics management that runs four times every 24 hours. And, as a side effect of this once-per-day strategy, it's more or less inevitable that one of the business hubs will be starting its busiest trading cycle just as the stats-collection job decides to hammer the database to death and confuse the optimizer.

Ideally, of course, you would want to design the system so that every significant table was partitioned by list, and collect statistics only on one set of partitions at any time, but this system was designed before table partitioning existed in Oracle.

Partitioning

Say that client Z—a large corporation, but without the international element—has some enormous tables partitioned by month. This client also allows Oracle's automatic stats-collection job to run every night at 10 p.m. Unfortunately, they find that some time around the middle of the month (after running perfectly well for the first couple of weeks), a few execution plans for the morning reports can vary quite dramatically from day to day—leading to delays in reporting and poor response times during the morning.

The problem is in the automation. The job gathers statistics if more than 10 percent of the data has changed based on comparing the number of rows inserted, updated, and deleted with the number of rows believed to be in the table. (11g allows the percentage to be configured at multiple levels.)

On the first day of the month, the partitions created for that month get loaded with a batch of data that means more than 100 percent of the data in the partition changes. On the second day of the month, the batch load is 100 percent of the size of the current dataset. On day 3, it is 50 percent of the size of the data set, and so on. For the first 11 days of the month, the automatic job collects new stats every night. On day 12, the batch load is roughly 9 percent of the size of the existing data—so Oracle doesn't refresh the stats.

The following morning, the optimizer gets to the suite of reports on "what happened yesterday," and the statistics say, "nothing happened yesterday—the dates go up to only the day before." By the end of the month, the statistics on that month's partitions are being collected only once every three or four days—and not necessarily all on the same day.

Batch Jobs

Various clients have batch processes that manipulate large amounts of data through the course of the night. There are always a few awkward pieces of code that behave badly at some point in the batch. Eventually, the batch code acquires lots of hints, a few index rebuilds, and a few places where dbms_stats has been called to collect stats for a specific table. That last step in patching up the batch job highlights the common misconception about statistics.

Getting the right statistics for the data is not a DBA job; it's a developer job. It's the developer who should know how the application behaves, what the data means, what the data looks like, what the relationships are between datasets, how dynamically the relationships change, and how the data is used. The DBA (and the procedures in dbms_stats) can query the database to get some idea of what the numbers look like at any one point in time, but that's expensive and potentially misleading.

Querying the data and recording the results can be good enough for a lot of the queries the database does. But when problems appear, the DBA should be able to go to the developer (or the designer if there is one) and ask questions such as the following:

- How many trades do we do each day?

- How long does it take the status to change from *new* to *closed*?

- For deals that are not *closed*, how many should we assume are in each status?

- How many deals does the typical customer do per month?

- Are there any products that are traded far more than others?

If the people writing the application don't know the answers to these questions, who should? Obviously, the DBA can write some queries to count rows and columns and find things out the hard way. But when a script runs for an extra 3 hours at 2 a.m., who is supposed to know how many rows were at status *x* at that moment, and why that status is (or is not) supposed to change, and to what, in how many cases?

A lot of the time, you can get away with sampling and brute force to gather statistics—if you pick the right moment. But if you want your systems to be stable and well behaved, you will need to add business intelligence to the mix. That intelligence will include knowledge of critical timing issues, patterns of data distribution, variation, and extremes.

Creating Statistics

The biggest block to obtaining good statistics on complex systems is time. If you let the computer run its standard stats-gathering routines, the time spent by the machine could be huge and unpredictable. If you try to identify the cases where you can take short cuts, avoid stats collection, use small samples, or write programs to create handcrafted stats, you can end up using a lot of your time.

As so often occurs with Oracle, you need to find a compromise position. Can you do something simple that's good enough most of the time, and then add a few refinements at critical points? I believe this is possible, and if you start with the right framework, the refinements can only improve over time.

The key ideas we have to hit with the strategy are as follows:

- We don't want to spend all our time creating and maintaining the stats-gathering code.

- We don't want the demand for machine resources to affect user activity.

- We would like to have a known upper limit on the work done collecting stats.

- Some statistics have to be created at specific points in time.

- Some statistics have to be carefully constructed lies.

A few guidelines that may be helpful in designing the strategy are as follows:

- Start by looking at the ideas Oracle Corp. has embedded in their automatic stats-collection job.

- Remember to exclude system-generated objects from any driving SQL.

- Make sure you don't exclude objects by accident.

- Some tables don't need to have their statistics changed very often.

- Some tables need statistics changed more than once every 24 hours, perhaps as part of a loading process.

- You probably have time to use compute to gather stats on small tables—where *small* is a fairly arbitrary limit that you decide for your system.

- You can often gather reasonable stats on large tables (or individual partitions) with a very small sample size.

- At a global level, partitioned tables probably need special treatment (custom code).

- A few indexes will need special treatment to adjust their clustering_factor.

- You may want to adjust the number of distinct values for a few columns.

- A few columns will need histograms, and it's probably best to write code to construct them.

■ **Note** Many people have a mental block about generating statistics outside some sort of official window, and I sometimes find DBAs sounding quite apologetic about having added code to generate statistics somewhere in the middle of a data-loading job. This approach is perfectly reasonable—whenever the data changes, especially if the change in volume is significant, the statistics may have to change. Gathering stats once every 24 hours in the middle of the night may be an adequate strategy for many systems, but it should be viewed only as a starting point (one of several possible) that is likely to need refining.

The most cost-effective strategy for ensuring that you have good statistics depends to a large extent on what you are doing at present, how effective it is, and how much (human) time you have to spare developing a new approach. Whatever your choice, remember that batch loading processes that make radical changes to the data probably ought to have built-in code that changes the statistics as the data changes. If you're lucky, the code that does the loading may know enough about the data to make the statistical adjustment very cheap.

Several years ago, a colleague asked me if there were any quick ways of building a histogram on a large dataset because his client had a program that took ages to load some data and just as long again to build a histogram on a critical column. I made a comment to the effect that it was a pity he didn't collect the relevant statistics as he loaded the data, and he replied, "We do." All he needed to do was make a couple of simple changes to the following code to create a suitable histogram in less than a second:

```
create table t1 (
        v1      varchar2(1),
        n1      number,
        padding varchar2(100)
)
;

insert into t1
select
        'X'                     v1,
        rownum                  n1,
        lpad(rownum,100)        padding
from
        all_objects
where
        rownum <= 10000
;

commit;

-- collect statistics without histograms before continuing

declare
```

```
        m_distcnt          number;       -- num_distinct
        m_density          number;       -- density
        m_nullcnt          number;       -- num_nulls
        m_avgclen          number;       -- avg_col_len

        srec               dbms_stats.statrec;
        c_array            dbms_stats.chararray;

begin

        m_distcnt          := 3;
        m_density          := 1/1000;
        m_nullcnt          := 0;
        m_avgclen          := 1;

        srec.epc           := 3;
        c_array            := dbms_stats.chararray('A','C','E');
        srec.bkvals        := dbms_stats.numarray(20, 180, 800);

        dbms_stats.prepare_column_values(srec, c_array);

        dbms_stats.set_column_stats(
                ownname            => user,
                tabname            => 't1',
                colname            => 'v1',
                distcnt            => m_distcnt,
                density            => m_density,
                nullcnt            => m_nullcnt,
                srec               => srec,
                avgclen            => m_avgclen
        );
end;
/
```

Reading through the anonymous PL/SQL block, you can see that I've defined a few variables, including two variables of array types defined in the dbms_stats package. In 10g, the package also has array types for numeric types, date types, raw types, floats, and doubles. The simple variables have names that match the parameter names in the set_column_stats() procedure, and are also similar to the names of the columns they will ultimately populate in the view dba_tab_colums, but there are other columns in the view that are derived from the arrays that you supply. In particular, the low_value and high_value are derived from the first and last entries in the arrays, respectively.

If you check the script that generates the dbms_stats package, you will find that the stats record (srec) includes three arrays that correspond to the three data columns in the view dba_tab_histograms (endpoint_number, endpoint_value, and endpoint_actual_value). If you want to generate a frequency histogram, you have to supply a set of values for the bkvals array, and these are used in the endpoint_number column. If you don't supply a set of values for the bkvals array, Oracle assumes you are supplying the boundary values for a "height-balanced" histogram. The array that you supply as the second parameter to the prepare_column_stats procedure is represented numerically in the endpoint_value column, and if this array is of character type, the data you supply may end up in the endpoint_actual_value column (but only if the values you supply are not "different enough" from each other).

In my example, I want to build a frequency histogram with three popular values ('A', 'C', and 'E'), but by supplying the density, I have also told Oracle that any value not in the array should be treated as having a selectivity of 1/1,000—if you're running 10.2.0.3 or earlier (things changed in 10.2.0.4 and 11g).

■ **Note** There was a significant change in the way that Oracle handled frequency histograms and "nonexistent" values in the upgrade from 10.2.0.3 to 10.2.0.4 or 11g that also had a knock-on effect on the treatment of "out of bounds" values. The side effects can be a big surprise.

To demonstrate the effect of the histogram, and to show things changed in the newest releases, I've created a couple of tables showing the critical line extracted from the execution plans for the simple query select * from t1 where v1 = '&1';. Each line comes from a plan with a different value for the substitution variable, and the value used is shown as the last column in the table:

```
-------------------------------------------------------------------
| Id  | Operation          | Name | Rows  | Bytes | Cost | Value |
-------------------------------------------------------------------
|*  1 |  TABLE ACCESS FULL | T1   |   200 | 21200 |   25 |  'A'  |
|*  1 |  TABLE ACCESS FULL | T1   |  1800 |  186K |   25 |  'C'  |
|*  1 |  TABLE ACCESS FULL | T1   |  7995 |  827K |   25 |  'E'  |
|*  1 |  TABLE ACCESS FULL | T1   |    10 |  1060 |   25 |  'B'  |
|*  1 |  TABLE ACCESS FULL | T1   |    10 |  1060 |   25 |  'G'  |
|*  1 |  TABLE ACCESS FULL | T1   |    10 |  1060 |   25 |  'X'  |
-------------------------------------------------------------------
```

Note how the Rows column shows values that are 10 times the size that we supplied in the call to set_column_stats. This is because Oracle has taken our figures and worked out that they represent a total of 1,000 (non-null) rows. Then, when optimizing the query, it sees that there are 10,000 rows in the table (from gather_table_stats), none of which are null for this column (according to our call to set_column_stats). Consequently, it has taken our histogram values and scaled them up to match the table value. This is one of the nice features of faking a histogram: we don't have to know the actual number of rows in the table; we need to know only the relative frequency of appearance of the different values. (I can't explain why 'C' produces a prediction of 7,995 rows rather than 8,000, but it's close enough that I'm not currently too worried about it.)

Note also how the Rows column reports 10 rows for values that I haven't included in the frequency histogram. That value comes from multiplying the number of rows in the table (num_rows = 10,000) by the density I supplied (density = 1/1000).

Now for the 11g results. The figures for values in the frequency histogram don't change, but look what happens to the other three:

```
select * from t1 where v1 = '&1';
```

Id	Operation	Name	Rows	Bytes	Cost	Value
* 1	TABLE ACCESS FULL	T1	200	21200	25	'A'
* 1	TABLE ACCESS FULL	T1	1800	186K	25	'C'
* 1	TABLE ACCESS FULL	T1	7995	827K	25	'E'
* 1	TABLE ACCESS FULL	T1	100	10600	25	'B'
* 1	TABLE ACCESS FULL	T1	50	5300	25	'G'
* 1	TABLE ACCESS FULL	T1	1	106	25	'X'

There are actually two changes in strategy visible here. The value 'B' is between the known low and high values recorded by the histogram, so Oracle has used half the least popular frequency (200/2) for that missing value.

The values 'G' and 'X' are outside the range of the known values, and 'X' is a lot further outside the range than 'G'. The optimizer has started by using the strategy *half the least popular frequency* and then scaled the value to give some indication of how far outside the known range the value is. Very roughly, 'A' to 'E' (the known range) is four letters (yes, I know it's five letters, but the number of *steps* is four), so the optimizer "suggests" that there is no data past 'I' (four more letters past the high value). Because 'G' is two letters past 'E' (half the distance), the estimated cardinality for 'E' is 100 × 2/4. Because 'X' is a long way past 'I', the optimizer estimates no data, and rounds up to one row.

There are a couple of important lessons to be learned from these results (both in absolute terms, and in the change in algorithm). First, if you allow Oracle to gather stats to create a histogram on a column with an extremely skewed data distribution, you may find that any sample size less than 100 percent may miss a couple of values on different days. This could result in extreme changes in execution plans from day to day as the optimizer flips between using a number it saw and the assumption it makes about missing values.

Second, and associated with the first problem, the timing of stats collection can make a big difference. If an overnight process clears thousands of rows from state 'X', say, and you collect statistics just after the batch runs, those statistics will show that there are no X values—and will still say there are no X values when the same batch job that is supposed to look for state 'X' runs the following night.

Finally, in the change between versions, we can see that it is dangerous to play games with statistics (or, in fact, any other Oracle feature) if we don't prepare test cases for our cunning code—and rerun those tests on every single upgrade.

Other Stats

Histograms are probably the most complex stats creation that you can do in Oracle. But fortunately, you probably won't find many cases where you need them. The "hacking" I do most commonly is to set high values on columns, change clustering factors on indexes, and roll forward partition stats.

The relevant procedures from dbms_stats come in pairs and are as follows: get_column stats and set_column_stats, get_index_stats and set_index_stats, and get_table_stats and set_table_stats. If you're wondering about the validity of using coding methods to avoid gathering statistics, you should be encouraged by the appearance in 11g of a new procedure called copy_table_stats that exists to enable you to roll statistics forward from one partition to another. (I haven't used this yet, but it may make some of the code I've written in the past much simpler.)

Without going into extreme detail of using these procedures, here's a typical use of each:

Column statistics are most prone to introducing errors when they are time-dependent or sequence-based. At the end of each day, you may know the latest high value for such columns (perhaps because you know the date or can check the current value of a sequence). Write a short piece of code that (in outline) does something like this:

```
dbms_stats.get_column_stats()          -- into pl/sql variables
adjust pl/sql variables                -- typically high-value, and num_distinct
dbms_stats.set_column_stats()
```

Problems with *index stats* tend to occur after a stats collection. The fact that the volume of data slowly changes with time may not be relevant for quite some time, but a new collection could leave Oracle with index and column stats that are not consistent with each other, or with an index clustering_factor that is misleading.

The consistency problem has a generic fix for single column indexes: query dba_tab_columns for the column stats, and copy the value into the distinct_keys of the index. This is a strategy that I have seen Oracle use in its own index-collection code, and it can be very useful with virtual columns in 11g. However, the problems of the clustering_factor and multicolumn indexes will need some business intelligence applied. Again in outline form, you might have something like the following (with suitable variables declared in the PL/SQL):

```
dbms_stats.get index_stats();          -- into pl/sql variables

m_clustfct := 1 + trunc(m_clustfct/50);
m_avgdblk  := 1 + trunc(m_clustfct / m_numdist);

dbms_stats.set_index_stats();
```

The sample is based on the assumption that you want to correct the critical statistics after allowing Oracle to do most of the collection on automatic. There are various ways to work out the best strategy for dealing with the clustering_factor (which I've described in Chapter 5 of *Cost-Based Oracle Fundamentals*, available as a PDF download from www.apress.com). It's important to note, though, that if you're going to adjust statistics, they need to be kept consistent, and the *average data blocks per key* is a restatement of the clustering_factor and should therefore be consistent with the clustering_factor. In fact, for some of your indexes, you may prefer to derive the clustering_factor from the average data blocks per key by using an argument such as this: "I know that there are about X distinct keys, and the data for any particular value will typically be scattered across Y blocks of the tables, so let's set num_distinct = X, avg_data_blocks_per_key = Y, and clustering_factor = X * Y."

Exactly the same change applies to tables: call `get_table_stats()` to copy current values into PL/SQL variables, fix the variables, and then `set_table_stats()` to write them back to the database. Of course, the stats that you can set for a table are very limited—numrows, numblks, and avgrlen—so you might decide that you can simply set the stats without first getting the stats. Things may change in the future, though, if Oracle starts to make use of the "local cache hit ratio" information that can be stored at the object level.

The biggest challenge comes from partitioning. All the get/set procedures I have mentioned so far include a `partname` parameter, so you can specify a partition or, though it's not immediately obvious, a subpartition of a table or index as the target for the change. Updating the individual stats for (say) one column of a subpartition is not difficult, but there are two other problems to address that really are quite significant.

First, if you do write programs to create statistics manually for a (sub)partition, there's an awful lot of code to write, but if you try to use Oracle's stats-gathering routines, you may have to spend a lot of time gathering stats across levels of granularity that you don't really need (or perhaps want) to do.

Second, if you write code to create or modify (sub)partition stats, you also have to consider modifying the stats for the higher levels of granularity. Consider, for example, a table of sales partitioned by date with a daily bulk load of data into a new partition. You may be able to produce a reasonable estimate for the number of rows in the partition, for the number of distinct customer IDs, and for the low and high sale dates, but how should these numbers affect the global (table-level) statistics? It would be reasonable to add the number of rows in the partition to the number of rows in the table; it would be sensible to make the table high-value for the sale date the same as the high value for the partition. The number of distinct customers is harder—possibly it should not change at all or should increase very slightly. Maybe you don't want a truthful number anyway. Or perhaps you want a number that represents the number of distinct customers over the last 12 months because most of your queries are targeted at date ranges in that 12 months.

There are no easy answers with partitions, but the best approach may simply be to copy forward the statistics for the "previous" partition and adjust the smallest number of things needed to make the statistics "good enough." This, at least, minimizes the amount of code you have to write, and the approach enables you to refine details over time.

Historically, I used to copy the stats by writing PL/SQL loops that generically read (get_xxx_stats) from one (sub)partition and write (set_xxx_stats) to another, and then followed this up with specific code to fix the few things that really made a difference. But I have had clients that handled the bulk of the copying by using the "statistics export" feature—using `dbms_stats.create_stat_table()` to create a table to hold statistics, calling `dbms_stats.export_xxx_stats()` to copy stats from one object into the table, hacking the contents of the table (to change partition names, and so forth), and then using `dbms_stats.import_xxx_stats()` to copy the stats to a new object. (One client even got approval from Oracle support for doing this, although another client was told that they wouldn't be supported if they tried it.)

An alternative to this bulk approach appeared in 11g with the `copy_table_stats()` procedure that copies statistics from a source (sub)partition to a destination (sub)partition. I haven't tried it yet, but it looks as if it might be useful. (For the eagle-eyed, this procedure appeared in 10.2, but in that version carried the following health warning: *The following procedure is for internal use only.*)

Baseline

As you have seen, it is easy to define, or adjust, any statistics you want—provided you are prepared to take the time and effort. Clearly, though, you don't want to spend the next few months making decisions and writing programs to produce reasonable statistics on a large database so, in the same way we needed a best starting point for partition statistics, we need to start from a simple baseline that is "good enough" and adjust a few details as needed. I think there are three candidates for the baseline:

- Oracle automatic stats-collection job and some stats locked (from 10g)

- Regular calls to `gather_schema_stats()` with `auto_sample_size` and some stats locked (from 10g)

- A simple table-driven PL/SQL loop with a driving table giving a sample percentage (default `auto_sample_size`) for each table

In all cases, you should disable the call to collect histograms, and in the first two cases lock stats (`dbms_stats.lock_table_stats()`) on partitioned tables because you're going to be running separate scripts for histograms and partitioned tables. And in all cases, you will have a table-driven mechanism to do some of the work. It's just that it needs to handle only the exceptions for the first two options, while handling everything in the last option.

The first option is particularly attractive if your current approach is simply to rely on the automatic stats collection (and you think it just doesn't do the job well enough). In effect, all you are doing is adding a list of jobs to run after the normal stats collection to correct mistakes, add special cases, and handle partitioned tables, and you could start by emulating exactly your current strategy by (a) not locking any stats and (b) by listing in your exception handler calls to create the histograms that you have found to be useful.

As far as the driving table is concerned, this can be a list of tables, indexes, and columns—with a flag identifying which type of object the row in the list represents—and a few directives about the action to be taken. A default directive (especially for the full, table-driven loop of option 3) would be to call `gather_table_stats()`, `gather_index_stats()`, or `gather_column_stats()` with input parameters supplied by further columns in the driving table, and in most cases you could allow null values to represent the default gathering options. Some of the rows, however, could simply name procedures that should be run for special cases, enabling you to make the code for handling exceptions as simple or as subtle as you wish.

After you have an initial framework in place to do the simplest possible job, it becomes much easier to correct problems caused by the odd effects that sometimes appear from special combinations of circumstances. Conversely, it is also easier to eliminate redundant work when you discover that a recent upgrade now handles a problem that you created a workaround for.

You can even use this table-driven/exception handling strategy to deal gracefully with that international site that has to deal with "end of day" four times in 24 hours. There's nothing stopping you from having a separate table for each business center—or even four separate views, where each view is a `union all` of a common driving table and a local driving table.

The bottom line in this strategy is simple: you can get pretty good statistics from a reasonable use of resources, and it's fairly easy to spot the terrible errors that have to be addressed. So find a cheap and simple way to implement a default collection strategy, and then bolt on a mechanism to handle the exceptions with precisely targeted code.

Summary

Even if your choice of hardware is appropriate, your data design is reasonable, your indexing is carefully thought out, your SQL is well structured, and you haven't introduced inefficiencies in the outer levels of code, you could still have performance problems because the optimizer can't cope with your SQL.

You have seen that you may be able to pinpoint a bug in the optimizer by stripping complicated production code back to the minimum. You have also seen that it's possible to find optimization strategies that are "obvious" to the human eye but not yet coded into the optimizer. Apart from these issues, you also know that the optimizer can pick the wrong path because it is simply not possible for it to determine how much data it is going to have to process.

Although some of the problems of estimating data volumes are inherently impossible for the optimizer to handle, in some cases we can supply statistical information that helps the optimizer produce better estimates of volume and (equally important) the pattern of data scatter. The critical strategy then is to do the minimum amount of work while ensuring that the optimizer gets good enough figures.

Whatever the problems the optimizer has with statistics, though, we need to recognize that a single, simple, strategy for gathering statistics is unlikely to produce an ideal set of statistics for anything other than the simpler applications. We need to design a mechanism that is easy to manage but allows special handling for critical objects at a detailed level. The obvious difficulty is that some applications have literally tens of thousands of tables (or partitions thereof) and indexes—and it would be undesirable to have to worry about every object (and subobject) separately.

Given the potential complexity (and sheer size) of a framework for controlling statistics, the best bet seems to be to use a basic generic approach to generate most statistics and then follow this up with a table-driven approach for exceptions. Although there are difficulties in implementing such a system, it can be done incrementally. Usually only a few special cases need to be corrected after an easily implemented driving mechanism has run (such as a call to Oracle's automatic stats-collection routine—with histogram collection disabled).

In a nutshell, the mechanisms you need to create are as follows:

- A default mechanism that generates statistics for objects that need them (for example, Oracle's gather stale)

- A mechanism to identify any objects that dropped out of sight of the default mechanism

- A mechanism for unlocking and locking stats on objects that must not be touched by the default mechanism

- A follow-up that checks whether any of the gathered stats need to be "fixed," or whether any special cases need handling

- A custom mechanism for dealing with each partitioned object

The final point to bear in mind is that the statistics must reflect the data—so when the data changes (enough), the statistics should change as well. This means that your process shouldn't be restricted to run once every 24 hours (as Oracle's automatic stats collection nearly does). The process may have to run once at the end of every business day (and international businesses may do end-of-day processing several times in 24 hours). In addition, you may have to allow for subsidiary mechanisms that execute after (or even during) every major batch process.

When implementing such a system, remember three key points:

- Keep it simple—don't let special cases proliferate.

- Think about how the system can be self-correcting.

- Keep an eye on how Oracle does the difficult bits. Don't get left behind as Oracle changes strategies.

Finally, if there's one thing you should remember above all others after reading this chapter, it's this: the task of maintaining appropriate statistics should be part of the application code. Leaving it as a DBA (or automatic) task is an abdication of responsibility that's begging for performance problems to appear.

CHAPTER 12

∎∎∎

Troubleshooting Latch Contention

by Riyaj Shamsudeen

In Oracle Database, latches are used to serialize changes on critical structures. While latches are crucial to maintain consistency, they also introduce contention points. Resolving these contention points will improve application scalability. Latch contention is a complex topic. This chapter explores the concepts behind latches and latch contention issues, and it offers a few methods to debug and resolve latch contention. Some of the most commonly occurring hot-spots of contention for latches are discussed in detail, including cache buffer chains, the shared pool, the library cache, and enqueue hash chains.

The following story from a client engagement illustrates just how important an issue latch contention can be. The client had moved a flagship application to a bigger Unix server hoping to improve scalability. After database migration, performance of the application was unbearable. The client reversed the migration to an older Unix server, with much down time. We were called in to analyze the situation. Our analysis showed that it was the combined storm of latch contention for cache buffers chains latches and library cache latches that caused very high CPU usage, in turn leading to the performance issue. We were able to understand the root cause of the problem, and we resolved it with very simple database configuration changes. Bigger projects such as this migration can fail because of poor understanding of latch contention. Thus it is essential for you to be able to debug latch contention accurately.

Latches and Why We Need Them

Latches are a serialization mechanism to protect critical resources in the system global area (SGA) from concurrent modifications. Specific latches must be acquired before inspection or modification of those critical resources. For example, a cache buffers chains latch must be held before a buffer cache chain is modified, preventing concurrent changes to the specified cache buffers chains resource. Another example is that before a chunk of memory can be allocated in the shared pool, one of the shared pool latches must be held.

Latches are handled exclusively by the Oracle RDBMS engine. Users have no ability to control latch operations directly. Internally, almost all SQL operations will one way or another access latches.

Latches are very different from *enqueues* (also termed *locks*). Enqueues are used to lock objects or rows to avoid simultaneous conflicting operations on tables or rows. Enqueues have their own complex data structures, and the resources in question can be locked in one of six available modes. In contrast, latches can be acquired only in either share mode or exclusive mode.

Another difference is that enqueues have queuing structures, and they are acquired in a strict serial fashion. By contrast, latches have no queuing structures.

Solitaire, Parent, and Child Latches

Latches can be grouped into two classes: solitaire and non-solitaire latches. The non-solitaire group can further be broken into parent and child latches.

A solitaire latch is a single latch that allows only one process to modify the critical resource it protects. For example, in Oracle Database version 11gR1, the granule operation latch is a solitaire latch, and only one process can hold that latch. Essentially, only one process can resize various areas such as the shared pool, and the granule operation latch protects such structures from concurrent resize operations.

The cache buffers chains latch (CBC latch) is a typical example of a non-solitaire latch. There are thousands of child latches for this parent latch. These child latches protect modifications to cache buffer chains (discussed later in this chapter), and there are many thousands of cache buffers chains in a System Global Area (SGA).

In a nutshell, before modifying a cache buffer chains structure, a specific CBC child latch protecting that structure must be acquired. Because there are many such child latches, another process can modify a different cache buffers chains structure by holding another CBC child latch, leading to improved concurrency.

Latches are externalized in dynamic views such as v$latch, v$latch_children, and v$latch_parent. The view v$latch_children maintains statistics for latches at the child level, while v$latch maintains aggregated statistics for all child latches, and v$latch_parent maintains statistics at the parent level.

You can use the code fragment in Listing 12-1 to see solitaire and non-solitaire latches. For example, the listing shows that there are 33 child latches for the KJCT flow control latch. The number of child latches depends upon the configuration and the Oracle Database version. The output in Listing 12-1 is from Oracle version 10.2.0.4.

Listing 12-1. Querying to see solitaire and non-solitaire latches

```
Rem Example of solitaire latches
col name format A35
select name, latch# , count(*) from v$latch_children group by name, latch#
having count(*) =1 order by 1;
NAME                                 LATCH#   COUNT(*)
----------------------------------- ---------- ----------
TLCR meta context                       126         1
channel handle pool latch                33         1
ges resource scan list                   51         1
granule operation                        42         1
redo allocation                         115         1

Rem Example of non-solitaire latches
select name, latch# , count(*) from v$latch_children group by name, latch#
having count(*) >1 order by 1;
NAME                                 LATCH#   COUNT(*)
----------------------------------- ---------- ----------
KCL freelist parent latch               120        10
KCL gc element parent latch             118       250
KCL name table parent latch             119       832
KJC message pool free list               58         3
KJCT flow control latch                  66        33
...
```

Operational Specifics

A latch is implemented as a few bytes of memory. The value of a latch's memory area indicates whether that latch is available or not. In multiprocessor systems, it is very important that acquisition and release of latches be atomic, since any processor *can* modify the given memory area, but only one process must be *allowed* to modify it. Most operating-system (OS) platforms provide atomic instructions such as test-and-set instructions or compare-and-swap (CAS) instructions, and latches are implemented using those instructions.

A test-and-set instruction checks a latch's memory area. If the memory area indicates that the latch is available, then that memory area is marked, indicating the acquisition of that latch. If the latch is not available, then one of several latch-acquisition algorithms kicks in.

So far, I've described the mechanism very simplistically. There are many more details to consider, such as latch recovery structures. The following sections describe the operational aspects of latches, also in a somewhat simplified manner. There are generally three modes in which latches can be requested: immediate, willing-to-wait, and latch-wait posting.

Before we dive into these modes, let's take a brief look at *sleeps* and *spins*. Algorithms presented in the following section use sleeps and spins if a latch is not available. If a latch is not immediately available, then the process might need to sleep before trying to acquire the latch again. Sleep is the process of giving up CPU cycles voluntarily and "sleeping" for a specific time-out period. Sleep results in costly context switches. Typically, latches are held for very short durations on the order of a few nanoseconds, and in many cases it is better to avoid the context switches. Thus, Oracle Database code makes a preset number of attempts to acquire a latch before going to sleep. This process is known as spinning.

There are statistics that keep track of these spins and sleeps. The spin_gets value indicates the number of times a process was able to acquire a latch with just spinning alone, without the need to sleep. The sleep_gets statistic indicates the number of sleeps encountered trying to acquire a latch. As the value of sleep_gets increases, performance worsens.

■ **Note** Spinning is not used on single-CPU servers. That's because spinning on such servers will starve the process that holds the latch already. On a single-CPU server, sleeping is the only option when another process holds a needed latch.

Immediate Mode

In the *immediate mode* of latch acquisition, Oracle code tries to acquire any of the available child latches (of a given latch family) without waiting, and it tries to acquire the last child latch in a willing-to-wait mode. For example, redo copy latches must be held before copying redo records to the log buffer. There are several Redo copy latches configured in an SGA, and it is sufficient to hold any one of the Redo copy latch children to copy the redo records to the log buffer. Oracle Database's internal code tries to acquire any of those child latches s in a round-robin fashion. If none of the child latches are available, then the code tries to acquire the last child latch in willing-to-wait mode.

Listing 12-2 presents a pseudo-algorithm written to explain the concepts of spinning and sleeping. Be aware that the exact algorithm used in the Oracle Database can change from one release to the next and between various operating systems. The intent of Listing 12-2 is to demonstrate the concepts behind the algorithm, but not to present the precise algorithm itself. In the case of Listing 12-2, the code tries to acquire any of the latch children in immediate mode, and it tries the last latch child in willing-to-wait mode.

Listing 12-2. A pseudocode algorithm to illustrate immediate-mode latch acquisition

```
Try to acquire first child latch selected pseudo randomly.
If latch acquired
    Increment gets counter
    Exit loop and proceed to modify critical resource
Else
        Step X: Try to acquire next child latch in a round-robin fashion.
        If latch is available then
            Increment immediate_gets counter
            Exit loop and proceed to modify critical resource.
        Else
            Increment immediate_misses counter
            Go to step X until all but one child latches tried.
        End
        If all the child latches except one has been tried, then
            Try that last child latch in willing-to-wait mode.
            While (latch is not available)
              Loop
                 if latch acquired
                    increment gets counter
                    exit loop and proceed to modify critical resource.
                 Else
                    For ( req_count=0;
                  req_count < spin_count && latch not acquired;
                  req_count++
                    )
                  Loop
                      Spin and try to acquire latch;
                  End loop;
                  If the latch is acquired
                      Increment misses counter
                      Increment spin_gets counter
                      exit loop and proceed to modify the critical resource
                 else
                    while (latch is not available)
                    loop
                        Sleep (sleep duration increases slowly until reaching
                      _max_exponential_sleep).
                        Increment sleeps counter.
                    End loop;
                    Increment misses counter.
                      Exit loop and proceed to modify the critical resource.
                 End if
              End if
           End loop;
       Increment gets counter;
       Exit loop and proceed to modify the critical resource
   End if
End if
```

Willing-to-Wait Mode

Willing-to-wait mode involves the practice of requesting a latch and waiting until the latch becomes available. Successful attempts to acquire the latch are termed *gets*. Failed attempts are termed *misses*.

With a solitaire latch, the resource being protected is protected by only that latch. Thus, the algorithm for latch acquisition is slightly different from that used to acquire latches in immediate mode.

Listing 12-3 shows how a process needs to wait for a latch to become available before modifying a critical resource. For example, before modifying a cache buffers chains in the SGA, the child latch protecting that hash chain must be held. The pseudo-algorithm in Listing 12-3 is really a subset of the algorithm in Listing 12-2.

Listing 12-3. Latch acquisition in willing-to-wait mode

```
Try to acquire the latch in willing-to-wait mode.
While (latch is not available)
Loop
   if latch acquired
      increment gets counter.
      Exit loop and proceed to modify critical resource.
   Else
      Increment misses counter.
      For ( req_count=0;
      req_count < spin_count && latch not acquired;
      req_count++
      )
      Loop
         Spin and try to acquire latch;
      End loop;
      If the latch is acquired
         Increment spin_gets counter.
         Increment misses counter.
         exit loop and proceed to modify critical resource
      else
         while (latch is not available)
            loop
                     Sleep (sleep duration increases slowly until
                     reaching _max_exponential_sleep).
                     Increment sleeps counter.
                     Try to acquire the latch.
            End loop;
            Increment misses counter.
              Exit loop and proceed to modify critical resource.
      End if
   End if
   Try to acquire the latch;
End loop;
Exit loop and proceed to modify critical resource
```

Latch-Wait Posting Mode

The third method of latch acquisition relies on *latch wait posting*. This method uses more sleeps, thus reducing spin. Excessive spin can lead to high CPU usage, and latch wait posting effectively addresses that problem. Oracle Database code differentiates latches into two general categories: *short-wait* and *long-wait* latches. For example, a cache buffers chains latch is a short wait latch, meaning that most probably this latch is held for a very short time. The library cache latch is a long-wait latch. It can take longer to search for a suitable object in library cache hash chain, and so the library cache latch may be held for longer time.

Oracle Database uses the preceding two methods of acquisition—immediate mode and willing-to-wait mode—for short wait latches. For long wait latches, the mechanism of acquisition is slightly different. There is spinning involved for long wait latches also, but there is a mechanism in place to reduce the amount of spinning. If the parameter _latch_wait_posting is set to 1 (the default), then processes go to sleep while waiting for long wait latches, thus reducing the CPU usage associated with latch spin. When the holder of a long wait latch is ready to release the latch, it will scan through the waiters list and post the processes waiting for the latch to indicate latch availability. The waiting processes largely sleep until the latch is available and posted.

Identifying and Analyzing Latch Contention

High CPU usage in user mode is a typical symptom of latch contention. This high CPU usage is a result of spinning associated with latch waits. The typical knee-jerk response to such spinning is to decrease the value of the initialization parameter _spin_count (default 2000), but that is often an incorrect response. It is essential to understand the root cause behind latch contention and resolve that root cause.

Latch contention can be observed using utilities such as Statspack, Automatic Workload Repository (AWR), and Active Session History (ASH) reports. Typically, events having names starting with "Latch Free" will be in the top five wait events if an instance is suffering from latch contention. Program-level latch contention can be observed and measured accurately using the SQL Trace facility with the waits parameter set to a value of TRUE.

There will always be latch-free waits in any database. Only when the time spent on these waits is a major contributor to slowness do they become a critical problem to be resolved. You need to realize that it is nearly impossible to remove latch-free waits completely.

The following subsections give a generic analysis approach that works for all types of latch contention. Later sections of this chapter will look in detail at some of the more common, specific types of contention.

Step 1: Identify Latches Causing Contention

The first thing you should do when you have latch contention is identify the specific type of latch involved in the contention. Prior to Oracle Database version 10g, all latch-related waits are grouped together in one wait event, Latch Free. From version 10g onward common latches have their own latch wait events. If a latch does not have a separate wait event, then statistics for that latch are accounted in the generic Latch Free wait event. Listing 12-4 shows that in a version 9i database, there are 12 wait events with the event name containing "latch," and in Oracle Database version 10.2.0.4 there are 39 such wait events. This increased use of the word "latch" in event names makes latch contention easier to diagnose.

Listing 12-4. Querying to compare wait events between Oracle version 9i and 10g

```
REM Version 9.2.0.8
select name from v$event_name where name like '%latch%' order by 1;
NAME
-----------------------------------------
PX qref latch
buffer latch
fib/fob latch
ges proc table latch - kjdrptref
...
13 rows selected.

REM Version 10.2.0.4
select name from v$event_name where name like '%latch%' order by 1;
NAME
----------------------------------------------------------------
PX qref latch
buffer latch
gcs remastering wait for read latch
gcs remastering wait for write latch
ges2 proc latch in rm latch get 1
ges2 proc latch in rm latch get 2
...
39 rows selected.
```

To see this for yourself, create an AWR or Statspack report and refer to the latch activity section. Then identify the latch that consumes the most time. Listing 12-5 shows that cache buffers chains latch contention induced a wait time of 1556 seconds. To improve performance in this SGA, you must resolve the contention for the cache buffers chains latch.

Listing 12-5. Statpack report with latch contention

Latch	Get Requests	Pct Get Miss	Avg Slps /Miss	Wait Time (s)	NoWait Requests	Pct NoWait Miss
begin backup scn array	259	0.0		0	0	
cache buffer handles	1,590,942	0.1	0.0	0	0	
cache buffers chains	543,412,587	0.1	0.2	1556	21,385,402	0.2
cache buffers lru chain	1,103,303	0.5	0.1	0	15,118,767	0.6
...						

Step 2: Review Distribution of Gets

Your next step is to review the distribution of gets among child latches. For non-solitaire latches, check to see if the distribution of gets among latch children is skewed. If all the gets are incurred for one child, then it is possible that one or a few objects are causing the latch contention that you are experiencing. You can then probe further to see which specific objects are involved.

Listing 12-6 shows a query to show the distribution for child latches for cache buffers chains. We identified the cache buffers chains latch as a contributor for latch contention in step 1. Child latches for that latch type are probed further to review the distribution of gets among child latches. You can also see that child 437962 has a very high number of gets. Those gets need to be further analyzed. I discuss the analysis for cache buffers chains latch contention later in this chapter, in the section "Cache Buffers Chains Latch Contention."

Listing 12-6. Querying to see the distribution of child latches

```
Select * from (
select child#, gets, misses,sleeps,
   rank() over (partition by latch# order by gets desc ) rnk_gets,
   rank() over (partition by latch# order by misses desc )rnk_misses,
   rank() over (partition by latch# order by sleeps desc ) rnk_sleeps
 from v$latch_children where name = 'cache buffers chains'
)
where rnk_gets <=20 and rnk_misses <=20 and rnk_sleeps <=20
order by rnk_gets
/
    CHILD#       GETS      MISSES      SLEEPS   RNK_GETS RNK_MISSES RNK_SLEEPS
---------- ---------- ---------- ---------- ---------- ---------- ----------
    437962  425447511     4218981       25183          1          1          3
    426176  117300404      780869        7891          5          4         15
    522827   59284925      284159        7597         15          9         17
    165842   55773949      281581        7372         17         10         19
    488282   50065301      177063       10513         18         18         10
    305548   47423058      314308       20591         19          8          4
...
```

Step 3: Check the Code Path

Check to see which code path incurred the most latch waits. The Latch misses section in an AWR report or Statspack report is useful here. The column where in that section provides the names of functions that are incurring latch misses. You can also use the view v$latch_misses to do this analysis, but it is a cumulative view and care must be taken to decipher the data from that view.

Listing 12-7 shows a portion of the Latch misses section from a Statspack report. From the output, you can see that for cache buffers chains latches, the function kcbgtcr: fastpath incurs the most sleeps. This is a common function call, but if the latch contention is for uncommon latch functions, then that function call needs to be searched in a metalink for a possible bug match.

Listing 12-7. Statspack report, a section showing latch misses

Latch Name	Where	NoWait Misses	Sleeps	Waiter Sleeps
...				
cache buffers chains	kcbgtcr: fast path	0	35,979	30,837
cache buffers chains	kcbgtcr: kslbegin excl	0	17,333	16,409
cache buffers chains	kcbzwb	0	16,858	6,399
cache buffers chains	kcbchg: kslbegin: bufs not	0	14,021	16,685
cache buffers chains	kcbgtcr: kslbegin shared	0	3,774	3,188
cache buffers chains	kcbgcur: kslbegin	0	3,470	1,091
cache buffers chains	kcbget: pin buffer	0	2,366	1,325
cache buffers chains	kcbzgb: scan from tail. no	0	1,508	0

The correct analysis and solution for a particular latch contention depend upon the type of latch involved in the contention. The following sections explore some commonly encountered latch contention problems. Possible remedies are given to correct the problems.

Cache Buffers Chains Latch Contention

Cache buffers chains (CBC) latch contention is the most common cause of latch contention in the real world. The Buffer cache is split into multiple data block buffers, and data blocks are read from the data files (disk) into these buffers.[1] Every data block buffer has an associated buffer header pointing to that buffer. These buffer headers (externalized in x$bh or in the dynamic view v$bh) are hanging from a hash chain. Multiple buffer headers are chained together to create a hash chain, and a hash bucket is in the head of this chain.

The buffer header associated with a database block can only be chained to a specific hash chain. Essentially, if a data block needs to be read or received from a remote cache (as in the case of real application clusters), then the Data Block Address (DBA) of the block is hashed to a hash bucket and a buffer header is linked to that chain.

Figure 12-1 shows a hash bucket at the beginning of a hash chain. You also see buffer headers that are linked to that hash chain. These buffer headers are pointing to buffer cache buffers. Inspection or modification to the hash chain must be done while holding the CBC child latch protecting that hash chain. That child latch must be acquired even if the operation is simply to inspect whether a block is in the buffer cache or not (in share mode from Oracle Database 10g onward). The child latch protecting that hash chain must be acquired in order to modify or inspect the chain.

There is one-to-many relationship between a child latch and hash buckets. One child latch can protect multiple hash chains, and a hash chain is always protected by the same latch.

---

[1] Or transferred from the remote cache in the case of real application clusters.

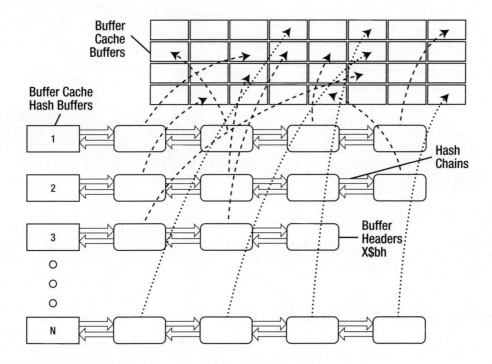

Figure 12-1. Buffer cache hash chains and buffer headers

Let's review how a database block is read into the buffer cache by Oracle Database code. Assume that code has identified a database block to read from the disk. The following algorithm gives a high-level overview of CBC latch operations. It is intended simply to clarify the concepts of CBC latch operations and is not precise.

1. Identify the database block to be read from the disk.

2. Check to see if the block is already in the buffer cache: Apply a hash function over the DBA of the block to identify the hash bucket. If that buffer is in the buffer cache, it will be in the hash chain associated with the bucket.

3. Acquire the CBC latch protecting that hash chain. Walk the hash chain to see if that block with a specific version can be found.

4. If a block is found in the hash chain, use that block. If the block is not found, find a free buffer in the buffer cache, delink the buffer header for that buffer from its current chain, and link that buffer header to the hash chain under the protection of the CBC latch. Pin the buffer header, release the latch child, and read the block into this buffer.

You can see that CBC latches are heavily used, and that high activity against CBC latches can lead to latch contention. It is essential to understand that this algorithm is executed by Oracle Database internal code, and that user code has no direct control over it. You can influence latch activity by writing efficient SQL statements, but you can't control it directly.

Common Causes of CBC Latch Contention

There are many reasons for CBC latch contention. It is impossible to discuss every possible cause, but following are the most common of them:

Longer cache buffers chains. It is possible that (at least, in Oracle Database versions prior to 9i) numerous buffers can be chained together into one hash chain. Processes that inspect this chain must hold the latch for a longer time, as many buffer headers must be inspected. That longer hold time leads to contention for CBC latches. Even if the processes are trying to access completely different objects, because the same latch is protecting all buffer headers linked in that hash chain, that child latch can inadvertently cause latch contention. This problem is mostly resolved from Oracle Database version 10g, since the number of hash buckets[2] configured by default increased dramatically in that release.

Heavy concurrent access of an index root block or branch blocks. In a tight, nested-loops join based upon a unique or primary key, the associated index's root block must be accessed very frequently. Consider the access path shown in Listing 12-8. For each row from the outer row source at step 130, probe the inner table through a unique key column. To find a specific join key, the database engine will access the root block of the RCV_SHIPMENT_HEADERS_U1 index. Next, the engine will access branch blocks, and then leaf blocks. If the query is executed by hundreds of concurrent processes, then each of those processes will access the root/branch/leaf blocks thousands of times per second. That heavy concurrent access can result in numerous processes trying to access the hash chain looking for the root block of the index, in turn leading to CBC latch contention.

Listing 12-8. A tight, nested-loops join

```
| 129 |    NESTED LOOPS                   |                             |   1  |
| 130 |      TABLE ACCESS BY INDEX ROWID  | RCV_TRANSACTIONS_INTERFACE  |1339  |
|*131 |      INDEX RANGE SCAN             | CUS_RCV_TXNS_INTERFACE_C3   |1339  |
|*132 |      TABLE ACCESS BY INDEX ROWID  | RCV_SHIPMENT_HEADERS        |   1  |
|*133 |        INDEX UNIQUE SCAN          | RCV_SHIPMENT_HEADERS_U1     |   1  |
```

Heavy concurrent access of a leaf block. Such access typically happens if concurrent inserts are made into a nonpartitioned table with a monotonically increasing sequence of primary or unique keys. Sequence-based values will be in a strict numeric order. Since primary or unique indexes are populated with these sequence values, recently generated values tend to be populated in the same leaf block. CBC latches protecting the hash chains of those buffers will be heavily accessed, leading to CBC latch contention.

Heavily accessed small table. In a nested loops join method, if the inner row source is a small table, and if it is not indexed, then for every row from the outer row source, the inner row source will be accessed using a full table scan. The result can be much higher concurrent access to the few blocks used by that table, which in turn may lead to CBC latch contention for the latches protecting that small table's blocks. While some amount of buffer access is done under the protection of a

---

[2] The number of buffer cache hash buckets is configured by _db_block_hash_buckets. The number of CBC latches is configured by _db_block_hash_latches. Underscore parameters should not be changed without Oracle Support's blessing.

buffer pin, still many sessions will be accessing very few blocks, and that can lead to CBC latch contention. Listing 12-9 shows the type of execution plan involved.

Listing 12-9. A heavily accessed small table

```
| 129 |   NESTED LOOPS                   |                           |    1 |
| 130 |     TABLE ACCESS BY INDEX ROWID  | RCV_TRANSACTIONS_INTERFACE |1339 |
|*131 |       INDEX RANGE SCAN           | CUS_RCV_TXNS_INTERFACE_T3  |1339 |
|*132 |     FULL TABLE SCAN              | MTL_PARAMETERS             |    1 |
```

High consistent block generation. A SELECT statement requires a database block to be in a specific version. In many cases, buffers have been modified already, and that SELECT statement cannot see the most recent changes. This makes it necessary to create buffer clones consistent with the SELECT statement. Buffer clones are created by applying undo records to a copy of the buffers being cloned, creating consistent versions of the blocks—known as *consistent read (CR) block generation*. The process of cloning buffers can result in higher access to the undo header block, and to undo blocks. As concurrency increases, the problem tends to magnify under stress. Furthermore, if many processes are accessing the same table, and with one or more uncommitted transactions, then each of the processes will clone and create a consistent version of the buffers by applying undo, thus increasing the demand for CBC latches.[3]

Many sessions performing full table scan on one or few tables. In a *full table scan*, table blocks are accessed from the first block to the last block under the high water mark. This means that many processes will compete for the same blocks or range of blocks, and that competition can in turn lead to CBC latch contention.

Analyzing CBC Latch Contention

This section provides a step-by-step method to analyze CBC latch contention. The steps are listed in what is usually the most logical order, but they can be switched around to fit the situation at hand.

Step 1: Review the Distribution of Gets

To analyze CBC latch contention, you need to find whether the latch contention is widespread across many child latches or is limited to a smaller set of child latches. You can use the view v$latch_children to determine which is the case. Please refer to the SQL in Listing 12-6 for further details.

Step 2: Identify the SQL Statements Involved

Your next step is to identify SQL statements involved in the latch contention. Use the SQL in Listing 12-10 to show the top SQL statements suffering from latch contention. Keep in mind that any given SQL

---

[3] This can get worse in the case of real applications cluster (RAC), since the undo blocks may need to be transferred as global cache services buffers, leading to latch contention or other wait-event problems such as global cache buffer busy waits, buffer busy waits, and so on.

statement identified by the query in Listing 12-10 could be merely a *victim* of latch contention, and not a root cause. You should not assume that every statement returned by the query is a problematic statement.

In the output shown in Listing 12-10, 58 processes are executing the SQL statement with a hash_value 1509082258 and waiting for the Latch Free event. This listing is taken from Oracle Database 9i release, and almost all latch event waits are grouped under one Latch Free event wait.

Listing 12-10. Querying to see Latch Free events and SQL hash values

```
select substr(w.event, 1, 28) event, s.sql_hash_value, count(*)
from v$session_wait w, v$session s, v$process p
where s.sid=w.sid
and p.addr = s.paddr
and s.username is not null
and w.event not like '%pipe%'
and w.event not like 'SQL*%'
group by substr(w.event, 1, 28), sql_hash_value
order by 3
/
EVENT                            SQL_HASH_VALUE   COUNT(*)
-------------------------------- --------------- ----------
enqueue                                 3740270          1
enqueue                               747790152          1
enqueue                              1192921796          1
latch free                           1807800540          1
global cache null to x                  3740270          1
global cache null to x               1473456670          1
global cache null to x               3094935671          1
db file sequential read               109444956          1
latch free                            622474477          3
latch free                           1509082258         58
```

You need to drill down to identify the specific latch type at the root of the contention. Column p2 in v$sesssion_wait identifies the latch number to reference in the v$latch dynamic performance view. Listing 12-11 shows how to query for the latch number (the nested SELECT) and how to use that number to query v$latch for the hash values of SQL statements suffering from contention. Listing 12-11 further shows that 56 sessions were waiting for the Latch Free wait event, and that the latch type waited on was the cache buffers chains latch.

Listing 12-11. Finding the latch type and SQL hash value

```
Set lines 160 pages 100
Column event format A35
Column name format A35
select x.event, x.sql_hash_value,
 case when x.event like 'latch%' then
   l.name
     else '                       '
```

```
end name,
x.cnt from (
  select substr(w.event, 1, 28) event, s.sql_hash_value, w.p2,count(*) cnt
  from v$session_wait w, v$session s, v$process p
  where s.sid=w.sid
  and p.addr = s.paddr
  and s.username is not null
  and w.event not like '%pipe%'
  and w.event not like 'SQL*%'
  group by substr(w.event, 1, 28), sql_hash_value,w.p2
  ) x,
  v$latch l
where
  x.p2 = l.latch#(+)
order by cnt
/
EVENT                                SQL_HASH_VALUE NAME                         CNT
------------------------------------ -------------- ---------------------------- ----
...
Latch free                           1509082258     cache buffers chains         56
```

From Oracle Database version 10g onward, Active Session History[4] (ASH) provides sufficient information to identify SQL statements suffering from CBC latch contention. The SQL statement in Listing 12-12 shows the sessions suffering from CBC latch contention in the past hour.

A word of caution, though: if an application uses literal values in its SQL, then each of that application's statements will be unique and will get a unique value for sql_id. In those cases, the output from the query in Listing 12-12 might be misleading. Still, the query gives clues about SQL statements suffering from CBC latch contention.

It is possible to acquire a latch without any associated SQL statement. In Listing 12-12, latch Session Allocation has no sql_id associated. This simply means that those sessions haven't started executing any SQL statements yet.

Listing 12-12. Querying Active Session History to identify SQL_IDs

```
select event, sql_id, sql_child_number, count(*) cnt
from v$active_session_history where event like 'latch%'
and sample_time > sysdate-(1/24)
group by event, sql_id, sql_child_number
order by 4 desc
/
EVENT                              SQL_ID          SQL_CHILD_NUMBER       CNT
--------------------------------- --------------- ---------------- ----------
latch: cache buffers chains       575pgrw7xwgy3                  0        392
latch: object queue header operation 7vs2dcaqkvn80              0        211
latch: session allocation                                        0        143
```

---

[4] Active Session History is a product licensed separately from Oracle Database version 10g.

```
latch: object queue header operation                              0        73
latch free                            gmxk70psu7ma5               0        71
latch: row cache objects              54658ggyqua91               0        62
latch free                                                        0        56
latch free                            ?tqd4wxg82v80               0        29
latch: cache buffers lru chain                                    0        27
```

It is possible that another process is holding the latches in Listing 12-12 and thus not allowing SQL from the application in question to acquire those latches. This scenario is rare but needs to be analyzed. You need to verify that the hash value acquiring or holding the latch matches the hash value from Listing 12-11. You should execute the SQL in Listing 12-13 repeatedly (at least 10 times) to verify that the hash values match.

Listing 12-13. Querying for SQL hash values acquiring or holding a latch

```
select s.sql_hash_value, lh.* from
v$latchholder lh, v$session s where
lh.sid=s.sid
order by s.sql_hash_value
/
SQL_HASH_VALUE     PID        SID LADDR            NAME                    GETS
--------------     -------    ---------- ----------------  --------------------  ----------
            0      418        10766 0000000ABBF5E3E8 library cache pin    16775103
   1509082258      418        10766 0000000ACA8A1158 cache buffers chains   461959
```

Step 3: Identify Objects Causing the Contention

In this step, you identify the buffer cache buffers that the child latches are protecting. As discussed earlier, blocks from many different objects can be hanging from the same hash chain, protected by a CBC child latch. Because that child latch is protecting all buffers in the hash chain, access to any one of the buffers in that hash chain could be a root cause of contention for the latch contention. We need to differentiate the specific buffer causing the contention. The column tch in x$bh[5] is helpful in identifying that buffer.

The script in Listing 12-14 queries to find objects that are hanging from the hash chain protected by those child latches. Output is sorted in part by the tch column, placing the more suspect objects first in the output. Objects with higher tch values are problematic and most probably causing the latch contention. You may need to execute the query a few times to get consistent data while latch contention is occurring. In the example output, you can see that the inv.mtl_onhand_quantities table is causing the contention.

---

[5] x$bh externalizes buffer headers. The tch column indicates the touch count of a given buffer. If a buffer is accessed frequently, that buffer will have a higher touch count.

■ **Note** The buffer cache is a very dynamic area. The output of the script in Listing 12-14 can be misleading if it is run even a few minutes after the latch contention has ended. Take care to run the script while the problem is ongoing.

Listing 12-14. Querying to find objects involved in latch contention

```
with bh_lc as
   (select
lc.addr, lc.child#, lc.gets, lc.misses, lc.immediate_gets, lc.immediate_misses,
lc.spin_gets, lc.sleeps,
bh.hladdr, bh.tch tch, bh.file#, bh.dbablk, bh.class, bh.state, bh.obj
  from
    v$session_wait sw,
    v$latchname   ld,
    v$latch_children lc,
    x$bh bh
  where lc.addr =sw.p1raw
  and sw.p2= ld.latch#
  and ld.name='cache buffers chains'
  and lower(sw.event) like '%latch%'
  and bh.hladdr=lc.addr
)
select bh_lc.hladdr, bh_lc.tch, o.owner, o.object_name, o.object_type,
bh_lc.child#,
           bh_lc.gets, bh_lc.misses, bh_lc.immediate_gets,
           bh_lc.immediate_misses, spin_gets, sleeps
from
  bh_lc, dba_objects o
where bh_lc.obj = o.data_object_id(+)
order by 1,2 desc
/
HLADDR             TCH OWNER   OBJECT_NAME                   OBJECT_TYP
---------------- --- ------- ------------------------------ ----------...
0000001029B81010 203 INV     MTL_ONHAND_QUANTITIES_DETAIL   TABLE...
0000001029B81010  81 ONT     OE_ORDER_HOLDS_ALL_C3          INDEX...
...
```

Step 4: Review Execution Plan of Problem Statements

In step 2, SQL statements causing latch contention were identified. In step 3 objects involved in CBC latch contention were identified. Data from steps 2 and 3 can be correlated and matched. This correlation can be done by reviewing the execution plans of the SQL statements from step 2. Query the access plans for those SQL statements using the dbms_xplan package. Listing 12-15 provides a query to print the execution plan of a cursor using dbms_xplan.

In Listing 12-15, the display_cursor procedure call displays the execution plan from the SGA, or more accurately from the v$sql_plan view. The second parameter to this call is cursor_child_number, which defaults to 0. The third parameter is to print all statistics of the last execution of that SQL.

Listing 12-15. Quering to find execution plan

```
Select * from table(dbms_xplan.display_cursor('&sqlid','','ALLSTATS LAST'));
```

Check whether the object from step 3 is participating in any of the execution plans. Read the earlier section "Common Causes of CBC Latch Contention" to see whether any of those common causes apply. Take appropriate action if one does apply. If not, then continue on to the next section, "Resolving CBC Latch Contention."

■ **Note** The dbms_xplan.display_cursor call is available from Oracle version 10g onward. In 9i, plan from memory can be queried using a script. Read about doing that at the following URL:
http://asktom.oracle.com/pls/asktom/f?p=100:11:0::::P11_QUESTION_ID:230338600346782894.

Resolving CBC Latch Contention

There are many techniques for resolving CBC latch contention. The following sections describe several that you should consider.

Eliminate Full Table Scan on Small Tables

If a small table is accessed in full table scan mode concurrently, then many processes will be accessing a small set of buffers. Access to these buffers is protected by CBC latches, leading to CBC latch contention. Even though the number of blocks in the table is small, comparing columns in every row is a CPU-intensive operation. In most cases, adding an index to that small table and eliminating full table scans will resolve the latch contention.

Eliminate Full Index Scan on Small Indices

Similar to full scans on small tables, full index scans on smaller indices also will result in many concurrent processes accessing a small set of buffers, in turn leading to CBC latch contention. Eliminate full index scans with proper indexing techniques such as careful selection of index columns and choosing proper index types (such as btree or bitmap indexes).

Eliminate Leaf Block Contention with Partitioning

Processes that insert rows with primary key values generated from a sequence will insert rows in the rightmost leaf block of the associated primary or unique index btree. All concurrent inserts will suffer from CBC latch contention accessing that leaf block. The root cause here is that synthetic keys are inserted in just a few leaf blocks of index. You can also see that, as the current block is filled, latch contention will move on to the next latch, protecting the next leaf block. This leaf block contention also will result in "buffer busy" and "read by other session" waits in a single instance.[6]

To eliminate leaf block contention, you can hash partition the involved table on the primary key. When you do that, make sure that your primary key or unique key index is created as a local index. For example, if a table is hash-partitioned with 32 partitions, then synthetically generated keys will hash into different partitions. Since the primary key is local to the partitions, the primary key values will distribute nicely among the leaf blocks of local index trees. This distribution results in an equivalent spread of 32 leaf blocks.

For example, Figure 12-2 shows that synthetic keys between 1801 and 2000 will go to the rightmost leaf block of the associated nonpartitioned index. Figure 12-3 shows that value 1701 will go into a leaf block of the first partition, 1702 will go into a leaf block of the second partition, and so on.

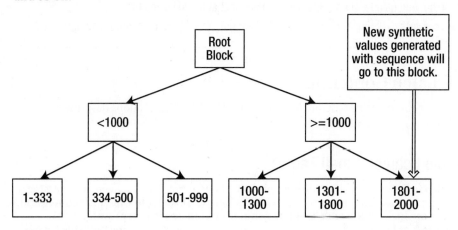

Figure 12-2. Nonpartitioned index

---

[6] In RAC, if the rows are inserted from multiple instances, the result will be many global waits, such as "buffer busy global."

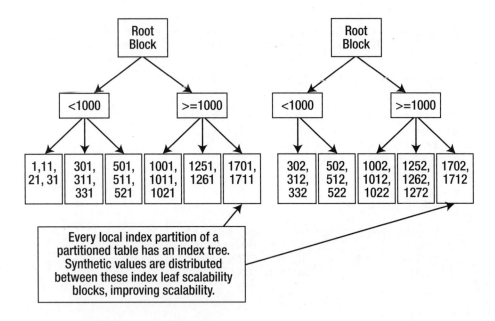

Every local index partition of a partitioned table has an index tree. Synthetic values are distributed between these index leaf scalability blocks, improving scalability.

Figure 12-3. Hash-partitioned local index trees

If you want to increase concurrency, then increasing the number of partitions is good enough. For example, if you expect to have 50 concurrent inserts into that table, you might want to consider hash partitioning that table with 64 partitions.[7] Also, if a table cannot be partitioned, you may be able to convert the primary key and unique key indices into hash-partitioned indices over the nonpartitioned table.[8]

Favor Hash Joins Over Tightly-Nested Loop Joins

If the number of rows from the outer row source in a nested loops (NL) join is very high, and the inner probed table is small, processes can contend for the latches that protect the small inner table. Sometimes you can resolve this contention by converting the nested loops join to a hash join.

Listing 12-16 shows that outer table RCV_TRANSACTIONS_INTERFACE returns 1339 rows, and that probed table RCV_SHIPMENT_CODES is accessed using an index unique scan. Furthermore, the query is executed by many processes concurrently.

RCV_SHIPMENT_CODES is a small table with just a few blocks for the index. Each execution of the query will result in at least 1339 accesses to the index blocks. With many processes executing the query concurrently, CBC latches protecting the buffers of probed table and index will be a contention point.

---

[7] Note that number of hash partitions must be a binary power of two for performance reasons.

[8] Note that hash-partitioned indices on a nonpartitioned table can be created from Oracle Database 10g onward.

Listing 12-17 shows the plan after it has been converted into a hash join. Now, with the hash join in place, RCV_SHIPMENT_CODES is accessed once per execution. Latch contention is thus resolved.

Listing 12-16. A nested-loops join that is a candidate for conversion to a hash join

```
| 129 |   NESTED LOOPS                  |                           |    1 |
| 130 |     TABLE ACCESS BY INDEX ROWID | RCV_TRANSACTIONS_INTERFACE |1339 |
|*131 |       INDEX RANGE SCAN          | CUS_RCV_TXNS_INTERFACE_C 3 |1339 |
|*132 |     TABLE ACCESS BY INDEX ROWID | RCV_SHIPMENT_CODES         |    1 |
|*133 |       INDEX UNIQUE SCAN         | RCV_SHIPMENT_CODES_U1      |    1 |
```

Listing 12-17. The resulting hash join

```
| 129 |   HASH JOIN                     |                           |    1 |
| 130 |     TABLE ACCESS BY INDEX ROWID | RCV_TRANSACTIONS_INTERFACE |1339 |
|*131 |       INDEX RANGE SCAN          | CUS_RCV_TXNS_INTERFACE_C 3 |1339 |
|*132 |     TABLE ACCESS BY INDEX ROWID | RCV_SHIPMENT_CODES         |   11 |
|*133 |       INDEX UNIQUE SCAN         | RCV_SHIPMENT_CODES_C3      |   11 |
```

Tune Inefficient Indices

Avoid inefficient index-based lookup. Table blocks are accessed for each row returned from an index scan. Excessive accesses to the table blocks can cause CBC latch contention. When too many blocks are scanned with index range scans (because of index inefficiency), concurrent processes will contend for the same set of buffers and latches, and that leads to CBC latch contention.

In Listing 12-18, you'll see that the step of scanning through MTL_MATERIAL_TRANS_N30 is reading 2.6 million rows, and that the next step accessing the table is returning just 13 rows. If many concurrent processes are executing the SQL statement in question, then CBC latch contention will be the result. In this specific example, adding one more column to the index reduced the cardinality of the index step and resolved CBC latch contention. Listing 12-19 shows the resulting, noncontentious plan.

Listing 12-18. Execution plan showing problem with inefficient index

```
HASH JOIN                         |                           |    1 | 107 |31   (7)|
  INLIST ITERATOR                 |                           |      |     |        |
    TABLE ACCESS BY INDEX ROWID   | MTL_MATERIAL_TRANSACTIONS |   13 | 884 |14   (8)|
      INDEX RANGE SCAN            | MTL_MATERIAL_TRANS_N30    |2669K |     | 5  (20)|
```

Listing 12-19. Execution plan after index change

```
HASH JOIN                         |                           |    1 | 107 | 9   (2)|
  INLIST ITERATOR                 |                           |      |     |        |
    TABLE ACCESS BY INDEX ROWID   | MTL_MATERIAL_TRANSACTIONS |   13 | 884 | 8   (2)|
      INDEX RANGE SCAN            | MTL_MATERIAL_TRANS_N30    |   18 |     | 2   (1)|
```

Reduce CPU Usage

If CPU usage is very high in the database server, that can also lead to latch contention. Ironically, high CPU usage is also a side effect of latch contention. Knowing whether high CPU usage is the cause or the result of contention can be a challenge. If you suspect latch contention from high CPU usage, you should reduce CPU usage and then measure for latch contention again.

Shared Pool Latch Contention

Shared pool latches are held while allocating or releasing space from the shared pool. Allocation and deallocation in the shared pool results in changes to shared pool free lists, essentially, shared pool child latches protect changes to the shared pool free lists.

First, you should understand the improvements beginning in Oracle Database version 9i. Prior to Oracle version 9i, the shared pool was just one big heap protected by just one shared pool latch, and it was a major contributor to latch contention. But from Oracle version 9i onward, the shared pool is split into multiple subheaps, and each subheap is protected by a shared pool child latch. This change has reduced the incidence of trouble with shared pool latch contention. Still, it is important to understand the problem of shared pool latch contention.

Structures in the Shared Pool

Each of the subheaps in the shared pool is further split into smaller subheaps. The fixed table x$ksmss externalizes shared pool subheaps. For example, Listing 12-20 shows that the shared pool is split into seven subheaps in the SGA of the database in question. The number of subheaps (and so the number of shared pool latches) is dependent upon initialization factors such as shared pool size, granule size, a few underscore parameters, the Oracle Database version, and even a few OS parameters. Listing 12-21 shows that there are seven shared pool latches, each protecting a subheap. (Results from the queries in Listings 12-20 and 12-21 might be different in your database.)

Listing 12-20. Query to list shared pool subheaps

```
select ksmdsidx, count(*) , sum(ksmsslen) from x$ksmss
where ksmdsidx>0
group by ksmdsidx
order by 1
/
  KSMDSIDX    COUNT(*) SUM(KSMSSLEN)
---------- ---------- -------------
         1        229     268435536
         2        237     268435520
         3        241     268435520
         4        235     268435512
         5        234     268439728
         6        247     268435616
         7        248     268435552
```

Listing 12-21. Query showing the number of shared pool latches

```
select count(*) from v$latch_children where name='shared pool'
  COUNT(*)
----------
         7
```

Shared Pool Free Lists

Allocation requests in the shared pool specify a size to allocate. Oracle's internal algorithm tries to find a chunk at least as big as the request, and the search for a free chunk is not cheap. From Oracle Database release 9i onward, these free chunks of memory are grouped by their size and arranged as free lists from a hash bucket. This arrangement of free chunks grouped by size improves free space search. A process looking for a chunk of free space can quickly locate a free chunk.

It is easier to explain shared pool free lists with a shared pool heap dump. Listing 12-22 uses the oradebug command to take a heap dump at level 2. The level 2 heap dump writes shared pool area details to a trace file. A few lines from that heap dump trace file are printed in the listing; they show the free list buckets for subheap 1.

Consider bucket 122 in the subheap 1 as shown in the listing. It points to chunks of size bigger than 1008 bytes and smaller than 1016 bytes. For example, if a process is trying to allocate a chunk with a size of 1008 bytes, the process will hold the shared pool child latch protecting subheap 1. The process will then search for a chunk of size at least 1008 bytes from bucket 122 onward.[9] Chunks with a size of 1008 bytes cannot be in the buckets below 122, so searching from bucket 122 is sufficient in this case.

Listing 12-22. A few lines from a heap dump trace file (version 10gR2)

```
sqlplus "/ as sysdba"
SQL> oradebug setmypid
SQL> oradebug dump heapdump 2
SQL> oradebug tracefile_name
...
 Bucket 119 size=984
 Bucket 120 size=992
   Chunk        4ebe06c00 sz=      992    free        "              "
 Bucket 121 size=1000
 Bucket 122 size=1008
   Chunk        4eb14c540 sz=     1008    free        "              "
   Chunk        4eaa6ede0 sz=     1008    free        "              "
   Chunk        4ebd8a118 sz=     1008    free        "              "
   Chunk        4ebd898d0 sz=     1008    free        "              "
 Bucket 123 size=1016
   Chunk        4eac77018 sz=     1016    free        "              "
   Chunk        4eac751b0 sz=     1016    free        "              "
```

---

[9] This is true because the minimum chunk size is 1008 bytes for bucket 122, and for bucket 121 it is 1000 bytes.

```
Chunk        4eac696e8 sz=    1016    free      "              "
Chunk        4ebe33f88 sz=    1016    free      "              "
Chunk        4eacfa298 sz=    1016    free      "              "
...
```

Shared Pool Reserved Free Lists

A small percentage of the shared pool is set aside as the *shared pool reserved area*.[10] Each subheap of the shared pool allocates a fraction of itself as part of the shared pool reserved area. And even though the shared pool reserved area has separate free lists, the latch for a given subheap also protects that portion of the subheap in the reserved area. Listing 12-23 shows some information on the shared pool reserved area from the heap dump trace file taken in Listing 12-22.

The reserved area is to serves to hold large chunks of memory that can be used when the space in the nonreserved area becomes fragmented. If there is no free space in the main part of the shared pool, and if a requested chunk size is above a threshold determined by the _shared_pool_reserved_min_alloc initialization parameter, then the chunk is allocated from the shared pool reserved area.

Listing 12-23. Shared pool reserved area trace file lines

```
RESERVED FREE LISTS:
 Reserved bucket 0 size=32
 Reserved bucket 1 size=4400
 Reserved bucket 2 size=8216
 ...
 Reserved bucket 10 size=20544
 Reserved bucket 11 size=20552
 Reserved bucket 12 size=32792
 Reserved bucket 13 size=65560
 Chunk         518000088 sz=  3358536  R-free      "              "
```

Common Causes of Shared Pool Latch Contention

Shared pool latch contention is almost always due to shared pool fragmentation. Processes will hold a shared pool child latch while searching for a free chunk suitable enough for allocation. If the shared pool is fragmented, then the shared pool latch will be held longer during this search. There are some other possible causes though. Following is a list of some of the root problems you might encounter:

Shared pool fragmentation. The shared pool may be fragmented with too many smaller chunks. While a process is trying to allocate a chunk big enough to satisfy an allocation request, recreatable or freeable chunks can be flushed off the shared pool and those chunks need to be coalesced to create a bigger chunk. That coalescing might involve walking shared pool freelists many times and flushing chunks until suitable chunks can be found or created. This activity is performed under the protection of the shared pool child latch leading to latch contention.

---

[10] The initialization parameter shared_pool_reserved_size controls the size of the shared pool reserved area.

Incorrect configuration. If a pool is incorrectly or inadequately configured, then chunks may be allocated from the shared pool instead of, say, the large pool. For example, if the large pool is not configured, then RMAN communication buffers or parallel query slave communication buffers may be allocated from the shared pool. Allocation of these buffers can deplete and fragment shared pool free space, leading to shared pool latch contention.

Reduced shared pool subheaps. Multiple shared pool subheaps are very important to performance, since it is critical to have multiple shared pool latches. Each shared pool subheap is protected by a shared pool child latch. If the number of shared pool subheaps is reduced, then the number of shared pool child latches also will be reduced. That reduction in turn has a detrimental effect on performance.

High CPU usage in the server. If CPU usage is very high in the server, then the process holding a latch might not get enough CPU cycles and go to sleep prematurely before completing the code path. That sleep can result in the process holding the latch longer than is ideal. Fortunately, this problem has been solved in many platforms through the use of facilities to prevent a process from being preempted on the CPU. Such an option is referred to as the *no_preempt* option. But the no_preempt option is not available in all platforms, and without such an option it becomes important to reduce CPU usage to resolve latch contention.

Too-frequently flushed shared pool. Flushing the shared pool too often can lead to latch contention. This typically happens in databases upgraded from Oracle Database version 8i or earlier. Flushing the shared pool involves flushing unpinned, recreatable chunks. Latches must be held during the time in which the flushing occurs. The result is increased activity on the shared pool latches.

Analyzing Shared pool Latch Contention

To analyze shared pool latch contention it is imperative to understand the contents of the shared pool. It is also important to understand type of allocation requests that are flushing existing chunks. It is worthwhile to investigate shared pool free lists also.

Step 1: Review Distribution Among Child Latches

Check whether the distribution among various child latches of the shared pool is uniform. If the distribution of gets and misses is skewed, meaning that a few child latches have much more demand than others in the shared pool, it may mean that those few subheaps are undergoing intense pressure.

Listing 12-24 shows a situation in which just a few shared-pool child latches are acquired much more frequently than other child latches. Such a situation suggests higher activity in a few shared pool subheaps.

Listing 12-24. A skewed distribution of gets for shared pool latch children

```
select child#, gets , misses, immediate_gets, immediate_misses
from v$latch_children where name='shared pool';

    CHILD#       GETS     MISSES IMMEDIATE_GETS IMMEDIATE_MISSES
---------- ---------- ---------- -------------- ----------------
         7        280          0              0                0
         6        280          0              0                0
         5        280          0              0                0
```

4	280	0	0	0
3	12907260	1035751	0	0
2	15153322	1276786	0	0
1	12826219	1154988	0	0

7 rows selected.

If the gets among children are skewed, then it is important to understand the type of chunks allocated in those subheaps. You can delve into the problem in at least two ways. Statspack and AWR reports have a section that will show the increase/decrease in various shared pool area sizes. Listing 12-25 shows that section from a Statspack report. The numbers in Listing 12-25 show no signs of abnormality, as no areas have grown abnormally. In abnormal conditions, you would see one area growing by leaps and bounds.

Listing 12-25. Statspack output showing SGA differences

```
SGA breakdown difference for DB: APDB  Instance: APDB3  Snaps: 242425 -242426

Pool   Name                             Begin value        End value  % Diff
------ -------------------------------- ---------------- ---------------- -------
shared library cache                      44,448,832       44,463,992    0.03
shared messages                            2,080,000        2,080,000    0.00
shared miscellaneous                      40,601,264       38,964,144   -4.03
shared parameters                            188,648          188,648    0.00
shared partitioning d                        228,600          228,600    0.00
shared pl/sql source                           3,288            3,288    0.00
shared processes                          13,760,000       13,760,000    0.00
shared qmps connections                    4,842,200        4,842,200    0.00
```

Another method of researching the problem is to query the fixed table x$ksmss. It can be queried to see which area has grown bigger. The SQL in Listing 12-26 prints the top 20 areas that are consuming space in the shared pool.

You may need to run a query or report multiple times. In some cases, it may necessary to monitor shared pool areas with a custom script to detect abnormal growth.

Listing 12-26. Query against x$ksmss to see which area is bigger

```
select  ksmdsidx,ksmssnam, size_area from(
select ksmdsidx, ksmssnam,sum(ksmsslen) size_area from x$ksmss
where  ksmssnam!='free memory'
group by ksmdsidx, ksmssnam
order by 3 desc
)
Where rownum<21;
```

Step 2: Inspect Shared Pool Fragmentation

In most cases, shared pool latch contention is caused by shared pool free list fragmentation. Inspect the free space fragmentation using the SQL in Listing 12-27.[11] A fragmented shared pool will have thousands of chunks in just a few buckets.

Listing 12-27. Query to inspect shared pool fragmentation

```
select
  ksmchidx,ksmchdur,
  case
        when ksmchsiz < 1672 then trunc((ksmchsiz-32)/8)
        when ksmchsiz < 4120 then trunc((ksmchsiz+7928)/48)
        when ksmchsiz < 8216 then 250
        when ksmchsiz < 16408 then 251
        when ksmchsiz < 32792 then 252
        when ksmchsiz < 65560 then 253
        when ksmchsiz >= 65560 then 253
  end bucket,
  sum(ksmchsiz) free_space,
  count(*) free_chunks,
  trunc(avg(ksmchsiz)) average_size,
  max(ksmchsiz) biggest
from
  sys.x$ksmsp
where
  inst_id = userenv('Instance') and
  ksmchcls = 'free'
group by
  case
        when ksmchsiz < 1672 then trunc((ksmchsiz-32)/8)
        when ksmchsiz < 4120 then trunc((ksmchsiz+7928)/48)
        when ksmchsiz < 8216 then 250
        when ksmchsiz < 16408 then 251
        when ksmchsiz < 32792 then 252
        when ksmchsiz < 65560 then 253
        when ksmchsiz >= 65560 then 253
  end ,
  ksmchidx, ksmchdur
order by ksmchidx , ksmchdur
/
```

---

[11] The query in Listing 13-27 accesses x$ksmsp. Access to x$ksmsp is also protected by a shared pool latch. In a database with a large SGA (in the order of GB), accessing this table itself might induce shared pool latch contention.

For example, the output in Listing 12-28 shows that number of chunks in what we might call "subheap 1 duration 1" is very small. For example, bucket 1 has just 33 chunks. This shared pool is not badly fragmented. There are big chunks in bucket 253, and the shared pool is unfragmented.

Listing 12-28. Output of query in Listing 12-27 for a nonfragmented shared pool

KSMCHIDX	KSMCHDUR	BUCKET	FREE_SPACE	FREE_CHUNKS	AVERAGE_SIZE	BIGGEST
1	1	1	1320	33	40	40
		2	2160	45	48	48
		3	1400	25	56	56
		4	2240	35	64	64
.....						
		13	4896	36	136	136
		14	2016	14	144	144
		15	3040	20	152	152
		16	2880	18	160	160
.....						
		252	98944	4	24736	27992
		253	528156120	40	13203903	15597568

By contrast, Listing 12-29 shows that bucket 1 has 18,133 chunks, and that bucket 253 has just one chunk. If a process allocating memory can't find a big enough chunk, then free chunks may need to be coalesced, in turn leading to shared pool latch contention (or worse, to the dreaded ORA-4031 error).

Listing 12-29. Output of query in Listing 12-27 for a fragmented shared pool

KSMCHIDX	KSMCHDUR	BUCKET	FREE_SPACE	FREE_CHUNKS	AVERAGE_SIZE	BIGGEST
1	1	1	1320	18133	40	40
		2	2160	19245	48	48
		3	1400	2025	56	56
		4	2240	35	64	64
		5	2448	34	72	72
.....						
		15	3040	20	152	152
		16	2880	18	160	160
		252	98944	1	24736	27992
		253	528156120	1	132039	157568

■ **Note** The query in Listing 12-27 gives an approximate idea of how much the shared pool is fragmented. In Oracle Database version 11g, the script still gives a good idea about fragmentation, but it looks like the bucket sizing algorithm has been changed in 11g, so only the heap dump trace file shown here is accurate for that version.

Step 3: Review Objects Causing Flushing

The fixed table x$ksmlru keeps track of the most recent flushes of the shared pool.[12] If there is no chunk big enough to accommodate an allocation request, then chunks that can be recreated or freed might need to be flushed. This object flushing also will increase the activity on the shared pool latches. In Listing 12-30, column KSMLRNUM indicates the number of items flushed to accommodate an allocation request. KSMLRCOM shows the allocation comment for the allocation request. Reviewing that column will provide valuable clues about why there is higher activity on shared pool latches.

Listing 12-30. Query to identify objects that are flushing the shared pool

```
Set lines 160 pages 100
Spool ksmlru.lst
Select * from x$ksmlru order by ksmlrnum;
Spool off
```

Step 4: Identify SQL Statements Using Literal Values

Another common reason—probably the most common—for shared pool fragmentation is repeated hard parsing of the SQL statements due to use of literal values in those statements. A hashing function is applied on the text of a SQL statement to create a hash value (or sql_id), and the library cache is searched with this hash value to identify any existing parsed representation. If there is no parsed representation, then a hard parse is incurred.[13]

If an application does not use bind variables in its SQL statements, the result can be a very high number of unsharable SQL statements. Parsed representation of these SQL statements will allocate space in the shared pool, potentially for each execution of a given statement, and such frequent allocations will result in higher activity on the shared pool latches.

The dynamic performance view v$sql is quite useful in identifying SQL statements that do not use bind variables. The query in Listing 12-31 identifies SQL statements using literals. Because literals are used, each statement will potentially hash to a unique hash value.[14] However, most of these SQL statements will have the same execution plan, and hence the same *plan hash value*. The SQL in Listing 12-31 uses that fact to identify SQL statements that do not use bind variables. In the query output, you can see that column plan_hash_value 703834417 has 4939 versions, meaning that 4939 distinct versions of the SQL statements are in the shared pool, and probably those SQL statements should be converted to use bind variables.

---

[12] Interestingly, querying x$ksmlru will remove rows from that fixed table. Thus, it is better to spool the output to a file.

[13] The initialization parameter cursor_sharing plays a major role here. The discussion in this paragraph assumes this parameter has been set to EXACT.

[14] This does not mean that we should never use literal values. Literal values have their use. For example, in a typical data warehouse application the proper use of literals enables the Cost Based Optimizer to optimize SQL statements by way of using histograms more effectively. In general, queries of the data warehouse type benefit from literal values, and OLTP queries benefit from bind variables.

Listing 12-31. Query to see the top 20 SQL statements that use literal values

```
select * from (
   select plan_hash_value, count(distinct(hash_value)), sum(executions),
      sum(parse_calls)
   from v$sql
   group by plan_hash_value
   having count(distinct(hash_value)) > 10
   order by 2 desc
) where rownum<21;

PLAN_HASH_VALUE COUNT(DISTINCT(HASH_VALUE)) SUM(EXECUTIONS) SUM(PARSE_CALLS)
--------------- -------------------------- --------------- ----------------
      511709263                       4939            4939             4939
     1438036477                       4907            4907             4907
     3532438726                       4814            4814             4814
     1130272986                       4798            4798             4798
     2751086974                       4677            4677             4677
              0                         48            3287             4341
...
/
```

The dynamic performance view v$sql can be queried to identify the SQL text associated with a given plan_hash_value. The query in Listing 12-32 accesses v$sql to find the SQL text associated with the plan_hash_value 511709263.

Listing 12-32. Mapping plan_hash_value to a SQL statement

```
select  sql_text from v$sql where plan_hash_value=703834417 and rownum<10;
SQL_TEXT
-------------------------------------------------------------------
select aa.spid   from fnd.f_audit aa  where aa.ask_kill_time >=↵
 to_date('10/09/2009_20:45:00','MM/DD/YYYY_HH24:MI:SS')

select aa.spid   from fnd.f_audit aa  where aa.ask_kill_time >=↵
 to_date('10/09/2009_20:50:00','MM/DD/YYYY_HH24:MI:SS')

select aa.spid   from fnd.f_audit aa  where aa.ask_kill_time >=↵
 to_date('10/09/2009_20:55:01','MM/DD/YYYY_HH24:MI:SS')
...
```

In a few cases, successive executions of a SQL statement may not be shared, creating many child cursors. If there are numerous child cursors for a SQL statement, then shared pool latch contention is inevitable. The query in Listing 12-33 identifies SQL statements with higher version counts. You need to review those SQL statements and understand why there are so many child cursors, and why they can't be shared. The view v$sql_shared_cursor lists the reasons why child cursors are not shared.

Listing 12-33. Query to see top 20 SQL statements with high version_count values

```
select * from (
    select hash_value,  module, action, executions, parse_calls,
    version_count, sharable_mem,persistent_mem from v$sqlarea
    where version_count>10
    order by version_count desc
) where rownum<21
/
```

Resolving Shared Pool Latch Contention

Shared pool latch contention is usually resolved by determining the reasons shared pool latches are being held for a longer period. The following sections provide an overview of common solutions.

Avoid Unnecessary Heaps

Avoid creation of unneeded heaps in the shared pool. If certain areas are not explicitly reserved, then heaps for those areas are allocated in the shared pool, in turn causing fragmentation. Query output from x$ksmlru is helpful in figuring out the type of chunks that are deallocating other chunks.

Avoid and Reduce Fragmentation by Sharing SQL Statements

SQL statements that are executed very frequently with literal values must be converted to use bind variables. SQL statements that use literal values cannot be shared, and each version of such a statement might consume space in the shared pool. That situation can lead to fragmentation and latch contention.

Use of the initialization parameter cursor_sharing is another option to minimize the effects of unsharable SQL statements. If cursor_sharing is set to force or similar, then all the literal values in SQL statements will be converted to system bind variables, and those SQL statements may be shared, thus avoiding fragmentation. There is ample documentation available about the cursor_sharing parameter.[15]

Avoid Setting _kghdsidx_count to 1

In earlier versions of Oracle 9i, there were a few issues with configuring multiple shared pool heaps. Now, because of the configuration issues and RDBMS software bugs, one subheap can grow to be much bigger than other subheaps. The likelihood of this happening increases with an incorrect SGA configuration. One workaround, mostly applicable only to the version in which the problem was encountered, is to set the _kghdsidx_count parameter to 1. This parameter controls the number of

---

[15] Use of the cursor_sharing parameter is only a workaround and not a solution. Setting this parameter to force has minor side effects such as an increase in CPU utilization due to increased soft parsing.

subheaps allocated for the shared pool, and setting it to 1 allocates just one shared pool heap with just one shared pool latch. This means that the shared pool latch becomes a solitaire latch, and this can lead to shared pool latch contention. After a software upgrade, it is prudent to remove this underscore parameter and check whether the original problem is encountered.

Avoid Flushing the Shared Pool

You can flush the shared pool with the `alter system flush shared_pool` command. Flushing a shared pool throws away recreatable and freeable chunks. These chunks must be added to shared pool free lists under the protection of a shared pool child latch. Flushing the shared pool will increase activity against shared pool latches artificially and can lead to shared pool latch contention.

Sometimes flushing the shared pool can improve performance. However, if you find that flushing the shared pool improves performance, the correct action is not to continue to flush, but to find the root cause of the fragmentation and resolve that.

Avoid Shared Pool Reserved Free List Fragmentation

The shared pool reserved free list is searched only if there is not enough contiguous space in the main free list, and if an allocation request is larger than the value specified by the _shared_pool_reserved_min_alloc parameter. Up until version 11g, this parameter defaults to 4200. The default value is sufficient in many cases. Setting the value of the parameter[16] lower can lead to fragmentation in the reserved pool, in turn leading to latch contention.

Library Cache Latch Contention

The library cache holds parsed representations of SQL statements, execution heaps of procedures, functions, and packages. There are many other items, such as table definitions, but we will talk mostly about SQL statements in this section.

Figure 12-4 shows the library cache and hash buckets.[17] The library cache is organized as an array of hash buckets. Hash chains are hanging from these hash buckets. Library cache objects are attached to these hash chains, and these objects point to various heaps in the shared pool. Changes and inspections to these library cache hash chains are protected by library cache latches. The library cache latch is a non-solitaire latch, and there are many child latches protecting changes to the hash chains.

---

[16] A common reason for modifying this parameter is a misconception about shared pool allocation. A shared pool free list is searched for suitable chunks; only if there is no suitable chunk is available in the shared pool *and* the allocation request size is more than the _shared_pool_Reserved_min_alloc parameter will the space be allocated in the reserved pool. The common misconception is that space is allocated in the shared pool reserved area even if there is free space in the shared pool.

[17] This figure is intended simply to clarify the operation of the library cache and is not an exact representation.

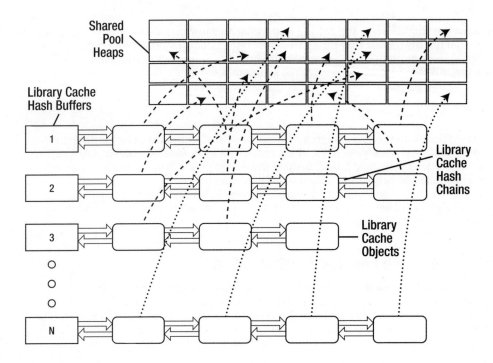

Figure 12-4. Library cache hash buckets

Before a new SQL statement can be executed, the statement must be parsed. The parsing step involves too many operations to discuss in detail, but following is a subset of what happens:

1. First, a unique hash value is created from the SQL text, or from the text of the library cache object.

2. Using that hash value, a library cache bucket number is derived.

3. That library cache bucket is protected by a library cache child latch. The parsing process holds that latch while searching the hash chain for a match on the hash value (together with a few other criteria).

4. If match is found, then the parsed representation of the SQL statement (or other object) exists, and no additional hard parsing is needed.

If there is no match for a hash value, then an additional hard parsing step must be completed. A new library cache object must be added to the hash chain with pointers to various heaps for the object being parsed. Any change to library cache hash chains is done under the protection of a library cache child latch. Hard parsing can lead to contention for those child latches.

Common Causes of Library Cache Latch Contention

Library cache latch contention is almost always caused by excessive parsing or by nonsharable child cursors. Use of literal values in SQL is the most common cause of library cache and shared pool latch contention. Following is a summary of these common causes:

Excessive parsing: If an application is using literal values, then each SQL execution can result in a unique hash value and cursors cannot be shared. Hard parsing of SQL statements is a costly step and leads to many gets and releases on library cache latches. Further, new heaps need to be allocated for each SQL statement parsed, thus polluting the library cache with unneeded heaps. Allocation and deallocation of those heaps leads to shared pool fragmentation.

Side effects of hard parsing: If there is no free space available to accommodate an incoming allocation request, existing cursor heaps might need to be flushed from the shared pool/library cache. This increases activity against shared pool and library cache latches.

Creation of excessive child cursors: Another reason for library cache latch contention is the creation of many child cursors. Child cursors cannot be shared if they are not suitable for sharing. For example, if there are many schemas in a database supporting multiple copies of an application, each of the application copies will generate SQL statements with the same hash value (assuming bind variables are in use), but those child cursors cannot be shared, since they are associated with different schemas. That lack of sharing will result in longer hash chains, and in many objects hanging from any one chain. Processes will be searching through these longer hash chains, increasing activity against library cache child latches.

Analyzing Library Cache Latch Contention

The process for analyzing library cache latch contention is almost identical to analyzing shared pool latch contention. The following subsections describe the process.

Step 1: Identify Cursors Using Literal Values

The most common cause of library cache latch contention is excessive parsing. Use Step 4 under "Analyzing Shared Pool Latch Contention" to probe this possible cause further.

Step 2: Understand the Reason for Unsharable Child Cursors

If child cursors are not shared, then determining why they are not shared is quite essential to resolving library cache latch contention. Fortunately, v$sql_shared_cursor (from 10g onward) provides a mechanism. There are over 30 reasons why child cursors may not be sharable, and this view provides the reason that applies to the situation with any given cursor of interest. Listing 12-34 shows how to query the view for a specific SQL statement.

Listing 12-34. Identifying reasons for unsharable child cursors

```
Select * from v$sql_shared_cursor where sql_id='5jxwda6s8nvc7';
```

Library Cache Latches and Mutexes

From Oracle version 10g onward, most library cache latches have been replaced by mutexes. Mutexes in Oracle are analogous to mutexes available at the OS level, but they are implemented as memory locations in the SGA. Starting in version 10gR2, latches such as the library cache lock and library cache pin are implemented as mutex latches. Library cache objects are locked and pinned under the protection of a mutex associated with the parent cursor. Still, library cache hash chains are protected by library cache latches, and having longer hash chains can result in library cache latch contention.

Version 11g improved this area further. Each bucket in the library cache has its own mutex, and scanning through the library cache hash chain is also performed under the protection of a mutex governing that specific bucket. The use of a mutex for each library cache hash chain increases scalability and reduces contention points. It also avoids false contention points, since a mutex generally covers a specific object.

The dynamic performance views v$mutex_sleep and v$mutex_sleep_history are useful in analyzing performance issues with mutexes. If there is a high number of sleeps for library cache mutexes, then the techniques discussed in this section for resolving library cache latch contention apply, too.

Resolving Library Cache Latch Contention

There are a few common reasons for library cache latch contention. The following action items are useful in resolving the problem.

Use Bind Variables

Using bind variables can help reduce contention. It's especially important to use bind variables for statements that have a high number of executions. If a SQL statement uses literals, then those statements are nonsharable. If an application cannot be changed to use bind variables, then a workaround is to use the cursor_sharing initialization parameter. Setting this parameter to a value of FORCE or SIMILAR will convert nonsharable literal SQL statements to sharable SQL, by replacing literal values with system bind variables. Using the cursor_sharing parameter is just a workaround. The correct—or at least better—approach is to modify the offending application to use bind variables.

Avoid Flushing the Shared Pool

Too much flushing of the shared pool can result in contention. Bear in mind that not only can you flush your shared pool manually, but you also flush it each time you restart your instance.

Unpinned recreatable chunks from the library cache are thrown away during a shared pool flush operation. Instance restart also throws away all the cursors. Flushing artificially induces a higher amount of hard parse calls. Avoid flushing and restarting if possible. A cold backup is the most common reason for scheduled instance restarts. Look into using RMAN backups or hot backups instead.

Adjust the session_cached_cursors Parameter

The parameter `session_cached_cursors` controls the maximum number of cursors a session can pin. With a default value of 200 (from version 9i onward), many cursors executed frequently can be reused. If a cursor is found in the session cursor cache, then the parsing step[18] is cheaper than otherwise. Increasing this initialization parameter to a more modest value such as 400 will improve parsing performance. Of course, if SQL statements are using literal values, then increasing this parameter will provide very little benefit. Further, increase of this parameter comes at a cost, since cursors that are in the session cursor cache are pinned in the shared pool, and this can result in higher space usage in the shared pool.

Adjust the cursor_space_for_time Parameter to True

The parameter `cursor_space_for_time` controls the behavior of the SQL heaps in the shared pool. If there is a cursor open pointing to a cursor heap, then that cursor heap is less likely to be flushed out. Retaining the cursor heap improves the performance of subsequent executions of that SQL statement at the cost of increased shared pool usage. The `cursor_space_for_time` parameter is a tool to combat excessive flushes and the resulting library cache latch contention. As of Oracle Database version 10.2.0.5 and 11.1.0.7, this parameter is deprecated.

Control and Limit Histograms

It is a common practice in some vendor applications to collect histograms on all columns, and that is not necessarily a good practice. Child cursors cannot be shared if the `cursor_sharing` parameter is set to `similar`, and if the optimizer detects bind variables as sensitive to the histograms. In such a case, with many table joins, it is possible to have thousands of child cursors, leading in turn to library cache latch contention. If your application is collecting histograms on all columns, then rethink that practice, and narrow the scope of collection to only those columns that matter.

■ **Note** I am not recommending against all use of histograms, just their overuse.

---

[18] This parsing is cheaper than soft parse itself.

Enqueue Hash Chains Latch Contention

Enqueue hash chain latches protect structures handling enqueues, commonly known as locks. Higher amounts of enqueue activity can lead to enqueue hash chains latch contention.

Resources are the structures that a process is trying to lock. For example, if a process is trying to acquire a table level lock (lock type TM), then the process allocates a resource structure having the combination of that table's object_id and lock type as a resource key. A lock is then allocated on that resource in an appropriate mode.

Following is a summary of the operational details of the enqueue latching mechanism. Please refer to Figure 12-5 while reading the list.

1. A hashing function is applied on a string with a combination of `<lock type, id>`. For example, if the table scott.emp is to be locked, and that table has an object ID of 6509, and if the object type is TM for table, then a hashing function is applied over the string "(TM, 6509)".

2. The result of the hashing function uniquely identifies a hash bucket to which the resource will always be chained. Changes to or inspection of the hash chain are protected by the enqueue hash chains child latches. So, while holding an enqueue hash chains child latch, that hash chain is searched to see if that resource is already allocated.[19]

3. If the resource exists in the hash chain, then the process tries to see whether the resource is locked in a compatible mode with the lock request mode (assuming that there are no other waiters). If the resource is available or if the resource is locked in compatible mode, then a locking structure is added to the holders' queue.

4. If there is another process waiting to lock the resource, then a locking structure is added to the waiters' queue, and the process waits until the resource is available.

5. If the resource does not exist in the hash chain at all, then a new resource structure is added to the enqueue hash chain. A locking structure is also added to the holders' queue.

6. Changes to the enqueue hash chain are protected by enqueue hash chains latches.

---

[19] This would mean that the resource is already locked by another process.

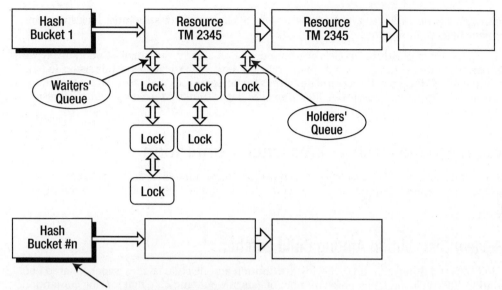

The length of this hash bucket array is determined by
the initialization parameter_enqueue_hash_buckets.
The number of latches is determined by the initialization
parameter enqueue_hash_chain_latches.

Figure 12-5. Resources, locks, and hash chains

If there is an enormous amount of locking activity, typically in the case of high-end OLTP applications, it is conceivable that there will be a higher amount of activity against enqueue structures and enqueue hash chains child latches. This leads to enqueue hash chains latch contention.

Common Causes of Enqueue Hash Chains Latch Contention

There are two common causes of enqueue hash chains latch contention, and they are often seen together:

Excessive locking activity: OLTP applications tend to have thousands of short transactions per second. Typically, these transactions insert one or two rows into a transaction table, and then commit the transaction. But these row updates will acquire a TM lock on that table or table partition in row share mode.[20] In addition, the start of a transaction also creates a TX lock.[21] Thousands of

---

[20] TM level locks are acquired for DML activity in row-share mode to avoid concurrent modifications to the table. For example, structural modifications to the table should not be allowed when there is an outstanding transaction.

[21] TX locks are the transaction locks, available in Oracle RDBMS, that implement row-level locking.

such short transactions will result in excessive activity against resource structures, lock structures, and enqueue hash chains latches.

Deadlock detection algorithm: Oracle's deadlock detection algorithm is invoked periodically, and it holds a parent enqueue hash chains latch (thereby holding all child latches) while searching for deadlocks between processes. If there are numerous processes, locks, and resource combinations in the database concurrently, then the deadlock detection algorithm can take long enough to result in contention for enqueue hash chains latches.

Analyzing Enqueue Hash Chains Latch Contention

Follow the process described in the next few subsections to detect enqueue hash chains latch contention. Once you've identified the root cause, you can look into applying one of the common solutions.

Step 1: Review Distribution Among Child Latches.

Refer to Listing 12-6 and the section on reviewing distribution among child latches under "Shared Pool Latch Contention." If a child latch has a high number of gets, it would indicate that locking contention on one resource is causing the issue. For example, the output of Listing 12-35 shows that child number 28 has much higher activity than other child latches. This condition implies that one specific enqueue has a much higher activity. If the activity on latch children is distributed across all child latches uniformly, then many enqueues are involved in the latch contention.

Listing 12-35. Skew among enqueue hash chains child latches

```
select * from (
select child#, gets, misses, sleeps
from v$latch_children where name like 'enqueue hash%'
order by gets desc )
where rownum <=20;

    CHILD#       GETS      MISSES      SLEEPS
---------- ---------- ---------- ----------
        28   12297672      211726           0
        20     284429        2151           1
        12     261698        2013           0
        16     212018        1390           0
        24     176909        1521           2
        17     140880        3089           1
         7     130085        1361           0
        27     113049        1251           1
```

Step 2: Identify the Enqueue Causing Latch Contention

Next, you need to find enqueues with high activity. An appropriate action is to enable SQL Trace at level 8 (with waits) on a process suffering from latch contention. Listing 12-36 shows lines from a SQL Trace output file. The event enqueue indicates that a process was waiting for an enqueue. We also see that this process is suffering from latch contention by the number of latch free waits that occur.

Listing 12-36. An example of SQL trace output lines (version 9.2.0.8)

```
WAIT #1: nam='enqueue' ela= 301 p1=1414332420 p2=9086 p3=0
WAIT #1: nam='latch free' ela= 1 p1=-1437405580 p2=19 p3=0
WAIT #1: nam='latch free' ela= 1 p1=-1437405580 p2=19 p3=1
WAIT #1: nam='latch free' ela= 1 p1=-1437405580 p2=19 p3=2
```

Next you need to find the latch type listed in the trace file. In the latch free wait event, parameter p2 tells us about the latch type. Listing 12-37 shows a query to get the latch type. In this case, the latch type is enqueue hash chains.

Listing 12-37. Querying to find the latch type and then the lock type

```
select name from v$latch where latch#=19;
NAME
--------------------------------------------------
enqueue hash chains
```

Check the lock type of the wait event enqueue using the SQL statement in Listing 12-38. In this example, TM is the enqueue that is causing enqueue hash chains latch contention.

Listing 12-38. Querying to find latch type and then lock type

```
select chr(bitand(1414332420,-16777216)/16777215) ||
       chr(bitand(1414332420,16711680)/65535) from dual
/
CH
--
TM
```

From the analysis in this section we can safely conclude that latches protecting TM enqueues are causing performance issues. We also know that the object_id causing trouble is 9086. Querying dba_objects for that ID will reveal the object_name and owner. You need to repeat this exercise for several times to confirm your analysis.

Step 3: Identify Lock Types with High Gets

Corroborate output from the previous two steps while querying statistics for enqueue activity. Listing 12-39 shows the top 20 enqueue types by activity. In this case, the TM lock type has high enqueue activity, confirming our analysis in earlier steps. Of course, in your case, you may have contention for some other lock type, and you might need further adjustments.

Listing 12-39. Top 20 lock types by activity

```
-- v$enqueue_statistics top 20 only..
select * from (
    select eq_name, eq_type, total_req#, total_wait#, succ_req#, failed_req#
    from  v$enqueue_statistics
    order by total_Req# desc)
where rownum<21
/
EQ_NAME                      EQ TOTAL_REQ# TOTAL_WAIT#  SUCC_REQ# FAILED_REQ#
--------------------------- -- ---------- ----------- ---------- -----------
DML                          TM     18554       17630      18155         400
Session Migration            SE     17709           0      17725           0
Job Scheduler                JS     12975           0      12975           0
Job Scheduler                JS     12970           4      12970           0
Controlfile Transaction      CF     12248        1493      12228          20
Transaction                  TX      6340         114       6340           0
...
```

Resolving Enqueue Hash Chains Latch Contention

This section provides some action items useful in resolving enqueue hash chains latch contention.

Avoid Excessive Short Transactions

Typically, OLTP applications suffer from having large numbers of very short transactions. Thousands of concurrent short transactions will increase activity against enqueues for TM and TX, leading to latch contention. If possible, modify the code to avoid or reduce this type of activity, and try grouping small transactions into bigger ones.

Note that worrying about short transactions only matters if the lock type behind the contention is TM or TX.

Disable Table Level Locks

In some cases, it may be beneficial to avoid table-level locks. Listing 12-40 provides an example of the syntax to use in doing so.

Listing 12-40. Disabling table level lock

```
Alter table emp disable table lock;
alter table backup.emp add (n2 number)
*
ERROR at line 1:
ORA-00069: cannot acquire lock -- table locks disabled for EMP
Alter table emp enable table lock;
```

Disabling table level locks means that there can be no DDL statements on the target table. But in a production OLTP database suffering from latch contention, not being able to issue DDLs against a table is a very small price to pay to resolve the problem. Of course, you can always enable locks during maintenance on that table.

Reduce or Avoid Activity Against the Lock Type Causing Contention

Reduce or avoid activity against the lock type underlying the contention. For example, if the lock type is DX, try to reduce distributed transaction by redesigning the application architecture. Creative use of materialized views will be helpful in this scenario. For example, if the application accesses remote tables using database links, then a distributed transaction needs to be created even in the case of a SELECT statement. With a materialized view, access can be localized, thereby avoiding the distributed transaction.

Advanced Help for Latch Contention Problems

There are a few exceptions and bugs that can cause excessive latch contention. This section tries to list them, but for informational and debugging purposes only. You should contact Oracle Support before trying any of the suggestions I provide here in a production database. Incorrect settings or incorrect use of these suggestions can lead to database crashes.

The v$latch_parent View

The v$latch_parent view maintains statistics at the parent latch level. In some cases, if there are many child latches, then the RDBMS code will need to acquire all the child latches. For example, deadlock detection code holds the parent latch of enqueue hash chains during execution of the deadlock detection algorithm, and no child latch can be acquired by any other process until that parent latch is released.

The spin_count Parameter

The parameter spin_count determines amount of time the process will spin on the CPU before going to sleep. This parameter affects the behavior of all latches. Rarely, adjusting the spin_count is a good solution. Adjusting the spin count is unnecessary, and there are only few situations in which it might need to be adjusted.

The _latch_classes and _latch_class_N Parameters

If it is not possible to resolve the root cause of the latch contention, then the _latch_classes and _latch_class_n parameters can be used to modify the spin count just for few latches from Oracle Database version 9iR2. For example, if you want to increase the spin count for library cache latches, you can use the method demonstrated in Listing 12-41. In the listing, which is from Oracle Database version 10.2.0.4. the spin_count for _latch_class_1 is set to 18000, and the _latch_classes parameter specifies that latch number 214 belongs to latch_class_1. Latch number 214 is for the library cache latch.

And again, take care to avoid setting underscore parameters in your database without first talking the problem through with Oracle Support.

Listing 12-41. _latch_classes and _latch_class_1 parameter changes for library cache latches

```
Select latch#, name from v$latch where name='library cache';
    LATCH# NAME
---------- -------------------------------------------------
       214 library cache

*._latch_class_1=18000
*._latch_classes='214:1'
```

The _latch_wait_posting and _enable_reliable_latch_waits Parameters

The parameter _latch_wait_posting controls how *long wait* latches such as library cache latches are handled. By default, this parameter is set to 1, and library cache or shared pool latches are acquired using the latch wait posting mode method discussed in the section "Latch-Wait Posting Mode." If a latch is not available after a certain period, the process sleeps until posted by the latch holder.

If _enable_reliable_latch_waits is set to true, then all latch posts are considered reliable. A process waiting for a latch will go to sleep and not wake up until posted. The result is reduced CPU usage, tending to reduce the symptoms of latch contention.

Summary

In this chapter, we've looked at various common latch contention issues faced in the real world. We've also looked at methods and techniques to resolve those issues. As always, it is best to understand the root cause of a problem, in this case a latch contention problem, and to resolve that root cause. It is always better to resolve a root cause than to apply a band-aid.

CHAPTER 13

■ ■ ■

Measuring for Robust Performance

by Robyn Sands

Cary Millsap was my mentor long before we ever met. Shortly after I began working with the Oracle database around 1996, I began to find papers he had written. The first one must have been his now famous "OFA *Standard: Oracle for Open Systems*" paper, but there were others that I read and reread those first few years. Although I was new to Oracle, his writings made complete sense to me when so much of the documentation and writings on Oracle were confusing or contradictory. I knew that I needed to master the concepts mentioned in these papers if I ever hoped to master Oracle, and unlike anything I'd come across in my studies or work experience, Oracle had grabbed my attention. There was so much to discover in how it worked and what it could do, and I intended to figure out absolutely everything I could about this new tool in my hands.

Years later, I had the opportunity to meet Cary and, eventually, to become one of his many friends. Listening to him present one day, I realized something. His writings and presentations made sense to me because he thinks like an engineer. Having studied operations research, manufacturing, and quality engineering in school, I found that listening to Cary was like listening to one of my professors or an engineering coworker. Of course his way of communicating and solving problems made sense to me—he was speaking my language and he used logical, repeatable methods very similar to those I use in the non-Oracle side of my work.

Once this little epiphany passed, a bigger one followed: although I had learned a great deal from Cary and other Oak Table members over the years, some of the techniques I used as a database administrator had originated from methods I had used when working in industrial engineering, manufacturing control, and quality engineering. Over the years, I had blended what I knew about statistics and process capability methods with the knowledge I'd gained from others, and had optimized Oracle performance in many systems by doing so. Therefore, it seems appropriate to begin this chapter with a story from *Optimizing Oracle Performance* by Cary Millsap and Jeff Holt (O'Reilly Media, 2003):

> *You can't extrapolate detail from an aggregate.*
>
> *Imagine that I told you that a collection of 1,000 rocks contains 999 grey rocks and one special rock that's been painted bright red. The collection weighs 1,000 pounds. Now, answer the following question: "How much does the red rock weigh?" If your answer is, "I know that the red rock weighs one pound," then, whether you realize it or not, you've told a lie. You don't know that the red rock weighs one pound. With the information you've been given, you can't know. If your answer is, "I assume that the red rock weighs one pound," then you're too generous in what you're willing to assume. Such an assumption puts you at risk of forming conclusions that are incorrect—perhaps even stunningly incorrect.*

The correct answer is that the red rock can weigh virtually any amount between zero and 1,000 pounds. The only thing limiting the low end of the weight is the definition of how many atoms must be present in order for a thing to be called a rock. Once we define how small a rock can be, then we've defined the high end of our answer. It is 1,000 pounds minus the weight of 999 of the smallest possible rocks. The red rock can weigh virtually anything between zero and a thousand pounds. Answering with any more precision is wrong unless you happen to be very lucky. But being very lucky at games like this is a skill that can be neither learned nor taught, nor repeated with acceptable reliability.

Finding the Red Rocks

The preceding analogy makes it clear that picking up the red rock and actually weighing it is the way to get the right answer. But what happens when that rock is not so easily found? We are talking about a lot of rocks if the entire collection weighs 1,000 pounds, and the red one is probably not sitting on top like a cherry on a sundae. If it were visible, you might have been able to make a reasonably accurate estimate. Do you have the time and strength to dig through 1,000 pounds of rocks to find the red one? And what if you got through the entire stack and didn't see it at all? Is it gone? Or did you just miss it? Or maybe, somewhere along the line, someone decided that painting the red rock grey would make it just like the others. Now you're faced with examining every rock to see whether it's really grey or just camouflaged. What if there are a million rocks instead of 1,000? How do you find that one red rock so you can measure it?

Why would someone hide the red rock or paint it grey? That's a good question, but when we're talking about database processes, it happens on a regular basis. Anytime someone is able to make a temporary improvement to processing time that doesn't address the root cause of the problem, they've camouflaged the red rock. It may blend in with the other processes for a little while, but it's likely to revert to its former behavior and may still have a detrimental impact on system resources. You can monitor performance from Statspack, Active Session History (ASH) or Automatic Workload Repository (AWR), and maybe you can see that something is wrong, but identifying the specific problem can be like trying to spot the red rock in the pile from a vantage point of 50 feet in the air. Depending on the kind of problem you are looking for and when you look for it, perhaps you'll see it, but then again, maybe you won't.

The business can't always identify the red rocks for you. The users may know which processes they wait on, but maybe the job they're watching isn't really the source of the problem. Their report may be suffering from a resource drain created by another process, and in that case, it's the process creating the bottleneck that needs to be measured and addressed. Management may know which processes are most important to the company as a whole, but that can be a very long list to work through, and answers are usually needed immediately for a performance issue. Perhaps there is an entire batch of processes that is necessary to support critical business functions, and the goal is for every process to complete within a specified time frame. You need to find the right processes to optimize in order to improve the system's overall throughput, allowing all the processes to complete within the required window. What if this performance problem occurs only intermittently? Perhaps the performance issue the user reported really was there but, by the time a problem report is made through the required channels, something in the system has changed, and the process is behaving differently when someone is finally able to check the database.

This chapter is about finding the red rocks. You still can't extrapolate detail from an aggregate. That's not how statistics are meant to be used. What you can do is use statistics to help identify the red rocks so you can fix the right problem the right way.

Understanding the Properties of Performance

Performance is a common topic of discussion among most database administrators, but what exactly does *performance* mean? Personally, I think solving a performance problem is one of the most challenging and interesting aspects of working with Oracle, second only to preventing a performance problem. But if I tell you that I *optimized performance* in a database today, what does that mean to you? Or more important, what does it mean specifically to the business and the users? After all, they are the stakeholders in any performance improvement project. If I've optimized performance in their system, I should be able to tell them specifically what has changed and what they will see from the system as a result of my work. So what does optimizing performance encompass? What exactly is the goal we want to achieve? What do we need to accomplish to achieve demonstrable results? And who should be able to see the results of our efforts? We need the answers to these questions before we can measure performance, much less begin to improve it.

Response Time Is Key

If there is one critical number in database performance, it's response time. *Response time* is a measure of time from the initiation of a process until its completion; it is the elapsed time of a transaction or the set of transactions that compose the process. There are two components to response time: service time and wait time, and performance can be improved by reducing either component.

The most complete method to measure the response time of a specific process is the 10046 trace. The trace file produces raw data that can be profiled to detail the components within the process and the amount of time spent on each of them. The most effective way to improve response time is to focus on improving the component that expends the most unnecessary time within the process. Not only does the profile provide the details needed to improve the process, but it also provides the means to measure and record the results. The response profile is then the proof that the performance has been improved, as well as the baseline measurement for how the process should perform in the future.

Throughput Counts

Throughput is a measure of how much work a system can complete in a given time period, but it's important to remember that a batch is just a group of individual processes. Trying to optimize throughput without optimizing individual processes and balancing the workload first is like attempting to maximize the return on your investments without paying attention to the individual performance of your stocks, mutual funds, and other assets. Perhaps you'll get lucky on some days, but how will you respond when you don't? You can wait to see whether the overall value moves up or down, but it may be too late to change a bad investment by then. And how would you decide which investment needs to change? Or when it should be changed?

Statspack and AWR are like the various stock market indices: these measurements give you an indication of performance across different sectors at a specific period in time, but if you take that measurement at the wrong time or out of context, the results can be misleading. ASH is more like the daily stock reports: you receive much more detailed data, but only for the most recent time period. That doesn't mean that you should totally ignore the indices or stop using the Oracle performance tools—just that you need to understand their intended purpose and use them accordingly.

To return to the investment analogy, if you've tracked individual performance and paid attention to how that investment helps or hinders the overall growth of your investments, you know exactly how that option contributes to the results. The overall performance measurement tells you whether your strategy is working. If it's not, you can return to the data on individual performance to point you to the right adjustment to make in your portfolio. In your database, if the Statspack report tells you there is a resource bottleneck and you have measurements of the individual processes that affected the time frame when the bottleneck occurred, you know definitively which process needs to be optimized to alleviate the contention.

Meeting Expectations Matters

Much has been written and discussed about the challenges of satisfying users. However, there is one simple truth: users are happier when a system performs as expected. If they have a monthly report that takes 10 minutes to process as it summarizes large quantities of data, they will generally accept that this report will take a while to complete, and plan to get another cup of coffee while it executes. But when a report that normally takes 10 minutes runs for 20 minutes and still hasn't completed, they become less understanding. They may not know or care about how the system works, but they know it's behaving differently than expected, slowing down their ability to complete the tasks that must be done before lunch, and that's when they get irritable (and rightfully so). Expectations are based on past performance, so process predictability should be considered when evaluating whether optimization goals have been met.

There is a larger justification for measuring consistency beyond meeting expectations: processes that perform inconsistently use resources outside of their expected window, impacting the resources available for other jobs. When a process that normally finishes by 3 a.m. runs until 3:30 a.m., the processes that start at 3:05 have an additional competitor on their playing field, and there's no guarantee that everyone is going to play nice. Perhaps the long-running process pushes the processors almost to capacity. If one of those 3:05 processes also requires a healthy percentage of CPU time, the system can reach saturation, resulting in a bottleneck that impacts multiple processes. This type of impasse slows the entire schedule, and in the morning, it's clear that something went wrong.

However, finding the process that needs to be optimized is not always an easy task. By morning, reports may show that everything ran past normal execution times. The business will have critical jobs that ran late: do you focus on optimizing those first? Or do you look for the longest-running process and hope that's where the problem lies? Somebody is bound to suggest it's the statistics, someone else will decide it was the network, and everyone will hope it was a random issue with a low probability of reoccurring. And when everything goes back to normal the next night, there's a collective sigh of relief. It must have been the statistics after all. But there may be a red rock in the system, and if you don't find it, odds are that that "random" issue will be back. Inconsistency makes your system less predictable, and unpredictably creates a host of management problems. If you don't know how long a process will run, how do you know how much of a system resource will be consumed? And if you don't know your resource consumption, how do you know that the system will be able to deliver the promised functionality and service levels?

All Together Now...

Response time, throughput, and predictability are interrelated functions of a complex system—a small change in one can have a large impact on another. Response time may be fine when there are no other active processes, but executing one process at a time is hardly an acceptable use of hardware. User reports may execute very consistently, except near month-end, when more users request more data. Or maybe throughput for a batch process was excellent until a new code module was added to the package, creating resource bottlenecks that didn't exist before. Each of these factors can present a system optimization challenge, but the more inconsistency there is within the processes themselves, the more complex it becomes to find and fix the suboptimal components.

"Tuning" a Data Warehouse

Now that we've discussed the impact an unpredictable process can have on a system, let me share a specific example of a process with variable performance. A daily sales and bookings (DSB) report tended to slow considerably toward the end of any quarter and especially at the end of the fiscal year, just when the report was most critical to business users as they worked toward meeting their targeted sales goals. Analysis of the trace data did not show problems with latches or locks until the report had failed several times and the impatient users had resubmitted multiple requests for the same data. The DSB report had been created years earlier and had been modified many times, resulting in layers of views and interrelationships with other reports that made changes to the code a scary proposition. Prior tuning attempts had helped temporarily, but the results never lasted very long.

Initial Tuning

In the fourth quarter of fiscal year 2007 (FY07), the data warehouse team decided that the job needed to be thoroughly investigated before the process hit critical mass at year-end. Monitoring individual user executions showed that response times were highly varied. At best, the report finished in about 12 minutes, but sometimes it failed after 20 minutes because of a timer on the report server. When the code was traced for a single execution, the predominant waits were read waits. The data was highly skewed as the sales numbers had trended upward over the years (good for the business, not so good for the database). In order to minimize the impact of the skewed data, the central table was partitioned by fiscal year and subpartitioned by month. Partition pruning minimized the reads, and the next round of trace files showed that the majority of the response time was now spent in CPU waits. This led to the discovery of a clever little function buried deep within a view that was being used to determine the months that should be included in a specific quarter. Unfortunately, this function clearly didn't pass the scalability test. Early in the quarter, the function performed well, but as the number of records to be processed increased, the function created a CPU bottleneck, and the more users that tried to retrieve the data, the more work backed up behind it.

The solution was simple: the function was eliminated and two columns were added to the calendar dimension to provide the fiscal month and quarter. After this change, CPU usage became negligible under any data load. The report was faster, but more important, it became more consistent. Response time predictably increased toward the end of the quarter, but execution times remained between 6 and 11 minutes. Not all variation could be removed from the process; users can still submit multiple requests, and data will always be skewed because of the natural fluctuations in sales, but the new queries are written to minimize the impact of these known variables.

Having seen the potential for variance to identify older code that no longer functioned well under current data loads, an analysis of the data warehouse job runtimes was needed to see whether variability could be used to identify other code issues. The data warehouse included a table of job completion times that was used to monitor successful job execution. This table provided all of the data necessary to calculate the variability in elapsed time.

The goal of this experiment was to compare average response times to variance, using an approach inspired by Genichi Taguchi's quality engineering methods. Collecting the mean, median, standard deviation, and variance for all jobs that had at least 12 successful executions over FY07 showed that some processes had enormous amounts of variance in their processing times. Following are the 20 least predictable jobs from that list. The analysis was done in July 2007, using Oracle Database Enterprise Edition 9.2.0.8.

JOB	EXECUTIONS	AVERAGE	MEDIAN	DEVIATION	VARIANCE	VMR	TOPN
736	15	20291.467	18266.0	7293.171	53190342.267	2621.316	1
244	24	14720.417	13235.5	5920.793	35055786.428	2381.440	2
654	327	220.933	53.0	660.884	436767.922	1976.927	3
810	314	5649.035	4559.0	3044.318	9267870.884	1640.611	4
685	49	26617.163	27231.0	6228.938	38799664.473	1457.693	5
371	325	1339.065	1069.0	1381.680	1909040.542	1425.652	6
236	324	3883.188	2740.5	2330.879	5432997.745	1399.107	7
297	23	1823.913	1117.0	1569.664	2463844.174	1350.856	8
546	388	5413.353	4882.0	2540.904	6456195.516	1192.643	9
510	12	10791.500	10759.5	3349.294	11217768.818	1039.500	10
483	323	2289.582	1931.0	1398.884	1956876.909	854.687	11
62	346	493.772	307.0	605.533	366670.206	742.591	12
457	326	881.810	722.5	790.901	625523.859	709.364	13
706	14	1640.143	940.0	1046.019	1094154.747	667.109	14
426	12	2025.000	1465.0	1111.136	1234623.455	609.691	15
298	23	592.043	355.0	595.571	354704.225	599.119	16
558	151	212.252	1.0	356.245	126910.390	597.924	17
001	261	280.092	127.0	398.075	158463.476	565.755	18
51	337	160.288	112.0	297.527	88522.253	552.271	19
272	866	202.936	147.0	318.676	101554.293	500.424	20

The variance-to-mean ratio (VMR) is a measure of the randomness of the individual data points within the set. When this calculation was applied to the job execution data, it resulted in a sort of *predictability factor*: the less dispersion within a process's execution times, the more consistently a job performed. The results were logically consistent with job performance history; jobs with the highest VMR were some of the biggest troublemakers in the job schedules. The data warehouse team concurred that the identified jobs held the most potential for tuning within the code but pointed out some notable absences from the top 20.

In the past, the team had focused on the long-running jobs as the performance issues. Further analysis showed that the jobs with long execution times and lower levels of variance were processing large amounts of data in a very efficient manner.

Repeating the Analysis

At the end of fiscal year 2008 (FY08), I decided to repeat the analysis of the prior year. I did this primarily to satisfy my own curiosity, because the data warehouse had been upgraded to a completely new platform and the users were reporting that overall system performance was very good. The servers had been replaced with new HP Itanium models, and everything had been rebuilt from the hardware up. The Oracle executables had been upgraded to Oracle 10g release 2, and as the SAP system that supplied most of the data had been upgraded to ECC 6, the majority of the tables in the data warehouse had been rebuilt and repopulated. Everything except the code was brand new and cleanly built, because code had been altered only when changes in SAP required it.

Following are the results from my repeat analysis. Again, I list the 20 least predictable jobs. This time the year is 2008, and the database version is 10.2.0.4.

JOB	EXECUTIONS	AVERAGE	MEDIAN	DEVIATION	VARIANCE	VMR	TOPN
736	12	42042.583	24508.5	59935.039	3592208846.000	85442.153	1
539	12	15840.833	14399.0	13497.970	182195186.000	11501.616	2
810	308	7337.919	6320.5	8418.195	70866008.300	9657.508	3
685	52	21318.250	17848.0	12162.038	147915167.000	6938.429	4
244	23	12465.696	11899.0	8764.807	76821849.300	6162.660	5
475	12	25853.417	25443.0	11019.209	121422958.000	4696.592	6
654	315	1033.270	379.0	2183.026	4765601.640	4612.156	7
478	12	31588.750	31520.5	10655.897	113548145.000	3594.575	8
477	12	2616.917	1525.0	3005.849	9035125.900	3452.584	9
706	14	1907.000	925.0	2394.294	5732645.540	3006.107	10
510	12	14935.667	13518.0	6626.314	43908032.600	2939.811	11
550	12	1734.000	1033.0	2077.257	4314996.360	2488.464	12
549	12	1768.000	1083.5	2071.642	4291702.360	2427.433	13
678	12	5551.333	5276.0	3520.410	12393283.700	2232.488	14

118	311	13.971	4.0	170.276	28994.041	2075.293	15
001	264	453.159	119.0	935.298	874781.427	1930.407	16
116	311	20.084	8.0	196.585	38645.470	1924.230	17
167	312	240.654	140.0	647.528	419292.021	1742.303	18
563	311	15.904	5.0	159.547	25455.242	1600.603	19
08	323	8.409	2.0	114.236	13049.808	1551.947	20

What I found was that although the majority of the processes had significantly improved on the new hardware, many of the highly variable processes from the prior year were still creating problems in the job schedules. The top twenty VMR jobs included repeat appearances by seven jobs seen in the previous analysis. Most of the others were a little further down the list by just enough to keep them out of the top 20. One brand new job showed up as the third most variable process, job number 810, and this was surprising. Taking a look at the code, I discovered that the developer had built the report from an existing bit of code and by doing so, he had reintroduced the same function we had worked to eliminate the prior year.

This second analysis increased my confidence that high levels of variance in relation to a process's average completion time is an effective way to identify code in need of optimization. The analysis also reaffirmed something I had learned many years earlier: not all performance problems can be fixed by better hardware. If the code has not been optimized, new hardware will at best have no effect, while improving the hardware component that is not causing the bottleneck could even make a performance problem worse by increasing the rate of arrival at the true bottleneck.

Exploring What Variance Can Tell Us About a Process

Although the idea of comparing the variance to the mean was inspired by Taguchi's concepts and methods, Taguchi's functions, arrays, and equations are far more complex. Yet a simple comparison of the variance in completion times to the mean completion time provided enough insight to highlight some serious problems. But why?

Refer back to the initial results from the data warehouse analysis and take a look at the numbers for the item labeled 654. This is not a terribly long-running process for a data warehouse: the average completion time is 220.9 seconds, or 3.7 minutes, with a sample size of 327 executions. That seems fine, or does it? Take a look at the next number, the median. The median is the center point of the distribution and gives us the midpoint completion time for the individual samples. The median for this process is 53 seconds, so half of the samples took longer than 53 seconds, and half of the samples executed more quickly. Think about that for a minute: half of the processes completed in less than 53 seconds, yet the average completion time was 220.9 seconds. This tells us that when process 654 goes bad, it goes really, really bad. Checking the variance and the VMR confirms our suspicions because those are some very big numbers, but a graph in Figure 13-1 makes it crystal clear.

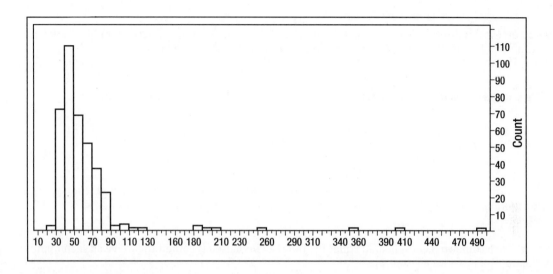

Figure 13-1. Distribution of elapsed time for process 654

■ **Note** Charts for this chapter were produced using JMP 8 software from SAS.

In case you're wondering, the longest execution time for process 654 was 5,380 seconds, or almost 90 minutes, which is a significant deviation from the average. (Figure 13-1 shows only about 12 percent of the complete distribution.) Numbers like these give you an idea of the kind of problem we're trying to solve. 50 percent of the time, process 654 completes in 53 seconds or less. The completion time for the remaining 50 percent of the processes could be much longer, meaning this process could unexpectedly require system resources for an extended period of time, and subsequently may impact many other processes when this happens.

If a user waits on this process, that user will expect the process to return in less than a minute based on past performance. If Murphy has anything to say about it, just when the user needs to get this data for an urgent meeting, the process will run for an hour and a half, easily outlasting the meeting. The end result may be an angry user or a whole room full of them. It could be one long-running process or it could be twenty long running processes, depending on the system resources that were used or saturated.

This is variance: a randomly occurring problem that impacts the business. The variance-to-mean ratio tells us that this "random" problem occurs too frequently to truly be random, and we've found our red rock. Actually, for the data warehouse, this was one of many red rocks, and considering the elapsed time and the levels of variance in the other process, this rock is on the smaller side. However, it does illustrate the point quite well: *variance in processing time creates problems.*

Distribution Analysis

A *distribution* is a dataset shown with the individual values and the frequency or relative frequency of occurrence. The distribution most of us are familiar with is the normal, or bell, curve. The formal name of such a curve is the *Gaussian curve*, named for Johann Carl Friedrich Gauss, a German mathematician and astronomer. In the *Oxford Dictionary of Statistics* by Graham Upton and Ian Cook (Oxford University Press, 2006) a normal curve is defined as follows:

The distribution of a random variable x for which the probability density function f is given by

$$f(x)= \frac{1}{\sigma\sqrt{2\pi}}\ \exp\left(-\frac{(x-\mu)^2}{2\sigma^2}\right),\ \ -\infty<x<\infty$$

The parameters μ and σ are, respectively, the mean and the variance of the distribution. The distribution is noted by N (μ,σ) and the random variable may be referred to as a normal variable.

Seems like a somewhat complicated equation, but the curve itself is something we've all seen many times. Figure 13-2 provides an example.

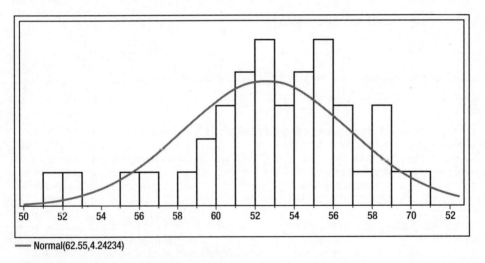

— Normal(62.55,4.24234)

Figure 13-2. Gaussian, or normal, distribution

Note that although the definition mentions variance, the equation uses the square root of variance, or the standard deviation. In a normal distribution, the curve is centered on the mean and extends equally to the left and the right, with 99.7 percent of the values in the dataset falling within three standard deviations from the mean. The normal distribution is the foundation of a large part of statistical analysis, but there are other distributions, such as the binomial distribution, the chi-squared distribution, the Poisson distribution, and the Student's t-distribution. Knowing a dataset's distribution is key to determining the types of analysis to use in evaluating it. When working with elapsed time data, the distribution is more likely to resemble a Poisson distribution. Again, the following is from the *Oxford Dictionary of Statistics*:

A random variable X, whose set of possible values consists of non-negative integers, with a probability function given by

$$P(X=r) = \frac{e^{-\lambda}\,\lambda^r}{r!}, \qquad r = 0, 1, \ldots ,$$

where λ is a positive constant, is said to have a Poisson distribution, or to be a Poisson variable, with a parameter λ.

Once again, the equation appears complex, but the curve itself should look very familiar, as similar curves are frequently seen in presentations on system performance, especially when one of the topics under discussion is skew. Figure 13-3 shows an example.

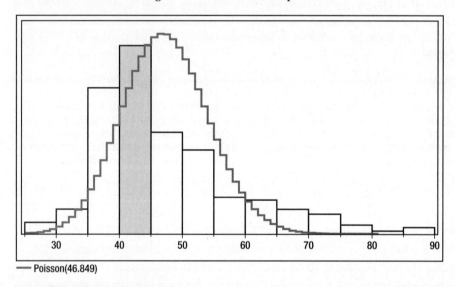

— Poisson(46.849)

Figure 13-3. Poisson distribution

■ **Note** The Poisson distribution was named for Simeon Denis Poisson, a French mathematician. The usage of the distribution is actually attributed to Abraham de Moivre, a French mathematical prodigy. de Moivre's paper, "*de Mensura Sortis*," was published in 1711, 120 years prior to Poisson's book, *Researches on the Probability of Criminal and Civil Verdicts*, published in 1837. de Moivre was also the first to study the normal distribution.

Distribution of Elapsed Time Data

There were a very specific set of common properties for the jobs used in the data warehouse analysis, and these properties are important to determining the appropriate measures to use for statistical analysis. These properties are common to most elapsed time datasets:

The dataset included every successful execution of a job over one year's time. Job completion times were available for prior years as well. This was not a random sample; instead it was *a complete sample of the total population over a specific window of time.*

The distribution of the elapsed time of an individual process typically is *not* a Gaussian curve, or normal distribution. Although processes can run significantly longer than average, a successful execution seldom runs significantly faster unless a change has been made. If you plot the completion times of a specific, repetitive process, you'll find that the elapsed time data points will produce a curve that more closely resembles a Poisson distribution, positively skewed with the long tail to the right.

Elapsed times are always a positive number. It is not possible for a job to complete any time except after it begins.

Of course, it is possible to have a dataset that is truly sampled data; i.e., a subset of observances that should be representative of the larger dataset. When you use ASH data, you are using sampled data. However, even when using sampled data, the other two properties will be true of elapsed time data. The only difference is that, with sampled data, the sample size is represented by $(n-1)$ instead of n. Based on my experiences and the levels of variances that will be present in most datasets, this adjustment is unlikely to impact your results unless you are using very small sample sizes or have already achieved exceptionally consistent performance, but you should still be aware of the difference and make the adjustment when appropriate.

■ **Note** In atomic and molecular physics, there is a measurement known as the Fano factor, discovered by Ugo Fano in 1947. This measure is also a variance-to-mean ratio for a dataset with the same properties described, plus one more: the window time being measured approaches infinity. Could an Oracle process run forever, if the server were connected to an unending source of electricity? Probably not, but it can certainly feel like forever to the user.

Variance

Variance is a measure of the dispersion of a dataset. The higher the variance, the more spread out the individual data points are. The lower the variance, the closer the data points are to one another and to the mean value of the dataset. It's important to note that variance is not measured in the same units as the variable being analyzed, unlike the average, median, or standard deviation. If the average completion time of a process is 7.953 seconds, it is incorrect to say that the sample population had a variance of 15.711 seconds. Instead, you would say that the average completion time is 7.953 seconds, with a variance of 15.711 and a standard deviation of 3.964 seconds.

The Index of Dispersion

The *index of dispersion* (*I*) is a measure of the level of dispersion within a Poisson distribution. A value below one indicates that the values are underdispersed and clustered closer to the mean. A value above one indicates that the levels are overdispersed, and possibly not representative of a truly random sample or process. The higher the index of dispersion, the more likely it is that there are clusters of reoccurring values distributed throughout the data. In process elapsed time data, these clusters may indicate the presence of a nonrandom "random" event. In the data warehouse, this is exactly what we found: reoccurring problems that occurred at unpredictable intervals.

The index of dispersion is calculated by dividing the sample variance by the sample mean—that is, the index of dispersion is a variance-to-mean ratio. It is intended to test a sample to confirm that (a) the distribution is a Poisson distribution, and (b) the sample is truly random. Although the elapsed time data in the data warehouse analysis was clearly skewed to the right and resembled a Poisson distribution, it fails the index of dispersion null hypothesis test on both counts. We already know this is not a random sample of a larger population. We also found that the processes with a high VMR tended to suffer from reoccurring performance problems. The fact that the problem reappears and creates clusters in the data is what tells us the code needs optimization. Approaching the concept from the other direction, as the elapsed time data for a single process gets closer to passing the index of dispersion test, the more likely it is that the code is already optimized.

What About Standard Deviation?

The same traits that indicate a Poisson distribution for analyzing elapsed time data contradict the use of the standard deviation to mean (coefficient of variation, or CoV), because the CoV is used to evaluate the level of dispersion within a normal curve. A normal curve by definition is equally skewed in both directions, with 99.7% of the observations falling within three standard deviations to the left and three standard deviations to the right. A normal curve can encompass negative values. And a normal curve typically results from a random sample of a large population. None of these things were true of the dataset used for the original test. Nor are they true for the data points of a typical single-process elapsed time profile.

In the data warehouse, the jobs with high CoV values fit a different profile. These jobs processed different amounts of data depending on when in the month, quarter, or year they were executed. Many of the high CoV processes were materialized view refreshes from the SAP system, which contained the manufacturing data. The materialized views themselves were very simple, but the amount of data to be refreshed was impacted by the amount of product that shipped, which always increased at the end of any revenue cycle. Early in the month, there was less data. As the month progressed, the number of records to be processed steadily increased, and the execution times increased with the data. When a new month began, once again there were fewer records to process, and the execution times returned to their lowest values. This resulted in a cyclical pattern to the elapsed time. In cases like this, if the window of time measured includes a full cycle, or a series of cycles, a graph of the elapsed times will be closer to a normal distribution. In the FY08 analysis, the elapsed times were much faster, and even less variation existed on the new platform for jobs with high CoV indicators, because the new hardware relieved the bottleneck for this type of process and increased throughput.

CoV is the appropriate measure for the distribution of a Gaussian curve, and although elapsed time data fits within a Gaussian curve only under certain conditions, other measurements within a database may be better suited for a CoV analysis, such as number of executions completed within a block of time. CoV may also highlight maintenance-type processes that are consuming more resources than you realize: backup jobs, statistics collection, or reoccurring data loads. Although it is important to understand the impact these processes have on the system, you should already be well aware of the maintenance tasks that execute within your databases and when they are executed. If not, there are already plenty of tools in the Oracle suite that can display this information for you.

Elapsed Time Data Sources

If you're curious and would like to try this type of analysis with your systems, job time data is readily available in most data center environments. Job scheduling tools record the actual start and completion time, along with the scheduled start time and other valuable information. Different scheduling products use different approaches to record their timestamps, and sometimes the values can be obscured, but it is possible to back-solve for a method to decipher them. Be cautious when calculating the elapsed time from these start and complete times; if you've misused an obfuscated timestamp, the resulting numbers will be wrong. A comparison of your calculated elapsed times to the values on the reports produced by the tool will tell you when you have it right.

There are a few additional guidelines you should keep in mind:

Create a table for the dataset you've selected for analysis. Data may be purged by the scheduling tool at regular intervals, or job data may be altered within the selected time window. If this happens, trying to determine why your numbers have changed can be very frustrating. If you've stored your analysis set, you can always refer back to it and compare it to the current view.

Include a reference to the time window in the table name. If the table includes the records for a fiscal year or specific quarter, include that designator so that two years from now, you know which dataset belongs to which time frame. If you retain the tables over time, you can determine whether the same processes continue to plague the schedule, or whether new issues are cropping up.

Include as many executions as is feasible. Results will be more meaningful the more executions you have per job, especially when you are measuring a live production system. In test situations where you have more control over the data being processed and system utilization, it is possible to gain the insight you need with fewer executions, but more is better.

Talk to the development team. After you've identified a list of jobs that you think need improvement, talk to the development team before announcing your results. Show some discretion, because you'll need to work together to solve the problem. In many cases, the team members will already be aware of the problems with optimizing a particular process and can offer insight into how to improve it. They might even think it's cool that you can confirm something they have been trying unsuccessfully to escalate to their manager.

Take care when changing schemas. Your job-scheduling tool schema may be proprietary. Read the fine print on your license and never make changes within the product schema. Creating a separate schema for your analysis tables, views, and code is recommended.

Following is some example code to create and populate an elapsed time table:

```
create table job_stats_2009
  as
select job_name,
       count(job_name)                               executions,
       round(avg(elapsed_time),3)                    average,
       round(median(elapsed_time),3)                 median,
       round(stddev(elapsed_time),3)                 deviation,
       round(stddev(elapsed_time)/avg(elapsed_time),3)  cov,
       round(variance(elapsed_time),3)               variance,
       round(variance(elapsed_time)/avg(elapsed_time),3) vmr
  from job_history
```

```
where start_dat_time > '2008-12-31 23:59:59'
  and start_dat_time < '2010-01-01 00:00:01'
  and elapsed_time != 0
group by job_name
order by job_name ;
```

■ **Note** The `job_history` table used as the source to create the stats tables is already one step removed from the job-scheduling tool, so the start/complete time translation is not shown. Any translation will be product specific.

And you can use the following query to generate a list of the top 20 processes with the highest VMRs:

```
select * from (
  select job_name, executions, average, median, deviation, variance, vmr, rank()
  over (
    order by vmr desc
  ) topn from job_stats_2009
)
 where topn <= 20
 order by vmr desc ;
```

Achieving Robust Performance

Although Genichi Taguchi is considered controversial in some statistical circles, the methods he defined are thought provoking. Taguchi contended that conventional sampling methods were incomplete because it is not possible to collect a random sample of future conditions. Traditional approaches sought to remove variation from the experiment. Taguchi made variation the focus of his experiments, and the goal became ensuring that a process was capable of performing consistently in the presence of expected variation. *Taguchi Methods for Robust Design* by Yuin Wu and Alan Wu (ASME Press, 2000) defines *robustness* as follows:

> ... *the condition used to describe a product or process design that functions with limited variability in spite of diverse and changing environmental conditions, wear, or component-to-component variation. A product or process is robust when it has limited or reduced functional variation even in the presence of noise.*

One of the core concepts of Taguchi Methods is that variance naturally occurs within all processes. *It is not possible to remove all variation from a process.* And although a system or a process may perform perfectly in a tightly controlled environment, maintaining a very high level of control can be cost-prohibitive. Taguchi advocated identifying the normal causes of variation within a process, and designing the process to be able to perform well in the presence of the expected variation.

Uncontrollable variables are referred to as *noise factors*. There are three types of noise factors, and they are usually explained in manufacturing or product design terms. However, these types can be easily associated to the "uncontrollable" variables that affect database systems:

External causes: Users or operators, any system issue external to the database

Internal causes: Data growth or changes to code within the database

Component-to-component factors: System resource contention or systemwide changes that affect more than the intended process

Given a large enough budget, building a system capable of withstanding all possible variants would be easy, but Taguchi had another important concept: the quality loss function. The goal is to balance the cost and effectiveness of the solution to an optimal state. We need to optimize performance without overspending on the solution, because overspending is just a different kind of inefficiency.

The goal of Robust Design is to create a product or process that is capable of consistently meeting its targeted goals within a cost-effective solution. The goal of robust performance is then a database system that consistently meets performance requirements while minimizing the total cost to do so. When determining *total cost*, it is critical to include all factors of the cost: hardware, software, design, implementation, and ongoing system maintenance. Too often, IT projects are overly focused on the development and implementation phases, without giving proper attention to designing the system to minimize ongoing support. Failing to plan for and minimize maintenance requirements can end up costing far more than expected: a small optimization deemed "too expensive" in the design phase may have reduced unplanned and unbudgeted support efforts over the life of the product. It is likely that the resulting support efforts are hundreds or thousands of times more costly than a timely optimization would have been. In an internal IT shop, excessive support requirements translate to having to devote too many hours to emergency calls and repairs. When building products for external customers, a difficult-to-maintain product translates to unhappy customers and reduced sales. In both cases, the end result is a much lower return on the initial investment. Robust Design and performance aims to avoid this undesirable ending by achieving a thorough understanding of system capability and making changes in the design or development phases to reduce future performance issues, support problems, and maintenance costs.

Designing an Experiment

Now let's review the analysis of another database with a variable performance problem, and in this case, we'll see how the concept of testing the impact of expected variation and measuring the results produces a more consistently performing system. This database is built for customers and installed at a large number of remote, unrelated sites. Each database collects between 15 and 25 million records per day, and each record represents strings of data values captured at subsecond intervals. Every night a series of summarization processes is executed via cron, producing views of trend-type data in charts and graphs. Summaries are calculated in 60-second intervals, and higher-level summaries are generated at daily, weekly, and monthly intervals.

The product is sold with an embedded license, meaning that the end customer is not licensed to access the database directly. Therefore, the systems are expected to be extremely low maintenance, and any emergency support is provided by the vendor's support team. There is no access to receive alerts or to monitor the database status. If a problem is reported, a VPN tunnel is opened for a brief window to permit troubleshooting and repair efforts. After the problem has been resolved, the tunnel is closed and the system is again expected to complete all processing without human intervention.

This system does have one thing in common with the data warehouse: nightly summaries need to complete within a specified window. Otherwise, customers will be unable to review the summary reports the next morning as expected. Plus, total application performance is severely impacted while the summaries are executing.

The product had been developed several years earlier and was originally deployed on Oracle 9.2. Because the existing version had some known performance issues and many of the customers needed the application to scale to larger amounts of data, it was time to replace the product with a new version using Oracle 10g. However, before the new product could be approved for distribution, it was necessary to confirm that several issues had been resolved in the new release. The prior version had experienced problems with the optimizer choosing an inappropriate execution plan for some of the summarizations depending on the quantity and the cardinality of the data collected for a given day. The problem had been managed in the existing product by using hints when it became apparent that a specific bit of code or a specific site needed a different execution plan than the one selected by the optimizer, but customizing the code on an as-needed basis was not a cost-effective solution. Nor would it make the customer happy if the product had to fail in order to be optimized.

Although there were multiple changes in the new product to test and verify, the primary goals of performance testing were as follows:

- Verify that the known optimizer issue had been resolved.

- Confirm that summarization processes would complete within a set time frame in spite of wide ranges of data quantities.

- Ensure that no new issues reduced the predictability of summary completion times.

- Verify expected performance improvements resulting from code changes.

Using Instrumentation

Part of the challenge in managing these sites was that problems were seldom reported when they were actually occurring. It could be several weeks before some problems were noticed, and if the performance had been gradually degrading, it was possible that the source of the degradation had begun months earlier. Although it was possible to determine how long a process took to execute by reading application logs, there was no way to quickly locate a problem or capture a trend specifically in summarization processing. The longer it had been since a performance problem began, the more difficult it was to determine the factors responsible for the decline. Statspack data was collected regularly but kept for only a 30-day period. The limitations of connecting over unique customer VPN tunnels meant that Enterprise Manager or other GUI administration tools were difficult to use or completely unavailable.

To improve the visibility of summary performance, the individual processes were instrumented with the Instrumentation Library for Oracle (ILO) available on SourceForge.net. The library provides the ability to correctly and easily enable 10046 tracing on an as-needed basis. The ILO procedures were altered to record the start and stop time for each instrumented process in an elapsed time table. This was done by making a call to DBMS_UTILITY.get_time at both the beginning and the end of the task. In 10g, it is possible to record the elapsed CPU time by using DBMS_UTILITY.get_cpu_time in the same manner. The resulting table included the following data values for every execution of an instrumented process:

ILO module: Name of the summarization process

ILO action: Calendar day of the dataset being processed

Start time: Execution recorded start timestamp

End time: Execution recorded end timestamp

Go time: DBMS_UTILITY.get_time (at start)

Stop time: DBMS_UTILITY.get_time (at stop)

Elapsed time: Stop time–go time

CPU go time: DBMS_UTILITY.get_cputime (at start)

CPU stop time: DBMS_UTILITY.get_cputime (at stop)

CPU elapsed time: CPU stop time–CPU go time

The elapsed time table is quite small yet provides an enormous value, making it possible to see at a glance the performance history of the entire summarization process, an individual process, or the details for a specific day. Simple reports using the analytical functions for mean, median, variance, and standard deviation are now part of each deliverable code set so trends in elapsed time and variance can be evaluated. If a performance problem is reported, the performance table can be referenced and compared to the Statspack data for a specific time frame to check for resource contention at the time that performance began to degrade. Storing the calendar date of the dataset being summarized makes it possible to compare trends in performance against the data growth by date or location.

■ **Note** CPU times are available in only Oracle 10g and higher.

Adding the instrumentation and timing data was even more beneficial to the development and test efforts. It was now possible to create an inexpensive performance test bed that could be used to test and verify the impact of a specific change. Using the concepts advocated by Taguchi, specific, targeted changes were made one at a time and tested against six different datasets of varying sizes, making it possible to provide a definitive answer for each of the performance goals that needed to be met prior to releasing the new version.

The tests completed for this exercise included the following comparisons:

- Measured performance on the 9.2 version, comparing results on the current and planned hardware platform.

- Confirmed that the known performance issues could be replicated with the test dataset.

- Confirmed that hardware alone did not significantly improve performance.

- Measured performance for the 10.2 version on both the current and planned hardware platform.

- Confirmed that the known performance issues were resolved by the upgrade and planned application changes.

- Confirmed that the minor improvements seen using the 9.2 version on the new hardware platform were also present with the 10.2 version.

- Measured performance with and without subpartitions in the summarization tables. Subpartitioning was expected to be beneficial for the application interface, but had the potential to slow the actual summarization process.

- Confirmed that any increase in elapsed time or variance for individual summarizations was negligible on the total processing time.

The end result of the testing process was that the new version was confirmed to perform significantly better than the existing version on either hardware platform, and no new issues were identified. The test process also provided more-complete system capacity and capability information than had been available in the past. Based on the levels of I/O usage noted during testing, it was clear that while the new hardware would support the current expectations for the number of records to be processed per day, any plans to increase the target would require an improved disk configuration to prevent I/O saturation. Having this information in advance is crucial, because altering the hardware configuration on the bill of material (BOM) for products shipped to customers creates long delays in release dates.

Measuring the Results

Instrumenting the code and using the instrumentation to collect the test data made it possible to build a low-maintenance test bed for repeatable testing under changing conditions. Depending on the system requirements, the test bed could be reset by truncating the tables that were populated by the test. In more-complex schemas, it is faster to use restore points to flash back to the test start point. The ability to repeat a test quickly under changing conditions is invaluable when you need to know that performance will be consistent and stable. The ILO_COMMENT field is used to label the results from a specific set, making it possible to build a report displaying all tests executed on that configuration and identify the combinations that performed best.

Some of the components of the instrumentations are shown next. A complete package is available for download from this book's catalog page on the Apress website (www.apress.com).

To create the elapsed time table, execute the following:

```
create table elapsed_time (
    id                  number          not null,
    spid                varchar2(12)    not null,
    ilo_module          varchar2(200)   not null,
    ilo_action          varchar2(200)   not null,
    ilo_client_id       varchar2(200),
    ilo_comment         varchar2(2000),
    start_time          timestamp,
    end_time            timestamp,
    go_time             number,
    stop_time           number,
    elapsed_time        number,
    go_cputime          number,
    stop_cputime        number,
    elapsed_cputime     number,
    error_num           number,
    parent_id           number,
    instance            varchar2(200),
    db_user             varchar2(200)
constraint elapsed_time_pk primary key (id));
```

Then make some modifications to the ILO timer code to record elapsed time:

```
-- first we need to make sure that the task being ended has a sequence assigned.
   if p_stack_rec.sequence is not null then
      -- get the start times that were set in begin_timed_task. delete when done.
      v_start_time      := g_start_time_info(p_stack_rec.sequence).start_time;
      v_go_time         := g_start_time_info(p_stack_rec.sequence).go_time;
      v_go_cputime      := g_start_time_info(p_stack_rec.sequence).go_cputime;
      g_start_time_info.delete(p_stack_rec.sequence);

      -- set the end time and prep for et calc
      v_end_time        := nvl(p_end_time, current_timestamp);
      v_stop_time       := dbms_utility.get_time;
      v_stop_cputime    := dbms_utility.get_cpu_time;
      v_elapsed_time    := ((mod (v_stop_time - v_go_time + power (2, 32),
                            power (2, 32)))/100);
      v_elapsed_cputime := ((mod (v_stop_cputime - v_go_cputime + power (2, 32),
                            power (2, 32)))/100);

      -- now lets insert into elapsed_time the values passed to us
      v_curr_rec := g_elapsed_time.count;
      g_elapsed_time(v_curr_rec).id := p_stack_rec.sequence;
      g_elapsed_time(v_curr_rec).spid := v_spid;
      g_elapsed_time(v_curr_rec).ilo_module := p_stack_rec.module;
      g_elapsed_time(v_curr_rec).ilo_action := p_stack_rec.action;
      g_elapsed_time(v_curr_rec).ilo_client_id := p_stack_rec.client_id;
      g_elapsed_time(v_curr_rec).ilo_comment := p_stack_rec.comment;
      g_elapsed_time(v_curr_rec).start_time := v_start_time;
      g_elapsed_time(v_curr_rec).end_time := v_end_time;
      g_elapsed_time(v_curr_rec).go_time := v_go_time;
      g_elapsed_time(v_curr_rec).stop_time := v_stop_time;
      g_elapsed_time(v_curr_rec).elapsed_time := v_elapsed_time;
      g_elapsed_time(v_curr_rec).go_cputime := v_go_cputime;
      g_elapsed_time(v_curr_rec).stop_cputime := v_stop_cputime;
      g_elapsed_time(v_curr_rec).elapsed_cputime := v_elapsed_cputime;
      g_elapsed_time(v_curr_rec).error_num := p_error_num;
      g_elapsed_time(v_curr_rec).parent_id := v_parent_id;
      g_elapsed_time(v_curr_rec).instance := v_instance;
      g_elapsed_time(v_curr_rec).db_user := v_db_user;
   end if;
```

Finally, you can summarize and report on the statistics:

```
select ilo_module,
       count(ilo_module)                              count,
       avg(elapsed_time)                              average,
       variance(elapsed_time)                         variance,
       round(variance(elapsed_time)/avg(elapsed_time),3)  vmr,
       round(stddev(elapsed_time)/avg(elapsed_time),3)    cov,
       avg(elapsed_cputime)                           cpu_average,
       variance(elapsed_cputime)                      cpu_variance,
```

```
        round(variance(elapsed_cputime)/avg(elapsed_time),3) cpu_vmr,
        round(stddev(elapsed_cputime)/avg(elapsed_time),3)    cpu_cov
  from elapsed_time
 group by ilo_module
 order by &ORDER_BY ;
```

Following are the pre-optimization results from six executions run on Oracle Database 9.2.0.6, each having a distinct dataset:

ILO_MODULE	AVERAGE	VARIANCE	VMR
Process 1	810.638	17036.220	21.016
Process 3	4109.603	4755461.770	1157.158
Process 4	12.005	195.974	16.324
Process 5	11.365	606.863	53.398
Process 6	4.498	86.205	19.164
Process 7	4.822	.815	.169
Process 8	16.778	15.266	.910
Process 9	88.532	1740.610	19.661
Process 10	15.607	4.312	.276
Process 11	60.815	63.733	1.048
Process 12	266.472	15910.780	59.709

And next are the post-optimization results on Oracle Database 10.2.0.4, also from six executions with distinct datasets:

ILO_MODULE	AVERAGE	VARIANCE	VMR	CPU_AVERAGE	CPU_VARIANCE	CPU_VMR
Process 1	220.563	851.481	3.860	47.237	47.337	.215
Process 3	124.693	783.041	6.280	93.632	504.290	4.044
Process 4	184.803	15476.636	83.747	184.578	15483.162	83.782
Process 5	79.745	1290.146	16.178	79.608	1289.177	16.166

Process 6	54.787	330.729	6.037	54.613	331.418	6.049
Process 7	2.792	2.046	.733	.038	0	0
Process 8	11.242	1.896	.169	.053	0	0
Process 9	88.833	1824.274	20.536	.047	0	0
Process 10	8.472	2.759	.326	.123	0	0
Process 11	30.752	32.355	1.052	.155	0	0
Process 12	152.943	5006.197	32.732	.222	.002	0

Finally, here are some results from an acceptably performing site after six months with four times more data:

ILO_MODULE	AVERAGE	VARIANCE	VMR	CPU_AVERAGE	CPU_VARIANCE	CPU_VMR
Process 1	3315.780	952321.352	287.209	371.028	59289.236	17.881
Process 2	497.045	33686.979	67.774	61.018	438.116	.881
Process 3	398.326	45203.021	113.482	9.755	26.669	.067
Process 4	35.636	162.640	4.564	1.009	.074	.002
Process 5	7.953	15.712	1.975	.656	.016	.002
Process 6	3.672	2.037	.555	.560	.007	.002
Process 7	1472.876	369669.824	250.985	.932	.045	0
Process 8	1723.979	411119.582	238.471	1.037	.006	0
Process 9	1894.774	525779.733	277.489	1.068	.009	0

Some processes were not available on specific analysis sets or site locations. Those process numbers are missing from the examples. However, the processes are consistently labeled to allow for comparison across datasets—that is, process 1 is the same code in all datasets.

Tolerance Ranges and Process Capability

After you have optimized your code and measured performance, you have specific information that tells you how long processes can be expected to run in the future. As Taguchi says, all systems are subject to uncontrolled variation, and this is especially true of a database system with a huge number of individual, intertwined components. Keeping this thought in mind, you would not expect a process to complete in the exact same amount of time every time, but you can set a tolerance range to assist in identifying processes that exceed a reasonable amount of variation. The precision you need for this exercise depends on the criticality of performance for a specific system and system resource limitations.

Let me share an example to illustrate the point. In both test cases referenced in this chapter, there is an acceptable window for the completion of nightly processes. For the instrumented test case, once the set of nightly processes had been optimized, the total nightly processing time took less than one-third of the allowed window when measured with the initial test dataset. A dataset with more than twice as many records as the original test data completed in less than half of the available window. Continued testing on increasingly larger datasets would have provided the definitive answer to our data-scaling questions; however, as frequently happens in development, there was not enough time to execute additional tests.

Although it's clear that processing more data requires more time, note that the time increase did not increase at the same rate as the data. Doubling the data resulted in an approximately 15 percent increase in processing times, not twice the processing time. If a customer location could be expected to process up to four times the data as used in testing, we can estimate an expected processing window by calculating a growth factor and adding in the longest completion time. If you store the maximum acceptable completion times in a table by process name, this creates a recorded upper limit that can be used to trigger an investigation by the database team. Depending on service-level requirements, it may be appropriate to send alerts when tolerances are exceeded. If alerts are not possible or service levels don't require that level of response, you can opt to use reporting to keep an eye on performance trends or problems that occur. In our case, alerts are not feasible, but the reports do provide information needed to track trends in performance.

The other limitation to keep in mind is the available system resources. If any of the required resources are approaching saturation, elapsed time will increase exponentially if you exceed that point. It would be wise to make your tolerances much more conservative as resources become more limited.

■ **Note** If you attempt to set tolerance limits without optimizing the code first, you will accomplish nothing. Basing upper limits on the unoptimized numbers will result in all executions appearing to complete within an acceptable tolerance range. The reports will say the system performs well, but your users will say otherwise.

In manufacturing and quality control, process capability is measured against a known part specification. Each part or sampled part is measured to ensure that critical characteristics fall within an acceptable range of variability. It would be possible to measure every part and throw away those that didn't meet specifications, but that would be a very expensive and wasteful approach. Instead, the goal of process capability is to ensure that the process will produce results consistently within the acceptable range. After it is known that the process is capable of meeting requirements, it is necessary to measure only enough samples to ensure that variance is not increasing and that quality is not drifting off target. Of course, database processes don't come with specifications, and even if they did, processing times that are unacceptable in one company's PeopleSoft system could be perfectly fine at another company. This means that it's up to the system architects and administrators to determine the service-level requirements and design a system that is capable of meeting them. It takes time and effort, but it's much more interesting work than responding to trouble tickets reporting problems after the fact.

What is "Too Much" Variation?

Never assign too much importance to a specific number, or even a range of numbers. Although in statistics the index of dispersion indicates that a dataset may be overdispersed if the ratio is higher than 1, no specific value of this index would be an appropriate target for all database systems. As you can see from the results for the acceptably performing site on page 465 it is possible to have much higher VMR values and still be well within your targeted performance level.

The goal in this analysis is not to achieve a certain number or to eliminate all variation. The goal is to obtain as much knowledge as possible of the system's capability and the potential influences of applicable noise factors: the variables that you have identified as most likely to impact your system. The earlier you can gather this information, the easier and more cost-effective it will be to plan your design and implementation appropriately. If your system is already in production but failing to meet performance targets, analyzing for variance can help you identify your best targets for measurement and improvement. If you know which processes have the highest VMR value, you know which processes are most likely to extend their runtime and create resource bottlenecks. If you know that elapsed time or variance values have increased inexplicably for some processes, you know to investigate and determine why. If you can confirm that the system is performing as expected right now, but additional growth is expected, you know it's time to revisit capacity planning efforts and determine whether additional optimizations in code or hardware will be needed to meet the new requirements. In the words of Cary Millsap, "Why guess when you can know?"

When using variance in the design phase, its best application is in identifying the architecture that will be the most stable and predictable for your expected conditions. When using variance to monitor a production system, think of it as a barometer of the conditions in and around your system. Sudden or extreme changes could indicate that trouble is brewing, but minor fluctuations are perfectly normal.

Measuring Variance Within Oracle Sample Sets

One of the questions I am asked most frequently after presentations is about using the Oracle sampled data for this type of analysis. Statspack, ASH, and AWR all contain a wealth of information about system performance, without anyone having to expend the effort to instrument the code. My first response is that I find the instrumentation effort to be extremely valuable because it allows you full control of what you choose to instrument, what you choose to measure, and how often you want to collect the samples. The end result is both a tool to identify problems in production and a test bed designed specifically for your needs—something you can't get from the sampled data or aggregated results collected by the Oracle tools.

Sampling from Samples

However, the primary reason that I caution people about performing analytic functions such as average, variance, or standard deviation on Oracle samples is that sampling from a sample set increases the standard error in your results: to put it plainly, you have a greater chance of analyzing a dataset that is not representative of the total population.

Think about a national poll. It collects a sample that is ideally a subsection of a specific population, because the goal is to choose a random sample that is representative of a category of individuals. However, anytime you sample a population, there is the chance that your sample may not be representative of the group you think it is. Careful planning is needed to make sure that you collect the information in an unbiased approach that will not slant your results.

In the 2008 U.S. elections, early polls showed that the conservative ticket had a strong lead, but a few months into the election season, someone realized the polls were being conducted over landline telephones. Younger voters tend to use cell phones, and an increasing number of people no longer have a hardwired phone at all. This mea culpa resulted in older voters being disproportionately represented in the early polls, and older voters tend to be conservative. As polls increased the calls to cell phone users, the statistics showed a very different result. However, even without oversights such as this, it's always possible to miss the target when collecting a sample. This isn't a reason to stop using the information, but it is critical to remain aware of any potential bias in the data you've collected.

Whenever you sample a sample, the odds of misleading results increase. This is also true of Oracle samples. For example, ASH data is sampled at a rate to prevent introducing a bias into the data. However, if you were to take a subsequent sample of the data and use that as your data source, the results you derived from your analysis would be more subject to error. Of course, it's not always possible to measure everything you want to analyze; that's why we need statistics in the first place. Just remember that the further removed you are from the population, the more you need to question and possibly retest to confirm your results. If you understand the intricacies of a specific system and the types of processes within it, you will be better equipped to recognize a good sample, or a bad one. Unfortunately, tools are usually needed to assist in finding problems in the systems we *don't* know. In those cases, stick with using the Oracle tools and performance data as Oracle intended them to be used and see if you can find another source for elapsed time data. Also, keep in mind that even if you find an algorithm that is working well for you on one system, the properties of the samples on a different system may not give you the same results.

■ **Note** Oddly enough, one place where the rules about sampling sample data are not followed is in the Poll of Polls during the U.S. elections. I can think of no other time that results are gathered and combined from multiple statistical studies and the standard error values of the individual studies cancel each other out to result in a standard error of 0 for the combined analysis.

Summary

Optimization requires knowledge about all of the components within a system: the software, the hardware, the application, and the data. It's also important to understand how the application is used. By understanding all of the pieces and how they work together and impact each other, you are able to design solutions that perform efficiently. When the right balance of system resources and code come together, processes perform faster *and* more consistently. When systems perform inconsistently, it is an indicator that something within the system is out of balance. These indicators are the red rocks we need to find, measure, and optimize if we want to achieve our goal of robust performance.

It requires knowledge of the system to design an effective test-and-measure approach, and at the same time, by measuring the system, we also gain more knowledge. By extending the effort to measure, we learn the reality of how the system functions. We get the opportunity to test our assumptions (maybe I should say *hypothesis*) about the performance of the database. Administering a database based on assumptions is a very precarious position because the system is bound to prove you wrong before too long.

To achieve robust performance, you need to seek the solution that performs best in the presence of the variation you are likely to see within your system. The specific cause of variance, or noise, will depend on the type of application and its usage. After you've identified the kinds of variance that are likely to occur, measure and benchmark the system under the influence of different levels of those variables. This process will show you the capability of the system: where it functions well and where it will break. Use this information to plan resource requirements and consider setting performance thresholds based on what you learn from your testing. Even if such thresholds aren't required by the business, you can learn even more by reviewing the system as it approaches these thresholds or stress levels. Sometimes you'll even discover a new red rock to optimize. Optimizing these random processes extends system capacity by preventing bottlenecks and resource saturation. Increasing the consistency of processing time can lead to more satisfied users and fewer problem reports. Variance does affect system performance: it is measurable and it cannot be eliminated, but you can minimize variance and you can design a database to perform well in spite of it.

CHAPTER 14

User Security

by Pete Finnigan

Protecting access to database user accounts is one of the most important aspects of securing data in an Oracle database. Unfortunately, the security landscape has not changed drastically in the ten years or so I have looked into the security of Oracle databases. Back in the early days, when no one really did much to secure their databases at all, there were obvious issues with weak user account design, privileges, and easy access to those accounts. For example, a database supporting an application may have had a schema owner who had DBA privileges or indeed completely excessive privileges.

In recent times, the excessive privilege problems have subsided quite a bit in respect to third-party applications, but the problems of easy unauthorized access to accounts have not. In addition, although it is true that the problems of excessive privileges are better and perhaps less targeted, the problems are still there.

In an Oracle database, usually lots of types of user accounts are created. The efforts by researchers and by Oracle over recent years seem to have focused more on the schema accounts. These accounts hold application objects. The database isn't just full of schema accounts, though; there are lots of other types of accounts, including normal business users, reporting users, batch users, power users, database administrators, and feed users, to name but a few. The list of user types is large, and as I have seen over the years, the focus on improving security is often not consistent.

There are still databases with all types of users having excessive privileges or having weak passwords, but there are also more subtle user security problems that must be understood and corrected. Security issues may arise, for example, when real people (users) share database accounts. Problems may also occur when database accounts are shared across multiple applications or administrative tasks or purposes. A final example is accounts in the database that are actually unused or unnecessary.

An even deeper level of subtlety with user security is that so-called obvious fixes such as the simple locking of an account don't actually work. If the account also has objects in the database, perhaps business logic, or perhaps functionality added for monitoring or administrative purposes, this functionality is potentially still available even if the account is locked. This subtle user security problem is amplified the most in relation to Oracle-installed accounts. These are the default accounts or the accounts provided to support functionality available within the database that are installed by Oracle when you install the software and build the database. Locking these accounts presents the same problem; in fact, the problem is made worse if security bugs are found in software supported by these schemas and exploits are released on public websites. Just having these accounts installed in your database effectively makes you vulnerable to the published exploits.

Almost always, the only fix available is to apply a Critical Patch Update (CPU). The area of CPUs is often seen as a minefield when any discussion starts on the subject of Oracle security. Really the answer to CPUs is very simple: either you apply the patch or you don't. In real terms, this is far more complicated, because in the world of databases there are often hundreds or thousands of databases that must be maintained and also protected. Applying a CPU is a major undertaking and costly when you consider testing the security fix, regression testing the application, and even deciding which databases must be patched. That's as far as the discussion of CPUs is going to go in this chapter and the next. This chapter focuses on the issues around user security; logically if an account is not installed, then even if a security bug is found in functionality provided by that schema, your database is not vulnerable to that issue—simple!

One final area of consideration is that the problem of securing user accounts within the database is not just technical; it is also a process- or policy-driven problem. If a company allows its users to share accounts within the database or to create database accounts for multiple purposes or, even worse, to not even create a database account for a business purpose but then simply use a built-in account, then the problem is procedurally related. Processes must be put in place to prevent procedural security problems that are related to technical user security types of problems.

Securing User Accounts

Providing security of user accounts should be one of the first steps taken in securing a database. Whether a database is brand new or it already exists, the tasks involved to secure the data are very similar. The only advantage available with securing a new database is that it is much simpler not to install software or user accounts or default schemas at the time of database installation, rather than trying to investigate and eradicate these surplus accounts at a later date when securing an existing database.

Before you investigate user security in your own database, I will first summarize the tasks and process involved. I will then go into much more detail in later sections of this chapter to enable you to review and potentially eradicate security issues from your database. The areas I'm going to discuss are as follows:

> **User enumeration:** Before attempting to secure users in the database, you must understand what accounts are actually installed, what the installed accounts are used for, and possibly who uses the accounts. It is a pointless exercise to correct problems with any particular database account if the answer is that the account should be just deleted. Therefore, first you must assess all the accounts within the database and understand their uses. Further, you must identify whether some of the accounts can be deleted, and some or all of each account's privileges removed, locked, or audited.

> **Feature analysis:** Closely related to user enumeration is the problem of feature analysis. Features installed in the database are often supported by default schemas. Assessing the features installed in the database against the requirements of the application is an important step. You must identify features that are not required so schemas can be removed that support these features.

> **Reduction of accounts:** The final step of the analysis phase is to remove accounts that are unnecessary for support and use of the application.

> **Account password strength:** All the accounts installed within the database must have strong passwords. Later in this chapter, you will analyze the current strength of your user account passwords and start to investigate the steps necessary to secure those remaining accounts within the database.

Roles and privilege assessment: Every account that remains in the database (either created by Oracle to support a built-in feature or function, or created by you to support the application) will have some level of privilege assigned to it. You will assess the privileges assigned to each user account in order to reduce those assigned privileges.

Password management: Making account authentication strong is an important task but is also a problem of subtlety. It is important that you prevent weak authentication from being re-implemented. Later in this chapter, you will decide on suitable password management settings to implement in your database.

Audit settings: In a very similar vein to password management, it is just as important to know what is going on with user accounts as it is to prevent security issues with user accounts from going on in the first place. Later in this chapter, you will assess current audit settings in relation to user accounts and develop suitable audit settings.

Assessing user account security is unfortunately not a trivial task because of the complex relationships between the purposes of a user account and who has access to the same user account, and the privileges assigned to that user account. The following sections present in more detail each of the areas I have just discussed.

User Enumeration

Enumerating the users within the database must be the first step in the process toward securing all the user accounts in the database. There is always an underlying tenet in database security, and that tenet is *reduction*. This security idea manifests itself in many forms, but the process toward a solution is always similar, and the intended result is always the same. Reduction is the sensible first step in any security project. If the database system—and in particular, the security configuration of the database—is simpler, then *modifying and hardening the database also has to be simpler*, because there is less to do to achieve security of users and to identify the tasks that need to be done.

This is a great effect of security: most of what security practitioners do is simple, and if we simplify the system, achieving a secure database has to become easier to understand and do. The added benefit with simplification actions is that the so-called *attack surface* is reduced. If you remove, in this case user accounts, you also remove the chance of attack against particular user accounts. Reduction in this scenario is in the first instance removing accounts that are not necessary for the successful operation and maintenance of the application. Drilling further into the process, the next logical stage after removing unnecessary database accounts is to remove unnecessary privileges from the database accounts that remain. There are further steps in terms of reduction that can be taken as part of database security (for instance, reducing data quotas per individual users), but these are not covered here because of space restrictions.

■ **Note** The *attack surface* is a term used in security circles that refers to the amount of threat you are under because of circumstances. In simple terms, imagine that you install a certain component in the database—this could be intelligent agent software or the external procedures feature or indeed any component. Now imagine that some mischievous person finds a security bug in one of these features and then publishes an exploit for the security bug that perhaps allows someone to escalate their privileges in the database to an administrator level. If you had not installed that specific feature, you would not be vulnerable to the published exploit. By installing the feature in the first place, you *increased the attack surface*. By uninstalling the same feature, you would *reduce the attack surface*. Security should be about reducing the attack surface.

Splitting the Task in Two

The first step in assessing users within the database is to split the task of user enumeration by defining two groups. These can be summarized as follows:

> **Oracle-installed users:** These are the users, schemas, and default schemas that Oracle creates as part of the database installation or as a subsequent upgrade or addition of a database feature. These Oracle-installed users would include accounts such as SYSTEM or SYS, which are core users. Oracle-installed accounts would also include users such as DBSNMP, which is required only if you are using the intelligent agent as part of Enterprise Manager. Then there are default example accounts such as the ubiquitous SCOTT, or IX, SH, and others.

> **Customer-installed users:** These are the user accounts that you have installed to support your application schemas, to provide additional functionality, to allow users or power users access to the database, for administration, or indeed lots of other uses that have been thought of in your organization that have resulted in the creation of database user accounts.

The next step is for you to understand which accounts you have created so you can split all installed accounts into these two groups. This grouping activity should be a fairly simple task, but the problem is that the Oracle database has an inordinate number of default accounts and roles that could have been installed at some point in any database. Oracle hosts a list of default accounts within the 11g database that includes some 600 default passwords; there is also a similar list of about 600 default accounts and passwords on my website. (This URL details the Oracle default password list in multiple forms: www.petefinnigan.com/default/default_password_list.htm.) There is a crossover between my published list and Oracle's that creates a list of almost 900 unique default accounts. In reality, most Oracle database systems are likely to have quite a small number of default accounts installed, usually a maximum of around 30 if the database started as a seed database.

This situation with default accounts leads to choices: should you be very thorough and attempt to locate every possible built-in account in your database (in this case, that could be some of the 900 or so accounts mentioned in the preceding paragraph) or should you take a high-level view and look for the more common default accounts? Fortunately, Oracle 11g is easier to analyze than earlier versions because it has a system table that lists the 600 accounts. This means that you can write SQL against this table to locate which accounts are defaults. Writing such a query is a good first step because this SQL accesses a bigger list of default accounts without having to type that big list in, and the SQL also includes the small, more-realistic list because that is part of the bigger list. The downside is that this table is not installed in the earlier versions of the database.

For this example, you will start with an 11g list because that's easier. The first step is to try to assess whether the DBA_USERS_WITH_DEFPWD view and its underlying system table are suitable. Listing 14-1 shows a query returning the definition of the DBA_USERS_WITH_DEFPWD view. It is that view that lists all of the default accounts known to Oracle.

Listing 14-1. Code to Show Where the Default User List Is Stored in Oracle 11g

```
SQL> select text from dba_views
  2  where view_name='DBA_USERS_WITH_DEFPWD';

TEXT
--------------------------------------------------
SELECT DISTINCT u.name
    FROM SYS.user$ u, SYS.default_pwd$ dp
   WHERE
     (u.type#  = 1
      AND bitand(u.astatus, 16) = 16
     ) OR
     (u.type#     = 1
      AND u.password = dp.pwd_verifier
      AND u.name     = dp.user_name
      AND dp.pv_type = 0)


SQL>
```

Great, the output shown in Listing 14-1 is ideal for identifying default accounts installed in your own database. If the DBA_USERS_WITH_DEFPWD view is not available because of permissions, log in as a database user for this query that has the SELECT ANY DICTIONARY system privilege. If on the other hand the view does not exist, please see the queries in Listings 14-3 and 14-4, in the next section.

The view itself is not suitable for locating installed default accounts because it shows only users who still have their password set to the default value. The underlying base table (SYS.DEFAULT_PWD$) is ideal for locating installed default accounts in your database because it includes a correlation between username and default password hash. In this case, the default password is not required, but this is a really useful list of default usernames. Listing 14-2 shows a SQL statement to identify default users within the database; quite clearly by default it also identifies accounts created by the customer.

Listing 14-2. SQL Code to Identify Built-in Users

```
SQL> col username for a30
SQL> col user_name for a30
SQL> select distinct u.username,nvl(d.user_name,'---') user_name
  2  from dba_users u,sys.default_pwd$ d
  3  where u.username=d.user_name(+)
  4  /

USERNAME                        USER_NAME
------------------------------  ------------------------------
DBSNMP                          DBSNMP
FLOWS_030000                    FLOWS_030000
MDSYS                           MDSYS
SYS                             SYS
SYSTEM                          SYSTEM
TSMSYS                          TSMSYS
WMSYS                           WMSYS
```

471

```
BB4                        ---
IMPORTER                   ---
ERIC                       ---
CC_GRANTABLE               ---
A2                         ---
TESTPWD                    ---
BI                         BI
DIP                        DIP
BILL                       ---
EMIL                       ---
AMIS                       ---
{output removed for space conservation}
RES_TEST                   ---
XX                         ---
A                          ---
BB2                        ---
AB                         ---
EVILUSER                   ---

85 rows selected.

SQL>
```

The output in Listing 14-2 shows default accounts that are still installed in this database and also the accounts installed by the customer. The customer accounts are identified by --- instead of using the account username for Oracle-installed accounts. For instance, in the preceding example output, the user EMIL was installed at the customer, and the user DIP was installed by Oracle.

Dealing with Oracle Database 10g and Prior

Listing 14-2's query works fine for Oracle Database 11g, but for 10g and lower the SQL in that listing will not work. There are a number of possible ways forward. To achieve the same level of checking as with 11g, you would have to install the 11g table into your 10g or lower database, or include the complete list of default accounts in the WHERE clause of your SQL, or alternately to include the list in a PL/SQL script. In the world of security—not just Oracle security—it is always the better option to *not* modify the system that is being checked because this could introduce new security issues. In this particular case, that means do not install a table of default users simply to perform security tests. In general, the tests described here should be performed against a single, suitably chosen production database. The purpose of the tests described in this chapter and the next is to establish a suitable security policy that can be applied to all the databases in an organization. In most organizations, there are often tens or hundreds or even thousands of databases, so considering any check that would involve installing data is not only bad practice, it is also time-consuming and expensive.

Back to the important task at hand, which is to find an easy way to split the users in your 10g and lower-version database into two groups. If an 11g database is available (and it should always be available, as Oracle kindly allows anyone to download and install the database software), the PL/SQL shown in Listing 14-3 can be executed to generate a nice SQL query that you can run in your 10g and lower database to generate a SQL script to test for installed default users in another database.

Listing 14-3. Code to Generate a SQL Query to Split Users into Groups

```
SQL> get split_use_derive.sql
  1  set feed off
  2  spool split_use_derive_output.sql
  3  declare
  4     lv_first boolean:=true;
  5     lv_second boolean:=true;
  6     cursor c_main is
  7     select distinct user_name
  8     from sys.default_pwd$;
  9  begin
 10     dbms_output.put_line('select username,''BIN'' from dba_users');
 11     dbms_output.put_line('where username in (');
 12     for lv_main in c_main loop
 13            if(lv_first) then
 14                   dbms_output.put_line(''''||lv_main.user_name||'''');
 15                   lv_first:=false;
 16            else
 17                   dbms_output.put_line(',''''||lv_main.user_name||'''');
 18            end if;
 19     end loop;
 20     dbms_output.put_line(') union ');
 21     dbms_output.put_line('select username,''---'' from dba_users');
 22     dbms_output.put_line('where username not in (');
 23     for lv_main in c_main loop
 24            if(lv_second) then
 25                   dbms_output.put_line(''''||lv_main.user_name||'''');
 26                   lv_second:=false;
 27            else
 28                   dbms_output.put_line(',''''||lv_main.user_name||'''');
 29            end if;
 30     end loop;
 31     dbms_output.put_line(');');
 32  end;
 33  /
 34  spool off
 35* set feed on
 36  .
SQL> @split_use_derive
select username,'BIN' from dba_users
where username in (
'ABA1'
,'ADS'
,'AK'
,'ALA1'
,'ALLUSERS'
,'AMF'
{output removed to conserve space}
,'WMSYS'
,'WSH'
```

```
,'WSM'
);
SQL>
```

You can now take the output from Listing 14-3's query and run it against any 10g or lower database. Example output is shown in Listing 14-4.

Listing 14-4. Running the Derived SQL to Locate Built-in Accounts

```
SQL> @split_use_derive_output.sql

USERNAME                      'BI
----------------------------- ---
A                             ---
A2                            ---
AB                            ---
AMIS                          ---
ANONYMOUS                     BIN
APEX_PUBLIC_USER              BIN
B                             ---
B1                            ---
BB1                           ---
BB10                          ---
BB11                          ---

USERNAME                      'BI
----------------------------- ---
BB2                           ---
BB3                           ---
BB4                           ---
{output removed to conserver space}
SYSMAN                        BIN
SYSTEM                        BIN
TESTPWD                       ---
TSMSYS                        BIN
WKPROXY                       BIN

USERNAME                      'BI
----------------------------- ---
WKSYS                         BIN
WK_TEST                       BIN
WMSYS                         BIN
XDB                           BIN
XMLT                          ---
XS$NULL                       BIN
XX                            ---
ZULIA                         ---

85 rows selected.

SQL>
```

Essentially, Listings 14-3 and 14-4 show how you can use the contents of the Oracle Database 11g's SYS.DEFAULT_PWD$ table in queries against Oracle Database 10g and lower releases. In the preceding example, the user ZULIA is added by the customer. The user WKSYS is added by Oracle.

The first stage of enumerating users is complete; and yes, it is simple. All that is required is to split the users that are installed in the database into two groups: those user accounts installed by Oracle and those installed by you. The next steps will use this list.

■ **Note** The accounts that Oracle installs (such as SYS, SYSTEM, DBSNMP, and many more) should not be modified by the customer—*you*. Doing so may seem like a good security solution, perhaps to remove a set of privileges from an account, but this may break existing functionality because Oracle may use the account either directly or indirectly within some of its other features. In reality, the only thing that is sensible to do to improve security in respect to Oracle-installed accounts is to uninstall them where possible. It is also acceptable to lock these accounts, but in reality the functionality that may be targeted by a hacker is not likely protected by locking because simply logging in to an account is unnecessary to use the functionality provided by that account.

Feature Analysis

One of the biggest problems assessing the accounts installed by Oracle is that it is hard to decide what to keep or remove. More to the point, it is hard to have the confidence to actually remove an account. The problem is that Oracle does not make it easy to discover whether a feature or function is used. If it was simple to isolate all of the Oracle install accounts that are not used, it would be simple to just remove them—but instead you need to take a step-by-step approach.

You will notice in security that often a step-by-step approach is the best. Often a black-and-white yes or no, or true or false, does not exist to answer security questions about accounts. However, it is possible to iterate through a list of accounts and establish with reasonable certainty that one group of items can safely be removed, another group definitely cannot be removed, and a third requires assessment in more depth to see which of the first two groups they may belong to. The best approach for this group of unclassified accounts is to use as much correlated evidence as possible and as little effort as possible. Because the Oracle database software is so large and complex, simple ideas and simple rules should be observed to help you secure it. If you were to analyze every little detail of database security in enormous depth, you might have to set aside many man years of effort. This is clearly not practical, so the 80/20 rule works fine in these cases. You will use most of your effort for closing out as big a chunk of problems as possible.

A PL/SQL script that can be downloaded from www.petefinnigan.com/use.sql is use.sql. This script is too large to show here; its function will be explained shortly, but first Listing 14-5 shows you how to run it. Pass in 0 when prompted.

Listing 14-5. Running the use.sql PL/SQL Script to Assess Built-in Accounts

```
SQL> @use


use.sql: Release 1.0.2.0.0 - Production on Thu Aug 20 21:09:17 2009
```

```
OUTPUT FLAG [A|O|C]                    [A]: O
```

Typ	USER	Rol	RSO	Sys	Ob	Tab	PL
ADM	SYS	49		200	15	881	1405
ADM	SYSTEM	9		5	211	154	5
DEF	OUTLN	1		3	1	3	1
DEF	DIP	0		1	0	0	0
DEF	TSMSYS	1		1	0	1	0
DEF	ORACLE_OC	0		1	2	0	6
DEF	DBSNMP	1		4	2	20	7
DEF	WMSYS	3		29	14	42	52
DEF	EXFSYS	1		9	7	47	71
DEF	CTXSYS	2		7	52	47	139
DEF	XDB	3		10	13	23	68
DEF	ANONYMOUS	0		1	12	0	0
DEF	ORDSYS	1		13	14	68	87
DEF	ORDPLUGIN	0		10	2	0	10
DEF	SI_INFORM	0		1	0	0	0
DEF	MDSYS	2		18	31	110	239
DEF	OLAPSYS	2		13	33	126	89
DEF	MDDATA	2		1	0	0	0
DEF	SPATIAL_W	3		8	0	0	0
DEF	SPATIAL_C	3		8	0	0	0
DEF	WKSYS	7		59	32	56	50
DEF	WKPROXY	0		3	0	0	0
DEF	WK_TEST	2		0	0	13	0
APX	FLOWS_FIL	0		0	6	1	0
APX	APEX_PUBL	0		1	11	0	0
APX	FLOWS_030	3		28	98	213	369
DEF	OWBSYS	10		23	43	0	0
SAM	SCOTT	2		3	1	6	4
SAM	HR	1		7	1	7	2
SAM	OE	2		7	14	10	1
SAM	IX	5		17	11	15	0
SAM	SH	3		12	4	17	0
SAM	PM	2		1	10	2	0
SAM	BI	1		9	23	0	0
ADM	SYSMAN	2		7	20	700	390
DEF	MGMT_VIEW	1		0	4	0	0
DEF	XS$NULL	0		0	0	0	0
Typ	USER	Rol	RSO	Sys	Ob	Tab	PL

```
PL/SQL procedure successfully completed.

SQL>
```

The output shown in Listing 14-5 needs to be explained in terms of what each column of data means. The first column, Typ, defines the type of the user account; SAM means *sample account*, DEF means *default account*, ADM means *admin account*. The Rol column shows how many database roles have been assigned to each user. The RSO column will be explained in a later section as no output is shown in Listing 14-5. The Sys column signifies the number of system privileges granted to each user. The Ob column signifies the number of object privileges granted to each user. The Tab column signifies the number of tables owned by each user. Finally, the PL column signifies the number of PL/SQL functions/procedures or packages owned by each user. All of the numbers displayed in Listing 14-5 are used to help assess what type of account exists. This will be explained further as we discuss the script's output in more detail.

The use program shown in Listing 14-5 is easy to run. It is a SQL*Plus script that accepts a single parameter that controls the output. The single parameter passed to use.sql can be set to O so that only Oracle-installed accounts are shown, or the parameter can be set to C to show customer-installed accounts, or finally it can be set to A to show all accounts in the database. The output in Listing 14-5 tries at a high level to identify some of the accounts and the three groups that they fall into. Remember, the first task is to identify accounts installed by Oracle and split them up further into *can keep, can remove*, or *don't know*.

Accounts That Can Definitely Be Removed

The task to identify accounts to be removed is an iterative process that is going to be different in every database, but you can use the lessons described here and apply them to every database you manage. Basic principles and methodologies are one of the important facets of security. Simply following a security checklist may seem effective, but experience and methods must be applied to the relevant situation at hand. Start by going through Listing 14-5 looking for accounts that are categorically not needed.

If you look at the output in Listing 14-5, the accounts identified as SAM in the first column are sample demonstration accounts that should never have been installed in a production database. However, my own experience has shown these accounts to be installed in many production databases. Sample accounts often appear in production databases because the person who created the database started with a seed database. Sample accounts are the easiest accounts to identify.

The next step is to look for installed accounts that support features of functionality that is definitely not used. There is a further requirement with the class of users that support unwanted features; that is, it is important to understand whether Oracle itself uses a feature even if the application does not. This internal usage factor makes the removal of accounts installed by Oracle difficult to assess because it is unclear what features are used by Oracle itself to support other features.

A walk through the output of the use.sql script in Listing 14-5 shows that there are some obvious candidates for removal. The application using my simple example database is written using PHP, and data is served using an Apache web server. The functionality I require means that the accounts APEX_PUBLIC_USER, FLOWS_030000, and FLOWS_FILES can be removed because APEX is not used by my database. Another good example is the SYSMAN, DBSNMP, and MGMT_VIEW accounts, which are used to support database manager/Oracle Enterprise Manager. My database is not administered using graphical tools, so it is a reasonably safe to remove these three accounts. As a final example, the account DIP is installed by default in my example database. The DIP account is used to synchronize changes in the Oracle Internet Directory (OID) with applications in the database. Because my sample database does not use OID or indeed single sign-on, this account can definitely be removed.

The same methodology can be used in your own database to identify accounts installed by Oracle and providing functionality that is definitely not used. Add accounts that you identify to this *can remove* group for your own database.

Accounts That Definitely Have to Remain in the Database

The second group of accounts to identify are those that must remain. These can be located in a similar manner to the preceding group. Your task is to review the report shown in Listing 14-5 and identify Oracle-installed accounts that provide functionality that definitely *is* used, or provide functionality used by other Oracle features and functions, so cannot be removed. The first accounts that can be added to this group are SYS and SYSTEM. These accounts cannot be removed from the database.

Review the rest of Listing 14-5 and identify functionality that is *not* required. If the functionality is not required, you must also assess whether that functionality stands alone in the database or whether it is used by other built-in features. As I said earlier, this is not easy. If you are not sure at this point, you must place each account you work on into the third group, which will be discussed next. The third group contains the *unknowns*.

The next step after identifying all accounts that can be deleted is to look up security solutions for those accounts that have to remain. If an account must remain in the database, limited actions can be performed to protect that account. Most of the accounts added by Oracle are installed to support functionality. Only a small number of installed accounts are for performing administrative tasks. The SYS and SYSTEM accounts clearly fall into this latter category.

Built-in administration accounts should not be used for day-to-day administration activities because these accounts are designed by Oracle and not by you or your organization. Oracle does not know your processes, practices, or requirements, so the accounts Oracle has provided are not suitable. That said, there are two basic rules to follow with built-in accounts:

- SYSTEM should not be used by your staff for administration. Each of your DBAs should have their own accounts that are designed with privileges suitable for your tasks and processes.

- The SYSTEM account should therefore be locked and not used. Your DBAs will use their own database accounts.

What should you design into your own DBA accounts? Well, each DBA account should be designed for day-to-day work, so the privileges added should suit the daily tasks at hand. The design task should not create a massive list of privileges but should include limited privileges for day-to-day tasks. Each DBA should have their own database user for accountability. Having each DBA have their own account implies that auditing must also be enabled; it must be. Auditing should be enabled for capturing connections to the database and also for the use of system privileges (all system privileges). One useful aspect of auditing system privilege use is that the audit trail can be used to help design your DBA roles. Turn on audit for a month or so and establish a list of core privileges used in your day-to-day work.

This leaves the SYS account to discuss. This account is key to Oracle's operation and cannot be locked; well, the SYSDBA connection cannot be locked anyway, so locking SYS is not an option. SYS can be used, but not day-to-day as a given. Using SYS is acceptable for jobs that require the power of SYS, but it should not be necessary to use it as a general DBA account. Auditing must also be enabled to assess who is connecting as SYS and who is making SYSDBA and SYSOPER connections to the database. You must also audit who is connecting as SYSTEM. You must understand who is making privileged connections to your database in general and then assess why and stop those who should not be doing it.

The other category of built-in accounts that must remain but must be protected comprises the accounts that support functionality within the database. These are hard to protect. You can lock them, but what is the point? Okay, there is some benefit to locking but it is not a golden-bullet solution, and you should take this into account. Locking an account does not lock out its functionality. A lot of the security bugs reported to Oracle often involve bugs in packages owned by default or built-in schemas installed for you by Oracle. Locking these accounts does not block access to the features, so you are still vulnerable should you not patch or should there be a new bug discovered.

The possible security solutions for default installed accounts are different in each case. For instance, the public execute privilege could be revoked for key functionality within each default schema so that access to the particular scheme can be granted back only to specific other schemas in the database that need it. This idea is flawed because removing the public execute privileges may break all of the functionality that uses a particular feature. One particular alternate solution is to identify the key packages of the schema that should remain. A good example would be to pick the package DBMS_RLS for the virtual private database (VPD) functionality. Auditing can be enabled on the DBMS_RLS package to understand who is using it and why. So the security solution is observation rather than encasement in this example. More-complex solutions could involve creating wrapper packages around the key functionality so your own rules can be enabled to prevent access where it is not necessary.

In summary, protecting built-in schemas that must remain in the database is fraught with problems mostly because the public privileges granted by Oracle cannot easily be turned off.

Accounts to Analyze Individually

The next category of accounts installed by Oracle are those that fall outside the *must be removed* and *must not be removed* categories. Either you are not sure of the functionality supported by the account or you are not sure whether the account and its functionality are used internally by Oracle itself.

Locating evidence of whether some functionality is used is hard to do. Reviewing the contents of database views such as DBA_FEATURE_USAGE_STATISTICS and DBA_HIGH_WATER_MARK_STATISTICS added in Oracle Database 10g seems like a great option. The two views were added primarily to track license usage, but there are no equivalent views provided in 9i and lower. Even though there are many reported cases in online forums of Oracle consultants performing audits for license infringements by using some scripts to locate feature usage information, the scripts they use are not public. The scripts that potential Oracle consultants run are likely to identify feature usage at the instance level. Detailed features within the database may also identify key additional cost options such as Oracle Label Security (OLS), where single schemas (LBACSYS, in this case, for instance) and code installed (that is, OLS policies) may be used to identify use of a feature; if feature data is present, that feature is probably used. It is hard to know exactly what any Oracle consultant possibly does without access to any scripts that they may use, if indeed these scripts actually exist.

If you are running 10g or above, the DBA_FEATURE_USAGE_STATISTICS view is useful to assess which features in your database are used. Listing 14-6 shows how to query the DBA_FEATURE_USAGE_STATISTICS view to assess which features are used.

Listing 14-6. Analyzing the Features Used in the Database

```
SQL> col name for a37 head "Name"
SQL> col version for a10 head "Version"
SQL> col currently_used for a6 head "Used"
SQL> col first_usage_date for a9 head "First"
SQL> col last_usage_date for a9 head "Last"
SQL> col detected_usages for 999 head "Det"
SQL> select      substr(name,1,37) name,
  2       version,
  3       currently_used,
  4       first_usage_date,
  5       last_usage_date,
  6       detected_usages
  7  from dba_feature_usage_statistics
```

```
  8  where first_usage_date is not null
SQL> /

Name                                Version     Used    First       Last         Det
----------------------------------- ----------  ------  ---------   ---------    ----
Segment Advisor                     11.1.0.7.0  TRUE    24-APR-09   20-AUG-09      15
Segment Advisor                     11.1.0.6.0  TRUE    12-MAR-08   19-APR-09      46
Automatic SQL Tuning Advisor        11.1.0.6.0  TRUE    03-MAR-08   19-APR-09      47
Automatic SQL Tuning Advisor        11.1.0.7.0  TRUE    24-APR-09   20-AUG-09      15
Virtual Private Database (VPD)       11.1.0.6.0  TRUE    19-MAR-09   19-APR-09       5
Virtual Private Database (VPD)       11.1.0.7.0  TRUE    24-APR-09   20-AUG-09      15
XDB                                 11.1.0.6.0  TRUE    03-MAR-08   19-APR-09      46
XDB                                 11.1.0.7.0  TRUE    24-APR-09   20-AUG-09      15
LOB                                 11.1.0.6.0  TRUE    03-MAR-08   19-APR-09      47
LOB                                 11.1.0.7.0  TRUE    24-APR-09   20-AUG-09      15
Object                              11.1.0.6.0  TRUE    03-MAR-08   19-APR-09      47
EM Database Control                 11.1.0.6.0  FALSE   03-MAR-08   03-MAR-08       1
Encrypted Tablespaces               11.1.0.6.0  TRUE    28-MAR-09   19-APR-09       4
Encrypted Tablespaces               11.1.0.7.0  TRUE    24-APR-09   20-AUG-09      15
{output removed for space considerations}
Oracle Text                         11.1.0.7.0  TRUE    24-APR-09   20-AUG-09      15
Oracle Text                         11.1.0.6.0  TRUE    03-MAR-08   19-APR-09      47
Recovery Area                       11.1.0.6.0  TRUE    03-MAR-08   19-APR-09      47
Recovery Area                       11.1.0.7.0  TRUE    24-APR-09   20-AUG-09      15
Resource Manager                    11.1.0.6.0  TRUE    03-MAR-08   19-APR-09      43
Resource Manager                    11.1.0.7.0  TRUE    24-APR-09   20-AUG-09      15
Server Parameter File               11.1.0.6.0  TRUE    03-MAR-08   19-APR-09      47
Server Parameter File               11.1.0.7.0  TRUE    24-APR-09   20-AUG-09      15

62 rows selected.

SQL>
```

The output in Listing 14-6 shows features in the database that have been used at least once since the database was created. The task of assessing default users whose features may or may not be needed in your database can again be split into two groups. In the first group, the feature has been used, and in the second group, the feature has not been used.

The output in Listing 14-6 shows the former group. Although this output is very nice, there is a problem: the output is related to features within the database, but they are not mapped to schemas installed in the database; the task of solving this problem is left to the customer. Some default accounts and features are obvious to map. For example, the XDB feature maps to the XDB schema. A more indirect example is the feature EM database control, which maps to the users SYSMAN, MGMT_VIEW, and DBSNMP. The particular example of EM highlights an issue with the DBA_FEATURE_USAGE_STATISTICS view. Database control is not being used in my database, but Oracle used it itself as part of the installation. Therefore, you must establish when the database was installed (March 3, 2008 in my case) and discount output if the first and last use was on the same day and that day is also the installation date. The DBA_FEATURE_USAGE_STATISTICS view also duplicates entries when there has been an upgrade of a feature. My database was upgraded to 11.1.0.7, so I have lots of duplicate entries that can be seen in Listing 14-6.

These are examples of features that have been used. Entries in Listing 14-6 that can be mapped to schemas in the database will show that either a feature is used natively in your application or it is used by Oracle in the background via another feature or schema. Schemas identified at this stage of the methodology should be moved to the *must remain* list.

The second group of schemas in this part of the exercise are those whose features have not been used. Modify the query in Listing 14-6 so it now returns records indicating that the feature has not been used. Listing 14-7 shows features that specifically have not been used.

Listing 14-7. Locating Features That Have Not Been Used

```
SQL> select      substr(name,1,37) name,
  2       version,
  3       currently_used,
  4       first_usage_date,
  5       last_usage_date,
  6       detected_usages
  7  from dba_feature_usage_statistics
  8  where first_usage_date is null
SQL> /
```

Name	Version	Used	First	Last	Det
Advanced Replication	11.1.0.7.0	FALSE			0
Externally authenticated users	11.1.0.7.0	FALSE			0
Automatic SQL Execution Memory	11.1.0.7.0	FALSE			0
Automatic Storage Management	11.1.0.7.0	FALSE			0
Automatic Workload Repository	11.1.0.7.0	FALSE			0
AWR Baseline	11.1.0.7.0	FALSE			0
AWR Baseline Template	11.1.0.7.0	FALSE			0
Backup Encryption	11.1.0.7.0	FALSE			0
Baseline Adaptive Thresholds	11.1.0.7.0	FALSE			0

```
{Output snipped for brevity}
```

Listing 14-7 should be reviewed in the same manner as Listing 14-6, except that this time any firm answers on default account status will result in the schema being added to the list of schemas that can be removed. Actually removing a default schema also brings yet another layer of complexity. It is not acceptable to simply drop a default schema, and again because there are literally hundreds of default schemas that could possibly be installed in each case, an uninstall script should be located on Metalink if it exists.

Finally, in this section, what if the database is pre-10g? The two great license views, and particularly DBA_FEATURE_USAGE_STATISTICS, are not available in earlier versions of the database, and there is no workaround because the data collected in the view is created by packages that are also not installed. Resolving the group of users who may or may not be removed is a time-consuming task, and there are a number of possible solutions that do work to establish whether the schemas are used. Hopefully, the process has become clearer. The easiest solution is to identify the key packages or views for each default schema or objects that are created and that are "part" of the feature. This is also not easy because each schema is completely different. A good example is the schema OUTLN; Listing 14-8 can be used to identify whether any outlines have been created with these queries.

Listing 14-8. Identify Whether Any Outlines Have Been Ccreated

```
SQL> select count(*) from ol$;

  COUNT(*)
----------
         0

SQL> select count(*) from ol$hints;

  COUNT(*)
----------
         0

SQL> select count(*) from ol$nodes;

  COUNT(*)
----------
         0

SQL>
```

The output in Listing 14-8 shows that no outlines have been created in my database. Therefore, we can be reasonably sure that this functionality is not used at the moment. There is no certainty that the feature has not been used in the past and will not be used in the future. The key package for the outline functionality is DBMS_OUTLN, so a good option would be to enable auditing on execution of the DBMS_OUTLN package and monitor it for a reasonable amount of time to assess whether the feature really is not used.

There are more possibilities for assessing built-in accounts, but these require more programming effort. The first option is to review all of the source code within the DBA_SOURCE view to assess whether any of the key packages from a particular schema are used. However, this could be flawed because the code may not be stored in the database, and if the feature is administrative, it is not likely to be stored in the database anyway. A second option, which is similar but actually solves part of the problems discussed earlier, is to parse the System Global Area (SGA) for the same packages or views. As you may expect, there is also a flaw with this solution in that the contents of the SGA are very time-dependent, so it should be done often over a period for true assessment.

Reduction of Accounts

The preceding section discussed the accounts installed by Oracle, but this is only half of the problem. The second half is all the accounts that you, the customer, have created in the database. The use.sql script can be used again, but this time with a different input parameter. Set the parameter to C to get a detailed analysis of the custom installation accounts. Listing 14-9 demonstrates the running of the use.sql script.

Listing 14-9. Running the use.sql PL/SQL Script to Assess Customer-Installed Accounts

```
SQL> @use


use.sql: Release 1.0.2.0.0 - Production on Thu Aug 20 21:16:39 2009
Copyright (c) 2007, 2009 PeteFinnigan.com Limited. All rights reserved.

OUTPUT FLAG [A|O|C]                     [A]: C
```

USER	Rol	RSO	Sys	Ob	Tab	PL
PETE	2	B,2,9,0	1	3	0	0
BILL	2	B,2,9,0	1	3	0	0
A	0		2	0	0	0
B	0		1	0	0	0
C	1	B,42,443,13862	3	0	0	0
RES_TEST	0		0	0	0	0
XX	0		0	0	0	0
ORASCAN	0		3	1	0	0
IMPOSS	0		0	0	0	0
D	0		0	0	0	0
AB	0		1	0	0	0
P1	2	N,4,4,2	3	1	0	0
P2	1	N,2,2,1	0	0	0	0
B1	2	B,44,443,13966	3	0	0	0
LT_EXP	0		1	0	0	0
CRACKER	0		1	1	0	0
EVILUSER	0		2	1	0	0
MONITOR	1	B,2,0,2130	3	0	0	0
PXF	0		5	4	1	1
PP	0		200	0	0	0
PRIV	0		3	0	0	1
ENC	0		3	0	2	0
ORABLOG	1	B,1,8,0	3	2	11	0
IMPORTER	1	B,5,80,2260	4	2	1	0
TESTPWD	0		2	1	0	1
PETE2	0		0	3	0	0
GRANTALL	0		1	11	0	0
CC_PER	0		1	3	0	0
CC_GRANTA	0		1	1	0	0
A2	0		0	1	0	0
BB1	0		0	1	0	0
BB2	0		0	1	0	0
BB3	0		0	1	0	0
BB4	0		0	1	0	0
BB5	0		0	1	0	0
BB6	0		0	1	0	0
BB7	0		0	1	0	0
BB8	0		0	1	0	0
BB9	0		0	1	0	0

USER	Rol	RSO	Sys	Ob	Tab	PL
BB10	0		0	1	0	0
BB11	0		0	1	0	0
DUAL_GRAN	0		0	2	0	0
ZULIA	1	N,1,0,1	0	0	0	0
ERIC	1	N,2,0,1	0	0	0	0
EMIL	1	N,1,0,1	0	0	0	0
AMIS	0		2	1	0	0
XMLT	2	B,43,443,13872	2	0	0	0
EVERYTHIN	1	B,42,443,13862	200	0	0	0

```
PL/SQL procedure successfully completed.

SQL>
```

Listing 14-9 shows the output for accounts created by the customer within the database. The column RSO needs to be explained, as this is the first listing that uses it. The RSO column is a summary column to aid the investigator in seeing the complete picture of all privileges assigned to users within the database. It does this by recursively counting privileges assigned via roles. The user XMLT shown in Listing 14-9 would seem to be a low-privileged user because it has one role assigned and two system privileges. The RSO column helps show the true picture: this user is in fact very powerful. The figures B,43,443,13872 are interpreted as follows:

- B means that the user has been assigned a built-in role. This field can also be N, which means it has not been assigned a built-in role.

- 43 indicates the actual number of roles assigned to this user. This is recursively counted by assessing which roles are assigned to the one role directly assigned.

- 443 indicates the total number of system privileges recursively assigned via roles.

- 13872 indicates the total number of object privileges recursively assigned via roles.

I use the use.sql script day-to-day in security audits. It is a reasonably simple script and very powerful in analyzing the type of user accounts installed in a database, correlating the accounts to real people, and finally, correlating the privileges each account has been assigned. I also use the use.sql script to match each account to its described purpose. The assessment process sounds complicated but is not, really. As you may have guessed already, the process involves a number of steps. Ideally, before you run the use.sql script in your database, it is best to isolate an individual and their database account for each job purpose that you know of within your company. For instance, for a fictional company I may create a list as follows. I am aiming to simply list the job description and database account name:

- Business users who have a database account: Mrs. Smith, account SMITHB

- Feed users: account FEED1

- Batch users: account BATCH1

- Reports users: account REP21

- Application administration users: Andy Brown, account ABRN1

- Schema accounts: account ORABLOG

- Developer accounts: Phil Gibbs, account PAG1

- DBA accounts: Mark Green, account MGDBA

- More...

You do not need to be 100 percent accurate in identifying real people, job purposes, and database account names. The purpose of the identification is to try to correlate real people with database accounts and ensure that you can correlate the privileges actually assigned to the database account with its intended purpose. Creating the list is easy to do and takes only 10 minutes.

Output from the use.sql script in Listing 14-9 is fairly simple. The script lists database account names, the number of roles granted to the account, the number of system privileges granted to the account, and the number of object privileges granted to the account. It also lists the number of tables and PL/SQL objects that the account owns. The section in the middle of the report, where the column is titled RSO, breaks down the granted roles more deeply in order to assess the true quantities of privileges granted to the user. A description is provided after Listing 14-9. The numbers shown in Listing 14-9 are all the roles granted (including roles granted to roles, granted to roles...) and all the privileges granted to each role in the hierarchy. The first letter in this section indicates whether the user has been granted any built-in roles.

Again, as in previous sections, this task can be split into two—see a pattern? The first group of customer-installed users to look into are those that you have identified in Listing 14-9, which are mapped to real people or jobs. Remember that my sample list of jobs/database accounts was made up; yours will be real. The second group of customer-installed accounts to look into are users that look odd, in the sense that unusual numbers of privileges have been assigned to the user. Also pay attention to names of database accounts. If an account is named DEV01 and it has the DBA role, then clearly there is a problem.

As an example, the user ORABLOG in Listing 14-9 could have been identified in the second group as an account with unusual privileges. If you look at the right-hand side of this example report, you will see very few users have any tables or PL/SQL objects in my sample database. Therefore, for ORABLOG the account looks like it could be a schema owner because the account has far more objects than other accounts. If your collation of account names included the ORABLOG account, for example, then correlating what was learned beforehand when making a list of people/accounts/jobs is important. The ORABLOG account also has some interesting numbers on the left-hand side. ORABLOG has a small number of roles and system and object privileges but interestingly it is also identified with B in the RSO section to show it has been granted a built-in role. At this point, it is worth using the find_all_privs.sql script available from www.petefinnigan.com/tools.htm to fully assess all the privileges of this account. Listing 14-10 shows how to use find_all_privs.sql to assess all privileges for an account.

Listing 14-10. Running find_all_privs.sql to Test the Privileges of the ORABLOG Account

```
SQL> @find_all_privs

find_all_privs: Release 1.0.7.0.0 - Production on Mon Aug 24 18:15:53 2009
Copyright (c) 2004 PeteFinnigan.com Limited. All rights reserved.

NAME OF USER TO CHECK              [ORCL]: ORABLOG
OUTPUT METHOD Screen/File             [S]: S
FILE NAME FOR OUTPUT          [priv.lst]:
OUTPUT DIRECTORY [DIRECTORY  or file (/tmp)]:

User => ORABLOG has been granted the following privileges
```

```
===================================================================
        ROLE => RESOURCE which contains =>
                SYS PRIV => CREATE CLUSTER grantable => NO
                SYS PRIV => CREATE INDEXTYPE grantable => NO
                SYS PRIV => CREATE OPERATOR grantable => NO
                SYS PRIV => CREATE PROCEDURE grantable => NO
                SYS PRIV => CREATE SEQUENCE grantable => NO
                SYS PRIV => CREATE TABLE grantable => NO
                SYS PRIV => CREATE TRIGGER grantable => NO
                SYS PRIV => CREATE TYPE grantable => NO
        SYS PRIV => CREATE SESSION grantable => NO
        SYS PRIV => CREATE TABLE grantable => NO
        SYS PRIV => UNLIMITED TABLESPACE grantable => NO
        TABLE PRIV => SELECT object => SCOTT.CREDIT_CARD grantable => NO
        TABLE PRIV => SELECT object => SCOTT.CVG4 grantable => NO
```

PL/SQL procedure successfully completed.

For updates please visit http://www.petefinnigan.com/tools.htm

SQL>

The find_all_privs.sql script is useful for giving a hierarchical listing of all the privileges granted to any particular user or role. The script is also easy to run: simply pass in the username and tell it whether you want the output to go to the screen or to a file. In the example in Listing 14-10, the ORABLOG user has been granted the built-in role, RESOURCE, and also three system privileges and two object privileges. The CREATE SESSION privilege is fine. The UNLIMITED TABLESPACE privilege indicates a legacy problem of granting the RESOURCE role, so it should be revoked because it is a systemwide privilege. The two table privileges can be ignored at this point of the assessment. The built-in role RESOURCE was not designed for the ORABLOG application; it is clear, therefore, that the privileges of the ORABLOG user are not relevant for its purpose. Listing 14-11 demonstrates that the privileges assigned to ORABLOG are not suitable.

Listing 14-11. Assessing the Objects Owned by ORABLOG

```
SQL> select distinct object_type
  2  from dba_objects
  3  where owner='ORABLOG';

OBJECT_TYPE
-------------------
SEQUENCE
LOB
TRIGGER
TABLE
INDEX

5 rows selected.

SQL>
```

If you compare the actual objects owned by ORABLOG shown in Listing 14-11 with the privileges granted to ORABLOG shown in Listing 14-10, there is quite a big difference. For instance, ORABLOG has privileges to create clusters, procedures, and types but does not actually have any of these objects. In my particular case, the application is fairly static so the list of objects actually owned is also fairly static. Testing assigned privileges against actual objects owned demonstrates that using built-in roles is about design decisions.

There is also one other interesting aspect of the ORABLOG user: ORABLOG has a duplicate privilege granted. The CREATE TABLE privilege has been granted via the RESOURCE role and also directly. One of these privileges must be removed. The RESOURCE role must also be removed because it is a built-in role. The best way to achieve the removal is to make a direct copy of the RESOURCE role, perhaps calling it ORABLOG_RESOURCE, and grant this role to the user ORABLOG. In the first instance, nothing will break; everything is the same in terms of privilege levels. Initially, all privileges that are currently granted to the ORABLOG_RESOURCE role that do not match existing objects can also be revoked. Reducing the privileges assigned to the ORABLOG user more closely matches its purpose. Going forward, it can also be possible to revoke all the privileges assigned to ORABLOG in a runtime mode simply by revoking the role ORABLOG_RESOURCE. When any maintenance or upgrades are necessary, the role can be granted back for the period of the upgrade. If the upgrade includes a change to privileges necessary for the application to work, the new privileges can also be granted as part of the upgrade to ORABLOG, either permanently if they are needed at runtime or to the role if they are needed simply to maintain the schema.

The same process must be applied to all of the users you have identified in advance (remember your job/user list) that match particular job types for purposes. Remember also to assess those accounts that are a bit strange in terms of numbers of granted privileges. As an example, the user EVERYTHING is a good candidate. The RSO column shows excessive privileges and roles granted. Because the user has been granted only one role and it is identified with B, even without looking you can be almost sure that this user has been granted the DBA role simply because of the quantity of privileges. Also the SYS column shows a very high number of granted system privileges (200). This user looks like an administrative user, a DBA. If the list of users you gathered does not include the EVERYTHING user (in my example), and the EVERYTHING user is not an account that has been assigned to a real DBA, then the EVERYTHING user must be locked and eventually removed because it is completely unacceptable to have users with this level of privilege who are not administrative users. Indeed, as discussed previously, DBAs should have their own accounts with privileges designed for day-to-day business, which clearly should not include 200 system privileges granted directly or tens of thousands of privileges granted via roles. This is a very dangerous account in my database.

Account Password Strength

Initially, it seems unnecessary to assess the password strength of every user in the database because the first step in improving user security is to reduce the available accounts within the database, as discussed in the previous sections. The problem is, we live in the real world full of time constraints and financial factors. In the real world, is unlikely that you will fix everything. It is also unlikely that you will fix the list of things you decide to fix quickly. Therefore, all the accounts in the database need to be tested for password strength because guessing the password is simply the easiest way to break into a database. Even if nothing else was fixed in terms of removing accounts or reducing privileges, password security issues must be solved, or at least all staff in your organization should be prevented from attempting to connect directly to the database.

■ **Note** The privileges necessary to run the PL/SQL and SQL scripts shown in this chapter are not excessive. One of the key things in security assessment is to not modify the database that is being assessed. Therefore, all the scripts have been designed to run with just three simple privileges: CREATE SESSION, SELECT ANY DICTIONARY, and SELECT ANY TABLE. The latter two privileges are dangerous because they allow access to system information and also potentially to any data within the business tables. Therefore, you should create a specific account to use for assessment of the database. This account should be created closely prior to the assessment and then should be removed immediately afterward. It is good practice not to run the types of queries shown in this chapter through normal DBA-type accounts or indeed to store the results on a DBA workstation. Imagine if you assessed hundreds of databases within your organization, including password cracking, and stored all of the results on your terminal. Your terminal would be a very valuable asset or target to somebody who wants to steal from your company.

Password cracking is an important and necessary step in securing database users. Because the passwords are not stored in the database, but instead hashes are stored, there is no simple way to test the strength of a user's password in terms of just looking at a clear-text version of it—unless you ask every database user to tell you their passwords. Heh, heh. If you attempt to ask users for their passwords and you are successful, you have a problem because users should not be divulging their passwords.

The following fundamental steps must be performed when testing the strength of passwords:

1. Test whether the password is the same as the username.

2. Test whether the password is a default password.

3. Test whether the password is a dictionary word.

4. Test whether the password is too short.

Cracking Passwords with a PL/SQL Password Cracker

The simplest way to test password strength is to use the PL/SQL password cracker available from www.petefinnigan.com/oracle_password_cracker.htm. The PL/SQL password cracker has a great advantage: it is simple to run because it is just a SQL*Plus script. This means there are no binaries or operating system libraries or anything else to install; it is just a PL/SQL script of the type DBAs are used to running. The script encompasses all the check types listed previously and also tests role passwords.

There are a couple of downsides to the script: it is much slower than a cracker written in the C language and it is also uses a lot of CPU (this is actually a problem of Oracle's encryption algorithm implementations rather than anything to do with the script), but the script is fine provided you understand how many accounts you are testing in advance and you understand there could be a load on the server for a short period. Listing 14-12 shows a demonstration of running the PL/SQL-based password cracker. Note that because the cracker uses the password column of the SYS.USER$ select table, access must be granted on SYS.USER$ to the user logged in to run the cracker script.

Listing 14-12. Running the PL/SQL Password Cracker

```
SQL> set serveroutput on size 1000000
SQL> @cracker-v2.0.sql
cracker: Release 1.0.4.0.0 - Beta on Wed Aug 19 20:03:19 2009
Copyright (c) 2008 PeteFinnigan.com Limited. All rights reserved.


T Username                 Password                CR FL STA
========================================================
U "SYS"                    [ORACLE1               ] DI CR OP
U "SYSTEM"                 [ORACLE1               ] DI CR OP
U "OUTLN"                  [OUTLN                 ] DE CR EL
U "DIP"                    [DIP                   ] DE CR EL
U "TSMSYS"                 [TSMSYS                ] PU CR EL
U "ORACLE_OCM"             [ORACLE_OCM            ] PU CR EL
U "XDB"                    [CHANGE_ON_INSTALL     ] DE CR EL
R "GLOBAL_AQ_USER_ROLE     [GL-EX {GLOBAL}        ] GE CR OP
U "DBSNMP"                 [ORACLE1               ] DI CR OP
U "WMSYS"                  [WMSYS                 ] DE CR EL
{some of the output removed to conserve space}
U "EXFSYS"                 [EXFSYS                ] DE CR EL
U "CTXSYS"                 [CHANGE_ON_INSTALL     ] DE CR EL
U "XS$NULL"                [                      ] -- -- EL
U "XMLT"                   [XMLT                  ] PU CR OP
U "XX"                     [123456                ] DI CR OP
U "ORASCAN"                [ORASCAN               ] PU CR OP
U "IMPOSS"                 [IMP {imposs123456789] IM CR OP
U "D"                      [                      ] -- -- OP
U "MGMT_VIEW"              [                      ] -- -- OP
U "ORABLOG"                [ORABLOG               ] PU CR OP
U "IMPORTER"               [IMPORTER              ] PU CR OP
U "TESTPWD"                [TESTPWD               ] PU CR OP
U "GRANTALL"               [GRANTALL              ] PU CR OP
U "BB8"                    [BB8                   ] PU CR OP
U "BB9"                    [BB9                   ] PU CR OP
U "BB10"                   [BB10                  ] PU CR OP
U "BB11"                   [BB11                  ] PU CR OP
U "DUAL_GRANT"             [DUAL_GRANT            ] PU CR OP
U "ZULIA"                  [ZULIA                 ] PU CR OP
U "ERIC"                   [ERIC                  ] PU CR OP
U "EMIL"                   [EMIL                  ] PU CR OP
U "EVERYTHING"             [EVERYTHING            ] PU CR OP


INFO: Number of crack attempts = [91039]
INFO: Elapsed time = [6.28 Seconds]
INFO: Cracks per second = [14490]

PL/SQL procedure successfully completed.

SQL>
```

As you can see, the script is easy to run. In my sample database, it tested 85 user and 6 role passwords. It ran for 6.28 seconds and cracked passwords at a rate of 14,490 per second. The speed is not bad, but nothing compared to the 1.5 million passwords per second that can be checked with a cracker written in C on the same hardware. The output in Listing 14-12 is fairly explanatory: the first column defines whether the row is for a user or a role; the second column is the username; the third is the password if it was cracked; and the next column defines how the password was cracked (PU is password = username, DE is password = default, DI is password = dictionary word, BF is password was brute forced, IM is password cannot be cracked).

Although the output shown in Listing 14-12 is a great start and often all that is needed to achieve a better level of password security, most likely you will need to crack passwords with a real password cracker. These are discussed in the next section.

As a general comment about the example in Listing 14-12, because almost all the passwords were cracked, there is absolutely no reason to go any further. We are not hackers and we are not trying to hack the database. Our task is to assess the security level and to define solutions to make the database more secure. Therefore, scripts such as the PL/SQL cracker give a view of the password security. For me, the output in Listing 14-12 is enough.

It is also worth mentioning at this stage that the password crackers such as my PL/SQL cracker and those discussed in the next section work only if the password hashes are available. If a hacker does not have a list of the password hashes from the database, none of the crackers discussed will work because the password hashes are mandatory input. Therefore, it should be really obvious that the password hashes must be protected at all costs and must not be readable by anyone. If password hashes are not available, the only way to break into the database is to guess passwords. This is very slow and time-consuming even if scripted. Password management would also prevent a guess-based attack from succeeding if failed_login attempts are set to a suitably low number. If a hacker cannot successfully guess passwords in fewer than 10 attempts, for instance, then having failed_login attempts set to 3 will enhance security.

Cracking Passwords with a "Real" Password Cracker

The first step in reviewing the strength of your database passwords should always be to use the PL/SQL cracker simply because it's much easier to use. When you need to assess passwords to a better level or simply have huge numbers of them to test, a real password cracker is needed. It is also worth noting that if passwords need to be cracked offline, a real password cracker is also needed.

Several options are available for "real" password crackers written to work with Oracle passwords. The following list summarizes some of them:

> **orabf:** This was one of the first password crackers for Oracle, and I used it for quite a long time. Written by 0rm, it is available from www.toolcrypt.org/tools/orabf/orabf-v0.7.6.zip. This is still a fast Oracle password cracker but it is not multithreaded. 0rm has told me that he may add multithreading in the future, so watch out.

> **woraauthbf:** This tool is written by Laszlo Tóth, and the latest version is available from www.soonerorlater.hu/index.khtml?article_id=513. This is the fastest software Oracle password cracker currently available and is multithreaded. Woraauthbf supports the Oracle 11g password algorithm and, notably, it also supports cracking the authentication packets in the TNS protocol (O3Logon and O5Logon).

checkpwd: This tool is written by Red Database Security and is closed source. Its distinguishing factor over orabf and woraauthbf is its capability to connect to the database and retrieve the details necessary to perform password cracking directly.

Cain and Abel: This tool is a more complex suite of security tools but also supports Oracle password cracking, TNS cracking, 11g password cracking, and generation of Oracle rainbow tables useful for fast offline password recovery.

Commercial alternatives: Most of the commercial Oracle database security auditing products such as PFCLScan from PeteFinnigan.com Limited, AppDetective from Application Security, Inc., or NGSSQuirrel from NGSSoftware all have built-in password crackers. These are generally easier to use because of the point-and-click interface.

■ **Note** One of the driving factors that encouraged me to write a password cracker in PL/SQL was the frustration of dealing with lots of clients who were not allowed to download binary or compiled programs such as password crackers to test the security of passwords within all of the databases. Often large companies have policies that prevent installation of any software and in particular prevent installation of software such as password crackers. That is not to say that these are not genuine valuable tools to be used by security practitioners; they are. If your company has such a policy, do not download these tools unless you obtain permission in advance to do so.

The choice of which password cracker to use is complex and is based on ease of use, ease of installation (including company issues), and availability of the source code. I recommend woraauthbf because it's the only free Oracle password cracker that includes the source code, so you can see how it works or even modify it to use company internal rules. The checkpwd cracker seems to be a good choice because it's the only free cracker that connects to the database and retrieves the password hashes and usernames for you ready for cracking, but there is a big downside in that it's only about one-third of the speed of woraauthbf.

You can download the chosen password cracker (woraauthbf) from www.soonerorlater.hu/index.khtml?article_id=513. Woraauthbf does not need to be installed. Simply unzip the contents to a suitable directory, and it is ready to run. The first step is to extract the usernames and hashes in a suitable format from the database. This can be done by using the script www.petefinnigan.com/cracker.sql. Listing 14-13 shows how to extract the hashes from the database.

Listing 14-13. This Is the SQL to Extract Password Hashes in a Form Suitable for Use in woraauthbf

```
select name||':'||password||':A:A:'
from sys.user$
where password not in ('GLOBAL','EXTERNAL')
and length(password)=16
/
```

It is worth downloading the file cracker.sql referenced before Listing 14-13, because it includes suitable formatting so the output works immediately in the password cracker. The code in Listing 14-13

491

tries to eliminate some passwords that cannot be cracked, such as GLOBAL and EXTERNAL accounts. The SQL in Listing 14-13 also leaves out passwords that are not the correct length, which indicates impossible passwords. An impossible password is set by the ALTER USER … IDENTIFIED BY VALUES… clause. The VALUES syntax allows a password to be set that does not represent a hashed password. The Oracle password algorithm is now suitably documented on the Internet but not by Oracle; a simplified overview is given here:

1. Concatenate the username and password while also making the string Unicode—for instance, for SYSTEM/MANAGER this would be S0Y0S0T0E0M0M0A0N0A0G0E0R0.

2. Pad out the string with zeros to be a multiple of eight characters. This is not necessary if the memory holding the string is zeroed first, because it is then implicitly padded.

3. Using an encryption key of 0123456789ABCDEF, use Data Encryption Standard Cypher Block Checksum (DES CBC) mode to encrypt the username/password string. Note that CBC mode means that the first 8 bytes are encrypted and the result is XOR'd with the next 8 bytes, and then that is encrypted, and so on. When completed, the last input vector (the last XOR result) is used as the new encryption key for the second round.

4. Repeat all the preceding steps but use the encryption key extracted in step 3. This time, the last input vector is the result; the password hash stored in SYS.USER$.PASSWORD. The result is a "hash," not an encrypted value, even though a very popular encryption algorithm is used. This is because of the two stages used that make the final output nonrevisable, that is, it cannot be decrypted.

If you would like to see an implementation in code, review the code in www.petefinnigan.com/testpwd.sql written in PL/SQL. For a version written in C, see the link for woraauthbf noted earlier and download the C source code. Listing 14-14 shows running the cracker.sql SQL script to create input for the woraauthbf cracker. It saves the output to a file as follows.

Listing 14-14. Creating the Password Cracker Input

```
SQL> @cracker
SYS:5C7AF4F0C16786C7:A:A:
SYSTEM:BE702D700B33808C:A:A:
OUTLN:4A3BA55E08595C81:A:A:
DIP:CE4A36B8E06CA59C:A:A:
TSMSYS:3DF26A8B17D0F29F:A:A:
ORACLE_OCM:6D17CF1EB1611F94:A:A:
XDB:88D8364765FCE6AF:A:A:
DBSNMP:CDB1CB3DD68BF4FD:A:A:
WMSYS:7C9BA362F8314299:A:A:
EXFSYS:66F4EF5650C20355:A:A:
CTXSYS:71E687F036AD56E5:A:A:
XS$NULL:DC4FCC8CB69A6733:A:A:
SPATIAL_WFS_ADMIN:32FA36DC781579AA:A:A:
ORDSYS:7EFA02EC7EA6B86F:A:A:
ORDPLUGINS:88A2B2C183431F00:A:A:
SI_INFORMTN_SCHEMA:84B8CBCA4D477FA3:A:A:
{output trimmed for space considerations}
```

Next run woraauthbf. The first steps normally in a cracking session are to assess whether the password is set to the username, assess whether the password is set to a known default, check the password against a dictionary, and finally check whether the password is too short. The woraauthbf password cracker is a *dictionary* and *brute-force* password cracker. A password cracker takes a "guess" of possible passwords and works out the password hash by using a combination of the username and the guess of the password. If the final hash created by the cracker is the same as that in SYS.USER$.PASSWORD, you have cracked the password.

A *dictionary cracker* takes a dictionary of words one at a time and feeds the words into the password algorithm implemented in the cracker. If the hashes match, the password is found. Instead of using a dictionary of words, a *brute-force cracker* uses every possible combination of characters to crack randomly created passwords such as fgv54dj. What you are trying to do here is to check whether the password is long enough. Although a brute-force cracker can test any password, even random ones, it takes a very long time to crack reasonably long ones. By choosing a long password, someone with reasonable hardware and the same software cracker that you can download cannot crack your password.

The woraauthbf cracker has a couple of tricks built in. First, it automatically tests whether the password is set to the username. Second, it tests whether the password is a default. The cracker comes with a list called default.txt extracted from my website. The first step you should try then is actually the third step—the dictionary phase. Listing 14-15 shows how to run woraauthbf to crack passwords by using a dictionary.

Listing 14-15. Running the woraauthbf Cracker in Dictionary Mode

```
C:\woraauthbf_0.22R3>woraauthbf -p cracker.lis -d cracker_dict.txt -t hash
Usernames will be permuted!
The number of processors: 2
Number of pwds to check: 4825604
Number of pwds to check by thread: 2412802
Password file: cracker.lis, dictionary file: cracker_dict.txt, type: hash
Start: 1 End: 2412802
Start array thread with 578 number of passwords!
Password found: OUTLN:OUTLN:A:A
Password found: DIP:DIP:A:A
Password found: TSMSYS:TSMSYS:A:A
Password found: ORACLE_OCM:ORACLE_OCM:A:A
Password found: WMSYS:WMSYS:A:A
Password found: EXFSYS:EXFSYS:A:A
Password found: SPATIAL_WFS_ADMIN:SPATIAL_WFS_ADMIN:A:A
Password found: ORDSYS:ORDSYS:A:A
Password found: ORDPLUGINS:ORDPLUGINS:A:A
Password found: SI_INFORMTN_SCHEMA:SI_INFORMTN_SCHEMA:A:A
Password found: MDSYS:MDSYS:A:A
Password found: MDDATA:MDDATA:A:A
Password found: SPATIAL_WFS_ADMIN_USR:SPATIAL_WFS_ADMIN_USR:A:A
Password found: WFS_USR_ROLE:WFS_USR_ROLE:A:A
Password found: SPATIAL_CSW_ADMIN:SPATIAL_CSW_ADMIN:A:A
Password found: SPATIAL_CSW_ADMIN_USR:SPATIAL_CSW_ADMIN_USR:A:A
Password found: CSW_USR_ROLE:CSW_USR_ROLE:A:A
Password found: WK_TEST:WK_TEST:A:A
Password found: OWBSYS:OWBSYS:A:A
Password found: AB:AB:A:A
```

```
Password found: PETE:PETE:A:A
Password found: BILL:BILL:A:A
{some output removed for space considerations}
Password found: D:XXXXXX:A:A
Password found: SYS:ORACLE1:A:A
Password found: SYSTEM:ORACLE1:A:A
Password found: DBSNMP:ORACLE1:A:A
Password found: SYSMAN:ORACLE1:A:A
Writing session files...
Elpased time: 70s
Checked passwords: 52544946
Password / Second: 750642


C:\woraauthbf_0.22R3>
```

The output in Listing 14-15 shows that the cracker accepts a parameter to specify the file you created earlier that contains the usernames and hashes to be cracked. It also accepts a parameter to specify the dictionary file; in my case, this is called cracker_dict.txt. My file is created over many years from many sources and contains around 5 million words. You can find a lot of sites via Google to create word lists. It is also feasible to use multiple dictionaries in steps.

An interesting thing to try is to permute the passwords in the dictionary file. *Permutation* is a trick whereby an existing dictionary word is modified in some way. This enables you to create much bigger dictionary files from a starting point of a small file. Woraauthbf supports only basic permutation as a standard, and this works only on the username. The readme file in the woraauthbf distribution gives many more details. Basically, usernames can be reversed, doubled, or added onto with numbers. This is controlled by the parameter --perm when running the cracker.

A more substantial permute program is available with orabf. Download the orabf tool and unzip the package; the permute program is called permute, and just running it shows the options. Listing 14-16 shows the parameters of the permute program.

Listing 14-16. Running the orabf Permute Program

```
C:\orabf>permute

permute v0.54, (C)2004 orm@toolcrypt.org
----------------------------------------

usage: permute infile outfile [options]

- for stdin/stdout

options:
-b      for basic rules
-y      for years
-n      for some numbers
-N      for lots of numbers (disables -n)
-e      for l33tsp3ll1ng (can be expensive)
-r      for word reversal
-c      for case permutation (can be expensive)
-f      toggle case for first character only
-i      write some statistics when done
```

```
output multiplier effect:
default: +1
-b        +39
-y        +40
-n        +29
-N        +210
-e        total x n, where 1 <= n <= 1958 (depends upon word composition)
          usually n is somewhere around 60
-r        total x 2
-f        total x 2
-c        total x 2^len

CAUTION! -b -y -N -e -r results in a multiplication factor of about 40000
don't write -b -y -N -e -r -c to file unless your input file is really small
```

After you're finished cracking with the dictionary mode, review the results of what you have found. Security is interesting and in general fairly simple, but you must also have a suspicious mind. Although the results may seem obvious (after all, a password has been cracked and therefore must be weak), you must also look out for the subtle problems.

If you review the output in Listing 14-15, you will see that the users SYS, SYSTEM, DBSNMP, and SYSMAN all share the same password. The subtle issue with sharing passwords is that this also implies sharing of passwords across all systems within the organization. If key accounts have the same password in one system, it is highly likely that the passwords are shared in all systems. Having shared passwords also implies that job sharing is occurring and that account sharing exists by individuals, not just across systems. So the solutions to fix weak passwords should not be limited to technical solutions but must also encompass procedure and policy. In the case of the SYS, SYSTEM, DBSNMP, and SYSMAN user accounts, the passwords are weak, easily guessed, and even the password used implies sequence—that is, the next password could be ORACLE2. (A useful check to perform at this point is to also run the password cracker against any password history if it exists. This would confirm your suspicion of whether a sequence is used for key passwords.)

The next step is to assess what was found in the dictionary cracking and then to remove the passwords that were cracked from the file cracker.lis created in Listing 14-15 so that a much smaller input file can be used for brute-force cracking. It is not necessary to recrack passwords already found, of course.

■ **Note** It is interesting to note that the PL/SQL cracker ran for about 6 seconds and cracked all but one of the passwords that woraauthbf did in 70 seconds. One of the key elements of password cracking in this database security scenario is that we are not hackers and we do not need to leave a password cracker running for days or even weeks to assess whether a password is stronger than, say, seven or eight characters. Depending on the character set used and the machine the cracker is running on, this may take a long time. In this scenario, it is necessary to get a view of the relative strength of passwords in the first instance. The preceding example of the PL/SQL cracker is great; about 97 percent of the passwords in my database were cracked in 6.28 seconds. I don't need to crack the rest; I now know the "state" of password security in my database and need to take the next steps. This is the idea I want you to understand when cracking your passwords.

As a demonstration of brute-force mode, I have removed all of the entries from the input file cracker.lis except the entry for the database user D. In my case, this is simply to demonstrate the cracker without it running forever. The cracker is then run in brute-force mode by setting the –m parameter for maximum password length of six characters, and the –c parameter to set the character set to alpha + numeric—that is, abcdefghijklmnopqrstuvwxyz0123456789—a character set of 36 characters. The dictionary file is now not necessary, of course. Listing 14-17 demonstrates brute-force cracking with woraauthbf.

Listing 14-17. Running woraauthbf in Brute Force Mode

```
C:\woraauthbf_0.22R3>woraauthbf -p cracker.lis -t hash -m 6 -c alpha
um
Usernames will be permuted!
The number of processors: 2
Number of pwds to check: 2238976116
Number of pwds to check by thread: 1119488058
Password file: cracker.lis, charset: alphanum, maximum length: 6, type: hash
Start: 0 End: 1119488058
Start: 1119488058 End: 2238976116
Start array thread with 489 number of passwords!
Writing session files...
Writing session files...
Writing session files...
Writing session files...
Writing session files...
Writing session files...
Writing session files...
Writing session files...
Password found: D:XXXXXX:Λ:Λ
Elpased time: 544s
Checked passwords: 749562520
Password / Second: 1377872

C:\woraauthbf_0.22R3>
```

Brute-forcing passwords is time-consuming, and extended cracking should be avoided. The example in Listing 14-17 ran for 9.06 minutes for just one user password. A simple calculation can be done to show how long any cracker attempt would take. For the example in Listing 14-17, the cracker was limited to a maximum password length of six. The total possible number of passwords is as follows:

$36^1 + 36^2 + 36^3 + 36^4 + 36^5 + 36^6 =$
$36 + 1,296 + 46,656 + 1,679,616 + 60,466,176 + 2,176,782,336 =$
$2,238,976,116$

■ **Quiz question** If you know Oracle and its password-naming conventions, you should have noticed that the preceding calculation is actually wrong. See if you can work out why it is wrong and by how much. The answer appears at the end of the chapter.

This is a huge number of possible passwords, but as you can see in Listing 14-17, the cracker was running at 1.37 million hashes a second. If I divide the total possible passwords by 1.37 million per second, I get 1,624.9 seconds = 27 minutes. It would only take 27 minutes *if* the actual final guess was my password. Clearly the cracker found the password after 9 minutes, so it's faster than the theoretical limit. This is because you would be very unlucky (or lucky) if the actual password was the last possible one tried. A reasonable figure to use for elapsed cracker time is 50 percent of the total possible time it would take to crack a password.

Why give this math lesson? Well, you need to know how long it would take if someone in your organization wanted to crack your passwords by using reasonable software and reasonable hardware. This is because when you look at password management, you have to ensure that the password is long enough that it cannot be cracked very quickly. More important, the password lifetime should be much shorter than the time taken to crack the password (theoretically).

Before embarking on a session of brute-force password cracking, you need to calculate a rough estimate of how many users you are going to crack multiplied by the character set you would like to use (that is, its length) multiplied by the hardware that you have. As you can see, the task of password cracking is easy, so this is something you must do in databases in your organization.

Fixing Weak Passwords

On the face of it, finding a weak password in a database is easy. As you've seen in this chapter, several password crackers are available, including one written by this author in PL/SQL that is easy to run. In simplistic terms, it should be simple to fix a weak password. If the password is set, for instance, to the username, this is obviously bad. The answer is to change the password to a strong password, perhaps to ghft56ak887. Fine and fixed—or is it?

The problem with passwords is that there are always hidden issues. In a general sense, just fixing the password is not enough. Password management must also be designed and enabled to prevent the weak password from being reset. Auditing must be enabled to understand who is attempting to connect to this user account or who is trying to guess the password, and worst of all, hard-coded passwords must be located. Often there is a reason that a password has been set to a username and never changed since the database was created. This is often because the password is hard-coded in a file somewhere. If you fixed the password, making it strong, and then the business stopped working, you would not be popular. Locating passwords that are hard-coded is not easy because there is no standard way to do it (because there is no standard place the passwords are hard-coded).

Simple file searches can be used—for instance, using grep and find commands on Unix. These need to be backed up with an understanding of who connects with each account. A good starting point is to analyze the listener log and extract accounts that are connected to not by people but by services. Again, there is no standard way to do this, but some things you can try include identifying locations that are known to be servers or terminals but are known not to be used by people or applications that are system executed.

Solutions to hard-coded passwords fall into a number of categories. The first step should always be to eradicate the job that requires the password. Second, attempt to move the job within the database as a database job so the password is no longer required. If the job must remain external to the database, use a solution such as Oracle Wallet to allow authentication using / (slash) connections. Alternately, an externally authenticated user (local, not remote) can be considered, but the privileges assigned to the user must be minimal.

Roles and Privilege Assessment

The assessment of user accounts does not stop at testing password strength or privileges assigned to accounts. More-detailed analysis must also be performed. One obvious test should be to show whether the account has actually been used. It's also worth testing to see whether accounts are being shared.

Have Accounts Been Used?

Checking whether accounts have been used is fairly easy if auditing is enabled. If it is not enabled, an analysis of the listener log could be used instead. As with the previous checks in earlier sections, this is a multistage process. First run the following queries in SQL*Plus. Listing 14-18 demonstrates looking for unused database accounts.

Listing 14-18. Looking for Unused Accounts

```
SQL> select u.username
  2  from dba_users u
  3  where u.username not in (select a.usernam
  4  from dba_audit_session a)
  5  /

USERNAME
-------------------------------
BB4
OWBSYS
ZULIA
FLOWS_030000
BB10
SI_INFORMTN_SCHEMA
{some output removed to conserve space}
WMSYS
BB6
FLOWS_FILES
DUAL_GRANT

44 rows selected.

SQL>
```

The first step is to cross-reference this list in Listing 14-18 with the lists you created earlier for built-in Oracle accounts and also customer accounts. Beware that just because an account has not been used does not mean that it is not needed. For instance, a built-in account may not have been logged in to, but the functionality is used. This check should be clearer for customer accounts because if an account has not been used and it is not a schema account, the account's purpose must be investigated and more than likely can be removed. Also beware that a check for unused accounts is very time-sensitive because it is based on the contents of the audit trail, which in a hardened and secure system should be purged regularly.

Another useful test is to confirm whether an account password has ever been changed. It is also easy to do using SQL. Listing 14-19 demonstrates looking for passwords that have never been changed.

Listing 14-19. Testing Whether Passwords Have Ever Changed

```
SQL> select name,ctime,ptime
  2  from sys.user$
  3  where password is not null
  4  and password not in ('GLOBAL','EXTERNAL')
  5  and length(password)=16
  6  and ctime=ptime;
```

NAME	CTIME	PTIME
OUTLN	15-OCT-07	15-OCT-07
DIP	15-OCT-07	15-OCT-07
TSMSYS	15-OCT-07	15-OCT-07
ORACLE_OCM	15-OCT-07	15-OCT-07
XDB	15-OCT-07	15-OCT-07
WMSYS	15-OCT-07	15-OCT-07
EXFSYS	15-OCT-07	15-OCT-07
XS$NULL	15-OCT-07	15-OCT-07
BILL	05-MAR-08	05-MAR-08
A	23-JUL-08	23-JUL-08
B	23-JUL-08	23-JUL-08
RES_TEST	25-JUL-08	25-JUL-08
AMIS	04-AUG-09	04-AUG-09
XMLT	04-AUG-09	04-AUG-09
PETE2	12-MAY-09	12-MAY-09
P1	17-SEP-08	17-SEP-08

```
{output removed to conserve space}
```

The contents of the report in Listing 14-19 are not surprising but must be correlated with the password management settings for the database. The check for accounts with unchanged passwords is more important when password management settings are enabled but the password has never changed. A password that has not changed when password management is enabled could indicate two things: password management settings are inadequate, or password management is not enabled for all accounts. Finally, if password management is suitable, unchanged passwords would indicate that accounts have been created and never accessed. Therefore, these unused accounts are most likely not needed and should be removed.

Have Accounts Been Shared?

One final check that is worth looking at is to test whether accounts are being shared. Sharing is another one of the subtle problems that relate to policy rather than just technical checks. Checking whether accounts are being shared can be done more easily if there is an audit trail enabled. Listing 14-20 SQL demonstrates looking for shared accounts.

Listing 14-20. Locating Shared Accounts

```
SQL> select username,count(distinct(terminal))
  2  from dba_audit_session
  3  having count(distinct(terminal))>1
  4  group by username;

USERNAME                         COUNT(DISTINCT(TERMINAL))
------------------------------   -------------------------
CTXSYS                                                   2
DBSNMP                                                   2
SCOTT                                                    2
SYSMAN                                                   2
SYSTEM                                                   3

5 rows selected.

SQL>
```

Correlating data is an important part of security. For instance, the results of the query in Listing 14-20 must be correlated with the results of the previous sections. Database accounts that are shared should fall into one of two groups: built-in or customer added. If the account was customer added, there should be some indication of what the account is used for as well as the detailed indication of the privileges assigned to the account. Often more-detailed analysis is required after running queries such as the code in Listing 14-20. A good example from Listing 14-20 is that the SCOTT account has been shared. This is a sample account, so we must identify who is using the SCOTT account and for what purpose. An analysis of the privileges assigned to this account is not necessary at this point, because it clearly should be removed.

Security is often about subtlety, about process and management, and about attitude toward the protection of the data, as well as being about testing individual parameters and settings. Don't forget this; this is very important.

Password Management

This journey into the security assessment of user accounts within the database has to come a long way before you get to assess password management. At this point, you should understand which accounts are in the database, which accounts should be removed, and the purpose and use of the accounts that remain. Also at this point, you must consider password management as a solution to provide additional protected access to the accounts that remain. In other words, the accounts must have strong passwords, and protections must be there to prevent anyone from cracking the passwords within a reasonable time.

The script profiles.sql is available from www.petefinnigan.com/profiles.sql and is useful for getting an overview of all of the profile settings within the database for all users. Most of the values in the report reveal password management restrictions but also included is sessions_per_user, which can be used to prevent multiple concurrent sessions. The sessions_per_user profile setting cannot totally prevent sharing of accounts but can help. Listing 14-21 demonstrates how to test the current profile settings within the database.

Listing 14-21. Running the profiles.sql Script

```
SQL> @profiles


profiles.sql: Release 1.0.0.0.0 - Production on Fri Aug 21 20:51:36 2009
Copyright (c) 2007, 2009 PeteFinnigan.com Limited. All rights reserved.

USER              Profile          F   T   S   L   M   G   L     V
==========================================================================
PP                DEFAULT          10  U   U   1   U   7   180 NULL
BB4               DEFAULT          10  U   U   1   U   7   180 NULL
PXF               DEFAULT          10  U   U   1   U   7   180 NULL
ZULIA             DEFAULT          10  U   U   1   U   7   180 NULL
MONITOR           DEFAULT          10  U   U   1   U   7   180 NULL
LT_EXP            DEFAULT          10  U   U   1   U   7   180 NULL
P2                DEFAULT          10  U   U   1   U   7   180 NULL
IMPORTER          DEFAULT          10  U   U   1   U   7   180 NULL
ORASCAN           DEFAULT          10  U   U   1   U   7   180 NULL
BB5               DEFAULT          10  U   U   1   U   7   180 NULL
BB8               DEFAULT          10  U   U   1   U   7   180 NULL
PM                DEFAULT          10  U   U   1   U   7   180 NULL
BI                DEFAULT          10  U   U   1   U   7   180 NULL
XS$NULL           DEFAULT          10  U   U   1   U   7   180 NULL
DBSNMP            MONITORING       U   D   D   D   D   D   D   D
SYSMAN            DEFAULT          10  U   U   1   U   7   180 NULL
WKSYS             WKSYS_PROF       U   D   D   D   D   D   D   D
OLAPSYS           DEFAULT          10  U   U   1   U   7   180 NULL
OWBSYS            DEFAULT          10  U   U   1   U   7   180 NULL
{some output removed to conserve space}
ANONYMOUS         DEFAULT          10  U   U   1   U   7   180 NULL
CTXSYS            DEFAULT          10  U   U   1   U   7   180 NULL
WMSYS             DEFAULT          10  U   U   1   U   7   180 NULL
MDSYS             DEFAULT          10  U   U   1   U   7   180 NULL
FLOWS_FILES       DEFAULT          10  U   U   1   U   7   180 NULL
SYSTEM            DEFAULT          10  U   U   1   U   7   180 NULL
SYS               DEFAULT          10  U   U   1   U   7   180 NULL
MGMT_VIEW         DEFAULT          10  U   U   1   U   7   180 NULL
OUTLN             DEFAULT          10  U   U   1   U   7   180 NULL
==========================================================================
USER              Profile          F   T   S   L   M   G   L     V

PL/SQL procedure successfully completed.

For updates please visit http://www.petefinnigan.com/tools.htm

SQL>
```

The output shown in Listing 14-21 needs to be explained. Taking the record for the OUTLN user, I will explain the columns shown in the report. The first column is the username. The second is the name assigned to the profile that has been allocated to OUTLN; the profile in this case is DEFAULT. The column F is the number of failed login attempts allowed; for OUTLN this is 10. The next column, T, is the amount of time allowed between password reuses. For OUTLN, this is set to U, which means *unlimited*; the password cannot be reused. The next column identified as S shows the sessions allowed per user; for OUTLN, this is set also to unlimited. The next column is L, which is the lock time for a password; for OUTLN, this is set to one day. The next column is M, which is the number of passwords that have to be set before a password can be reused; for OUTLN, this is also set to unlimited, which means passwords cannot be reused. The next column is G, which is the password grace time; for OUTLN, this is set to 7 days. The next column is L, which is the password lifetime; for OUTLN, this is set to 180 days. The final column is V, which is the name of the assigned password complexity function; for OUTLN, this is NULL, not set.

The output shown in Listing 14-21 is unfortunately very common in almost all systems this author audits. Very rarely do I see password management enabled, although Oracle is improving the situation by enabling some default settings for you in the DEFAULT profile. It should be said now that although the settings provided by Oracle are better than nothing, they are absolutely inadequate.

You must design different profiles for different types of accounts within your database. A one-size-fits-all policy doesn't work for a number of reasons. Do not go overboard on the design of password policies, though, because the permutations of settings are not that broad anyway.

As an initial step, the following groups of user accounts in the database (you should be able to identify these by now) should have separate profiles:

- Application schemas

- Default accounts

- Administrative accounts

- Power users such as those running or creating reports

Finally, ensure that the default profile contains the strongest setting for each resource name taken from all the profiles that have been designed. This ensures that any account created without a profile specifically assigned gets the strongest settings because all accounts are assigned the DEFAULT profile if one is not specifically assigned. Having a strong DEFAULT profile also ensures all users falling to a catchall of the strongest settings. Designing profiles is often very specific to each individual organization, or certain design decisions can be taken into consideration. Internal access and use policies must also be taken into consideration; most companies have a policy such for "access and use" that defines password management settings. For instance, some of the specific settings for the preceding profiles could include those listed in Table 14-1.

Table 14-1. Showing Suitable Profile Settings for Classes of Users

Profile	Failed Login	Reuse Time	Sessions per User	Lock Time	Max Reuse	Grace Time	Lifetime
SCHEMA	1	Infinite	1	10 days	Never	0	Calculate
BUILTIN	1	Infinite	1	10 days	Never	0	Calculate
ADMIN	3	Infinite	3	0.5 day	Never	1 days	Calculate
POWER	5	Infinite	2	1 day	Never	3 days	Calculate
DEFAULT	1	Infinite	1	10 days	Never	0 days	Calculate

Finally, you must also consider complexity rules for the password. Each profile must have a password complexity function attached to it. In general, there are no reasons to allow different password complexity rules for different classes of users, because the risk is just as high for any user that the password is guessed. The password verification function that is shipped with the database before 11g is better than nothing but is completely inadequate—for instance, the 10g and lower function enforces a password length of four characters, which is clearly far too small. The password verification function shipped with 11g has much better features than the 10g function; even if you are running a database of a lower version, start with the 11g password verification function and improve on it.

The password length must be set to a number that is long enough that normal software and hardware cannot be used to crack the password in a reasonable time. The calculations earlier will help you with this. It is generally considered that eight characters is long enough, but this is seriously doubted at the current time because much faster password crackers are waiting in the wings that utilize graphics card accelerators and FPGA hardware. Even an eight-character password can be cracked in a reasonably short amount of time. Therefore, you should consider a minimum length of 10 characters or ideally at least 15 characters for passwords.

A second important point must be made: if you want to use a grace time with the password management, then when calculating a suitable password lifetime based on cracker speed, subtract the grace time from the figure you come up with rather than adding it to the lifetime, because this will just artificially extend the lifetime password.

The settings shown in Table 14-1 are just for illustration. Your own settings should be derived from your own access and use policy and other factors from assessing the database security. If your calculations show profiles with the same settings for most groups of users, it is still valuable to create them as separate profiles for identification purposes. This also allows you to change the settings in the future without affecting the second group of users.

Audit Settings

Auditing is a valuable weapon in your fight against potential breaches of your data. Oracle has finally enabled auditing by default with version 11g, primarily to support their own Audit Vault product. All production databases in this day and age should have auditing enabled within the database at least to log connections to the database and ideally also to log use of system privileges.

Ensure that auditing is enabled by selecting the audit_trail parameter. This parameter has numerous possible settings allowing audits to be sent to the operating system or stored within the database. This parameter also allows the audit trail to be written to syslog or as XML files or as raw text trace files. Any of these settings are suitable, but for ease of reporting, quite clearly an audit trail written to the database is simple to use. There is a downside in writing the audit trail to the database: the audit trail can be manipulated by administrative staff. For sites that have no auditing enabled at all, it is probably still better to start with audit trails written to the database, even accepting a potential security problem of doing this, because it makes configuration and setup of reports and processes to manage the audit trail easier. The audit trail should then be migrated to a more secure solution as soon as possible.

Ensure that auditing is enabled to capture connections to the database. Listing 14-22 shows how to test whether auditing is enabled within your database.

Listing 14-22. Checking Audit Settings

```
SQL> col user_name for a10 head "User"
SQL> col audit_option for a14 head "Option"
SQL> col success for a10 head "Success"
```

```
SQL> col failure for a10 head "failure"
SQL> select nvl(user_name,'*') user_name,
  2       audit_option,
  3       success,
  4       failure
  5  from dba_stmt_audit_opts
  6  where audit_option='CREATE SESSION';

User       Option         Success    failure
---------- -------------- ---------- ----------
*          CREATE SESSION BY ACCESS  BY ACCESS

1 row selected.

SQL>
```

The output shown in Listing 14-22 is an ideal setting, but as usual with security, there are more things that you will think about than just turning the audit on. Turning on auditing is the first step, but you must also consider archiving the audit trail for future reference and also purging the audit trail on a regular basis to ensure that it is not manipulated or deleted. Reports must also be created that highlight incorrect use of database accounts. This could include testing access at times that are not normal, it could include sharing of accounts as shown earlier; it could also include checking for failed login attempts and detection of individuals trying to guess passwords if possible. Many types of reports can be created, but the most important aspect of this is that you must start with the reports, not the audit technical settings. Start with a business requirement that says, "I want to know..." and then design reports, the purging mechanisms, and the management processes to surround the audit.

Summary

This chapter has covered a lot of ground with lots of steps. In general, Oracle security is not a complicated process. The problem is, the steps are easy but there are lots of them. It is also important to work the steps in a methodical manner. There are two main messages that I have tried to get across in this chapter: remove and reduce.

You should remove what is not needed, either because it was installed by Oracle and you don't need it, or because it was installed by you but again you don't need it. Anything in the database that is not needed is simply increasing risk. So at the highest level, *remove* means to remove accounts from the database, but the same idea permeates through the whole process.

This leads to the second idea, which is *reduce*. Reduce the privileges from the accounts that remain in the database to the absolute minimum necessary and reduce to only the privileges necessary to do the job that the accounts are designed for. This means that every account in the database must have an owner, someone who uses that account or owns the business that uses it. That physical person must have one account only; she must not share the account with other people, and of course the account must be used for one purpose only. If an account is shared by people or shared among tasks, the account cannot have been designed for the specific purpose; this sharing implies that there would have to be a compromise.

After the removal of accounts has been completed and the reduction of privileges phase has simplified the users and their privileges, what is left must be locked and secured. Accounts that are not used on a day-to-day basis should not be open and should not be connectable.

All accounts must be audited, and the audit trail must be acted upon when breaches of process and protocol occur. Management must also be considered. The task of securing an Oracle database is not just about fixing technical parameters and settings; it's also about process and people. The correct management processes must be in place to ensure that database accounts are not abused.

Security, if done properly, is a time-consuming task, and contrary to popular belief is not simply a case of following hints in a checklist but is a methodical and logical process. If you follow the ideas and principles in this chapter, you will have secure users and privileges within your database. Simply following a checklist will not achieve this because there is no thought process involved and there is no correlation involved.

Quiz Answer

As you may remember, in the brute-force password-cracking section, I pointed out that the calculation I used for the total number of passwords can be slightly incorrect in some cases. The reason is that a password in Oracle that is not encased in quotes cannot start with a digit; for instance, a password of 0FRED is not valid, but "0FRED" is. This means that the length of the first character set is actually only 26, not 36. This modifies the possible passwords downward. The actual password cracker, though, is correct because it must cater to the case of a password encased in quotes and having no limitations on its first character.

So for a six-character password, the calculation becomes this:

26	= 26	+
26*36	= 936	+
26*36*36	= 33,696	+
26*36*36*36	= 1,213,056	+
26*36*36*36*36	= 43,670,016	+
26*36*36*36*36*36	= 1,572,120,576	
	= 1,617,038,306	

Compare this with the original number of possible passwords seen earlier. If you calculate the difference ($2,238,976,116 - 1,617,038,306 = 621,937,810$), you will see there's a 28 percent reduction in the number of passwords that must be cracked. The cracker used in this chapter does not support this mode, but someone could easily add it. Therefore, this must be considered when designing password management settings. The commercial audit tool PFCLScan does support this now in its built-in password cracker.

■ ■ ■

CHAPTER 15

Securing Data

by Pete Finnigan

Attempting to secure an Oracle database by using just a checklist is a flawed idea. I say this even after creating some of the checklists that exist. I wrote the SANS Security Consensus Operational Readiness Evaluation (SCORE) checklist and the SANS Step-by-Step guide, and my step-by-step guide was used as the basis for the Centre for Internet Security benchmark version 1. So I speak with authority. Using checklists per se is not flawed; the measures and details in them are still useful and if followed will in general result in a more hardened database than if you didn't follow the steps in them. But imagine that you download the CIS benchmark version 3; hundreds of pages and an even bigger number of checks are included. If you diligently sit down and follow and apply all recommendations, you would most likely be looking at man years of effort to complete all the checks. But after all of that effort, would your credit card data be secure? No! Why is that?

Well, because checklists such as the CIS benchmark are lists, not methodologies. The CIS benchmark does not say anything about your data or in this case specifically about your credit cards. The lack of focus on the data in checklists is a problem that must be solved in a different manner.

Checklists are useful from a general hardening point of view but they must not be the focus of the database security process. It is sad to say the checklists could be likened to the problem in the tuning world known as *compulsive tuning disorder*. Checks in the security checklists are just a random list of checks and advice.

Even worse, in later versions of some checklists, suitable fixes for each of the entries have been included. A cursory look through these security fixes shows that some have issues. A good example is the check that states, "File system privileges in $ORACLE_HOME/bin must be set to 0755 or less." While the setting of 0755 is fine as a requirement, the change suggested is actually incorrect as the checklist states `chmod 0755 $ORACLE_HOME/bin/*`.

■ **Quiz question** Why is the command `chmod 0755 $ORACLE_HOME/bin/*` incorrect in this case? The answer is at the end of the chapter. But see if you can work out why the command is incorrect without looking first.

A more general problem with checklists, even if they suggest a fix for a particular problem, is that fixes required for Oracle databases are often not consistent. There are lots of different versions of Oracle running on different platforms supporting a myriad of different applications. In general, security fixes suggested in checklists can be applied across combinations of platforms, versions, and applications. However, in some cases a fix will not work for a specific combination of platform/Oracle database version/application. This is a rather tricky problem of Oracle security in that consistent solutions should be found that work on most platforms. The reason generally is because companies have large numbers of databases, and applying different fixes to different databases becomes very expensive. A good example of differences in fix strategies would be that for Oracle Database version 9i and lower, it is advisable to set a password for the Oracle listener, but for Oracle database versions 10g and later, this is much less relevant because the listener uses host-based security.

This discussion seems negative against checklists but it is not meant to be. General hardening should always be part of the solution for securing Oracle databases; checklists are required to support this activity. Good examples of general hardening include things such as enabling audit, enabling password management, password cracking, and many more. This leads the discussion to a fundamental question. Are you trying to secure Oracle, the software, or are you trying to secure the data? In my opinion, it is impossible to secure the Oracle software; this is often what checklists are trying to do. This is because the software is immensely complex with seemingly infinite combinations of parameters, settings, and configurations that can be made; securing it is impossible because without focusing on something to secure, there is no focus. There is no starting point and there is no end point, because without a target to focus the security at, there is no way to know whether you've finished. In other words, how is it possible to tell if the database is secure?

The fundamental purpose of any database is to store, manage, and serve the data in a format that suits the business and enables it to operate. Therefore, when security is applied to the equation, security must focus on the data first. Although in my view it is impossible to secure the Oracle software, it is possible to secure the data in your database. To create an effective security plan for your Oracle database, you have to start with the *data*. Unless you know exactly which data you want to secure, there is no way you can secure that chosen data. The idea of focusing on the data first is common sense, but the underlying story of security is common sense.

The focus of this chapter is the data. To enable you to secure your database, you have to start with the data; to start with the data, you have to know which data to target. This is the process you will look into next; you will identify key data and then investigate in depth how the data you have chosen is protected and controlled from a security perspective.

Identifying Key Data

The starting point to the whole process of securing data *is* to choose some data. Even if the database has hundreds of tables or even thousands of tables, it is only necessary at this stage to pick one or two tables. In fact, what you will pick at this stage is a business object or piece of data, not a database table. The process will convert that to tables in the database. You may ask, "What about the rest of the tables in the database if I pick only one or two tables at this stage?" The data selection process is intended to give a clear picture of the access models employed in the whole database by analyzing a specific set of data. The final task in this chapter is to generalize these detailed data access ideas presented for a chosen group of data across the whole database. As you will see, analyzing a single table (or rather a piece of data) is complex and time-consuming if done properly, so it is completely impractical to analyze to the same depth for all data in the database. The output from any such data analysis process would in fact be completely overwhelming.

The data you choose to analyze doesn't really matter in terms of what that data is. The important point is that you choose relevant data for your situation. In other words, the data must be production data and not static data or configuration data or other periphery data. Nonproduction data is not likely to have the same access model as the real data. In a business system that, for instance, supports the storage of credit card details to allow the purchase of the organization's products, choosing the credit card details data as the target of this analysis would be a great choice. But, the data you choose for your investigation can be anything so long as it is relevant production data. You can choose more than one piece of data, but a good starting point is to just choose one.

A final point worth making at this stage is that although the data you choose does not really matter (apart from the proviso I gave earlier about it being production data and not configuration static data), the data choice will provide more impact for management if that data is critical or important data for the business. For instance, if your business is based on credit card sales, choosing credit card details is a great choice because there is then a much larger chance of a budget being made available to correct the access model after that access model is analyzed because everyone understands the threat to credit card details. Your choice of data to analyze could equally be banking details, sales targets, nationally sensitive data, customer lists, or indeed any critical data that is relevant to your organization.

Locating the Database Table

To move this chapter along, I need to make a choice for the example I am going to present to you. Because the theft of credit card details seems to be in vogue with the media and specifically in terms of data security because of recent publicized breaches of large numbers of credit card details, it makes a great choice for me to analyze as an example.

Every site and every application and every database are different, so the starting point is always going to be different for you compared to the example laid out in this chapter. However, the processes described to you will be the same.

One of the big problems you will come across immediately is that people don't really know where their sensitive data is within the database. They think they know with reasonable certainty, but what you will discover quite quickly is that they probably don't. Because you are not trying to hack the database, you have the great advantage of being able to talk to the right people to locate data of interest. If the application and database were designed in-house, you can simply talk to the designers and ask where the credit card details are stored. If your application is provided by a third-party vendor, contact the vendor and ask where the credit card details are stored. Also solicit advice from DBAs or application developers or support teams who are likely to know where the chosen data is stored. If none of these avenues of investigation result in you locating a database table in which credit card details are stored, then there are still options available. I will discuss these options now.

If the source code for the applications is available, the source code can be parsed in the area of the routines that affect credit card details to look for the table name that stores the credit card details. Another alternate solution to locate the data is to enable a database trace using event 10046 and then have a business user do something related to processing credit card details—for instance, viewing a customer's credit card details. This trace file should reveal the table name where the credit cards details are stored. If none of these ideas work or no access to the source code is available, you can resort to searching the database looking for tables that may store credit card details.

If a table is not found via an obvious table name or column names, more-complex solutions can be used. You could, for example, implement the *Luhn algorithm* (http://en.wikipedia.org/wiki/Luhn_algorithm), which is used to verify that a credit card number is valid. Data can then be sampled for each database table column where the data type is character based and is the correct length for a credit card number. The numbers retrieved can then be tested with the algorithm to check whether they are valid credit cards. There is a flaw with this idea: if the credit card details, particularly the personal access numbers (PAN), are encrypted, the Luhn algorithm is not useful. Getting to this stage to have to find credit card details (my example data, don't forget) is rare and indicates a worrying, but subtle issue: if this much effort is needed to find the data, either it is stored very securely or no one in the organization understands the database properly, which means that your credit card data is almost certainly insecure. One final idea that could be tried in the case of credit card details of course is to assume that the credit card data is encrypted, and then look for any database procedure that has implemented the Oracle encryption routines DBMS_CRYPTO or DBMS_OBFUSCATION_TOOLKIT, and then look for correlations between database tables and the routines.

In my sample database, I will also use an example of credit card data. The designers have been unable to tell where the data is stored. I was unable to enable trace. The DBAs are part of an external organization, and I am unable to get access to them to find out the information. So I will demonstrate one of the harder methods to find the data. This method is to use SQL to search in the database for any table that may hold credit card details. The first query I can try is shown in Listing 15-1.

Listing 15-1. Searching for the Credit Card Data

```
SQL> col object_name for a20 head "Name"
SQL> col object_type for a20 head "Type"
SQL> col owner for a20 head "Owner"
SQL> select owner,object_name,object_type
  2  from dba_objects
  3  where object_name like '%CREDIT%';

Owner                Name                 Type
-------------------- -------------------- --------------------
ORABLOG              CREDIT_CARD          TABLE

SQL>
```

Locating the table in Listing 15-1 was relatively easy because the developer has called the table by a really obvious name. Although it isn't the number one security problem of a typical data installation, consideration should be given to the naming of key tables. Changing the name to something innocuous like S45 would not prevent a determined hacker from finding the data, but it would certainly prevent an unskilled or casual thief.

It is also worth noting that I am in England and speak English so I searched with an English word, *credit*, but if I was working in, say, France, I would need to search for the French word *crédit* and also the English word *credit*. Developers in non-English-speaking countries still tend to use English words in computer code, so searching in both languages is important. If I didn't find the table immediately with a simple word like *credit*, my next check would have been to sample columns in tables using the view DBA_TAB_COLUMNS and look for columns that could be part of a credit card implementation with names such as PAN or CVV or CVV2. I will not demonstrate this now because I will show it later in the chapter for a different reason.

I just want to reiterate at this point that the query in Listing 15-1 seems very simple, but remember in your own organization you may not be searching for credit card details, you may be searching for banking details or sales lists or customer lists, so substitute the relevant word used in Listing 15-1. Also, as you will see, Oracle security is often about using very simple queries with powerful effect.

Direct Table Privileges

I had a dilemma while writing this chapter: whether to tell you now the whole problem or to leak it to you as the chapter evolves. So I decided the best option is to give you an overview of the complete picture at this stage and cover the details as I progress through the rest of the chapter.

The problem with data is that it is not static. Data moves from users through applications, web servers, application servers, database tiers, and out again to backup tapes, other databases, reports, feeds, and many other processes and actions. In simple terms, data can be said to *flow* throughout a complete application. During all this movement, data can be viewed in transit and can be viewed at rest at any of the stages. What this means at a high level is that simply securing a single table that reputedly holds the data within a database is not enough to secure the same data. After all, the task of securing "your data" should drive all of your Oracle security work. Drilling deeper inside the database layer, the problems get worse. It is possible to have multiple paths to the same data, and of course the data can be replicated, causing the problem again to widen.

Going back to the plot of this chapter, I've chosen a single entity of data—the credit card details—and located a table within my database that holds these details. I have to start somewhere, and the first step is to assess the privileges granted on the single table identified earlier. Later sections in this chapter will illustrate the reality of where the data actually is available within the database and also will build on the access rights map you start right here.

Download the script who_can_access.sql from www.petefinnigan.com/tools.htm and use it to produce a hierarchical listing of all the privileges assigned to the ORABLOG.CREDIT_CARD table. Run the script as shown in Listing 15-2.

Listing 15-2. Running who_can_access.sql to Assess the Privileges on ORABLOG.CREDIT_CARD

```
SQL> @who_can_access

who_can_access: Release 1.0.3.0.0 - Production on Thu Aug 27 16:01:35 2009
Copyright (c) 2004 PeteFinnigan.com Limited. All rights reserved.

NAME OF OBJECT TO CHECK        [USER_OBJECTS]: CREDIT_CARD
OWNER OF THE OBJECT TO CHECK          [USER]: ORABLOG
OUTPUT METHOD Screen/File                [S]: S
FILE NAME FOR OUTPUT              [priv.lst]:
OUTPUT DIRECTORY [DIRECTORY  or file (/tmp)]:
EXCLUDE CERTAIN USERS                    [N]:
USER TO SKIP                        [TEST%]:

Checking object => ORABLOG.CREDIT_CARD
====================================================================


Object type is => TABLE (TAB)
        Privilege => ALTER is granted to =>
        User => EMIL (ADM = NO)
        Privilege => INSERT is granted to =>
        User => EMIL (ADM = NO)
        Privilege => SELECT is granted to =>
        User => EMIL (ADM = NO)

SQL>
```

The report in Listing 15-2 is easy to run and simply requires you to enter the table name and the owner of the table, and to decide whether the output should go to the screen or to a file. In the preceding example, I am sending output to the screen. If I choose to send the output instead to a file, I must also provide a location or directory object and the name of the file.

The output is hierarchical and is also separated on each privilege granted against the table (actually the script can be run against any objects in the database, not just tables) to users or roles. This is neat because it allows you to see the end users who have been assigned the privilege even if the privilege is assigned by a role or via multiple roles. A second script called get_tab2.sql can be downloaded from www.petefinnigan.com/get_tab2.sql that gives a more succinct view of the privileges assigned to an individual table. Run the script now, passing in the table name and the owner of the output format, as shown in Listing 15-3.

Listing 15-3. Running get_tab2.sql to Analyze Privileges

```
SQL> @get_tab2

get_tab2: Release 1.0.0.0.0 - Production on Thu Aug 27 16:30:59 2009
Copyright (c) 2004,2009, PeteFinnigan.com Limited. All rights reserved.

OBJECT TO CHECK                      [XXX_XXXX]: CREDIT_CARD
SCHEMA/OWNER OF THE OBJECT TO CHECK    [USER]: ORABLOG
OUTPUT METHOD Screen/File                 [S]: S
FILE NAME FOR OUTPUT              [priv.lst]:
OUTPUT DIRECTORY [DIRECTORY  or file (/tmp)]:

Testing root object => [ORABLOG.CREDIT_CARD]


GRANTOR        GRANTEE        S I U D A F D I R Q C
-------------  -------------- - - - - - - - - - - -
ORABLOG        EMIL           X X     X

SQL>
```

The output from the script in Listing 15-3 shows the same information as the first script, but all the privileges are collapsed into a single line.

The output of running the script get_tab2.sql shown in Listing 15-3 seems quite verbose on first inspection, but the output is quite simple to interpret. The columns in Listing 15-3 labeled with letters are as follows:

- S = Select privilege has been granted

- I = Insert privilege has been granted

- U = Update privilege has been granted

- D = Delete privilege has been granted

- A = Alter privilege has been granted

- F = Flashback privilege has been granted

- D = Debug privilege has been granted

- I = Index privilege has been granted

- R = References privilege has been granted

- Q = Query Rewrite privilege has been granted

- C = On Commit Refresh privilege has been granted

Therefore, for the output shown in Listing 15-3, the user EMIL has been granted SELECT, INSERT, and ALTER privileges on the database table ORABLOG.CREDIT_CARD.

I tend to use both scripts (who_can_access.sql and get_tab2.sql) when reviewing the security of a database. The second script gives a more compact view of the privileges, but the first script allows me to view the privileges in the hierarchy so I can see exactly where they came from.

At this point in the review, a DBA with a naive view of security would say that security of the credit card information is pretty good. Only the user EMIL has any sort of access to the data, and he only has read and insert access on the data—indeed he cannot even delete or update. The ALTER privilege is interesting because this user could modify the structure of this credit card table. Modification privileges clearly should not be allowed for nonadministrative staff and should generally be available to only the schema owner. The ALTER privilege should be revoked. That's the naive view. In the next section, we'll dig deeper and get a more realistic appraisal of our credit card data security.

Understand the Hierarchy

The preceding section showed that only a single user has access to the credit card data for a small handful of privileges. I isolated one privilege that should be revoked, the ALTER privilege. As I have said, this is a very naive view. Let me now show you the other users who have access to the data. Listing 15-4 shows how to locate other objects (procedures, views, and so forth) that have access to the credit card table.

Listing 15-4. Locating Any Objects That Access ORABLOG.CREDIT_CARD

```
SQL> col name for a20 head "Name"
SQL> col owner for a20 head "Owner"
SQL> col type for a20 head "Type"
SQL> select owner,name,type
  2  from dba_dependencies
  3  where referenced_name='CREDIT_CARD'
  4  and referenced_owner='ORABLOG';

Owner                Name                 Type
-------------------- -------------------- --------------------
ORABLOG              REP_CC_COUNT         FUNCTION
ORABLOG              CC1                  VIEW

2 rows selected.

SQL>
```

Already the problem has become more complex. The simple query in Listing 15-4 shows that two objects depend on the credit card details table that I have chosen as the target. The next step is to assess the privileges assigned to the two objects, to the function and the view. Run the get_tab2.sql script as shown in Listing 15-5.

Listing 15-5. Review the Privileges Granted to REP_CC_COUNT and CC1

```
get_tab2: Release 1.0.0.0.0 - Production on Thu Aug 27 17:26:18 2009
Copyright (c) 2004,2009, PeteFinnigan.com Limited. All rights reserved.

OBJECT TO CHECK                       [XXX_XXXX]: CC1
SCHEMA/OWNER OF THE OBJECT TO CHECK    [USER]: ORABLOG
OUTPUT METHOD Screen/File                 [S]: S
FILE NAME FOR OUTPUT               [priv.lst]:
OUTPUT DIRECTORY [DIRECTORY  or file (/tmp)]:

Testing root object => [ORABLOG.CC1]


GRANTOR         GRANTEE        S I U D A F D I R Q C E
-------------   -------------  - - - - - - - - - - - -
ORABLOG         FRED           X     X
ORABLOG         BILL           X   X X
ORABLOG         ERIC           G X
ORABLOG         BB             X
ORABLOG         AA             X X

SQL> @get_tab2

get_tab2: Release 1.0.0.0.0 - Production on Thu Aug 27 17:26:36 2009
Copyright (c) 2004,2009, PeteFinnigan.com Limited. All rights reserved.

OBJECT TO CHECK                       [XXX_XXXX]: REP_CC_COUNT
SCHEMA/OWNER OF THE OBJECT TO CHECK    [USER]: ORABLOG
OUTPUT METHOD Screen/File                 [S]: S
FILE NAME FOR OUTPUT               [priv.lst]:
OUTPUT DIRECTORY [DIRECTORY  or file (/tmp)]:

Testing root object => [ORABLOG.REP_CC_COUNT]


GRANTOR         GRANTEE        S I U D A F D I R Q C E
-------------   -------------  - - - - - - - - - - - -
ORABLOG         REP                            X

SQL>
```

■ **Note** When the children of a base table such as the ORABLOG.CREDIT_CARD are views or procedures, it is also necessary to review the columns exposed in each view or procedure. This takes security analysis down to a lower level. The purpose is to protect credit card details in this example, which are in a table called CREDIT_CARD. The data in this table is not focused purely on the credit card number itself, though. More-detailed analysis should take into account the level of detail actually in the database table. Perhaps a regulatory requirement controls the access to the credit card number or the CVV, but if a child view exposes only the forename or surname on the card, this must be taken into account.

The output of the two reports in Listings 15-4 and 15-5 clearly show that the problem of securing credit card data is much bigger than that of securing just the one base table. Our further analysis has shown that another six users of the database have access to the credit card data in some form or other.

The problem doesn't stop here, though; I can feel the weight of collective heads sighing and sagging at the moment. The next step is to repeat the process until the complete hierarchy has been resolved. So run the query in Listing 15-6, which shows digging deeper into the credit card hierarchy.

Listing 15-6. Digging Deeper into the Credit Card Heirarchy

```
SQL> col name for a20 head "Name"
SQL> col owner for a20 head "Owner"
SQL> col type for a20 head "Type"
SQL> select owner,name,type
  2  from dba_dependencies
  3  where referenced_name='CC1'
  4  and referenced_owner='ORABLOG';

Owner                Name                 Type
-------------------- -------------------- --------------------
ERIC                 CREPORT              VIEW
ORABLOG              CCNAME               VIEW
ORABLOG              CCEXP                VIEW

3 rows selected.

SQL> select owner,name,type
  2  from dba_dependencies
  3  where referenced_name='REP_CC_COUNT'
  4  and owner='ORABLOG'
  5  /

no rows selected

SQL>
```

The view CC1 has two other views that use it as a source, but the function REP_CC_COUNT has no further dependencies. The same test used in Listing 15-6 now must be repeated for CCNAME and CCEXP, as shown in Listing 15-7.

Listing 15-7. Completing the Heirarchy

```
SQL> select owner,name,type
  2  from dba_dependencies
  3  where referenced_name='CCNAME'
  4  and owner='ORABLOG'
  5  /

no rows selected

SQL> select owner,name,type
  2  from dba_dependencies
  3  where referenced_name='CCEXP'
  4  and owner='ORABLOG'
  5  /

no rows selected

SQL> select owner,name,type
  2  from dba_dependencies
  3  where referenced_name='CREPORT'
  4  and referenced_owner='ERIC'
  5  /

Owner                   Name                    Type
--------------------    --------------------    ----------------
ERIC                    CC_LIST_CC              PROCEDURE

1 row selected.

SQL> select owner,name,type
  2  from dba_dependencies
  3  where referenced_name='CC_LIST_CC'
  4  and referenced_owner='ERIC'
  5  /

no rows selected

SQL>
```

All of the objects in the hierarchy have now been located. The next step is to look at the privilege model for each of the objects displayed within the hierarchy. These include CCNAME, CREPORT, CCEXP, and CC_LIST_CC. So use the get_tab2.sql script again as shown in Listing 15-8.

Listing 15-8. Review the Remaining Privileges

```
SQL> @get_tab2

get_tab2: Release 1.0.0.0.0 - Production on Thu Aug 27 18:32:58 2009
Copyright (c) 2004,2009, PeteFinnigan.com Limited. All rights reserved.
```

```
OBJECT TO CHECK                    [XXX_XXXX]: CCNAME
SCHEMA/OWNER OF THE OBJECT TO CHECK   [USER]: ORABLOG
OUTPUT METHOD Screen/File                [S]: S
FILE NAME FOR OUTPUT              [priv.lst]:
OUTPUT DIRECTORY [DIRECTORY  or file (/tmp)]:

Testing root object => [ORABLOG.CCNAME]


GRANTOR        GRANTEE        S I U D A F D I R Q C E
-------------  -------------- - - - - - - - - - - - -
ORABLOG        CC             X

SQL> @get_tab2

get_tab2: Release 1.0.0.0.0 - Production on Thu Aug 27 18:33:12 2009
Copyright (c) 2004,2009, PeteFinnigan.com Limited. All rights reserved.

OBJECT TO CHECK                    [XXX_XXXX]: CCEXP
SCHEMA/OWNER OF THE OBJECT TO CHECK   [USER]: ORABLOG
OUTPUT METHOD Screen/File                [S]: S
FILE NAME FOR OUTPUT              [priv.lst]:
OUTPUT DIRECTORY [DIRECTORY  or file (/tmp)]:

Testing root object => [ORABLOG.CCEXP]


GRANTOR        GRANTEE        S I U D A F D I R Q C E
-------------  -------------- - - - - - - - - - - - -

SQL> @get_tab2

get_tab2: Release 1.0.0.0.0 - Production on Thu Aug 27 18:34:49 2009
Copyright (c) 2004,2009, PeteFinnigan.com Limited. All rights reserved.

OBJECT TO CHECK                    [XXX_XXXX]: CREPORT
SCHEMA/OWNER OF THE OBJECT TO CHECK   [USER]: ERIC
OUTPUT METHOD Screen/File                [S]: S
FILE NAME FOR OUTPUT              [priv.lst]:
OUTPUT DIRECTORY [DIRECTORY  or file (/tmp)]:

Testing root object => [ERIC.CREPORT]


GRANTOR        GRANTEE        S I U D A F D I R Q C E
-------------  -------------- - - - - - - - - - - - -
ERIC           IX             X
ERIC           HR             X

SQL> @get_tab2
```

```
get_tab2: Release 1.0.0.0.0 - Production on Thu Aug 27 18:35:05 2009
Copyright (c) 2004,2009, PeteFinnigan.com Limited. All rights reserved.

OBJECT TO CHECK                    [XXX_XXXX]: CC_LIST_CC
SCHEMA/OWNER OF THE OBJECT TO CHECK   [USER]: ERIC
OUTPUT METHOD Screen/File                [S]: S
FILE NAME FOR OUTPUT              [priv.lst]:
OUTPUT DIRECTORY [DIRECTORY  or file (/tmp)]:

Testing root object => [ERIC.CC_LIST_CC]


GRANTOR        GRANTEE        S I U D A F D I R Q C E
-------------- -------------- - - - - - - - - - - - -
ERIC           ORABLOG                            X
ERIC           EMIL                               X
ERIC           CC                                 X

SQL>
```

We now have a comprehensive picture of the access model for the credit card data in our database. What is left to do is to summarize all the privileges into one table so that a distinct picture can be provided of the true access to the credit card details for this example database. It is not necessary in this final table to isolate the actual objects as each underlying grant is against a base table anyway. Listing 15-9 shows a summary of all direct and indirect access privileges to the CREDIT_CARD table.

Listing 15-9. A Complete Picture of the Privilege Access Model Implemented for the CREDIT_CARD Table

GRANTOR	GRANTEE	S	I	U	D	A	F	D	I	R	Q	C	E
ORABLOG	EMIL	X	X		X								
ORABLOG	FRED	X			X								
ORABLOG	BILL	X			X	X							
ORABLOG	ERIC	G		X									
ORABLOG	BB	X											
ORABLOG	AA	X		X									
ORABLOG	REP									X			
ORABLOG	CC	X											
ERIC	IX	X											
ERIC	HR	X											
ERIC	ORABLOG											X	
ERIC	EMIL											X	
ERIC	CC											X	

The output shown in the report (Listing 15-9) shows some interesting features. First, there are no duplicate privileges within the database. This is unusual in my experience; normally there are lots of duplications of privileges in production databases I review. Another interesting factor is that the user ERIC was given SELECT privilege on the base table with the grant option. This user has then regranted this privilege to two other users directly and three other users indirectly via EXECUTE privileges on PL/SQL procedures. Without even seeing the source code of the procedures that have been granted, it is possible to deduce that they must select data from the base table ORABLOG.CREDIT_CARD or from a view on the base table. In total at this point in the chapter, 11 users have access to the single credit card table. Note that the user ERIC has granted EXECUTE privileges to three users on his PL/SQL. These additional users have actually implicitly got SELECT privileges on the data also as these procedures are created as definer rights. If these procedures were invoker rights, explicit privileges would be needed on the table directly for each user. Having invoker rights PL/SQL code would be a better security model as the currently implemented solution means there could be a way to get ERIC to execute the procedure on your behalf.

■ **Note** Remember that the owners of each of the objects in the hierarchy also have privileges on their own objects. ORABLOG, who owns the base table CREDIT_CARD in this example, has all privileges on that same table. ERIC, who owns views on the CREDIT_CARD base table, has all privileges on his views as normal, but his privileges are actually implicitly restricted on the CREDIT_CARD data exposed to those granted by ORABLOG. The user ERIC's views are based on the table owned by ORABLOG, and this restricts the allowed privileges to just select on the base table. This makes the analysis slightly more complex, as you can see some privileges are red herrings.

What I've described in this section is the reality of access to data and what I see on a day-to-day basis when performing security analysis for clients. Often the client naively assumes that the data is only in the base table and that only users granted access to the base table can see the data. Hopefully, you will see from the discussion so far in this chapter that this is clearly not the case.

Other Methods to Read Data

Unfortunately, the problem of securing credit card data is not resolved at this point. Our analysis so far has shown that the data is accessible, not just in the base table but also from objects that sit above the base table in the hierarchy; these objects are PL/SQL functions and also database views. The problem now gets even worse, because there are many other ways to get at the data we are analyzing (in this case, credit card details) than just the base table and related objects such as views and stored procedures.

Oracle provides many sweeping privileges; these are identified by the keyword ANY in the middle of their names. In Oracle Database 11g Release 1 there are 132 such privileges; although not all of these sweeping system privileges will allow access to the credit card data (in this case), a lot will. Often quite devious ideas have to be used by hackers and researchers to show how system privileges can be used to read data.

The first example (perhaps the most obvious one) I want to show is the SELECT ANY TABLE privilege, which will allow any user with that privilege to see any production data and in this case the credit card details. Checking which users have this privilege is easy with the script who_has_priv.sql from www.petefinnigan.com/tools.htm. Download the script and run it to show a hierarchical view of the users who have the SELECT ANY TABLE system privilege. Listing 15-10 shows an example run of the script.

Listing 15-10. Looking for Users Who Have the SELECT ANY TABLE Privilege

```
who_has_priv: Release 1.0.3.0.0 - Production on Thu Aug 27 19:05:33 2009
Copyright (c) 2004 PeteFinnigan.com Limited. All rights reserved.

PRIVILEGE TO CHECK          [SELECT ANY TABLE]: SELECT ANY TABLE
OUTPUT METHOD Screen/File              [S]: S
FILE NAME FOR OUTPUT           [priv.lst]:
OUTPUT DIRECTORY [DIRECTORY  or file (/tmp)]:
EXCLUDE CERTAIN USERS                  [N]:
USER TO SKIP                      [TEST%]:

Privilege => SELECT ANY TABLE has been granted to =>
======================================================================
        Role => DBA (ADM = YES) which is granted to =>
            User => SYS (ADM = YES)
            User => SYSMAN (ADM = NO)
            User => AA (ADM = NO)
            User => SYSTEM (ADM = YES)
            Role => APPROLE (ADM = NO) which is granted to =>
                User => BB (ADM = NO)
                User => AA (ADM = NO)
                User => SYSTEM (ADM = YES)
            User => IMPORTER (ADM = NO)
    User => MDSYS (ADM = NO)
    User => SYS (ADM = YES)
    Role => IMP_FULL_DATABASE (ADM = NO) which is granted to =>
        User => SYS (ADM = YES)
        User => WKSYS (ADM = NO)
        User => IMPORTER (ADM = NO)
        Role => DBA (ADM = NO) which is granted to =>
            User => SYS (ADM = YES)
            User => SYSMAN (ADM = NO)
            User => AA (ADM = NO)
            User => SYSTEM (ADM = YES)
            Role => APPROLE (ADM = NO) which is granted to =>
                User => BB (ADM = NO)
                User => AA (ADM = NO)
                User => SYSTEM (ADM = YES)
            User => IMPORTER (ADM = NO)
        Role => DATAPUMP_IMP_FULL_DATABASE (ADM = NO) which is granted to =>
            Role => DBA (ADM = NO) which is granted to =>
                User => SYS (ADM = YES)
                User => SYSMAN (ADM = NO)
                User => AA (ADM = NO)
                User => SYSTEM (ADM = YES)
                Role => APPROLE (ADM = NO) which is granted to =>
                    User => BB (ADM = NO)
                    User => AA (ADM = NO)
                    User => SYSTEM (ADM = YES)
                User => IMPORTER (ADM = NO)
            User => SYS (ADM = YES)
```

```
       User => WKSYS (ADM = NO)
       User => ORASCAN (ADM = NO)
       Role => EXP_FULL_DATABASE (ADM = NO) which is granted to =>
               User => WKSYS (ADM = NO)
               Role => DATAPUMP_EXP_FULL_DATABASE (ADM = NO) which is granted to =>
                       User => SYS (ADM = YES)
                       Role => DBA (ADM = NO) which is granted to =>
                               User => SYS (ADM = YES)
                               User => SYSMAN (ADM = NO)
                               User => AA (ADM = NO)
                               User => SYSTEM (ADM = YES)
                               Role => APPROLE (ADM = NO) which is granted to =>
                                       User => BB (ADM = NO)
                                       User => AA (ADM = NO)
{output snipped for space considerations}

SQL>
```

The output shown in Listing 15-10 highlights that there is a massive duplication of privileges. The granting of the SELECT ANY TABLE system privilege used within this database has been done many times. With just this one privilege, a further 10 users in the sample database have access to the CREDIT_CARD table; this does not even consider the duplication of privilege grants. The users shown are mostly built-in users. You should address those by using the ideas presented in the preceding chapter. Removing the duplication is harder because this is something Oracle must do.

SELECT ANY TABLE is an easy system privilege to understand. Another good example to discuss is the CREATE ANY TRIGGER privilege, which would allow an assailant to create a trigger on a table he has no rights to access and from that trigger code simply select all of the data from the table. Sweeping privileges are a major issue and must be addressed. Of course, SELECT is not the only dangerous privilege. INSERT ANY TABLE, DELETE ANY TABLE, and UPDATE ANY TABLE are just as dangerous.

Another common issue is that data is often found outside the database—on the database server, for instance, or on application servers, or on client desktops or indeed in other databases. A cursory search on the server is very specific to each situation and also is implicitly linked to the type of data searched for. As an example, on the Unix server supporting my sample database, a search through the application owner's home directory shows possible data leakage. Listing 15-11 shows the contents of the ORABLOG users home directory.

Listing 15-11. A Listing of the ORABLOG Users Home Directory

```
[root@vostok orablog]# ls -ltr
total 692
-rw-r--r-- 1 orablog oinstall    172 Mar  4  2008 fix_wp.sql
-rw-r--r-- 1 orablog oinstall   3509 Mar  4  2008 fix_wp.lis
-rw-r--r-- 1 orablog oinstall     81 Mar  7  2008 su.out
-rw-r--r-- 1 orablog oinstall    359 Mar  7  2008 su.sql
-rw-r--r-- 1 orablog oinstall 155648 Mar  7  2008 orablog.dmp
-rw-r--r-- 1 root    oinstall 399249 Aug  1  2008 out.tar.gz
-rw-r--r-- 1 orablog oinstall 139264 Nov 28  2008 crypt.dmp
-rw-r--r-- 1 oracle  oinstall     10 Nov 28  2008 test.txt
-rw-r--r-- 1 oracle  oinstall     85 Nov 28  2008 cards.lis
[root@vostok orablog]#
```

The file cards.lis and also the export file crypt.dmp both look suspicious as the names suggest that they could contain credit card data. Listing 15-12 shows the contents of the cards.lis file.

Listing 15-12. The Contents of the cards.lis File

```
[root@vostok orablog]# cat cards.lis
4049877198543457
3742345698766678
4049657443219878
3742112366758976
4049990855468731
[root@vostok orablog]#
```

Our discovery of credit card numbers in text files is interesting on a number of levels. At the highest level, it indicates that either bug fixing or development or some form of administration is going on on the server that involves fixing data. Modifying data outside of change control is a separate issue in itself and should be resolved as part of your security review. The focus of this chapter is to show you that you must secure the data first. Therefore, every possible method for staff to view data must be considered and locked. On a more detailed level, our security problem is now worse because, although the data is actually encrypted within the database table, it is clearly not encrypted on the file system. Whoever has created those files needs access to encryption and decryption routines. The data *must* be locked down and encrypted. If the system needs to be Payment Card Industry Data Security Standard (PCI DSS) compliant, then the lack of encryption would be an issue.

The other file of interest in the directory listing shown in Listing 15-12 is the export dump file called crypt.dmp. Listing 15-13 shows some of the contents of that file.

Listing 15-13. A Dump of the Export File crypt.dmp

```
...
METRICSUXDB Schemas by user
METRICEU 27
TABLE "CREDIT_CARD"
CREATE TABLE "CREDIT_CARD" ("NAME_ON_CARD" VARCHAR2(100), "FIRST_NAME"
VARCHAR2(50), "LAST_NAME" VARCHAR2(50), "PAN" RAW(100))  PCTFREE 10 PCTUSED 40
INITRANS 1 MAXTRANS 255 STORAGE(INITIAL 65536 FREELISTS 1 FREELIST GROUPS 1
BUFFER_POOL DEFAULT) TABLESPACE "ORABLOG_DATA" LOGGING NOCOMPRESS
INSERT INTO "CREDIT_CARD" ("NAME_ON_CARD", "FIRST_NAME", "LAST_NAME", "PAN")
VALUES (:1, :2, :3, :4)
^D^@^A^@d^@Â²^@^A^@^A^@2^@Â²^@^A^@^A^@2^@Â²^@^A^@^W^@d^@^@^@^@^@^M^@Pete
Finniga^@Pete^H^@Finnigan^X^@Ã<95>Ã©^Y<9a>x<98><8f>=7]R<97>Â®Ã^CBÂªÃ´Ã£/Ã¢<8a>-
^@^@^N^@Finnigan^E^@Zulia^H^@Finnigan^X^@Ã¦4ÃgÃUÃ
ÃÃ¼^FÃ¸Ã¼^@vid Litchfield^E^@David        cH<8f>-{<91>Â±Ãª¨<92>0\Ã³Ã<9d>)Ã<8a>Ã
<92>^CvÂµÂ±^@^@^L^@Aaron Newman^E^@Aaron^F^@Newman^X^@ ^K^K=^DÂ½gÃ©G<96>Ã¢-
Ã<80><99>22
Ã¾=ÃÃ^NÃt<98>^@^@^K^@Laszlo Toth^F^@Laszlo^D^@Toth^X^@%Xw^^<97>0^WÃªg
~<89>ÃsvÃ¬
   Ã^@^@Ã¿Ã¿
GRANT SELECT ON "CREDIT_CARD" TO PUBLIC
```

```
ANALSTATS TR "CREDIT_CARD"
6); END;
DBMS_STATS.SET_TABLE_STATS(NULL,'"CREDIT_CARD"',NULL,NULL,NULL,5,5,53,
ANALSTATS TR "CREDIT_CARD"
@
...                                                                      776
```

The output shown in Listing 15-13 is slightly corrupted by special nonprintable characters. The corruption is simply caused by the terminal used in the example. The data shown below the INSERT statement contains the credit card details from the database table, including credit card numbers in an encrypted form. Both this export file and the file cards.lis shown in Listing 15-12 are world readable. This means any person logging on to the server can read the credit card numbers in clear text for the cards.lis file shown in Listing 15-12 or as encrypted text of the export file shown in Listing 15-13. The exposure of data on the server clearly must be resolved by removing the data and also addressing the administrative processes that allowed the data to be removed from the database.

Locations to check on the server for suspicious files that may contain data should include any directories pointed at by directory objects within the database itself, or by the utl_file_dir parameter, or by locations identified by Java JVM privileges. Add to that list all server users' home directories, common Oracle software directories such as $ORACLE_HOME/bin, /network/admin, and more. Then add all key application directories.

A final example of an area of concern is that all SQL statements also end up in the SGA of the database. If the SQL statements include inserting data or are in SELECT statements that have a SQL WHERE clause that includes a credit card number, or alternately an UPDATE statement has a WHERE clause that includes a credit card number, then these SQL statements would also expose credit card details. Any SQL statements that include credit card details must also be protected. Even if bind variables are used in statements that could include credit card details, the contents of bind variables can still be found within the SGA. First search the SGA for SQL text that may include credit card numbers. Listing 15-14 shows how to do that.

Listing 15-14. Locating Credit Card Numbers in the SGA

```
SQL> select sql_id,sql_text
  2  from v$sqltext
  3  where sql_id in(
  4  select sql_id
  5  from v$sqltext
  6  where upper(sql_text) like '%PAN%')
  7  order by sql_id,piece
  8  /

SQL_ID          SQL_TEXT
-------------   ----------------------------------------------------------------
01fxrwu6vzngy   select table_name,column_name,owner from dba_tab_columns where c
01fxrwu6vzngy   olumn_name = 'PAN'
080na0k5tahm5   select sql_id,sql_text from v$sqltext where sql_id in( select sq
080na0k5tahm5   l_id from v$sqltext where upper(sql_text) like '%PAN%') order by
080na0k5tahm5   sql_id,piece
{output snipped for space considerations}
1v55cbq0g3v3d   insert into credit_card(name_on_card,first_name,last_name,pan) v
1v55cbq0g3v3d   alues ('Eric Finnigan','Eric','Finnigan',orablog_crypto.encrypt(
```

```
1v55cbq0g3v3d '4049987688654564'))
58m2h83vggg0q select table_name,column_name,owner from dba_tab_columns where c
58m2h83vggg0q olumn_name like '%PAN%'
63k7v7snq2qny SELECT NAME_ON_CARD,PAN FROM CREPORT
{output snipped for space considerations}
7zyzh73qpx9ck select count(*) from sys.type$ t, sys.obj$ o, sys.user$ u
7zyzh73qpx9ck     where o.owner# = u.user# and o.oid$ = t.tvoid and
7zyzh73qpx9ck         u.name not in (select schema_name from v$sysaux_occupants)
7zyzh73qpx9ck  and                  u.name not in ('OE', 'IX', 'PM')
8y569rxzuc4bz select name_on_card,orablog_crypto.decrypt(pan) from credit_card
8y569rxzuc4bz  where orablog_crypto.decrypt(pan) like '4049%'
9uk9v3wf554cn select * from credit_card where orablog_crypto.decrypt(pan) = '3
9uk9v3wf554cn 742112366758976'
c13zqu0c6jr50 select * from credit_card where pan='3742112366758976'
{output snipped for space considerations}
ggn6qfs1kbfwf select * from credit_card where pan=orablog_crypto.decrypt('3742
ggn6qfs1kbfwf 112366758976')

69 rows selected.

SQL>
```

The output in Listing 15-14 clearly shows a number of credit card numbers in clear text (remember that the credit card numbers are stored encrypted within the table itself). The V$SQLTEXT view is just one view that allows access to the shared memory of the Oracle instance and is used as an example. There are more data dictionary views to worry about that also expose data. A detailed analysis should consider all possible views.

In this example, the next step is to review permissions on the view in question to assess which users could access credit card numbers via the method shown in Listing 15-14. Listing 15-15 shows how to generate that list of users.

Listing 15-15. Review Which Users Can Access v$sqltext

```
SQL> @get_tab2

get_tab2: Release 1.0.0.0.0 - Production on Thu Aug 27 20:19:11 2009
Copyright (c) 2004,2009, PeteFinnigan.com Limited. All rights reserved.

OBJECT TO CHECK                    [XXX_XXXX]: V_$SQLTEXT
SCHEMA/OWNER OF THE OBJECT TO CHECK   [USER]: SYS
OUTPUT METHOD Screen/File              [S]: S
FILE NAME FOR OUTPUT             [priv.lst]:
OUTPUT DIRECTORY [DIRECTORY  or file (/tmp)]:

Testing root object => [SYS.V_$SQLTEXT]


GRANTOR        GRANTEE        S I U D A F D I R Q C E
-------------  -------------  - - - - - - - - - - - -
SYS            WK_TEST        X                          ↵
```

```
[,D][WKUSER][SELECT_CATALOG_ROLE]
SYS          SYS          X                    ↵
[A,D][WKUSER][SELECT_CATALOG_ROLE]
SYS          SYS          X                    ↵
[A,D][DBA][SELECT_CATALOG_ROLE]
SYS          SYSMAN       X                    ↵
[,D][DBA][SELECT_CATALOG_ROLE]
SYS          AA           X                    ↵
[,D][DBA][SELECT_CATALOG_ROLE]
SYS          SYSTEM       X                    ↵
[A,D][DBA][SELECT_CATALOG_ROLE]
{output removed to conserve space}
```

The output from the query in Listing 15-15 is excessive in this sample database and again illustrates the problem of Oracle's massive duplication of privileges. This problem manifests itself mostly around system privileges and the privileges granted on data dictionary objects. The report in Listing 15-15 shows more than 70 records in total for a reasonably small number of actual users (although I have removed most of them to conserve space), but none of the users shown in this report is new for this analysis of credit card data access.

This section of the chapter has shown that the data is not just available via a single database table that it is stored in. There are many other methods to get to the same data, including views and procedures that access the same base table and then also via data leakage and sweeping privileges. The investigation has shown so far that it is not enough to secure just the base table itself, because all other aspects of data access must be considered.

Access to Access

Just when you thought the problem couldn't get deeper, unfortunately I can assure you that it really does. You saw in earlier sections that the data is stored in a table called CREDIT_CARD, and the privilege model did not include just the one person who had been granted direct privileges on this table but many users who were being granted privileges on views and PL/SQL that also accesses this table.

In security, you need to have a devious mind because there are always more ways to get what you want than the designers of the system thought they were allowing. Another issue to consider is the problem of privileges that grant privileges. A good example is the system privilege GRANT ANY OBJECT PRIVILEGE. Any user who has this privilege may not already have direct access to the credit card table, but because of this privilege he could simply grant himself direct access to the credit card table. Therefore, we must consider privileges that grant privileges as part of the security process. Listing 15-16 shows how you can run the script who_has_priv.sql (which is available from www.petefinnigan.com/tools.htm) to find out which users have a given privilege. Listing 15-16 checks which users are granted the GRANT ANY OBJECT PRIVILEGE.

Listing 15-16. Check Which Users and Roles Have Been Granted the GRANT ANY OBJECT System Privilege

```
SQL> @who_has_priv

who_has_priv: Release 1.0.3.0.0 - Production on Thu Aug 27 20:22:32 2009
Copyright (c) 2004 PeteFinnigan.com Limited. All rights reserved.

PRIVILEGE TO CHECK        [SELECT ANY TABLE]: GRANT ANY OBJECT PRIVILEGE
```

```
OUTPUT METHOD Screen/File                    [S]: S
FILE NAME FOR OUTPUT              [priv.lst]:
OUTPUT DIRECTORY [DIRECTORY  or file (/tmp)]:
EXCLUDE CERTAIN USERS                        [N]:
USER TO SKIP                           [TEST%]:


Privilege => GRANT ANY OBJECT PRIVILEGE has been granted to =>
====================================================================
        Role => DATAPUMP_IMP_FULL_DATABASE (ADM = NO) which is granted to =>
                Role => DBA (ADM = NO) which is granted to =>
                        User => SYS (ADM = YES)
                        User => SYSMAN (ADM = NO)
                        User => AA (ADM = NO)
                        User => SYSTEM (ADM = YES)
                        Role => APPROLE (ADM = NO) which is granted to =>
                                User => BB (ADM = NO)
                                User => AA (ADM = NO)
                                User => SYSTEM (ADM = YES)
                        User => IMPORTER (ADM = NO)
                User => SYS (ADM = YES)
        Role => DBA (ADM = YES) which is granted to =>
                User => SYS (ADM = YES)
                User => SYSMAN (ADM = NO)
                User => AA (ADM = NO)
                User => SYSTEM (ADM = YES)
                Role => APPROLE (ADM = NO) which is granted to =>
                        User => BB (ADM = NO)
                        User => AA (ADM = NO)
                        User => SYSTEM (ADM = YES)
                User => IMPORTER (ADM = NO)
        User => WKSYS (ADM = NO)
        User => SYS (ADM = NO)
{output snipped to preserve space}


SQL>
```

The report shown in Listing 15-16 shows a large number of users who have access to the GRANT ANY OBJECT PRIVILEGE system privilege. The good news in this particular example is that no new users over and above those I have identified so far have gained access to the credit card table, but all the users within this report *could gain access* to any of the data that they perhaps already do not have access to.

The focus of this section is really to highlight the idea of thinking outside the box—that security is not flat, the data model is not flat, and the access paths to the data are not flat. Devious people will always find the easiest way to steal what they want to steal. This section highlighted one single system privilege, but there are many others that would allow similar actions. These include but are not limited to GRANT ANY PRIVILEGE, GRANT ANY ROLE, and GRANT ANY OBJECT PRIVILEGE. Clever people can also use privileges such as ALTER USER, which would allow you to log in as any user who already has privileges on the table or who has a privilege to grant a privilege. This highlights the importance of having auditing enabled to capture the use of system privileges.

Duplicating Data

Not more, I hear you say. Yes, unfortunately, there are even more ways to get the data. This whole chapter has focused on the credit card data that supposedly is stored in the ORABLOG.CREDIT_CARD table. I showed that there is a hierarchy above this table in my sample database of various views and other objects, but also in real systems it is almost certain that the data has been copied. In one system that I audited, in which I also happened to choose credit cards as the target data, I found 17 copies of the credit card data within the database in a short period of time.

Locating duplicate data should be just as difficult as finding the initial data storage in some sense, although after you have found the initial set of data, it should be easier to find duplicate copies because the table structure is now known and the real data can be sampled to look for exact copies. A simplistic approach to locate copies is to initially choose a key column from the starter table. For this example, I have chosen the PAN column because it stores the credit card number and is unique. Another initial approach could be to look for tables that have exactly the same structure as the table you started with. Finally, it is also possible to sample data from all tables in the database irrespective of table names and then test every column in every table in the database with the same sizing characteristics as the sample data to see whether the same records are held. Listing 15-17 shows how you may search the database for additional copies of the credit card data.

Listing 15-17. Looking for Copies of the Credit Card Data

```
SQL> col owner for a15 head "Owner"
SQL> col table_name for a30 head "Table Name"
SQL> col column_name for a20 head "Column Name"
SQL> select owner, table_name,column_name
  2  from dba_tab_columns
  3  where column_name='PAN'
  4  /

Owner           Table Name                      Column Name
--------------- ------------------------------- --------------------
ORABLOG         BIN$SFVOAmZ7LGngQAB/AQB5+w==$0  PAN
ORABLOG         BIN$SFV2LPPq6wHgQAB/AQB6GA==$0  PAN
ORABLOG         BIN$SFYmOpXjnWngQAB/AQAFSg==$0  PAN
ORABLOG         BIN$SFYqtq+wTp3gQAB/AQAGEA==$0  PAN
ORABLOG         BIN$SFYv3FNLroDgQAB/AQAGQA==$0  PAN
ORABLOG         BIN$SFY2dIAeFVTgQAB/AQAGeA==$0  PAN
ORABLOG         BIN$SFY3HrgmcFrgQAB/AQAGgQ==$0  PAN
ORABLOG         BIN$SFY5dvNjVRrgQAB/AQAGlw==$0  PAN
ORABLOG         BIN$SFY74g46F9fgQAB/AQAG8w==$0  PAN
ORABLOG         BIN$SFY/AtrNeRngQAB/AQAHGw==$0  PAN
ORABLOG         BIN$SFZJq3Itvb7gQAB/AQAHtw==$0  PAN
ORABLOG         BIN$SFZNmEOKfpjgQAB/AQAH+g==$0  PAN
ORABLOG         BIN$SFZSz8RAdAPgQAB/AQAIZg==$0  PAN
ORABLOG         BIN$SFZUh/pQIyfgQAB/AQAIew==$0  PAN
ORABLOG         BIN$SFZYZjtXVwngQAB/AQAIoQ==$0  PAN
ORABLOG         BIN$SFZZhezhGdPgQAB/AQAIsA==$0  PAN
ORABLOG         CREDIT_CARD                     PAN
ORABLOG         CC1                             PAN
```

```
IMPORTER        C23                      PAN
ORABLOG         CCEXP                    PAN
ERIC            CREPORT                  PAN

21 rows selected.

SQL>
```

This initial analysis shown in Listing 15-17 has located three of the views of tables that were already found in the initial phases of this chapter's analysis, but it also found a new table called C23 owned by the user IMPORTER. This is clearly a copy of the credit card data. Also it is worth noting that the tables with strange names are recycle bin objects that also could contain copies of the data.

The analysis now enters another level of complexity because everything that has gone before in this chapter in terms of hierarchy now has to be applied again to the copy of the data. So run the SQL in Listing 15-18 to create privilege reports to understand which objects are providing additional access to the data in this table.

Listing 15-18. Resolving the Heirarchy for IMPORTER.C23

```
SQL> col owner for a20 head "Owner"
SQL> col name for a20 head "name"
SQL> col type for a20 head "Type"
SQL> select owner,name,type
  2  from dba_dependencies
  3  where referenced_name='C23'
  4  and referenced_owner='IMPORTER'
  5  /

Owner                name                 Type
-------------------- -------------------- -------------------
IMPORTER             C34                  VIEW

1 row selected.

SQL>
```

In the particular case shown in Listing 15-18, the hierarchy is very small because there is only a single view that utilizes the C23 table. The next step is, as I am sure you can guess, to test the privileges against this table and the view that uses it. Use the script get_tab2.sql as shown in Listing 15-19 to review the privilege access model for the C23 and C34 objects.

Listing 15-19. Assess the Privileges on C23 and C34

```
SQL> @get_tab2

get_tab2: Release 1.0.0.0.0 - Production on Fri Aug 28 15:21:12 2009
Copyright (c) 2004,2009, PeteFinnigan.com Limited. All rights reserved.

OBJECT TO CHECK                  [XXX_XXXX]: C23
SCHEMA/OWNER OF THE OBJECT TO CHECK    [USER]: IMPORTER
```

```
OUTPUT METHOD Screen/File                 [S]: S
FILE NAME FOR OUTPUT              [priv.lst]:
OUTPUT DIRECTORY [DIRECTORY  or file (/tmp)]:

Testing root object => [IMPORTER.C23]


GRANTOR         GRANTEE         S I U D A F D I R Q C E
-------------   -------------   - - - - - - - - - - - -
IMPORTER        ORABLOG         X
IMPORTER        BB              X
IMPORTER        AA              X

SQL> @get_tab2

get_tab2: Release 1.0.0.0.0 - Production on Thu Aug 27 20:35:10 2009
Copyright (c) 2004,2009, PeteFinnigan.com Limited. All rights reserved.

OBJECT TO CHECK                 [XXX_XXXX]: C34
SCHEMA/OWNER OF THE OBJECT TO CHECK   [USER]: IMPORTER
OUTPUT METHOD Screen/File             [S]: S
FILE NAME FOR OUTPUT          [priv.lst]:
OUTPUT DIRECTORY [DIRECTORY  or file (/tmp)]:

Testing root object => [IMPORTER.C34]


GRANTOR         GRANTEE         S I U D A F D I R Q C E
-------------   -------------   - - - - - - - - - - - -
IMPORTER        SCOTT           X

SQL>
```

The output in Listing 15-19 shows that two more sets of privileges have been discovered. One new user who was not included in the earlier analysis of ORABLOG.CREDIT_CARD has been located who can access the credit card data (against the copy in C23, but it is still the credit card data). Listing 15-19 also highlights privilege duplication, but this is complex duplication: three users who have SELECT privilege on the table C23 also have SELECT privilege on the original table. Although this is a distinct new privilege, it is still a duplicate access path to the same credit card data. Rather than consider the issue of a duplicate privilege, the primary focus for security should be to remove the duplicate data, not the privilege.

At the beginning of this chapter, it seemed as though only one user had access to the credit card data in addition to the owner of the table. In reality, I have shown the complete hierarchy, and 23 users have been located who can access the credit card data. This is 47 percent of the total users of this database, and this figure indicates a common trend found on most databases. This number does not include operating system users who can access credit card data. Furthermore, the analysis is not complete; other areas I've identified could be reviewed if I had more space. Having 23 users capable of accessing the data is a very big difference from the original notion of having only one. Unfortunately, such a difference is common in my day-to-day work.

Generalizing Across the Database

The sample analysis of a single piece of data—in this case, credit card data—has been completed. But remember, this was just a single piece of data, not the complete database. Although this analysis is very valuable in that it has focused on the most critical data in the database, the complete database should be secured. This is a problem because performing the same analysis shown in this chapter for every table in the database is impractical.

The focus has been on the key data because this is important, and the key data will be secure if all of the security issues located are resolved. The resolution should follow steps outlined in the preceding chapter: removal and then reduction. First, identify users of data who can be removed and identify data that can be removed. The security solution strategy should also include files on the operating system that may contain the key data you chose to analyze. If duplicate copies of data are found outside of the database, these should also be removed. The second step in the security process is reduction. Reduce the privileges that are being granted against the remaining data to the minimum necessary for the business to operate.

The sweeping privileges that were highlighted as possible paths to the data should also be reviewed and revoked. In general, no users of the database except administrative users should have any sweeping privileges. Indeed, the removal of system privileges from nonadministrative users is even more important with the privileges that grant privileges. In general, even system privileges should not be granted to the day-to-day accounts used by database administrators. System privileges should be available to only built-in accounts such as SYS and SYSTEM. Solving the issues around system privileges for the credit card data implicitly solves a problem for every other piece of data in the database because these are system-level privileges, not object-level privileges.

Consideration should be given to the rest of the data within the database as some efforts must be made to secure it. Keep in mind that it is not appropriate to use the techniques described in this chapter on all data, so generalizations are required. As you may expect from the preceding chapter, I'm going to tell you to break the problem down into pieces. Identify true production data as opposed to configuration data or static data or similar. The identification of true production data is very application-specific. In general, all the solutions (not complete analysis, remember) we define for your specific data must be applied to the rest of the data, but usually the two are entwined. If, for instance, a solution specifically for the credit card data is to remove a layer of privileges on a layer of views, that solution is likely to be the same on many of the other tables in the database. In fact, I have worked with systems where removing a role used for access to the key data has actually been the solution for many of the other tables as well; so the solution was, in this example, simple. This simplicity in terms of solutions is often borne out by the fact that most users of the system are granted the same or similar roles, so even though you investigated a single table, you often find that a chosen solution benefits the whole system.

Listing 15-20 shows a simple test to try to assess how many tables in production schemas have dependencies.

Listing 15-20. Summarizing Dependencies for a Schema

```
SQL> col cnt for 9999 head "Cnt"
SQL> col name for a30 head "Name"
SQL> col type for a20 head "Type"
SQL> select count(*),name,type
  2  from dba_dependencies
  3  where referenced_owner='ORABLOG'
  4  group by name, type
  5  /
```

```
COUNT(*) Name                            Type
-------- ------------------------------- --------------------
       2 WP_POSTS_TRIG                   TRIGGER
       2 WP_USERMETA_TRIG                TRIGGER
       2 WP_USERS_TRIG                   TRIGGER
       2 BIN$R56OHs5SzeXgQAB/AQBbfA==$0  TRIGGER
       1 CC1                             VIEW
       1 DAY                             FUNCTION
       1 ORABLOG_CRYPTO                  PACKAGE BODY
       1 CREPORT                         VIEW
       2 BIN$R56OHs59zeXgQAB/AQBbfA==$0  TRIGGER
       1 CCEXP                           VIEW
       1 CCNAME                          VIEW
       2 WP_LINKCATEGORIES_TRIG          TRIGGER
       2 WP_POST2CAT_TRIG                TRIGGER
       2 BIN$R56OHs47zeXgQAB/AQBbfA==$0  TRIGGER
       2 BIN$R56OHs4szeXgQAB/AQBbfA==$0  TRIGGER
       2 BIN$R56OHs5tzeXgQAB/AQBbfA==$0  TRIGGER
       1 CCDEC                           FUNCTION
       2 WP_COMMENTS_TRIG                TRIGGER
       2 BIN$R56OHs51zeXgQAB/AQBbfA==$0  TRIGGER
       2 BIN$R56OHs5ezeXgQAB/AQBbfA==$0  TRIGGER
       2 BIN$R56OHs6XzeXgQAB/AQBbfA==$0  TRIGGER
       2 BIN$R56OHs6fzeXgQAB/AQBbfA==$0  TRIGGER

COUNT(*) Name                            Type
-------- ------------------------------- --------------------
       1 CCEN                            FUNCTION
       2 WP_LINKS_TRIG                   TRIGGER
       2 WP_POSTMETA_TRIG                TRIGGER
       2 BIN$R56OHs6QzeXgQAB/AQBbfA==$0  TRIGGER
       1 REP_CC_COUNT                    FUNCTION
       2 WP_CATEGORIES_TRIG              TRIGGER
       2 WP_OPTIONS_TRIG                 TRIGGER

29 rows selected.

SQL>
```

The output shown in Listing 15-20 does not show the complete hierarchy (*hint: use a* connect by prior *query to do this*) but gives a high-level view of the issue across the complete schema and is a good starting point. Assess the complete schemas by using summarized queries and then assess the roles and privileges assigned against these schema objects again at the summary level and revoke at the role level.

Summary

To secure an Oracle database, you must modify your mindset to think about securing the data and not about securing the software. To secure the software is literally impossible, because the software is almost infinitely configurable and the software does not know anything about your system (apart from what you tell it), your applications, or the versions you are running. Relying on checklists alone is also futile; checklists are useful as a general hardening guide but not as a guide for complete security of data. To secure the data completely, you must understand the data; you must understand how the data flows into the database and how the data flows out of the database. You must also understand who has access to the data and where and how. Only with complete information can you form a security policy that will enable you to secure the data.

This chapter started with an abnormally naive approach of thinking that the data is simply within a single table; this is wrong. Extending the problem to also include security means that the security is not just the privileges on that single table but it is the privileges of every object that also accesses that table. The problem does not stop there because there are many other ways to get at the same data, and that is why it is important to understand how the data flows into and out of the database. With this knowledge, you will be able to think in a devious manner, in the same manner as someone who wants to steal your data. Learn to *think like a hacker*.

If you can understand the true privilege model and access model to the data within the database, you can secure it. Therefore, you can secure the data and, with it, Oracle.

Combine the processes described in this chapter with the knowledge from the preceding chapter around securing users, and then your database will be much harder to break into. If no one who should not be able to access the data can even attempt to enter the database, and you have hardened the privileges on the data to the level of an authorized user, you will be really secure. Good luck!

Quiz Answer

As you may remember, in the first section of this chapter I asked why the file permissions in the $ORACLE_HOME\bin directory should not be fixed by using the command chmod 0755 $ORACLE_HOME/bin/*. Did you get it?

The issue is simple, really. There are file permissions in the directory that are already set stronger than 0755, so issuing the command that I asked about would actually weaken some of the permissions. Verify file permissions first before correcting them. A more general comment is to never blindly apply solutions from checklists. Always research the issue yourself first and understand exactly what you're doing.

Index

■E

■W

You Need the Companion eBook

Your purchase of this book entitles you to buy the companion PDF-version eBook for only $10. Take the weightless companion with you anywhere.

We believe this Apress title will prove so indispensable that you'll want to carry it with you everywhere, which is why we are offering the companion eBook (in PDF format) for $10 to customers who purchase this book now. Convenient and fully searchable, the PDF version of any content-rich, page-heavy Apress book makes a valuable addition to your programming library. You can easily find and copy code—or perform examples by quickly toggling between instructions and the application. Even simultaneously tackling a donut, diet soda, and complex code becomes simplified with hands-free eBooks!

Once you purchase your book, getting the $10 companion eBook is simple:

❶ Visit **www.apress.com/promo/tendollars/**.

❷ Complete a basic registration form to receive a randomly generated question about this title.

❸ Answer the question correctly in 60 seconds, and you will receive a promotional code to redeem for the $10.00 eBook.

THE EXPERT'S VOICE™

233 Spring Street, New York, NY 10013

Offer valid through 6/10.